Cognition
and conditionals
Probability and
logic in human thinking

Cognition and conditionals
Probability and logic in human thinking

Edited by

Mike Oaksford
Professor of Psychology
Department of Psychological Sciences
Birkbeck College London

Nick Chater
Professor of Cognitive and Decision Sciences
Department of Cognitive,
Perception and Brain Sciences
University College London

OXFORD
UNIVERSITY PRESS

OXFORD

UNIVERSITY PRESS

Great Clarendon Street, Oxford OX2 6DP

Oxford University Press is a department of the University of Oxford.
It furthers the University's objective of excellence in research, scholarship,
and education by publishing worldwide in

Oxford New York

Athens Auckland Bangkok Bogotá Buenos Aires Cape Town
Chennai Dar es Salaam Delhi Florence Hong Kong Istanbul Karachi
Kolkata Kuala Lumpur Madrid Melbourne Mexico City Mumbai Nairobi
Paris São Paulo Shanghai Singapore Taipei Tokyo Toronto Warsaw

with associated companies in Berlin Ibadan

Oxford is a registered trade mark of Oxford University Press
in the UK and in certain other countries

Published in the United States
by Oxford University Press Inc., New York

British Library Cataloguing in Publication Data

Data available

Library of Congress Cataloguing in Publication Data

Data available

Typeset by Glyph International, Bangalore, India
Printed in Great Britain
on acid-free paper by the
MPG Books Group, Bodmin and King's Lynn

ISBN 978–0–19–923329–8

10 9 8 7 6 5 4 3 2 1

Contents

Contributors

Nilufa Ali
Cognition, Perception and
Brain Sciences,
University College London, UK

David O'Brien
Baruch College and the
Graduate Center of the City
University of New York, USA

Jean-François Bonnefon
CNRS – Université de Toulouse,
Toulouse, France

Ruth M.J. Byrne
School of Psychology and Institute of
Neuroscience, Trinity College Dublin,
Ireland

Nick Chater
Cognition, Perception and
Brain Sciences,
University College London, UK

Denise Cummins
Departments of Psychology
and Philosophy,
University of Illinois,
Champaign-Urbana, USA

Shira Elqayam
School of Applied Social Sciences,
De Monfort University, UK

Jonathan St. B.T. Evans
School of Psychology,
University of Plymouth, UK

Sonja M. Geiger
University of Western Australia,
Australia

Vittorio Girotto
University IUAV of Venice,
Italy

Philip N. Johnson-Laird
Department of Psychology, Princeton
University, USA

Gernot D. Kleiter
Department of Psychology,
University of Salzburg, Austria

Robert Kowalski
Department of Computing,
Imperial College London, UK

Michiel van Lambalgen
Department of Philosophy,
Amsterdam University,
Netherlands

In-mao Liu
National Chung-Cheng University and
National Taiwan University,
Taiwan

Andrea Manfrinati
Università di Padova,
Italy

Henry Markovits
Department of Psychology, Université du
Québec à Montréal,
Montreal, Canada

Wim De Neys
CNRS – Université de Toulouse,
Toulouse, France

Mike Oaksford
Department of Psychological Sciences,
Birkbeck College,
University of London, UK

Klaus Oberauer
Department of Psychology,
University of Zurich,
Switzerland

David E. Over
Department of Psychology,
Durham University, UK

Niki Pfeifer
Department of Psychology,
University of Salzburg,
Austria

Guy Politzer
CNRS – Institut Jean-Nicod,
Paris, France

Walter Schaeken
University of Leuven,
Belgium

Anne Schlottmann
Developmental Science,
University College London, UK

Walter Schroyens
Laboratory for Experimental Psychology,
University of Ghent,
Belgium

Abigail Shaw
Developmental Science,
University College London, UK

Keith Stenning
Human Communication Research Centre,
Edinburgh University,
Scotland, UK

Valerie A. Thompson
University of Saskatchewan,
Canada

Niki Verschueren
University of Leuven,
Belgium

Part 1

Introduction

Chapter 1

Cognition and conditionals: An introduction

Mike Oaksford and Nick Chater

The conditional construction, 'if *p* then *q*' in English, is the probably the most important term in human language. It occurs in all human languages (Comrie, 1986) and allows people to express their knowledge of the causal or law-like structure of the world and of others' behaviour, e.g., *if you turn the key, the car starts, if John walks the dog, he stops for a pint of beer*; to make promises, e.g., *if you cook tonight, I'll wash up all week*; to regulate behaviour, e.g., *if you are drinking beer, you must be over 18 years of age*; to suggest what would have happened had things been different, e.g., *if the match had been dry, it would have lit*, among many other possible uses. The way in which the conditional is modelled also determines the core of most logical systems. Unsurprisingly, it is also the most researched expression in the psychology of human reasoning.

There is a large array of theoretical proposals for how people reason in general and with conditionals in particular. Indeed, from outside the psychology of reasoning, it is perhaps difficult to discern much progress in an area where there would appear to be a different theory adopted by every major figure in the field. After almost 50 years of research, rather than converging on the one true theory of reasoning, the area continues to fractionate with new approaches developing every 10 years or so, e.g., mental logic, mental models, heuristic approaches, dual process theory, pragmatic reasoning schemas, probabilistic approaches, and so on.

However, the concentration of research over the last 10 to 15 years on the conditional may mark the beginnings of something more like a consensus. To be clear, we are not arguing that researchers are converging on any one of the particular theories so far put forward. Rather, as the research on conditionals reveals the complexity of the phenomena to be explained, researchers are gaining a better appreciation of what is important about each theoretical perspective, and perhaps of how they may fit together to provide a complete theory of the how people reason with conditionals. Moreover, recently different theoretical proposals are becoming precise enough for it to be possible to formally compare different theories and combinations of theories, to see how well they can explain the experimental results (Klauer, Musch, & Naumer, 2000; Klauer, Stahl, & Erdfelder, 2007; Oaksford & Chater, 2003; Oberauer, 2006).

To understand the current state of the psychology of conditional reasoning requires looking at two interlocking histories: the history of the psychology of conditional reasoning, and the history of conditional logic and its formal semantics. At times, these histories have proceeded relatively independently and it is really only in the last 10 to 15 years that advances in the logic of the conditional have found their way in to the psychology of how people reason with this connective (Evans & Over, 2004; Oaksford & Chater, 2007; Oaksford, Chater, & Larkin, 2000; Stenning & Lambalgen, 2005). In this introductory chapter, we will briefly trace some of the relevant history of the two areas to provide the reader with an appropriate overview of the relevant issues. In doing so, we have chosen not to review each area separately but to intertwine developments in both areas, so that we can trace both their interactions and their failures to interact, which have affected where we find ourselves today.

A brief joint history of the logic and psychology of the conditional

The goal of the psychology of reasoning is to explain the patterns of inference that underpin human behaviour. Reasoning can occur within the individual, when for example someone infers that they will need their umbrella on looking out the window to see that it is raining. It also occurs between individuals, when a speaker tries to argue for a particular point of view. Moreover, it is clear that not just any old process counts as reasoning. For example, in arguing with others, there are implicit standards to which reasoning should conform to count as a rational attempt at persuasion rather than mere coercion or bluster. This suggests that the psychology of reasoning needs to provide not only a descriptive account of the patterns of reasoning that people use, but also an evaluative account of what is and what is not a good argument.

As far back as Aristotle, philosophers have been cataloguing patterns of inference, and in particular the patterns of inference that attach to a few particular words in natural languages. These are the structure building words that take other sentences and join them together to make more complex sentences. These include *and, or,* and *not* but in particular, the focus of this book, *if...then.* They also include quantifiers such as *all* and *some.* Aristotle's attempts at an evaluative theory were explicit, in the sense that for quantified syllogistic reasoning – e.g., *All ravens are black, Some birds are ravens,* therefore, *Some birds are black* – he simply listed the valid and the invalid syllogisms. However, he had no method for showing why some were valid (i.e., that the conclusion must be true, if the premises are true) and some were not. For more than two thousand years, Aristotle's theory of the syllogism almost exhausted logical theory – and indeed, Kant considered all logical questions to have been decisively resolved by Aristotle, stating: 'It is remarkable also, that to the present day, it has not been able to make one step in advance, so that, to all appearance, it [i.e., logic] may be considered as completed and perfect'. (Kant, 1961, p. 501). Generations of scholars, from the Greeks to the medieval period, and in some traditions, to the present day, have learned the valid syllogisms by rote as part of their education.

Within mathematics, the need for anything more than Aristotle's explicit formulation of logic was not apparent until the nineteenth century. What conclusions followed with certainty in a mathematical derivation were regarded as simply self-evident to the intelligent mathematician. But mathematical reasoning itself came into question with the development of puzzles in geometry, previously the paradigm of mathematical certainty. Attempts to prove Euclid's fifth postulate (that parallel lines never meet) from Euclid's first four postulates led to confusion and failure. Some mathematicians, such as Gauss and Riemann, began to suggest that such a proof was impossible, and therefore that there were perfectly consistent non-Euclidean geometries, in which the fifth postulate does not hold. The resulting crisis led to a profound re-evaluation of the nature of mathematical proof, as itself requiring a mathematical analysis to resolve apparently conflicting intuitions (deLong, 1970).

The attempt to provide a certain foundation for mathematics gave a huge impetus to the development of logic. But a particularly important and, from the point of view of cognitive science, startlingly prescient, early pioneer of the new logical techniques was Boole. For the first time, he proposed explicit mathematical rules for logical reasoning; and he also extended the scope of logic outside of the syllogism. Intriguingly, Boole's motivations were more psychological than mathematical. His aim was less to resolve problems in the foundations of mathematics than to characterise 'The Laws of Thought' (Boole, 1854). With more mathematical goals in mind, Frege further revolutionized Boole's logic, developing 'predicate logic,' which for the first time provided a mathematical theory of syllogistic reasoning, and much more besides. Frege's programme of providing a rigorous foundation for mathematics was followed by Russell and Whitehead's logicist philosophy of mathematics, which attempted to reduce mathematics to logic. A related, but distinct, viewpoint was pioneered by Hilbert, who viewed mathematics as a process of explicit symbol manipulations, where the rules of symbol manipulation were defined without any reference to what the symbols were about. This 'formalist' tradition provided the starting point for the branch of logic called proof theory, concerned with rigorous specifications of the rules of proofs in terms of formal operations on symbols, and which later underpinned the developed of digital computers, as well as providing a core hypothesis about the operation of the human mind (e.g., Fodor & Pylyshyn, 1988; Newell & Simon, 1976). These developments in formal logic fed directly into developments in philosophy. Frege and Russell began to apply the formal systems that they had devised for understanding mathematical argument to informal philosophical argument, framed in natural language. This was the beginning of the enterprise of formal semantics – specifying precisely the meaning of sentences in terms of their underlying logical form.

The notion of the conditional that emerged from considerations in philosophy about the foundations of mathematics was the material conditional (Whitehead & Russell, 1910, 1912, 1913). The material condition is, crucially, truth functional: that is, whether a conditional sentence is true or false is a function of the truth or falsity of the antecedent and consequent sentences from which it is composed. Specifically, according to the material interpretation of the conditional, a conditional *if p then q* is true if *p* is false or *q* is true (or both), otherwise it is false. That is, it is only false when *p* is true and *q* is false (the case of a clear counterexample to the conditional), and it is true otherwise. These truth conditions can be represented as a truth function, a mapping from pairs of truth values of the constituent sentences *p* and *q*, to the truth value of the conditional sentence *if p then q*. Specifically, it maps TF (an ordered pair meaning '*p*' is true and '*q*' is false) to F (meaning '*if p then q*' is false); and the other three pairs, TT, FT, and FF map to T. This truth function also has a straightforward set-theoretic interpretation in terms of set-inclusion. If it is true that set *p* is included in set *q*, then there cannot be an *x* that is *p* but not *q*. Moreover, if this is true then if *x* is not *q* it cannot be *p*. So, for example, the set of integers is included in the set of positive real numbers and if a number is not a positive real, it cannot be an integer. These properties of the material conditional meant that it seemed well-suited to provide an account of mathematical reasoning (but see Brouwer, 1992/1927).

This account of the conditional was also used outside the mathematical contexts in which it was first derived. For example, it was used by the logical positivists in their characterisation of natural laws in their account of scientific theories (Suppe, 1977). A scientific law was taken to be a universally quantified material conditional, e.g., *all swans are white* ($\forall x(if\ x$ is a swan then *x* is white)). This is given exactly the same interpretation as the set theoretic account of the material conditional, so that it has the consequence that there can be no non-white swans, and if a bird is not white it cannot be a swan. This same conception of natural laws was adopted by Popper (1959), although he criticized the logical positivist's reliance on verification. Popper argued that the logic of the material conditional meant that we can never be certain that a natural law is true, only that it is false. However many white swans we find, the next may not be white. Consequently, it is only rational to seek falsifying evidence in the attempt to disprove our conjectures about natural laws.

Within psychology, and particularly developmental psychology, the idea that people are capable of logical reasoning was a standard assumption (Inhelder & Piaget, 1955). The goal of cognitive development, according to Piaget, was the attainment of the formal operational stage where abstract logical reasoning was possible. While the psychology of reasoning had some earlier precursors (e.g., Woodworth & Sells, 1935), it is generally agreed that the first systematic attempts to experimentally test people's logical reasoning abilities began with Wason's (1960) tests of the assumptions underlying Piagetian theory. Perhaps what is most surprising about these first attempts, in retrospect, is that they were not directly aimed at logical inference, but rather at scientific inference. The principal tasks Wason developed, the 2-4-6 task (Wason, 1960) and the selection task (1968) were about evidence *selection* and whether it followed Popperian falsificationist prescriptions. So, in the 2-4-6 task, participants were told that the experimenter has a rule in mind of which the number triple 2-4-6 is an instance. The participant must then discover the rule, by proposing number triples and receiving feedback on whether they too are instances of this rule or not. Participants showed a strong tendency to propose triples that fitted whatever candidate rule they were currently considering, rather than proposing candidate triples that potentially violated the rule. For example, if a participant considers the candidate rule that the number triples ascend by twos, a typical item that might be tested would be 3-5-7, which would fit with this conjecture, rather than 2-3-4, which violates it.

The 2-4-6 task did not directly address the logical positivist and Popperian conception of a scientific law as a universally quantified material conditional. This was left to the selection task, which seemed to explicitly require participants to employ their knowledge of the logic of the conditional to test a hypothesis. In this task, participants are shown four cards which have a number printed on one side and a letter printed on the other (and participants know this). They are told that these cards obey the rule that *if there is an A on one side then there is 2 on the other side*. They are then shown four cards of which they can only see the uppermost side. One card shows an A, one shows a K, one shows a 2, and the final card shows a 7. They are then asked to select the cards that they must turn over to determine whether the rule is true or false. On the logical falsificationist strategy, participants should select the A and the 7 card as either could be a falsifying instance of the form p is true but q is false. However, participants tend to select the A and the 2 card or the A card alone, which seems to reveal a preference for confirmatory data. Indeed, work on both the 2-4-6 task and the selection task were interpreted as indicating that people possess a 'confirmation bias', in contrast to the dictates of Popper's falsificationist view of science.

The concentration in psychology on scientific inference, and the logical interpretation provided by Popper and the logical positivists, is perhaps understandable given that the first English translation of Popper's *The Logic of Scientific Discovery* (originally, 1934) only became available in 1959. Moreover, Piaget's developmental work had been following this path, taking a logical perspective on the child's problem of gaining empirical knowledge of the world. Hence, focussing on experimental analogues of scientific inference must have seemed a natural starting point from which to evaluate, and potentially to critique Piagetian assumptions about the nature of the adult mind. It was not until the 1970s that experimental work (Roberge, 1970, 1971; Kodroff & Roberge, 1975;) explicitly and directly addressed the formal inference rules that the material conditional prescribes and proscribes, and which are the main focus of this book.

Early accounts of Wason's experimental results did not treat them as denying that people are logical. Rather, theorists made appeal to other aspects of cognitive processing that might explain why, in this task, the cognitive system failed to engage its presumed logical knowledge. This is a common feature of many attempts to explain deviations from logical performance and it is a perfectly reasonable explanatory strategy. By analogy with Chomsky's (1965) influential distinction between linguistic competence (knowledge of the grammar) and linguistic performance (the error-prone processes by which the grammar is recruited to understand and produce language), it was natural to propose that logic provides an appropriate competence level theory of human reasoning and to seek explanations for behavioural deviations from that theory by considering performance limitations on the reasoning system.

Early accounts of this type borrowed the notion of 'insight' from Gestalt problem solving theory (Wertheimer, 1959) and speculated that logical knowledge was only fully engaged when insight into the logical structure of the problem is gained. This theoretical perspective led to experiments that attempted to encourage insight into the problem. For example, so-called 'therapy' experiments were used to try to help participants to see the importance of the falsifying cases (Wason, 1969). Such 'therapy' took a variety of forms, the most concrete of which involved the experimenter turning over the not-q card and showing the participant a p instance and persuading them to agree that this card falsified the rule. Even then, however, in a subsequent selection task, only 42% made the logically correct, p and not-q card selection (Wason, 1969).

The selection task was originally introduced as a problem in hypothesis testing (Wason & Johnson-Laird, 1972), although it has been re-interpreted as an inferential problem (e.g., Rips, 1994). In its original guise, however, there were already good reasons to question the task's core assumption that the material conditional provides an adequate interpretation of scientific laws. In the philosophy of science during the 1950s, the material conditional interpretation of scientific laws and falsificationism had been shown to be problematic.

One particularly important source of problems stemmed from the Quine-Duhem thesis (Duhem, 1914/1954; Quine, 1953): that a scientific hypothesis cannot be decisively falsified by data, however apparently damning, because the data can always be explained away by adjusting so-called auxiliary hypotheses (e.g., about other forces that may be acting; about the operation of the data collecting equipment, and so on), and leaving the theory under test intact. For example, early predictions concerning the orbit of Uranus relied on the auxiliary assumption that there were only seven planets. The failure of Newton's celestial mechanics to successfully predict Uranus' orbit, should according to the falsificationist logic, have lead to the rejection of Newtonian theory. However, the discovery of an eighth planet, Neptune, which turned out to be influencing Uranus' orbit, showed that it was the auxiliary assumption about the number of planets that should be rejected, not Newtonian mechanics.

The fact that prediction from scientific laws requires a body of unstated further assumptions also figured in Goodman's (1954) critique. Goodman's work focussed on two issues. First, he noted that scientific laws must also satisfy Hume's second definition of causation, which is counterfactual, i.e., *if* the cause had occurred, *then* the effect would also have occurred. For example, if the match had been struck, it would have lit. Goodman noted that the truth of such a statement cannot be captured by the logic of the material conditional since the antecedent of a counterfactual is always false and so, on this analysis, counterfactual conditionals are always true. But clearly *if the match had been struck, the moon would have been made of cheese* is simply not true. Moreover, statements like, *if the match had been struck, it would have lit*, also depend on a range of auxiliary assumptions, e.g., that there is oxygen present, the match is struck sufficiently hard, the match is not wet, and so on. These assumptions have to be what Goodman described as 'co-tenable' with the antecedent of the counterfactual before its truth can be affirmed. 'Co-tenable' conditions are those which taken together with the antecedent would logically entail the consequent of a conditional (see also Rescher, 2007 on the 'enthymematic basis' of a conditional). However, there is a problem with cotenability theories as a definition of the counterfactual conditional. For a condition to be co-tenable seems to depend circularly on the truth of another counterfactual, e.g., *if the match had been dry, it would have lit* (but see Kvart, 1985). These problems aside, such a contenability account can also be applied to the standard 'indicative' conditional. When used to describe a law, the antecedent of a conditional is perhaps better characterized as the conjunction of the proximate cause with the co-tenable conditions: *if the match is struck and it is dry and there is oxygen...etc., then it lights*. As with our example concerning planetary orbits and Newtonian mechanics above, the observation of a struck match not lighting on some specific occasion does not falsify the hypothesis that it should light because this evidence most likely bears on the co-tenable conditions and not on the law-like relation itself.

Second, Goodman also noted that even if co-tenability accounts of the counterfactual could not be made to work, it is still the case that intuitively, good scientific laws should in any case be counterfactual supporting. So, we believe that if the match *had* been struck, it *would* have lit, when, all other things being equal (i.e., all co-tenable conditions are in place), you believe that 'if a match is struck it lights' describes a real, i.e., causal, relation in the world. However, the material conditional analysis cannot guarantee this as it says nothing about such relationships. Consequently, such an analysis cannot distinguish between counterfactual supporting conditionals that describe causal laws, like 'if a match is struck it lights', from non-counterfactual supporting accidental generalizations, like 'if this is a coin in my pocket today, then it is silver'. Via his famous 'grue' problem, Goodman argued that this difference could not depend on any superficial characteristic, like temporal specificity (indexing to 'today'). Rather, the difference was an issue of *content*, i.e., the nature of the predicates used in a law-like statement, not of the form of the conditional. Predicates like 'being a struck match' have a history of being used to make predictions about future events; it is 'projectable'. However, predicates like 'being a coin in my pocket today' have no such history and consequently are not projectable. A non-circular account of projectability, which does not merely define projectable predicates as those that reliably support generalizations is, though, difficult to come by.

Goodman also pointed out that adopting the material conditional creates problems for the nature of the confirmation relation between evidence and a hypothesis about a causal law. The logical positivist position on confirmation could be viewed as, in a sense, the reverse of deduction. Thus, according to this viewpoint, predictions follow from a scientific theory by processes of deduction (or, rather, these predictions follow from the theory, conjoined with auxiliary hypotheses concerning initial conditions of the system under study, the operation of the measuring instruments with which data is gathered, and so on). To the extent that these predictions, derived by deduction, are correct, then the theory is viewed as receiving 'inductive confirmation'. One set of difficulties for this perspective concerns the troublesome auxiliary hypotheses. Just as auxiliary hypotheses can be modified to save a theory, when its predictions appear to go astray, similarly it is not clear how much credit should be assigned to the auxiliary hypotheses, rather than the theory itself, when predictions are observed (the "credit apportionment" problem [Holland, Holyoak, Nisbett, & Thagard, 1986]).

Another potential source of concern is Hempel's (1945a,b) well-known 'ravens paradox'. If a theory or hypothesis is confirmed when its deductive consequences are observed to be correct, then the statement *All ravens are black* (or, if you wish to frame this sentence in terms of the conditional, *if something is a raven, then it is black*, which is equivalent, according to the material conditional) must presumably be confirmed by the observation of a raven that is black (the deductive consequence is: suppose we observe a raven; then the theory predicts that it should be black; and so it is). But *All ravens are black* is, of course, according to the material conditional at least, equivalent to *All non-black things are non-ravens* (or, to again give the equivalent sentence in terms of conditionals, *if something is not black, then it is not a raven*), which is surely, by the same logic, confirmed by the observation of one of *its* instances – e.g., a white sock (once the object has been observed to be white, the hypothesis implies that it is not a raven; and indeed it is not). But according to some minimal assumptions at least, it seems difficult to escape the strange conclusion that observing a white sock confirms the hypothesis that *all ravens are black*, rather than being entirely irrelevant to it.

And indeed there may be an even more direct challenge to the idea that confirmation can be viewed as the inverse of deduction – cases where an instance of a generalization can actually disconfirm it! Howson and Urbach (1993), for example, consider the following type of case. Consider the generalization *All beetles of species X are found in Ecuador*. Observing such a beetle, in Ecuador, but a matter of a few meters from the border with Peru, would surely throw the generalization into severe doubt. If the beetles have spread this far, we would naturally argue, then surely they must have spread across the border too. But if this is right, then an observation which is in line with the deductive consequences of a theory (we observe the beetle; predict, using the hypothesis, that it should be in Ecuador; and duly observe that, yes, indeed it is), can *dis*confirm, rather than confirm the hypothesis. The more general problem is that questions of confirmation or disconfirmation of the conditional is not a matter purely of their truth functional properties, That is, it is not important merely that a particular piece of data is *consistent* with a conditional; the nature of the data, the nature of the claim made by the conditional, and our relevant background knowledge, all seem to contribute to determining whether or not an apparent instance of the conditional generalization serves to make that generalization more or less plausible. But this viewpoint only make sense on the assumption that conditionals do much more than make truth functional claims over a domain of possible instances – rather, they seem to make claims about the laws by which the world is governed (in the terminology of the philosophy of language, their claims are intensional, rather than purely extensional).

In the light of these problems, the assumption that experimental participants should seek falsifying evidence in the selection task could have been questioned on sound philosophical grounds at the time of Wason's original studies. There were some voices of discontent (Wetherick, 1962) with the interpretation that people were behaving irrationally in the 2-4-6 task but they were in the minority. The general consensus was that this behaviour on the selection task was a manifestation of a general 'confirmation bias', a bias that was to be found again and again in experiments on human cognition (see Nickerson, 1998 for a review).

At around the same time as the publication of Wason and Johnson-Laird's (1972) seminal book, Evans and Lynch (1973) showed that people's behaviour on the selection task may be even less rational than first thought. He systematically varied negations in the antecedents and consequents of conditionals, for example, if A then not-2. For this rule, people selected the falsifying *p* (A) and not-*q* (2) cards. But of course this meant selecting exactly the same A and 2 cards as they did to apparently confirm the if A then 2 rule! This seemed to show that rather than confirming, people were simply matching the letters and numbers in the rule to the letters and numbers on the cards. Evans (1972) referred to this behaviour as 'matching bias'.

As these examples demonstrate, the bulk of research up to this point had been done using abstract alphanumeric stimuli. The reason for this was straightforward: the idea was to examine the phenomena unpolluted by world-knowledge. Similar strategies had been pursued in a variety of cognitive domains, such as memory (paired associate learning, Ebbinghaus & Meyer, 1908) and problem solving (Tower of Hanoi, Wertheimer, 1959), because of the concern that exponent results could be driven almost entirely by general world knowledge, rather than experimental manipulations of interest (Oaksford, Chater, & Stenning, 1990). However, a result that, with the benefit of hindsight, one might argue is consistent with Goodman's analysis, was that content did seem to matter. For example, Wason and Shapiro (1971; see also, Johnson-Laird, Legrenzi, & Legrenzi, 1972), used rules like, *If I travel to Manchester, then I take the train*, which led to considerably greater falsification rates in the selection task. The interpretation put on this behaviour was that it is due to familiarity with the content (Griggs & Cox, 1982). Such an interpretation suggests that different hypothesis testing strategies are adopted, depending on how familiar people are with the content used in the putative law-like relation. Again, with hindsight, this is consistent with Goodman's observation that law-like relations, even everyday ones, rely on their content being 'projectable', i.e., having a history of being projected in one's linguistic community. *If I travel to Manchester, then I take the train* seems to describe a sensible counterfactual supporting disposition, i.e., it supports the claim *if I had travelled to Manchester, I would have taken the train*. This contrasts with the situation in the standard, abstract selection task. The rule *if there is a an A on one side of the card, then there is a 2 on the other side of the card*, which does not seem to support the counterfactual claim that if there *had* been an A on one side, then there *would* have been a 2 on the other. In the later case, there would appear to be no mechanism or process that can guarantee this, which contrasts with the behavioural disposition in the train example. It is also now commonly agreed, that content eliminates the matching bias effect (Evans, 1998), although this was not initially thought to be the case (Manktelow & Evans, 1979).

This apparent confluence of empirical findings of content effects in hypothesis testing and Goodmans's analysis of the problems for confirmation is, of course, a post hoc observation. In the history of the psychology of reasoning, research on content effects took a different turn. Some researchers noted that content effects seemed more marked for certain types of conditional, for example, rules such as, *if the letter goes first class, it must have a 50 lire stamp on it*, or, *if you are drinking beer, you must be over 21*. These rules describe *deontic* regulations, i.e., rules about what you can and cannot do (Cheng & Holyoak, 1985; Cosmides, 1989). As such, they are not candidates for confirmation or falsification, for the simple reason that they cannot be true or false at all. Rather their claims are about how the world should be, not about how the world actually is. So, even if *all* the people drinking beer were under 21 years old, the law that they should not be drinking would still be in force (Manktelow & Over, 1987). This development highlighted the fact that conditional sentences can be used for many purposes (see also Johnson-Laird, 1986). It therefore provided one of the reasons for the current emphasis on conversational pragmatics in reasoning (see Bonnefon & Politzer, this volume). However, such content has not been used extensively in investigating conditional inference, although that situation is beginning to change (e.g., Bonnefon & Hilton, 2004; Hilton, Kemelmeier, & Bonnefon, 2005; Thompson & Mann, 1995).

So far, we have concentrated on the evaluation of conditionals rather than on their use in conditional inference. The truth conditions for the material conditional prescribe two inference rules: modus ponens (MP) and modus tollens (MT), and proscribe two fallacies: denying the antecedent (DA) and affirming the consequent (AC).

$$\text{(MP)} \quad \frac{p \Rightarrow q, p}{\therefore q} \qquad\qquad \text{(MT)} \quad \frac{p \Rightarrow q, \neg q}{\therefore \neg p} \qquad\qquad (1.1)$$

$$\text{(DA)} \quad \frac{p \Rightarrow q, \neg p}{\therefore \neg q} \qquad\qquad \text{(AC)} \quad \frac{p \Rightarrow q, q}{\therefore p}$$

These inference schemata read that if the premises above the line are true, then so is the conclusion below the line. Actually, the truth conditions for the material conditional prescribe many more inference rules than these, as we shall see, but these are the four most commonly investigated in the psychology of reasoning. So, in experiments where people are presented with these four inferences, the logical expectation is that people will endorse MP and MT but not DA and AC. Some of the first experiments on conditional inference were conducted in the early 1970s by Roberge (1970, 1971; Kodroff & Roberge, 1974), who also manipulated negations in this task (Roberge, 1971) in the same way as Evans and Lynch (1973) in the selection task and Evans (1972) in the related evaluation task.

The principal findings from these early studies was that people endorse MT a lot less than MP and that they also endorse the fallacies AC and DA, although subsequent results showed that AC was endorsed more than DA. This 'MP-MT inferential asymmetry' seems to have an immediate explanation in terms of Goodman's co-tenability account. People know that an instrumental causal relation such as, if I strike the match, it lights, relies on the other unstated co-tenable conditions, as we discussed earlier. However, we rarely take these into account when striking the match in the expectation that it will light, i.e., we are likely to *predict* that the match will light (MP), even in ignorance of the status of the co-tenable conditions. But if one were told that the match does not light, it would be perverse to conclude that the match was not struck – that is, it would typically be inappropriate to draw an inference using MT. This is because, in everyday life, we expect matches to light only if they are struck and hence when one comments that the match did not light this is only surprising and worthy of comment if an attempt to strike it has been made. Indeed, this observation leads to the interesting and almost paradoxical conclusion that, on being told that the match did not light, one can conclude that it was struck, and one can conclude this only on the basis of the rule to which the present case is itself a counterexample.

For this reason, on being told that the match did not light, we tend, instead, to suppose that perhaps the match was wet, was not struck sufficiently hard, and so on, rather than applying MT. This type of pragmatic account provides a competence model of the MP-MT asymmetry, but a competence model that is based on the nature of everyday conversational interaction, rather than purely on principles of logic.

Later we will see that the factors suggested by co-tenability accounts have been experimentally investigated (Byrne, 1989; Cummins, Lubarts, Alksnis, & Rist, 1991). However, in the psychology of reasoning, explaining these differences followed the earlier pattern found in the selection task of seeking performance level explanations. The competence theory remained standard logic, and deviations from logic were to be explained as performance errors. For example, *Mental Logic* theorists (Rips, 1994; see also O'Brien, this volume) argued that the reason for the MP-MT inferential asymmetry was that people do not possess a formal mental inference rule for MT (as in 1.1). This had the consequence that to draw an inference like MT required them to use a more long winded *reductio ad absurdum* proof in which they assume the antecedent, p, is true, and derive the conclusion, q, using MP (see 1.1); since this contradicts the categorical premise of the MT argument, *not-q*, the assumption must be false and so the conclusion *not-p* follows. Because this is a more complex inference it is completed less often which explains the empirical asymmetry. This basic form of the explanation for the asymmetries is still used in some mental logical theories (e.g., Rips, 1994).

Throughout the 1970s, there was, however, increasing debate about the way in which logic might be implemented in the mind. Were the formal, syntactic, representations postulated by mental logic the only way in which logical reasoning could be implemented? Might there be some more concrete, and perhaps to some degree imagistic, style of mental representation of the meaning of statements. Perhaps reasoning might be defined over such image-like representations rather than purely syntactic formulae. Such possible representations included Euler circles (Erickson, 1974; Guyote & Sternberg, 1981) and, most influentially, Johnson-Laird's (1983) concept of a *mental model*. In quantified syllogistic reasoning, it seemed that mental models, together with the performance limitations imposed by working memory capacity, could remarkably explain more of the empirical phenomena on reasoning (Johnson-Laird & Steedman, 1978).

Mental model theory was readily applied to conditionals (Johnson-Laird, 1983; Johnson-Laird & Byrne, 1991; see also Byrne & Johnson-Laird, this volume; Girotto & Johnson-Laird, this volume). The assumption is that people represent, probably imagistically, the truth conditions for connectives like the conditional. In doing so, a mental model only represents the conditions under which a complex proposition is true (this is called the principle of truth). From the truth function for the material conditional, there are three conditions under which the conditional, *if p then q*, is true: p is true and q is true (p, q), p is false and q is true (not-p, q), p is false and q is false (not-p, not-q). The theory appeals to working memory limitations to propose that initially people only represent the conditions under which both p and q are true, rather than representing all possibilities plus a schematic representation for an initial mental model of the conditional *if p then q* has the form:

$$[p] \quad q \qquad (1.2)$$
$$\ldots$$

The square brackets indicate that p can be paired with nothing else, except a q. Note that the ellipsis forms an important part of this initial representation of the conditional, indicating that there are other conditions that can be made explicit. Making these conditions explicit is called 'fleshing-out' in the theory. The fleshed-out mental model for a conditional is shown in 1.3:

$$p \quad q \qquad (1.3)$$
$$\neg p \quad q$$
$$\neg p \quad \neg q$$

Of course, in the actual world only one of these cases can hold. For example, suppose your friend tells you that 'if it is sunny tomorrow, I will play tennis'. Obviously, only one of these cases will obtain if she has said something true (of course if it is sunny and she doesn't play tennis, she has lied): either it's sunny and she plays tennis, or if it's not sunny she can do what she likes without being accused of lying. Consequently, the cases in 1.3 represent *possibilities* the actual occurrence, of any one of which, according to the material conditional, guarantees that your friend said something true. Both 1.2 and 1.3 warrant the MP inference because p can only be paired with q. However, only 1.3 warrants the MT inference because 1.2 provides no match to the categorical premise $\neg q$ but 1.3 does and it can only be paired to $\neg p$.

Both mental logic and mental model theories explain the fact that people endorse the DA and AC 'inferences' by allowing that people may misinterpret a conditional as a *bi-conditional*. Conditional promises are typically interpreted as bi-conditionals, e.g., *if you mow the lawn, I'll pay you £5*, is taken to entail that *if I pay you £5, you mowed the lawn*. MP and MT on the latter is equivalent to AC and DA on the former. An equivalent way of framing this would be that *if you mow the lawn, I'll pay you £5*, invites the inference to the obverse, *if you don't mow the lawn, I won't pay you £5*. Mental logicians argued that this is a pragmatic phenomenon (Grice, 1975). This is because telling participants that there was an alternative rule, e.g., *if you clear the gutters, I'll pay you £5*, overrides the tendency to endorse the DA inference. This alternative rule indicates that you may still get the £5 even if you don't mow the lawn (Rumain, Connell, & Brain, 1983). Logical rules of inference can not be overridden by the addition of further information (as we discuss in more depth later on), indicating that this must be a pragmatic effect.

If pragmatic factors are indeed the explanation for people's tendency to endorse DA and AC, mental logicians could strive to preserve a role for immutable syntactic rules in human reasoning by viewing pragmatics as a source of 'performance' error in experimental reasoning tasks. However, Byrne (1989) went on to show that even inferences such as MP could be effectively 'suppressed' by the provision of additional pragmatic world knowledge. She used rule pairs like 1.4a and 1.4b:

If it is sunny tomorrow, John will play tennis (1.4a)

If the baby sitter is on time, John will play tennis (1.4b)

Participants would then be told that it is sunny tomorrow and asked whether they would endorse the MP inference to the conclusion that John plays tennis. Participants endorsed the MP inference far less when both 1.4a and 1.4b were presented than then 1.4a was presented on its own. What such a 'suppression effect' seems to show, in Goodman's terms, is the potential failure of a co-tenable condition. The fundamental difference between these cases and the types of case that Goodman considered is that 1.4a is not a scientific law or indeed law-like at all. It is a specific conditional tied to a particular space-time location, describing a particular behavioural intention. It could be backed up by a more enduring behavioural disposition, i.e., whenever it is sunny, John plays tennis, which one may be inclined to regard as counterfactual supporting. That is, if John has this disposition, then one might be inclined to view the claim that *if it had been sunny yesterday, John would have played tennis* as true.

People's sensitivity to manipulations like Byrne's (1989) and the above example suggests that the factors discussed by Goodman with respect to scientific laws may be of more general applicability. The same factors that affect scientific laws – additional 'co-tenable' conditions and the relationship between indicative conditionals and counterfactual conditionals – may apply to conditionals more generally (Thompson & Mann, 1995). The principal philosophical issue concerns the status of scientific, i.e., causal, laws, behavioural dispositions, intentions, and the like. Where, contra Hume, we may be inclined to view causal laws as ontologically respectable, i.e., as a part of the physical world, we may perhaps be less inclined to treat behavioural dispositions and intentions in the same way. However, psychologically, with respect to how people think about the world and interpret conditional statements, this may not be a relevant distinction. Perhaps people are as inclined to project their habits of inference onto the world whether they relate to causes (as Hume suggested) or to behavioural dispositions. That is, the way people think about the world may incline them to be as realist about behavioural dispositions as they are about causes.

Initial studies in the psychology of reasoning demonstrating the impact of alternative or additional causes on human reasoning, mentioned these possible causes explicitly to participants. The manipulations in Rumain et al. (1983) and Byrne (1989) were of this kind, i.e., the information was provided in the materials as in 1.4a. and 1.4b. Cummins et al. (1991) showed importantly that, for causal conditionals, the factors such as alternative and additional information can affect conditional inference even when it is implicit. Cummins et al. (1991) pre-tested causal conditionals for possible additional or co-tenable conditions and for possible alternative causes of the effect. Cummins et al.'s (1991) methodology, and the focus on causal conditionals, has been a feature of much of the empirical work on conditionals over the last two decades and of much of the work reported in the chapters in this book. But, as we have noted, it is quite possible that insights derived from the study of causal conditionals may extend much more broadly.

With this in mind, we now return to the discussion of the logic and formal semantics of the conditional. One consequence of the suppression results may be that we need alternative normative theories of when people are reasoning correctly. There are two approaches to reconciling suppression effects with normative theories of reasoning: revisionist and non-revisionist. The latter, including mental models, by and large retain a standard logical interpretation. The essence of the non-revisionist approach is to make the representation of a conditional more complex, to include information about additional or co-tenable conditions (r) and alternative causes (s). Thus, the general form of a conditional was now (where, $\wedge$ = and; $\vee$ = or):

$$(p \vee s) \wedge r \Rightarrow q \tag{1.5}$$

MP can only be applied if one of the alternatives p or s is true (or they both are) and the co-tenable condition (r) holds.[1]

---

[1] We leave aside the complexity that there are potentially many co-tenable conditions ($r_1...r_n$) and alternative causes ($q_1...q_n$).

The main phenomenon that motivates this theoretical choice is the finding that conditional inferences are *defeasible* (Oaksford & Chater, 1991, 1993, 1995), a phenomenon that we have just encountered in the context of the suppression effects. So, thinking about your friend, 1.4a, and noting that it was sunny on the day in question (p), would incline you to infer that she played tennis (q). However, if you were then told that your friend's babysitter did not turn up ($\neg r$) you would be inclined to withdraw this inference. 1.5 will not allow this behaviour because it would not let you draw the MP inference in the first place because it is not initially known whether r is true. So 1.5 is not capable of capturing the sequence of inferences we have just described. This sequence is as follows (1.6):

$$\frac{\dfrac{p \rightarrow q, p}{\therefore q}}{\dfrac{\neg r}{\therefore \neg q(?)}} \tag{1.6}$$

This behaviour is called *defeasibility* because the subsequent information, $\neg r$, *defeats* the conclusion that appeared to follow from the previous premises, but without casting doubt upon those premises. However, according to the material interpretation of the conditional, this leads to incoherence, because of another valid rule of inference which attaches to the conditional: the law of strengthening the antecedent:

$$(\text{Strengthening}) \qquad\qquad \frac{p \Rightarrow q}{\therefore p \wedge r \Rightarrow q} \tag{1.7}$$

That is, adding information cannot overturn the conclusion of a logically valid argument. The sequence in 1.6 appears to violate this logical law. Consequently, this seemingly innocuous chain of inferences cannot be captured by the material conditional.

Logic-based theories like mental models address these problems by proposing that people's mental representations in working memory are modulated by semantic and pragmatic information. However, according to revisionist theorists (Ali, Schlottman, Shaw Chater, & Oaksford, this volume; Bonnefon & Politzer, this volume; Oaksford & Chater, this volume; Pfeifer & Kleiter, this volume) without a theory of how such modulation *should* affect inference, we simply don't know if the resulting behaviour is correct.

The phenomenon of 'suppression effects' seems to show how Goodman's philosophical observations about co-tenable conditions have direct parallels in the inferential behaviour of participants in causal conditional reasoning tasks. The main problem for a co-tenability account was the lack of a formal normative theory of inference like standard logic to provide an evaluative theory by which to judge people's inferential performance as errorful or not (although see Kvart, 1985). More generally, problems like the apparent failure of strengthening the antecedent and other inference rules that attach to the material conditional suggest that a different account is required (Cohen, 1981). In logic and formal semantics, it is generally agreed that serious attempts to account for the meaning of the conditional of natural language, as opposed to the conditional of mathematics, did not really start until about 40 years ago with the Lewis-Stalnaker possible world semantics (Lewis, 1973; Nute, 1984; Stalnaker, 1968).

In briefly outlining this formal semantic theory, we will not concentrate too much on the formal detail but rather on what Haack (1978) refers to as the 'depraved' semantics, i.e., the semantic intuitions that motivate the formal theory. With respect to a possible worlds semantic theory, the most relevant interpretation psychologically is to view possible worlds as a consistent state of knowledge, a standpoint championed by Stalnaker (1984). As we will see, Stalnaker's 'conceptualist' interpretation of possible worlds provides an interesting connection between counterfactuals and indicative conditionals.

The intuition behind most contemporary accounts of the conditional come from attempting to formalize Ramsey's (1990, originally 1931) famous test:

> 'If two people are arguing 'if A will C' and are both in doubt as to A, they are adding A hypothetically to their stock of knowledge and arguing on that basis about C…We can say that they are fixing their degrees of belief in C given A'.
>
> (Ramsey, 1929: p. 143)

For Stalnaker, the Ramsey test amounts to the claim that in assessing a conditional, people first add the antecedent hypothetically to their current set of beliefs. They then make minimal adjustments to accommodate the new belief. They then consider whether the consequent of the conditional is true in their revised set of beliefs. To idealise, before adding the consequent, they will have a belief about every matter of fact and after adding the antecedent they will have a revised set of beliefs about every matter of fact. These epistemically ideal states are what Stalnaker refers to as 'possible worlds'. In the statement of the Ramsey test, it is explicit that the truth or falsity of the antecedent in the actual world is unknown.

There are some aspects of the formal theory that are central to understanding the conceptualist interpretation offered by Stalnaker (1984). In possible worlds semantics, the proposition expressed by a sentence is the subset of possible worlds in which the sentence is true. The core of the theory as it applies to the conditional is the *selection function*. If we take a conditional, *if p then q*, the selection function, s, takes the set of worlds in which the antecedent, p, is true, which is written $[p]$, as one argument, and the actual world, α, as another argument, $s([p], \alpha)$, and it returns the subset of $[p]$ which is most similar to α. If this subset is non-empty and is included in the set of possible worlds in which the consequent is true, $[q]$, then the conditional is true. For example, suppose someone asserts that:

> *If it's sunny at Wimbledon today, John will be playing tennis.* (1.8)

Being, say, in Bloomsbury, we don't know whether it's sunny in Wimbledon or not. Nonetheless, our interpretation of the antecedent is the set of all possible worlds in which it is sunny in Wimbledon. The selection function then picks the subset of these worlds that are most similar to the actual world. If in all of these worlds John is also playing tennis, then the original conditional will be regarded as true.

The factors that affect the selection function depend on the actual world. So, for example, a possible world in which it is sunny at Bloomsbury but there is a blizzard at Wimbledon is less like the actual world than one where it is sunny at both locations due to their physical proximity. This could be expressed as another conditional,

> *If it's sunny in Bloomsbury, then it's sunny in Wimbledon.* (1.9)

In particular, the *specific* conditional (1.8) about what John does today may be underwritten by the general claim that:

> *If it is sunny at Wimbledon, John plays tennis* (1.10)

1.10 describes one of John's enduring behavioural dispositions. Stalnaker refers to 1.9 and 1.10 as 'open' indicative conditionals (where the truth or falsity of the antecedent may be unknown), which describe people's *methodological policies* to change their beliefs. The selection function is an abstract characterization of people's dispositions to alter their beliefs in response to new information. It is these dispositions or methodological policies that determine how we alter our beliefs when the antecedent is hypothetically added as in the Ramsey test.

Central to Stalnaker's account is the relation between open indicative conditionals like 1.9 and 1.10 and counterfactual conditionals, like,

> *If it had been sunny at Wimbledon today, John would have played tennis.* (1.11)

Our methodological policy in 1.10 gives us good grounds to believe 1.11 and if we do so, it must be because we believe that 1.10 is a real behavioural disposition of John's. The relationship between 1.10 and 1.8 is simply that of a general rule to an instance respectively, so if 1.10 is one of our methodological policies to change our beliefs then we are bound to believe 1.8. As Stalnaker points out, our inclinations to believe specific claims like 1.8 and 1.11 depend not only on our methodological policies to change our beliefs (1.9 and 1.10) but also on our other factual knowledge. For example, if we know that *John has a broken leg* then we would not infer 1.11 based on 1.10. This behaviour is directly related to the fact that strengthening the antecedent is not valid in Stalnaker's semantic theory. Before the addition of the extra information that John had a broken leg, the subset of worlds closest to the actual world in which it is sunny at Wimbledon, $s([\text{sunny at Wimbledon}], \alpha)$, will be included in the set of worlds where John plays tennis, [John plays tennis]. However, after this information about John's injury becomes known, the subset of worlds closest to the actual world in which it is sunny at Wimbledon *and* John has a broken leg, $s([\text{sunny at Wimbledon \& John has a broken leg}], \alpha)$, will not be included in the set of worlds where John plays tennis, [John plays tennis]. Of course, this depends on our further use of the information, that if your leg is broken, then you can't play tennis. The fact that strengthening is not valid in this semantic theory reflects the empirical data we have reviewed on suppression effects.

The possible worlds semantics for the conditional has never had a great direct influence on the psychology of reasoning (although, Oaksford [1989] discussed this theory at length, and more recently Evans and Over [2004] have discussed its consequences). Given that in the areas of logic and formal semantics, the emergence of these theories marked the first real attempts to account for the meaning of natural language conditionals (see, for example, Nute, 1984), this is perhaps surprising. One possible explanation is provided by the relatively swift dismissal of the psychological relevance of possible worlds semantics in Johnson-Laird's (1983, pp. 58-59) groundbreaking book, *Mental Models*:

> '" Possible worlds"...are highly abstract, and since any proposition is either true or false in a given possible world, each possible world goes far beyond what any individual can comprehend...The real problem, however, is that universes of possible worlds are metaphysical luxuries that have nothing to do with the way in which people ordinarily understand conditionals'.

So given that each possible world is a specification of the truth or falsity of every possible matter of fact, it might seem that such astonishingly rich representations could not possibly fit 'inside the head'.

Stalnaker's (1984) conceptualist interpretation may not be completely devoid of psychological relevance, however. Such an interpretation proposes that the selection function is an abstraction from the collection of open conditional sentences that describe an individual's world knowledge and which constrain the way in which they alter their beliefs in response to new information. Thus, these methodological policies or habits of inference constrain the possibilities we can consider. For example, consider the methodological policies that support 1.4a and 1.4b, i.e., 1.12a and 1.12b respectively:

> *If it is sunny, John plays tennis* (1.12a)
>
> *If the baby sitter is on time, John plays tennis* (1.12b)

Suppose John's friend A does not know that John's playing tennis depends on his baby sitting arrangements (1.12b is not one of A's methodological policies). She is likely to evaluate the counterfactual *if it had been sunny yesterday, John would have played tennis* as true. Friend B, on the other hand, knows of 1.12a and of John's reliance on the baby sitter (1.12b) and moreover saw the baby sitter at the beach yesterday when John usually plays tennis. Consequently, B won't evaluate the counterfactual as true. Moreover, Friend C, who knows about the baby sitter, also knows that he is unreliable, often failing to turn up without warning. Consequently, C will only endorse the counterfactual as *probable* depending on their estimate of how likely the baby sitter is to turn up.

So once we move away from epistemically ideal states, different epistemic agents, with different sets of methodological policies and other factual knowledge will evaluate the same counterfactual differently. That is, *prior knowledge matters* in the evaluation of conditionals. Moreover, people's prior knowledge may not incline them to endorse a counterfactual as true but only as probable. Such considerations also apply equally to indicative conditionals like 1.4a and 1.12a. We may endorse 1.4a because we possess the methodological policy in 1.12a. So when we add the antecedent, *it is sunny tomorrow*, to our set of beliefs, 1.12a will generate a new belief state in which the consequent of 1.4a is true. Alternatively, of course, we may believe it to be true because John made a conditional promise to this effect and we know John is trustworthy. Or if we believe that John is untrustworthy or just generally unreliable, we may only assign a greater that chance probability to John playing tennis in our revised set of beliefs and hence to the conditional. Of course, we would evaluate an assertion of 1.12a as true if we also possess it as one of our methodological policies. If we did not, then it can still be assessed by adding its antecedent to our stock of beliefs and making adjustments based on our other methodological polices and factual knowledge: perhaps we know John is a keen tennis player and that his tennis club has no indoor courts and so this sounds like a perfectly reasonable methodological policy for John to possess. Alternatively, we may have accumulated enumerative evidence for this proposition, i.e., recollections of many instances of John playing tennis on sunny days.

Consequently, the intuitive motivation for possible worlds semantics (about truth and falsity) makes direct appeal to people's knowledge states. From a psychological point of view, this is probably where we should be looking to find an account of how people, who possess different knowledge, evaluate and draw inferences from conditionals. This is a point recently emphasised by Rescher (2007, Preface) who proposes a 'treatment of conditionals based on epistemological principles rather than upon semantical principles...[which] makes it easier to understand how conditionals actually function in our thought and discourse'. Rescher attributes this approach to Ramsey's earlier proposal (see above on the Ramsey Test) and makes a second intriguing suggestion, that to understand conditionals requires moving, 'into the realm claimed by theorists in artificial intelligence as they try to simulate our actual information-processing practices' (Rescher, 2007, Cover).

Rescher's two key points regarding an epistemological approach and regarding the relevance of AI models have been anticipated in the psychology of reasoning. For example,

> Like most everyday problems that call for reasoning, the explicit premises leave most of the relevant information unstated. Indeed, *the real business of reasoning in these cases is to determine the relevant factors and possibilities, and it therefore depends on knowledge of the specific domain.* Hence the construction of putative counterexamples calls for an active exercise of memory and interpretation rather than formal derivation of one expression from others.
>
> (Johnson-Laird, 1986:45).

Moreover, the consequences of taking AI knowledge representation seriously as potential models of human reasoning have been discussed in the literature (Oaksford & Chater, 1991, 1993, 1998, 2007) and empirical investigations of the influence of world knowledge on human inference have become very prominent in conditional reasoning research (e.g., Cummins, 1995; Cummins et al., 1991; De Neys, Schaeken, & d'Ydewalle, 2003; Geiger & Oberauer, 2007; Markovits & Quinn, 2002; Schroyens, Schaeken, Fias, & d'Ydewalle, 2000; Simoneau & Markovits, 2003).

As we now argue, there are some interesting parallels between the issues that arise in AI knowledge representation and the focus of much recent empirical research. As we have discussed, the dependence of conditional reasoning on prior knowledge is most evident in the phenomenon of defeasibility. What we know will affect our willingness to draw inferences and our willingness to defeat conclusions in the light of new information. So in possession of my methodological policy 1.12a, on learning that it is a sunny day today, I will likely infer that John will play tennis today. Within the AI approach to knowledge based reasoning proposed by Reiter (1985), reaching this conclusion requires a further step. It must also be shown that it cannot be proved from what you know that John will not play tennis (see Oaksford & Chater, 1991). That is, my methodological policy 1.12a, has an additional conjunct in the antecedent:

If it is sunny AND you can't prove ¬(John plays tennis), John plays tennis   (1.12a')

For example, nothing you know currently leads you to believe that John's baby sitter is not going to turn up today. In part, this inference has the form of a double negation inference, i.e., the conclusion that John will play tennis is licensed by the fact that it is a sunny day and that it can't be proved from what you know that ¬(John will play tennis). The second conjunct seems to allow the conclusion that John will play tennis and so seems equivalent to ¬¬(John will play tennis), which means John will play tennis by double negation. However, just because you cannot prove *x* from what you know does not mean that *x* is false (and so John will play tennis). The expression 'it can't be proved from what you know' is called "negation as failure", or constructive negation, and it relies on 'closed world reasoning', i.e., the assumption that, unless a proof to the contrary can be found, all that is relevant to the inference is assumed to be known (Harper, 2005; see also Kowalski, this volume; Stenning & Van Lambalgen, this volume).

This argument has the form of the classical reasoning fallacy, the *argument from ignorance*, for example, 'You cannot prove that ghosts do not exist, therefore ghosts exist'. Such an argument is fallacious because it conflates matters of *fact* with matters of *knowledge*: just because you do not *know* that *not-p*, does not mean you can infer that *p* is *true*. In the psychology of reasoning, there have been proposals similar to Reiter's (1985). For example, the idea that people conduct a *validating search* (Schroyens, Schaeken, Fias, & d'Ydewalle, 2000) of long term memory for a counterexample. Suppose that with the methodological policy 1.12a, you learn that it is sunny. You search your long term memory, i.e., the repository of your beliefs about the world, and come up with the memory that you saw John's baby sitter at the beach that day. You have therefore constructed a putative counterexample, where it is sunny but John does not play tennis. On this view if your validating search was unsuccessful you should endorse the conclusion, i.e., exactly the same recommendation as provided by Reiter's (1985) default logic. While this is a variety of inference that Rescher (2007) calls 'doxastic implication', it is not a logical inference, there is no transfer of truth from the premises to the conclusion, at least not absolute truth as required in standard logic. Not being able to recall a good reason for John not playing tennis does not mean that he does play tennis even though it is a sunny day. This does not, of course, mean that you, personally, would be unjustified in acting on the plausible hypothesis that John will play tennis if, for example, you were trying to track him down.

Much recent empirical research in the psychology of reasoning has focussed on the processes involved in this form of doxastic inference. That is, it has investigated the way in which people's prior beliefs affect reasoning. The original work on causal reasoning, in which co-tenable conditions and alternative causes were manipulated, implicitly investigated this type of inference

(Cummins et al., 1991; Cummins, 1995). Failure of a co-tenable condition for *if p then q* just is a situation in which *p* may be true but *q* is false, i.e., a counterexample. There is now a body of work showing that the efficiency of retrieval of co-tenable or 'disabling' conditions directly affects inference (De Neys et al., 2003; Markovits & Quinn, 2002). There is also evidence showing that the frequency of counterexamples matters more in suppressing inferences than the range of different types of counterexamples (Geiger & Oberauer, 2007). Moreover, there is evidence that people can inhibit the process of retrieving counterexamples (Simoneau & Markovits, 2003; De Neys, Vartanian, & Goel, 2008) when knowledge and logic conflict, in order to arrive at the responses that look more 'logical'.

This empirical work continues to be described in the psychology of reasoning in terms of standard logic. The consequences of treating doxastic inference, as governed by standard logic, motivates some of the alternative views discussed in this book. Suppose you are assessing 1.4 by retrieving 1.12 from world knowledge but this time you recall seeing John's babysitter at the beach. Note that 1.12 is not flagged as a default rule by any linguistic marker, but is just a standard, implicitly universally quantified conditional. The additional knowledge about the baby sitter provides a counterexample not only for 1.4 but also for 1.12. Consequently, retaining a purely logical concept of the inferential behaviour involved would entail rejecting not only 1.4 as false, but also 1.12 which would have to be excised from long term memory for world knowledge. Consequently, this useful methodological policy would no longer be available to draw inferences, indicative and counterfactual alike, about the world. In consequence, allowing standard logic to govern the management of information in LTM may be undesirable in the light of the failure of strengthening the antecedent for the conditionals that make up everyday world knowledge.

Another approach to the problems of defeasible inference has more recently become popular in the psychology of reasoning. Paralleling the developments we have discussed in logic and in the psychology of reasoning, *probabilistic* approaches have been proposed (for discussion of the wider application of probabilistic ideas across cognitive science see, for example, Chater & Oaksford, 2008; Chater, Tenenbaum, & Yuille, 2006). From the probabilistic perspective, defeasability should be expected to be the norm in human reasoning, on the grounds that almost all reasoning involves making plausible, but not certain, conjectures on the basis of partial information. Such conjectures will always be vulnerable to the possibility of later additional evidence which may undermine them (for discussion see, e.g., Oaksford & Chater, 1998, 2007).

Indeed, in logic and formal semantics a probabilistic perspective on the Ramsey test has a fairly long history, this important approach being developed by Adams (1968, 1975, 1998) at the same time as the creation of the Lewis-Stalnaker possible worlds semantics (Lewis, 1973; Stalnaker, 1968, 1984). The essential idea behind the *Adams Conditional* is the identification of the probability of a conditional $P(if p then q)$ with the conditional probability, $P(q|p)$. The resulting identity, $P(if p then q) = P(q|p)$, is simply called 'the Equation' (Edgington, 1995). On a subjective interpretation of probability, the conditional probability is then defined by the Ramsey test. As Bennett (2003, p. 53) says:

> 'The best definition we have [of conditional probability] is the one provided by the Ramsey test: your conditional probability for *q* given *p* is the probability for *q* that results from adding $P(p) = 1$ to your belief system and conservatively adjusting to make room for it'.

This account immediately contrasts with the probability of a conditional provided by standard logic for which $P(if p then q) = P(\neg p) + P(p, q)$. The main contrast here is that on the conditional probability view the probability of a conditional does not depend on the probability of *q* when *p* is not present. In a critical set of experiments Evans and Over and their colleagues (Evans, Handley, & Over, 2003; Over, Hadjichristidis, Evans, Sloman, & Handley, 2007) confirmed that people appear to interpret the probability of a conditional as the conditional probability and not as recommended by the material conditional, a result also found by Oberauer and colleagues (Oberauer, Weidenfeld, & Fishcer, 2007; Oberauer & Wilhelm, 2003).

These experimental findings, though, were not on conditional inference directly; rather, people were asked to estimate the probability of the antecedent, consequent, and the full conditional, with the goal of relating to these to Adams' account of the Equation. Formally, turning the adoption of the Equation into a theory of inference has pursued several routes and many are represented in this book (Oaksford & Chater, this volume; Pfeifer & Kleiter, this volume). One route is to define a notion of probabilistic validity along the lines of logical validity. Probabilistic validity or 'p-validity' is more economically formulated using the concept of *uncertainty*. The uncertainty of a proposition p, $U(p)$, is simply $1 - P(p)$ (Adams, 1975). Adams observed that, '*in a classically valid argument the uncertainty of the conclusion cannot exceed the sum of the uncertainties of the premises*' (Bennett, 2003, p. 131). That is,

$$\text{If } p_1 \ldots p_n \text{ entails } q, \text{ then } U(q) \le \sum_{i=1}^{n} U(p_i) \tag{1.13}$$

An argument fulfilling this condition, Adams (1975) calls p-valid. Armed with the concept of p-validity, it was possible to show that many of paradoxes that result from applying the material conditional of mathematics to everyday conditionals disappear. For example, the material conditional licenses the inference from *the moon is not made of cheese* to the conclusion that *if the moon is made of cheese, then the sea is red*. This inference is clearly not p-valid because if the premise is true, i.e., $U(\neg p) = 0$, then $P(p) = 0$ and hence the probability of the conclusion, $P(q|p)$, is undefined. *Strengthening the antecedent* is also not a p-valid inference. Suppose, for example, that I hear that Mary has lost her watch during a boat trip on Loch Ness. I may fear that it is lost in the icy depths, and, with high probability, will never be seen again. Hearing a faint ticking noise coming from the bottom of the boat, however, may cause me to radically revise this gloomy conclusion; finding that the ticking noise is actually coming from some other source may lead to a further revision of belief, of course, and this process may continue indefinitely. P-validity is nonetheless not defeasible.

However, Adams (1998) also outlined a dynamic view of conditional inference as belief revision by conditionalisation which is defeasible. This dynamic view of probabilistic conditional inference was also adopted in the psychology of reasoning by Oaksford, Chater, and Larkin (2000; see Oaksford & Chater, 2007). For example, one's prior degree of belief in 1.4, a specific conditional will be based on the conditional probability one assigns to the methodological policy 1.12, i.e., $P_0(John$ $plays\ tennis|it\ is\ sunny)$. In an MP inference, one is given new information in the categorical premise, i.e., $P_1(it\ is\ sunny) = 1$. By Bayesian conditionalisation, the new probability of the conclusion, $P_1(John\ plays\ tennis)$, will be the prior conditional probability, $P_0(John\ plays\ tennis|it\ is\ sunny)$.

This dynamic view of conditional inference cannot be extended directly to MT and the fallacies (DA and AC) because the premises do not provide the relevant conditional probability for the categorical premise to conditionalize on, e.g., $P_0(\neg p|\neg q)$ for MT. However, just knowing that $P_0(John\ plays\ tennis|it\ is\ sunny) = a$ and that $P_1(John\ does\ not\ play\ tennis) = b$ does permit a probability interval for $P_1(it\ is\ not\ a\ sunny\ day)$ to be deduced solely in terms of a and b, i.e., solely in terms of the information given in the premises (Wagner, 2004).[2] Pfeifer and Kleiter (this volume)

---

[2] This depends on allowing the unknown probability required to define a complete probability model (2 by 2 contingency table) to vary between 0 and 1.

have developed this idea in their *mental probability logic*. Constructing probability intervals assumes we do not know $P_0(it\ is\ not\ a\ sunny\ day)$ or $P_0(John\ plays\ tennis)$. Oaksford et al. (2000) assumed that people will also have background beliefs about these probabilities that they can use to infer point values for the posterior probabilities. This involves using $P_0(p|q)$, $P_0(p)$, and $P_0(q)$, to calculate values for, for example, $P_0(\neg p|\neg q)$ on which the categorical premise can conditionalize in a probabilistic version of MT (see Liu, this volume; Oaksford & Chater, this volume; Over, Evans, & Elqayam, this volume).

These recently emergent probabilistic approaches seem to be in direct opposition to previous logic-based accounts. If so, then their emergence seems to contradict the integrative approach that we argued might emerge from this book. And it does seem that psychological theories of conditional inference based on logic or probability theory are typically compared, as if they are necessarily in opposition (e.g., Oberauer, 2006). However, one way of understanding probability theory is as an enrichment of conventional logic to provide an *inductive* logic, a system of logic that extends deduction to less-than-certain inferences (Hawthorn, 2008). To a good approximation, modern inductive logic just *is* Bayesian probability (Earman, 1992), with some additional discussion of the measure of the confirmation relation (see Chater, Oaksford, Hahn, & Heit, 2009). Since Carnap (1950), this Bayesian inductive logic *includes* classical logic – if a statement has a probability of 1, then any logical consequence of that statement also has a probability of 1. Similarly, if a statement has an implication with a probability of 0, then that statement has a probability of 0. Note, however, that probability theory does not readily represent the *internal* structure of propositions, but rather focusses on the influential relationships *between* propositions. Thus, standard probabilistic methods contain no theory of key logical and representational notions such as quantification and modality. Indeed, the methods of modern logic appeared to be indispensable in understanding how to represent the internal structure of complex propositions, which may make claims about possibility, necessity, desirability, time, the existence of objects and properties of many types, and many more. It is in understanding *representation* that the centrality of logic to the project of cognitive science is most evident.

Proponents of a Bayesian inductive perspective argue that logical methods need to be supplemented with probabilistic notions not because classic logic is incorrect, but because they contend that outside of mathematics, it rarely, if ever, applies to real human inference and arguments (Oaksford & Chater, 2009; Oaksford & Hahn, 2007). That is, they view the inferential relations between propositions as relentlessly uncertain (Jeffrey, 1967). One could therefore argue, that amongst those researchers who see a role for normative theories, all are agreed that logic is important, the question is only which aspect of inductive logic, including classical logic, better captures human thought on the tasks people confront in everyday life.

The subtitle of this volume – *and Probability Logic in Human Thinking* – makes the assumption that normative theories do indeed have a role in the exercise of constructing descriptively accurate psychological theories of conditional reasoning. However, one conclusion of an investigation into the role of logic and probability in human thinking could be that they play little or no role. Indeed, recently some authors have argued that, in principle, neither logic, nor probability, nor any normative theory forms a proper part of a psychological theory of human reasoning (Schroyens, 2009; Evans, 2009).

These radical arguments merit serious consideration, although detailed treatment is unfortunately beyond the scope of an introductory chapter. Nonetheless, it is worth considering two issues that bear on this question. The first concerns the evolution of reasoning processes. As for most adaptations, it is safe to assume that reasoning has emerged in those organisms capable of it because it confers an adaptive advantage, i.e., it leads to greater success. Even if people achieve their reasoning competence via heuristics adapted to our particular ecological niche, assessing how successful they are will entail assessing how closely these heuristics approximate a normatively appropriate solution (Martignon & Blackmond-Laskey, 1999). Consequently, normative theories still play pretty much the role they have always done in cognitive theory: defining the computational level theory of the task the cognitive system is trying to perform.

The second issue is more specific: the possibility that treating normative theories as relevant to theory choice in the psychology of reasoning commits a reasoning fallacy: Moore's *naturalistic fallacy* (Moore, 1993/1903). While the irony of this argument in itself may be compelling to the postmodern mind, we don't believe the fallacy is actually committed. Moore warned against the error of inferring a norm of behaviour or reasoning from a matter of mere fact, i.e., inferring an *ought* from an *is*. In particular, any proposal to prefer one normative theory as a better descriptive account of human reasoning than another is accused of this fallacy because that decision is based on empirical evidence about what *is* the case. However, it is argued, theoreticians then conclude that the theory thereby selected governs how people *ought* to reason on the experimental tasks used in evidence.

Yet this is not what the relevant theoreticians conclude. For example, when proposing an alternative Bayesian account of hypothesis testing in inductive confirmation, Oaksford and Chater (1996) argued that, 'the purpose of rational analysis is to characterize the task participants *think* they have been assigned'. So the empirical question is the nature of the reasoning task, *from the point of view of the experimental participant.* Yes, in the selection task, if participants are implicitly viewing their goal as to find as much information as possible about whether a conditional rule is true, or whether on the other hand there is no connection between the information on each side of the card, then it may reasonably be argued that participants *should* use the Bayesian theory of optimal data selection (or employ heuristics that approximate this theory in their normal environment). That is, the normative force behind such claims is itself purely conditional. That is, *if* your goal is X, *then* you *should* reason according to normative theory Y, or use heuristics that well approximate Y in our ecological niche, because this will allow you to succeed. In the philosophical literature, exactly the same observation has been made by Papineau (2003) who argues that such conditional claims are perfectly naturalistically respectable. In sum, the assumption of this book's subtitle, which implies that much recent work in the psychology of conditional reasoning is an extended dialogue on the roles of logic and probability, is untouched by the naturalistic fallacy. Moreover, if, as we have also just considered, logic and probability have complementary and compatible roles in helping to explain human reasoning, then there may be no need to decide between them on empirical grounds: both may be needed to fully understand human reasoning, normatively and psychologically.

Indeed, such a view permits us to resolve a problem that has nagged us both for almost 25 years. This is what we will call here the problem of ter Meulen's Mule, which at one time we took to refute a probabilistic view of defeasible reasoning (Oaksford & Chater, 1991). In the 1986 volume, *On Conditionals*, Alice ter Meulen (1986) introduced the problem of encountering a complaisant donkey when you have the background belief that *all donkeys are stubborn* (or *if x is a donkey, x is stubborn*). The probabilistic view seems to recommend that you make a small downward adjustment in your conditional probability,[3] $P(x = \text{stubborn}|x = \text{donkey})$, and then you should proceed on your way. We argued that this response must be wrong because surely one would want to inquire into why this particular donkey was complaisant? And if, for example, you discovered it was circus-trained, you would want to record this information in a suitable representational scheme that would allow you to make the right predictions when, say, encountering donkeys the next time you are at the circus. In logic, this information would be embodied structurally as in (1.5), i.e., the antecedent is conjoined with co-tenable conditions (i.e., *if x is a donkey and x is not*

---

[3] We assume all the N donkeys you have observed were stubborn and that N is reasonably high.

circus-trained, x is stubborn), which leads to the problems discussed earlier. But if the relationships defined over this structure are probabilistic then these problems may not arise (see Oaksford & Chater, this volume). The problem with a pure logical analysis is that *all* possible co-tenable conditions would have to be listed. But an individual epistemic agent, such as a person, will never be able to discover what these are in their lifetime: they are in the so-called 'finitary predicament' (Cherniak, 1981, 1986). This inescapable ignorance manifests itself as the need to represent most of these relationships probabilistically. That is, our default hierarchies are likely to be shallow *and* probabilistic (see Oaksford & Chater, this volume) rather than deep and logical (see also Holland, Holyoak, Nisbett, & Thagard, 1986).[4]

In this introductory section, we have sought to show how the major theories of the conditional in logic and formal semantics bear on the psychology of reasoning. We have shown that many of the issues that have arisen in one area are reflected in the other. For example, the importance of content, rather than mere logical form, to inductive confirmation; the importance of prior beliefs to the interpretation of conditionals; and the consequent deviations from standard logic captured in the Stalnaker-Lewis and the Adams conditionals and observed in the lab, especially with respect to defeasibility. In particular, the conceptualist interpretation of the Stalnaker-Lewis conditional (Stalnaker, 1984) is relevant to the psychology of reasoning when we move away from epistemically ideal states to considering the actual cognitive repertoire of methodological policies and world knowledge that a person is likely to possess. The Adams conditional reminds us that the ways this cognitive repertoire bears on our interpretation of conditionals is very often probabilistic. This is useful because managing world knowledge in LTM – particularly the conditional beliefs that underpin our methodological policies – using standard logical inference would excise most useful knowledge in the light of the problem of defeasibility.

Cognition and conditionals: The structure of the book

Imposing an organization on the papers in a volume such as this is bound to have some Procrustean outcomes: inevitably, some chapters will fit better than others. The chapters in this volume represent what are frequently argued to be competing theoretical positions. From our perspective, in many cases, these accounts are addressing different aspects of the cognitive system – and how cognitive systems interact with each other, i.e., in verbal communication – that must ultimately underpin conditional inference. Consequently, we have fought the temptation to simply list the chapters under the headings corresponding to the current theoretical commitments of the authors, e.g., mental logic, mental models, dual process theories, or probabilistic approaches. This is because most of these theories are radically incomplete: none comes close to specifying everything about the cognitive system that is required to explain the current data we have on conditional inference, both experimental and linguistic. Moreover, as the papers themselves reveal, a far more sophisticated and integrated view of the cognitive architecture of reasoning is beginning to emerge. It therefore seems more fruitful to classify chapters under headings corresponding to those aspects of the cognitive system primarily addressed in each chapter. As we introduce each chapter below, we will also provide comments on how logic and probability fit into the arguments presented.

---

[4] We think this view is obscured by Fodor's (1983) arguments about the isotropy of central cognition, which can be thought of as the claim that such hierarchies *can* be extended at will. For example, all donkeys are stubborn unless drugged, hypnotized, or else had a conversation with a mule whisperer, etc. That we appear able to extend these hierarchies at will does not mean that we permanently record them. Although, we agree that this leaves the problem of how our central cognitive system *can* extend these hierarchies at will.

The nature of the cognitive system required for conditional inference must conform to general theories of cognitive architecture. At the most general level there is the putative distinction between working memory (WM) and long term memory (LTM). That is the distinction between the workspace in which current incoming information is processed (WM) and the repository of world knowledge (LTM) that enables us to do interesting things with this incoming information, like draw inferences. Even if one were the most committed proponent of a logic-based approach, the logical rules used in inference would need to be stored in LTM and accessed when needed in WM.[5] Theoretical positions in the psychology of reasoning typically concentrate on WM or LTM processes, even if they suggest that both are needed. For example, mental logic and mental models theory concentrate primarily on the nature of the representations of logical terms (or the inferential schemata that attach to them) in WM and the processes that operate over them to draw inferences. In contrast, probabilistic approaches have been accused of focussing largely on LTM processes and ignoring WM processes (a conclusion explicitly endorsed in, for example, Oaksford and Chater [2003]). Dual process theories, perhaps more realistically, see a role for both WM and LTM processes, which they refer to as System 2 and System 1 processes respectively (Stanovich & West, 2000; Evans & Over, 2004). Proponents of these theories (Verschueren & Schaeken, this volume; Thompson, this volume; Evans, Over, & Elqayam, this volume) argue that the nature of the processes carried out in these two systems may be very different. Moreover, their interaction explains the typical patterns of performance (Oberauer, 2006), although task instructions can focus on one system more than another.

Dual process theorists are almost by definition proposing an *integrative* approach to human reasoning, one that appeals to both WM and LTM processes. However, this is an algorithmic level distinction. As we just argued for logic, WM and LTM might be involved even if both are playing a role in computing only one function, e.g., logical inference. Kowalski (this volume) suggests that logic programming can provide the algorithmic framework that plays both roles and which can handle defeasibility and probabilities (this approach is directly related to Stenning & van Lambalgen's [this volume] appeal to non-monotonic logic and closed world reasoning). Whether people are attempting to reason logically or probabilistically – using both or only one of WM or LTM – is a computational level distinction. Most dual process theories invoke the distinction between WM and LTM because they view the functions of each to be fundamentally different. Crudely, WM processes perform logical (or analytic) functions and LTM processes perform probabilistic (or associative, or perhaps heuristic) functions. Thus, they are dualist at both levels of description. However, some dual process theorists (e.g., see Over, Evans, & Elqayam, this volume), argue that analytic processes in WM are best characterised by probability logic (Adams, 1998). This opens the possibility that both WM and LTM processes are probabilistic (see Oaksford & Chater, in press). The very idea of a 'probability logic' suggests that integrative approaches are possible that integrate logic and probability directly at the computational level (see Pfeifer & Kleiter, this volume). Moreover, this leads to the further possibility that there may be other formalisms that can achieve a similar integration, which might be psychologically relevant (see Politzer & Bonnefon, this volume) and which has been explored in the literature on artificial intelligence (e.g., Pollock, 2001; see also Hahn & Oaksford, 2007).

---

5 It is important not to conflate the processes that control what happens in WM and which accesses LTM when needed with logic. As Kowalski (1979) reminds us, a programme = logic + control, thus logic and control processes are quite different things, e.g, we expect logical statements to have a declarative semantics in a way that we don't expect this for control processes.

In the light of these theoretical distinctions, we have organized this book into those chapters that predominantly deal with WM processes (Section 1), those that deal predominantly with LTM processes (Section 2), and those that are explicitly proposing an integrative approach (Section 3) either at the algorithmic level, the computational level, or both. Sections 1 and 2 are further subdivided in to those chapters that have logic or probability as their primary focus. We close the book with an epilogue considering some of the questions left open by the contributions to this volume.

Section one – *Working memory: Function, representation and process* – begins with four chapters whose primary focus is on logical thinking. In Chapter 2, *The mental logic theory of conditional propositions*, one the world's leading advocates of the mental logic approach, David O'Brien, and his colleague, Andrea Manfrinati, make the case for the existence of various formal syntactic inference schemata (like 1.1 above) in the human cognitive system. These inferential schemata must be applied to incoming verbal information in WM to draw conditional inferences. O'Brien and Manfrinati point out that our evolved mental logic is not the same as standard textbook logic in which *ex falso quodlibet* holds, i.e., anything follows from a contradiction. In mental logic, reaching a contradiction just indicates something has gone wrong in the chain of reasoning and that therefore a premise needs to be rejected, as in *reductio ad absurdum* reasoning. Thus, the response to the problem of defeasiblity is that, e.g., on reaching a contradiction by having inferred *Tweety can fly* and then discovering that *Tweety is an Ostrich* one must reject the original conditional, *birds fly* (*if x is a bird, then x flies*). O'Brien and Manfrinati also observe that logical inferences are always made in the context of other pragmatic inferences. However, they do not go on to outline the nature of the representations and processes that make up this pragmatic component which must also influence performance especially with everyday real world content.[6] They outline the evidential support for the existence of inferential schemata and then examine the ability of other accounts of conditional reasoning to explain these results and find them wanting.

In Chapter 3, *Conditionals and possibilities*, Ruth Byrne and Phil Johnson-Laird, the creators and leading proponents of mental model theory, outline how this theory relates to the conditional. As we have seen, they observe that the core of the theory is the representation in WM of the possibilities ruled in and ruled out by the statement of a conditional. Bryne and Johnson-Laird specifically address the representation of counterfactual conditionals using exactly the same mechanism, and discuss the relationship between these conditionals and the indicative conditional. The important topic of semantic and pragmatic modulation is also introduced. As we have suggested by placing this chapter in this section on working memory processes, the discussion focusses on how modulation leads to the representation of one of ten possible mental models in WM. They do not discuss the nature of the representations and processes in LTM that support semantic/pragmatic modulation. They conclude with a set of ten principle phenomena that they argue must be accounted for by any complete theory of the conditional.

In Chapter 4, *Logic and/in psychology: The paradoxes of material implication and psychologism in the cognitive science of human reasoning*, Walter Schroyens addresses recent critiques of the mental models theory because of its apparent endorsement of the paradoxes of material implication as valid inferences. Schroyens suggests that these critiques are guilty of *psychologism*, the claim that logic is descriptive of the laws of thought. He argues that this fallacious interpretation

---

6 'Pragmatics' takes on two distinct meanings in the psychology of reasoning and this ambiguity is reflected elsewhere in the cognitive sciences. First, we label as 'pragmatic' aspects of inference that rely on prior world knowledge. Second, we label 'pragmatic' aspects of inference that rely on the communicative function of language.

of logical systems is rife in the psychology of reasoning and leads to a confounding of logical validity and psychological validity. Just because an inference, e.g., p to *if p then q* (one of the paradoxes), is logically valid does not mean it is psychologically valid. As we have seen there are many logics in which it is not logically valid either (see discussion of the Stalnaker-Lewis and Adams conditionals). Schroyens traces the textual evidence for various authors making an apparent commitment to psychologism. He concludes by arguing that there is a functional mismatch between classical logic at the computational level and the mental models algorithmic level theory. On pain of rejecting the standard multilevel approach to computational level explanation in the cognitive sciences (Marr, 1982), he argues that classical logic can not provide the computational level theory of mental models – a conclusion reached in many of the other chapters in this book, including the next chapter in this section.

In Chapter 5, *The logical response to a noisy world*, Keith Stenning and Michiel van Lambalgen argue that one need not retreat directly to probability theory in order to account for the uncertainty of the world in which we live, and about which we want to draw inferences. A nonmonotonic logic using closed world reasoning may also account for uncertainty, as we discussed above. Stenning and van Lambalgen introduce an important element of human reasoning which may have been missed from extant theories. This element is the need to reason to an interpretation of the premises before drawing inferences. They argue that the logics that apply in each case may be different. We include this chapter in this section because of the explicit claim that these interpretations are built up in WM and that with respect to drawing inference, it is only the statements in WM that make up the relevant data-base. On this view, the interpretation of 1.4a in WM is *If it is sunny tomorrow AND **nothing is abnormal**, John will play tennis*. In the absence of 1.4b, there is no reason to assume anything is abnormal and so in the closed world of the contents of WM, it is safe to conclude *John will play tennis*. Once a reasoner interprets 1.4b, the possibility of an unreliable baby-sitter renders the situation abnormal and so the conclusion that *John will play tennis* is withdrawn. Stenning and van Lambalgen remain neutral on the nature of the representations and processes required to implement this account in WM, as they argue that a rule based or a model based account could achieve the same result. After presenting this account, they turn their attention to probabilistic views of the 'suppression' effects, and conclude that because these fail to draw the distinction between reasoning to and from an interpretation they fail to adequately account for these effects.

The next four chapters in this section focus primarily on probabilistic inference or on probability logic accounts of the conditional. In Chapter 6, *Conditionals and probability*, Vittorio Girotto and Phil Johnson-Laird apply the mental model theory to the assessment of *extensional* probabilities. These are probabilities that rely on some random process in the world that defines an event space or possibility space. The probability of x can then be calculated in terms of the proportion of events or possibilities in which x occurs. Girotto and Johnson-Laird assume that these possibilities are represented by mental models in WM and they assess the predictive success of this theory in accounting for people's probability estimates. In particular, their theory draws a distinction between the probability of a conditional, $P(if\ p\ then\ q)$, and the conditional probability, $P(q|p)$, such that, *pace* the assumptions of probability logic (i.e., The Equation), these are not always equal. They present evidence that people interpret extensional conditional probabilities in the way the mental model theory describes. Consequently, they argue that the relationship between conditional sentences and conditional probabilities is not that given by the application of the Equation and the Ramsey Test.

In Chapter 7, *Causal discounting and conditional reasoning in children*, Nilufa Ali, Anne Schlottman, Abigail Shaw, Nick Chater, and Mike Oaksford present a developmental study of causal conditional reasoning. They appeal to the *mental mechanisms* account (Chater & Oaksford,

2006) which assumes that people interpret causal and diagnostic conditionals in terms of small-scale dynamic representations in WM that behave like causal Bayesian networks. These interpretations suggest a sequential pattern of inferences that depend on causal discounting.[7] They argue that this pattern is not predictable under a logical interpretation or mental models theory. In adults, most of the predicted effects were observed but one was not and this appeared to be because adults see some multiple possible causes as correlated. The experiment reported in this chapter used children who were presumed not to have sufficient experience to perceive the possible correlation between causes. The results seem to support this conclusion. Ali et al. conclude with a discussion of other findings that have seemed to question whether when reasoning with causal conditionals, people do discount in the way predicted by causal Bayes nets.

In Chapter 8, *Conditionals and non-constructive reasoning*, David Over, Jonathan Evans, and Shira Elqayam present arguments and evidence to distinguish the mental model interpretation of the conditional from that provided by probability logic. Their argument depends on distinguishing between elimination inferences for conditionals, like MP and MT, and introduction inferences, i.e., inferences that introduce a conditional. For example, according to standard logic if *p OR q* is true then *if ¬p then q* can be introduced as they are mutually entailing. *p OR q* itself can be introduced constructively, e.g., because *p* true, or non-constructively, because of prior knowledge indicating that *p OR q* is the case. Over et al. point out that, according to the Equation, if $P(p \: OR \: q)$ is believed to be high only because $P(p)$ is high, then $P(if \: ¬p \: then \: q)$ can be much lower than $P(p \: OR \: q)$ and so the inference to *if ¬p then q* from *p OR q* cannot be *p*-valid (see 1.13). Over et al. discuss evidence apparently showing that $P(if \: ¬p \: then \: q)$ is frequently evaluated as lower than $P(p \: OR \: q)$. They then report an experiment showing that inferring *if ¬p then q* from *p OR q* is a relatively strong inference when *p OR q* depends on non-constructive reasoning, and a relatively weak inference when *p OR q* is itself introduced by constructive reasoning. We include this chapter in the section on WM because this computational level discussion must be implemented in Evans and Over's *epistemic mental models* theory, which is an account of the mental representation of conditionals in WM.

In Chapter 9, *The conditional in mental probability logic*, Niki Pfeifer and Gernot Kleiter introduce *coherence* based probability logic as an account of people's mental rules of inference which, as in mental logic theory, can be applied to incoming information in WM to draw inferences. That is, they specifically propose formal rules justified by probability logic as a specific theory of human inference. Their chapter demonstrates that a probabilistic approach does not preclude a deductive approach based on formal rules of inference, thus Pfeifer and Kleiter are very firmly in both the mental logic *and* the probabilistic camps. They point out that on a probabilistic interpretation, the rules of inference will define a probability interval; more information than is provided by the premises would be needed to infer a point value. They also present experimental work on the probabilistic interpretation of a variety of inference rules, including MP and strengthening (see 1.7), and show that people's endorsements fall within the prescribed intervals.

Section two – *Long term memory: Function, representation and process* – again begins with chapters whose primary focus is on logical thinking. In Chapter 10, *Semantic memory retrieval, mental models, and the development of conditional inferences in children*, Henry Markovits presents a multinomial process tree model of conditional reasoning that can account for the typical developmental trajectory observed in conditional inference. This model assumes that people produce inferences from a set of mental models, in which the basic elements are determined by

---

[7] That is, where there are multiple possible causes of an effect which is known to have occurred, finding out that one cause occurred leads to the other possible cause to be discounted as having not occurred.

information about the premises retrieved from LTM. For example, people can access information on cases which create counterexamples (p AND $\neg q$), like co-tenable conditions, or information on cases that indicate alternative causes, ($\neg p$ AND q). Accessing this information will affect the sets of mental models people construct. The multinomial modelling allows Markovits to quantitatively assess how well his model, which differs from Byrne and Johnson-Laird's account (this volume), of how semantic/pragmatic modulation of mental models works. According to this model, there is always a probability that a counterexample will be retrieved from LTM and so the situation will most often be regarded as abnormal (see Stenning & van Lambalgen, this volume) even in the absence of a further explicit premise (like 1.4b).[8] Markovits does not provide a model of LTM, but shows how the differential availability of information in LTM might affect the processes responsible for logical inference in WM.

In Chapter 11, *Counterexample retrieval and inhibition during conditional reasoning: Direct evidence from memory probing*, Wim De Neys presents direct evidence that people access, or inhibit access to counterexamples in LTM during conditional reasoning. Accessing alternative causes ($\neg p$ AND q) should prevent people from drawing the DA and AC fallacies, whereas inhibiting access to co-tenable conditions (p AND $\neg q$) should allow people to draw the MP and MT inferences. De Neys had participants perform a lexical decision task after a reasoning task, using probes that were associated with co-tenable conditions or alternative causes. For the DA and AC fallacies, words associated with alternative causes were accessed faster than unrelated words, whereas for the MP and MT inferences, words associated with co-tenable conditions were accessed more slowly than unrelated words. These results seem to show that people are inhibiting access to counterexamples for valid inferences but accessing counterexamples for invalid fallacies during conditional inference. Consequently, it would appear that logical behaviour in this task requires active suppression of the knowledge that most situations are likely to be abnormal. Again we include this chapter in the *logic* section because its focus is on how memory processes of activation and inhibition can facilitate logical or logic-like reasoning.

The next three chapters in this section focus on inference processes that the authors' conceive of as probabilistic or decision theoretic, and explores how LTM access might affect these processes. In Chapter 12, *How semantic memory processes temper causal inferences*, Denise Cummins, who pioneered the use of causal conditionals in reasoning research, and whose early results first demonstrated that access to counterexamples was automatic, presents a model of how this process affects causal inferences. Like Markovits, Cummins provides a parameterized model of how access to the different types of counterexample affects the process. In particular, she accords a role to the overall plausibility of the proposed causal link in an *if cause then effect* conditional. She proposes that counterexample information is automatically accessed but that the plausibility of the causal conditional affects the degree to which this information is utilized. This parameterized model is applied to a re-analysis of the data from Cummins (1995).

In Chapter 13, *A successive-conditionalization approach to conditional reasoning*, In-mao Liu outlines the successive-conditionalization approach (Liu, 2003; Liu, Lo, & Wu, 1996) to conditional reasoning. In this approach people are assumed first to compute the probability of the conclusion using the categorical premise to conditionalize on prior world knowledge in LTM (the knowledge based component of reasoning). People then conditionalize on the conditional premise (the assumption-based component of reasoning). Liu's experimental procedure, which introduces incomplete problems without the conditional premise, provides a method of

---

[8] Indeed, defeasibility appears graded because as De Neys et al. (2003b) put it, "every counterexample counts."

explicitly assessing the prior degree of belief in the conclusion given the categorical premise without further assuming the truth the conditional premise. Liu argues that this procedure measures the knowledge-based component, which represents the inductive strength of a conditional inference (Oaksford & Hahn, 2007; Rips, 2001), separately from the assumption-based component, which represents the deductive correctness of a conditional inference. Liu contrasts this successive-conditionalization approach with the mental models approach and with approaches based on conditional probability.

In Chapter 14, *Pragmatic conditionals, conditional pragmatics, and the pragmatic component of conditional reasoning*, Jean-Francois Bonnefon and Guy Politzer argue that the pragmatic knowledge based component of the human reasoning system remains relatively unexplored. Moreover, they point out that the conversational *use* to which conditionals are put must also be addressed by the psychology of reasoning. They categorize pragmatic conditionals, pointing out that their practical uses usually entail a decision-theoretic interpretation, in which actions and their consequences may vary in utility for a speaker or a hearer. They examine a range of utility conditionals, including promises, inducements, deontic conditionals, pointing out the pragmatic commitments they licence. They then go on to investigate conditional pragmatics, i.e., the pragmatic implicatures that conditionals might invite. They then introduce the *conditional field*, the complex of factors including co-tenable conditions and alternatives that make up what Rescher (2007) calls the 'enthymematic background' to a simple conditional statement, and which provides the most investigated pragmatic effects on human conditional reasoning. Bonnefon and Politzer's closing section on interactions between these pragmatic components provides fertile ground for further explorations of pragmatic effects in conditional inference

The next section, *Integrative approaches,* comprises seven chapters whose primary focus is on the integration of WM and LTM processes and logical and probabilistic factors, but at different levels of description and sometimes by proposing an integration of specific, apparently competing, theories of reasoning. In Chapter 15, *Reasoning with conditionals in artificial intelligence*, Bob Kowalski, one of the founders of the logic programming movement in artificial intelligence, argues that this approach can address some of the issues confronting the psychology of conditional reasoning. In particular, Kowalski shows how closed world reasoning and negation as failure (see above) is used to deal with defeasibility, an approach also explored by Stenning and Lambalgen (this volume). A logic programme is a representation of stored world knowledge on a topic, and the underlying inference engine, based on unification, follows logical principles. Moreover, logic programming provides a highly specific process theory of a level of detail and sophistication barely imagined in the psychology/cognitive science of reasoning. Kowalski also argues that probabilities can be smoothly integrated into the framework of *abductive logic programming* (ALP). Such programmes—with probabilistic, abducible predicates—have apparently been shown to have the expressive power of discrete Bayesian networks (Poole, 1993, 1997). Thus a single framework may have the power to integrate both the apparently logical and probabilistic features of human inference.

In Chapter 16, *Towards a reconciliation of mental model theory and probabilistic theories*, Sonja Geiger and Klaus Oberauer propose a similar reconciliation of logical and probabilistic processes using theories with a longer psychological pedigree. In a detailed review of the recent empirical literature on conditional reasoning, Geiger and Oberauer observe that studies on the interpretation of the conditional seem to support the probabilistic account, whereas studies on conditional inference seem to support a mental models view. However, they also observe that the data on inferential performance is rendered more complex by their own findings, showing that people are highly influenced by probabilities but in a way that depends on response mode. They then propose a revised mental model theory that argues that the basic meaning of a conditional is a procedure for constructing a particular mental model and that this procedure can be revised by prior knowledge in a similar way to semantic/pragmatic modulation. Prior knowledge can also provide probabilities as annotations to mental models that can be processed as part of the reasoning process.

In Chapter 17, *Conditional inference and constraint satisfaction: Reconciling mental models and the probabilistic approach?* Mike Oaksford and Nick Chater propose a very different reconciliation of mental models and probabilistic approaches. They argue that mental models are a by-product of the need to store representations in WM of the results of probing LTM for world knowledge modelled as a constraint satisfaction neural network. Interrogating the network with the minor premise of an MP inference, for example, by clamping on its representation in the network, letting it settle, and then reading off the activation of the conclusion, provides a process model of performing a Ramsey test, albeit over a highly simplified knowledge-base. Such operations on these neural networks can be interpreted as computing real posterior probabilities given certain assumptions. Oaksford and Chater present only a toy model which can be conceived of as a *mental mechanism* (Chater & Oaksford, 2006) or as the active part of LTM, where such a mechanism provides a tentative model of the causal structure of a relevant part of the environment. It also provides a representation of a shallow but probabilistic default hierarchy (see above). If further possibilities, i.e., cues, are used to probe LTM, then from, a probabilistic perspective, errors will result. But if the activation levels (probabilities) are ignored in the stored retrieval cues in WM used to probe LTM, then the possibility of logical responding emerges. Oaksford and Chater argue that this behaviour is consistent with experimental results on drawing conditional inferences under time pressure. They go on to show how this integrative model might account for a variety of other findings on conditional inference.

In Chapter 18, *Towards a metacognitive dual process theory of conditional reasoning*, Valerie Thompson proposes that a metacognitive theory is required to address the important question of how the System 1 processes in LTM and the System 2 processes in WM interact. To quote the founder of the dual process approach, Jonathan Evans, such an account is necessary to 'define more precisely the nature of the interaction between the two processes (S1 and S2) and to assist the generation of experimental predictions about particular reasoning tasks', (Evans, 2006, p. 379). Thompson argues that, in terms of predicting the outcome of any given reasoning attempt, the crucial questions for dual process theory are: (i) what is the nature of the System 1 output? (ii) when and in what way, does System 2 intervene? and (iii) how does this intervention produce the final answer? Thompson argues that metacognitive processes mediate the degree of System 2 involvement. In particular, she proposes that a *feeling of rightness* (FOR) is involved: if the conclusion recommended by System 1 has a high FOR, then System 2 involvement will be low, if FOR is low then System 2 WM processes will be invoked to check the conclusion.

In Chapter 19, *A multi-layered dual-process approach to conditional reasoning*, Niki Verschueren and Walter Schaeken propose that what is important about dual process theories is that they propose that more than one process is involved in any particular attempt at reasoning. In this chapter, they argue for three processing levels, each of which introduces a particular choice. We introduce their levels in reverse order. At level 3, inference can be contextualized, i.e., it engages prior knowledge; or de-contextualized, not engaging prior knowledge. At their Level 2, contextualized inference can be either probabilistic – based on likelihood estimates – or employ mental models and so be based on counterexample retrieval. At this level, just as with ter Meulen's mule, they observe that counterexamples and probabilities provide different information and that both are needed. At their Level 1, information retrieval can be either automatic – driven by semantic association – or strategic – driven by active cue generation. Verschueren and Schaeken discuss the nature of the processes at each level in detail and then apply the account to a typology of everyday pragmatic inferences, showing how the distinctions they have drawn can account for the very different response profiles observed with these different materials.

In Chapter 20, *Two aspects of reasoning competence: A challenge for current accounts and a call for new conceptual tools*, Guy Politzer and Jean-Francois Bonnefon review the history and results on human reasoning and conclude that while people have a facility for deductive reasoning they frequently need to deal with the uncertainty of premises and how these ramify to affect conclusions. Rather than seek a rapprochement between logic and probability theory they argue that there are alternative formalisms for integrating proof and uncertainty that remain largely unexplored in the psychology of conditional reasoning (for the exception, see George's [1997] work testing Dempster-Schafer belief functions). In particular, they propose that a *plausibilist* approach (Pollock, 2001; Rescher, 1976; see also Hahn & Oaksford (2007), for discussion). An important difference is with 1.13, i.e., the uncertainties of the conclusion cannot be less than the sum of the uncertainties of the premises. This contrasts with plausibility, where the plausibility of the conclusion cannot be less than the plausibility of the least plausible premise. In sum, Politzer and Bonnefon propose an integrative formal theory at the computational level that they argue may fare better as a standard of reasoning than either classical logic or probability theory. Finally, in Chapter 21, *Open issues in the cognitive science of conditionals*, we briefly summarise some of the outstanding issue in the area.

Many of the chapters in this book were first presented at the 2nd London Reasoning Workshop on The *Psychology of Conditionals* held at Birkbeck College, University of London , 27th - 28th August, 2007. We thank all the contributors to both the workshop and to this book for their enthusiasm for the project and for their attention to producing such an excellent set of chapters. We also thank Martin Baum of Oxford University Press for his continued support and the whole production team for their diligence in correcting our mistakes. Finally, as always, we thank our families for their forbearance while we were engrossed in this project. The chapters in this volume provide evidence of a varied and vigorous field, bringing together insights from a range of disciplines to understand the nature of perhaps the most central aspect of human reasoning: the conditional. We hope that both the contrasts and the common themes that emerge in this work indicate that the analysis of the conditional is becoming ever more sophisticated. We hope that the study of the conditional may prove to be a key case study in cognitive science, allowing us to see, in microcosm, the full complexity and subtlety of human thought.

References

Adams, E. W. (1968). Probability and the logic of conditionals. In F. Suppes & J. Hintikka (Eds.), *Aspects of inductive logic* (pp. 265–316). Amsterdam: North Holland.

Adams, E. (1975). *The logic of conditionals: An application of probability to deductive logic*. Dordrecht: Reidel.

Adams, E. W. (1998). *A primer of probability logic*. Stanford: CLSI Publications.

Bennett, J. (2003). *A philosophical guide to conditionals*. Oxford England: Oxford University Press.

Bonnefon, J. & Hilton, D. (2004). Consequential Conditionals: Invited and Suppressed Inferences From Valued Outcomes. *Journal of Experimental Psychology: Learning, Memory, and Cognition*, **30**, 28–37.

Boole, G. (1854). *An investigation of the laws of thought on which are founded the mathematical theories of logic and probabilities*. Cambridge, U.K.: Macmillan & Co.

Brouwer, L. E. J. (1992). *Intuitionismus*. (Ed. D. van Dalen), Mannheim: BI-Wissenschaftsverlag (originally 1927).

Byrne, R. (1989). Suppressing valid inferences with conditionals. *Cognition*, **31**, 61–83.

Carnap, R. (1950). *The logical foundations of probability theory*. (1962 edition), Chicago: University of Chicago Press.

Chater, N. & Oaksford, M. (2006). Mental mechanisms. In K. Fiedler, & P. Juslin (Eds.), *Information sampling and adaptive cognition* (pp. 210–236). Cambridge: Cambridge University Press.

Chater, N. & Oaksford, M. (Eds.) (2008). *The probabilistic mind: Prospects for Bayesian cognitive science.* Oxford: Oxford University Press.

Chater, N., Oaksford, M., Heit, E., & Hahn, U. (2009). Inductive logic and empirical psychology. In S. Hartmann (Ed.), *The Handbook of the History of Logic: Induction* (Volume 10) (pp. 549–620). Amsterdam: North Holland.

Chater, N., Tenenbaum, J., & Yuille, A. (2006). Probabilistic models of cognition: Conceptual foundations. *Trends in Cognitive Sciences,* **10**, 287–291.

Cheng, P.W. & Holyoak, K.J. (1985). Pragmatic reasoning schemas. *Cognitive Psychology,* **17**, 391–416.

Cherniak, C. (1981). Minimal rationality, *Mind,* **90**, 161–183.

Cherniak, C. (1986). *Minimal rationality.* Cambridge MA: MIT Press.

Chomsky, N. (1965). *Aspects of the theory of syntax.* Cambridge. MA: MIT Press.

Cohen, L. (1981). Can human irrationality be experimentally demonstrated? *Behavioral and Brain Sciences,* **4**, 317–370.

Comrie, B. (1986). Conditionals: A typology. In E. C. Traugott, A. Ter Meulen, J. S. Reilly, & C. A. Ferguson (Eds.), *On conditionals* (pp. 77–99). Cambridge: Cambridge University Press.

Cosmides, L. (1989). The logic of social exchange: Has natural selection shaped how humans reason? Studies with the Wason selection task. *Cognition,* **31**, 187–276.

Cummins, D. D. (1995). Naive theories and causal deduction. *Memory & Cognition,* **23**, 646–658.

Cummins, D. D., Lubart, T., Alksnis, O., & Rist, R. (1991). Conditional reasoning and causation. *Memory & Cognition,* **19**, 274–282.

DeLong, H. (1970). *A profile of mathematical logic.* Reading, MA: Addison-Wesley.

De Neys, W.D., Schaeken W., & d'Ydewalle G. (2003a). Causal conditional reasoning and strength of association: The disabling condition case. *The European Journal of Cognitive Psychology,* **15**, 161–176.

De Neys, W.D., Schaeken W., & d'Ydewalle G. (2003b). Inference suppression and semantic memory retrieval: Every counterexample counts. *Memory and Cognition,* **31**, 581–595.

De Neys, W., Vartanian, O., & Goel, V. (2008). Smarter than we think: When our brains detect that we are biased. *Psychological Science,* **19**, 483–489.

Duhem, P. (1914). *The aim and structure of physical theory.* Princeton, NJ: Princeton University Press (English trans. 1954).

Earman, J. (1992). *Bayes or bust?* Cambridge, MA: MIT Press

Ebbinghaus, H. & Meyer, M. (1908). *Psychology: An elementary text-book.* Boston, MA: D C Heath & Co Publishers.

Edgington, D. (1995). On conditionals. *Mind,* **104**, 235–329.

Erickson, J. (1974). A set analysis theory of behavior in formal syllogistic reasoning tasks. *Theories in cognitive psychology: The Loyola Symposium.* Oxford England: Lawrence Erlbaum.

Evans, J. St.B. T. (1972). Interpretation and 'matching bias' in areasoning task. *Quarterly Journal of Experimental Psychology,* **24**, 193–199.

Evans, J. St.B. T. (1998). Matching bias in conditional reasoning: Do we understand it after 25 years? *Thinking and Reasoning,* **4**, 45–82.

Evans, J. St.B. T. (2006). The heuristic-analytic theory of reasoning: Extension and evaluation. *Psychonomic Bulletin and Review,* **13**, 378–395.

Evans, J. St.B. T. (2009). Does rational analysis stand up to rational analysis? *Behavioral and Brain Sciences,* **32**, 88–89.

Evans, J. St.B. T., Handley, S. H., & Over, D. E. (2003). Conditionals and conditional probability. *Journal of Experimental Psychology: Learning, Memory and Cognition,* **29**, 321–355.

Evans, J. St.B. T. & Lynch, J. S. (1973). Matching bias in the selection task. *British Journal of Psychology,* **64**, 391–397.

Evans, J. St.B. T. & Over, D.E. (2004). *If.* Oxford, England: Oxford University Press.

Fodor, J. A. (1983). *Modularity of mind.* Cambridge, MA: MIT Press.

Fodor, J. A. & Pylyshyn, Z. W. (1988). Connectionism and cognitive architecture: A critical analysis. *Cognition*, **28**, 3–71.

Geiger, S. M. & Oberauer, K. (2007). Reasoning with conditionals: Does every counterexample count? It's frequency that counts. *Memory & Cognition*, **35**, 2060–2074.

George, C. (1997). Reasoning from uncertain premises. *Thinking and Reasoning*, **3**, 161–190.

Goodman. (1954). *Fact, fiction, and forecast*. London: The Athlone Press.

Grice, P. (1975). Logic and conversation. In P. Cole & J. Morgan (Eds.), *Syntax and semantics. Volume 3: Speech Acts* (pp. 41–58). New York: Academic Press.

Griggs, R. & Cox, J. (1982). The elusive thematic-materials effect in Wason's selection task. *British Journal of Psychology*, **73**, 407–420.

Guyote, M. & Sternberg, R. (1981). A transitive-chain theory of syllogistic reasoning. *Cognitive Psychology*, **13**, 461–525.

Haack, S. (1978). *Philosophy of logics*. New York: Cambridge University Press.

Hahn, U. & Oaksford, M. (2007). The rationality of informal argumentation: A Bayesian approach to reasoning fallacies. *Psychological Review*, **114**, 704–732.

Harper, R. W. (2005). Constructive negation. *Supplementary Notes 15–399, Department of Computer Science, Carnegie Mellon University*.

Hawthorn, J. (2008). Inductive logic. *Stanford Encyclopedia of Philosophy*, http://plato.stanford.edu/entries/logic-inductive/

Hempel, C. G. (1945a). Studies in the logic of confirmation I. *Mind*, **54**, 1–26.

Hempel, C. G. (1945b). Studies in the logic of confirmation II. *Mind*, **54**, 97–121.

Hilton, D., Kemmelmeier, M., & Bonnefon, J. (2005). Putting Ifs to Work: Goal-Based Relevance in Conditional Directives. *Journal of Experimental Psychology: General*, **134**, 388–405.

Holland, J. H., Holyoak, K. J., Nisbett, R. E., & Thagard, P. R. (1986). *Induction*. Cambridge, MA: MIT Press.

Howson, C. & Urbach, P. (1993). *Scientific reasoning: The Bayesian approach* (2nd edition). La Salle, Illinois: Open Court Publishing Company.

Inhelder, B. & Piaget, J. (1955). *De la logique de l'enfant à la logique de l'adolescent*. Paris: Presses Universitaires de France. (English version: The growth of logical thinking from childhood to adolescence. London: Routledge, 1958).

Jeffrey, R. C. (1967). *Formal logic: Its scope and limits*. New York: McGraw-Hill.

Johnson-Laird, P. N. (1983). *Mental models*. Cambridge: Cambridge University Press.

Johnson-Laird, P. N. (1986). Conditionals and mental models. In C. Ferguson, J. Reilly, A. ter Meulen, and E. C. Traugott (Eds.), *On Conditionals* (pp. 55–75). Cambridge: Cambridge University Press.

Johnson-Laird, P.N. & Byrne, R.M.J. (1991). *Deduction*. Hillsdale, NJ: Lawrence Erlbaum Associates.

Johnson-Laird, P. N., Legrenzi, P., & Legrenzi, M. (1972). Reasoning and a sense of reality. *British Journal of Psychology*, **63**, 395–400.

Johnson-Laird, P. N. & Steedman, M. (1978). The psychology of syllogisms. *Cognitive Psychology*, **10**, 64–99.

Kant, E. (1787). *Critique of the pure reason*. (trans. Norman Kemp Smith), London: Macmillan (1961).

Klauer, K. C., Musch, J., & Naumer, B. (2000). On belief bias in syllogistic reasoning. *Psychological Review*, **107**, 852–884.

Klauer, K. C., Stahl, C., & Erdfelder, E.(2006). The abstract selection task: An almost comprehensive model. *Journal of Experimental Psychology: Learning, Memory & Cognition*, **33**, 680–703.

Kodroff, J. & Roberge, J. (1975). Developmental analysis of the conditional reasoning abilities of primary-grade children. *Developmental Psychology*, **11**, 1–28.

Kowalski, R. (1979). Algorithm = Logic + Control. *Communications of the Association for Computing Machinery*, **22**, 424–436.

Kvart, I. (1985). *Theory of Counterfactuals*. Indianapolis, IN: Hackett Publishing Company Inc.

Lewis, D. (1973). *Counterfactuals*. Cambridge, MA: Harvard University Press.

Liu, I. M (2003). Conditional reasoning and conditionalisation. *Journal of Experimental Psychology: Learning, Memory & Cognition*, **29**, 694–709.

Liu, I.M., Lo, K. C., & Wu, J. T. (1996). A probabilistic interpretation of "If–then". *The Quarterly Journal of Experimental Psychology*, **49A**, 828–844.

Manktelow, K. & Evans, J. St.B. T. (1979). Facilitation of reasoning by realism: Effect or non-effect? *British Journal of Psychology*, **70**, 477–488.

Manktelow, K. I. & Over, D. E. (1987). Reasoning and rationality. *Mind and Language*, **2**, 199–219.

Markovits, H. & Quinn, S. (2002). Efficiency of retrieval correlates with "logical" reasoning from causal conditional premises. *Memory and Cognition*, **30**(5), 696–706.

Moore, G. E. (1993). *Principia ethica*. New York: Prometheus Books (originally 1903).

Newell, A. & H. A. Simon. (1976). Computer science as empirical inquiry: Symbols and search. *Communications of the Association for Computing Machinery*, **19**, 11–26.

Nickerson, R. (1998). Confirmation bias: A ubiquitous phenomenon in many guises. *Review of General Psychology*, **2**, 175–220.

Nute, D. (1984). Conditional logic. In D. Gabbay and F. Gunthner (Eds.), *Handbook of Philosophical Logic Volume 2* (pp. 387–439). Amsterdam: Kluwer Academic Publishers.

Oaksford, M. (1989). *Cognition and inquiry: The pragmatics of conditional reasoning*. Unpublished doctoral dissertation, Centre for Cognitive Science, University of Edinburgh.

Oaksford, M. & Chater, N. (1991). Against logicist cognitive science. *Mind and Language*, **6**, 1–38.

Oaksford, M. & Chater, N. (1993). Reasoning theories and bounded rationality. In K. I. Manktelow & D. E. Over (Eds.) *Rationality* (pp. 31–60). London: Routledge.

Oaksford, M. & Chater, N. (1995). Theories of reasoning and the computational explanation of everyday inference. *Thinking & Reasoning*, **1**, 121–152.

Oaksford, M. & Chater, N. (1998). *Rationality in an uncertain world: Essays on the cognitive science of human reasoning*. Hove, Sussex: Psychology Press.

Oaksford, M. & Chater, N. (2003). Optimal data selection: Revision, review and re-evaluation. *Psychonomic Bulletin & Review*, **10**, 289–318.

Oaksford, M. & Chater, N. (2007). *Bayesian rationality: The probabilistic approach to human reasoning*. Oxford: Oxford University Press.

Oaksford, M. & Chater, N. (2009). The uncertain reasoner: Bayes, logic and rationality. *Behavioral and Brain Sciences*, **32**, 105–120.

Oaksford, M., & Chater, N. (in press). Dual systems and dual processes but a single function. In K. I. Manktelow, D. E. Over, & S. Elqayam (Eds.), *The science of reason: A Festschrift for Jonathan St. B. T. Evans*. Hove, Sussex: Psychology Press.

Oaksford, M., Chater, N., & Larkin, J. (2000). Probabilities and polarity biases in conditional inference. *Journal of Experimental Psychology: Learning, Memory and Cognition*, **26**, 883–889.

Oaksford, M., Chater, N., & Stenning, K. (1990). Connectionism, classical cognitive science and experimental psychology, *AI & Society*, **4**, 73–90.

Oaksford, M. & Hahn, U. (2007). Induction, deduction and argument strength in human reasoning and argumentation. In A. Feeney, & E. Heit (Eds.), *Inductive reasoning* (pp. 269–301). Cambridge: Cambridge University Press.

Oberauer, K. (2006). Reasoning with conditionals: A test of formal models of four theories. *Cognitive Psychology*, **53**, 238–283.

Oberauer, K., Weidenfeld, A., & Fischer, K. (2007). What makes us believe a conditional? The roles of covariation and causality. *Thinking & Reasoning*, **13**, 340–369.

Oberauer, K. & Wilhelm, O. (2003). The meaning(s) of conditionals: Conditional probabilities, mental models, and personal utilities. *Journal of Experimental Psychology: Learning, Memory, and Cognition*, **29**, 680–693.

Over, D., Hadjichristidis, C., Evans, J., Sloman, S., & Handley, S. (2007). The probability of causal conditionals. *Cognitive Psychology*, **54**, 62–97.

Pollock, J. L. (2001). Defeasible reasoning with variable degrees of justification. *Artificial Intelligence*, **133**, 233–282.

Poole, D. (1993). Probabilistic horn abduction and Bayesian networks. *Artificial Intelligence*, **64**, 81–129.

Poole, D. (1997). The independent choice logic for modelling multiple agents under uncertainty. *Artificial Intelligence*, **94**, 7–56.

Popper, K. (1959). *The logic of scientific discovery*. New York: Basic Books (originally 1935).

Quine, W. V. O. (1953). *From a logical point of view*. Cambridge, MA: Harvard University Press.

Ramsey, F. P. (1990). *The foundations of mathematics and other logical essays*. London: Routledge and Kegan Paul (originally 1931).

Reiter, R. (1985). On reasoning by default. In R. Brachman & H. Levesque (Eds.), *Readings in knowledge representation* (pp. 401–410). Los Altos, CA: Morgan Kaufman.

Rescher, N. (1976). *Plausible reasoning*. London: Macmillan Press.

Rescher, N. (2007). *Conditionals*. Cambridge, MA: MIT Press.

Rips, L. J. (1994). *The Psychology of proof*. Cambridge, MA: MIT Press.

Rips, L. J. (2001). Two kinds of reasoning. *Psychological Science*, **12**, 129–134.

Roberge, J. (1970). A study of children's abilities to reason with basic principles of deductive reasoning. *American Educational Research Journal*, **7**, 583–596.

Roberge, J. (1971). Some effects of negation on adults' conditional reasoning abilities. *Psychological Reports*, **29**, 839–844.

Rumain, B., Connell, J., & Braine, M. (1983). Conversational comprehension processes are responsible for reasoning fallacies in children as well as adults: If is not the biconditional. *Developmental Psychology*, **19**, 471–481.

Schroyens, W. (2009). On is an ought: Levels of analysis and the descriptive versus normative analysis of human reasoning. *Behavioral and Brain Sciences*, **32**, 101–102.

Schroyens, W., Schaeken, W., Fias, W., & d'Ydewalle, G. (2000a). Heuristic and analytic processes in propositional reasoning with negatives. *Journal of Experimental Psychology: Learning, Memory, and Cognition*, **26**, 1713–1734.

Simoneau, M. & Markovits, H. (2003). Reasoning with premises that are not empirically true: Evidence for the role of inhibition and retrieval. *Developmental Psychology*, **39**, 964–975.

Stalnaker, R.C. (1968). A theory of conditionals. In N. Rescher (Eds.), *Studies in logical theory* (pp. 98–112). Oxford: Blackwell.

Stalnaker, R. C. (1984). *Inquiry*. Cambridge, MA: MIT Press.

Stanovich, K. E. & West, R.F (2000). Individual differences in reasoning: Implications for the rationality debate? *Behavioral and Brain Sciences*, **23**, 645–665.

Stenning, K. & van Lambalgen, M. (2005). Semantic interpretation as reasoning in non-monotonic logic: The real meaning of the suppression task. *Cognitive Science*, **29**, 919–960.

Suppe, F. (1977). *The structure of scientific theories*. Urbana, IL: University of Illinois Press.

Ter Meulen, A. (1986). Generic information, conditional contexts and constraints. In E. C. Traugott, A. ter Meulen, J. Snitzer Reilly, & C. A. Ferguson (Eds.), *On Conditionals* (pp. 123–146). Cambridge: Cambridge University Press.

Thompson, V. & Mann, J. (1995). Perceived necessity explains the dissociation between logic and meaning: The case of 'Only If.'. *Journal of Experimental Psychology: Learning, Memory, and Cognition*, **21**, 1554–1567.

Wagner, C. G. (2004). Modus tollens probabilized. *British Journal for Philosophy of Science*, **55**, 747–753.

Wason, P. C. (1960). On the failure to eliminate hypotheses in a conceptual task. *Quarterly Journal of Experimental Psychology*, **12**, 129–140.

Wason, P. C. (1968). Reasoning about a rule. *Quarterly Journal of Experimental Psychology*, **20**, 273–281.

Wason, P. C. (1969). Regression in reasoning? *British Journal of Psychology*, **60**, 471–480.

Wason, P. & Johnson-Laird, P. (1972). *Psychology of reasoning: Structure and content*. Oxford England: Harvard U. Press.

Wason, P. C. & Shapiro, D. (1971). Natural and contrived experience in a reasoning problem. *Quarterly Journal of Experimental Psychology*, **23**, 63–71.

Wertheimer, M. (1959). *Productive thinking*. Oxford England: Harper.

Wetherick, N. (1962). Eliminative and enumerative behaviour in a conceptual task. *The Quarterly Journal of Experimental Psychology*, **14**, 246–249.

Whitehead, A. N. & Russell, B. (1910, 1912, 1913). *Principia mathematica*, 3 vols, Cambridge: Cambridge University Press.

Woodworth, R. S. & Sells, S. B. (1935). An atmosphere effect in syllogistic reasoning. *Journal of Experimental Psychology*, **18**, 451–460.

Part 2

Working memory: Function, representation, and process

Chapter 2

The mental logic theory of conditional propositions

David O'Brien and Andrea Manfrinati

The mental logic theory of conditional propositions

There is an *a priori* reason to expect human cognition to include a mental logic. Human cognition records propositional information in a declarative memory, e.g., *Brazzaville is across the river from Kinshasa, Socrates is wearing a yellow shirt*. Braine and O'Brien (1998) and O'Brien (2004) argued that in order for information to be recorded in a declarative memory, there must be a format in which to record it (see Fodor, 1975 and Macnamara, 1986 for similar arguments), and this format needs to be able to distinguish between properties and the entities that have those properties. Put simply, the format needs to include some logical structure that includes a predicate/argument structure.

It would be useful for the format to be able to represent alternatives and conjunctions among the properties, as well as among the entities that have those properties (e.g., *Gombe and Kintambo are across the river from Brazzaville, Socrates is wearing a yellow shirt and blue shorts*). Such a format also needs some way to distinguish between those propositions that are true and those that are false (e.g., *Ilford is across the river from Brazzaville*). In order for a species to be considered intelligent, it would need some way to make inferences about propositions that go beyond the information as received, and it would need to assess which inferences are sound, that is, to ensure that an inference based on true premises is also true (see O'Brien, 1993). It also would be useful to be able to make hypothetical inferences in situations in which the truth status of a proposition is unknown, that is, when one can suppose that some proposition is true without knowing it to be the case. A species without such ability would not be able to reason about situations that might yet occur, and thus would be unable to think through plans or to consider alternatives among possibilities. An important feature of such a reasoning system thus would include ways of keeping track of which propositions are assumed true, which are assumed false, and which are supposed true. Conditional reasoning concerns reasoning from and about suppositional propositions, and keeping track of when and how a supposition can be discharged.

Mental logic is not identical to the logic found in standard logic textbooks

Just because one expects there is a mental logic, one need not assume it is identical to logic as presented in standard logic textbooks. For example, in textbook logic, anything follows from a contradiction, whereas in mental logic nothing follows from a contradiction except that some error has been made.

Standard logic textbooks typically treat conditionals as material implication, that is, $p \supset q$ is true unless p is true and q is false, implying that $p \supset q$ is true when p is false. Yet, at the time that

Philo of Megara first suggested material implication as a way of viewing conditionals, his contemporaries viewed his proposal as counterintuitive (Kneale & Kneale, 1962). Mental logic theory understands *if* as conveying supposition, and truth-functional assignments of the sort that define the material conditional play no role.

A psychological theory for a logic particle requires not only a representational format, but also procedures that allow one to introduce and discharge the logic term in lines of reasoning. Again, there is no reason to assume that any particular procedures presented in logic textbooks correspond to those used in ordinary reasoning. Indeed, logic textbooks provide a wide array of inference-making (and inference-checking) procedures, and it would be surprising if many of them correspond to the ways in which people ordinarily make inferences. Logic *per se* does not provide any reasoning programme that constructs lines of reasoning. A theory of mental logic, however, would be unable to make precise predictions without a reasoning programme to implement the proof procedures.

Logical reasoning is embedded in a pragmatic architecture

We assume that the representational format, and the inference procedures that operate with it, are a result of human evolutionary history. Our logical reasoning skills thus exist to serve practical purposes. Our Pleistocene ancestors needed neither to make metalogical inferences nor to construct complex proofs of completeness. The construction of complex arguments probably arrived only with the advent of literate professional classes, such as theologians, mathematicians, and lawyers. Our Pleistocene ancestors instead would have gained an advantage from making short, rapid, direct logical inferences about matters of practical interest. For example, a woman who knew that her son was either with the fishermen or with the hunters, and then discovered that he was not with the hunters, would find it useful to be able to infer that her son thus must be with the fishermen. Without such an inference, this woman would be unable to limit the search when she needed to find her son.

Our assumption that mental logic evolved to meet practical needs also makes it unlikely that ordinary logical skills would include the setting aside of pragmatic influences. Although lawyers are skilled at setting aside the intentions of people in order to find loopholes in the words themselves, ordinary people do not do so, and most often it is of practical value to consider the intentions of a speaker (see Braine, 1990). Logic inferences cohabit in the same lines of reasoning with pragmatic inferences and with inferences from many other sources, including those based on real-world knowledge, story scripts, semantic memory, etc. This intermingling of inferences from various sources holds for inferences made in a line of reasoning under a supposition. Although cognitive scientists are interested in the sources of inferences made in a line of reasoning, ordinary reasoners typically do not attend to the sources of the inferences they are making, but only to the output of the inferences.

Asserting, evaluating, and reasoning from conditional propositions

Braine and O'Brien (1991) described three aspects of conditional reasoning: A set of inference schemas, a reasoning programme that implements the schemas to construct lines of reasoning, and a pragmatic architecture in which reasoning is embedded. They proposed that the basic meaning of a logic particle – its lexical entry – is provided by the inference schemas and reasoning programme that introduce and eliminate suppositions and conditionals in lines of reasoning.[1]

---

[1] The philosophical literature (e.g., Block, 1987; Field, 1977; Gentzen, 1934; Harmon, 1982; Loar, 1981; Peacocke, 1992; Quine, 1960; Woods, 1981) includes an inferential-role approach (or conceptual

Of course, how a term is understood in any particular utterance can differ as a function of context and pragmatics from what is provided in the lexical entry alone.

Two schemas are directly concerned with reasoning with and about *if*. A *schema for conditional proof* allows one to assert or evaluate a conditional proposition: When one can derive the consequent of a conditional from a set of premises taken together with the antecedent of the conditional as a hypothetical assumption, one can assert the conditional on the premises alone. In other words, to derive or evaluate *if p then q*, one first supposes *p*; when one then can derive *q* from the supposition taken together with other background premise information, one can assert *if p then q*. A second schema, *modus ponens* holds that when both a conditional (*if p then q*) and its antecedent (*p*) are known to be true, one can assert the truth of the consequent (*q*). The *modus ponens* inference follows from the *schema for conditional proof* in that when the suppositional status of a conditional's antecedent is replaced with its assertion, the consequent of the conditional inherits the assertability of the antecedent on which it is based.[2]

These schemas, and a more complete set for mental logic as a whole, are implemented with a reasoning programme to construct lines of reasoning (see Chapters 6 and 11 of Braine & O'Brien, 1991, for descriptions of the complete sets of schemas and the reasoning programmes at both sentential and predicate-logic levels). The reasoning programmes includes a part – the direct-reasoning routine (DRR) – that is simple and that we claim is universal, as well as some more sophisticated reasoning strategies that are not universal, although they are common among university students. Put simply, in the DRR, when a schema's conditions of application are satisfied, the schema is applied. Thus, modus ponens will be applied when both *if p then q* and *p* are held conjointly in working memory.

The DRR provides a procedure that concerns how the schema for conditional proof is applied. To evaluate a conditional given as a putative conclusion, the procedure adds the antecedent of the conditional to the premise set and then treats the consequent as the conclusion to be tested. As we shall note later, this procedure leads to some differences in judgement from what would follow if people reasoned according to standard logic.

The DRR is rudimentary – as one might expect given its Pleistocene-era roots – and does not include ways to make a supposition in the service of constructing a complex argument. Indeed, what impresses the reader in Sherlock Holmes's reasoning is the use of suppositions in the service of argument construction (e.g., suppose the criminal were a stranger; then the watchdog should

---

role approach) to semantics that proposes that the meaning of a term is provided by the pattern of inferences that it sanctions. Advocates of this approach present logic particles as paradigmatic of how meanings can be found in patterns of implication. Although there may be problems with this approach to account for the entire lexicon (Fodor & Lepore, 1991), we see no reason that it cannot provide a semantics for logical connectives. For logical particles such as *if*, *and*, *not*, and *or*, and quantifiers such as *all* and *some*, etc., an inferential-role semantics needs to specify their rules for introduction and elimination. To provide an empirically testable theory of the semantics of a logical term, such as *if*, the inference procedures need to be specified in detail, and mental-logic theory provides such descriptions. What distinguishes the mental-logic proposal from other inferential-role semantics is its integration of the inference schemas and the reasoning routines that apply these schemas in lines of reasoning – a matter that is particularly important for conditionals. For this reason we have referred to it as a procedural semantics (Braine & O'Brien, 1991; O'Brien et al., 1998). (See Johnson-Laird, 1975, for a similar proposal.)

[2] The schema for conditional proof illustrates that the meaning of *if* is profoundly suppositional. There is an additional schema that concerns suppositions, although it does not concern *if* directly. The *Schema for Negation Introduction* states that when a supposition taken together with a known set of premises leads to a contradiction, one can assert that the supposition is false.

have barked, but did not, so the criminal must not have been a stranger). Note that although people typically are limited in the use of suppositions to set up reasoning strategies, they tend to be able to recognize the soundness of inferences that follow from complex arguments under suppositions – readers are impressed rather than puzzled by Sherlock Holmes's inferences. Similarly, someone who makes a pragmatically based supposition has no trouble following a line of reasoning that follows under the supposition, even though the supposition was not set up for strategic reasons. Bowerman (1986) provided an example of understanding of the *schema for negation introduction* in the spontaneous speech of a two-year old, who told her mother not to kiss her, because if she gets kissed then her paper hat will fall off and get wet in the bath. In this example, the supposition (being kissed) leads to a contradiction (between the desire to keep the paper hat dry and the fact that it will get wet), leading to the negation of the supposition (don't kiss me). We assume that no intention was made in advance to set up a *reductio* argument, but the child clearly seems to understand such an implication.

Constraints that apply to the schema for conditional proof

In mental logic nothing follows from a contradiction except for a realization that some assumption was wrong. This notion that nothing follows from a contradiction entails two constraints on how the schema for conditional proof can be applied. (See Braine & O'Brien, 1991, for a detailed discussion.) First, a supposition can be the antecedent of a conditional conclusion reached via the schema for conditional proof only if the supposition is consistent with prior assumptions (i.e., premise assumptions plus any previously made suppositions). Second, an assumption reiterated into a conditional argument cannot contradict the supposition that is to be the antecedent of the conditional. Note that these latter two constraints reflect the ordinary meaning of the term *suppose*: One cannot suppose something and simultaneously refer to information that is incompatible with the supposition.

How one determines whether a set of premise assumptions is compatible with a supposition, and thus whether some premise can be imported into a suppositional line of reasoning, is outside the scope of the mental logic *per se*. People are notoriously poor at making incompatibility or completeness judgements, as noted earlier, and such matters often are in dispute among interlocutors.

Mental logic at the sentential and predicate-logic levels

Construction of a theory for a mental sentential logic is a much simpler matter than it is for a mental predicate logic. A sentential logic includes only inferences that can be made on the basis of logic particles like *if, and, or,* and negation, whereas a predicate logic requires additional analyses of the internal composition of propositions, including their predicate-argument structure, quantifiers, and ways of marking quantificational scope. At the sentential level, conditionals can be represented as *if p then q*. At the predicate level, logic textbooks tend to represent universally quantified conditionals as $(\forall x)(Px \supset Qx)$. Quite apart from the counterintuitive use of $\supset$, this standard-logic representation presents a counterintuitive way of representing the scope of quantification, using domain-free quantifiers with outside scope. A detailed discussion of the differences in representational format at the predicate-logic level between the standard-logic and mental-logic formats is beyond the scope of this chapter. A sense of the difference, however, is provided by considering how standard logic represents a universally quantified disjunction: $(\forall x)(Px \vee Qx)$. Our system places the quantification inside the sentence, e.g., S_1[All X] OR S_2[PRO-All X], using a pronominal device to mark that the universally quantified Xs that are predicated on S_2 are the same Xs that are predicated on S_1, e.g., the boys went by bus or *they* went by train, where *they* is an anaphoric reflex of *the boys*, and both clauses are marked for universal quantification. Note that in this notational system, the predicates (S_1, S_2), rather than the quantifiers, have outside position, and the quantifiers attach directly to the arguments and thus come within the boundaries of a proposition's content. (See Braine & O'Brien, 1998, Chapter 11, for a detailed discussion of how such quantified propositions are represented in mental logic.)

Basic predictions and supporting evidence concerning conditionals

Braine and O'Brien (1998) and O'Brien (2004) provide reviews of much data in support of mental logic theory, and we present only a few data here to illustrate some issues concerning conditionals. The most basic predictions concern whether people – both children and adults – make judgements that are consistent (a) with *modus ponens* and (b) with the schema for conditional proof, as both are implemented by the DRR. Turning first to modus ponens, a large number of laboratory studies show that both children and adults endorse modus ponens inferences almost universally, and that these inferences tend to be immune task features such as the presence and absence of negation that often influence judgements of other non-basic argument forms (see reviews in Braine & O'Brien, 1991; Braine & Rumain, 1983; Evans, 1982; see also developmental data reported, e.g., by Lecas & Barrouillet, 1999; Markovits, 2000).

The mental logic prediction concerning evaluation of conditional conclusions differs from what would be predicted by the "⊃" of standard logic. When a reasoner evaluates a proposition of the form *if p then q* against a premise set, the preliminary procedure of the DRR adds the antecedent of the conditional, *p*, to the premise set and then treats the consequent, *q*, as the conclusion to be tested. This procedure leads to a judgement that *if p then q* is 'true' when *q* follows, but 'false' when *q* is false under the supposition of *p*. Note that this is judgement is not supported by the '⊃' of standard logic, because *p* might be false.

Problems that require such evaluations were presented to adults by Braine, Reiser, and Rumain (1984) and to children by O'Brien, Dias, Roazzi, and Braine (1998). For example, consider two problems from O'Brien et al., which referred to toy animals in a box:

There is either a Cat or a Rabbit in the box. (2.1)

∴ If there is not a Cat in the box, then there is a Rabbit.

There is either a Cat or a Rabbit in the box. (2.2)

∴ If there is not a Cat in the box, then there is not a Rabbit.

Note that both of these problems share the same single premise (*cat or rabbit*), and both have conditional conclusions with the same antecedent (*not cat*). On both problems the DRR adds the antecedent to the premise set, which leads to derivation of *rabbit*. For Problem (2.1), the DRR then terminates with a 'true' response, so the output of mental logic is the same as what follows in standard logic, and most six to eight-year olds made this response. On Problem (2.2), however, this is incompatible with conclusion to be tested – i.e., that there is not a Rabbit – which yields a 'false' response. This latter response would not follow in standard logic, where one cannot make a definite judgement because there might be a Cat. Research participants, however, consistently made the 'false' response predicted by the mental logic procedure. This finding held up across a large number of similar problems that counterbalanced the presence vs. absence of negatives, and varied the logical terms in the premises.

O'Brien, Roazzi, and Athias (2010) found that illiterate indigenous populations in an isolated region of the Brazilian Amazon also made judgements that were consistent with the mental logic procedures. Problems that were structurally similar to those of Braine et al. (1983) and O'Brien et al. (1998) were constructed, referring to baskets and bracelets. For example, an experimenter placed two baskets and one bracelet under a blanket and told participants (in their native language, Tukano) that the bracelet was being placed into one of the two baskets. The following two propositions then were presented: (a) If the bracelet is not in this basket (pointing to one of the two baskets), then it is in this basket (pointing to the other of the two baskets); (b) If the bracelet is not in this basket, then it is not in this basket. Responses by all participants were consistent with the mental logic predictions. A second set of similar problems was presented with two coloured baskets (one red and one yellow) and a cord. The cord was placed in the red basket, and the baskets then were placed under a blanket. A bracelet then was put inside one of the baskets. Two sentences were presented: (a) If the bracelet is not in the yellow basket, then it is in the basket that contains the cord; (b) If the bracelet is not in the yellow basket, then it is not in the basket that contains the cord. Again, responses universally were those predicted by the mental logic procedures. In summary, for both children and adults in New York and for illiterate adults in an isolated region of the Brazilian Amazon, responses to reasoning problems with conditional conclusions were consistent with the basic predications of mental logic theory rather than with standard logic.

Theories without a mental logic are inadequate

Mental models theory. Johnson-Laird et al. (1992) argued that mental models theory accounts for valid deductions without a mental logic, using the modus ponens argument as an example. These two premises, *if p then q* and *p*, lead to the following models:

$$[p] \; q; \; p; \; p \; q \qquad (2.3)$$

$$\cdots$$

where the sets of models for each of the premises and then their combination are separated by semicolons. The conditional premise is represented by the two models in the left-hand column. One includes both *p* and *q*; the square brackets around the token for *p* in this model indicate that *p* cannot occur in other models with tokens for ~*q* (Johnson-Laird & Byrne, 1991, p. 119). The second model of the first set is an ellipsis that functions as a mental footnote that there may be alternative models in which *p* is false. When the single model for the second premise is combined with the two models for the first premise, the ellipsis is lost, leaving a single final model that would support the conclusion *p and q*; however, *p* is not included in a response because of a pragmatic constraint not to restate the obvious, so subjects give *q* as the conclusion. Thus, say the modellers, a valid deduction need not rely on a mental logic, and requires only models.

Braine et al. (1995) explored some related problems on which this sort of pragmatic constraint would not apply. These related problems presented the same two premises, but either with *p and q* or with *not both p and q* as a final premise. Note that if people are responding on the basis of mental models, the first of these conclusions should lead straightforwardly to a response that the conclusion is valid because it matches exactly the final model for the problem and the second of these conclusions should lead straightforwardly to a response that the conclusion is not valid because it is completely inconsistent with the final model set. Mental logic theory, however, predicts an intermediate reasoning step that is not predicted by models theory for these two problems: The first two premises lead by the *modus ponens* schema to an intermediate conclusion of *q*, which only then can be combined with the second premise, using an AND-introduction schema, to infer *p and q*. Only following this two-step line of reasoning can a response be made to either of these two problems. Braine et al. presented these two problems to participants as part of a set of problems that required participants to write down each intermediate inference made on the way to making a final judgements about a conclusion, and the vast majority of participants wrote down *q* as an intermediate conclusion, even though models theory provides no way to explain such an intermediate inference. Models theory has no way to account for this apparent application of *modus ponens* on the way to making a judgement of the presented conclusion.

More recently, Johnson-Laird and Byrne (2002) argued that children will tend to interpret *if* as having the meaning of a conjunction rather than a conditional because the initial model for *if* has tokens only for *p* and for *q*, and children are unlikely to attend to the information in the ellipsis in the initial model shown in (2.3). Johnson-Laird and Byrne cited data reported by Kuhn (1977) and by Barrouillet and Lecas (1999) to support this claim. When one inspects these studies, however, the data fall short of support for the claim that children think *if* means *and*. Kuhn (1977) reported what can appear at first sight to be a conjunction interpretation of universally quantified *if*-sentences by children. The problems presented pictures of three kinds of bugs – big striped bugs, small striped bugs, and small black bugs – and eight conditionals of the form *If a bug is ___ then it is ___* (*If a bug is big then it is striped, If a bug is small then it is striped*, etc.). When the children were asked to judge each conditional as true or false of the bugs, the second and fourth graders responded as though the sentence form meant, 'There is a bug that is both ___ and ___'. O'Brien et al. (1989) showed that the response tendency that had been reported by Kuhn did not stem from the conditional form of the sentences, but instead from the use of the indefinite article, *a*, as a reflex of the universal quantifier ("If *a* bug..."). O'Brien et al. discovered that the children tended to interpret *a* not as a marker of universal quantification, but as an existential, that is, *a bug* was taken as referring to some particular bug. Note that, for instance, *There is a bug such that if it is small it is striped* is equivalent (in the task presented by Kuhn, where there are some small bugs) to *There is a bug that is small and striped*. O'Brien et al. found in a similar task that using *all* or *if any* rather than *if a* to express the quantifier greatly reduced this response tendency. O'Brien et al. also reported the same response tendency on similar problems that did not present conditionals at all, thus demonstrating that the response tendency did not stem from a tendency to interpret *if* to mean *and*.

Inspection of the study reported by Barrouillet and Lecas (1999) reveals that children were not interpreting *if* as a conjunction. They presented a falsification task that presented a conditional, *if p then q*, with all four of its possible instances, *p and q*, *not-p and q*, *p and not- q*, and *not-p and not-q*, and asked children to identify which case or cases were impermissible. If the children were representing the *if*-sentences as conjunctions as Johnson-Laird and Byrne (2002) suggested, i.e., with a single model that includes a token for *p* and a token for *q*, then they ought to choose instances of *p and not-q*, *not-p and q*, and *not-p and not-q* equally as impermissible, because none of these instances are included in the model. They would have no reason to prefer choosing instances of *p and not-q* more often than instances of the other two types. Inspection of the data presented in Table 2.1 of Lecas and Barrouillet, however, shows that instances of *p and not-q* were chosen far more often than *not-p and q* or *not-p and not-q*, however, with 99% of the nine-year olds judging such instances as impermissible; the other two types of instances were selected as impermissible only 66% of the time. Note that if children really were interpreting *if p then q* as equivalent in meaning to *p and q* as claimed both by Lecas and Barrouillet and by Johnson-Laird and Byrne, there would be no reason for this strong preference for choosing instances of *p and not-q* as impermissible. The data reported by Barrouillet and Lecas thus are consistent with the use of the mental logic, rather than the mental models, procedures.

Even stronger evidence that children do not interpret *if* as a conjunction comes from a study of three and four-year old children in O'Brien, Dias, Roazzi, and Cantor (1998). The children were shown a puppet of Pinocchio, who was making conditional assertions about what children in a park were wearing. In one problem Pinocchio said, 'If a boy is playing basketball, he is wearing sneakers'. The children were asked to choose which of four pictures (corresponding to *p and q*, *not-p and q, p and not-q*, and *not-p and not-q*) would make Pinocchio's nose grow. Children chose the pictures that represented *p and not-q* 67% of the time. If these children were representing *if* with the single explicit model that is equivalent to treating *if* as *and*, there would be no reason for them systematically to prefer the selection of *p and not-q* instances over selections of *not-p and q* and *not-p and not-q* instances. Indeed, the chance level for selection of *p and not-q* should be equal to.33 given that *p and not-q, not-p and q* and *not-p and not-q* all are absent from the conjunction-like model set. Put simply, these data simply do not support the claim that children interpret *if* to have the same meaning as *and*, as they should if the children were representing *if* with the single model with a token for *p* and a token for *q*.

The most serious deficit for models theory for conditionals, we think, concerns the absence of anything in the models *per se* that would cause a reasoner to assert a conditional conclusion. We are told only that a reasoner will 'read off' a conclusion from the final model set for a set of premises, yet these model sets contain only tokens. Granted, the form of models representations is isomorphic to the normal disjunctive form (see Post, 1921), with each row listing a set of conjunctions and the various possible rows disjunctively related. Nothing about such a normal disjunctive form, however, is sufficient to invite a conditional conclusion. Put briefly, models per se are lacking a mechanism to represent that a proposition is being considered suppositionally, and without such a representational mechanism, it is difficult to know why anyone would assert a conditional.

Content-dependent theories

Various proposals that have emphasized the influence of content on reasoning have expressed generally negative views of mental logic. Cosmides (1989), for example, claimed that people do not reason according to 'the canons of logic' (p. 191), arguing instead that the environmental pressures faced by our hunter/gatherer ancestors led to the evolution of a special reasoning module for finding violators of social contracts. These contracts refer to costs and benefits that have the general form that *if one is to take a benefit, one must pay the cost*. This explains, she claimed, why problems that require identification of violators of such regulations often lead to responses that correspond to responses that would be made on the material conditional of standard logic, whereas such responses are comparatively rare when such content is absent.

Alternatively, Cheng and Holyoak and their colleagues (e.g., Cheng & Holyoak, 1985; Cheng, Holyoak, Nisbett, & Oliver, 1986; Holland, Holyoak, Nisbett, & Thagard, 1986; Kroger, Cheng, & Holyoak, 1993) proposed that people typically apply content-dependent pragmatic schemas that are inductively acquired and are defined in terms of goals and actions. According to the pragmatic-schemas approach, any content-general schemas – such as those of a mental logic – could emerge from content-specific ones, but would be rare, so the pragmatic-schemas theorists thus are generally negative about the sorts of schemas we propose. As yet, however, only two pragmatic schemas have been described – one for permissions and one for obligations – and the schemas are claimed to be used in identifying potential violators of rules for permissions and obligations. Again, responses on problems presenting such regulations and requiring identification of rule violators often are equivalent to what would follow on the material conditional of standard logic, but are limited to the specific sort of content that corresponds to the schemas.[3]

Manktelow and Over (1991) and Over and Manktelow (1993) proposed that identification of potential violators of rules such as those described by Cosmides and by Cheng and her associates are governed by the utilities with which such rules are perceived, i.e., by the perceived importance

---

[3] The social-contract and pragmatic-schemas theories also predict some instances in which responses systematically will diverge from the material conditional.

of the constituent activities and regulations. Again, responses based on such utilities often can be the same as those that follow on the material conditional, although such responses are limited to the specific pragmatic sorts of content.

Evidence in favour of these content-dependent theories comes almost entirely from performance on variants of Wason's selection task (e.g., Wason, 1968). In its standard form, the task presents four cards showing, for example, *A*, *D*, *4*, and *7*, respectively, together with a tentative conditional rule, e.g., *if a card has an A on one side, it has a 4 on the other side*, and requires identification of those cards, and only those cards, whose inspection could test whether the rule is true or false. Although identification of the logically appropriate cards is rare, people often succeed in identifying those instances that are potential violators of the sorts of regulations described by these theorists.

Do these theories, or the evidence gathered in their support, present a problem for our mental logic theory? For two reasons, we think not. First, the scope of these theories and the evidence cited in their favour is extremely limited. The theories explain only a limited set of findings that relate mostly to a single task and a single reasoning procedure: identifying violators of certain sorts of conditional regulations. They say nothing of reasoning about a broader class of situations, including, for example, reasoning about alternatives. Indeed, they say nothing about conditional reasoning except with these extremely limited content types. In particular, these theories have no way of accounting for any but an extremely small fraction of the data that exist in support of the mental logic schemas. Note that much of the published data concerns content like letters written on an imaginary blackboard, or toy animals and fruits randomly assigned to small boxes, or beads and various shapes and colours in bags, and none of the content-dependent processes of the social-contract, pragmatic schemas, and utilities theories are applicable in any obvious way to such content. Further, none of these approaches explain why widely varying content are expressed with the same logical formatting, e.g., as conditionals, as alternatives, or as universally quantified.

Second, the pragmatic anchoring of mental logic guarantees a rich variety of content effects. We have illustrated how factual knowledge enriches the knowledge base for inferences (see Braine & O'Brien, 1998; O'Brien, 1993, 2004). Moreover, knowledge of a topic may provide additional inferences from scripts, case inferences, causal inferences, inferences from story grammars, and so forth. In so far as some of the knowledge available from declarative memory is stored as alternatives, conjunctions, conditionals, and negations, it readily could feed the mental logic schemas. Topical knowledge thus would provide additional inferences that pertain directly to the logical particles; for example, situations in which *or* clearly is exclusive would sanction *not q* from *p or q* and *p*. In addition, we have no problem with the claim that people acquire some content-appropriate inference rules. Thus, certain sorts of conditionals, such as those presented by the social-contract, pragmatic-schemas, and utilities theorists, could sanction inferences beyond those available on the skills of the basic mental logic alone. What these theories cannot do, and what a mental logic can, is provide a reason that such regulations all have the form of conditionals. One thus needs a mental logic to account for those sorts of reasoning that go beyond finding violators of a narrow set of conditional regulations, and to understand why these regulations have the form of conditionals.

We agree with Cosmides that human bioevolutionary history has provided some innate reasoning abilities, but we see no *a priori* reason to expect nature to have provided domain-specific inference processes and not domain-general ones. A species with overly specified behavioural traits is at a disadvantage when a situation changes, and a species with reasoning processes that are over-specified in terms of content is at a disadvantage when it encounters a widening set of content domains. (See also O'Brien, Roazzi, & Athias (2010)). As Braine and O'Brien (1998, Chapter 4) argued, an innate representational format provides a unified basis for propositional reasoning, language, and declarative memory, which includes much of what one would consider intelligence. A species with such intelligence would be prepared better for survival than would be a species with only domain-specific inference-making procedures.

Are the content-dependent theories adequate without a mental logic? Thus far the social-contract theory has described only a single social-contract algorithm and only two pragmatic schemas have been described by pragmatic-schemas theory, and their effects have been investigated mainly only for a single sort of task. Only a small variety of conditionals have been considered and reasoning about alternatives has been ignored entirely. Without proliferating an extraordinary number of content-specific rules, it is difficult to see how these theories could account for reasoning over the wide variety of content that can be expressed with particles such as *or* and *if*, including algebraic content. A mental logic provides exactly what is needed – a set of basic inferences for the logical particles that apply across all sorts of content. Without a mental logic the content-dependent theories seem to exist largely as extremely broad promissory notes.

The biases-and-heuristics approach

Several research programmes have claimed that human judgements do not correspond to normative standards, but typically are guided instead by non-normative heuristics and response biases (e.g., Kahneman & Tversky, 1973; Kahneman, Slovic, & Tversky, 1982). The best known advocate of this position in the deductive-reasoning literature is Evans (e.g., Evans, 1982, 1989, 1993), who concluded that the large number of errors reported across a variety of logical-reasoning tasks demonstrates that reasoning is rarely, if ever, governed by logic principles; instead, responses were claimed to reflect primarily a variety of biases, such as a matching bias, a confirmation bias, a set of content biases, a negative-conclusion bias, and so forth, together with some content-specific effects.

The mental logic approach provides no reason to exclude biases and heuristics in the account of human reasoning. We take issue, however, with claims against a mental logic by heuristics-and-biases theorists. According to mental logic theory, when a problem can be solved using the core schemas and the DRR it generally will be, but when a problem is beyond the scope of these basic mental logic skills, people must rely on other resources. Many such problems will elicit 'can't tell' responses, but, as we have discussed elsewhere, there is a bias against 'can't tell' responses (e.g., Braine & Rumain, 1983; O'Brien, et al., 1989; Rumain et al., 1983), and some people (particularly children) are thereby motivated to find a basis for giving a determinate response. Sometimes a determinate response can be supported by an invited inference or by a content-specific process; sometimes it can stem from a guess influenced by a response bias. Evans (1989) reported that responses based on biases occur more often on invalid than on valid argument forms, a finding that is quite consistent with mental logic theory; many valid arguments can be solved by the basic mental logic skills, whereas the basic mental logic inferences usually are of little help on invalid arguments.

Just as we have no problem admitting response biases in the mental logic account, we can see no reason that mental logic should be excluded from the biases-and-heuristics approach. Research programmes in the biases-and-heuristics tradition have found their evidence primarily on problems that subjects find difficult; such findings overlook, as we said above, that there is a set of logical inferences that people (including children) make regularly and easily, and biases and heuristics alone could not account for them.

Probability-based accounts of conditional reasoning

We turn first to Evans, Over, and Handley (Evans, Handley & Over, 2003; Evans & Over, 2004; Evans, Over & Handley, 2005; Over & Evans, 2003), who proposed that in understanding conditionals, people proceed by adding p to their stock of knowledge and then evaluating on that basis the status of their belief in q. Evans et al. (2003) wrote, 'when people assess conditionals, they do so through hypothetical thinking in which they try to construct mental models of the antecedents and, on that basis, assess the believability of the consequents' (p. 323). When one encounters a conditional, *if p then q*, one's attention is focused on the antecedent, p, and mental models are constructed as follows:

    p q

    p not q

To the extent that the first model is assigned a higher probability than is the second, *if p then q* is assigned a high probability. Alternatively, to the extent that the second model is assigned a higher probability than is the first, *if p then q* is assigned a low probability. From the perspective of their proposal, *if p then q* is functionally equivalent to a conditional probability, $P(q|p)$, and one works out $P(q|p)$ from the probabilities assigned to the two models that include tokens for p.

In so far as the procedure described by Evans et al. begins with the supposition of p, it has much in common with our theory of conditionals, although the two theories differ about what happens after one supposes p. According to mental logic theory, *if*-propositions are evaluated by adding the antecedent to the premise set and treating the consequent as the conclusion to be tested. Evans and Over (2004) argued that because we reject the inclusion of a logical semantics – either of a Stalnaker possible-worlds sort or of a mental models sort – and instead ground the meaning of *if* only on its inference procedures, it is impossible in the Braine and O'Brien approach to give any account of the probability of a conditional. As Evans and Over wrote, the mental logic theory could not account for a probability judgement for the conditional 'until they had semantics for their conditionals in term of the possible state of affairs that are fundamental to probability judgement' (p. 59). For Evans and Over, the necessary logical semantics is provided by the two mental models that have tokens for p and q, and for p and *not q*, respectively. Without such a logical semantics, they argued, the conditional proof schema cannot make a probability judgement.

To understand how the two proposals differ in the treatment of probability judgements concerning conditionals, imagine a scenario in which there are two boxes, one large and one small. In the large box are 80 red balls and 20 green balls, and you are asked to evaluate whether *a ball will be red if it is taken from the large box*. Following the proposal of Evans and his associates, you might construct two models and assign probability assignments to each of them, as follows:

    large red   .80

    large not red .20

The differential probability assignments to the two models would lead to the judgement that *it is probably true that if a ball comes from the large box, then it is red*. From the perspective of our mental logic theory, however, you would begin by supposing that a ball is drawn from the large box and then would reason about what would be entailed under that supposition about whether the ball would be red. Remember that one can introduce inferences from a variety of cognitive resources when constructing a line of reasoning, including reasoning under a supposition, so you likely would realize by knowing that 80% of the balls are red so there is an 80% chance that a ball drawn from the large box would be red. The Schema for Conditional Proof thus would allow you to conclude that *if the ball comes from the large box, then it probably is red*. The difference between the account provided by Evans, Over and Handley and the account provided by mental logic concerns where probability would be placed. Following the procedures described by Evans and his colleagues, one would place probability outside the conditional proposition (*it is probably true that …*), which is tantamount to a metalogical inference about the conditional, whereas following the procedures described by the mental logic procedures, one would place probability inside the conditional proposition by attaching it to the consequent clause (*… then it probably is red*).[4] Clearly, Evans and Over (2004) were wrong in suggesting that without a separate semantics provided by the sorts of models they describe the mental logic procedures have no way to make judgements about probabilities.

We turn now to a proposal made by Oaksford and Chater (e.g., Oaksford & Chater, 1994, 1996, 1998, 2003a, 2003b, 2003c, 2003d; Oaksford, Chater, & Larkin, 2000) for conditional reasoning. Their basic proposal was that the probability that someone will accept an inference depends on the strength of their conditional belief in the conclusion given the premises and other background information. The approach can be illustrated with a modus ponens argument that has the major premise, *if Tweety is a bird, then Tweety flies* and the minor premise that *Tweety is a bird*. The inference that *Tweety flies* will depend on the degree of belief in the premises. To the extent to which belief in the premises is weakened, acceptance of the conclusion becomes less probable. For example, when the minor premise states that *Tweety is a penguin*, belief in the major premise will be weakened so that the conclusion is unlikely to be accepted. Oaksford and Chater provided formulae that can make predictions about the probabilities that conclusions will be accepted for particular sorts of conditional arguments. For example, the probability that a modus tollens inference will be accepted is equal to $[1 - P(Fx) - P(Bx)(1 - P(Fx|Bx))]/1 - P(Fx)$, although Oaksford and Chater stated, 'we doubt that people make these actual calculations' (2003b, p. 364).

Oaksford and Chater also argued against a role for a mental logic in human reasoning. First, they argued that a mental logic theory would view logic connectives in a truth-functional way; in particular, they claimed that the Braine and O'Brien theory of *if* assumes the truth-functional material conditional (e.g., Oaksford & Chater, 2003b, p. 360). Of course, as described earlier, we always have argued that the material conditional does *not* provide a psychologically plausible account of *if*, and our theory of *if* makes predictions that differ from what would be predicted from adopting the material conditional as a psychological model, making moot this argument by Oaksford and Chater.

An additional argument that Oaksford and Chater have made against a mental logic stems from the fact that human reasoning is nonmonotonic, that is, adding premises does not always increase the number of conclusions that can be drawn. Instead conclusions can be defeasible, and 'putative conclusions can be defeated by subsequent information' (Oaksford & Chater, 1993, p. 34). For example, the conclusion that *Tweety can fly* that follows from the premises that *If Tweety is a bird, then Tweety can fly* and *Tweety is a bird* will be withdrawn when one discovers that Tweety is a penguin. Oaksford and Chater argued that such instances of defeasibility present a problem for mental logic theories; standard logic is monotonic and thus is unable to account for defeasible arguments. Mental logic theorists, wrote Oaksford and Chater, tend to dismiss the defeasibilty problem as resulting from 'interfering pragmatic or performance factors' (1993, p. 41).

Seeing defeasibility as a problem for mental logic overlooks our proposal that mental logic is not equivalent to standard logic. In particular, we have argued that unlike standard logic, in which anything can be derived from a contradiction, nothing can be concluded in mental logic from a contradiction except that some mistake has been made, and the example that *Tweety is a penguin* seems to be just such an example that some mistake has been made. Oaksford and Chater

---

4 We doubt ordinary reasoners would appreciate a difference between the inside and outside placement of probability in these surface-structure conditionals; as Braine and O'Brien (1991) noted, plausibility is a more important determinant of how meaning is interpreted than is surface-structure adjacency.

are correct in pointing out that mental logic theorists often refer to pragmatics, but this is not a reference to something that interferes in the reasoning process. As we argued earlier, mental logic is profoundly embedded in a pragmatic architecture and evolved to serve pragmatic needs. Thus, inferences from a wide variety of processes can co-habit comfortably with inferences from the logic schemas. Let us consider the example of the discovery that Tweety is a penguin, which leads one – on the basis of world knowledge about penguins as a special case of flightless birds to withdraw the inference – that Tweety can fly – that followed from the conditional that *if Tweety is a bird, then Tweety can fly*. From the mental logic perspective this presents no problem. The contradiction between the discovery that Tweety is a penguin (who thus cannot fly) and the earlier conclusion that Tweety can fly, leads us to conclude simply that the conditional premise was mistaken. Because the mental logic schemas can be applied only to premises that are assumed to be true (see O'Brien, 1993), we realize that the modus ponens schema was applied erroneously, and so the erroneous inference should be withdrawn. Although Oaksford's and Chater's criticism would apply if one proposed standard logic as a psychological model, it does not apply to our mental logic proposal.[5]

We turn now to the question of whether the conditional-probabilities model of Oaksford and Chater could provide an adequate theory of deductive reasoning without a mental logic. One way of posing this question is to ask how well their approach could account for the data that exist in support of mental logic theory. The Oaksford and Chater account is dependent on the assumption that people have prior beliefs about the premises, which raises the question of its applicability in situations in which people are presented a reasoning problem for which they are unlikely to have prior beliefs. To address this issue, Oaksford and Chater (2003b; see also Schroyens, Schaeken, Fias, & d'Ydewalle, 2000), proposed that even when people are presented abstract reasoning problems they will refer to prior beliefs about the domain, e.g., beliefs about the frequencies of letters or numbers in the original Wason's selection task. What prior beliefs would people be able to bring to bear, however, on problems with materials like those reported in Yang, Braine, and O'Brien (1998, Table 2.6), that referred to beads of various colours, sizes, and shapes? Yang et al. reported that people not only evaluate conclusions across dozens of reasoning problems correctly, but that their judgements about relative problem difficulties can be predicted by the schemas that mental logic theory proposes, with two-thirds of the variance accounted for when observed difficulty ratings are correlated with predicted difficulty ratings. Clearly, prior beliefs about the probabilities of colours, sizes, and shapes of beads cannot account for such reasoning data. To promise that prior beliefs about letters and numbers, or about any other sort of content, might help account for these data, or for the ordinal sequences of inferences that participants wrote down in both sentential- and predicate-level reasoning problems as reported by Braine et al. (1995), O'Brien et al. (1994), or O'Brien et al. (2007), requires that one describe what such prior beliefs are and how they then lead to probability computations that could account for the data. Finally, the Oaksford and Chater proposal has been applied only to two types of tasks that present conditionals – to the four conditional-syllogisms tasks and to Wason's selection task – and would need to be developed so that it could be applied to reasoning about conjunctions, alternatives, quantifiers, etc., that are included in the schemas and reasoning programmes

---

[5] The Oaksford and Chater argument also seems to miss the fact that in order for the modus-ponens inference to be withdrawn, it had to be made in the first place, which is explained parsimoniously in mental logic theory through the application of the modus ponens schema. Nothing in the Oaksford and Chater theory accounts for the initial modus ponens inference.

presented in Chapter 6 and 11 of Braine and O'Brien (1998). Nothing indicates that this could be done, indicating that their approach cannot provide an alternative to our theory.

Conclusions

This chapter concentrated on making the following points. First, we should expect the existence of a mental logic because (a) some sort of logical predicate/argument structure is needed in order to represent propositional information, (b) such a logical format needs some way to keep track of which propositions are true, which are false, and which are being considered as suppositionally true, and (c) an intelligent species needs procedures to make inferences that go beyond the information as given. Second, mental logic is not identical to the logic found in standard logic textbooks. Third, mental logic theory provides a sufficiently detailed hypothesis about the mental logic representational format, about the inference schemas, and about the implementation procedures, to make detailed predictions about the introduction and discharge of propositions in lines of natural reasoning. Fourth, ample evidence exists in support of these predictions. Fifth, alternative theories of human deductive reasoning are inadequate unless they include a mental logic. We also have argued that a separate logical semantics is not needed, because an adequate semantics for logic terms is provided by an inference-role semantics.

References

Barrouillet, P. & Lecas, J. -F. (1999). Mental models in conditional reasoning and working memory. *Thinking & Reasoning*, **5**, 289–302.

Bowerman, E. (1986). First steps in aquiring conditionals. In E. Traugott, A. ter Meulen, J. S. Reilly, & C. A. Ferguson (Eds.). *On conditionals.* Cambridge, UK: Cambridge University Press.

Braine, M. D. S. (1990). The natural logic approach to reasoning. In W. F. Overton (Ed.). *Reasoning, necessity, and logic: Developmental perspectives.* Hillsdale, NJ: Erlbaum.

Braine, M. D. S. & O'Brien, D. P. (1991). A theory of if: A lexical entry, reasoning program, and pragmatic principles. *Psychological Review*, **98**, 182–203. Reprinted in M. D. S. Braine and D. P. O'Brien (Eds.). (1998). *Mental logic.* Mahwah, NJ: Lawrence Erlbaum Associates.

Braine, M. D. S. & O'Brien, D. P. (Eds.) (1998). *Mental logic.* Mahwah, NJ: Lawrence Erlbaum Associates.

Braine, M. D. S., O'Brien, D. P., Noveck, I. A., Samuels, M., Lea, R. B., Fisch, S. M., & Yang, Y. (1995). Predicting intermediate and multiple conclusions in propositional logic inference problems: Further evidence for a mental logic. *Journal of Experimental Psychology: General*, **124**, 263–292. Reprinted in M. D. S. Braine and D. P. O'Brien (Eds.) *Mental logic.* (pp. 145–196). Mahwah, NJ: Lawrence Erlbaum Associates.

Braine, M. D. S., Reiser, B. J., & Rumain, B. (1984/1998). Some empirical justification for a theory of natural propositional logic. In G. H. Bower (Ed.). *The psychology of learning and motivation: Advances in research and theory.* New York: Academic Press. Reprinted in M. D. S. Braine & D. P. O'Brien (Eds.). (1998). *Mental logic.* Mahwah, NJ: Lawrence Erlbaum Associates.

Braine, M. D. S. & Rumain, B. (1983). Logical reasoning. In J. H. Flavell & E. M. Markman (Eds.). *Handbook of child psychology: Vol. 3. Cognitive development.* New York: Wiley.

Cheng, P. W. & Holyoak, K. J. (1989). On the natural selection of reasoning theories. *Cognition*, **33**, 285–313.

Cheng, P. W., Holyoak, K. J., Nisbett, R. E., & Oliver, L. M. (1986). Pragmatic versus syntactic approaches to training deductive reasoning. *Cognitive psychology*, **18**, 293–328.

Cosmides, L. (1989). The logic of social exchange: Has natural selection shaped how humans reason? Studies with the Wason selection task? *Cognition*, **31**, 187–276.

Evans, J. St.B. T. (1982). *The psychology of deductive reasoning.* London: Routledge & Kegan Paul.

Evans, J. St.B. T. (1989). *Bias in reasoning: Causes and consequences.* Hove, UK: Erlbaum.

Evans, J. St.B. T. (1993). Bias and rationality. In K. I. Manktelow & D. E. Over (Eds.). *Rationality: Psychological and philosophical perspectives*. London: Routledge.

Evans, J. St.B. T. Handley, S. J., & Over, D. (2003). Conditionals and conditional probability. *Journal of Experimental Psychology: Learning, memory, & cognition*, **29**, 321–335.

Evans, J. St.B. T. & Over, D. E. (2004). *If*. Cambridge, UK: Cambridge University Press.

Evans, J. St.B. T., Over, D. E., & Handley, S. J. (2005). Supposition, extensionality and conditionals: A critique of the mental model theory of Johnson-Laird and Byrne (2002). *Psychological Review*, **112**, 1042–1052.

Fodor, J. (1975). *The language of thought*. Cambridge, MA: Harvard University Press.

Fodor, J. & Lepore, E. (1991). Why meaning (probably) isn't conceptual role. *Language and Mind*, **6**, 328–343.

Holland, J. H., Holyoak, K. J., Nisbett, R. E., & Thagard, P. (1986). *Induction: Processes of inference, learning, and discovery*. Cambridge, MA: MIT Press.

Johnson-Laird, P. N. & Byrne, R. M. J. (2002). Conditionals: A theory of meaning, pragmatics, and inference. *Psychological Review*, **109**, 646–678.

Johnson-Laird, P. N. & Byrne, R. M. J. (1991). *Deduction*. Hove, UK: Lawrence Erlbaum Associates.

Johnson-Laird, P. N., Byrne, R. M. J., & Schaeken, W. (1992). Propositional reasoning by models. *Psychological Review*, **99**, 418–439.

Kahneman, D., Slovic, P., & Tversky, A. (1982). *Judgment under uncertainty: heuristics and biases*. Cambridge, UK: Cambridge University Press.

Kahneman, D. & Tversky, A. (1973). On the psychology of deduction. *Psychological Review*, **80**, 237–251.

Kneale, W. & Kneale, M. (1962). *The development of logic*. Oxford, UK: Oxford University Press.

Kroger, J. K., Cheng, P. W., & Holyoak, K. J. (1993). Evoking the permission schema: The impact of explicit negations and a violations-checking context. *Quarterly Journal of Psychology*, **46A**, 615–635.

Kuhn, D. (1977). Conditional reasoning in children. *Developmental Psychology*, **13**, 342–353.

Lecas, J.-F. & Barrouillet, P. (1999). Understanding of conditional rules in childhood and adolescence: A mental models approach. *Current Psychology of Cognition*, **18**, 363–396.

Macnamara, J. (1986). *A border dispute: The place of logic in psychology*. Cambridge, MA: MIT Press.

Manktelow, K. I. & Over, D. E. (1990). Social roles and utility in reasoning with deontic conditionals. *Cognition*, **39**, 85–105.

Markovits, H. (2000). A mental model analysis of young children's conditional reasoning with meaningful premises. *Thinking and Reasoning*, **6**, 335–347.

Oaksford, M. & Chater, N. (1993). Reasoning theories and bounded rationality. In K. I. Manktelow & D. E. Over (Eds.) *Rationality: Psychological and philosophical perspectives*. London, UK: Routledge.

Oaksford, M. & Chater, N. (1994). A rational analysis of the selection task as optimal data sselection. *Psychological Review*, **101**, 608–631.

Oaksford, M. & Chater, N. (1996). Rational explanation of the selection task. *Pscyhological Review*, **103**, 381–391.

Oaksford, M. & Chater, N. (1998). *Rationality in an uncertain world: Essays on the cognitive science of human reasoning*. Hove, UK: Psychology Press.

Oaksford, M. & Chater, N. (2003a). Modelling probabilistic effects in conditional inference: Validating search or conditional probability? *Psychologica*, **32**, 217–242.

Oaksford, M. & Chater, N. (2003b). Conditional probability and the cognitive science of conditional reasoning. *Mind & Language*, **18**, 359–379.

Oaksford, M. & Chater, N. (2003c). Computational levels and conditional reasoning: A reply to Schroyens and Schaeken. *Journal of Experimental Psychology: Learning, Memory and Cognition*, **29**, 150–156.

Oaksford, M. & Chater, N. (2003d). Probabilities and pragmatics in conditional inferences: Suppression and order effects. In D. Hardman & L. Macchi (Eds.). *Thinking: Psychological perspectives on reasoning, judgements and decision making*, (pp. 95–122). Chichester, UK: John Wiley and Sons, Ltd.

Oaksford, M., Chater, N., & Larkin, J. (2000). Probabilities and polarity biases in conditional inference. *Journal of Experimental Psychology: Learning, Memory, and Cognition*, **26**, 883–899.

O'Brien, D. P. (1993). Mental logic and irrationality: We can put a man on the moon, so why can't we solve those logical reasoning problems? In K. I. Manktelow & D. E. Over (Eds.). *Rationality: Psychological and philosophical perspectives*. London: Routledge. Reprinted in M. D. S Braine & D. P. O'Brien (Eds.). (1998). *Mental logic*. Mahwah, NJ: Lawrence Erlbaum Associates.

O'Brien, D. P. (2004). Mental-Logic theory: What it proposes, and reasons to take this proposal seriously. In J. Leighton R. J. & Sternberg (Eds.), *The nature of reasoning* (pp. 205–233). New Haven, CT: Cambridge University Press.

O'Brien, D. P., Braine, M. D. S., Connell, J., Noveck. I. A., Fisch, S. M., & Fun, E. (1989). Reasoning about conditional sentences: Development of understanding of cues to quantification. *Journal of Experimental Child Psychology*, **48**, 90–113.

O'Brien, D. P., Dias, M. G., Roazzi, A., & Braine, M. D. S. (1998). Conditional reasoning: The logic of supposition and children's understanding of pretense. In M. D. S. Braine and D. P. O'Brien (Eds.). *Mental logic*. Mahwah, NJ: Lawrence Erlbaum Associates.

O'Brien, D. P., Dias, M. G., Roazzi, A., & Cantor, J. B. (1998). *Pinocchio's nose knows: Preschool children recognize that a pragmatic rule can be violated, an indicative conditional can be falsified, that a broken promise is a false promise*. In M. D. S. Braine & D. P. O'Brien (Eds.). *Mental logic*. Mahwah, NJ: Lawrence Erlbaum Associates.

O'Brien, D. P., Grgas, J., Dias, M. G., Roazzi, A., & Brooks, P. J. (2007). Predicting Multiple Inferences on Predicate-Logic Reasoning Problems: Direct Evidence in Support of a Theory of Mental Predicate Logic. Manuscript in preparation.

O'Brien, D. P., Roazzi, A., Athias, R., & Brandão, M. C. (2007a). What Sorts of Reasoning Modules Have Been Provided by Evolution? Some Experiments Conducted Among Tukano Speakers in Brazilian Amazônia Concerning Reasoning About Conditional Propositions and About Conditional Probabilities. In M. Roberts (Ed.). *Integrating the Mind: Domain General vs. Domain Specific Processes in Higher Cognition*, (pp. 59–81). Hove, UK: Psychology Press.

O'Brien, D.P., Roazzi, A, & Athias, R. (2010). An Experimental Investigation of Logical Reasoning by Tukano (Daseá) Speakers in Brazilian Amazonia and by North American University Students. Manuscript in preparation.

Over, D. E. & Evans, J. St.B. T. (2003). The probability of conditionals: The psychological evidence. *Mind and Language*, **18**, 340–358.

Over, D. E. & Manktelow, K. (1993). Rationality, utility, and deontic reasoning. In K. I. Manktelow & D. E. Over (Eds.). *Rationality: Psychological and philosophical perspectives*. London: Routledge.

Rumain, B., Connell, J., & Braine, M. D. S. (1983). Conversational comprehension processes are responsible for reasoning fallacies in children as well as adults: If is not the biconditional. *Developmental Psychology*, **19**, 471–481.

Schroyens, W., Schaeken, W., Fias, W., & d' Ydewalle, G. (2000). Heuristic and analytive processes in propositional reasoning with negatives. *Journal of experimental Psychology*: Learning, memory and cognition, **26**, 1713–1734.

Wason, P.C. (1968). Reasoning about a rule. *Quarterly Journal of Experimental Psychology*, **20**, 273–281.

Yang, Y., Braine, M. D. S. & O'Brien, D. P. (1998). Some empirical justification of the mental-predicate-logic model. In M. D. S Braine & D. P. O'Brien (Eds.). *Mental logic*. Mahwah, NJ: Lawrence Erlbaum Associates.

Chapter 3

Conditionals and possibilities

Ruth M.J. Byrne and Philip N. Johnson-Laird

Introduction

If Bush wants to end the war then it is not evident in his press conferences.

This conditional assertion is true, at least at the time of writing (July 2007). And, as an example of an everyday conditional, it seems unexceptional. Such conditionals are so ubiquitous that they prompt the question to those who haven't studied them: what's so special about conditionals? In fact, conditionals are deeply problematic: no consensus exists about what they mean, how they are understood, or how reasoning is carried out from them. Our aim in this chapter is to try to answer these three questions from the standpoint of one psychological theory – the theory of *mental models*. According to this theory, human thinking rests on the ability to imagine possibilities. This hypothesis has been explored in a variety of domains from intuitive inferences to reverse engineering, but nowhere is it more pertinent than to reasoning based on conditionals. Our aim in what follows is to integrate an earlier account of conditionals (Johnson-Laird & Byrne, 2002), a theory of counterfactual thinking (Byrne, 2005), and a general explanation of reasoning (Johnson-Laird, 2006).

When you imagine a situation, such as that Bush wants to end the war, you are engaged in an exercise crucial to human rationality. Without this ability to imagine possibilities, you wouldn't be able to reason, to plan, to predict, to formulate strategies, or to solve problems. And you wouldn't understand conditionals either. But, your ability to imagine possibilities is constrained by various factors, including the capacity of your working memory. Hence, the key to unlocking the workings of conditionals is to consider the general factors constraining comprehension and reasoning. Indeed, what we show in this chapter is that the complexity of conditionals arises from interactions among a small set of separate and simple components. The plan of this chapter is accordingly to begin with grammar, to consider the interpretation of basic conditionals, to describe semantic and pragmatic factors that affect this interpretation, and to end with a consideration of the strategies that individuals use to reason from conditionals.

The grammar of conditionals

The first component that affects conditionals is grammar. Their interpretation in English depends on their tense, mood, aspect, and the auxiliary verbs that they contain. They also have a grammatical structure that differs from sentences formed with other connectives, such as 'and' and 'or'. The if-clause in a conditional is subordinate to the main then-clause, whereas 'and' and 'or' can interconnect two main clauses. One simple test illustrates this difference. Certain phrases, such as 'it is necessary that' normally apply to a sentence as a whole. For example, the assertion:

It is necessary that the troops leave and that the President resigns means that both actions are necessary. But, when such phrases occur at the head of a sentence containing a subordinate and a main clause, they apply only to the main clause. Hence, an assertion using 'before' in a subordinate clause, such as:

It is necessary that before the troops leave the President resigns

is synonymous with:

Before the troops leave it is necessary that the President resigns.

The two assertions may differ in connotations, but when one of them is true so is the other. Exactly the same phenomenon occurs with conditionals. Hence, the assertion:

It is necessary that if the troops leave then the President resigns

is synonymous with:

If the troops leave then it is necessary that the President resigns.

One reason why this grammatical point is important is that it may have misled theorists about the probabilities of conditionals (see Girotto & Johnson-Laird, this volume).

Other peculiarities of grammar also occur with conditionals (see, e.g., Dudman, 1984). Indo-European languages often contain special moods for the clauses in conditionals. In English, the equivalent of the subjunctive may occur in a conditional, e.g.,:

If the President *were* to resign then the troops *would* leave.

This conditional concerns hypothetical events in much the same way as a conditional in the indicative mood:

If the President resigns then the troops will leave.

But, in the past tense, an important ambiguity occurs. An assertion such as:

If the President had resigned then the troops would have left

has two distinct interpretations. One interpretation leaves open whether or not the President resigned, but states a consequence if he had done so. The other interpretation is *counterfactual*. It means that once it was possible that the President would resign and the troops would leave, but this possibility did not occur: it is contrary to the facts, which are that the President did not resign and the troops did not leave. Counterfactual conditionals have led to developments in philosophical semantics (Stalnaker, 1968; Lewis, 1973; Pollock, 1986). The creation of counterfactual alternatives to reality underlies emotions, such as regret, guilt, and hope (e.g., Roese & Olson, 1995). It also underlies social ascriptions, such as blame, fault, and responsibility (e.g., Mandel, Hilton, & Catellani, 2005). And it calls for the imagination of situations that were once possible but are so no longer. Such interpretations yield some striking psychological phenomena to which we return presently.

Basic conditionals

Consider, again, the conditional with which we began: *If Bush wants to end the war then it is not evident in his press conferences.* What does the 'it' in the then-clause refer to? The answer is: Bush wanting to the end the war. The reference is made explicit in this paraphrase: if Bush wants to end the war then his wanting to end the war is not evident in his press conferences. You make this interpretation of 'it' in the conditional without a second's thought, but how you assign referents to pronouns is not well understood, and in this case it illustrates an important fact about many conditionals: the if-clause and the then-clause may both refer to something in common. This co-reference can have drastic effects on the meaning of conditionals. And so we start our analysis with *basic* conditionals, those in which there are no relations between the if-clause and the then-clause beyond their co-occurrence in the same conditional.

The theory of mental models – or the model theory, for short – distinguishes between the meaning of an assertion, and its interpretation. The meaning of an assertion refers to a set of possibilities consistent with the assertion, whereas its interpretation consists of one or more mental models, which usually represent just some of these possibilities (Johnson-Laird & Byrne, 1991). This contrast is clear in the case of a basic conditional, such as:

If there are daisies then there are poppies

Its meaning refers to three possibilities, which concern the presence or absence of the flowers:

1. daisies   poppies
2. no daisies   no poppies
3. no daisies   poppies

A computer program that implements the model theory has this information about conditionals, and comparable information about other connectives, such as 'and' and 'or'. Given a compound assertion such as: *If there are daisies or there are poppies then there are roses and there are daffodils,* it can spell out the full set of possibilities consistent with the assertion from a recursive use of its representation of the meanings of the different connectives. We refer to this set as the 'fully explicit models' of the assertion to contrast them with its mental models.

Human reasoners can spell out the fully explicit models of the possibilities consistent with basic conditionals. As Barrouillet and his colleagues have shown, they gradually develop this ability from childhood (e.g., Barrouillet & Leças, 1999; Barrouillet, Grosset, & Leças, 2000). Children list only the first possibility above: they interpret 'if' as though it meant 'and'. Young adolescents list the first two possibilities. And only older adolescents and adults list all three possibilities. The processing capacity of working memory, however, is a better predictor of performance than age. The ability to list the possibilities compatible with sentences containing connectives seems trivial, but human performance breaks down with sentences containing just a handful of connectives.

A different task is to evaluate whether a basic conditional is true or false given a particular state of affairs in the world. In the laboratory, participants can evaluate a conditional, such as:

If there is an 'A' then there is a '2'

in the light of a contingency in which, say, there is an *A* and 2. In this case, the majority respond that the conditional is true. Likewise, given an *A* and 3, the majority respond that the conditional is false. But, for cases in which the if-clause is false, such as *B* and 2, or *B* and 3, most participants respond that these cases are irrelevant to the truth or falsity of the conditional (see, e.g., Evans, 2007, for a review).

There is an apparent inconsistency between the task of listing possibilities and the task of judging truth values. For the conditional above, which we abbreviate as, *if A then 2*, individuals judge that the case of *B* and 2 is irrelevant to the conditional's truth value, whereas they list this case as possible given the truth of the conditional. When these observations were first made, one of the present authors suggested a 'defective truth table' for conditionals, that is, they had no truth value when their if-clauses were false. This idea was due to a well-known logician, Quine (1952), and it has had several recent defenders (e.g., O'Brien, 1999; Evans & Over, 2004). But, it fails for a reason that we failed to notice until recently. Consider this inference:

The following assertion is true or false. If Bush wants to end the war then it is not evident in his press conferences.
Therefore, Bush wants to end the war.

The conditional premise is either true or false, and so according to the defective truth table its if-clause must be true too, because that is the only way in which the conditional as a whole can be either true or false. Hence, the preceding inference is valid, that is, if its premises are true then its conclusion must be true. In fact, both of its premises are true, and so its conclusion is true too. In other words, all true conditionals (and all false conditionals) validly imply the truth of their if-clauses. But, that's absurd. Hence, the theory of defective truth tables for conditionals is not viable. It also fails to explain performance in listing possibilities consistent with conditionals.

How are we to explain the judgments of truth and falsity? The answer depends on mental models, which are based on a principle of truth. This principle encapsulates a widespread phenomenon in human thinking: individuals tend to think about what is true rather than false (Johnson-Laird & Byrne, 1991), about what is possible rather than impossible (Goldvarg & Johnson-Laird, 2000), about what is permissible rather than impermissible (Bucciarelli & Johnson-Laird, 2005), and about what are positive instances rather than negative instances of hypotheses, concepts, and outputs of systems (Klayman & Ha, 1987; Goodwin & Johnson-Laird, 2007; and Lee & Johnson-Laird, 2007).

When individuals think about the basic conditional, 'if there are daisies then there are poppies', they envisage the possibilities in which it is true. They do not normally think about the possibility in which it is false: daisies and no poppies. But, the principle of truth also applies within the conditional to its subordinate if-clause: individuals do not normally think about the possibilities in which the if-clause is false, either. Hence, their mental models of the conditional represent one possibility explicitly, and other possibilities only implicitly:

> daisies   poppies
> ...

The ellipsis in this diagram denotes an implicit model – one that has no explicit content – representing the possibilities in which the if-clause is false. If individuals retain this information about the if-clause then they should be able to flesh out the mental models into *fully explicit* models of the three possibilities. Likewise, they can construct a model of the situation in which the conditional is false: daisies and no poppies. Mental models are accordingly much more parsimonious than fully explicit models, and so individuals rely on mental models because they reduce the load on working memory.

A simple explanation of the difference between evaluating truth or falsity and listing possibilities is that individuals rely on mental models of the conditional in the evaluation task but are able to flesh them out into fully explicit models when they are asked to list possibilities (Johnson-Laird & Byrne, 2002). The first task is more complex because it calls for the use of the meta-linguistic terms, 'true' and 'false' and for a comparison between language and the world. Barrouillet and his colleagues take this argument one step further: they make an epistemic distinction between evaluating the truth of a conditional given a situation and reasoning about possibilities given the truth of a conditional (Barrouillet, Gauffroy, & Leças, 2008). A corollary of their hypothesis is that children who list as possible only one case – daisies and poppies – should judge that the other three cases make the conditional false. Because children develop, listing an increasing number of cases as possible, there should be a mirror-image decline in the number of cases that they judge as making the conditional false. Barrouillet and his colleagues corroborated this prediction experimentally.

A basic conditional, as we have seen, is consistent with three possibilities. A basic biconditional, such as:

> If and only if there are daisies then there are poppies.

is consistent with only two possibilities:

> daisies   poppies
> no daisies no poppies

The key difference between the basic conditional and the basic biconditional concerns this possibility:

> no daisies poppies

It is consistent with a basic conditional but inconsistent with a basic biconditional. The distinction yields a prediction. According to the model theory, people think about true possibilities rather than false possibilities. Hence, they should be more likely to represent the preceding possibility when they understand a conditional than when they understand a biconditional.

How can experimenters find out whether individuals have thought about a possibility? Early studies relied on the inferences that they made (see Manktelow, 1999 for a review). They reasoned better from basic biconditionals, which are consistent with two possibilities, than from basic conditionals, which are consistent with three possibilities (Johnson-Laird, Byrne, & Schaeken, 1992). Likewise, there was a difference with inferences of the form known as *modus tollens*, such as: If there are daisies then there are poppies; there are no poppies; therefore, there are no daisies. These inferences are easier when the categorical premise was presented prior to the conditional premise rather than vice versa. The model theory predicts this phenomenon: when the categorical premise occurs first, it blocks the representation of the explicit mental model in which the if-clause is true and thereby makes it easier to represent the possibility in which it is false (Girotto, Mazzoco, & Tasso, 1997).

A recent method provides a subtler but more direct measure of the possibilities individuals have in mind when they understand a conditional. It does so without the risk of prompting them to think of possibilities that would not otherwise occur to them. The participants read a story containing both a conditional and a subsequent conjunction describing a possibility, e.g.,:

> Carmen went shopping to the market. When Carmen looked at the poster she saw written on it, 'if there are daisies there are poppies'. When she looked at the shelves she saw that there were daisies and there were poppies. Carmen checked her list of purchases.

The participants read the story in their own time, and the length of time they spend reading each sentence provides evidence about whether they have thought of a possibility beforehand. If they have, they should read the description of the possibility faster than otherwise. The procedure has provided evidence about individuals' understanding of various sorts of conditional, both indicative (Santamaria & Espino, 2002) and counterfactual (Santamaria, Espino, & Byrne, 2005).

In a recent experiment using this method, the participants read 48 stories containing either a basic conditional or a basic biconditional, and subsequent conjunctions describing various possibilities (Espino, Santamaria, & Byrne, 2009, Experiment 2). The sentences in each story were presented one at a time on a computer under the participants' control. To ensure that they understood the stories, they answered simple questions at the end of each story, such as: 'Did Carmen go to the market?'. The results corroborated a predicted interaction. The participants were about a quarter of a second faster to read a conjunction, such as: 'There were no daisies and there were poppies', in a story containing a conditional than in a story containing a biconditional. The conjunction is consistent with the conditional, but not with the biconditional. Yet, there was no reliable difference in the times to read a conjunction consistent with both the conditional and the biconditional, such as: 'There were daisies and there were poppies'. Hence, individuals read a description of what was possible (according to an earlier conditional) faster than a description of what was impossible. In accordance with the principle of truth, when they understood the conditional, they thought of what was possible rather than what was not possible.

Most studies of reasoning from conditionals have examined four traditional inferences from basic conditionals of the form, *If A then C,* when they are combined with an additional categorical premise as shown here:

Modus ponens: *A;* therefore, *C.*
Affirmation of the consequent then-clause: *C;* therefore, *A.*

Modus tollens: *not C*; therefore, *not A*.
Denial of the antecedent if-clause: *not A;* therefore, *not C*.

Affirmation of the consequent and denial of the antecedent are valid only if the conditional is interpreted as a biconditional.

Many studies of these four inferences have been carried out, and meta-analyses have shown that the model theory gives a better account of the results than other theories (Schroyens, Schaeken, & d'Ydewalle, 2001; Schroyens & Schaeken, 2003). Chronometric studies have shown that the model theory predicts the time course of conditional inferences more accurately than other theories (Barrouillet et al., 2000). And Oberauer (2006) formalized various theories of conditionals, fitted them to data, and showed that the model theory gives a better account of the four inferences than either a suppositional theory (Evans & Over, 2004) or a probabilistic theory (Oaksford, Chater, & Larkin, 2000). To do so, however, the model theory must take into account that it is easier to reason forwards from the if-clause than to reason backwards from the then-clause.

Mental models also predict the occurrence of compelling but illusory inferences from conditionals and other connectives. Consider this premise as an example:

If there's a king then there's an ace, or else if there isn't a king then there's an ace.

Its mental models do not represent what is false and they imply that there's an ace. Most individuals draw this conclusion (Johnson-Laird & Savary, 1999). But, the force of 'or else' is that one of the conditionals may be *false*. However, individuals tend not to think about what's false, and so they overlook that when either conditional is false, there isn't an ace. Hence, mental models imply a compelling but invalid conclusion.

Basic counterfactual conditionals

According to the principle of truth, mental models represent only what is true and so you normally think about what is true rather than about what is false. You also tend to be parsimonious in the number of models that you represent, in order to reduce the load on working memory (Goodwin & Johnson-Laird, 2005). Hence, by default, you tend to think about a few true possibilities – ideally just one (see Schroyens, this volume). Yet, in some circumstances you do think about false possibilities and about more than one possibility. One such circumstance is when you understand a conditional as counterfactual, e.g.,:

If Tim had been handsome, then Peg would have married him.

You create a representation of a situation that was once possible but that did not occur, i.e., a representation of a proposition that is false: Tim was handsome and Peg married him. This ability is important, and Byrne (2005, p. 35) proposes a principle of counterfactual possibilities: you can think about possibilities that once were true possibilities but that are no longer true. In addition, you should also represent the facts of the matter: Tim was not handsome and Peg did not marry him. You may know these facts to be true, or assume that the speaker presupposed them whether or not you believe them. You keep in mind models of the two possibilities and keep track of which one is a conjecture contrary to the facts and which one is a fact or presupposition. We now turn to the evidence for this account.

One source of evidence is the study of reading times (Santamaria et al., 2005). After participants read an indicative conditional such as, 'If Tim was handsome, Peg married him', they read the conjunction: Tim was handsome and Peg married him, faster than the conjunction: Tim was not handsome and Peg did not marry him. In contrast, after they read a counterfactual conditional, such as, 'if Tim had been handsome, Peg would have married him', they read both these conjunctions faster than a conjunction, such as 'Tim was handsome and Peg did not marry him', which is inconsistent with the counterfactual claim. Further evidence for a counterfactual interpretation comes from a study in which the participants stated what they believed in the light of given assertions (Thompson & Byrne, 2002). Given a counterfactual, such as the preceding example, they tended to believe that the speaker is implying that Tim was not handsome and that Peg did not marry him.

The interpretation of an indicative conditional, as we showed earlier, tends to elicit only one explicit mental model, in which both the if-clause and the then-clause hold, and one implicit mental model. It is therefore easy to infer both modus ponens and the affirmation of the consequent, but harder to infer modus tollens and the denial of the antecedent. Neither of these latter inferences can be made in a simple way from the single explicit mental model of the conditional. Reasoners must therefore use some other strategy to make these inferences. For example, they can flesh out the mental models of the conditional into fully explicit models (Johnson-Laird et al., 1992) or they can make an assumption that the if-clause is true and derive a contradiction (Van der Henst, Yang, & Johnson-Laird, 2002). In contrast, the interpretation of a counterfactual conditional should elicit two models, one representing the counterfactual possibility in which Tim was handsome and Peg married him, and the other representing the fact that Tim was not handsome and Peg did not marry him. This model enables individuals to infer the modus tollens inference and the denial of the antecedent. Experiments have indeed shown that they make these inferences more often from counterfactual conditionals than from indicative conditionals, whereas the two sorts of conditional have no effect on the frequencies with which they make modus ponens and affirmation of the consequent (Byrne & Tasso, 1999).

A recent series of experiments tested whether people think about the two possibilities for different sorts of conditional (Dixon, Guttentag, & Byrne, 2009). It compared indicative conditionals with two sorts of counterfactual conditionals. One sort were regular counterfactuals, but the other sort introduced the word, 'only', as in:

If only Tim had been handsome then Peg would have married him.

'Only' can serve several communicative purposes. In a sentence such as, 'only the handsome get married', it is a quantifier, so the sentence is equivalent to: None of those other than the handsome gets married. In a sentence such as, 'the handsome only get married', it quantifies over events, so the sentence is equivalent to: the handsome do nothing other than get married (Johnson-Laird & Byrne, 1989). Its function in counterfactuals is more mysterious. It does not change the conditions in which the counterfactual would be true or false, but rather emphasizes the presupposed facts of the matter: Tim (alas!) was not handsome and Peg did not marry him. To test this account, the participants in one experiment were divided into three groups, with each group receiving a different sort of conditional – indicatives, regular counterfactuals, or 'if only' counterfactuals, e.g.,:

If Tim went to Wexford then Peg went to Donegal.
If Tim had gone to Wexford then Peg would have gone to Donegal
If only Tim had gone to Wexford then Peg would have gone to Donegal.

In an inferential task, the participants decided what followed given an additional categorical premise, such as: Peg did not go to Donegal. They were given a choice of three options:

Tim went to Wexford.
Tim did not go to Wexford.
Tim may or may not have gone to Wexford.

The second of these options is the conclusion of a valid modus tollens inference. As the theory predicts, the participants made this inference more often with either sort of counterfactual than with the indicative conditional. When the categorical premise denied the antecedent clause: Tim did not go to Wexford, they inferred that Peg had not gone to Donegal in a reliable trend: most often from the 'if only' conditional, then from the regular counterfactual, and least often from the indicative conditional.

A further task showed that a difference occurs in individuals' understanding of the two sorts of counterfactual conditional (Dixon et al., 2009). The participants had to judge whether or not a possibility was consistent with a conditional, and they made the judgment about four possibilities, such as:

> Tim went to Wexford and Peg went to Donegal.
> Tim did not go to Wexford and Peg did not go to Donegal.
> Tim went to Wexford and Peg did not go to Donegal.
> Tim did not go to Wexford and Peg went to Donegal.

The participants judged that the possibility corresponding to the presupposed facts – the second possibility above – was consistent with the counterfactuals, whereas they were barely above chance in making this judgement for indicative conditionals. However, a clear difference between the two sorts of counterfactuals occurred in their judgements of the counterfactual possibility (the first possibility in the list above). The participants overwhelmingly judged this possibility as consistent with regular counterfactuals (and with indicative conditionals), but they were at chance for the 'if only' counterfactuals. The overall pattern of results has a simple explanation. Indicative conditionals are likely to elicit an explicit mental model in which both the if-clause and the then-clause hold. Counterfactuals tend to elicit two models, but regular counterfactuals are more likely to elicit both of them than 'if only' counterfactuals. The latter are more likely to elicit a model of the presupposed facts than a model of the counterfactual possibility. This hypothesis has a further corroboration. When an additional categorical premise affirmed the if-clause, e.g.,:

> Tim went to Wexford

participants drew the modus ponens conclusion that Peg went to Donegal more often from a regular counterfactual (and from an indicative conditional) than from an 'if only' counterfactual. Individuals do think about what is false when they grasp a counterfactual conditional, but they focus more on what is presupposed to be true, when they grasp an 'if only' counterfactual.

Modulation and complex conditionals

We have so far considered *basic* conditionals, whether indicative or counterfactual, and they have a neutral content as independent as possible from knowledge and with no semantic or referential relations between their if-clauses and then-clauses other than their co-occurrence in the same conditional. As we showed earlier, they are consistent with three possibilities. But, as Johnson-Laird and Byrne (2002) argued, in the ordinary conditionals of daily life, the meaning of the clauses and co-referential relations between them often *modulate* their interpretation: a process of 'semantic modulation'. Likewise, knowledge about the context or the topic of the conditional can modulate their interpretation: a process of 'pragmatic modulation'. The effects of the two sorts of modulation are similar: they can block the construction of models, they can add information to models about the relations between the states of affairs in the if-clause and the then-clause, and they can increase the probability that mental models are fleshed out into fully explicit models. We refer to conditionals modulated by meaning or knowledge as 'complex' conditionals.

One effect of modulation, whether from meaning or knowledge, is to block the construction of models of possibilities. For instance, the conditional, 'if it rained then it poured', does not yield three possibilities: 'poured' means 'to rain heavily, and so it blocks the possibility in which it didn't rain but poured. You can therefore infer from the conditional alone that either it didn't rain or else it poured. Given a conditional of the form, *If A then possibly C*, its interpretation as a tautology is consistent with all four possibilities: *A* and *C*, *A* and *not-C*, *not-A* and *C*, and *not-A* and *not-C*. The theory of modulation postulates that any conditional referring to more than one possibility must include the case in which the if-clause and the then-clause are true, and that any conditional referring to only one possibility cannot refer to the possibility in which the conditional is false (Johnson-Laird & Byrne, 2002). It follows that conditionals can refer to ten different sets of possibilities. Table 3.1 summarizes them, and gives examples of conditionals corresponding to them, including those consistent with only one possibility, which usually depend on irony. The same ten patterns also occur with 'deontic' conditionals, which concern what is permissible, impermissible, and obligatory.

Several studies have examined the effects on inferences of whether a conditional, *if A then C*, states that *A* is a necessary condition for *C* or that *A* is a sufficient condition for *C* (Thompson, 1994, 2000), or, equivalently, whether there are alternatives to *A* that bring about *C*, or additional conditions that prevent *A* from bringing about *C* (Byrne, 1989; Cummins, Lubart, Alksnis, & Rist, 1991). These effects are consistent with the model theory, which accounts for necessity and sufficiency in terms of models of possibilities: *A* is necessary for *C* if no model of *C* occurs without *A*, e.g., an instance of the enabling interpretation in Table 3.1, and *A* is sufficient for *C* if no model of *A* occurs without *C*, e.g., an instance of the conditional interpretation in Table 3.1.

A recent study has corroborated the occurrence of the tautological, conditional, enabling, and biconditional interpretations, and showed that the *order* in which the participants listed the possibilities conformed to the model theory's predictions. It also confirmed that the patterns of possibilities in Table 3.1 predicted which of the four sorts of conditional inference individuals

Table 3.1 Modulation blocks the construction of models of possibilities, yielding different interpretations of conditionals of the form: *If A then C*. The table presents the set of possibilities referred to by each sort of conditional ('¬' denotes negation), and gives an everyday example of a corresponding conditional (based on Johnson-Laird & Byrne, 2002)

	Tautology	
	a c	
	a ¬ c	
	¬ a c	
	¬ a ¬ c	
	If the dessert is made with apples then it may be pie.	

	Presence of ¬a ¬c	Presence of a c	Presence of ¬a c
Three possibilities	Conditional	Enabling	Disabling
	a c	a c	a c
	¬a c	a ¬c	a ¬c
	¬a ¬c	¬a ¬c	¬a c
	If the dish is kidney beans then it is based on beans.	If the dish is made with meat, then it may be a stew.	If the workers settle for lower wages then the company may still go bankrupt.
Two possibilities	Biconditional	Strengthen antecedent	Relevance
	a c	a c	a c
	¬a ¬c	a ¬c	¬a c
	If the animal is a lion then the female is a lioness .	If gravity exists then your apples may fall.	If you need money then there's $10 in the teapot.
One possibility	Tollens	Ponens	Deny antecedent and affirm consequent
	¬a ¬c	a c	¬a c
	If it works then I'll eat my hat.	If my name is Phil then Viv is engaged.	If Bill Gates needs money then I'll lend it to him.

tended to make, e.g., the enabling interpretation tends to elicit affirmation of the consequent then-clause and denial of the antecedent if-clause rather than the other two inferences (Quelhas, Juhos, & Johnson-Laird, 2009).

Another important effect of modulation is to add information to the models of possibilities. Modulation can add a temporal relation between the states referred to in the if-clause and the then-clause. The default interpretation of the past tense in the two clauses is that the event in the if-clause happened before the event in the then-clause, e.g., 'if she fell off her bike then she broke her leg'. This interpretation can be overruled, however, in the case that the two clauses refer to the same event, e.g., 'if it rained then it poured'. These effects do not occur with disjunctions, and so, 'she fell off her bike or she broke her leg', does not imply a temporal order for the events. Knowledge or an appropriate tense of auxiliary verbs can reverse the usual temporal order, e.g., 'if she broke her leg then she had fallen off her bike'.

The examples of temporal order are superficial effects of modulation. But, consider the following complex conditional:

If Tim got into the subway train then Peg got off at the next stop.

When you understand this assertion, you envisage that in one possibility Tim got into a car of the subway train, by default at a station, the train then went on to the next station, the doors opened, and Peg got off. The construction of this kinematic sequence of spatio-temporal events depends on your prior knowledge of subway trains and stations. If you doubt it, then you should try to formulate a proof of the sequence of events using only the literal information in the conditional. It cannot be done. For example, you are told that Peg got off, but not what she got off from: you use your knowledge to infer that she got off the subway train. The assertion is also compatible with another possibility: Tim didn't get into the subway train. What did Peg do in this case? One possibility is that she was on the subway train, Tim was standing on the platform, but then did not get on the train. In this case, Peg may or may not have exited the train at the next stop. But, another possibility is that Tim was not even in a subway station – in which case, the noun phrase 'the next stop' has no referent. In this interpretation, there are just two possibilities: one in which Tim got on and Peg got off at the next stop, and one in which Tim did not get on. Conditionals *are* complex.

Here is a problem:

If someone pulled the trigger then the gun fired.
Someone pulled the trigger.
But the gun did not fire.
How come?

You may have envisaged the following sort of explanation:

A prudent person unloaded the gun and there were no bullets in the chamber.

The majority of participants in a series of experiments did so (Johnson-Laird, Girotto, & Legrenzi, 2004). Such explanations typically imply that the conditional is false rather than that the categorical assertion is false. They also make a more than minimal change to the scenario – a manifestly lesser change would be merely to propose that there were no bullets in the chamber. The participants rated this minimal explanation as less probable than the preceding one – an instance of the well-known 'conjunction fallacy' (Tversky & Kahneman, 1983). These judgments depend on the same machinery as modulation. A computer program implementing the theory demonstrates this point. It uses a model of the facts – the gun did not fire – to reject whichever premise has a mental model that fails to match the facts – in this case, the conditional. The conjunction of the remaining propositions:

Someone pulled the trigger and the gun did not fire.

matches various models in the program's knowledge of guns and firing. It makes an arbitrary choice amongst them, and uses the resulting model to extend the preceding conjunction:

There were no bullets in the chamber and someone pulled the trigger and the gun did not fire.

This putative explanation itself stands in need of explanation, and so the program uses the same procedure to extend the conjunction still further:

A prudent person emptied the gun and there were no bullets in the chamber.

The key similarity to pragmatic modulation is in the use of a mental model of a proposition to trigger a matching model from a set in general knowledge. In modulation, the resulting model blocks the construction of a possibility or adds information to the triggering model. In explanation, it adds information to the triggering model.

Strategies and suppositions

You might suppose that individuals have a single strategy for reasoning that unwinds in a deterministic way like a piece of clockwork. But, several phenomena count against this view. For example, experiments in which the participants had to make inferences from three or four premises revealed that they spontaneously developed a variety of inferential strategies (Van der Henst, Yang, & Johnson-Laird, 2002). They had to think aloud as they reasoned, and they were allowed to use paper and pencil. One strategy was quite prevalent when they had to evaluate a conditional conclusion. They made a supposition, i.e., an assumption corresponding to a single possibility, in order to start their inferences rolling. Here's a typical problem from the experiment in an abbreviated form:

There's a red if and only if there's a black.
Either there's a black or else there's a green.
There's a green if and only if there's a blue.
Does it follow that: if there's not a red then there's a blue?

A typical protocol began with a supposition 'Assuming we have no red'. The participant then drew a sequence of conclusions from it, starting with, 'So there is no black', and leading eventually to 'There is blue'. At which point, the participant accepted the conditional conclusion: If there's not a red then there is a blue. The participants did not always use suppositions correctly. They sometimes made a supposition corresponding to the then-clause of a conditional conclusion, constructed a chain of inferences leading to the if-clause, and announced that the conditional followed from the premises. They also made suppositions corresponding to clauses in disjunctions (pace Evans, 2007, p. 51), and in general were much less disciplined in their use of suppositions than is acceptable in logic.

The participants used various other strategies, and the most frequent was one in which they listed all the possibilities compatible with the premises, often in the form of a diagram. One strategy was totally unexpected: given a conditional conclusion, the participants converted all the premises, including disjunctions, so that they made a chain of conditionals leading from one clause in the conclusion to the other. In the inference above, for example, a participant constructed this chain:

If there's not a red there there's not a black.
If there's not a black then there's a green.

If there's a green then there's a blue.
So, if there's not a red then there's a blue.

The participants switched from one strategy to another, even sometimes in the middle of a problem. There were no fixed sequences of inferential steps that anyone invariably followed. Yet, regardless of strategy, problems that needed only one mental model were easier than those that needed two mental models, which in turn were easier than those that needed three mental models.

Conclusions

The model theory distinguishes between meaning and interpretation, and its account of conditionals reflects this distinction. The theory's starting point is *basic* conditionals that have no relations between their if-clauses and their then-clauses beyond their co-occurrence in the same conditionals.

What do conditionals mean?

The answer according to the model theory is that their meanings refer to sets of possibilities. Basic conditionals refer to three possibilities; complex conditionals can refer to other sets of possibilities, and the meanings of individual clauses, coreference, and knowledge, can all modulate the basic meaning. One consequence of modulation is that conditionals have an indefinite number of meanings – ten sets of possibilities and a variety of relations between the antecedent if-clause and the consequent then-clause (Johnson-Laird & Byrne, 2002, p. 674). And so, as we also wrote (p. 673):

> If the interpretative system has access only to the truth values of the antecedent and consequent, then it is unable to take into account either temporal or spatial relations or to determine which of the ten different sets of possibilities is applicable. Conditionals are not truth functional.

In other words, the meanings of conditionals cannot be captured in a 'truth-functional' way, which is concerned solely with the truth or falsity of their clauses. Such a treatment may be feasible for the three possibilities of basic conditionals (see Grice, 1975, for such an approach), but it fails utterly for conditionals in general, and indeed for all sentential connectives in natural language.

How are conditionals understood?

Individuals use the meaning of conditionals to construct mental models of possibilities, and mental models follow the principle of truth: they represent what is true rather than what is false. In some circumstances, however, models can be fleshed out to represent what is false, and this happens systematically when individuals understand a counterfactual alternative to reality.

How do individuals reason from conditionals?

In the same way that they reason from other sorts of assertion: they infer that a conclusion is necessary if it holds in all their mental models of the premises, possible if it holds in some of the models of the premises, and probable if it holds in most of the models of the premises. They use a variety of strategies to reach these conclusions.

In this chapter, we have tried to refrain from arguments against other theories. But, if you are faced with a putative theory of conditionals, you should ask yourself whether it accounts for the ten principal phenomena that we have described:

- ◆ the listing of possibilities given a conditional.
- ◆ the judgments of whether or not a conditional is true in different possibilities.
- ◆ modulation and the patterns of different possibilities for different conditionals (in Table 3.1).
- ◆ the faster reading times of the descriptions of possibilities consistent with an earlier conditional in the text, and the shift in these patterns with counterfactual conditionals.
- ◆ the relative frequencies of the four traditional forms of inference from conditionals.

- the improvement in modus tollens with counterfactual conditionals.
- the change in patterns of inference that modulation creates.
- the systematic illusions in reasoning from conditionals.
- the resolution of inconsistencies among propositions containing a conditional.
- the use and misuse of suppositions, and other strategies in conditional reasoning.
- any theory that is unable to explain these phenomena is incomplete(Byrne & Johnson-Laird, 2009).

Acknowledgements

We are grateful to Walter Schroyens for a careful reading of an earlier draft of this chapter, and whose criticisms helped to improve it. Thanks to our many collaborators for allowing us to describe our joint work in this chapter: their names are too numerous to be listed here but can be found in the publications below.

References

Barrouillet, P., Gauffroy, C., & Leças, J-F. (2007). Mental models and the suppositional account of conditionals *Psychological Review*, **115**, 760–772.

Barrouillet, P., Grosset, N., & Leças, J- F. (2000). Conditional reasoning by mental models: Chronometric and developmental evidence. *Cognition*, **75**, 237–266.

Barrouillet, P. & Leças, J- F. (1999). Mental models in conditional reasoning and working memory. *Thinking & Reasoning*, **5**, 289–302.

Bucciarelli, M. & Johnson-Laird, P. N. (2005). Naïve deontics: a theory of meaning, representation, and reasoning. *Cognitive Psychology*, **50**, 159–193.

Byrne, R. M. J. (1989). Suppressing valid inferences with conditionals. *Cognition*, **31**, 61–83.

Byrne, R. M. J. (2005). *The Rational Imagination: How People Create Alternatives to Reality.* Cambridge: MIT press.

Byrne, R. M. J. & Tasso, A. (1999). Deductive reasoning with factual, possible, and counterfactual conditionals. *Memory & Cognition*, **27**(4), 726–740.

Byrne, R. M. J. & Johnson-Laird, P.N. (2009). 'If' and the problems of conditional reasoning. *Trends in Cognitive Sciences.* **13**, 282–287.

Cummins, D. D., Lubart, T., Alksnis, O. & Rist, R. (1991). Conditional reasoning and causation. *Memory & Cognition*, **19**, 274–282.

Dixon, J.,Guttentag, R., & Byrne, R. M. J. (2009). Counterfactual conditionals based on 'if' and 'if only'. *In preparation.*

Dudman, V. H. (1984). Conditional interpretations of *if*-sentences. *Australian Journal of Linguistics*, **4**, 143–204.

Espino, O., Santamaría, C., & Byrne, R (2009). People think about what is true for conditionals not what is false: Only true possibilities prime the comprehension of 'if'. *Quarterly Journal of Experimental Psychology*, **62**, 1072–1078.

Evans, J. St.B. T. (2007). *Hypothetical Thinking: Dual Processes in Reasoning and Judgement.* Hove, UK: Psychology Press.

Evans, J. St.B. T. & Over, D. E. (2004). *If.* Oxford: Oxford University Press.

Girotto, V., Mazzocco, A., & Tasso. A. (1997). The effect of premise order in conditional reasoning: A test of the mental model theory. *Cognition*, **63**, 1–28.

Goldvarg, Y. & Johnson-Laird, P. N. (2000). Illusions in modal reasoning. *Memory & Cognition*, **28**, 282–294.

Goodwin, G. P. & Johnson-Laird, P. N. (2005). Reasoning about relations. *Psychological Review*, **112**, 468–493.

Goodwin, G. P. & Johnson-Laird, P. N. (2007). Models as the representations of Boolean concepts. Under submission.

Grice, H. P. (1975). Logic and conversation. In Davidson, D. & Harman, G. (Eds.) *The Logic of Grammar.* (pp. 64–75). Encino, CA: Dickenson.

Johnson-Laird, P. N. (2006). *How We Reason*. Oxford: Oxford University Press.

Johnson-Laird, P. N. & Byrne, R. M. J. (1989). *Only* reasoning. *Journal of Memory and Language*, **28**, 313–330.

Johnson-Laird, P. N. & Byrne, R. M. J. (1991). *Deduction*. Hove, UK: Lawrence Erlbaum Associates.

Johnson-Laird, P. N. & Byrne, R. M. J. (2002). Conditionals: a theory of meaning, pragmatics and inference. *Psychological Review*, **19**, 646–678.

Johnson-Laird, P. N., Byrne, R. M. J., & Schaeken, W. (1992). Propositional reasoning by model. *Psychological Review*, **99**, 418–439.

Johnson-Laird, P. N., Girotto, V., & Legrenzi, P. (2004). Reasoning from inconsistency to consistency. *Psychological Review*, **111**, 640–661.

Johnson-Laird, P. N. & Savary, F. (1999). Illusory inferences: A novel class of erroneous deductions. *Cognition*, **71**, 191–229.

Klayman, J. & Ha, Y. W. (1987). Confirmation, disconfirmation, and information in hypothesis testing. *Psychological Review*, **94**, 211–228.

Lee, N. Y. L. & Johnson-Laird, P. N. (2007). The psychology of reverse engineering. *Under submission*.

Lewis, D. (1973). *Counterfactuals*. Oxford: Blackwell.

Mandel, D. R., Hilton, D. J., & Catellani, P. (Eds). (2005). *The Psychology of Counterfactual Thinking*. London: Routledge.

Manktelow, K. (1999). *Reasoning and Thinking*. Hove: Psychology Press.

Oaksford, M., Chater, N., & Larkin, J. (2000). Probabilities and polarity biases in conditional inference. *Journal of Experimental Psychology: Learning, Memory, and Cognition*, **26**, 883–899.

Oberauer, K. (2006). Reasoning with conditionals: A test of formal models of four theories. *Cognitive Psychology*, **53**, 238–283.

O'Brien, D. P. (1999). If is neither *and* nor material implication. Commentary on Lecas & Barrouillet (1999). *Current Psychology of Cognition*, **18**, 397–407.

Pollock, J. L. (1986). *Subjunctive Reasoning*. Dordrecht, The Netherlands: Reidel.

Quelhas, A. C., Juhos, C., & Johnson-Laird, P. N. (2007). The modulation of conditional assertions and its effects on reasoning. *Under submission*.

Quine, W. V. O. (1952). *Methods of Logic*. London: Routledge.

Roese, N. J. & Olson, J. M. (1995). *What Might Have Been: The Social Psychology of Counterfactual Thinking*. Mahwah, New Jersey: Erlbaum.

Santamaría, C. & Espino, O. (2002). Conditionals and directionality: on the meaning of 'if' versus 'Only if'. *Quarterly Journal of Experimental Psychology*, **55ª**, 41–57.

Santamaría, C., Espino, O., & Byrne, R (2005). Counterfactual and semifactual conditionals prime alternative possibilities. *Journal of Experimental Psychology: Learning, Memory and Cognition*, **31**(5), 1149–1154.

Schroyens, W. & Schaeken, W. (2003). A critique of Oaksford, Chater and Larkin's (2000) conditional probability model of conditional reasoning. *Journal of Experimental Psychology: Learning, Memory, and Cognition*, **29**, 140–149.

Schroyens, W., Schaeken, W., & d'Ydewalle, G. (2001). The processing of negations in conditional reasoning: A meta-analytical case study in mental models and/or mental logic theory. *Thinking & Reasoning*, **7**, 121–172.

Stalnaker, R. C. (1968). A theory of conditionals. In N. Rescher (Ed.), *Studies in Logical Theory*. Oxford: Basil Blackwell.

Thompson, V. A. (1994). Interpretational factors in conditional reasoning. *Memory and Cognition*, **22**, 742–758.

Thompson, V. A. (2000). The task-specific nature of domain-general reasoning. *Cognition*, **76**, 209–268.

Thompson, V. A. & Byrne, R. M. J. (2002). Reasoning counterfactually: Making inferences about things that didn't happen. *Journal of Experimental Psychology: Learning, Memory, and Cognition*, **28**(6), 1154–1170.

Tversky, A. & Kahneman, D. (1983). Extensional versus intuitive reasoning: The conjunction fallacy in probability judgment. *Psychological Review*, **90**, 292–315.

Van der Henst, J-B., Yang, Y., & Johnson-Laird, P. N. (2002). Strategies in sentential reasoning. *Cognitive Science*, **26**, 425–468.

Chapter 4

Logic and/in psychology: The paradoxes of material implication and psychologism in the cognitive science of human reasoning

Walter Schroyens

Cognitive science research about 'if' is most propitious in yielding insight into the marvels of the human mind. Imagine what would happen if imagining 'what if' were no longer possible. You would be stuck in the here and now; you would not even be able to imagine this. We regularly express our beliefs about causal relationships in terms of conditionals, and make inferences about them; We use conditional statements in expressing threats, commitments, obligations, permissions; We frequently engage in counter-factual thinking of what might have been, if only something else would have been different; We engage in constructing or understanding elaborate chains of conditional inferences in making predictions and evaluating evidence against hypotheses expressed in conditional relations between antecedent and consequent events. Reasoning about conditionals accordingly attracted the interest of cognitive scientists: linguists, philosophical-logicians, artificial-intelligence workers, and experimental/cognitive psychologists. Literally thousands of manuscripts and dozens of books have been devoted to understanding that illusive word 'if'.

I here address a border dispute between the logic and psychology of conditionals. In recent psychological literature we see an upsurge of straw-man arguments that reflect *psychologism*. The term *Psychologism* is used in two ways, depending on the point of departure regarding the relation between logic and psychology: actual thinking and reasoning constrains logic, or logic constrains thinking and reasoning theories (Notturno, 1989). In the latter case, logical systems are supposed to capture the 'laws of thought'; not in the sense of an idealized normative system of how people *should* reason, but in the sense of a descriptive system of how people actually *would* reason.

> Naïve psychologism says that the task of logic is to describe the ways in which people think. It makes logic into a branch of descriptive psychology, and the laws of logic into psychological laws, 'laws of thought'.
>
> (Musgrave, 1989, p. 315)

Both uses of 'psychologism' reflect the same idea: Logic systems are psychological, and have to be psychological. In the literature on human reasoning we accordingly see what we call psychologism arguments. One considers some derivations within a logical system and then extrapolates these derivations as psychological predictions. By itself there is no problem with this. Anything goes in being creative in making conjectures and seeking refutations. It means that the processing principles of the psychological model and the basic axioms of the logical system are one and the same. We are no longer concerned with goals proper to logic, but are doing cognitive psychology.

Psychologism is, however, most problematic and the consensus is towards anti-psychologism when it concerns classic first-order logic.

> Frege's influential review of Husserl (Frege, 1894, see also Frege, 1884) persuaded almost all theorists that psychologism was false of mathematics and logic (in particular), so that logic was seen not to be a 'subjective' enterprise but instead it concerns objective relations amongst propositions, predicates, and terms. *Nowadays, one would be hard-pressed to find anyone who holds psychologism with regards to logic, mathematics, geometry, and the like.*
>
> (Pelletier & Elio, 2005, p. 20)

Logic has evolved considerably since the classical debate over psychologism in the early days of the past century. In that era it came as far that '107 professors of philosophy from Germany, Austria and Switzerland signed a letter to the German Ministry of Education in 1913 in which they demanded elimination of experimental psychologists as candidates for professorships in philosophy' (Wolenski, 2003, p. 191). Nowadays, we see a rapprochement between logic and psychology with the development of non-monotonic, relevance, default, para-consistent and other contemporary logics. It is difficult to imagine how it would be possible to interpret epistemic logic without taking psychology into account. Many philosophical-logicians accordingly consider Husserl's anti-psychologism arguments are a curse on the development of logic (Kusch, 1995).

Many psychologists, however, still take the idealized systems of classic logic as 'the' logic. This makes these psychologists susceptible to misguided psychologistic arguments. Even if we accept the general idea of psychologism, the logical system these psychologists (i.e., classic logic) adopt without doubt lags behind developments in psychological modelling. Psychologism arguments thus become straw-man arguments which are misguiding when the predictions of the straw-man theory (i.e., classic logic) are associated with a psychological (vs. logical) theory that actually does not support the predictions. One criticizes not the extant psychological theory, but an oversimplified straw-man version of it.

Schroyens and Schaeken (2004) already uncovered such misguided psychologistic arguments. For instance, some theorists argue that the mental-models theory of human reasoning (Johnson-Laird & Byrne, 2002) is falsified because of the failed prediction that people would judge the probability of a conditional 'if A then C' and its contrapositive 'if not-C then not-A' to be the same. This equivalence prediction is a clear straw-man argument (cf. Schroyens, 2007). It is a relatively simple *logical* fact that the conditional *[if A then C]* is *logically* equivalent with its contrapositive *[if not-C then not-A]*.[1] This however, does not imply that they are psychologically equivalent. For instance, people almost universally accept the *Modus Ponendo Ponens* argument <A therefore C> while they much less frequently accept the *Modus Tollendo Tollens* argument <not-C, therefore not-A> about an abstract indicative <if A then C> conditional (see Schroyens & Schaeken, 2003, Schroyens et al., 2001, for meta-analyses). If the conditional and its contrapositive were psychologically equivalent, then MP and MT would be about equally difficult. MT would in fact be an MP argument on the contrapositive. The fact that MT is more difficult than MP shows that psychologism does not hold for classical logic. Of course, using actual behaviour

---

[1] The critical reader will notice the seed of psychologism in this simplified claim. Though close to being true – and true enough to most – it is strictly speaking incorrect to state that the conditional <if C then A> and its contrapositive <if not-C then not-A> are logically equivalent. The logical equivalence is one between the truth-functionally defined material implication <p → q> and its contrapositive <not-q → not-p>. For the sake of accessibility we often need to sacrifice the potential exactitude of our language. These simplifications have the potential danger of leading to oversimplifications, i.e., psychologism arguments that obscure the difference between logic and psychology.

to evaluate 'logic' presupposes 'psychologism'. When we start with a given system like propositional calculus, we can actually make the hypothesis that psychologism holds to consider the hypothesis refuted in virtue of the contradictions (i.e., failed predictions) it yields. Classical propositional calculus is vastly inadequate as a theory about how people reason. Whatever merits one (e.g., a logician) wants to attribute to the propositional calculus, one merit it cannot possess is being a descriptively adequate theory of human reasoning.

In the following I present an analysis of the so-called paradoxes of material implication. The above equivalence prediction is based on the logical fact that 'if not-C then not-A' can be derived from 'if A then C', provided <if A then C> is taken to be a truth-functional material implication. The paradoxes of material implication similarly reflect logically valid derivations, at least within propositional calculus. And, indeed they have also been used to construct misguided psychologistic arguments against mental-models theory, which both friend and foe consider 'one of the most influential theories of human reasoning' (Evans et al., 2003, p. 324).

The logic of conditionals and the paradoxes of material implication

Psychologistic arguments become straw-man arguments when predictions based on logical systems (i.e., classic first-order logic) are attributed to a psychological theory (i.e., mental models theory). To recognize the misguided nature of psychologistic arguments one needs to have some insight in both the logic and psychology of conditional reasoning. We first introduce the general reader to the mental-models theory of conditional reasoning, i.e., the theory that has been the subject of most straw-man arguments. Johnson-Laird and Byrne (2002) left their presentation of this theory open for interpretation as regards several debatable issues. We also take up this opportunity to resolve some of these potential ambiguities (see Evans et al., 2005) and to highlight some other properties that other interpreters/readers seem to have missed.

The psychology of conditional reasoning: Reasoning by model

The general idea behind reasoning by model is relatively straightforward. Mental-models theory postulates that individuals understand sentences by representing the possibilities that are compatible with them. In accordance with the Gricean principles of conversation (Grice, 1975, also see Levinson, 2000), people will assume that the information they are confronted with is true: They will initially not consider possibilities that are incompatible with the conditional and make it false. This is the so-called *truth-principle*. 'Individuals minimize the load on working memory by tending to construct mental models that represent explicitly only what is true, and not what is false' (Johnson-Laird, 1999, p. 116). Moreover, since people have limited processing resources they cannot and hence will not even consider all true possibilities from the outset. This is the *implicit-model principle*. Applying the truth-principle and implicit-model principle to <if A then C> conditionals yields an explicit representation (i.e., a mental model of the possibility) of <A> in relation to <C>.[2]

    [A] {C}

---

[2] Our notation deviates from Johnson-Laird and Byrne's (2002). Their notation did not reflect the idea that <C> occurs within the context of <A>. We place <C> in rounded brackets to reflect this – as if the 'C' is an argument of the function "A". As Johnson-Laird and Byrne (2002) expressed it: 'The antecedent refers to a possibility, and the consequent is interpreted *in that context*' (p. 649) or 'the antecedent of a basic conditional describes a possibility, at least in part, and the consequent can *occur in this possibility*' (p. 650). This notation reflects the directional nature of the initial mental representations of conditionals.

Other possibilities remain implicit, which is denoted by the elliptical empty <...> model. The square brackets are used as a notion for the 'mental footnote' that <A> is represented exhaustively in relation to <C>. There are no other instances of <A> than those in which <C> is also the cases, which implies that <A{not-C}> is not a true possibility. 'According to the theory, people will make a mental footnote that A occurs only in the explicit model, and so they should infer a probability of 0% for A and not-B (Johnson-Laird, Legrenzi, et al., 1999, p. 71)'; 'A mental footnote indicates that the ellipsis represents entities other than [<A> events]' (Johnson-Laird & Byrne, 2002, p. 655).

The explicit initial-model reflects the bare minimum. Content and context will aid the construction of alternative possibilities that are not represented *ab initio*. Context and content will also instigate the semantic enrichment of the above bare minimum initial model.[3] For instance, 'If the cardinality of the set matters, then models can be tagged with numerals, just as they can be tagged to represent numerical probabilities' (see Johnson-Laird & Byrne, 2002, p. 655; Johnson-Laird, Legrenzi, et al., 1999). The processes of enriching models and/or constructing additional models with the aid of pragmatic context and semantic content are referred to *semantic and pragmatic modulation* (Johnson-Laird & Byrne, 2002), which accounts for the well known belief effects (a.k.a. counterexample effects; Cummins et al., 1991).

The initial-model principle implies that people are reasoning *towards* an interpretation, not *from* an interpretation, which means that 'the' interpretation of a conditional does not exist (Schroyens, Schaeken, & Dieussaert, in press). The initial models reflect an initial representation and in treating the syntax and semantics of contextually embedded propositions; people are reasoning towards one or the other interpretation. The so-called conditional interpretation, however, deserves some special attention because of its conceptual link with the problematical material-implication and associated paradoxes of material implication we are considering here. When having (i.e., coming to) a so-called conditional interpretation of <if A then C>, people would represent three possibilities: everything is possible, except <A_not-C>. That is, when reasoning towards a conditional interpretation, people end up representing the following model set: {<A_C>; <not-A_C>; <not-A_not-C>}. This conditional interpretation is linked to the core-meaning principle of mental-models theory: 'The core meaning of If A then C is the conditional interpretation ...'(Johnson-Laird & Byrne, 2002, p. 650). The special status of the conditional interpretation, as the interpretation corresponding to the presumed core-meaning of basic conditionals, has been the subject of many criticisms.

It is easily shown that many arguments against the core-meaning principle and/or conditional interpretations are straw-man arguments in which one ignores the initial-model principle. Any interpreter of Johnson-Laird and Byrne (2002) must deal with the relationship between the implicit-model and core-meaning principle. The first one states that (*ab initio*) there is one explicit model; the latter states there are three explicit models. So what is it: one or three? The solution to the one-versus-three problem is simple (Schroyens, 2007). People *always* start with one model and *can* reason towards a three-model interpretation (or, depending on context/ context, a multitude of other interpretations). That is, people *never* start reasoning from a conditional interpretation and neither *must* they even aim to reach that interpretation. It follows

---

[3] In the abstract of Johnson-Laird and Byrne (2002) we read that 'modulation can add information about temporal and other relations between antecedent and consequent' (p. 646). That is, (pace Evans et al., 2003), Johnson-Laird and Byrne (2002, p. 651) 'do not deny that many conditionals are *interpreted* as conveying a relation between their antecedents and consequents'. Also see Footnote 2.

that critics can *never* claim mental-models theory makes predictions which presume that presuming people have or must have a material-conditional like interpretation.

The above mentioned logical equivalence between <if A then C> and <if not-C then not-A> is one example of a straw-man argument created by considering the core-meaning principle in isolation i.e., in neglect of basic processing principles (i.e., the initial-model principle) that are at the core of mental-models theory. The logical compatibility of <if A then C> and <if A then not-C> is another example (Handley, Evans, & Thompson, 2006). The initial-model principle implies these conditionals will tend to be judged incompatible. The paradoxes of material implication are similarly not endorsed by mental-models theory, even though paradoxically they are accepted as logically valid by mental-models theorists (note the difference between theory and theorists, which is conceptually linked to the difference between descriptive and normative theories).

The classic logic of conditionals and the paradoxes of material implication

Material implication, $<p \rightarrow q>$, is a truth-function whose truth is completely determined by the truth-value of its constituent propositions, $<p>$ and $<q>$. It is only false when the antecedent $<p>$ is true, while the consequent $<q>$ is false. That is, the true possibilities are:

> p . q
> not-p . q
> not-p . not-q

This makes it clear that there is a close link between material implication and the conditional interpretation: Material implication is in effect taken to be the core meaning of basic conditionals. Such basic conditionals are not ordinary natural language conditionals, but are conditionals 'with a neutral content that is independent as possible from context and background knowledge, and which have an antecedent and consequent that are semantically independent apart from their occurrence in the same conditional' (Johnson-Laird & Byrne, 2002, p. 648). Of course, as soon as we are dealing with real language utterances (whether abstract or realistic), this core meaning is not a given. Real language utterances are interpreted and people reason *towards*, not *from* an interpretation. The initial interpretation is not the conditional (i.e., material-implication like) interpretation.

Material implication has some paradoxical properties, which show that material implication *is not* the natural language connective 'if ... then...'. This, however, does not exclude the possibility that a conditional can yield a material-implication like conditional interpretation. Conditional interpretations are just one of many possible *interpretations* (vs. meanings). Given the material implication, the following arguments are logically valid. This does not mean that they are psychologically acceptable within mental-models theory:

P1:	Not-p therefore p $\rightarrow$ q
P2:	q, therefore p $\rightarrow$ q
P3:	p $\rightarrow$ q, therefore p & r $\rightarrow$ q

The following more realistic instantiations of these arguments illustrate their counterintuitive nature:

Paris is not in France; therefore, if Paris is in France, the world is round.
Walter will always love Erin; therefore, if pigs can fly, then Walter will always love Erin.
If it is a bird, then it can fly; therefore, if Tweety, the bird, is an ostrich, then it can fly.

Johnson-Laird and Byrne (1991, 2002) accept the logical validity of the paradoxes. In Evans et al., (2005) we see the claim that this is a problem for mental-models theory:

> The claim that P1 and P2 are valid for such an ordinary conditional like 1 is highly counterintuitive and quite simply absurd.

> (p. 1041)

I will show that the argument in Evans et al., (2005; also see e.g., Oaksford & Chater, 1998) is mistaken. It is a psychologistic argument in which one fails to take account of the well established fact that logical validity is not the same thing as psychological validity. The notion of validity laid down in classic logical systems is not the notion of validity adopted by naive reasoners (vs. idealized logicians). That is, I agree that the claim that P1 and P2 are *psychologically valid* for ordinary conditionals is 'highly counter-intuitive and quite simply absurd'. This is trivial, and but a mere description of accepted fact. I do not agree, however, that the claim that P1 and P2 are *logically valid* is highly counter-intuitive and quite simply absurd. On the contrary, it is quite simply absurd to claim P1 and P2 are not logically valid. Persons claiming this have failed to pick up much from their basic logic course.

> That truth-functional logic allows us to do that is certainly a fact. It does permit the inference from 'not-p' to 'if p then q' and from 'q' to 'if p then q'. And a supporter of the logic must then be willing to say that these inferences are valid. But he need not say that it would be reasonable actually to draw them, or to acquiesce in someone else's drawing them. Consider a parallel case ...: A says to B, 'I heard from John; he's in Rapallo', and B replies, 'Oh. It follows then that he's either in Rapallo or somewhere in the Shetlands'. B's remark will now be found puzzling and pointless. Why does he bother to say that? *But to criticize his remark on such grounds as these is one thing; to say he has committed a logical mistake, argued fallaciously, is quite something else.*

> (Thomson, 1990, p. 65)

The logical versus psychological validity of the paradoxes

What does it actually mean for something to be a paradox? A paradox is an apparent contradiction: It is a contradiction, which is only apparent. Thus, the first question to ask is: What is the contradictory nature of the paradoxes of material implication? This is not too difficult a question. Indeed, the contradiction lies in the fact that in classic logic the inferences are valid whereas in commonsense reasoning they are invalid. This is the contradiction: How can something be invalid and valid at the same time? But, it is truly only an apparent contradiction. Indeed, the question is not how something can be valid and invalid at the same time. The actual question/problem is, how can something be *logically valid* and *psychologically invalid* at the same time?

There is and can be little doubt that logical validity is not the same as psychological validity.[4] There is abundant evidence of this. Logically valid inferences are inferences that are necessarily true if the premises are true. This definition includes the concept of necessary inferences, as compared to inferences that are only possibly correct. It also includes the notion of hypothetical truth. The conclusions of the inferences are only true, given that the premises are true. (A valid argument with factually true premises and, hence a factually true conclusion, is called a sound argument). Any effect of explicating the notion of necessity or hypothetical truth therefore

---

[4] While there exists a precise definition of logical validity – one which is abandoned in non-monotonic logics – we do not need to be given an exact definition of psychological validity to draw the negative conclusion that 'psychological validity'; whatever it is, it is *not* the same as logical validity.

demonstrates that at least some people will not spontaneously reason in accordance with the notion of logical validity. Schroyens, Schaeken, and Handley (2003) accordingly demonstrated that stressing the necessity constraint increases the abovementioned logical validity effect in the conditional inference task (also see Schroyens, 2005; Schroyens & Schaeken, 2005). Schroyens (2004; Schroyens & Schaeken, 2005) also demonstrated that the logical validity effect in the conditional inference task with realistic materials increases when the truth-assumption is stressed.

Given that not a single theorist – being human as much as other participant in a proper experiment – has doubted the unacceptable nature of the paradoxes, I will accept it as a given that they are considered unacceptable by the vast majority of people. The crux of my argument is, however, that 'unacceptable' and 'paradoxical' do not mean the same thing and that a lack of conceptual rigour has led to straw-man arguments. The paradoxes will only be paradoxical (vs. contradictory and hence unacceptable) for those people who can bring to mind both the intuitive notion of validity and the idealized notion of logical validity. For the logically untutored person, the paradoxes are simply unacceptable.

Solutions to the paradoxes of material implications

The paradoxes of material implication are only a problem for philosophical-logicians or psychologists who want to extend classical logic to psychology; they only exist in virtue of psychologism. If logical validity did not exist as a well-defined notion in classic logic, then neither would the paradoxes exist. The 'paradoxes' would simply be unacceptable arguments. But classical logic exists (and it is the only logic that exists in the mind of many psychologists), and so does psychologism. The paradoxes therefore reflect a failed psychological prediction that can be phrased as follows:

Hypothesis:	if the conditional is a material implication and	
	if people aim to establish logical validity	
	then people should accept the paradoxes.	<if A and B, then C>
Fact:	People do not accept the paradoxes	<Not-C>

Phrased as such, we immediately see the only way out of dealing with the problem. Indeed, it follows – logically, by *Modus Tollendo Tollens* – from the fact that people do not accept the paradoxes (<not-C>), that the conditional is not a material implication and/or that people do not aim to establish logical validity: <not-C>, hence, <*not (A and B)*>, that is, <not-A and/or not-B>. Let me consider in turn, these two sides of the solution.

Logical versus psychological validity

The paradoxes of material implication teach us that any psychological theory that aims to capture commonsense reasoning will need to consider psychological vs. logical validity and/or will need to consider alternatives to the material implication. Chater and Oaksford (1999), for instance, delineated the notion of p-validity, referring to the idea that psychologically valid inferences need not be strictly valid, but can be probabilistically valid. Probabilistic validity makes sense from an adaptive point of view (see e.g., Anderson, 1990). Knowing whether something is possibly true gives us some information to act upon: something is better than nothing. We would not get far in our world if we were only to act upon certain knowledge. Though Oaksford and Chater beg to differ (Oaksford, personal communication; Oaksford & Chater, 1998), Johnson-Laird and Byrne's notion of validity similarly differs from that of logical validity. As noted by Stanovich and West (2000, p. 664):

> At the heart of the rational competence that Johnson-Laird and Byrne (1993) attribute to humans is not perfect rationality but instead just one meta-principle: People are programmed to accept inferences as valid provided that they have constructed no mental model of the premises that

contradict the inference. Inferences are categorized as false when a mental model is discovered that is contradictory.

The model theory proffers a conclusion validation stage during which (at least some) people (at least sometimes) search for counterexamples to conclusions drawn on the basis of the initial representation. Not all people, however, will engage in a search for counterexamples. Some will satisfice. As noted by Johnson-Laird and Byrne (1991, p. 206) 'the model theory allows that the inferential process itself can be influenced by motives: the search for alternatives that refute a putative conclusion can be thorough or cursory depending on motivational factors'.

The model theory also explains why the paradoxes are considered psychologically invalid (unacceptable) while they are logically valid (see e.g., Johnson-Laird and Byrne, 2002, p. 652). All the paradoxes involve a loss of semantic information, and the model theory holds that people will tend not to throw away semantic information. Semantic information refers to the number of possibilities that are ruled out by a proposition (see De Keyser, Schroyens, et al., 2000). For instance, the proposition <not A> has a semantic informativeness of 1/2. Something is either true or false, and as such <not-A> rules out the possibility that <not-A> is the case. Something is either true or false. When we have a two-place compound proposition, there are therefore (2 x 2) four possibilities: The proposition <if A then C> rules out only one out of four possibilities. It is falsified by the <A and not-C> case. The semantic informativeness of the conditional is thus 1/4. This illustrates that the conclusion of paradox P1 <not-A therefore if A then C> throws away semantic information.

Theorists who criticize the model theory on the basis of the paradoxes of material implication succumb to a fallacy of equivocation (Whyte, 2004), of which psychologism is a special case. One equivocates logical validity and psychological validity. Consider the following statements:

> As we have pointed out above, if Johnson-Laird and Byrne (2002) really do mean to claim that non-basic conditionals are (semantically) non-truth functional, then they cannot hold that the paradoxes, P1 and P2, are *[psychologically or logically?]* valid for these conditionals.

(Evans et al., 2005, p. 1048)

Are they talking about logical of psychological validity, or muddling the two – as one might suggest Johnson-Liard and Byrne have done in not making a clear distinction between the two? Johnson-Laird and Byrne (2002) or any other theorists – philosophical logicians and cognitive psychologists alike – who consider classical logic can state that the paradoxes of material implication are logically valid if the conditional is a material implication. Unless one wants to rewrite history and every basic introductory logic text book one actually has to state that the so-called paradoxes are logically valid if the conditional is a material implication.

In summary, it is a matter of fact that the paradoxes are logically valid, given a truth-functional material implication. It is something else to claim that the paradoxes are psychologically valid. The paradoxes only exist in virtue of the notion of logical validity. They do not exist for the laymen, however. For the laymen there is no apparent contraction. There is not even a contradiction. The concept of a contradiction reflects an opposition between two ideas. Lacking knowledge of logical validity, the layman generally only has one of the two potentially conflicting ideas or concepts. Hence, there can not be a contraction and neither can there be, a fortiori, an apparent contradiction. Holding that the paradoxes are logically valid, given a material implication, does not imply that the paradoxes would be psychologically valid, and neither does it imply that the conditional is only (vs. can be) interpreted as a material-implication like connective. It is a clear example of psychologism when one thinks it does. Classical first-order logic by itself does not allow any predictions about what people actually do.

'The' interpretation(s) versus meaning of 'if'

The paradoxes are only logically valid given that the conditional is taken to be a material implication. This is trivial. Critics of the mental-model theory might have taken issue with the statement that the paradoxes are valid, because they did not think theoretical narratives can also include trivial statements. Mental-models theory implies that conditionals *can* yield so-called conditional interpretations, which are conceptually linked to material implication. That is, though *some* people might indeed *sometimes* treat at least *some* conditionals as if they were the truth-functional material implication, often and indeed in most situations most people will not do so and will behave in line with less strict standards:

> The heart of the process is interpreting premises as mental models that take general knowledge into account, and searching for counter-examples to conclusions trying to construct alternative models of the premises. The only truth-functions that people think about in daily life are those that arise when the world behaves in a truth-functional way, e.g., in the 'logic' of electrical circuitry and simple switches. Real assertions in real contexts only occasionally give rise to truth-functional conclusions.

> (Johnson-Laird, 1983, p. 54)

The conditional interpretation is only one of many possible interpretations of iffy propositions. That is, even if Johnson-Laird and Byrne (2002) were to claim that people invariably aim to establish logical validity (which they do not) and were to presume that the interpretational process is distinct from the conclusion validation process (which it is not), then the theory does not necessarily predict the psychological validity (i.e., acceptability) of the paradoxes. The paradoxes are acceptable under some interpretations but not others. Let us rephrase the issue in a direct response to a critics' comment:

> You make comments like '...the paradoxes of material implication are logically valid IF the conditional is the material implication'. *No one can disagree with that!* It's utterly trivial. ...the paradoxes are logically invalid for the Adams conditional, the Stalnaker conditional, and every other non-extensional conditional. So your 'if' is a big 'IF'! It begs the question of whether the ordinary indicative conditional of natural language is a material implication, or an Adams conditional, or a Stalnaker conditional, or other. What is your view on that? Never mind that ordinary people don't know logic, you do! *So what is your position on which of these conditionals is the ordinary indicative conditional of natural language?*

Putting on his mental-model theorist's hat I responded 'none and all of the above'.[5] That is, none of them (the Adams conditional, Stalnaker conditional, etc. : see Bennett, 2003) *IS* the ordinary conditional; all of them *CAN BE* the ordinary conditional.

> In short, conditionals are not creatures of a constant hue. Like chameleons, as I once put it, they take on the colour suggested by their surroundings. Their logical properties are determined in part by the

---

[5] The trivial claim that the paradoxes are logically valid *if* the conditional is the material implication is not begging the question whether the ordinary indicative conditional is a material implication. First, the statement answers the question when, how and within which limitations one can justifiably express that the paradoxes are logically valid while psychologically unacceptable. Second, we agree it is another question whether the ordinary conditional is the material implication. Evans and Over (2004) cogently argued that people have a general tendency to accept the antecedent of an 'if' as a given instead of a hypothetical. The critique that we are begging the question is grounded by exactly such a misinterpretation of 'if'. Our suggestion to imagine a hypothetical world in which some things are true, does not imply that this world is supposed to be the real world – whatever 'real' might mean.

nature of the propositions that they interrelate. The crux is, not that *if* is ambiguous, though some critics have taken that to be my point, but rather that *if* has a single unequivocal semantics that leaves a role to be played by the interpretation of the clauses that it connects. It is the varying nature of the known links between them that gives rise to the chameleon-like properties of the conditional'.

(Johnson-Laird, 1983, p. 62)

It might be frustratingly 'slippery' but mental-models theory holds that *some* people *sometimes* interpret conditionals as material implication. Sometimes, and indeed probably most of the time, the ordinary conditional is 'probabilified' — to use Morris and Sloutsky's, (1998) term. That is, as argued and demonstrated by Schroyens et al., (2007), within mental-models theory 'the' interpretation of conditionals does not exist. Moreover, when we are talking 'psychology' we only have interpretation. The question 'which of these conditionals *is* the ordinary indicative conditional' can not be answered without considering what is meant by '*is*'. Is one asking for a timeless '*is*', or does one allow for the contingencies of our subjective reality to have an import on what the ordinary indicative conditional '*is*' to a particular person at a particular moment in space and time?

Evans et al.'s (2003, 2005; Handley et al., 2006) psychologism arguments are most likely due to a failure to follow the implications of Johnson-Laird and Byrne's (2002) distinction between ('timeless') *meaning* and ('contingent') *interpretation*. Meaning is not use. 'Meaning as model theoretic interpretations are idealizations – abstract theoretical fictions, though none the less useful for all that' (Johnson-Laird, 1983, p. 182). This implies that there is no core meaning that exists in the minds of ordinary people: it only exists in the minds of idealized people (like classic logicians) and it is only reified to the extent people are idealizing, e.g., by abstracting from content and context.

Johnson-Laird and Byrne (2002) were quite explicit regarding the need to distinguish meaning from interpretation:

> The article begins with a theory of the core meanings of conditionals... We develop a model theory of conditionals below, but in our account of their meaning, we refer to possibilities, not to models. *Our aim is to make the theory of meaning independent of the theory of comprehension,* which relies on models as mental representations.

(Johnson-Laird & Byrne, 2002, p. 648)

In our view, to discuss the psychological processes of human reasoning one could almost completely ignore Johnson-Laird and Byrne's stance as regards the 'core meaning of basic conditionals' (Johnson-Laird & Byrne, 2002, p. 648-652). Our primary concern, as cognitive psychologists, is first and foremost with the specification of descriptively adequate processing models of how modal reasoners go about, e.g., conditional thinking and reasoning. Whether some idealized reasoner has, or should have, one or the other interpretation is not our primary concern. That is, for most matter and purposes of psychological research we can almost completely forget about the model theory's thesis that material implication is the presumed core-meaning of basic conditionals. Cognitive psychology deals with processing systems in which representations are created and transformed from input to output states. When we are considering psychological processes of reasoning and thinking about conditional utterances, we are considering interpretational and representational processes. The conditional interpretation is just one of many interpretations people reason *towards* in constructing and manipulation representations of possible worlds.

The idea that the core-meaning assumption about basic conditionals is of limited relevance to psychological research does not mean it has 'no relevance'. Indeed, the core-meaning assumption has some explanatory import. The core-meaning assumption is an idealization. Speaking at the level of conceptual idealizations, the strongest argument in favour of material implication is the 'Semantic Occamism' argument, as it was labelled by Bennett (2003). An utterance of the form <*If A then C*> does not mean the same as <*if A then possibly C*> or <*If and only if A then C*>. That is, if – and this is a real, socio-cultural debatable 'if'; not a given – we want to have a language in which sentential connectives correspond to unique well-formed formulae, then the material implication seems to be a good candidate for 'if'. Our natural language is no such language and one can even question whether we should strive towards the conceptual rigour and reduced ambiguity of such a language, to the extent such is possible within the limits of our human condition.

A theory of meaning is not completely devoid of the actual interpretational processes in reasoning. An idealization still finds its source in reality. That is, as an idealization, the core-meaning assumption has some explanatory import nonetheless. Schroyens et al., (2007) accordingly specified an idealization-hypothesis, for which they provided empirical evidence in people's probability judgements of conditionals: When we approach the idealization, e.g., by imposing contextual constraints that bring us nearer to the idealized language game, then we should observe behaviour that more closely approaches the strictures and implications of that language game. That is, the very same comparative contrast that delineates <*if A then C*> as meaning something different from [*if A then possibly C*] or [*if and only if A then C*] can also steer people in their interpretation. Schroyens and Byrne (1998) observed, for instance, that when 'if A then C' is contrasted with '*If and only if* A then C', people are more likely behave in line with a highlighted consequence of this contrast, i.e., that with <if A then C> there might be alternative 'causes' (cf. supra) or situations in which <C> occurs without <A> being the case. Also, as mentioned before, when logical validity is stressed by explicating the notion of necessity (vs. possibilities) and/or highlighting the hypothetical truth of logical valid inferences, we see an increase in deductive rationality (Schroyens et al., 2003). In the general discussion we will come back to the issue of idealization (as in the core meaning of basic conditionals).

General Discussion

There is nothing really special about the paradoxes of material implication – psychologically speaking, that is. They are at the extreme end of a continuum of more or less intuitively acceptable arguments, but they are in most regards much like other arguments people have more difficulty with. Classic first-order logic deals with reasoning under certainty; necessary inferences derived from certain information; information that is supposed to be true even though in the 'real' world we know or believe it is not. Any mismatch between 'correct' performance according to one or the other system, which for one or the other reason happens to be elevated to a normative status, merely indicates that the axioms of the normative system are not shared by human reasoners and/or that they do not have the computational power to live up to the standard set out by the more or less idealized system (Stanovich & West, 2000). In the following, it being a *general* discussion, I will briefly touch on some conceptual issues that are often taken for granted but which are fundamental to any cognitive science project. That is, we will explore potential implications for the foundational multi-level approach to explanation in cognitive science.

Logic and/in psychology: idealization and competence

Psychologism is especially problematical when linking classic logic and psychology. The degree of idealization in classic first-order logic is the prime reason for anti-psychologism. Contemporary logics are much less idealized (i.e., there is less abstraction, generalization, and/or simplification involved) and using them as the intentional (Dennett, 1987) or computational (Marr, 1982) level description of our explanations is less problematical (see e.g., Macnamara, 1987, 1994; Stenning

& van Lambalgen, 2001, 2004). Compare for instance non-monotonic logic(s) and classic logic. The latter is monotonic in nature: once a conclusion is validly inferred it can not be retracted; it is and remains a valid inference. This stands in contrast – or apparent contrast: Schroyens, 2004a, 2006 – with the defeasible nature of commonsense reasoning. We readily withdraw the conclusion that Tweety the bird can fly (inferred from 'if it is a bird, then it can fly') when finding out that Tweety is an ostrich. The idealization is embodied by the assertion 'if it is a bird, then it can fly'. It is a false claim, but in classic logic we have to reason from the assumption (i.e., idealization) that it is (counterfactually) true. With the development of non-monotonic logics, we see that logic attempts to create systems that more closely map onto natural language reasoning, which is defeasible (see e.g., Elio & Pelletier, 1997; Schroyens & Dieussaert, 2005).

Theorizing in cognitive psychology is grounded on a multi-level approach to explanation. Best known to psychologists is Marr's (1982) distinction between the computational, algorithmic and implementation level. The computational level theory, specifies 'what is being computed and why' (Marr, 1977, p. 129). The algorithmic level theory specifies a 'representation for the input and output and the algorithm to be used to transform one into the other' (Marr, 1982, p. 25). The implementation level theory provides 'the details of how the algorithm and representation are realized physically' (Marr, 1982, p. 25). As we move down through these levels, our explanations become progressively more detailed; we understand first what function a system computes, then the procedure by which it computes it, and finally how that procedure is implemented physically in the system. Classic logic has been considered, justly or unjustly, the computational level description of psychological theories of human *deductive* reasoning. That is, it has been considered to specify 'what' is computed and why. A more general consideration of how this relates to explanation in the cognitive science of human reasoning is therefore in order.

Oaksford and Chater (2003b), for instance, make a comparison between predictions derived from classic logic and those derived form probability calculus. That is, they feel justified abstracting from algorithmic level specifications provided by mental-model theorists. The problematical nature of an attempt to divorce the 'pure' computational level theories form their algorithmic level specification (McClamrock, 1991), is illustrated by the fact that some algorithmic level assumptions were mixed in with what Oaksford and Chater (2003b) presented as the 'logical model'.

Briefly: Classic logic (i.e., the material implication hypothesis) dictates that the *Modus Ponendo Ponens* argument ('A therefore C') and *Modus Tollendo Tollens* ('not-C therefore not-A') argument are logically valid about <if A then C>. The Affirmation of the Consequent argument ('C therefore A') and the Denial of the Antecedent argument ('not-A therefore not-C') are logically invalid because the material implication allows for the falsifying possibility that <not-A> co-occurs with <C>. That is, the computational function of classic logic transfers the input (the four basic conditional arguments) into two output bins: valid or invalid. This is not the function Oaksford and Chater (2003b) considered. Indeed, it is too simple and would not make for a serious contender to their Bayesian model. Instead they 'generously' added some psychology (i.e., processes) by allowing for different interpretations of 'if A then C'. It makes it less obviously incongruous to treat classic logic as if it were a psychological theory (at the computational level) about how people actually reason. Indeed, AC and DA are logically valid under a bi-conditional interpretation and a large proportion of people reason in accordance with such an interpretation (Schroyens & Schaeken, 2003b). But this is beyond classic logic, in which 'if A then C' receives a single truth-functional meaning that differs from the meaning of 'if and only if A then C'. This case of Oaksford and Chater (2003b) illustrates that the multi-level approach to explanation is not as self-evident as one often takes it to be, and would like it to be (also see Oaksford and Chater's, 2003a, response to Schroyens and Schaeken, 2003).

Dennett (1987, p. 227) notes that explanation in classical cognitive science can be viewed as a 'triumphant cascade' through the three levels of description. The computational/intentional level provides a set of predictive relations between inputs and outputs, but it adds no explanation to that mapping. The algorithmic level provides a sequence of states which can map intervening states on to each other, allowing finely grained predictions, but not specifying the causal process properties of the states. The implementation level provides the causal account. As noted by Franks (1995, p. 479, also see Franks, 1999, Patterson, 1999):

> A basic requirement on a successful cascade can be termed the 'inheritance of the superordinate': given a particular [computational/intentional] Level 1 starting point, any algorithm must compute the same function, and any implementation must implement the same algorithm and compute the same function. Lower levels inherit their superordinates. Where this fails, a mismatch results between the description of the faculty at one level, and the description employed at the lower level. For example, failing to inherit a Level 1 specification results in the function computed by the algorithm specified at [algorithmic] Level 2 being a completely different function-there is a *functional mismatch* between levels.

When taking classic logic as their computational-level specification, theories of human reasoning become swamped with such functional mismatches.[6] Franks (1995) cogently argued that such functional mismatches are caused by idealizations, which block the classic cascade of explanation. We have accordingly tried to show that the paradoxes of material implication result from the idealized meaning of 'if' and have also shown how the outlines of the mental-model theory delineate a functional mismatch in comparison with the strictures of logic.

Acknowledgements

I gratefully acknowledge the support of the Flanders (Belgium) Fund for Scientific Research (G.0320.05) and the Canadian Natural Sciences and Engineering Research Council (NSERC 297517).

---

[6] Critics of mental-models theory consider classic logic to be its computational level theory. There is potential for an 'attribution error': we know of not a single mental-model theorist who holds or defends this position. Some mental-models theorist might (implicitly or explicitly) hold the evaluative stance that people *should* reason logical. This does not mean however that the theories of these theorists suppose people actually *do* reason logically. Normative issues are to be distinguished from descriptive issues and the computational-level description of a theory is descriptive in nature. Consider, for instance, which norms should apply in providing a computational-level description of a psychological theory of vision or memory? Space does not allow me to engage in an extensive quotation practice to demonstrate the rejection of classic logic as the computational-level description of reasoning by model. It is a textual fact that a validating search for counter-examples is at the heart of mental-models theory. This implies that defeating inferences is at the heart of mental-models theory. Critics (those who muddle the defeasibility of a conclusion and the non-monotonicity of an argument) have argued mental-models theory is fundamentally flawed because it has classic logic as its competence theory. They argue that if a theory has classic logic as its competence theory, it cannot account for the defeasible nature of human reasoning: <if C then not-D>. This claim is based on the fact that classic logic is non-monotonic in nature. These critics must therefore, given <D> (by force of logic, i.e., Modus Tollendo Tollens) accept/believe that mental models theory does not have classic logic as its competence theory.

References

Anderson, J. R. (1990). *The adaptive character of thought*. Hillsdale, NJ: Lawrence Erlbaum.

Bennett, J. (2003). *A philosophical guide to conditionals*. Oxford: Clarendon Press.

Chater, N. & Oaksford, M. (1999). The probabilistic heuristics model of syllogistic reasoning. *Cognitive Psychology*, **38**(2), 191–258.

Cummins, D. D., Lubart, T., Alksnis, O., & Rist, R. (1991). Conditional reasoning and causation. *Memory & Cognition*, **19**, 274–282.

Dekeyser, M., Schroyens, W., Schaeken, W., Spitaels, W., & d'Ydewalle, G. (2000). Preferred premise order in propositional reasoning: Semantic informativeness and co-reference. In W. Schaeken, G. De Vooght, A. Vandierendonck, & G. d'Ydewalle (Eds.), *Deductive reasoning and strategies* (pp. 73–95). London: Lawrence Erlbaum.

Dennett, D. (1987). The intentional stance. Cambridge, MA: MIT Press.

Evans, J. St. B. T., Handley, S. J., & Over, D. (2003). Conditionals and conditional probability. *Journal of Experimental Psychology: Learning, Memory and Cognition*, **29**(2), 321–335.

Evans, J. St. B. T., Over, D. E., & Handley, S. (2005). Supposition, extensionality, and conditonals: A critique of the mental model theory of Johnson-Laird and Byrne (2002). *Psychological Review*, **112**(4), 1040–1052.

Franks, B. (1995). On Explanation in the cognitive sciences: competence, idealization, and the failure of the classical cascade. *The British Journal of the Philosophy of Science*, **46**(4), 475–502.

Franks, B. (1999). Idealizations, competence and explanation: A response to Patterson. *British Journal of the Philosophy of Science*, **50**, 735–746.

Grice, H. P. (1975). Logic and conversation. In P. Cole, & J. L. Morgan (Eds.), *Studies in syntax: Speech acts* (Vol. 3, pp. 41–58). New York: Academic Press.

Jackson, F. (1987). *Conditionals*. Oxford: Blackwell.

Johnson-Laird, P. N. (1983). *Mental models: Towards a cognitive science of language, inference, and consciousness*. Cambridge: Cambridge University Press.

Johnson-Laird, P. N. (1999). Deductive reasoning. *Annual Review of Psychology*, **50**, 109–135.

Johnson-Laird, P. N. & Byrne, R. M. J. (1991). *Deduction*. Hillsdale, NJ: Erlbaum.

Johnson-Laird, P. N. & Byrne, R. M. J. (2002). Conditionals: A theory of meaning, pragmatics, and inference. *Psychological Review*, **109**(4), 646–678.

Johnson-Laird, P. N., Legrenzi, P., Girotto, V., Legrenzi, M., & Caverni, J.-P. (1999). Naive probability: A mental model theory of extensional reasoning. *Psychological Review*, **106**, 63–88.

Levinson, S. C. (2000). *Presumptive meanings: The theory of generalized conversational implicature*. Cambridge, MA: MIT Press.

Marr, D. (1977). Artificial Intelligence — A personal view. In J. Haugland (Ed.), *Mind Design*. Cambridge, MA: MIT Press.

Marr, D. (1982). *Vision: A computational investigation into the human representation and processing of visual information*. San Francisco: W.H. Freeman and Company.

McClamrock, R. (1991). Marr's three levels: A re-evaluation. *Minds and Machines*.

Morris, A. K. & Sloutsky, V. M. (1998). Understanding of logical necessity: Developmental antecedents and cognitive consequences. *Child Development*, **69**(3), 721–741.

Musgrave, A. (1989). Deductivism versus psychologism. In M. A. Notturno (Ed.), *Perspectives on psychologims* (pp. 314–340). New York: E. J. Brill.

Notturno, M. A. (Ed.). (1989). *Perspectives on psychologism*. Leiden, The Nederlands: E. J. Brill.

Oaksford, M. & Chater, N. (1998). *Rationality in an uncertain world*. Hove, UK: Psychology Press.

Oaksford, M. & Chater, N. (2003). Computational levels and conditional inference: Reply to Schroyens and Schaeken (2003). *Journal of Experimental Psychology: Learning, Memory, and Cognition*, **29**, 150–156.

Oaksford, M. & Chater, N. (2003). Conditional probability and the cognitive Science of conditional reasoning. *Mind & Language*, **18**(4), 359–379.

Patterson, S. (1998). Competence and the classical cascade: A reply to Franks. *British Journal for the Philosophy of Science*, **49**(4), 625–636.

Pelletier, F. J. & Elio, R. (2005). The case for psychologism in default and inheritance reasoning. *Synthese*, **146**, 7–35.

Schroyens, W. (2004). Conceptual muddles: Truth vs. Truthfulness, Logical vs. Psychological Validity, and the non-monotonic vs. defeasible nature of human inferences. In K. Forbus, D. Gentner, & T. Regier (Eds.) *Proceedings of the 26th Annual Conference of the Cognitive Science Society*. Hillsdale, NJ: Lawrence Erlbaum. http://www.cogsci.rpi.edu/CSJarchive/Proceedings/2004/CogSci04.pdf

Schroyens, W. (2004). Deductive rationality in human reasoning: Speed, validity and the assumption of truth in conditional reasoning. In K. Forbus, D. Gentner, & T. Regier (Eds.), *Proceedings of the 26th Annual Conference of the Cognitive Science Society* (pp. 1225–1230). New Jersey: Lawrence Erlbaum.

Schroyens, W. (2005). Issues in reasoning about iffy propositions: Deductive rationality in testing and revising conditional inferences. In B. Bara, L. Barselou, & M. Bucciarelli (Eds.), *Proceedings of the 27th Annual Conference of the Cognitive Science Society*. New Jersey: Lawrence Erlbaum.

Schroyens, W. (2005). Issues in reasoning about iffy propositions: The initial representation of conditionals. In B. Bara, L. Barsalou, & M. Bucciarelli (Eds), *Proceedings of the 27th Annual Conference of the Cognitive Science Society* (pp. 1967–1972). New Jersey: Lawrence Erlbaum.

Schroyens, W. (2007). *The Principle of Charity in Interpreting Scientific Theory: A Meta-Theoretical Polemic Against Theoretical Polemics*. In D. S. McNamara, & J. G. Trafton (Eds.), Proceedings of the 29th Annual Cognitive Science Society (p. 57). Austin, TX: Cognitive Science Society.

Schroyens, W. & Byrne, R. (1998). *The role of a conditional or bi-conditional interpretation in conditional reasoning about 'if'*. (Report No. 242). Leuven: University of Leuven, Laboratory of Experimental Psychology.

Schroyens, W. & Dieussaert, K. (2005). Issues in reasoning about iffy propositions: The secondary inference model of revising conditional beliefs and inferences. In B. Bara, L. Barsalou, & M. Bucciarelli (Eds.), *Proceedings of the 27th Annual Conference of the Cognitive Science Society* (p. 2550). Hillsdale, NJ: Lawrence Erlbaum.

Schroyens, W. & Schaeken, W. (2003). A critique of Oaksford, Chater and Larkin's (2000) conditional probability model of conditional reasoning. *Journal of Experimental Psychology: Learning, Memory and Cognition*, **29**, 140–149.

Schroyens, W. & Schaeken, W. (2004). Guilt by association: On iffy propositions and the proper treatment of mental-models theory. *Current Psychology Letters: Behaviour, Brain & Cognition*, **12**(1), http://cpl.revues.org/document411.html.

Schroyens, W. & Schaeken, W. (2005). Issues in reasoning about iffy propositions: The development of deductive rationality in conditional reasoning. I. In B. Bara, L. Barsalou, & M. Bucciarelli (Eds.) *Proceedings of the 27th Annual Conference of the Cognitive Science Society* (p. 2551). Hillsdale, NJ: Lawrence Erlbaum.

Schroyens, W., Schaeken, W., & Dieussaert (in press). Issues in reasoning about iffy propositions: "The" interpretation(s) of conditionals. *Experimental Psychology*, **55**(2), 113–120.

Schroyens, W., Schaeken, W., & d'Ydewalle, G. (2001). The processing of negations in conditional reasoning: A meta-analytic study in mental model and/or mental logic theory. *Thinking and Reasoning*, **7**(2), 121–172.

Schroyens, W., Schaeken, W., & Handley, S. (2003). In Search of Counter Examples: Deductive Rationality in Human Reasoning. *Quarterly Journal of Experimental Psychology*, **56A**(7), 1129–1145.

Stanovich, K. E. & West, R. F. (2000). Individual differences in reasoning: Implications for the rationality debate? *Behavioral and Brain Sciences*, **23**, 645–726.

Stenning, K. & van Lambalgen, M. (2001). Semantics as a foundation for psychology: A case study of Wason's Selection Task. *Journal of Logic, Language and Information*, **10**, 273–317.

Stenning, K. & van Lambalgen, M. (2004). A little logic goes a long way: Basing experiment on semantic theory in the cognitive science of conditional reasoning. *Cognitive Science*, **28**, 481–529.

Thomson, J. F. (1990). In defence of 'hook'. *Journal of Philosophy*, **87**(2), 57–70.

Whyte, J. (2004). *Crimes against logic: Exposing the bogus arguments of politicians, priests, journalists and other serial offenders*. New York: McGraw-Hill.

Wolenski, J. (2003). Psychologism and metalogic. *Synthese*, **137**, 179–192.

Chapter 5

The logical response to a noisy world

Keith Stenning and Michiel van Lambalgen

Introduction

We live in a noisy world and our premises are subject to doubt. There is a thriving school of opinion in the psychology of reasoning that this means that it is both desirable, and inevitable for realism's sake, that theories of human reasoning should be framed in probability theory rather than mental process theories in logical frameworks; a prominent recent example is Oaksford and Chater (2007). A forceful earlier statement of this position is:

> … it is, in fact, rational by the highest standards to take proper account of the probability of one's premises in deductive reasoning … performing inferences from statements treated as absolutely certain is uncommon in ordinary reasoning. We are mainly interested in what subjects will infer from statements in ordinary discourse that they may not believe with certainty and may even have serious doubts about …

> (Stevenson & Over, 1995, p. 615)

This approach assumes that reasoners come with their interpretations of materials already fixed. How otherwise could they have any ideas about the probabilities of component propositions? When subjects hear, to take a famous example we will return to, 'If she has an essay, she is in the library' how could they have any idea about a probability without knowing anything about who 'she' might be or anything else about the situation? As Cummins (1995) has shown, there is a strong correlation between subjects' willingness to draw for example a modus ponens inference from such conditionals, and the ease with which they can retrieve 'additional' and 'alternative' conditionals, such as 'If the library is shut, she isn't in the library', or 'If she has a reference book to read, she's in the library'. Does this mean that subjects come to such experiments with an estimate of the probability of all such propositions which they merely need to retrieve? Or does it mean that there is a process of discourse interpretation which can explain how discourses composed of these conditionals give rise to interpretations on the basis of which subjects are willing to hazard likelihoods? A process of interpretation, moreover, which is endlessly sensitive to subtleties of the kind of discourse subjects believe they should engage in? Does Cummins' result suggest, rather than an archive of probabilities, that subjects estimate likelihoods from the ease of retrieving schematic knowledge about alternatives and defeaters? At least in the situations where they construe the task as interpreting a kind of fiction about typical students and typical libraries? Our most basic claim is that what subjects cannot do is to engage in *no* process of interpretation. We cannot study some 'central' process of inference, without studying its 'front end' process of interpretation.

So, in contrast to the probabilists, we believe that the loudness of the world is one important reason why human reasoning is a two component process (Stenning & van Lambalgen (2008)). We impose interpretations on discourse before we can reason from those interpretations, and we generally start by reasoning to interpretations as if their assumptions were perfectly certain *within those interpretations*. That is, our guiding question as discourse comprehenders is

'What would it be like for the speaker's discourse to be absolutely true?' Only when we have constructed an intended interpretation, can we derive any consequences *from* the interpretation, or decide how it relates to the world. Needless to say, we believe the twin theories of reasoning *to* interpretations and reasoning *from* them must be couched in logic, though in very different logical frameworks than have hitherto figured in the psychology of reasoning. Our aim in this paper is to motivate such a logical account, by showing that probability cannot provide the kind of defeasible framework within which interpretations can be established. Our positive logical account has appeared elsewhere (Stenning & van Lambalgen, 2005, 2008); here we concentrate on the shortcomings of probabilistic analyses of defeasible reasoning. We start by discussing a number of faulty assumptions about logic that have hindered its application to actual human reasoning.

Dusting off logic

The probabilistic critique of 'logicist' accounts of the psychology of reasoning trades on several assumptions about logic that may perhaps be reasonably applied to logic's applications in some psychological theories (mental logics, mental models, …), but are quite foreign to a modern logical approach to human reasoning and discourse. First there is an assumption that logic is to be identified with classical logic whose logical forms can be read directly from natural language sentence forms. Second, the interpretative component of logic is ignored at the expense of total concentration on the derivational component. Third, it is assumed that using probability theory as a basis for rational analysis does not involve using a logic, and so avoids the criticism levelled at 'logicist' cognitive science.

The first assumption, that logic must be identified with classical logic, is unfortunately still rather common. On the formal side, it overlooks the great wealth of logical systems currently explored. More to the point, it unjustifiably takes classical logic to be the only logic with normative force (Stenning & van Lambalgen (2008), Chapters 2, 11). Once one drops this assumption, we must assume instead that the process of interpretation of natural language sentences is a substantial one, and is best viewed as involving the setting of parameters not only for the syntactic form of natural language sentences, but for their semantics, and for the concept of validity inherent in the reasoning task at hand. The end result of parameter setting is to fix on what we call a *logical form* (Stenning & van Lambalgen (2008), chapter 2). Here we will concentrate on the contrast between defeasible logics of interpretation and classical logics of derivation, but many other logics are often involved. A notable further example is deontic logic as involved in some selection task variants (Stenning & van Lambalgen (2004)).

The second assumption was that logic is to be identified with its formal, derivational component. The probabilistic approach identifies 'logicist' approaches with certainty of conclusions given premises and sees the central advantage of probabilistic approaches as their capacity to handle uncertainty. But even traditional logic always assumed that uncertainty was to be accommodated in its interpretative component. Traditional logic (that is, logic as it was practised and taught before the era of formalization) had no formal account of interpretation but, as we shall see, it shares this property with current probabilistic approaches, and besides traditional logic had a substantial informal account of the criteria for coherent interpretation. This problem perhaps arises from identifying logic with its applications in the foundations of mathematics, a late 19C employment. Traditional logic was developed as a theory of the discourse of argumentation – a subject matter as prone to uncertainty as it is possible to find.

On the third assumption, that the relevant properties of logic do not apply to probabilistic approaches, one must counter that probability theory simply is a (family of) logic(s) – probability logics – and as such qualifies as a target of all the criticisms levelled at 'logicist' approaches. In fact probability logic is a deductive theory which vastly extends the range of *certainty* of inference. For example, classical probability theory assures us that if the probabilities of events X and Y are both .5 and are independent, then the probability of $X \wedge Y$ is .25 – exactly. Even when probability theories only licence inferences of probability intervals rather than point probabilities, they often give exact bounds on the confidence intervals of our conclusions.[1] Everywhere uncertainty retreats before a tidal wave of exactitude. We agree entirely that handling uncertainty is of great importance, but we feel that this militates strongly against probabilistic frameworks. We agree entirely that we must give accounts of how content affects reasoning, but for precisely this reason we propose that a 'defeasible logic of interpretation' is required to explain reasoning over long-term knowledge *to* an interpretation.

In the next section, we will provide a brief sketch of our own positive logical approach through its account of the suppression task in the next section (Byrne (1989), Stenning & van Lambalgen (2005, 2008)). The last reference gives an overview of the reanalysis of several psychology of reasoning tasks in this interpretative framework: the selection and suppression tasks, categorial syllogisms and some non-linguistic executive function tasks. In the middle section we will examine the Oaksford and Chater probabilistic account of the suppression task and show, first that they too require an additional initial interpretative component which cannot be couched in probability theory and second, that even when this interpretative component is added, the resulting probabilistic treatment cannot cover all the argument patterns which people readily employ.

A logic of discourse interpretation

Whilst traditional logic had a substantial but informal understanding of interpretation, it had no formal account of the reasoning involved. Its formal accounts, such as they were, were of derivations within an interpretation – examples of which are known and loved by every introductory student. Interpretation figured mostly in the injunction that it must be held constant throughout an argument – no equivocation (surreptitious shifting of interpretation) was to be allowed. Since, with the advent of symbolic logic, teachers were often content to teach the formal manipulation of the symbols within systems, the process of interpretation was backgrounded in introductory courses, often to the point of disappearance.

Since the 1970s, artificial intelligence researchers have provided formal accounts of defeasible logics of interpretation (McCarthy, 1980; Reiter, 1980). Defeasibility, the capacity to withdraw earlier conclusions on the arrival of new evidence, is clearly a criterial requirement for any process of interpretation, even though it is equally obviously anathema to classical derivational processes. Unfortunately, despite their invention by those interested in computer implementation, the motivating belief that these 'natural' logics must be easier for people to use turned out to be disappointed. These logics are provably seriously computationally intractable – more so even than classical logic which was already known to be highly intractable. Out of the frying pan into the fire. This impasse had a baleful effect on the application of defeasible logics in psychology.

Fortunately, in the eighties and early nineties, the more tractable alternative logics of interpretation which we will use here became generally available. It is of some interest that they originated obliquely from the very practical research programme of adapting logic as a computer programming language, issuing in languages such as PROLOG. Whilst the practitioners saw themselves as

---

[1] There are important differences among probabilistic approaches (for example, Pfeiffer and Kleiter (2005) and Oaksford and Chater (2007) differ significantly), but they share the property of assuming prior interpretation.

using fragments of classical logic to achieve efficient computations, later logical study of the resulting systems revealed that they could more perspicuously be conceptualized as computing in defeasible logics. The particular logic we will introduce here is known as 'logic programming with negation as failure'.

Needless to say, the tractability of these new defeasible logics is purchased at a certain price. In this case, as one should expect, in expressiveness of the languages concerned. Logic programming (Doets, 1994) restricts conditionals to ones that are of the form $L_1 \wedge .... \wedge L_n \rightarrow A$, where A is atomic, and the L_i are either atoms or negated atoms.[2] However, we believe this loss of expressiveness is well worth the price. The fact that the resulting languages can be used in programming is a good indication that they are expressive enough to get lots done, and some of the restrictions (such as that against some syntactic iteration of the implication) also arguably apply to natural language conditionals. We think this is a good compromise balance between expressiveness and tractability. This is a stark contrast to the intractability of probability theory, which is acknowledged also by those advocating the probabilistic approach. This acknowledgment forces them back to a position where probability is a distant competence theory whose relation to the data we will argue is hard to understand, and whose implementation they have little to say about. Our defeasible logic can be shown to have a direct neural implementation and so brings competence and performance dramatically closer together (Stenning & van Lambalgen, 2005; 2008, chapter 8).

These defeasible logics specify valid patterns of reasoning over *databases* of default conditional rules. We conceive of these rules as representing long term general knowledge of environmental regularities, and of connections between the agent's beliefs and his actions.[3] Since we are concerned with modelling discourses, we conceive of the new statements of the discourse arriving sequentially and being incorporated into the 'hearer's' working memory (WM) which is conceived of as the activated part of long term memory, rather in the style in which ACT-R would model this relation (Anderson & Lebiere, 1998).

We model conditionals whose surface form is 'if p then q' as *default rules*, which are defined as logic programming clauses of the form: '$p \wedge \neg ab \rightarrow q$' read as 'If p and nothing is abnormal is the case, then q'.[4] The abnormality (and possibly other propositions as well) is governed by *closed world reasoning* (CWR), which says that if a proposition is not known to be true, it may be assumed false. Thus, if there is no information that an abnormality will occur, we may assume that none will occur, and the above conditional reduces to $p \rightarrow q$. CWR is the logic that one often applies in planning and prediction. There is an unlimited number of events – abnormalities – which could interfere with our goal to be in London on August 28, 2007 (ranging from major natural or man-made disasters, to strikes, to waking up too late and missing the plane). The vast majority of these events are not accounted for in our plan to go to London at said date – that is, they are treated as if they will not occur. CWR leads to a *non-monotonic* logic. New information may become available which forces us to consider an event as an abnormality which was not previously classified as such.

With this much logical background, we can introduce the main reasoning task to be studied in this chapter, the suppression task (Byrne, 1989). When subjects are presented with the modus ponens material 'If she has an essay she studies late in the library. She has an essay' they almost

---

2 The restrictions on the antecedent can be liberalised somewhat, but it is not allowed to have conditionals in the antecedent.

3 Stenning and van Lambalgen (2007) discusses the role of default conditionals in 'executive function', an umbrella term for processes involving planning of actions to achieve a given goal.

4 Strictly speaking we would have to write $p \wedge \neg ab_{pq} \rightarrow q$, a notation that emphasizes that the abnormality is specific to the conditional. We ask the reader to remember that this is the intended interpretation and we will continue using the less cumbersome notation.

universally draw the conclusion she studies late. When instead they are presented with the same premises *plus* the premise: 'If the library is open she studies late in the library', about half of them withdraw the inference. Byrne concludes that inference rules cannot be used to explain the former performance since they evidently cannot explain the latter non-inference. Rules, if they are to be invoked must be invoked universally and uniformly. So much the worse for mental logics – roll on mental models, concludes Byrne.

Stenning and van Lambalgen (2005) analyse this task in terms of CWR. In the condition of the suppression task where we are given that 'she has an essay' and 'if she has an essay she's in the library', the argument proceeds as follows. The underlying logical form of the premise set is $\{p, p \wedge \neg ab \rightarrow q\}$. By itself this does not justify the modus ponens inference, but now we invoke CWR, in the guise of the assumption that since no abnormalities are mentioned we may assume them not to be present, to conclude that $\neg ab$ is in fact true; whence q follows.

When, in the second condition of the experiment we get the extra premise that 'if the library is open she is in the library', it is conceived of as triggering the relevance of an abnormality – namely that the library may be closed (along with the relevance of other general knowledge conditionals such as 'if the library is closed, readers are not inside' etc.). Now we do have information that something abnormal may be the case, and from $p \wedge \neg ab \rightarrow q$ and ab we can no longer conclude q, though we, along with lots of subjects, may be happy to make the weaker conclusion that 'if she has an essay *and* the library is open she'll be in the library'.

Because of closed world reasoning over abnormalities, some patterns of reasoning are valid in this logic which are invalid in classical logic, notably affirmation of the consequent and denial of the antecedent. So from 'If she has an essay she is in the library' and 'She doesn't have an essay', it is valid to conclude that 'She isn't in the library', but again only by closed world reasoning. This is a valid move if this is all there is in the database concerning essays or libraries, because we can conclude that this is the only conditional with the relevant consequent. If we then add the 'alternative' premise 'If she has a textbook to read she's in the library' then this defeats the conclusion because the world is now large enough to contain another explanation for her presence in the library. Similarly, affirmation of the consequent is valid in this logic in the right context. From 'If she has an essay then she's in the library', and 'She is in the library' we can conclude that 'she does have an essay', but only providing the world is closed against abnormalities such as the library being closed. For a fuller exposition of the suppression task treated in this logic see Stenning and van Lambalgen (2005).

As an aside which we return to below, it is worth raising the question 'What is worth modelling in the suppression task?' Stenning and van Lambalgen (2005) show that each of the four conditional inference forms can be valid in the proposed logic, depending on context, and therefore why non-monotonic revisions of conclusions should or should not occur with the arrival of different kinds of premises. It is not unreasonable to fit this to group data such as Byrne's, showing that indeed the changes in proportion of subjects making or retracting conclusions fits well with the logical model. But it is important we don't forget that this is a very weak sort of data. What we would really like is longitudinal data on the same subject's revisions of belief in each of the conditions studied – the model is about belief revision, not about the development of group belief. Of course there are problems of interference between conditions measures which forced the original design. Our point is that other methods of investigation need to be brought to bear.

Lechler (2004) used Socractic dialogue to show that the range of interpretations subjects adopted was much wider than allowed for in Byrne's analysis, and that the classification of premises as 'alternative' or 'additional' was far from reliable.[5] So the logical model as it stands only models a

---

[5] Stenning and van Lambalgen (2008), chapter 7 features extracts of Lechler's (2004) data.

particular small range of the interpretations people adopt, but it is also clear, even from Byrne's data, that different subjects are doing different things and it makes little sense to model the details of their average mental processes.

We mention here in passing that there is a highly significant difference in performance between autistic children and normal controls, in that the former do *not* engage in closed world reasoning with respect to abnormalities, although they are capable of other forms of CWR. Thus autists suppress MP and MT much less, although they are indistinguishable from normals with respect to AC and DA. See Stenning and van Lambalgen (2007) for more details.

Defeasibility is achieved in this logic by closed world reasoning, and this is central to why the logic is tractable. In fact the semantics assigned to the logic guarantees that a unique minimal 'intended' model (valuation of all the atomic propositions) for the discourse is derivable at each step of incorporation of a new discourse sentence. The semantics is three-valued (true, false, so-far-undecided) but not truth functional and the concept of validity is not the classical 'truth of conclusion in *all* models of the premises' but rather 'truth of conclusion in the intended model of the premises'. The non-truth functionality of the system is clear for all to see. The defaults in long term memory cannot be shown to be false because of their robustness to exceptions invoked as abnormality conditions. Genuine counterexamples would require relearning – repair of the database which is a process outside this logic. None of this is surprising as long as we keep in mind that this is a logic of (*credulous*) discourse processing in which our goal as hearer is to make the speaker's statements true. That is, to find a model that makes them true. The three-valued semantics is required to allow negation-as-failure ($\neg p$ is adopted as true if we fail to prove p from the given premises; since an extended premise set may make p provable, the adoption of ($\neg p$ is always provisional, whence the non-monotonicity).

Interestingly, this three-valued semantics allows a neural network implementation of the logic in which a feedforward spreading activation network computes the intended model of a discourse in linear time (Stenning and van Lambalgen (2008), chapter 8). It should be obvious that this is not a logic of cogitation – slow deliberate derivation of conclusions. In psychological terms it is rather a logic of System 1 processes (Evans, 2003) – fast automatic processes of inference operating over general knowledge, often well outside of conscious control, or indeed awareness – exactly appropriate for the processes of discourse understanding for simple well-wrought discourse.

So why is discourse processing still hard?

Computational linguistics tells us that discourse processing is hard because discourses are massively ambiguous and require continual backtracking in their processing. How can a defeasible logic deliver a unique minimal intended model at each stage? We do not pretend to have solved the computational linguistic problem. What we are claiming is that the human problem is solved by the mobilization of general knowledge by the human processor. Human processors do not normally experience these ambiguities because they can apply commonsense knowledge to avoid them. The logical theory shows how this can happen in example cases but does not explain how LTM can be organized on a global scale to achieve this in a computer. Baggio, van Lambalgen and Hagoort (2007) show how ERP data can provide some evidence that the invocation of abnormalities in the logic leaves traces in brain activity in psycholinguistic experiments.

Let us take an example that is used by Oaksford and Chater to argue against the applicability of defeasible logics: *Birds fly. One-minute-old birds don't fly. Can the bird Tweety at one-minute-old fly?*

Here there is a conflict between defeasible rules. Our response would be that defeasible logical databases allow the mobilization of general knowledge 'theories' to resolve such impasses and this gives a plausible explanation as to how humans resolve them. The database also contains conditionals such as *Birds hatch from eggs, Helpless chicks take weeks to mature*, and lots of other linking materials ... which are sufficient to arrive at the conclusion *So Tweety can't fly, yet. Contra* Oaksford and Chater, this tractable defeasible logic really does solve some versions of the frame problem (Shanahan, 1997).

This problem of conflict between two applicable rules is only one kind of impasse. The other kind of impasse the credulous discourse processor may hit is where no models can be found i.e., where the speaker's utterances appear to contradict each other. *Socrates is mortal. Socrates lives forever in the dialogues of Plato.* Given a small amount of inference about living for ever and immortality, we have a contradiction. No model is available. Here, we propose, the credulous processor interrupts its activity while classical reasoning attempts to repair: 'Something is wrong. There must be equivocation in the interpretation. We must find an interpretation in which these two statements are consistent'. The intended (unique) model of the discourse, thus far, now has to be inflated into a set of classical models representing various possibilities. The single truth valuation of the atoms of the discourse fragment defines a set of all possible valuations. Now we have to find some modification of this interpretation which will allow an intended model in which the rogue statements are both true. Is the first Socrates perhaps the Brazilian football player? Or are there two senses of immortality involved? The reasoning is only classical in the sense that we *may* have to explore all possible classical models in order to repair the impasse by finding some one that will do. Failure to do so will turn the discourse from credulous cooperative to classical adversarial, at least until some mutually acceptable repair is found.

Our claim is that we have provided a logical framework for interpretation whose known properties make it plausible that these problems can be solved and will scale up. Much of the empirical psychology remains to be done. Note that in this account of 'suppression', nothing is suppressed, and the account is completely neutral as to whether the reasoning is done over syntactic rules or over models. Both proof-theoretic and equivalent model-theoretic expositions can be given. The task cannot provide any evidence whatsoever for resolving debates about rules versus models.

This concludes our survey of what we believe is the proper setting of the suppression task: defeasible reasoning on discourse interpretations. We now turn to a critical examination of a very different probabilistic analysis of the same task, that of Oaksford and Chater, 2003, reprinted in Oaksford and Chater, 2007). Our purpose here is general however: we believe the potential of probability theory to model defeasible reasoning has been overestimated, and the suppression task allows us to show why.[6]

A probabilistic model for the suppression task

Oaksford and Chater (2003) attempt to show that a probabilistic model can account for the observed suppression effects in conditional reasoning. We will carefully analyse the assumptions underlying the model because they are fairly typical of applications of probability to human reasoning. These assumptions can be divided into four broad categories:

  i philosophical assumptions forcing a close connection between uncertainty and probability (while denying a role for logic)

---

[6] Since this article was written, Oaksford and Chater have published a *précis* of Oaksford and Chater (2007) in the journal *Behavioral and Brain Sciences* (Vol. 32, Issue 1 (2009). The present authors contributed a commentary to this target article, mainly a condensed version of the following section 3, to which Oaksford and Chater gracefully responded. We have decided, in order not to interrupt the flow of argumentation, to put Oaksford and Chater's responses, and our rejoinders, in a series of footnotes attached to the relevant places in this article.

ii largely implicit assumptions about what is and what is not to be included in the model

iii coordinating definitions linking the probabilistic model to the task at hand

iv assumptions concerning what counts as validation of the model.

In our discussion below we indicate the category of assumptions at issue by the corresponding Roman numeral.

Probability and logic

The following quote from Oaksford and Chater (2003) provides much material for reflection on:

> [M]uch of our reasoning with conditionals is uncertain, and may be overturned by future information; that is, they are non-monotonic. But logic based approaches to inference are typically monotonic, and hence are unable to deal with this uncertainty. Moreover, to the extent that formal logical approaches embrace non-monotonicity, they appear to be unable to cope with the fact that it is the content of the rules, rather than their logical form, which appears to determine the inferences that people draw. We now argue that perhaps by encoding more of the content of people's knowledge, by probability theory, we may more adequately capture the nature of everyday human inference. This seems to make intuitive sense, because the problems that we have identified concern how uncertainty is handled in human inference, and probability is the calculus of uncertainty.
>
> (Oaksford & Chater, 2003 p. 100)

The argument sketched here is that logic is not useful as a model of reasoning because it is either monotonic, in which case it flies in the face of data such as suppression, or non-monotonic, in which case it is closer to the data, but still far off, because it cannot account for the difference between additional and alternative conditionals, which is supposed to be one of content not form. Probability fares much better in this respect, because it can incorporate changes in content as changes in the values of probabilities.[7] Furthermore, and most importantly, there are *a priori* arguments to show that probability theory is *the* normatively justified calculus of uncertainty. We will discuss this issue first.

Probability and uncertainty

The standard justification for probability – interpreted subjectively – as representation of uncertainty proceeds via so-called 'Dutch Book arguments', a simplified version of which goes as follows.[8] Assume given a sample space X and a set A of events on X, which has a Boolean structure. For ease of exposition we take A to be the powerset of X. What is important to note,

---

[7] Oaksford and Chater (2009) write (p. 108): 'As noted in [Oaksford & Chater, 2007] and elsewhere, there are, however, fundamental problems for non-monotonic logics in the crucial case where different 'lines of argument' clash. Thus, *if it is sunny, John goes to the park*, and *it's sunny* appears to provide a powerful argument that John goes to the park. But adding the premise, *John is arrested by the police in a dawn raid*, together with background knowledge, appears to yield the conclusion that John does not go to the park', and argue that 'that resolving such clashes is not typically possible by looking only at the structural features of arguments'. We disagree: this is precisely what our logical analysis of the suppression task (Stenning & van Lambalgen (2005, 2008) does (see section 2). Moreover, the logical modelling of 'clashing lines of arguments' turns out to be extremely useful in describing executive functioning and therefore disorders; see Stenning and van Lambalgen (2008), Chapter 9 for an application to autistic children reasoning in the false belief task.

[8] For an excellent exposition, see Paris (1994).

however, is that the Boolean structure of the set of events is given not derived; in other words, one must assume that the events satisfy classical logic. This severely restricts the kinds of uncertainty to which probability theory can be applied.

In the next step it is assumed that one's degree of belief in the occurrence of an event E in A can be determined via betting. In very rough outline, the agent's degree of belief in E equals the price of a promise to pay \$1 if E occurs, and \$0 otherwise. The phrase 'a promise to pay' refers to a subtlety in the wager: the bookmaker decides *after you have set the price* which side of the bet will be the agent's. Thus, the agent knows that the bookmaker will either buy such a promise from him at the price set, or will require the agent to buy such a promise, again at the price set by the agent. The price set by the agent is the subjective probability assigned to E. A *Dutch Book* is a betting scheme which guarantees a gain for the bookmaker. A famous foundational result in subjective probability then says that the following are equivalent:

(i) no Dutch Book can be made against the agent

(ii) the agent's degrees of belief satisfy the axioms of probability

Since it is supposedly irrational to engage in a bet in which you are sure to lose, the result is often glossed as: a rational assignment of degrees of belief is one which satisfies the axioms of probability theory. This is a so-called *synchronic* Dutch Book theorem; the *diachronic* Dutch Book theorem is concerned with Bayesian updates of beliefs and justifies the rule of Bayesian conditionalization (BaCo).

The absolute subjective probability of event D given that evidence E has been observed is equal to the conditional probability $P(D|E)$. Here E should encompass *all* available evidence.

(BaCo) will be important in constructing probabilistic analogues for the standard propositional inference patterns MP, MT, AC, DA.

An objection against justifications of this type is that the agent is all-knowing and 'all-willing' as well: he must be willing to bet on any event in A and he must fix a unique price for the promise, instead of, say, an upper and a lower bound. While these idealizations may be alright in some philosophical contexts, they are definitely out of order when it comes to cognition. It is not impossible that agents reason with subjective probabilities in some situations, but there is no guarantee that they assign probabilities to every event of interest.

There exists a way out of these problems, at least technically, by considering finite approximations to the space of all events. To fix ideas, suppose the space of all events corresponds to the denumerable set of propositions $p_0, p_1, p_2, p_3, \ldots$ An agent is aware of only finitely many propositions at any one time, but over time this set may increase. For the sake of argument we may suppose that the above betting procedure assigns a joint distribution P_n over the Boolean algebra generated by $\{p_0, p_1, p_2, p_3, \ldots, p_n\}$ for all $n > 0$.

In principle, however, the $P_n(p_i)$ can be different for all n, and hence there is no guarantee that there exists a limit distribution $\lim P_n$ (where n goes to infinity) which defines a joint distribution over the whole algebra generated by $\{p_0, p_1, p_2, p_3, \ldots, p_n\}$. The reader may wish to consider the special case where the P_n are actually truth value assignments to the $\{p_0, p_1, p_2, p_3, \ldots, p_n\}$; in this case $\lim P_n(p_i)$ exists only if the truth value of p_i changes finitely many times. That is, incoming information about propositions not considered so far may non-monotonically change the truth value of p_i, but only for finitely many propositions – the last change must be monotonic.

The general case in which the P_n are probability distributions is a difficult mathematical problem (Rao (1971) much studied in the Bayesian literature, for example in connection with 'hierarchies of beliefs' (see Brandenburger and Dekel (1993) for an interesting example). In order for the limit $\lim P_n$ to exist for all events, a complicated coherence condition must be satisfied.

A special case of this condition will be of interest later when discussing the suppression task. Suppose P_2 is the joint distribution over $\{p, q\}$ and P_3 the joint distribution over $\{p, q, r\}$. The coherence condition then implies the following relation among conditional probabilities:

$$P_2(q \mid p) = P_3(q \mid p \wedge r) \, P_3(r \mid p) + P_3(q \mid p \wedge \neg r) \, P_3(\neg r \mid p) \tag{5.1}$$

This property is the probabilistic analogue of monotonicity.

Summing up the discussion so far: we have seen that many assumptions are necessary to conclude that probability theory is the uniquely designated formalism to deal with every form of uncertainty. In fact the assumptions can be glossed by saying that the application of probability assumes quite a bit of certainty: the structure of events must be of a very specific type described by classical logic, the agent must be certain about the price he wants to set for any bet, and the agent must also be certain that his future probabilities conform to the coherence condition. This is too much to ask for a real cognitive agent. Of course, we do not deny that the brain uses *frequency* information about the environment – e.g., the frequency with which a given word occurs – in processing. We just doubt that, where frequency information is lacking, subjective probability can always do duty for frequencies.

It is therefore unclear why subjective probability can claim the status of a computational model (in the sense of Marr) for dealing with uncertainty (Oaksford & Chater, 2003, p. 103). Note that Marr did not intend his computational level to be an idealized model only. This level specifies the inputs and outputs – and their relation – of a given cognitive function, and thus functions as a declarative specification of the algorithm at the next level. Its character as specification of an algorithm means that the computational level is not just idealization and is connected in a lawlike manner to the algorithm.

Setting up the model

Of course, for the purposes of the argument we grant Oaksford and Chater the assumption that subjects do indeed assign degrees of belief to the events of interest in the suppression task. This assumption (of type III.) can be divided into two components:

(i) reasoning with a conditional $p{\rightarrow}q$ is *de facto* reasoning with the conditional probability $P(q \mid p)$ – which is assumed to be known exactly[9]

(ii) subjects assign precise probabilities to atomic propositions

Three parameters then suffice to determine a joint probability on the algebra generated by $\{p,q\}$: $a := P(p)$, $b := P(q)$, $\varepsilon := P(\neg q \mid p)$. This last parameter is the 'exception parameter', which models the defeasibility of the conditional $p{\rightarrow}q$. We will see below that suppression of MP and MT in the presence of an additional conditional is explained via modulation of ε, but we first discuss the two-premise inference patterns.

MP is viewed as (BaCo) applied to $P(q \mid p)$. That is, if p is given as the categorical premise, it is assumed this premise constitutes all the available evidence, so that (BaCo) can be applied. This way of justifying probabilistic MP gives it a nice non-monotonic flavour, for if in addition to p the categorical premise r is given, (BaCo) can no longer be applied to $P(q \mid p)$. Thus, it would seem that a probabilistic analysis is in principle suitable to model the suppression task.[10] In a similar

---

9   As a consequence, some reasoning with iterated conditionals cannot be represented, as is also the case in closed world reasoning.

10   This is not the justification given in Oaksford and Chater (2003) where it is simply observed that subjects, when given p, seem to rate the probability of q as proportional to $P(q \mid p)$. The present exposition makes it clearer why a probabilistic analysis of the suppression task is prima facie plausible.

way, MT is viewed as (BaCo) applied to $P(\neg p \mid \neg q)$, AC as (BaCo) applied to $P(p \mid q)$, and lastly DA as (BaCo) applied to $P(\neg q \mid \neg p)$. The three parameters a, b, ε suffice to generate the required conditional probabilities via the probabilities of conjunctions. For example, $P(p \wedge \neg q)$ is computed as $P(p)P(\neg q \mid p) = a.\varepsilon$, $P(p \wedge q) = P(p)P(q \mid p) = a.(1\text{-}\varepsilon)$, $P(\neg p \wedge q) = P(q)\text{-}P(p \wedge q) = b\text{-}a.$ $(1\text{-}\varepsilon)$. It follows that e.g., $P(p \mid q) = P(p \wedge q)/P(q) = a.(1\text{-}\varepsilon)/b$, and so on for the other conditional probabilities.

Validating the model for two premises

Why is it plausible to assume that subjects reason according to such a probabilistic model? Oaksford and Chater attempt to show this by fitting the model to characteristic data on two premise inferences (here taken from Byrne (1989)).

The fitting[11] proceeds as follows: ε was set to .1, and values of a, b were sampled[12] in the interval $[.1, .9]$.[13] The values of the four conditional probabilities were averaged over the b in the sample. Just to give an example, the value of the average for $P(q \mid p)$ obtained in this way was 90.00%. As a number, this is not dramatically different from the 97.36% rate of endorsement in Byrne's data, which are also averaged over subjects. This is a validation of sorts (if the problem indicated in the previous footnote can be solved) but it would be much stronger if the model were fitted to individual subjects – after all it's they who are supposed to reason with subjective probabilities. Further principled objections to this procedure will be discussed on p. 98.

Incorporating additional and alternative conditionals

There are two motivations for using probability theory as a model of reasoning in the suppression task. One is that Bayesian conditionalization is itself a non-monotonic principle: an extension of the evidence p may invalidate a previous posterior probability for q derived by (BaCo) applied to $P(q \mid p)$. The second motivation is that the conditional probability $P(q \mid p \wedge r)$ may differ from $P(q \mid p)$, so that strengthening the antecedent of a conditional has a real effect. Thus there is face validity in the attempt to model suppression via change in conditional probability. As we will see, however, it is not straightforward to give a probabilistic account of the processes involved in changing the conditional probabilities.

There is also a weak probabilistic explanation of the suppression task, which is content with observing that because (BaCo) is a non-monotonic principle, expansion of the original evidence p with an additional conditional invalidates the probability assignment to q, so that suppression of MP is expected. Such an explanation would need to show how (the antecedents of) additional conditionals differ from (the antecedents of) alternative conditionals, and in any case requires an account of how a conditional, i.e., a conditional probability, can be incorporated into the evidence. Since Oaksford and Chater do not take this road, we shall not explore it either.

---

[11] The assumptions used here are of type IV.

[12] If the probabilities a, b were frequencies, there would be no need to sample because they would be uniquely determined by the environment.

[13] Actually the sampling space was also restricted by the requirement that $a < b$. This is an assumption which should also count as a parameter of the model, so that we now have four parameters and four data points. The requirement is somewhat peculiar in a context where $P(q \mid p) < 1$. Note also that the rarity assumption prominent in Oaksford and Chater (1994) is now dropped, since a, $b > 0.1$, because '[conditional] inferences are specific to context' (Oaksford and Chater (2003), p. 103).

Additional conditionals

It is worth quoting Oaksford and Chater in full on suppression of MP:

> Additional antecedents (or exceptions), for example that there is petrol in the tank with respect to the rule *if you turn the key, the car starts*, concern the probability of the car's not starting even though the key has been turned – that is, they concern ε. If you do not know there is petrol in the tank, you cannot unequivocally infer that the car will start (MP). Moreover, bringing to mind additional factors that need to be in place to infer that the car starts – for example the battery must be charged – will increase this probability [i.e., ε] [...] [I]f there are many additional antecedents, that is, ε is high, the probability that the MP inference will be drawn is low.
>
> (Oaksford & Chater, 2003, p. 104)

In more formal terms, the argument for the suppression of MP seems to be the following. Initially the subject works with the conditional probability $P(q \mid p)$, derived from a joint distribution on $\{p, q\}$. The antecedent of the additional conditional enlarges this space to $\{p,q,r\}$ (where r stands for 'there is petrol in the tank'), and this leads to a new representation of $P(q \mid p)$. One may write

$$P(q \mid p) = P(p \wedge q)/P(p) = P(p \wedge q \wedge r)/P(p) + P(p \wedge q \wedge \neg r)/P(p) =$$
$$P(p \wedge q \wedge r)/P(p) = P(p \wedge q \wedge r)/P(p \wedge r)].[P(p \wedge r)/ P(p) = P(q \mid p \wedge r)P(r) \qquad (5.2)$$

where the last equality follows under the plausible assumption that p and r are independent.

In an orthodox Bayesian approach, $P(q \mid p \wedge r)P(r)$ is simply a different representation of $P(q \mid p)$, and the values of these expressions must be the same, since it is assumed that the subject had access to the joint distribution over $\{p, q, r\}$ in computing $P(q \mid p)$. But this is not how Oaksford and Chater use probability. They assume that the subject assigns a lower probability to $P(q \mid p)$ in the enlarged representation $P(q \mid p \wedge r)P(r)$; the quote suggests that this is because the subject lowers $P(r)$ from 1 to a value smaller than 1 when becoming aware of possible exceptions. This requires the kind of transition between algebras of events that we studied in section 3.1, but now we are in great difficulty, because such transitions must be governed by equation (1), which in the case at hand boils down to:

$$P_2(q \mid p) = P_3(q \mid p \wedge r)P_3(r) \qquad (5.3)$$

Thus, in Oaksford and Chater's model the subject must change his probabilities in a manner that *conflicts* with the Bayesian desideratum of striving toward a coherent probability distribution over all events. As a consequence, no Bayesian explanation of the transition $P(q \mid p \wedge r)P(r)$ and $P_3(q \mid p \wedge r)P_3(r)$ can be given – this transition must remain outside the model (a type II assumption).[14]

----

14 Oaksford and Chater (2009) seem to agree when they write (p. 106): 'In this light, we agree with Stenning and van Lambalgen's claim that 'pure' Bayesian analysis, working from the premises alone, cannot capture suppression effects in conditional reasoning (see sect. R3.6) – we view this as illustrating the knowledge-rich character of reasoning, rather than challenging a Bayesian account'. In the section R3.6 they refer to (p. 109), we read: 'Stenning & van Lambalgen argue that our account of suppression effects is not Bayesian because coherent Bayesian revision of the probability space assumes "rigidity": that is, the conditional probability $P(q \mid p)$ remains the same if we learn the truth of a categorical premise: $p, q, not\text{-}p$, or $not\text{-}q$ (and no other information). We agree. But this does not imply that $P(q \mid p)$ remains the same if we are told that p, because pragmatic factors allow us to infer a great deal of additional information; and this information can legitimately change $P(q \mid p)$. It is this latter case that is relevant for reasoning with verbal materials. Thus, suppose I believe if the key is turned, the car starts; and I am told: "the car didn't start this morning". This would be a pragmatically pointless remark if the key had not been turned. I therefore infer that the key was turned, and the car didn't start for some other reason. Thus, I revise

In order to account for the phenomena the model therefore needs to be supplemented with a theory about non-monotonic changes in degrees of belief.

A technical aside The reader might be tempted to object that the above representation of the increase of information is obviously not what is intended. More to the point would be a construction in which the probability spaces remain the same, but the probability distributions change. For our running example this would mean that the probability space is in both cases $\{p, q, r\}$, but that the probability distribution first assigns probability 0 to $\neg r$ and upon becoming aware of the additional conditional $r \rightarrow q$ a non-zero probability. The trouble with such a suggestion is twofold. Firstly, from a Bayesian point of view, the transition from the *a priori* probability $P(\neg r) = 0$ to the *a posteriori* probability $P(\neg r) > 0$ is not allowed, since this cannot be achieved via (BaCo): conditionalizing on more evidence cannot make a null probability positive. Secondly, one would like to have the assurance that incoming information generates a stable probability distribution in the limit. However, the convergence theorems that guarantee this[15] also require a null probability to remain null. Clearly it does not help to assume that the initial probability of $\neg r$ is very small, because this would bring us back to the situation where the probability is essentially defined on the set of all propositions, and not on a finite subset.

Again the conclusion must be that Bayesian probability has too much monotonicity built in to account for non-monotonic belief change as witnessed in the suppression task. A form of closed world reasoning with probabilities must be developed which allows an agent to set conditional probabilities to 0 by default, and to change these to a positive value if relevant new information comes in.

Alternative conditionals

Let us now look at distinction between additionals and alternatives: additionals are related to $P(\neg q \mid p)$, alternatives to $P(q \mid \neg p)$ – note that this is determined by a, b, ε. The effect of incorporation of an alternative conditional is that $P(q \mid \neg p)$ must increase, but ε must remain constant to account for MP with alternative conditional. This could mean that b increases – more alternative antecedents 'means' there are more possibilities for the antecedent to occur, and the probability of the given antecedent a decreases.

We find the same mixture of probabilistic and non-probabilistic modelling assumptions in Oaksford and Chater's account of the suppression of DA:

> Alternative antecedents, such as information that the car can also be started by hot-wiring, with respect to the rule *if you turn the key, the car starts*, concern the probability of the car starting even though the key has not been turned; that is $P(q \mid \neg p)$. If you know that a car can be started by other means, you cannot unequivocally infer that the car will start even though the key has not been turned. Moreover, bringing to mind other alternative ways of starting cars, such as bump-starting, will increase this probability. [...] It is therefore an immediate consequence of our model that if there are many alternative antecedents, that is, $P(q \mid \neg p)$ is high, the probability that the DA inference should be drawn is low.
>
> (Oaksford and Chater (2003), p. 104)

---

down the probability of the relevant conditional P(car starts|key turned) dramatically. So the violation of rigidity, notably in this type of Modus Tollens (MT) inference, does not violate Bayesian precepts, but merely applies them to the pragmatics of utterances'. This was not quite the point we intended to make, since we worried about the change in $P(q \mid p)$ when enlarging the probability space to include r. In the case envisaged by Oaksford and Chater the new value of $P(q \mid p)$ can simply be computed by applying the definition of $P(q \mid p)$, and no extensions of the probability space have to be considered. Problems for Bayesianism arise when the mere incorporation of an additional antecedent lowers the probability $P(q \mid p)$.

[15] The so-called 'martingale convergence theorems', see Williams (1995), Chapter 10.

Bearing in mind the analysis we gave above of the suppression of MP, it is now easy to see that what the Bayesian model *prima facie* predicts (via (BaCo)) is the following:

if the conditional probability $P(q \mid \neg p)$ increases, *then* the probability of DA decreases.

The essential question is, however, whether the Bayesian model also covers the first stage of the subject's reasoning, in which the presence of alternative antecedents increases the initial $P(q \mid \neg p)$. The argument seems to be this, using the same notation as in section 3.3.1: the subject makes a distinction between $P_2(q \mid \neg p)$ and $P_3(q \mid \neg p)$ given by:

$$P_3(q \mid \neg p) = P_3(q \mid r \wedge \neg p)P_3(r \mid \neg p) + P_3(q \mid \neg r \wedge \neg p)P_3(\neg r \mid \neg p) \tag{5.4}$$

which, in the example discussed though not always, can be simplified to:

$$P_3(q \mid \neg p) = P_3(q \mid r)P_3(r \mid \neg p) + P_3(q \mid \neg r \wedge \neg p)P_3(\neg r \mid \neg p) \tag{5.5}$$

since $r \to p$. In this formula, the term $P_3(q \mid r)$ is large, since it represents the conditional $r \to q$, and the term $P_3(q \mid \neg r \wedge \neg p) = P_3(q \mid \neg(r \vee p))$ is much smaller, especially when $P_3(\neg r \mid \neg p) = 1$, since it then represents $P_3(q \mid \neg p)$.

Oaksford and Chater then appear to argue as follows. In the case of one conditional premise $p \to q$ only, the subject works with the conditional probability $P_2(q \mid \neg p)$ on the probability space $\{p, q\}$. This probability is then identified with $P_3(q \mid \neg p)$ on the probability space $\{p, q, r\}$ under the assumption that $P_3(\neg r \mid \neg p) = 1$.

Consideration of the alternative antecedent $r \to q$ then leads to a decrease in $P_3(q \mid \neg p)$, so that a larger proportion of the large term $P_3(q \mid r)$ contributes to $P_3(q \mid \neg p)$, whence $P_3(\neg q \mid \neg p)$, i.e., the probability that $\neg q$ is concluded, decreases. But we can now see that this reasoning is not Bayesian, since it requires the subject to update $P_3(r \mid \neg p)$ from zero to strictly positive. This update must necessarily remain outside the model.

Validating the model for three premises

The hypothesis to be tested is that subjects reason with subjective probabilities in order to solve the suppression task. It is in the nature of this hypothesis that it does not concern the exact values of the subject's degrees of belief in concrete conditionals and categorical propositions. The hypothesis is that whatever these values are, they obey the Bayesian inference rules. This makes it difficult to test the hypothesis directly.

Above we have seen that Oaksford and Chater take the revision of conditional probabilities in going from simple MP to MP with additional premise to lie outside the scope of the probabilistic model. Thus the model provides no constraints on the values of the probabilities in the simple condition versus the three premises conditions. To fit the model it is therefore sufficient to estimate a, b, ε from the data in each condition of a suppression task; Oaksford and Chater (2003), p. 105 take Byrne's (1989) data for this purpose. Under the assumption that subjects apply (BaCo) when making an inference, the data supply information[16] about the conditional probabilities $P(q \mid p)$, (MP), $P(\neg p \mid \neg q)$ (MT), $P(\neg q \mid \neg p)$ (DA) and $P(p \mid q)$ (AC). Given these conditional probabilities, the parameters of interest, a, b, and ε, can be computed. The exception parameter ε is obtained from the rate of endorsement of MP (which is equal to $P(q \mid p)$). The parameter $a = P(p)$ is obtained from the rates of endorsement of MP, AC and DA via the following computation:

$$x := P(q \mid p) / P(p \mid q) = P(q)/P(p)$$

---

[16] It will soon become apparent why we use a deliberately vague expression here.

$$y := P(q \mid \neg p) / P(\neg p \mid q) = P(q)/(1 - P(p))$$
$$\text{hence } x.P(p) = y.(1-P(p)) \text{ and so } P(p) = y/x - y$$

where the right hand side is supplied by the data. The computation for b is similar and yields

$$P(q) = x.y/x+y$$

Observe that the parameters are computed using only three conditional probabilities: $P(\neg p \mid \neg q)$ is nowhere used, and can be computed from the remaining conditional probabilities. This puts a consistency requirement on the four data points, thus allowing the experimenter to check whether subjects are coherent in the probabilistic sense.

The result is that in every condition the three parameters can be fitted from the four data points MP, MT, DA, AC, where one is looking for a fit at .01 significance level. The question arises however whether the estimates of the parameters a, b, ε can be interpreted as *probabilities*: what is the event which is supposed to have probability $a = P(p)$? Recall the definition of $P(p)$: p does not stand for any specific proposition, but it refers to a particular role: the antecedent of the main conditional, the content of which differs from one conditional to the next. Similarly for the conditional probabilities used to estimate $P(p)$: these are in fact averages of the conditional probabilities hypothesised to be used by the subjects with the various experimental materials. Now suppose that the parameters were estimated using the data for a single subject. What would the estimated value $P(p)$ (or $P(q \mid p)$) mean in this situation? It would be an average over the very different contents occurring in the antecedent (and consequent) of the main conditional, not a degree of belief assigned by the subject to a particular event. What the model fitting procedure does, therefore, is construct a joint probability distribution (from a, b, ε) of which we can be certain that it represents the degrees of belief of no subject at all. This seems a weak justification for the model.

To summarize, we have not claimed that Bayesian probability plays no role at all in subjects' reasoning in the suppression task. Especially when the formulation of the task explicitly introduces qualitative probabilistic expressions like 'almost always' or 'rarely', as in Stevenson and Over's (1995) graded suppression task, a probabilistic model may be appropriate.[17] We do claim, however, that it cannot be the whole story in those reasoning tasks in which non-monotonic (degree of) belief revision plays an important part. If one does not incorporate this form of belief revision into the model, one is in effect saying it falls outside the scope of explanation. This is giving up too soon. If one is convinced that the last part of subjects' reasoning is indeed Bayesian conditionalization, there arises the challenge of combining closed world reasoning with probabilistic reasoning.

More generally, the discussion points to the necessity of distinguishing between 'reasoning to an interpretation' and 'reasoning from an interpretation', as we have done in Stenning and van Lambalgen (2008). Once the subject fixes the interpretation of the task at hand as 'reasoning with uncertainty, more particularly probability', and assigns probabilities to the propositions of interest, reasoning may proceed entirely within (Bayesian) probability theory. The reasoning process that leads up to fixing the interpretation as probabilistic, and to fixing the probabilities, may well be of a very different nature. Here we have argued that this reasoning to an interpretation is best seen as a form of closed world reasoning, perhaps applied to probabilities. In any case it seems

---

[17] We do not take performance in the graded suppression task to indicate that subjects *always* reason according to a probabilistic model in a suppression task.

more fruitful to investigate how logic and probability must interact than to view them as rival approaches.

System P?

The reader acquainted with the literature might think that a fruitful interaction between non-monotonic logic and probability theory already exists, in the form of **System P** (Kraus, Lehman, & Magidor, 1990; Pfeiffer & Kleiter, 2005). This is a logic for reasoning with exception-tolerant conditionals written as $\alpha \copyright \beta$ and interpreted as 'if α, then *normally* β'. A highly appealing feature of **System P** is that it allows probabilistic semantics, which are of two kinds:

1. '$\alpha \copyright \beta$ is true' is interpreted *as* $P(\beta \mid \alpha) > \theta$, where $\theta < 1$ but $1\text{-}\theta$ is infinitesimal (Adams, 1975).
2. '$\alpha \copyright \beta$ is true' if $P(\beta \mid \alpha) > \theta$ takes a value in a suitable interval (Gilio, 2002). The details need not concern us here. It suffices to say that the semantics introduces a new kind of object, 'conditional events' $B|A$, corresponding to $\alpha \copyright \beta$, allowing the possibility that the (absolute) probability of A is 0; and that the inference rules of **System P** in this semantics correspond to rules for transforming probability intervals.

It thus seems that **System P**, together with the interval semantics, is ideally suited to address the issues we raised above: it seems to allow a rational treatment of events with probability 0, and it is not wedded to the assumption that probabilities must be known precisely. This is not the case however, as can be seen when we look at **System P**'s rules, presented as sentences of the form 'premises $\Rightarrow$ conclusion':[18]

1. $\Rightarrow \alpha \copyright \alpha$	*Reflexivity Axiom*
2. $\models \gamma \leftrightarrow, \gamma \copyright \alpha \Rightarrow \beta \copyright \alpha$	*Left Logical Equivalence*
3. $\models \alpha \rightarrow \beta, \gamma \copyright \alpha \Rightarrow \gamma \copyright \beta$	*Right Weakening*
4. $\alpha \copyright \gamma, \beta \copyright \gamma \Rightarrow \alpha \vee \beta \copyright \gamma$	*Or*
5. $\alpha \wedge \beta \copyright \gamma, \alpha \copyright \beta \Rightarrow \alpha \copyright \gamma$	*Cut*
6. $\alpha \copyright \beta, \alpha \copyright \gamma \Rightarrow \alpha \wedge \beta \copyright \gamma$	*Cautious monotonicity*

It is now immediately obvious that one rule of **System P** dashes all hopes of treating the suppression task: the rule *Or*, which forces one to treat additional and alternative premises on the same footing.[19] **System P** therefore reinforces the point made earlier, that probability is too much tied to classical logic to model the truly non-monotonic reasoning that occurs in the suppression task.

Conclusion

Interpretation processes are necessary, whether one then applies probability theory or some other logic in reasoning from the resulting interpretations. In the case of suppression, understood in probabilistic terms, interpretation shows up as the necessity to change one's probabilities in ways not sanctioned by Bayesianism. We claim that a computational level analysis in the sense of Marr must also incorporate the interpretation process, not only the reasoning, once the interpretation is chosen. This is not to deny the role of Bayesian probability in a characterization of the computational level. If a subject construes the task as involving uncertain conditionals, in the sense of positive probability of exceptions, principles like Bayesian conditionalization may well form part

---

[18] '$\models$' indicates provability in classical logic.
[19] If one drops *Or* from **System P** one gets Makinson's 'cumulative logic' (Makinson (1989)) which however has no close relationship to probability.

of the computational level. In this case competence theory is needed of how judgements of probabilities can change in non-Bayesian ways. This we regard as one of the most interesting technical challenges issuing from the present analysis. We do deny that the entire computational level can be characterized in this manner, and also that the same computational level analysis applies to all subjects engaged in this task.

Classical logic forced a single competence model upon reasoning tasks, and one of the merits of the Bayesian approach is to have loosened the grip of classical logic. But the danger exists that Bayesian probability is itself promoted to the absolute standard of competence. The arguments purporting to show that probability is *the* calculus of uncertainty are too weak to establish this, hence absoluteness of the Bayesian standard cannot be defended in this way. On the empirical side it is clear that different subjects are interpreting tasks very differently, and although Bayesianism has some built-in mechanisms to deal with individual differences via variation in assignments of subjective probabilities, this does not capture the full range of differences. For instance, closed world reasoning, for which there exists evidence in our tutorial data (Stenning & van Lambalgen, 2008, chapter 7), cannot be modelled in this way.

Oaksford and Chater view their work as an instance of 'rational analysis' and consider that giving an account of the economics of information processing tasks should occupy centre stage. Our own work adopts a very different computational level analysis of reasoning tasks, assimilating them to discourse understanding. The familiar laboratory deductive reasoning tasks are interesting, important and potentially psychologically insightful precisely because subjects assimilate them to this overall process of discourse processing. Because the normal cues as to how to make this assimilation are removed, subjects make it in a variety of ways, many of which are not the classical logical one the experimenter expects. So we absolutely agree with Oaksford and Chater that the classical logical computational model is generally not a reasonable choice for data analysis. Where we disagree is that we believe discourse processing has to be understood as at least a two-component process, and the rational analyses of these two processes cannot be the same. Trying to make them the same leads to the invocation of probability theory as an overall framework, and that makes the computational theory distant from the data, and inappropriate for dealing with the kinds of uncertainty that permeate interpretation.

References

Adams, E. (1975). *The logic of conditionals*. Dordrecht Netherlands: Reidel.

Anderson, J. R. & Lebiere, C. (1998). *The atomic components of thought*. Mahwah NJ: Lawrence Erlbaum.

Baggio, G., van Lambalgen, M., & Hagoort, P. (2007). Language, linguistics and cognition. In N. Asher, T. Fernando, & R. Kempson (Eds.) *Handbook of the Philosophy of Linguistics*. Amsterdam: Elsevier.

Brandenburger, A. & Dekel, E. (1993). Hierarchies of beliefs and common knowledge. *Journal of Economic Theory*, **59**(1), 189–198.

Byrne, R. M. J. (1989). Suppressing valid inferences with conditionals. *Cognition*. **31**, 61–83.

Cummins, D. D. (1995). Naive theories and causal deduction. *Memory and Cognition*, **23**(5), 646–58.

Doets, K. (1994) *From logic to logic programming*. Cambridge, MA: The MIT Press.

Evans, J. St.B. T. (2003). In two minds: dual-process accounts of reasoning. *Trends in Cognitive Sciences*, **7**(10), 454–459.

Gilio, A. (2002). Probabilistic reasoning under coherence in System *P*. *Annals of Mathematics in Artificial Intelligence*, **34**: 5–34.

Kraus, S., Lehman, D., & Magidor, M. (1990). Non-monotonic reasoning, preferential models and cumulative logics. *Artificial Intelligence*, **44**, 167–207.

Lechler, A. (2004). Interpretation of conditionals in the suppression task. MSc thesis. University of Edinburgh: HCRC.

Makinson, D. (1989). General theory of cumulative reasoning. In M. Reinfrank, (Ed.) *Proceedings Second International Workshop on Non-Monotonic Reasoning*, volume 346 of *Lecture Notes in Computer Science*. Berlin, Germany: Springer.

McCarthy, J. (1980). Circumscription – a form of non-monotonic reasoning. *Artificial Intelligence*, **13**, 27–39.

Oaksford, M. & Chater, N. (1994). A rational analysis of the selection task as optimal data selection. *Psychological Review*, **101**, 608–631.

Oaksford, M. & Chater, N. (2003). Probabilities and pragmatics in conditional inference: Suppression and order effects. In D. Hardman & L. Macchi, (Eds.) *Thinking: psychological perspectives on reasoning, judgment and decision making*, chapter 6, pages 95–122. Chichester: John Wiley & Sons.

Oaksford, M. & Chater, N. (2007). *Bayesian rationality*. Oxford: Oxford University Press.

Oaksford, M. & Chater, N. (2009). Précis of: Bayesian rationality: The probabilistic approach to human reasoning. *Behavioral and Brain Sciences*, **32**, 69–120.

Paris, J.B. (1994). *The uncertain reasoner's companion*. Cambridge: Cambridge University Press.

Pfeiffer, N. & Kleiter, G. (2005). Coherence and non-monotonicity in human reasoning. *Synthese*, **146**, 93–109.

Rao, M.M. (1971). Projective limits of probability spaces. *Journal of Multivariate Analysis*, **1**, 28–57.

Reiter, R. (1980). A logic for default reasoning. *Artificial Intelligence*, **13**, 81–132.

Shanahan, Murray P. (1997). *Solving the Frame Problem: A Mathematical Investigation of the Common Sense Law of Inertia*. Cambridge MA: MIT Press.

Stenning, K. & van Lambalgen, M. (2004). A little logic goes a long way: Basing experiment on semantic theory in the cognitive science of conditional reasoning. *Cognitive Science*, **28**(4), 481–530.

Stenning, K. & van Lambalgen, M. (2005). Semantic interpretation as reasoning in non-monotonic logic: The real meaning of the suppression task. *Cognitive Science*, **29**(6), 919–960.

Stenning, K. & van Lambalgen, M. (2008). *Human reasoning and cognitive science*. Cambridge MA: MIT Press.

Stenning, K. & van Lambalgen, M. (2007). Logic in the study of psychiatric disorders: Executive function and rule-following. *Topoi*, **26**(1), 97–114. Special issue on Logic and Cognitive Science.

Stevenson, R. & Over, D. (1995). Deduction from uncertain premisses. *Quarterly Journal of Experimental Psychology* A, **48**(3), 613–643.

Williams, D. *Probability with martingales*. (1995). Cambridge: Cambridge University Press.

Chapter 6

Conditionals and probability

Vittorio Girotto and Philip N. Johnson-Laird

Consider the following problem. Paolo and Vittorio are playing cards, and there are three cards face down on the table. They know that the three cards are a three, a six, and an eight, but they don't know which card is which. Paolo takes a card at random, and then he takes another at random. Vittorio says: 'If one of the cards that Paolo picked up is the eight then the other card that he picked up is the three'. How do naïve individuals – those who haven't mastered the probability calculus – assess the probability that such a conditional is true? Our aim in what follows is to answer this question. One reason that the question matters is that many theorists, following Ramsey (1990), suppose that a subjective probability is an index of degrees of belief.

Like most researchers, we assume that two main ways exist to estimate probabilities. One way is *extensional*: the probability of an event is estimated from the different possible but mutually exclusive ways in which the event could occur. The branch of mathematics that concerns probability, i.e., the probability calculus, is a normative theory of extensional estimates. It tells us the correct probabilities given that certain idealizations hold true (Nickerson, 1999). For the problem above, there are three possible pairs of cards that Paolo could have picked up from the table: three and six, three and eight, and six and eight; and only the last of these pairs violates the conditional assertion. Hence, if each pair was equally likely to end up in Paolo's hand, the probability calculus tells us that the probability of the conditional is 2/3. A similar but subtly different problem is as follows: Paolo picked up the eight, and so what is the probability that he picked up the three? This question asks for a *conditional* probability. The probability calculus tells us that the answer is ½, because given the eight, the other card is either the six or the three, and, as Paolo chose the cards at random, they should be equally likely.

Another way to estimate a probability is *non-extensional*: the estimate relies on some relevant heuristic, index, or evidence, as, for example, when reasoners infer that because an exemplar is typical of a category, it has a high probability of being a member of the category. These heuristics have been identified in the seminal work of Danny Kahneman and the late Amos Tversky (see, e.g., Gilovich, Griffin, & Kahneman, 2002; Kahneman, Slovic, & Tversky, 1982). The probability of the conditional about the cards cannot be readily assessed in a non-extensional way, but the probabilities of many assertions are amenable to either (or both) methods of assessment. Our main concern in this chapter, however, is with extensional estimates of the probabilities of conditionals. They depend, we argue, on a mental representation of the prior possibilities, and then the computation of the proportion of these possibilities in which the assertion holds. It follows that estimation should be difficult when it requires individuals to construct a large set of possibilities. It also follows that individuals should in some cases infer a different value for the probability of a conditional than for the corresponding conditional probability of its then-clause given its if-clause. This view is controversial because some psychologists argue, contrary to Ramsey (1990, p. 76), that the probability of a conditional *is* this conditional probability.

The plan of the chapter is as follows. It begins with a theory of how naïve individuals can esti-mate extensional probabilities in general. It then shows how this theory, which is based on mental models, applies to conditional assertions. It considers next how individuals estimate conditional probabilities. It examines the hypothesis that naïve individuals compute them when they have to estimate the probability of a conditional. Finally, it draws some general conclusions about the probabilities of conditionals.

The model theory of extensional probabilities

If a fair coin is tossed twice, what is the probability of getting first 'heads' and then 'tails'? If you are familiar with the probability calculus, you are likely to answer: ¼. Given that the two events in question are independent, i.e., the first outcome has no effect on the second outcome, you can apply the multiplication rule and obtain the required result: ½ x ½. Even if you do not know the probability calculus, however, you can still reach the same answer by considering all the possible outcomes of the two tosses:

First toss	Second toss
Heads	Tails
Heads	Heads
Tails	Tails
Tails	Heads

The outcome that you have to assess, first heads and then tails, is one of these four possible outcomes, and so you can conclude that its probability is ¼. This way of answering the question without using the probability calculus is an example of an *extensional* estimate of a probability, and the hypothesis that individuals represent the different possibilities in estimating probabilities is part of a general theory of probabilistic reasoning based on mental models (Johnson-Laird, Legrenzi, Girotto, Legrenzi, & Caverni, 1999). This theory – the model theory, for short – makes three main assumptions about extensional estimates of probabilities. First, individuals represent each possibility in a mental model. Second, they assume that each possibility is equiprobable by default, that is, events are equiprobable unless there are reasons to the contrary. For example, gamblers know that some horses are better than others, so they do not assume that all the horses in a race have the same probability to win. Likewise, if they believe that the coin in the previous example is biased so that it tends to land 'heads' three out of four times, they can represent the relative frequencies in the models:

First toss
Heads
Heads
Heads
Tails

Alternatively, they can tag models with appropriate numerical values. Third, they compute the probability from the proportion of possibilities in which the required outcome holds.

As a general account of how naïve individuals assess extensional probabilities, the model theo-ry makes predictions that experiments have corroborated. For example, if individuals are told that a box contains a red marble or a green marble or both, they tend to estimate the probability that it contains both marbles as approximately a third: the disjunction, red or green or both, yields three possibilities and the required outcome holds in one of them (Johnson-Laird et al., 1999). Likewise, untutored individuals can solve otherwise difficult probability problems provided that they are presented to them in versions to which they can apply extensional procedures (e.g., Fox & Levav, 2004; Girotto & Gonzalez, 2001; Sloman, Over, Slovak, & Stibel, 2003). The most telling evidence is that infants' expectations are based on their evaluations of possibilities. For example, given a container in which three identical objects and one different in colour and shape bounced randomly, 12-month-olds looked longer at the display – usually a sign of an unexpected event – when the different object, rather than one of the three identical objects, exited from the pipe at the base of the container (Teglas, Girotto, Gonzalez, & Bonatti, 2007). The infants' reaction cannot be a result of experience, because they had not seen any previous outcomes before the trial in which the improbable object came out of the pipe. The result implies that from early in their development individuals base their expectations on an extensional assessment of possibilities. As we describe below, preschoolers are able to solve extensionally tasks that call for more complex probabilistic inferences (Girotto & Gonzalez, 2008).

The occurrence of extensional intuitions about probability does not imply that individuals reason about probabilities without error. Indeed, intelligent adults err even in problems that in principle they could solve extensionally, e.g.,:

> Suppose that *only one* of the following assertions is true about a specific hand of cards:
>
> If there is a jack in the hand, then there is a queen in the hand.
>
> If there is an ace in the hand, then there is a queen in the hand.
>
> Which is more likely to be in the hand: the queen or the jack?

Most individuals answer: the queen (see Johnson-Laird & Savary, 1996). But, their answer is an illusion. The correct answer depends on bearing in mind the false contingencies, that is, when one conditional is true the other is false. The only assumption that one then needs to make is that a conditional is false when its antecedent is true and its consequent is false – a view that is common to various accounts of the meaning of conditionals, though not all, and that is borne out by the judgments of naïve individuals (see, e.g., Johnson-Laird & Bryne, 2002, for a review; and also the following section). Hence, the first conditional is false when there is a jack but not a queen, and the second conditional is false when there is an ace but not a queen. Either way, there is not a queen: it is impossible, but the jack is not impossible, and so the correct answer is that the jack is more probable than the queen. The model theory predicts this and other illusions on the grounds that mental models represent what is true, not what is false. Extensional thinking therefore does sometimes lead individuals to draw incorrect inferences. The illusions, however, are a sign of their use of mental models. We now turn to the probability of conditionals.

Estimating the probability of conditional assertions

The application of the model theory to estimates of the probability of conditionals seems straightforward at first sight. Individuals should represent the prior possibilities, assume that they are equiprobable unless they have evidence to the contrary, and estimate the probability of a conditional as the proportion of these possibilities in which the conditional holds. Indeed, some estimates of the probabilities of conditionals are simple. Consider the following problem:

> (1) There are two cards face down on a table: an ace and a queen. Paolo takes both cards. Vittorio says:
>
> 'If Paolo has the ace, then he also has the queen'.
>
> What is the probability that Vittorio's assertion is true?

In this case, there is just one possible hand that Paolo can draw, and it contains the ace and the queen. Hence, Vittorio's assertion must be true, and so it has a probability of one.

When the number of possibilities increases, the task of assessing probabilities should become harder, and conditionals themselves present additional sources of difficulty. A conditional such as, 'If there is an ace then there is a queen,' is *basic* in that the situations to which its two clauses refer are not related in a significant way apart from their co-occurrence in the same conditional (for an account of basic conditionals, see Johnson-Laird & Byrne, 1991, 2002; and Byrne & Johnson-Laird, 2010). Basic conditionals are consistent with three possibilities, which we show here in a fully explicit way:

Ace	Queen
No ace	Queen
No ace	No queen

'Ace' denotes that an ace is present, and 'No ace' denotes that an ace is not present. Naïve individuals do list these possibilities when they are asked what is possible given the conditional (e.g., Barrouillet, Grosset, & Leças, 2000). But, three such possibilities overload the capacity of working memory, and so the model theory postulates that individuals usually represent a conditional as one explicit possibility, in which both its clauses are true, and one implicit possibility that allows for other possibilities, in which its if-clause is false. The two mental models of the conditional are accordingly:

Ace	Queen
. . .	

where the ellipsis denotes the implicit model representing the possibilities in which it is false that there is an ace. Of course, real mental models are not just words, but representations of states of affairs. Individuals who keep track of the information about the implicit model should be able to enumerate the three *fully explicit* possibilities shown above, and to envisage the possibility in which the conditional is false:

Ace	No queen

When individuals are asked to evaluate the truth or falsity of a basic conditional in the light of various contingencies, they tend to assert that the conditional above is true when there is an ace and a queen, that it is false when there is an ace but not a queen, and that it is irrelevant in those cases in which its if-clause is false, i.e., there is no ace. The task of evaluating the truth or falsity of an assertion is more complicated than merely listing the possibilities compatible with it, and so individuals appear to rely only on mental models rather than fully explicit models in order to evaluate truth or falsity (see Byrne & Johnson-Laird, this volume).

Another source of difficulty in estimating the probability of a conditional is that in all but the simplest of cases, naïve individuals at first do not know how to carry out the task. They have to devise a *strategy* for coping with it, and different individuals are likely to devise different strategies, just as they do in deductive reasoning (see, e.g., Schaeken, De Vooght, Vandierendonck, & d'Ydewalle, 2000). We can illustrate their likely strategies using the problem with which we began this chapter:

(2) There are three cards face down on a table: a three, a six and an eight. Paolo takes one card at random, and then he takes another at random. Vittorio says:

'If Paolo has the eight then he also has the three'.

What is the probability that Vittorio's assertion is true?

One potential **strategy** is to treat the estimate of a conditional's probability as akin to the evaluation of its truth **or** falsity, and accordingly to rely only on the mental models of the conditional, and to infer that the conditional is true in just the case corresponding to its explicit mental model in which both its if-clause and then-clause are true. Individuals then have an option. They may treat the conditional as false only in the case in which its if-clause is true and its then-clause is false, and ignore the other possibilities. Hence, they estimate the probability of Vittorio's conditional as ½. We refer to this method as the *equiprobable* strategy. A more sophisticated option is to consider the model in which the if-clause and then-clause are true (8 3) in relation to the three possible hands that Paolo could have:

8	3
6	3
8	6

In other words, they treat the conditional as though it were a conjunction – a tendency that has been observed independently in children (Barrouillet et al., 2000) and adults (Barres & Johnson-Laird, 2003; Johnson-Laird et al., 1999). It is true, they infer, in only one possibility. This *conjunctive* strategy yields a probability for Vittorio's conditional of 1/3.

In contrast, individuals may treat the conditional as true in all the possibilities that are consistent with it, and false in the one possibility that is inconsistent with it. This *complete* strategy yields a probability of 2/3 for Vittorio's conditional, because only one possible hand out of the three yields a violation of the conditional. Granted that a basic conditional of the form *If A then C* is treated as equivalent to a disjunctive statement of the form: *Not A and/or C*, then the complete strategy yields a correct estimate according to the probability calculus. Many theorists may not grant this assumption, and so we proceed without it.

Consider a third illustrative problem:

(3) There are two cards face down on a table: a seven and a five. Paolo takes one card at random, and then Maria takes the other card. Vittorio says:

'If Paolo has the seven, then Maria has the five.'

What is the probability that Vittorio's assertion is true?

There are just two possible results of the card drawing:

Paolo: 7   Maria: 5
Paolo: 5   Maria: 7

The equiprobable strategy yields a probability of one for Vittorio's conditional, because the first of these possibilities is a true instance of the conditional, and there is no possibility in which the conditional is false, i.e., in which Paolo has 7 and Maria doesn't have 5. The conjunctive strategy yields a probability of ½, because the conjunctive model corresponding to the first possibility has an alternative corresponding to the second model. The complete strategy also yields a probability of one because the conditional is consistent with both of the two possibilities. The three strategies could reflect different interpretations of the conditional: the conjunctive strategy is akin to a conjunctive interpretation, the equiprobable strategy is akin to an interpretation with a 'defective' truth table, and the complete strategy is akin to an interpretation as a basic conditional (see Byrne & Johnson-Laird, this volume). But, the strategies are compatible with different approaches to the basic interpretation of the conditional, e.g., the conjunctive strategy treats the task as akin to evaluating the truth or falsity of a basic conditional.

The theory predicts a trend over the three problems. Problem 1 should be most likely to yield estimates corresponding to the complete strategy because the problem elicits just a single possibility. Problem 3 should be the next most likely to yield them because it depends on two possibilities, and the estimate corresponding to the complete strategy will also be made using another strategy (the equiprobable one). Problem 2 should be the hardest because it depends on three possibilities, and the complete estimate can be made only by using the complete strategy. Girotto and Johnson-Laird (2004) corroborated this trend. All the participants in an experiment made the complete estimate for problem 1, 55% made it for problem 3, and only 10% made it for problem 2. Moreover, as the various strategies predict, most of the participants (85%) made more responses overestimating the complete probabilities for problems 2 and 3. Different participants did make different estimates, and the estimates concurred with those predicted by the three strategies reliably better than chance. In sum, individuals who have not mastered the probability calculus tend to estimate the probability of a conditional using strategies that depend on the possibilities compatible with the conditional.

Estimating conditional probabilities

We illustrated a conditional probability with the question: given that Paolo picked up the eight, what is the probability that he picked up the three? A conditional probability is accordingly the probability of one event (he picked up the three) conditional on another event having occurred (he picked up the eight). Conditional probabilities are on the border of the competence of individuals who haven't mastered the probability calculus. The calculus allows several ways in which to compute them, and perhaps the best-known method relies on Bayes's theorem. It shows how one conditional probability, the probability of C given A depends on the converse conditional probability of A given C, and the absolute probabilities of A and of C. These absolute probabilities are known as the 'base rates' of A and of C. The formula for the simplest version of Bayes's theorem is:

$$\text{Probability (C given A)} = \frac{\text{Probability (A given C)} \times \text{Probability (C)}}{\text{Probability (A)}}$$

Do naïve individuals have a tacit or unconscious access to Bayes's theorem? Although there has been some controversy about the matter, few psychologists have supposed that they do – if only because they err in estimating conditional probabilities. One common tendency, for example, is not to take sufficient account of the base rates (see, e.g., Kahneman & Tversky, 1973). This claim has been challenged (Koehler, 1996), and Gigerenzer and his colleagues have argued that when problems are expressed in frequencies based on naturally occurring samples, such errors disappear and individuals can make Bayesian inferences (see, e.g., Gigerenzer & Hoffrage, 1995). Likewise, Cosmides and Tooby (1996) have argued that evolution has led to the development of a specific inductive module in the brain that can make Bayesian inferences from natural frequencies.

In contrast, at least one experiment shows that individuals do not truly grasp the significance of base rates. The participants were presented with a series of problems based on conditional assertions, such as:

> If individuals have Pel Ebstein disease then they test positive 99 times out of a hundred.
> You test positive. What's the probability that you have the disease?

Readers are invited to think about what their answer would be. Most participants in the experiment responded with a high probability (this experiment was carried out by Jennifer Adams, and it is described in Johnson-Laird, 2006, p. 203). Of course, anyone with a knowledge of

Bayes's theorem will realize that the problem is ill-posed. You cannot estimate a conditional probability merely from its converse conditional probability. You need other information, such as the base rates of positive tests and of Pel Ebstein disease. Yet, the participants in the experiment carried out a series of such inferences and never refused to make any of them. They didn't assume that the two conditional probabilities were necessarily the same. In the example about Pel Ebstein disease, it is difficult to think of a reason why a person would test positive without having the disease. But, the experiment included other problems, such as:

> If an object is put into boiling water, then the chances that it becomes hot are 99 out of 100. An object is hot. What is the probability that it was put into boiling water?

It is easy to think of alternative ways in which an object might have become hot, and so the participants tended to give much lower estimates than the probability stated in the conditional premise. After the experiment was over, they reported that they had indeed considered the possibility of alternative ways of reaching the same outcome and lowered their estimates appropriately. The moral of these results is that naïve individuals do have difficulty in assessing conditional probabilities and do not spontaneously make use of Bayes's theorem (see also Gilovich et al., 2002).

Yet, naive individuals are not doomed to err. There are other ways in which to estimate conditional probabilities. If you know the probability of each relevant possibility, then it is feasible for you to estimate a conditional probability. Suppose, for example, Paolo has one of three possible hands, which are each equally likely:

8	3
8	6
3	6

and your task is to infer the conditional probability that given that he has an eight, he has a three. Only the first two possibilities are relevant, and in one of them he has a three and in one of them he doesn't. The required conditional probability is therefore: ½.

In general, the model theory postulates that individuals can make correct estimates of conditional probabilities when they can reason about a *single* set of possibilities, and the mental arithmetic is simple (Johnson-Laird et al., 1999). In these conditions, they estimate the conditional probability of C given A by considering the *subset* of possibilities of A in which C occurs. Experiments have confirmed that, for example, individuals do infer the probability that a person has a specific disease, if she has tested positive, by considering the subset of chances of testing positive in which the disease occurs (e.g., Girotto & Gonzalez, 2001). In analogous conditions, even preschoolers are able to make correct qualitative responses. Given a box containing four square chips (all black) and four round chips (three white and one black), preschoolers correctly make the simple inference that a random drawing is more likely to yield a black chip than a white chip. And, when they are told that a randomly drawn chip is round, they correctly infer a qualitative conditional probability: it is more likely to be white than black (Girotto & Gonzalez, 2008).

Adults are able to solve the conditional probability versions of the problems discussed in section 2 above. The conditional probability version of problem 1 is as follows:

> (1) There are two cards face down on a table: an ace and a five. Paolo takes both cards. Paolo shows one of his cards: it is the ace. Vittorio says:
>
>   'Paolo also has the five.'
>
> Given that, indeed, Paolo has the ace, what is the probability that Vittorio's assertion is true?

In order to answer this question, individuals have simply to consider the only possibility in which Paolo has the ace, and so correctly infer that the probability that Vittorio's assertion is true is one.

Likewise, the conditional probability version of problem 2 is as follows:

> (2) There are three cards face down on a table: a three, a six and an eight. Paolo takes one card at random, and then he takes another at random. Paolo shows one of his cards: it is the eight. Vittorio says:
>
> 'Paolo also has the three.'

Given that, indeed, Paolo has the eight, what is the probability that Vittorio's assertion is true?

Reasoners have to consider the two possibilities in which Paolo has the eight: eight and six, and eight and three. They can then infer that the required conditional probability is ½.

Finally, the conditional probability version of problem 3 is:

> (3) There are two cards face down on a table: a seven and a five. Paolo takes one card at random, and then Maria takes the other card. Paolo shows his cards: it is the seven. Vittorio says:
>
> 'Maria has the five.'

Given that, indeed, Paolo has the seven, what is the probability that Vittorio's assertion is true?

There is only one possibility in which Paolo has the seven and in that possibility Maria has the five. Hence, individuals can correctly answer that the conditional probability is one.

Girotto and Johnson-Laird (2004) reported a study in which the vast majority of participants correctly answered these three conditional probability problems. The percentages of correct estimates were as follows: 100% for problem 1, 85% for problem 2, and 90% for problem 3. Hence, untrained individuals are able to estimate conditional probabilities in situations in which they can easily consider subsets of possibilities.

Conditional probabilities and the probability of conditionals

An influential view about the probability of a conditional of the form *if A then C* is that naïve individuals estimate it by computing the conditional probability of *C* given *A*. We refer to this view as the *conditional-probability* hypothesis, and it is defended most notably by Jonathan Evans, David Over, and their colleagues (see e.g., Evans, Handley, & Over, 2003; Evans, Handley, Neilens, & Over, 2007; Over & Evans, 2003; Stevenson & Over, 1995). They derive the hypothesis from a well-known footnote in a paper published in 1929 by the philosopher, economist and logician, Frank Ramsey (1990, p. 155):

> If two people are arguing 'If p will q?' and both are in doubt as to p, they are adding p hypothetically to their stock of knowledge and arguing on that basis about q; so that in a sense 'If p, q' and 'If p, not q' are contradictories. We can say they are fixing their degrees of belief in q given p. If p turns out to be false, these degrees of belief are rendered *void*.

Ramsey (1990, p. 76) himself rejected the view that a conditional probability is the probability of the corresponding conditional. But, according to the conditional-probability hypothesis, Ramsey's suppositional method is used to estimate the probability of a conditional. Individuals suppose that its if-clause is the case, and then compute the probability of its then-clause.

One reason that such estimates may occur arises from the grammar of conditionals. The if-clause is subordinate to the main then-clause in a conditional, and so phrases, such as 'it is surprising that', which normally apply to a sentence as a whole are often interpreted as applying only to the main clause (for the details of this argument, see, e.g., Byrne & Johnson-Laird, this volume). For example, the assertion:

> It is surprising that if Paolo has the eight then he has the three

is taken to be synonymous with:

> If Paolo has the eight then it is surprising that he has the three.

In general, when adverbials, sentence operators, and even phrases posing a question, occur at the head of sentence consisting of a subordinate and a main clause, they tend to be interpreted as applying only to the main clause (Girotto & Johnson-Laird, 2004; see also Byrne & Johnson-Laird, this volume). This phenomenon occurs with phrases, such as, 'what is the probability that'. The question:

What is the probability that if Paolo has the eight then he has the three?

may therefore be interpreted as:

If Paolo has the eight then what is the probability that he has the three?

This latter question is tantamount to a request for the conditional probability: given Paolo has the eight, what is the probability that he has the three? And so individuals are likely in some instances to respond to a question that appears to ask for the probability of a conditional with the conditional probability of the then-clause given the if-clause.

One way to try to block the re-interpretation is to attribute the conditional assertion to a particular person, such as Vittorio, and then to ask participants to estimate the probability that Vittorio's assertion is true. We illustrated this procedure in the problems above, and other authors have also used it (e.g., Hadjichristidis, Stevenson, Over, Sloman, Evans, & Feeney, 2001). Yet, it does not guarantee that individuals understand the question as seeking the probability of the conditional. When the participants in a study had to think aloud as they solved problems, their remarks showed that they sometimes did assume that the if-clause of a conditional was true, and that their task was to estimate the conditional probability (Girotto & Johnson-Laird, 2004). A typical remark of this sort, for example, was, 'Given that Paolo has the seven, then the probability that Maria has the five is …'. We conclude that it is this interpretation of the question, which is by no means universal, rather than a general method of estimating the probability of conditionals, that yields those results that appear to corroborate the conditional-probability hypothesis.

The proponents of the conditional-probability hypothesis have questioned this conclusion. They argue that an assertion, such as:

If Paolo has the eight then what is the probability that he has the three?

is not a request for a conditional probability (Over, Hadjichristidis, Evans, Handley, & Sloman, 2007, p. 65). But, if the preceding question does not request a conditional probability, we are at loss to see how such a request might be framed directly. The conditional seems to be synonymous with the standard way of framing such a request:

Given that Paolo has the eight, what is the probability that he has the three?

Over et al. (2007) argue in turn that this question is confusing to the participants in experiments. We doubt it, because adults interpret it correctly (e.g., Girotto & Johnson-Laird, 2004; Oberauer & Wilhelm, 2003). And even children can respond to it with a correct judgment (Girotto & Gonzalez, 2008). Advocates of the conditional-probability hypothesis have sometimes accepted that individuals may re-interpret a question about a conditional to make it a question about a conditional probability (e.g., Hadjichristidis et al., 2001). Recently, however, they have denied it, claiming that individuals answer a question about a conditional with a conditional probability that does not depend on any re-interpretation (Over et al., 2007). Unlike the conditional-probability hypothesis, the model theory allows that the re-interpretation of the question is just one of several strategies that individuals use to estimate the probability of a conditional.

The model theory makes three crucial predictions. First, the greater the number of possibilities that individuals have to represent, the less often they should make an estimate corresponding to the use of the complete strategy. Second, because the estimate of a conditional probability calls for a simple subset strategy, these estimates should be correct more often than estimates of the probability of conditionals corresponding to the use of the complete strategy. Third, granted the use of various strategies, individuals should not always make the same estimates for both the probability of a conditional and the conditional probability of its then-clause given its if-clause.

The evidence corroborates all three predictions. We have already described the corroboration of the first prediction: the greater the number of possibilities that individuals have to take into account, the less often they arrive at a estimate corresponding to the use of the complete strategy. Girotto and Johnson-Laird (2004/Study 2) showed that that the correct estimates of conditional probabilities are more frequent than the complete estimates of the probabilities of conditionals (87% vs. 32%, respectively). And the same study showed that 100% of the participants made the same estimates for the two sorts of probability in problem 1, 50% did so for problem 3, but only 30% did so for problem 2.

Other studies have reported analogous results. For example, only about half of the participants in Hadjichristidis et al. (2001/Study 2) estimated the probability of a conditional as the correct value of its conditional probability. Likewise, Oberauer and Wilhelm (2003, p. 685) reported that 52% of the participants made the same estimates for both the probability of the conditional and the conditional probability in their Experiment 1B, but only 23% of participants did so in their Experiment 1A.

The conditional-probability theory cannot easily explain the corroboration of the model theory's three predictions. It proposes a single result for the estimate of the probability of a conditional, namely, the conditional probability, and it appears to have no machinery that takes into account the representation of the problem and the number of possibilities that need to be considered in its solution. Hence, the effect of this number on the use of the complete strategy is inexplicable on this account, and so too are the occurrence of different estimates of the probability of a conditional and of the divergence between these estimates and those of the conditional probability of the then-clause given the if-clause.

The model theory and the conditional-probability hypothesis make different predictions about the development of the abilities considered in this chapter. The model theory predicts that children should be able to estimate a conditional probability before they are able to make a complete estimate of the probability of a conditional. The prediction follows because the estimate of a conditional probability calls for the simple subset strategy, whereas the complete estimate of the probability of conditional depends on a more complicated strategy and a grasp of meta-linguistic terms, such as 'true' and 'false'. Children appear to understand these terms only after they have acquired the ability to reason about possibilities (see Barrouillet et al., 2000). Indeed, preschoolers can use the subset strategy (Girotto & Gonzalez, 2008). The conditional-probability hypothesis appears not to make predictions about developmental trends, other than perhaps that children should estimate the probability of a conditional before they can estimate a conditional probability, because the question about the latter is confusing.

Conclusions

In this chapter, we have focused on basic conditionals – those whose content does not depend on context or background knowledge (see Johnson-Laird & Byrne, 2002). Conditionals in daily life, however, are often not basic. For instance, the conditional:

> If she picked up a court card then it wasn't an ace

is not consistent with a possibility in which she didn't pick up a court card but did pick up an ace. Your knowledge of the meaning of 'court card' entails that an ace is a court card, and so this possibility, which would be consistent with a basic interpretation, is blocked. She either picked up a court card (king or jack) or a card that wasn't a court card. The same principles of extensional reasoning should apply mutatis mutandis to the estimates of the probabilities of such conditionals. They should also apply to cases in which the possibilities do not have equal probabilities of occurrence. However, studies have yet to test these predictions.

Many everyday conditionals are not susceptible to extensional reasoning. Consider how you might estimate the probability of a conditional, such as:

> If the cost of petrol increases then traffic congestion will improve.

One way, according to the conditional-probability hypothesis, is to imagine that the cost of petrol does increase, and then to infer the consequences: hence, people will buy less petrol; hence, they won't be able to drive so much; hence, there will be less traffic on the roads; hence, there will be less congestion. This sort of chain of reasoning has been implemented in a computer programme simulating a model-based account of how individuals resolve inconsistencies by using their general knowledge (Johnson-Laird, Girotto, & Legrenzi, 2004). To account for the resulting probability, however, it would be necessary to invoke some machinery for assessing the probability of each link in the chain. Yet, as readers will have noticed, this treatment takes for granted that the conditional-probability hypothesis is correct at least for non-extensional reasoning. Studies of causal conditionals, such as the preceding example, have provided corroboratory evidence for the hypothesis (see Over et al., 2007). Ramsey's test *is* plausible, even though psychologists do not have a working model of it (Oaksford & Charter, 2007, p. 166). But, it does not appear to be the full story.

Consider this claim:

> If Wordsworth alone wrote *The Ancient Mariner*, then Coleridge didn't write it.

This conditional is certainly true and has a probability of one. But, its if-clause is false, and so you cannot apply Ramsey's test to this conditional. Philosophers have shown how the test might be generalized to deal with such cases (e.g., Stalnaker, 1968). You add the if-clause to your beliefs, adjust them to accommodate the false intruder, and then assess the probability of the then-clause. In this case, however, there is a simple alternative. You know that Wordsworth and Coleridge were two different individuals. Ergo, if Wordsworth alone wrote *The Ancient Mariner*, Coleridge didn't.

Do individuals evaluating a conditional ever consider the possibility in which the if-clause of the conditional is false? According to the conditional-probability hypothesis, they do not. According to the model theory, they do. Evidence supports the model theory. One way to examine the contrasting predictions for a conditional of the form *if A then C* is to hold the probability of *C* given *A* constant and to manipulate the converse probability of *A* given *C*. The conditional-probability hypothesis predicts that the manipulation should have no reliable effect on performance. Studies have shown to the contrary that the manipulation does yield differences in the estimates of the probability of the conditional (Hasson, Walsh, & Johnson-Laird, 2005). Indeed, a re-analysis of the results in Evans et al. (2003) revealed a reliable effect. When the probability of *A* given *C* is high, *A* in effect tends to be necessary for *C* to occur, and individuals rate the probability of the conditional as higher than when *A* is not so necessary for *C* to occur (Hasson et al., 2005).

A conditional such as:

> If it doesn't rain today then it will rain next tomorrow.

implies that it will rain today or tomorrow, and naïve individuals are able to paraphrase conditionals as disjunctions, and vice versa (Richardson & Ormerod, 1997). But, they are unlikely to estimate the probability of a disjunction of the form, *A or C*, by inferring a conditional probability. Instead, they should consider the proportion of possibilities in which at least one of the clauses in the disjunction holds. Some individuals also use this complete strategy for estimating the probability of a conditional.

The extensional theory outlined in this chapter postulates that individuals estimate the probability of an event in three steps. They represent the possibilities; they assume by default that the possibilities are equiprobable; and they compute the proportion of possibilities in which the event occurs. This theory applies to estimates of the probability of conditionals. But, as we have shown, naïve individuals adopt a variety of strategies in coping with conditionals. They may treat the task as akin to assessing the truth or falsity of a conditional, and consider that the only relevant positive possibility is when both the if-clause and then-clause are true. They may contrast this possibility with the one in which the conditional is false (the equiprobable strategy), or with all the other possibilities (the conjunctive strategy). Another strategy, however, is to consider all the possibilities consistent with the conditional, and to work out the proportion of prior possibilities in which they hold (the complete strategy). The evidence that we reported bears out the use of a variety of strategies, because different individuals do make the different predicted estimates of the probability of a conditional.

Acknowledgements

Preparation of this chapter was funded in part by a COFIN (2005117840_003) grant from the Italian Ministry of Universities to Vittorio Girotto. We thank Nick Chater and David Over for comments on a previous version of the chapter. We also thank all colleagues with whom we have collaborated in the studies described in the present chapter.

References

Barres, P. & Johnson-Laird, P. N. (2003). On imagining what is true (and what is false). *Thinking & Reasoning*, **9**, 1–42.

Barrouillet, P., Grosset, N., & Leças, J- F. (2000). Conditional reasoning by mental models: chronometric and developmental evidence. *Cognition*, **75**, 237–266.

Cosmides, L. & Tooby, (1996). Are humans good intuitive statisticians after all? Rethinking some conclusions from the literature on judgment under uncertainty. *Cognition*, **58**, 1–73.

Evans, J .St.B. T., Handley, S. H., & Over, D. E. (2003). Conditionals and conditional probability. *Journal of Experimental Psychology: Learning, Memory and Cognition*, **29**, 321–335.

Evans, J. St.B. T., Handley, S. H., Neilens, H., & Over, D. E. (2007). Thinking about conditionals: A study of individual differences. *Memory & Cognition*, **35**, 1772–1784.

Fox, C. R. & Levav, J. (2004). Partition-edit-count: Naive extensional reasoning in judgment of conditional probability. *Journal of Experimental Psychology: General*, **133**, 626–642.

Gigerenzer, G., & Hoffrage, U. (1995). How to improve Bayesian reasoning without instruction: Frequency formats. *Psychological Review*, **102**, 684–704.

Gilovich, T., Griffin, D., & Kahneman, D., (Eds.) (2002). *Heuristics and Biases. The Psychology of Intuitive Judgment*. Cambridge: Cambridge University Press.

Girotto, V. & Gonzalez, M. (2001). Solving probabilistic and statistical problems: A matter of information structure and question form. *Cognition*, **78**, 247–276.

Girotto, V. & Gonzalez, M. (2008). Children's understanding of posterior probability. *Cognition*, **106**, 325–344.

Girotto, V. & Johnson-Laird, P. N. (2004). The probability of conditionals. *Psychologia*, **47**, 207–225.

Hadjichristidis, C., Stevenson, R. J., Over, D. E., Sloman, S. A., Evans, J. St.B. T., & Feeney, A. (2001). On the evaluation of 'if p then q' conditionals. *Proceedings of the 23rd Annual Meeting of the Cognitive Science Society*, Edinburgh.

Hasson, U., Walsh, C. R., & Johnson-Laird, P. N. (2005). What underlies the assessment of conditionals? *Proceedings of the 27th Annual Conference of the Cognitive Science Society*. Mahwah, NJ: Lawrence Erlbaum Associates. (pp. 911–916).

Johnson-Laird, P. N. (2006). *How We Reason*. Oxford: Oxford University Press.

Johnson-Laird, P. N. & Byrne, R. M. J. (1991). *Deduction*. Hillsdale, NJ: Lawrence Erlbaum Associates.

Johnson-Laird, P. N. & Byrne, R. M. J. (2002). Conditionals: A theory of meaning, pragmatics and inference. *Psychological Review*, **109**, 646–678.

Johnson-Laird, P. N., Girotto, V., & Legrenzi, P. (2004) Reasoning from inconsistency to consistency. *Psychological Review*, **111**, 640–661.

Johnson-Laird, P. N., Legrenzi, P., Girotto, V., Legrenzi, M., & Caverni, J. P. (1999). Naive probability: A model theory of extensional reasoning. *Psychological Review*, **106**, 62–88.

Johnson-Laird, P. N. & Savary, F. (1996). Illusory inferences about probabilities. *Acta Psychologica*, **93**, 69–90.

Kahneman, D., Slovic, P., & Tversky, A., (Eds.) (1982). *Judgment under Uncertainty: Heuristics and Biases*. Cambridge: Cambridge University Press.

Kahneman, D. & Tversky, A. (1973). On the psychology of prediction. *Psychological Review*, **80**, 237–251.

Koehler, J. J. (1996). The base rate fallacy reconsidered: Descriptive, normative, and methodological challenges. *Behavioral and Brain Sciences*, **19**, 1–53.

Nickerson, R. S. (1999). Ambiguities and unstated assumptions in probabilistic reasoning. *Psychological Bulletin*, **120**, 410–430.

Oaksford, M. & Chater, N. (2007). *Bayesian Rationality: The Probabilistic Approach to Human Reasoning*. Oxford: Oxford University Press.

Oberauer, K, & Wilhelm, W. (2003). The meaning(s) of conditionals: Conditional probability, mental models, and personal utilities. *Journal of Experimental Psychology: Learning, Memory and Cognition*, **29**, 680–693.

Over, D. E. & Evans, J. St.B. T. (2003). The probability of conditionals: The psychological evidence. *Mind & Language*, **18**, 340–358.

Over, D. E., Hadjichristidis, C., Evans, J. St.B. T., Handley, S. J., & Sloman, S. A. (2007). The probability of causal conditionals. *Cognitive Psychology*, **54**, 62–97.

Ramsey, F. P. (1990). *Philosophical Papers*. Mellor, D. H. (Ed.). Cambridge: Cambridge University Press.

Richardson, J. & Ormerod, T. C. (1997). Rephrasing between disjunctives and conditionals: Mental models and the effects of thematic content. *Quarterly Journal of Experimental Psychology*, **50A**, 358–385.

Schaeken, W., De Vooght, G., Vandierendonck, A., & d'Ydewalle, G., (Eds.). (2000). *Deductive Reasoning and Strategies*. Mahwah, NJ: Erlbaum.

Sloman, S. A., Over, D., Slovak, L., & Stibel, J. M. (2003). Frequency illusions and other fallacies. *Organizational Behavior and Human Decision Processes*, **91**, 296–309.

Stalnaker, R. C. (1968). A theory of conditionals. *American Philosophical Quarterly Monograph Series*, **2**, 98–112.

Stevenson, R. J. & Over, D. E. (1995). Deduction from uncertain premises. *Quarterly Journal of Experimental Psychology*, **48A**, 613–643.

Teglas, E., Girotto, V., Gonzalez, M., & Bonatti, L. L. (2007). Intuitions of probabilities shape expectations about the future at 12 months and beyond. *Proceedings of the National Academy of Sciences*, **104**, 19156–19159.

Chapter 7

Causal discounting and conditional reasoning in children

Nilufa Ali, Anne Schlottmann, Abigail Shaw, Nick Chater, and Mike Oaksford

Introduction

Conditional reasoning is widely viewed as central to human inference and a paradigm case of logical thought. Perhaps the most natural use of the indicative conditional is to express relationships between cause and effect, either in reasoning predictively from causes to effects (*if I cut my finger, then I bleed*); or reasoning diagnostically from effects to causes (*if I bleed, then I cut my finger*). To the extent that conditionals are used to describe cause-effect relationships, the study of cause and effect may help illuminate the function of conditionals.

Many studies of conditional reasoning have used experimental materials which participants are likely to interpret in causal terms. Indeed, unless the domain of reasoning is highly abstract (e.g., about numbers and letters printed on cards), it seems inevitable that people will recruit causal knowledge (about fingers, cuts, bleeding, etc) to solving conditional reasoning problems. But in the majority of studies causal *structure* has been *incidental*, rather than the focus of inquiry (but see Griffiths & Tenenbaum, 2005; Sloman & Lagnado, 2005). In this chapter we suggest that the causal structure described by the premises may be more important than its logical structure – the traditional focus of research in the psychology of conditional reasoning – in determining the inferences people draw.

More specifically, we consider that conditional inference patterns should differ when reasoning from cause-to-effect (predictively) than when reasoning from effect-to-cause (diagnostically). Accordingly, the present approach will develop a probabilistic view of indicative reasoning about cause and effect. There have been many studies marshalling evidence for a probabilistic approach to understanding conditionals, (e.g., Chan & Chua, 1994; Liu, Lo, & Wu, 1996; Oaksford & Chater, 1994, 1998; Oaksford, Chater, & Larkin, 2000; Quinn & Markovits, 1998). Nonetheless, no current psychological theory of conditional reasoning based on probability make the predictions described here concerning how causal *direction* affects patterns of conditional reasoning. But if participants interpret the premises as causal, then a theory of causal inference may fare better.

In fact, an influential normative account of causal reasoning recently developed in artificial intelligence (Pearl, 2000) allows us to make predictions about the effects of causal direction not made by existing conditional reasoning theories. Our previous research with adults (Ali, Chater, & Oaksford, 2008) broadly confirms the predictions of this account. However, there was an anomaly that we interpreted as being caused by the experience of our adult participants and which may be absent in children with less experience with causal relations. Accordingly, the aim of the experiment reported here was to investigate the influence of causal direction on conditional reasoning in children.

We first outline the conditional reasoning paradigm and the standard results. We then describe Pearl's (2000) normative theory from which we develop the current account.

Conditional inference

The starting point for the psychology of conditional inference has been the formal analysis of the conditional provided by standard logic. According to standard logic, a conditional *if p then q* is true, and so can be accepted if, and only if, either the *antecedent* (*p*) is false or the *consequent* (*q*) is true. This semantics for the conditional licenses two formal rules of inference called *modus ponens* (MP) and *modus tollens* (MT):

$$\text{MP} \quad \frac{p \rightarrow q, p}{\therefore q} \qquad\qquad \text{MT} \quad \frac{p \rightarrow q, \neg q}{\therefore \neg p} \qquad\qquad (7.1)$$

These inference schemata read that if the propositions above the line are true, then it can be inferred that the propositions below the line are true. For example, for MP, if it is true that *if Johnny has a runny nose* (*p*), *he has a cold* (*q*) and that *Johnny has a runny nose*, then it is true that *Johnny has a cold*. According to standard logic both MP and MT inferences are *valid*. Consequently, if people are logical then they should endorse both inferences and reject the inferential fallacies of *denying the antecedent* (DA) and *affirming the consequent* (AC):

$$\text{DA} \quad \frac{p \rightarrow q, \neg p}{\therefore \neg q} \qquad\qquad \text{AC} \quad \frac{p \rightarrow q, q}{\therefore p} \qquad\qquad (7.2)$$

However, rather than exhibiting the predicted symmetry between MP and MT, participants tend to endorse MP far more than MT. For example, in a recent meta-analysis involving 65 conditional inference experiments and 2774 participants, 97% (SD = 3.6%) on average draw the MP inference but only 72% (SD = 13.5%) the MT inference (Schroyens & Schaeken, 2003; see also Oaksford & Chater, 2003). Over the 65 studies, this result represents a highly significant asymmetry, $t(64) = 15.44$, $p < .0001$, between MP and MT. Moreover, participants also endorse DA and AC and there is a similar asymmetry such that AC is drawn more than DA.

Causal conditional reasoning

The results we described in the last section almost all relate to abstract alphanumeric stimuli rather than the causal conditionals that are the focus of the current study. However, there has been much work investigating the effects of causal conditionals on people's reasoning. Causal conditionals, in particular, have been used to show that the inferences, MP and MT, and the fallacies, DA and AC, can be *suppressed* by providing information about possible *defeaters, i.e., about additional enabling conditions or alternative causes*. For example, if you are told that *if the key is turned the car starts* and that *the key is turned*, you are likely to endorse the MP inference to the conclusion that *the car starts*. However, if you are also told that *the petrol tank is empty*, you are less likely to endorse this conclusion, because the car will *not* start if the petrol tank is empty. A full petrol tank provides an enabling condition that allows turning the key to start the car. The petrol tank being empty will also affect MT. If you knew that *the car didn't start* you may not infer that *the key was not turned* because the empty petrol tank may be the cause of the car not starting.

Information about alternative causes can suppress DA and AC. For example, if you are told that *if the key is turned the car starts* and that *the key is not turned*, you might endorse the DA inference to the conclusion that *the car does not start*. However, if you are also told that *the car was hot-wired*, you may be less likely to endorse this conclusion because the car may start even though the key was not turned because it has been hot-wired. This alternative cause would also mean that you are less likely to endorse AC. If you knew that *the car started* you may not infer that *the key was turned* because the car starting may have been caused by being hot-wired.

These kinds of effects have been investigated using two paradigms, the *explicit* and the *implicit* paradigms. We describe each, as features of both will figure in the design of our experiment. Although Byrne (1989) did not originally use causal materials, she demonstrated all the above effects by providing participants with additional conditional statements containing the new information:

Enabling Conditions (affecting MP)	*Alternative Causes (affecting AC)*
If the key is turned the car starts	If the key is turned the car starts
If there is fuel in the tank the car starts	If it is hot-wired the car starts
The key is turned	The car starts
The car starts?	The key was turned?

Cummins, Lubarts, Alksnis, and Rist (1991), see also Cummins (1995) and Thompson (1994), report results that were very similar to Byrne (1989). However, they left information about additional and alternative antecedents *implicit*. That is, unlike Byrne (1989), these authors pre-tested their conditional rules for how many alternative and additional antecedents came to mind, then they used these rules in the experimental task without explicit cueing concerning the relevance of alternative and additional antecedents. Cummins (1995) also used diagnostic conditionals, e.g., *if the car starts then the key was turned*, and showed a reversal of these effects. That is, now alternative causes affected MP and MT and enabling conditions affected AC and DA. Such effects are not predicted by logic and demonstrate clear effects of causal factors on conditional reasoning; although it has been argued that such effects can be incorporated in logic based models (see Byrne, Espino, & Santamaria, 1999).

Pearl's normative theory and predictions

Pearl's (2000) normative theory of causal reasoning provides a rich conceptual and mathematical framework for dealing with a wide range of issues in causal reasoning. Here we will focus on its broad structure, and its key predictions.

Pearl's account shows how causal relationships can be represented in terms of graphical structures (see also Pearl, 1988), such as those in the second row of Table 7.1. The structure for condition 1 and 3 shows two possible causes, C1 and C2, of a common effect, E. The structure for condition 2 and 4 shows a common cause, C, of two effects, E1 and E2. The direction of an arrow represents the direction of causality. The 'nodes', which are connected by the arrows, represent variables, which interact causally. In these experiments, these two structures are described using causal and diagnostic conditionals. So the common effect structure is described as *if C1 then E* and *if C2 then E* (causal conditionals in CE direction) and the common cause structure is described as *if E1 then C* and *if E2 then C* (diagnostic conditionals in EC direction) (see Cummins, 1995). In other words, the cause is either stated as antecedent or consequent of the conditional.

Given these descriptions, which form two premises in the inferences we investigate, there are four inferential patterns shown in Table 7.1. They arise from two binary factors: direction (cause-to-effect or effect-to-cause); and whether the consequent of the conditional is added as an additional premise or not (this is explained shortly). Rather than trace through the formal predictions of Pearl's theory here, we focus on the task given to the participant, and the rationale for the pattern of results that would be expected if participants are following Pearl's (2000) normative account.

Table 7.1 Problem structure and predictions for four experimental conditions (with concrete examples in light gray)

	Condition 1 CENC — Causal — Cause to Effect Direction; Consequent Not Asserted	Condition 2 ECNC — Diagnostic — Effect to Cause Condition; Consequent Not Asserted	Condition 3 CEC — Causal — Cause to Effect Direction; Consequent Asserted	Condition 4 ECC — Diagnostic — Effect to Cause Direction; Consequent Asserted
Causal structure	C1, C2 → E	C → E1, E2	C1, C2 → E	C → E1, E2
Background information given to participants, B	If C1 then E (*Premise 1*) If C2 then E (*Premise 2*)	If E1 then C (*Premise 1*) If E2 then C (*Premise 2*)	If C1 then E (*Premise 1*) If C2 then E (*Premise 2*) E is the case (*Premise 3*)	If E1 then C (*Premise 1*) If E2 then C (*Premise 2*) C is the case (*Premise 3*)
	If it rains, then the grass is wet. *If the sprinklers are on, then the grass is wet.*	*If it is warm outside, then it is sunny.* *If there are shadows, then it is sunny.*	*If it rains, then the grass is wet.* *If the sprinklers are on, then the grass is wet.* *The grass is wet.*	*If it is warm outside, then it is sunny.* *If there are shadows, then it is sunny.* *It is sunny.*
Rating 1	How likely is C1? (Corresponding to Prob(C1|B))	How likely is E1? (Corresponding to Prob (E1, B))	How likely is C1? (Corresponding to Prob (C1|E, B))	How likely is E1? (Corresponding to Prob (E1/C, B))
	How likely do you think it is that it rains?	*How likely do you think it is that it is warm outside?*	*How likely do you think it is that it rains?*	*How likely do you think it is that it is warm outside?*
Information given to participants	C2 is the case (*Premise 3*)	E2 is the case (*Premise 3*)	C2 is the case (*Premise 4*)	E2 is the case (*Premise 4*)
	The sprinklers are on.	*There are shadows.*	*The sprinklers are on.*	*There are shadows.*
Rating 2	How likely is C1? (Corresponding to Prob(C1|C2, B))	How likely is E1? (Corresponding to Prob (E1|E2, B))	How likely is C1? (Corresponding to Prob (C1|C2, E, B))	How likely is E1? (Corresponding to Prob (E1|E2, B, C))
	How likely do you think it is that it rains?	*How likely do you think it is that it is warm outside?*	*How likely do you think it is that it rains?*	*How likely do you think it is that it is warm outside?*
Prediction after Pearl (2000)	$P(C1\|C2) = P(C1)$ Independence	$P(E1\|E2) > P(E1)$ Augmenting	$P(C1\|C2, E,) < P(C1\|E)$ Discounting	$P(E1\|E2, C,) = P(E1\|C,)$ Independence

We first consider the Non-Consequent condition in the left columns of Table 7.1. Participants are first given the two causal conditional premises ('background' information, B), then asked to rate the probability of the first antecedent (Rating 1). Participants are then told that the second antecedent is true. What we are interested in is whether the additional information about the second antecedent raises or lowers the rated probability of the first antecedent or leaves it unchanged. Note that in conditions 1 and 2, for the cause-to-effect and effect-to-cause case, the problem has exactly the same logical form, but according to Pearl's causal analysis, these cases are very different.

In the cause-to-effect case, the key question is whether the addition of the new knowledge of one cause (C2) has an impact on the rated probability of another cause (C1), given the background knowledge that both causes give rise to effect E. We do not know whether E has occurred, so the first rating of C1, whether it rains, ought to simply reflect the base rate of the event. When we then learn that C2 occurred, i.e., that the sprinklers are on, this should have no effect on the second probability rating for C1, because rain and sprinklers are independent of each other (at least if the sprinklers are controlled automatically). Thus the occurrence of one event has no impact on the occurrence of the other. Formally, in terms of Pearl's theory, the only path between the two causes (see Table 7.1) passes through a 'collider' where the two arrows meet at a single node, thus $\text{Prob}(C1|B) = \text{Prob}(C1|C2, B)$.

In contrast, consider the effect-to-cause case of condition 2. Here, knowing one effect (that there are shadows) of it being sunny should raise the probability of other effects (that it is warm outside). This is because it being sunny causes both shadows and warmth, and hence the presence of one effect is informative about the presence of another. This is a case of causal augmentation. In terms of Pearl's theory, the two effects are joined by a path that does not include a 'collider' and thus $\text{Prob}(E1|B) < \text{Prob}(E1|E2, B)$.

The pattern changes subtly, but significantly, when a further premise (the 'consequent', see the right hand columns of Table 7.1) is added to the two background conditional statements. In the cause-to-effect case (condition 3), Rating 2 should decrease from Rating 1. Now that we are told initially that the grass is wet, we can reason that this is likely to have been caused either by rain or sprinklers. Hence, for the initial judgement, both causes are equiprobable and reasonably likely, leading to a higher Rating 1 than in condition 1. However, once one cause is confirmed (sprinklers), this suffices to explain that the grass is wet, thus the effect ceases to provide evidence for rain. Hence Rating 2 should decrease, to the base rate of rain. This is a case of causal discounting. In terms of Pearl's theory, the collider linking two causes 'unblocks' the path between C1 and C2 and thus $\text{Prob}(C1|E, B) > \text{Prob}(C1|C2, E, B)$.

Turning now to our final effect-to-cause case (condition 4), here the addition of the consequent (the cause, 'it is sunny') has a different result. Without the consequent, in condition 2, learning about one effect (shadows) increases the probability of another (warmth), because one effect increases the probability that the cause was present which in turn makes other effects more probable. But if the cause is given initially, then Rating 1 should already be at ceiling, and cannot be raised further by learning about the other effect. That is, the path between E1 and E2 is 'blocked' by the value of C being specified; once C is known, E2 carries no further information about E1, i.e., $\text{Prob}(E1|C, B) = \text{Prob}(E1|E2, C, B)$.

These predicted equalities and inequalities form the basis of our experimental predictions. Using the Rating 2 (RH side of each equality/inequality) minus Rating 1 (LH side of each equality/inequality) difference (ΔR) as the dependent variable, the experiment is a 2 (causal direction: CE, EC) by 2 (consequent: consequent (C), non-consequent (NC)) factorial design. At the highest level we predict two main effects, effect-cause > cause-effect (EC > CE) and non-consequent > consequent (NC > C). More detailed predictions correspond to the four simple effects

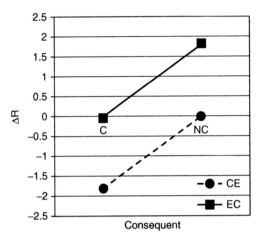

Fig. 7.1 Predictions showing the main effects for causal direction (cause-effect [CE], effect-cause [EC]) and consequent (Consequent [C], Non-Consequent [NC]) conditions.

(ECC > CEC, ECNC > CENC, ECNC > ECC, CENC > CEC). The most detailed level of predictions correspond directly to the equalities and inequalities outlined above (ECNC > 0, CEC < 0, CENC = 0, ECC = 0). These predictions are shown in the interaction plot in Figure 7.1. These predictions show no interaction effect. However, the underlying probabilities depend on the particular contents used in the experimental materials. Consequently, the lack of an interaction is not a direct prediction as one may arise as a result of the particular materials used.

These predictions can be derived directly from Pearl's normative theory of causality, but could not be made simply by considering the logical form of these conditional arguments (see Sloman and Lagnado [2005] for a similar argument). Ali, Chater, and Oaksford (2008: Experiment 1) tested these predictions with 10 different scenarios. The overall results are shown in Figure 7.2. These results show that most of the predicted effects were observed. However, there were some discrepancies. These related to conditions 1 and 4, where ΔR is predicted to be zero. In condition 4, ΔR was significantly lower than zero, i.e., ECC < 0 ($P(E1|E2, C, B) < P(E1|C, B)$). In condition 1, ΔR was close to being significantly lower than zero, i.e., CENC < 0 ($P(C1|C2, B) < P(C1|B)$). Thus causal discounting was observed more widely than predicted by Pearl's theory, in three rather than just one of four conditions.

We interpret this finding as relating to the effects of prior knowledge indicating independence of the effects of a common cause, or (negative) dependence of the causes of a common effect.

Take the case of the common cause structure in a diagnostic conditional. In condition 4, producing the ECC anomaly, one is told that the cause is present, i.e., it is sunny, from which one would expect both effects. However, you are then informed about only one of these effects, there are shadows. A possible pragmatic implicature is that the other effect did not occur, otherwise why explicitly mention only one of them? Another example would be 'The gong was struck, it vibrated...*but made no sound*'. That is, explicit mention of one effect may trigger the expectation that another did not occur. Moreover, people will be aware of cases in which normally positively correlated effects become uncorrelated: indoors, warmth and shadows do not have a common cause, at the poles when it is sunny there will be shadows but it will not be warm. This implicature depends on having the additional information that it is actually sunny; as long as this is not known (condition 2), mention of one effect augments the probability of the other. But when it is stated explicitly that it is sunny, implying both effects, then mention of only one of them pragmatically suggests an exception.

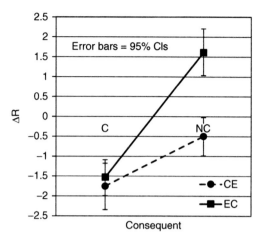

Fig. 7.2 Results of Ali et al.'s (2008) Experiment 1 showing the main effects for causal direction (cause-effect [CE], effect-cause [EC]) and consequent (Consequent [C], Non-Consequent [NC]) conditions.

So world knowledge — that even if effects are normally correlated there can be exceptions — together with conversational pragmatics leads to a reduced Rating 2.

In the common effect, causal conditional case of condition 1, producing the CENC anomaly, the events are independent and occurrence of one should not affect the other. However, although the mechanisms producing rain and those controlling the sprinklers are independent, the events can be correlated due to human intervention. In particular, some causes come into play typically when the *normal* cause has failed (Oaksford & Chater, 2003, 2008). Thus sprinkler systems are installed in areas where it does not rain a lot and predominantly used when it does not rain. In other words, world knowledge also suggests that physically independent causes of a common effect may in practice be negatively correlated. This would produce discounting rather than independence in the CENC condition, with a reduced Rating 2.

Children's reasoning with causal conditionals: The present study

Recent developmental work on simple causal conditionals in children shows that suppression of the conditional fallacies occurs in children as in adults, that it improves developmentally, and that it depends on how easy it is to generate alternative cases (Barrouillet, Markovits, & Quinn, 2001; Janveau-Brennan & Markovits, 1999). We also know that even pre-school children are capable of learning the more complex causal structures of the type assumed in the causal Bayes net framework (e.g., Gopnik, Sobel, Schulz, & Glymour, 2001; Gopnik, Glymour, Sobel, Schulz, Kushnir, & Danks, 2004; Schulz, Gopnik, & Glymour, 2007). These results suggest that children might also be capable of reasoning about conditionals involving common cause or effect structures, and that they might be sensitive to the factors that underpin the predictions tested by Ali et al. (2008).

One might further conjecture that with less experience of the real world exceptions to the assumptions of such structures, children might more closely follow the prescriptions of Pearl's theory. However, the previous explanations suggest an asymmetry between condition 1 (CENC = 0) and condition 4 (ECC = 0). Whereas one might expect considerable experience of conversational conventions and knowledge of causes not stated in the problem to be required for the sophisticated pragmatic implicatures involved in producing condition 4's deviation from 0, condition 1 only requires a general idea of alternative causes – one precluding the other – without additional world knowledge being required to come up with an example. Consequently, we might expect that young children might not show the ECC anomaly, because they do not have the necessary knowledge, i.e., ΔR will not deviate from zero for condition 4, but we may still observe a CENC anomaly, i.e., ΔR may still be less than zero in condition 1. The present study, therefore, investigated how children interpret similar situations to those described in Table 7.1 and whether they show the same pattern of results as predicted for Ali et al.'s (2008) Experiment 1.

Children are unlikely to perform well with purely verbal material; therefore we adapted the task to a simpler, concrete form, where the causal structure was physically seen. The cause-to-effect condition was represented by a box with two buttons turning on one light and the effect-to-cause condition was represented by a box with one button turning on two lights (see Table 7.2). The boxes were decorated with pictures illustrating two scenarios, with two versions each for the two causal structures. In the common effect version of the flower scenario, one cause button represented the sun shining and the other button represented the presence of water. The effect light represented a flower, which 'sparkled' if one or both buttons were pressed. In the common cause version, the single cause button for the shining sun made both a blue flower and a red flower light up. The other scenario concerned a ship and how the captain or engineer could work the anchor and its light, or how the captain could work lights on the anchor and the top of the stack. The adult study used different verbal scenarios for different causal structures, making it difficult to separate the effects of causal structure from scenario effects. In the child study, in contrast, the two scenarios were counterbalanced across children, so that we may observe 'pure' effects of causal structure.

In each condition, children were shown one of the boxes and then questioned in a similar way to Ali et al. (2008), but all verbal statements were accompanied by corresponding actions with the box. For example, to illustrate the background conditional premises,

> If the sun is shining, then the flower sparkles
> If there is water, then the flower sparkles,

the sun button was pressed, leading to the flower light sparkling, then the water button was pressed, also leading to the flower light sparkling.

To vary children's knowledge or ignorance about the state of the world/box, a scarf covered up parts of the apparatus and only the information known at that point in time was revealed. For example, when the initial R1 rating of the antecedent was made, there were no additional premises and the whole apparatus was covered, so that children did not know about the state of any of the lights/buttons.

Table 7.2 Diagrams showing the causal relationships between the variables within each scenario

Causal Direction	Scenario	
	Flower	**Ship**

Cause-to-effect	Sun ⟍
	     ⟶ Flower
	 Water ⟋
		Captain ⟍
		     ⟶ Anchor
		 Engineer ⟋

Effect-to-cause	⟶ Blue Flower
	 Sun ⟨
	     ⟶ Red Flower
		⟶ Blue Light
		 Captain ⟨
		     ⟶ Anchor

For the second R2 rating, additional information was given, e.g.,

Now you can see that the sun is shining. How sure are you that there is water?

Here, the sun button was revealed and the children saw it pressed, but the water button and flower light remained covered. In this way, the questions could be asked in the same way as in the adult study, but the verbal information was amplified visually by showing the children the corresponding state of the box.

Method

Participants

The participants were 48 children drawn from a school in Harrow, North London. Half of the children were in Year 2 (mean age = 7 yrs 1 month, range = 6 yrs 5 months to 7 yrs 9 months) and half were in Year 3 (mean age = 8 yrs 0 months, range = 7 yrs 6 months to 8 yrs 6 months).

Design

Each child saw all four conditions of interest. The CE version of one scenario was used together with the EC version of the other scenario. In each, the child first rated the non-consequent, then the consequent condition. Which scenario and which causal direction came first was counterbalanced across children. Thus the experiment was a mixed 2 × 2 × 2 × 2 × 2 design with causal direction (CE, EC) and (consequent (C), non-consequent (NC)) as within subject factors and year (Year 2, Year 3), consequent order (CE first, EC first) and scenario order (flower first, ship

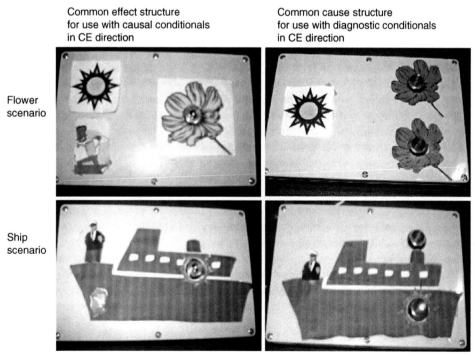

Fig. 7.3 The button-and-light boxes used to illustrate common effect and common cause structures for children; both structures were implemented in two different scenarios; each child saw the common effect version of one scenario and the common cause version of the other.

first) as the between subjects factors, and with the Rating 2 minus Rating 1 difference (ΔR) as the dependent variable.

Materials

The boxes of Figure 7.3 were used to illustrate different causal scenarios. They could be covered with a thick black scarf, as the problem demanded. Children responded by pointing/marking 10 cm rating bars, with shading continuously graded from dark to light. The dark end was marked 'yes', the light end 'no', and 'not sure' appeared in the middle. Ratings were read to the nearest .5 cm.

Procedure

Participants were tested individually. Before the boxes were presented children first practiced use of the rating bar. The children were told that they would be asked how sure they were that certain things were happening and would have to answer by pointing along the scale. They were told that the surer they were that the answer was 'yes' or 'no', the further they should point to the corresponding end of the scale. If they were not sure at all they could mark in the middle.

To practice, children were asked to point to how sure they were that a white button would be picked from an envelope with different numbers of white and blue buttons inside. First the children were shown five white buttons and all children pointed to the 'yes' end. Then the children were shown five blue buttons, then three of each colour, and finally five white buttons and one blue button. The next stage did not take place until the children were able to show that they understood how to use the rating scale.

The children were then shown the first box. The experimenter began explaining the causal scenario and said to the child, for instance in the cause-to-effect flower condition, '*My magic box has a big flower in the middle which shimmers and sparkles. Would you like to see it sparkle?*' When the children responded, the button was pressed to demonstrate its action. The experimenter then told the child that the flower only sparkles when it is happy. Pointing to the sun button and watering can button, the experimenter explained that both the sun and water will make the flower happy. Then the background conditional premises were introduced and the child was told that, '*If the sun is shining, then the flower sparkles*' and '*If there is water, then the flower sparkles*'. The corresponding buttons were pressed to demonstrate.

The non-consequent condition was always presented first, so children were then asked for an initial rating of the antecedent; in this example, how sure they were that there was water, without any knowledge of the state of the box. To illustrate, the box was completely covered by the scarf. Children were then told about the other antecedent, here, the alternative cause, the sun, with only the corresponding button revealed and pressed, and again asked to rate the antecedent.

The children were then tested in the same manner in the consequent condition of the same scenario, introduced as events happening on another day. In this condition, prior to their R1 rating children were told about the consequent. To illustrate, the flower was uncovered and the children saw it sparkling, whilst the cause buttons remained covered. The rest of the procedure was as before, except that the flower remained uncovered. The children were then presented with the second scenario illustrating the other causal direction and the procedure was repeated.

Results and discussion

We first calculated ΔR for each causal direction. We then carried out a $2 \times 2 \times 2 \times 2 \times 2$ mixed ANOVA with causal direction and consequent as within subject factors and year, direction order, and scenario order as the between subjects factors, with ΔR as the dependent variable. None of the between subjects factors produced significant main effects or interacted significantly with any combination of other factors. Therefore, the counterbalancing was effective and the age differences in the sample did not affect the results. Consequently, we only report the results of a within subjects 2 × 2 ANOVA with causal direction (CE, EC) and consequent (consequent (C), non-consequent (NC)) as factors, and with ΔR as the dependent variable.

The results are shown in Figure 7.4. Both main effects were in the predicted directions. ΔR was significantly higher in the effect-cause direction than for the cause-effect direction (EC > CE), $F(1, 47) = 20.16$, $MSe = 12.28$, $\eta^2 = .30$, $p < .0001$. ΔR was also higher in the non-consequent condition than in the consequent condition (NC > C), although this effect was only marginal, $F(1, 47) = 2.41$, $MSe = 15.22$, $\eta^2 = .05$, $p = .063$. As Figure 7.4 shows, unlike Ali et al. (2008: Experiment 1) there was no significant interaction effect, $F(1, 47) < 1$.

At the next level, we looked at all the simple effects using planned t-tests. In the effect-cause direction, ΔR was significantly higher in the non-consequent condition than in the consequent condition (ECNC > ECC), $t(47) = 1.77$, $p < .05$. However, in the cause-effect direction, ΔR was not significantly higher in the non-consequent condition than in the consequent condition (CENC > CEC), $t(47) = .45$, ns. In the non-consequent condition, ΔR was significantly higher in the effect-cause direction than in the cause-effect direction (ECNC > CENC), $t(47) = 3.59$, $p < .001$. Moreover, in the consequent condition, ΔR was significantly higher in the effect-cause direction than in the cause-effect direction (ECC > CEC), $t(47) = 2.26$, $p < .025$.

At the next level, we checked for the predicted differences from ΔR = 0, which amounts to testing the original equalities and inequalities in Table 7.1. In the non-consequent condition 2 (effect-cause direction), ΔR was significantly greater than zero (R1 = .59, R2 = .73 ECNC > 0), $t(47)$ = 1.89, $p < .05$, as for adults, and in line with the augmenting prediction based on Pearl's theory. For condition 1 (cause-effect direction), ΔR was significantly less than zero (R1 = .58, R2 = .44, CENC = 0), $t(47) = 2.22$, $p < .025$, i.e., children showed an anomaly, with discounting instead of independence, similar to adults in Ali et al. (2008). In the consequent condition 3 (cause-effect direction), ΔR was significantly lower than zero (R1 = .67, R2 = .49, CEC < 0), $t(47) = 2.66$, $p < .01$, as for adults, and in line with Pearl's discounting prediction. In condition 4 (effect-cause direction), ΔR did not differ significantly from zero (R1 = .80, R2 = .80, ECC < 0), $t(47) = .08$, $p = .47$

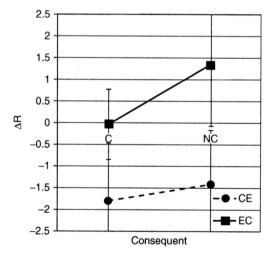

Fig. 7.4 Results of the Experiment showing the main effects for causal direction (cause-effect [CE], effect-cause [EC]) and consequent (Consequent [C], Non-Consequent [NC]) conditions.

(one-tailed). In other words, children did not show the anomaly that Ali et al. (2008) found for adults, and behaved in line with the independence prediction of Pearl's theory instead.

In summary, at all levels of statistical analysis the majority of the predictions of the hypothesis that children take causal knowledge into account in conditional inference have been confirmed. As expected, the ECC anomaly for condition 4 observed by Ali et al. (2008) was removed by moving down the age range. This result suggests that, at age 7 to 8, children are yet to acquire the knowledge required for the sophisticated pragmatic implicatures that may underpin this case of non-normative causal discounting in adults. However, children at this age continue to reveal the CENC anomaly.

The ECC results found here suggest that children of primary school age appreciate the idea of causal independence to the extent that they will apply it correctly in some circumstances in which adults' pragmatic knowledge misleads them. This is a novel finding in the literature on children's causal understanding. Gopnik and colleagues (e.g., Gopnik et al., 2001; Schulz et al., 2007) have shown that even preschoolers can infer causality from patterns of conditional dependence and independence, in line with Pearl's theory, in simple cases that seem equally intuitive to adults and children. Our finding goes beyond this to show that children can, on occasion, be more correct than adults, who are mislead by experience to over-apply the idea of causal discounting.

It is an open question, however, whether by pushing further down the age range, we may observe all the patterns of inference predicted by a causal Bayes approach, i.e., whether even younger children with even less experience will apply the idea of causal independence even more widely and even more appropriately. As argued above, if non-normative causal discounting depends only on specific knowledge – of the rules of conversation, of unstated other potential causes at work in the situations described, of specific instances of negatively correlated causes – then children may ultimately not show the anomalies found in adults.

Alternatively, it may be that causal discounting, over-generalized in adults (Ali et al., 2008) and children here, may reflect a stronger or perhaps earlier idea than independence, over-generalized from its first appearance. In particular, children might have an early idea that causes are negatively correlated, such that one cause precludes another. In fact, they might apply this interpretation not just to the CENC, but also the CEC case, where discounting would be expected for negatively correlated and for independent causes. In other words, children, and perhaps even adults, might show normative discounting for a non-normative reason in the CEC case.

In line with this view, a large literature on children's causal attributions from the 70s and 80s shows that children from at least 3 years have no difficulty at all with the idea that one, but not another cause produced an effect, while the possibility of two causes never seems to be considered. In addition, Sobel, Tenenbaum, and Gopnik (2004) showed backwards blocking in children as young as 3 years.

A similar debate also exists in the literature on children's understanding of logical connectives. The traditional view here is that children initially interpret the connective 'or' exclusively, with the inclusive interpretation only achieved several years later (Brain & Rumain, 1981; 1983). However, this view has recently been challenged (see Crain et al., 2000). These authors argue that even young children are capable of understanding that 'A or B' can refer to either or both items, and that children assume the exclusive interpretation only as a result of pragmatic implicature. Further empirical work is clearly necessary to decide whether equivalent pragmatic factors are at work in the case of causal discounting.

In evaluating the wider import of this work we now assess whether and how Mental Models and Causal Bayes theories of reasoning can explain the children's pattern of results. We then look at the relation of these results to other research using a causal Bayes approach to investigate the relationship between causal and conditional reasoning. Finally we look at some of the more theoretical issues raised concerning structure and strength in causal reasoning and in reasoning and argumentation more generally.

Logic and mental models theories

Sloman and Lagnado (2005) have worked through the ability of a variety of theories in the psychology of reasoning to explain the causal discounting effects. These explanations also apply to the common cause condition (CEC) in the present experiment. The common effect condition (ECNC) produces augmentation effects because the occurrence of an effect that shares a common cause with other effects raises the probability that they also occur. Augmentation is as inexplicable as discounting from the perspective of logic-based theories.

In the present experiments, participants are asked for probability ratings. Logical probability involves counting the possibilities in which a proposition is true and dividing by the number of possibilities. This account underlies the mental models approach to probability and hence should underpin how mental models explain these data (Johnson-Laird, Legrenzi, Girotto, Legrenzi, & Caverni, J.P, 1999). The only alternative is to argue that the models are annotated with probabilities, which places the processes responsible outside the explanatory purview of mental models theory. We now show in detail why discounting cannot be predicted by mental models theory.

The eight logical possibilities for the ECC and CEC cases are shown below in (A) and (B), respectively. Those that must be false assuming the truth of the background premises, B, are listed in bold. The premises additionally ruled out by the assertion of the consequent, C or E, respectively, are shown in italic. Logically, no other information is available and so the remaining possibilities must be equiprobable, yielding predictions to compare with our Bayesian predictions and with the data.

Following Byrne (1989) and Byrne et al. (1999) we encode the background premises in the alternative cause CEC case as a disjunctive antecedent, i.e., if C1 or C2, then E. We also allow that although the diagnostic ECC conditionals place the cause in the consequent and the common effects in the antecedent clauses, participants may convert the clauses of these conditionals and represent them as a single conditional with a conjunctive consequent, i.e., if C, then E1 and E2. Such conversion is a familiar explanatory manoeuvre in the psychology of reasoning, but of course logically it is an error. Conversion is also consistent with Goldvarg and Johnson-Laird's (2001) account of causal reasoning in which left to right order of a model reflects causal order, not antecedent-consequent order. Accordingly, with conversion, seven and six of the eight possibilities are ruled out in (A) and (B), respectively.

(A)	(condition 4, ECC)				(B) (condition 3, CEC)			
	C	E1	E2	1		C1	C2	E	.25(.5)
	¬C	E1	E2	0		¬C1	C2	E	.25(.5)
	C	¬E1	E2	0		C1	¬C2	E	.25
	¬C	¬E1	E2	0		¬C1	¬C2	E	.25
	C	E1	¬E2	0		C1	C2	¬E	0
	¬C	E1	¬E2	0		¬C1	C2	¬E	0
	C	¬E1	¬E2	0		C1	¬C2	¬E	0
	¬C	¬E1	¬E2	0		¬C1	¬C2	¬E	0

In (A) those possibilities ruled out by the truth of the conditional, *if C, then E1 and E2*, are in bold only; those possibilities further ruled out by the truth of *C* are shown in bold and italics. As we can see for ECC in (A) only one possibility is left, so R1 should be high, with $P(E1|B, C) = 1$. This is because this is simply a logically valid MP inference. Moreover, being then told that *E2* is the case, cannot change this probability as it is only true in the same possibility, i.e., for R2, $P(E1|B, C, E2) = 1$. So for ECC, ΔR should be zero and the ratings should be high, which is consistent with the data, $P(E1|B, C) = P(E1|B, C, E2) = .80$.

In (B), the possibilities ruled out by the truth of the conditional, *if C, then E1 and E2*, are in bold only; those possibilities further ruled out by the truth of *E* are in bold and italic; finally those possibilities additionally ruled out by the truth of *C2* are in bold and are underlined. From (B) for the CEC case, it is clear that $P(C1|B, E) = P(C1|B, E, C2) = .5$. So for CEC, ΔR should be zero and the ratings should be mid-range. However, consistent with our Bayesian analysis $P(C1|B, E) = .67 > P(C1|B, E, C2) = .49$.

For ECNC and CENC, we simply make the same calculations but without assuming the truth of the consequent of the original conditionals. For ECNC, in (A), the four possibilities in which *C* is false ($\neg C$) are also now possible true instances of the conditional, i.e., *B*, making 5 in all and *E1* is the true in three of these, so $P(E1|B) = .6$. Once *E2* can be assumed to be true, then only 3 possibilities remain and *E1* is true in two of these and so $P(E1|B, E2) = .67$. Consequently ΔR should be marginally greater than 0, which is consistent with the data: $P(E1|B) = .59 < P(E1|B, E2) = .73$.

For CENC, by similar reasoning, $P(C1|B) = .4$ and $P(C1|B, C2) = .5$, i.e., ΔR should be marginally greater than zero. This prediction is in the opposite direction to the data: $P(C1|B) = .58 > P(C1|B, C2) = .44$. In sum, this plausible mental models approach does not make the right predictions.

One might argue that without conversion mental models would fare better. However, without conversion the CE and EC cases would have to be treated identically as they are logically equivalent. Consequently, mental models would have to make the same predictions for both causal orders, which is not consistent with the highly significant main effect of causal order.

The idea that regardless of the order in the premises, people build a mental mechanism (Chater & Oaksford, 2006) consistent with the causal order, provides some motivation for why people may convert these premises. The converted conditional provides the most natural description of the directed mental representation of the premises B. Oaksford and Chater (this volume) also discuss how directed or ordered representations may emerge from interrogating a mental mechanism like a causal Bayes net. However, they used a constraint satisfaction neural network to implement the relations that conditionals may describe. Moreover, they explicitly include connections that build in knowledge of correlated causes (although not of correlated effects). This implementation raises the issue of how far a rational, computational level model can go in explaining causal conditional reasoning. This is because correlated causes violate the independence assumptions of causal Bayes nets (Pearl, 2000).

Of course, it has been a totally standard explanatory tool in cognitive science to appeal to the algorithmic or performance level to explain discrepancies with the computational/competence/rational level. This is the strategy pursued by Oaksford and Chater (this volume). The hypothesis we have explored here is that in human conditional reasoning, people build a mental mechanism (Chater & Oaksford, 2006) that is a dynamic representation of the dependencies described by a conditional which people can actively interrogate (see also Oaksford & Chater, this volume).

The relationship between causal and conditional reasoning

Besides our causal Bayes approach, there is also a related approach by Sloman and Lagnado (2005). These authors, however, argued that conditional reasoning differs in quality from causal reasoning, based on evidence showing that causal descriptions and corresponding conditional descriptions produced various systematic differences. In particular, conditional statements tended to produce weaker effects than causal statements. However, we believe there are several issues with Sloman and Lagnado's (2005) experiments, to do with an important element of Causal Bayes models, the distinction between structure and strength (Griffiths & Tenenbaum, 2005).

We believe that conditionals, 'if C then E', are structure building operators in the same way as 'C causes E', i.e., they suggest that some dependency exists between C and E. Different information about enablers, common causes or effects, will alter the local mental structure people build in working memory (Oaksford & Chater, this volume). However, to perform further inferences, the various parameters of these structures, or mental mechanisms (Chater & Oaksford, 2006), must be set from linguistic or environmental cues or from prior world knowledge. The mental structures built will be the same for causal and other dependencies, reflecting the idea in situation semantics (Barwise & Perry, 1983) that causal dependencies are regarded as the core meaning of the conditional. However, the parameters of these models, their strength, and whether additional machinery, perhaps to do with utilities, are needed will vary between different types of conditional sentences.

We argue that the differences between causal and conditional reasoning that Sloman and Lagnado (2005) observe are due to variations in strength but not in structure. We look at two cases. In their Experiment 1, a structure A → B → C is introduced concerning three billiard balls. This structure is described using causal terminology, e.g., Ball 1's (A) movement causes Ball 2 (B) to move, causal conditionals, e.g., If Ball 1 moves, then Ball 2 moves, or logical conditionals, which use the same conditionals but with the preamble, 'Someone is showing off her logical abilities. She is moving balls without breaking the following rules'. Participants are then told that there is an intervention on B which prevents it from moving, which should lead to the structure A→ B→ C. So if asked, 'Imagine that Ball 2 could not move, would Ball 1 still move?' participants should say 'Yes', but if asked, 'Imagine that Ball 2 could not move, would Ball 3 still move?' participants should say 'No'. For all three descriptions participants said that Ball 3 would not move but for the 'logical' conditionals about 45% said that Ball 1 would still move whereas 90% endorsed this statement for causal and causal conditional descriptions.

The only difference in the logical condition relates to the possible causes of Ball 1 moving. In the 'causal' cases, a causally open system is described where the normal causes of Ball 1 moving are in operation which should be unaffected by Ball 2 being prevented from moving. However, for the 'logical' case a closed system is described in which the only cause of balls moving and so of Ball 1 moving is an intentional action of the person showing off her logical abilities. With no knowledge of the rule governing whether she moves Ball 1, participants assume she moves it at random, i.e., the probability is approximately .5. So this is not an instance of people adopting a fundamentally different interpretation of conditional and causal statements. The 'logical' preamble simply changes the interpretation of the initiating causes of Ball 1 moving, from an open system to a closed system concerning the intentional actions of an agent.

Differences between causal and conditional reasoning in their Experiment 3 (Sloman & Lagnado, 2005, p.20) can also be explained by the difference between strength and structure:

> Germany's undue aggression has caused France to declare war. Germany's undue aggression has caused England to declare war. France's declaration causes Germany to declare war. England's declaration causes Germany to declare war. And so, Germany declares war.
>
> (1) If England had not declared war, would Germany have declared war?
> (2) If England had not declared war, would Germany have been aggressive?

Thus the causal statements categorically assert that Germany's undue aggression was the cause of France going to war. They are in the past tense describing events that have already occurred.

This is in contrast with the conditional statements, using materials like: 'if Germany is unduly aggressive, then France will declare war'. The consequent of the conditional statement is in the future tense describing an event that may happen in the future given the antecedent event occurs. The future is uncertain in a way that the past is not. Consequently these descriptions differ in strength but relate to the same causal structure. To compare like with like would involve using causal statements like 'Germany's undue aggression will cause France to declare war'. The difference in strength accounts fully for the lower endorsement of questions 1 and 2 for the conditional case. In sum, Sloman and Lagnado's (2005) data are entirely consistent with the present Causal Bayes approach to both conditional and causal reasoning.

Conclusions

This chapter has emphasized that patterns of verbal reasoning with conditionals may, in some cases, be understood in terms of causal, rather than logical, structure. Moreover, we have focused on a case in which the broad pattern of reasoning data observed is predicted by a normative theory of causal reasoning (Pearl, 2000). This approach may apply more generally: indeed, there has been a recent surge of interest in relating normative theories of causal reasoning to a wide range of cognitive phenomena, ranging from reasoning to learning, and aiming to capture the behaviour of participants including adults (Glymour, 2001; Sloman, 2005; Tenenbaum, & Griffiths, 2006) children (Gopnik et al., 2001, 2004) and rats (Daw, Courville, & Dayan, 2008; Waldmann, Cheng, Hagmayer, & Blaisdell, 2008). To pick a particularly elegant example, Blaisdell, Sawa, Leising, and Waldmann (2006) trained rats, in separate trials, to associate a light with either food or a tone. On hearing the tone they expected food; but when they pressed a bar to cause the tone, the tone elicited reduced expectation. Blaisdell et al.'s interpretation was that the rats had inferred that the light was a common cause of the food and tone, and hence that hearing the tone provided evidence that the food might also be present. But when the rat judged its own behaviour to have caused the observation of the food, this inference is blocked.

There is, though, also considerable interest in apparent departures of rational causal reasoning. For example, Quattrone and Tversky (1984) asked people to see how long they could hold their arms in cold water, with the cover story that tolerance was associated either with a healthy, or an unhealthy, heart. Those in the former condition tolerated the cold water for longer, suggesting that people tended to behave in a way that signals good, rather than bad, news about their health. But, of course, by manipulating a putative *effect* of the condition of their heart, they could not reasonably hope to influence the *cause* – i.e., the actual condition of their heart. Such apparent irrationality may be less stark, though, if we allow that people take account of the negative psychological impact of receiving 'bad news'. Thus, rather than test my endurance to the limit, possibly signalling bad news for my future health, I may not unreasonably choose to drop out early. The extent to which this and other apparent departures from normative standards of causal reasoning can be explained in rational terms, if we take a wider perspective on the reasoning problem, one that also includes the issue of reasoning in children and animals, is an interesting question for future research (cf. Hilton, 1990; McKenzie & Nelson, 2003).

References

Ali, N., Chater, N., & Oaksford, M. (2008). *Causal Interpretations Affect Conditional Reasoning*. Manuscript, Division of Psychology and Language Sciences, UCL.

Barwise, J. & Perry, J. (1983). *Situations and attitudes*. Cambridge, MA: MIT Press.

Braine, M. D. S. & Rumain, B. (1981). Development of Comprehension of 'Or': Evidence for a Sequence of Competencies. *Journal of Experimental Child Psychology*, **31**, 46–70.

Braine, M. D. S. & Rumain, B. (1983). Logical Reasoning. In J. Flavell and E. Markman (Eds.), *Handbook of Child Psychology: 3, Cognitive Development*, (pp. 261–340). New York: Academic Press.

Byrne, R. M. J., Espino, O., & Santamaria, C. (1999). Counterexamples and the suppression of inferences. *Journal of Memory and Language*, **40**, 347–373.

Byrne, R. M. J. (1989). Suppressing valid inferences with conditionals. *Cognition*, **39**, 71–78.

Blaisdell, A. P., Sawa, K., Leising, K. J., & Waldmann, M. R. (2006). Causal reasoning in rats. *Science*, **311**, 1020–1022.

Barouillet, P., Markovits, H., & Quinn, S. (2001). Developmental and content effects in reasoning with causal conditionals. *Journal of Experimental Child Psychology*, **81**, 235–248.

Chan, D. & Chua, F. (1994). Suppression of valid inferences: syntactic views, Mental Models, and relative salience, *Cognition*, **53**, 217–238.

Chater, N. & Oaksford, M. (2006). Mental mechanisms. In K. Fiedler, & P. Juslin (Eds.), *Information sampling and adaptive cognition* (pp. 210–236). Cambridge: Cambridge University Press.

Crain, S., Gualmini, A. & Meroni, L. (2000). The Acquisition of Logical Words, *LOGOS and Language*, **1**, 49–59.

Cummins, D. D., Lubart, T., Alsknis, O., & Rist, R. (1991). Conditional reasoning and causation. *Memory and Cognition*, **19**, 274–282.

Cummins, D. D. (1995). Naive theories and causal deduction. *Memory & Cognition*, **23**, 646–658.

Daw, N. D., Courville, A. C., & Dayan, P. (2008). Semi-rational models of conditioning: The case of trial order. In M. Oaksford & N. Chater (Eds.) *The Probabilistic Mind* (pp. 485–500). Oxford: Oxford University Press.

Glymour, C. (2001). *The mind's arrow: Bayes nets and graphical causal models*. Cambridge, MA: MIT Press.

Goldvarg, E. & Johnson-Laird, P. N. (2001). Naïve causality: A Mental Model theory of causal meaning and reasoning. *Cognitive science*, **25**, 565–610.

Gopnik, A., Sobel, D. M., Schulz, L. E., & Glymour, C. (2001). Causal Learning Mechanisms in Very Young Children: Two-, Three- and Four-Year-Olds Infer Causal Relations From Patterns of Variation and Covariation. *Developmental Psychology*, **37**, 620–629.

Gopnik, A., Glymour, C., Sobel, D. M., Schulz, L. E., Kushnir, T., & Danks, D. (2004). A theory of causal learning in children: Causal maps and Bayes nets. *Psychological Review*, **111**, 1–31.

Griffiths, T.L. & Tenenbaum, J.B. (2005). Structure and strength in causal induction. *Cognitive Psychology* **51**, 334–384.

Hilton, D. J. (1990). Conversational processes and causal explanation. *Psychological Bulletin*, **107**, 65–81.

Janveau-Brennan, G. & Markovits, H. (1999). The Development of reasoning with causal conditionals. *Developmental Psychology*, **35**, 904–911.

Johnson-Laird, P. N., Legrenzi, P., Girotto, V., Legrenzi, M. S., & Caverni, J. P. (1999). Naïve Probability: A mental model theory of extensional reasoning. *Psychological Review*, **106**, 62–88.

Liu, I., Lo, K. & Wu, J. (1996). A probabilistic interpretation of "If…Then." *The Quarterly Journal of Experimental Psychology*, **49A**, 828–844.

McKenzie, C. R. M. & Nelson, J. D. (2003). What a speaker's choice of frame reveals: Reference points, frame selection, and framing effects. *Psychonomic Bulletin and Review*, **10**, 596–602.

Oaksford, M. & Chater, N. (1998). *Rationality in an uncertain world*. Hove, England: Psychology Press.

Oaksford, M. & Chater, N. (2003). Computational levels and conditional reasoning: Reply to Schroyens and Schaeken. *Journal of Experimental Psychology: Learning, Memory & Cognition*, **29**, 150–156.

Oaksford, M. & Chater, N. (2008). Probability logic and the Modus Ponens-Modus Tollens asymmetry in conditional inference. In N. Chater, & M. Oaksford (Eds.), *The probabilistic mind: Prospects for Bayesian cognitive science* (pp. 97–120). Oxford: Oxford University Press.

Oaksford, M. & Chater, N. (this volume) Conditional Inference and Constraint Satisfaction: Reconciling Mental Models and the Probabilistic Approach? In M. Oaksford & N. Chater (Eds.), *Cognition and conditionals: Probability and logic in human thinking* (pp. 295–320). Oxford: Oxford University Press.

Oaksford, M., Chater, N., & Larkin, J. (2000). Probabilities and polarity biases in conditional inference. *Journal of Experimental Psychology: Learning, Memory and Cognition*, **26**, 883–899.

Pearl, J. (1988). *Probabilistic reasoning in intelligent systems*. San Mateo, CA: Morgan Kaufmann.

Pearl, J. (2000). *Causality: Models, reasoning, and inference*. Cambridge, UK: Cambridge University Press.

Quattrone, G. & Tversky, A. (1984). Causal versus diagnostic contingencies: On self-deception and on the voter's illusion. *Journal of Personality and Social Psychology*, **46**, 237–248.

Quinn, S. & Markovits, H. (1998). Conditional reasoning, causality, and the structure of semantic memory: Strength of association as a predictive factor for content effects. *Cognition*, **68**, 93–101.

Schroyens, W. & Schaeken, W. (2003). A critique of Oaksford, Chater and Larkin's (2000) conditional probability model of conditional reasoning. *Journal of Experimental Psychology: Learning, Memory and Cognition*, **29**, 140–149.

Schulz, L. E., Gopnik, A., & Glymour, C. (2007). *Developmental Science*, **10**, 322–332.

Sloman, S. A. (2005). *Causal models: How people think about the world and its alternatives*. Oxford: Oxford University Press.

Sloman, S. A. & Lagnado, D. A. (2005). Do we do? *Cognitive Science*, **29**, 5–39.

Sobel, D. M., Tenenbaum, J. S., & Gopnik, A. (2004). Children's causal inferences from indirect evidence: Backwards blocking and Bayesian reasoning in preschoolers. *Cognitive Science*, **28**, 303–333.

Tenenbaum, J. B., Griffiths, T. L., & Kemp, C. (2006). Theory-based Bayesian models of inductive learning and reasoning. *Trends in Cognitive Sciences*, **10**(7), 309–318.

Thompson, V. A. (1994). Interpretational factors in conditional reasoning. *Memory and Cognition*. **22**, 742–758.

Waldmann, M. R., Cheng, P. W., Hagmayer, Y., & Blaisdell, A. P. (2008). Causal learning in rats and humans: A minimal rational model. In M. Oaksford & N. Chater (Eds.) *The Probabilistic Mind* (pp. 453–484). Oxford: Oxford University Press.

Chapter 8

Conditionals and non-constructive reasoning

David E. Over, Jonathan St. B.T. Evans, and Shira Elqayam

Introduction

A key feature of human intelligence is the facility for *hypothetical thinking*. By this we mean the ability to run mental simulations by making suppositions and exploring their consequences. We engage in hypothetical thinking whenever we test hypotheses, evaluate the likely consequences of possible decisions, generate forecasts, or draw inferences from assumptions or beliefs (Evans, 2007). This is a very special ability that enables us, among other things, to generate imaginary scenarios, while at the same time de-coupling suppositions about the way things might be from actual beliefs about the way things are. Dual-process theorists have also argued that hypothetical thinking is a form of intelligence that is distinctively human (Evans & Over, 1996).

Indicative conditionals, 'if p then q', are found everywhere in natural language and ordinary discourse. There have been many psychological studies of such *ordinary conditionals* (see Evans & Over, 2004, for a review), but until recently, most have failed, in our opinion, to recognize the true *hypothetical* nature of the ordinary conditional and its significance in our mental life. The great majority have focussed on deductive reasoning from conditional statements and what logicians call *elimination* inferences. It would be hard to count the number of papers on just four elimination inferences from conditional premises: the two valid inferences, Modus Ponens (MP) and Modus Tollens (MT), and the two invalid inferences, Affirmation of the Consequent (AC) and Denial of the Antecedent (DA). To read all these papers with close attention may be beyond the ability of the most dedicated Ph.D student. In experiments on the four inferences, one has to decide whether a conclusion validly follows from the conditional, 'major' premise, 'if p then q', plus a categorical, 'minor' premise. In performing the inference, the conditional premise is said to be 'eliminated'. Consider a conditional about a psychology examination that will have only one question:

    (8.1)   If the question is not on learning, then it will be on perception.

Participants might be given (8.1) as the major premise and 'The question is not on learning' as the minor premise. The object would to see whether the participants inferred the conclusion, 'The question will be on perception'. MP is the logically valid inference of inferring this conclusion from the two premises.

The ordinary conditional of everyday natural language is *not* the material, truth functional conditional of extensional logic. The material conditional 'p $\supset$ q' is logically equivalent to the disjunction 'not-p or q', and the material conditional 'not-p $\supset$ q' is logically equivalent to the disjunction 'p or q'. For example, if the ordinary conditional (8.1) were a material conditional, (8.1) would mean exactly the same as the disjunction:

    (8.2)   The question will be on learning or it will be on perception.

But clearly (8.1) and (8.2) have different logical properties. The statement that the question will be on learning logically implies (8.2) but not the stronger ordinary conditional (8.1). To claim that a statement p logically implies an ordinary conditional 'if not-p then q' is indeed one of the intuitively unacceptable 'paradoxes' of treating the ordinary conditional as the material conditional (Bennett, 2003; Evans & Over, 2004). However, the ordinary conditional logically implies the material conditional, and MP and MT are logically valid, and AC and DA logically invalid, for both the ordinary and the material conditionals (Evans & Over, 2004). In fact, when studying only these four elimination inferences, psychologists are unable to separate ordinary from material conditionals. We hence propose a shift of focus to *introduction* inferences for the conditional. These inferences allow us to draw a conditional as a *conclusion*. Now we find some important differences between ordinary conditionals and material conditionals. As we have just pointed out, the material conditional (8.2), but not the ordinary conditional (8.1), can be introduced by inferring it from the statement that the question will be on learning.

There are few experiments on introduction inferences for conditionals in the psychology of reasoning. Psychologists who claim that there is a mental logic, rather than mental models, for reasoning have contributed the most to the study of introduction inferences in general (Braine & O'Brien, 1991, 1998; Rips, 1994; Rips & Marcus, 1977). But in this chapter, we will make a new departure by considering how the premise of an introduction inference has itself been derived. We will firstly consider inferring a conditional, 'if not-p then q', as a conclusion from a disjunction, 'p or q'. Under what conditions is this inference justified? Will people endorse this inference when it is justified and refuse to endorse it otherwise? We will argue secondly that the justification of this inference depends on how the premise 'p or q' has been justified. There are some experiments on inferring a conditional from a disjunction (Ormerod & Richardson, 2003), but they have not really questioned the justification of this inference, let alone investigated whether its justification depends on how the disjunction has itself been justified.

Let us ask how the disjunction (8.2) has been inferred, which is an important question on a little reflection. Imagine an occasion on which a speaker has asserted (8.2), and a hearer asks herself what she can infer from this assertion. To answer this question, the speaker would be interested to learn whether the only reason the speaker had for asserting (8.2) was that he believed:

(8.3)   The question will be on learning.

Of course, it would usually be pragmatically infelicitous for the speaker to assert (8.2), when the only reason he had for believing (8.2) was that he inferred it from (8.3). But even if it is misleading on pragmatic grounds, speakers sometimes do assert less than they believe. For example, the speaker and hearer may be students, and the speaker might have a reasonably confident, but still uncertain, belief that (8.3) is true, based on what he thinks he overheard the lecturer saying in an unguarded moment. The speaker might not wish to share his precise information with other students. He also has to balance the pragmatic requirement to be informative with that of speaking the truth (Grice, 1989), and he might decide to be cautious and to assert (8.2) as more likely to be true than (8.3). But no matter why the speaker asserts (8.2) rather than (8.3), our prediction is that the hearer would not be inclined to infer (8.1) from (8.2) if she suspected that the main reason the speaker had for asserting (8.2) was that he believed (8.3). To explain this prediction more fully, we must first review our theoretical position on ordinary conditionals of natural language, like (8.1).

The Ramsey test

In formal logic, the elimination inference for the conditional is called 'if-elimination' and is MP. The introduction inference for the conditional is simply called 'if-introduction' (or sometimes 'conditional proof'). In classical extensional logic, if-introduction is the rule that allows us to infer the material conditional 'p ⊃ q' when we have a classically valid proof of q from p. The material conditional is also called the 'truth functional conditional' or the 'extensional conditional': it is logically equivalent to 'not-p or q'. Some psychologists have rightly tried to modify extensional if-introduction for a mental logic that contains a conditional more like that of natural language (Braine & O'Brien, 1991; see Evans & Over, 2004, Ch. 4, for critical comment). But of course, most ordinary conditionals, 'if p then q', are not introduced by a logically valid proof, but rather as a result of causal, diagnostic, inductive, or heuristic inferences (compare Braine & O'Brien, 1991, p. 190). There has long been an influential proposal in philosophical logic for describing how people can introduce an ordinary conditional into their beliefs by means of these many types of inference: the *Ramsey test* (see Ramsey, 1931/1990). Rips and Marcus (1977) were the first psychologists to suggest a procedure like the Ramsey test for conditionals (followed by Braine & O'Brien, 1991). Stalnaker (1968) extended the Ramsey test, and we will adopt his version of it (see Evans & Over, 2004).

In a Ramsey test, people decide how much confidence to have in a conditional, 'if p then q', by supposing that p holds and making minimal changes to preserve coherence in their beliefs. They then judge how confident they are that q holds. This test ends in a *suppositional* conditional that expresses a degree of confidence in q given p, which is technically the conditional subjective probability of q given p. The Ramsey test can be compared to the simulation heuristic of Kahneman and Tversky (1982) applied to conditionals. We can call the test a 'simulation' in a technical sense, and sometimes the word can be used in its ordinary sense for the test. In either case, the conditional introduced by mental simulation or the Ramsey test is the kind that we call 'suppositional' (Evans & Over, 2004), rather than the material conditional 'p ⊃ q'. We have now amassed considerable evidence that people predominantly understand ordinary conditionals to be suppositional (Evans, Handley, Neilens, & Over, 2007; Evans, Handley, & Over, 2003; Handley, Evans, & Thompson, 2006; Over, Hadjichristidis, Evans, Handley, & Sloman, 2007) and have found none at all to support the view that they regard ordinary conditionals, of the form 'if p then q', as material or truth functional and so logically equivalent to 'not-p or q'. The suppositional conditional is used to expresses a degree of belief that q holds on the supposition of p. It is not truth functional and is stronger than merely asserting 'not-p or q'.

Our students may wish to make a judgement about how much confidence to have in (8.1) for an examination we have set. Using the Ramsey test, they will hypothetically suppose that the question will not be on learning, setting aside any beliefs they have that conflict with this supposition. They will then try to make a judgment about how much confidence to have in the conclusion that the question will be on perception. They may 'simulate', in an ordinary sense, our decision making processes given what they know about our interests. They might decide that our first interest is learning, with memory a close second and perception far down the list. This simulation would result in low confidence in (8.1), and they would not introduce (8.1) as a highly confident belief to use as a premise for further inferences. They would be unlikely to perform MP, with (8.1) as the major premise, when they learn that the examination question will not be on learning. People resist inferences from premises that they judge to be uncertain (as many studies stimulated by Byrne, 1991, have shown – see Evans & Over, 2004, Ch. 6, for a review.)

Other, lower level heuristics can be applied in a simulation, e.g., the availability heuristic (Kahneman and Tversky, 1982). But there is not yet a detailed account of the simulation heuristic. It and the Ramsey test cover a wide range of lower level mental processes. The Ramsey test can include logical or probabilistic inferences that would not be called 'simulations' in a non-technical sense. For example, a conditional with familiar content such as 'if Anne's pet is a dog then it barks' might be judged true by a rapid and non-reflective process that exploits a learnt association between dogs and barking. On the other hand, a conditional such as 'if there is life on Mars then there is life all across the universe' would require a good deal of explicit thinking and reasoning to evaluate. Psychologists might regard the first process as associative and the second as a mental simulation, but they are both simulations from a technical viewpoint. Much work has to be done to give a detailed account of all the mental processes that can occur in a Ramsey test.

It is clear, nevertheless, that the Ramsey test does have a far-reaching implication. Since the result of a Ramsey test is a suppositional conditional that expresses a conditional degree of belief, the test implies the *conditional probability hypothesis*: that people's subjective degree of belief in a conditional, P(if p then q), will equal their conditional subjective probability of q given p, P(q|p). We now know that the modal response is to assign the conditional probability as the probability of the conditional in a wide range of experiments on a number of different kinds of conditional. These include 'basic' indicative conditionals about simple frequency distributions, conditional bets, causal conditionals and related counterfactuals, and diagnostic conditionals (Evans et al., 2003; Evans et al., 2007; Evans, Handley, Hadjichristidis, Thompson, Over, & Bennett, 2007; Handley et al., 2006; Oberauer & Wilhelm, 2003; Over et al., 2007; Over & Evans, 2003; Politzer & Baratgin, 2006; Weidenfeld, Oberauer, & Hornig, 2005). People rarely, if ever, judge the probability of the ordinary conditional to be the probability of the material conditional, P(not-p or q). Girotto and Johnson-Laird (2004) report that people tend to interpret a question about the probability of a conditional as a request for the conditional probability, no matter how the question is framed. The conditional probability hypothesis can also be used to explain many results in the study of conditional reasoning (Hahn & Oaksford, 2007; Oaksford & Chater, 2007; Oaksford, Chater, & Larkin, 2000; Pfeifer & Kleiter, 2005, 2006).

Experimental evidence for the conditional probability hypothesis supports the Ramsey test. But as we have pointed out, much research is needed to understand the Ramsey test in detail. One supposes p in the test and tries to make minimal changes to preserve coherence, and then one tries to assess the degree to which q follows. Describing how people make minimal changes is itself a daunting problem. One difficulty is that, if we need to set aside a belief b in order to make the supposition, we must also set aside all other beliefs that depend on b. This may be simple, or very difficult to do. After a cricket captain loses the toss, he may say, 'If I had won the toss then I would have batted first'. To understand this we need only set aside the belief that he in fact lost the toss. But when someone asserts, 'If terrorists had not attacked New York then the USA would not have invaded Iraq', this is an extraordinarily difficult conditional to assess. The 9/11 attack had vast geopolitical implications. To undo this event in suppositional thought, we would have to set aside a huge number of things we believed about the world at the time of the Iraqi invasion. The use of a counterfactual like this one is hard to explain, but we will be concerned with indicative conditionals in what follows. Counterfactuals would be more problematic and call for much more discussion (Evans & Over, 2004, Ch. 7.)

There is the question of how people assess the *degree* to which q follows from p. People can sometimes try to represent many cases in which p holds and estimate the proportion in which q also holds (Evans et al., 2003). They may often try to construct a causal model linking p to q and estimate their subjective degree of belief in this causal link (Sloman, 2005). There are many other possibilities. The mental processes that implement Ramsey tests may well make up a 'baroque mishmash' (Oaksford, 2006) and take some considerable describing. We will make a start in this chapter by focussing on a relatively simple, but an important case: inferring a conditional from a disjunction. We will argue that the strength of this inference depends on how the disjunction has itself been justified as a premise.

Inferring a conditional from a disjunction

Before some students make a judgement about (8.1), they might acquire a high degree of belief in the disjunction we have already used as an example:

(8.2) The question will be on learning or it will be on perception.

A vital question is whether the students will give up their belief in (8.2) when they perform the Ramsey test on (8.1), as this would reflect on the outcome of the Ramsey test. This in turn depends on whether their belief in (8.2) depends on what is changed by the supposition in the Ramsey test or whether it holds independently. For example, they might have such a strong belief in (8.2), given their more general causal or epistemic beliefs, that they could apply a causal or epistemic 'must' to (8.2), making it of the form 'must-(p or q)'. In that case, when they supposed the antecedent of (8.1), 'the examination will not be on learning', for a Ramsey test, their minimal changes would not then affect their belief in (8.2). From 'p or q' and 'not-p', they could trivially infer q and come to have high confidence in (8.1) as a result of the Ramsey test. There could hardly be a simpler Ramsey test than this example. To account for the introduction of the conditional, we only have to explain how it is possible to infer q from 'p or q' and 'not-p', and a simple system of mental inference rules or mental models will do that. We will not, however, specify such a system, as we wish to make more general points in this chapter.

The crucial question is therefore whether the students *will* give up (8.2) when they come to suppose the antecedent of (8.1) for a Ramsey test. In our view, the answer to this question depends on *how* (8.2) has been justified as a belief or an assertion. Let us return to and extend our earlier example. There is a student speaker who asserts (8.2) because he has overheard the class lecturer apparently asserting (8.3) in an unguarded talk with another lecturer. It is a trivial (if sometimes pragmatically anomalous) inference that, if some proposition p holds, then any statement of the form 'p or q' holds. This is indeed the logically valid inference of or-introduction. In this inference form, we can say that 'p or q' has been inferred from 'below', meaning that it has been inferred from p. We can also note that the speaker can identify (if he wishes) which of p or q he believes to be true – the speaker in our example could simply assert (8.3), if he judged that to be all right pragmatically. In technical terms, the speaker has a *constructive* justification of (8.2) in this case (Dummett, 1978). We can say that 'p or q' is here 'constructed' from p – it is built up from p and has p as its support or foundation.

With this constructive justification of (8.2), the speaker will hypothetically set aside his belief in (8.2), when he performs a Ramsey test on (8.1). It would not be coherent to hang on to (8.2) under the supposition that the question will not be on learning, when the only basis for (8.2) is the belief that the question will be on learning. Suppose that the hearer has good reason to infer that the speaker has only a constructive justification for (8.2) - that the only grounds he has for asserting (8.2) is that he believes (8.3) strongly. Then the hearer will also set aside her belief in (8.2) when she performs a Ramsey test on (8.1). The result will be that neither the speaker nor the hearer will have any confidence in (8.1). Under the supposition that the examination question will not be on learning, and with (8.2) set side, there are no grounds for inferring that the question will be on perception. The result of this Ramsey would even be strong disbelieve in (8.1) when the lecturer's favourite topics were learning and memory with perception nowhere.

Now consider what is technically called a *non-constructive* justification of a disjunction (Dummett, 1978). We can say that this justification of 'p or q' is *not* constructed from 'below' on the foundation of p (or of q). In this kind of case, a speaker or hearer infers 'p or q' from 'above', from more general beliefs, and he or she cannot identify either p or q as what they believe. They believe only 'p or q' and cannot say more than that. To elaborate our example in a different way, suppose now that the speaker who asserts (8.2) inferred it from general knowledge of the lecturer, who has shown enthusiasm for learning and perception as subjects and boredom with other topics. The speaker has good reason, from 'above', for inferring that (8.2) is true, but cannot assert anything more definite than that. His justification is 'non-constructive' because it is suspended from 'above' by general reasons and does not rest on the foundation of a belief in (8.3). Let also suppose that the hearer knows that this is the speaker's justification for asserting (8.2). Now the speaker and hearer will be prepared to infer (8.1) from (8.2). For when they suppose in a Ramsey test that the question will not be on learning, they will *not* set (8.2) aside, but will continue to hold it because of the general reasons. These general reasons could even lead them to attach a 'must' to (8.2). With this level of confidence in (8.2), the minimal changes in the Ramsey test will not affect (8.2), and they will use (8.2), of the form 'p or q', and their supposition that the question will not be on learning, of the form 'not-p', to infer that it will be on perception, of the form q. Such a Ramsey test will thus give them high confidence in (8.1).

Non-constructive reasoning

We have just relied on the distinction between *constructive* and *non-constructive* reasoning and justification, as applied to a disjunction. In constructive reasoning about a disjunction, we introduce 'p or q' from 'below': we infer 'p or q' from p (or from q). In non-constructive reasoning about a disjunction, we infer 'p or q' from 'above', from more general principles or beliefs. Such an inference from above often allows us to use 'must' with the disjunction. Using non-constructive reasoning, we can be very highly confident in 'p or q', but often fail to have a highly confident belief in p or a highly confident belief in q.

Sometimes non-constructive reasoning is purely logical, and we will give an example of this type, which illustrates some basic points. The example comes from Toplak and Stanovich (2002), who made a systematic study of individual differences in disjunctive reasoning, inspired by Shafir's seminal paper on disjunctions (1994; they also refer to Levesque, 1989):

> There are five blocks in a stack, where the second one from the top is green and the
>
> fourth is not green. Is a green block directly on top a non-green block?
>
> A) Yes   B) No   C) Cannot tell

Most participants answer C), 'Cannot tell', even though the correct answer is A), 'Yes'. This problem requires difficult reflective reasoning of a type that dual-process theories call type 2 or System 2 (Saunders & Over, 2009). It also violates the singularity principle of hypothetical thinking theory (Evans, 2007). That is, people must grasp the relevance of making inferences from two possibilities, the alternatives of a green third block or a non-green third block. As Evans (2007) has shown with many examples, any explicit reasoning or decision task that requires people to make inferences from a disjunction of possibilities tends to be very hard to solve, as people can only run mental simulations one at a time. By contrast, notice how easy the problem would be if it we presented it constructively. In that case, we would show a stack of blocks to the participants. We would have had to arrange the stack so that the third block was green or, alternatively, not green. If the third block were green, the participants could use constructive inference from 'below', from perception of the stack, to answer the question. If the third stack were not green, the participants could again use constructive inference from perception to answer the question. The constructive reasoning in this version of the 'problem' is little more than perception itself.

Few participants solve the original problem in Toplak and Stanovich (2002) because that calls for non-constructive reasoning. This reasoning is more difficult than a simple inference direct from perception, but Toplak and Stanovich demonstrate, in a very interesting result, that people's tendency to engage in it is more associated with thinking style than cognitive ability. The participants must grasp for themselves the relevance of the logical law of the excluded middle: the third block must be either green or not green (Over, 2007a). The 'must' here is logical, and the participants who solve the problem reason from the highest logical level. The participants must use effortful System 2 processes to reason from 'above' by hypothetically supposing that the third block is green and consequently the answer is 'Yes', and then by covering the alternative by hypothetically supposing that the third block is not green and consequently the answer is again 'Yes'. Therefore, the participants reason, the answer must be 'Yes'. In pure mathematics, a constructive proof conveys more information than a non-constructive proof, and that holds generally for constructive and non-constructive reasoning (Dummett, 1978). Non-constructive reasoning does not allow the participants to identify the colour of the third block: it only allows them to infer that the answer is 'Yes' whatever the colour of the third block.

As we have already pointed out, non-constructive reasoning about ordinary affairs will often contain a weaker 'must' than the logical one, a causal or epistemic 'must'. We can find examples of this 'must' in standard murder mysteries about isolated country houses, or in board games about such mysteries, in which it is said that the butler or the maid, or one named character or another, *must* have committed the murder. We can also find this 'must' in historical studies of actual murder mysteries. After research in the archives, an historian might contend that George Chapman or Montague John Druitt *must* have committed the Whitechapel murders of 1888. This use of 'must' is sometimes based on deeply held beliefs about causation or space and time, e.g., these men were perhaps the only suspects in the locality when the murders took place. But it is worth being explicit that non-constructive reasoning can be irrational. For instance, a general prejudice against foreigners may have played a role in inferring that some men 'must' be treated as suspects in the Whitechapel case. Constructive inference and even perception itself can also be biased in various ways. The two types of reasoning or justification do not differ in the extent to which they can be rational or irrational, but constructive thought is generally the more informative. The Whitechapel murders would fascinate few people if the police had constructively identified George Chapman as the murderer by catching him in the act. Nevertheless, non-constructive reasoning can be very useful, if one is not lucky enough to have the more precise information from a constructive inference.

Still more generally, non-constructive reasoning does not always result in a conclusion of the form 'must-(p or q)', in which the probability of 'p or q', P(p or q), is 1 or near 1 given deeply held belief. Often P(p or q) is high but not taken to be close to 1 at the end of non-constructive reasoning, and we will consider an example of this type. But first let us make some points, at the computational level of analysis, about probability and logical validity. Tversky and Kahneman (1983) pointed out that the probability of a conjunction P(p & q) should not be greater than the probability of one of its conjuncts, P(p). This normative point depends on the fact that 'p & q' logically implies p. More generally, an inference with a single premise logically implies a conclusion if and only if the probability of the premise is not greater than the probability of the conclusion in *any* coherent probability assignment. We can use disjunction as well as conjunction to illustrate this definition: that p logically implies 'p or q' is logically equivalent to saying that, in all coherent probability assignments, P(p) is not greater than P(p or q). The necessary relation between logical validity and probability also extends to inferences with more than one premise. (See Adams, 1998, for the general account of logical validity in terms of probability, and Over, 2007b, on applications to psychological work on conditional reasoning.)

With this brief background, we can consider our example in which P(p or q) is less than 1. We might send our students off to do an assignment that they can probably complete only by using the library or the computer lab, which are in different parts of the university. We know that Anne is a conscientious student who will probably work hard on the assignment, and we infer non-constructively that she will probably be in the library or the computer lab. There is no chance, given what we know about the university, that she will be at both places, and we judge it equally likely that she is at one or the other. There is also a small chance that she can do the assignment without using either place or that she has decided uncharacteristically not to do it. Our probability judgements about where she is are:

P(library & lab) = 0

P(library & not-lab) = .45

P(not-library & lab) = .45

P(not-library & not-lab) = .1

Consider inferring 'if Anne is not in the library, then she is in the lab' from 'Anne is in the library or she is in the lab'. By the conditional probability hypothesis, the probability of the ordinary conditional is P(lab|not-library) = .45/(.45 + .1) = .82, and the probability of the disjunction is P(library or lab) = .9. This inference about Anne is not logically valid, as .9 is greater than .82, but we can say that it is quite a strong probabilistic inference. Many probabilistic strong inferences are not logically valid. Most scientific inferences are of this type. Our position is that inferring the conditional about Anne from the non-constructively justified disjunction is not logically valid, but is a strong probabilistic inference.

Compare an example in which we set no assignment, but look out the window and see a student who looks very like Anne entering the library. This observation gives us grounds for a constructive inference that she is in the library or in the lab. Our probability judgements about where Anne is are now:

P(library & lab) = 0

P(library & not-lab) = .9

P(not-library & lab) = .01

P(not-library & not-lab) = .09

Again consider inferring the conditional from the disjunction. By the conditional probability hypothesis, the probability of the conditional is now low at P(lab|not-library) = .01/(.01 + .09) = .1, but the probability of the disjunction is still high at P(library or lab) = .91. So inferring the conditional from the constructively justified disjunction is not just logically invalid: it is a very poor, weak probabilistic inference.

An elementary derivation in probability theory gives us the general relation between P(p or q) and P(q|not-p) in the equation:

$$P(p \text{ or } q) = P(p) + P(q|\text{not-}p) - P(p)P(q|\text{not-}p)$$

Inferring 'if not-p then q' from 'p or q' is not logically valid since P(p or q) can be higher than P(if not-p then q), given the conditional probability hypothesis. Moreover, P(p or q) can be much higher than P(if not-p then q) when the *only* reason that P(p or q) is high is that P(p) is high, and then the inference is probabilistically very weak. Notice that there is a constructive justification for 'p or q' when the only reason its subjective probability is high is that p has high subjective probability.

Pfeifer and Kleiter (2006) point out the importance, for the psychology of reasoning, of deriving probability intervals for inferences from the conditional probability hypothesis. We can do this, using the above equation, for inferring the conditional from the disjunction. Let P(p or q) be x. Then P(if not-p then q) will be in the interval [0, x]. Going the other way, let P(if not-p then q) be x. Now P(p or q) will be in the interval [x, 1]. We can also infer a point value for P(q|not-p) given both P(p or q) and P(p):

$$[P(p \text{ or } q) - P(p)]/P(not\text{-}p) = P(q|not\text{-}p)$$

With coherent probability judgements, P(if not-p then q) must be less than or equal to P(p or q), by the conditional probability hypothesis. This result in turn means that, although it is logically invalid to infer 'if not-p then q' (understood as the suppositional conditional) from 'p or q', it is logically valid to infer 'p or q' from 'if not-p then q'. Indeed it is logically valid to infer 'p or q' from 'if not-p then q' under in any acceptable interpretation of the ordinary conditional. When 'p or q' is false, 'not-p' is true and q false, and the ordinary conditional, 'if not-p then q', is false when its antecedent is true and its consequent false (Evans & Over, 2004). Therefore, inferring 'p or q' from 'if not-p then q' can never lead from truth to falsity. To repeat, the other direction, inferring 'if not-p then q' from 'p or q', is not logically valid, but can be probabilistic strong when the belief in 'p or q' itself results from non-constructive rather than constructive reasoning.

Our prediction about subjective degrees of belief is that, when people can make coherent probability judgements, their judgement of P(q|not-p) will be no greater than their judgement of P(p or q). However, to make a prediction about inferences in spoken or written language, rather than in belief, we must take account of pragmatic points. It would quite often be pragmatically misleading for speakers to assert 'p or q' when the only reason that they had confidence in 'p or q' was the constructive one that they had confidence in p (or q). People will infer 'p or q' from p at rates above chance although lower, for example, than typical rates for MT (Braine, Reiser, & Rumain, 1984; Rips, 1983, 1994; Rips & Conrad, 1983). The relatively lower rate for inferring 'p or q' from p is probably the result of pragmatic factors.

To assert 'p or q' merely on the basis of p can be pragmatically misleading. Speakers would usually tend to assert the stronger p (or q), when they can do so, rather than the weaker 'p or q', for otherwise they would violate Grice's maxim of quantity. There is also Grice's maxim of quality, which requires an assertion to be (probably) true. Speakers should balance these maxims (Grice, 1989), and that can mean that a speaker will sometimes assert 'p or q' when he believes p, as we noted above. However, when 'p or q' is used in an experiment, without any indication of how 'p or q' has been justified as a premise, the natural presupposition is that it is not known that p (or q) holds, for otherwise the stronger p (or q) would be given as a premise. We consequently predict that participants will be relatively confident in 'if not-p then q' when given only 'p or q' as a premise on its own. In contrast, we predict that participants will be relatively less confident in 'if not-p then q' when they can see that 'p or q' has been inferred constructively from p. (Compare Stalnaker, 1975, and Edgington, 2003, on inferring a conditional from a disjunction. Their positions are different from ours, but have influenced us.)

An alternative view

Johnson-Laird and Byrne (2002, p. 650) claim that given the premise, 'In a hand of cards, there is an ace or a king', it is valid to infer the conclusion, 'if there is not an ace in this hand of cards, then there is a king'. They add, 'Everyone to whom we have given this inference informally has accepted its validity'. Against Johnson-Laird and Byrne, we predict that people will often be more confident in P(p or q) than in P(if not-p then q), and they will judge P(if not-p then q) to be relatively low when 'p or q' is inferred from p before 'p or q' is used as a premise for inferring 'if not-p then q'.

Johnson-Laird and Byrne refer to research by Ormerod and his collaborators (see most recently Ormerod & Richardson, 2003). That research is interesting and relevant to our topic. But in it, pragmatic inference is not distinguished from logically valid inference, the probability judgements we have described are not investigated, and the possibility that 'p or q' was inferred from p, before it was used as a premise for inferring 'if not-p then q', is not considered. Only a highly irrational person would tend to believe 'p or q', or to assert 'p or q', without some justification, either from constructive or non-constructive reasoning. It is also a serious limitation in Johnson-Laird and Byrne's informal approach that they did not tell the people they questioned why 'p or q' was asserted as a premise. The people could only infer pragmatically that 'p or q' had not been derived from p, but depended on more general, non-constructive grounds.

We have pointed out above that, in all acceptable theories of the conditional, 'p or q' can be validly inferred from 'if not-p then q', and this holds in Johnson-Laird and Byrne's account as well. In *all* these theories, and not just Johnson-Laird and Byrne's, 'if not-p then q' is consistent with the 'p or q' possibilities, and 'if p then q' is consistent with the 'not-p or q' possibilities. But as we have just pointed out, Johnson-Laird and Byrne also incorrectly claim that 'if not-p then q' can be validly inferred from 'p or q'. Putting these points together, we see that Johnson-Laird and Byrne are logically committed to holding that the ordinary conditional, 'if not-p then q', is logically equivalent to 'p or q'. And by the double negation rule, making p and 'not-not-p' logically equivalent, they are logically committed to the following result: the ordinary conditional, 'if not-p then q', is logically equivalent to the truth functional or material conditional, 'p or q' (which is the same as 'not-p $\supset$ q'), and the ordinary conditional, 'if p then q', is logically equivalent to the truth functional conditional, 'not-p or q' (which is the same as 'p $\supset$ q'). Johnson-Laird and Byrne (2002) deny in places that their view of the ordinary conditional is truth functional, but as Evans, Over, and Handley (2005) have already demonstrated, other principles that they endorse, and the mental models they actually present, logically imply a truth functional account of the ordinary conditional (see also Evans & Over, 2004). In this section, we have noted yet another way in which claims they make lead logically to a truth functional account.

Johnson-Laird and Byrne (2002, p. 673) say that what they call semantic and pragmatic modulation can introduce non-truth functional relations, like temporal relations, into a conditional and other sentential forms, like disjunctions and conjunctions But this claim is not consistent with other principles that they endorse (Evans et al., 2005), and it is inconsistent with their statement (p. 647) that 'and' and 'or' sentences are truth functional. And it is inconsistent with their view of the relation between a disjunction and a conditional. The improbable conditional, 'if he does not smoke any longer, his health will get worse', might imply (semantically or pragmatically) a temporal relation between its antecedent and consequent, but for that very reason, we could not infer it from the disjunction, 'he is continuing to smoke or his health will get worse'. This disjunction could be highly probable merely because his health is very likely to get worse. Johnson-Laird and Byrne may claim that a disjunction can also assert a temporal relation between its components. We do not think that our disjunctive example states a temporal relation between someone's smoking and his health getting worse. But even if it did, it would not imply a temporal relation, expressed in the conditional, between his not smoking and his health getting worse.

The mental model theory of Johnson-Laird and Byrne (2002) is hard to interpret because some of the positions taken in the paper are inconsistent. However, they are very clear in claiming that everyone accepts the supposed validity of inferring 'if not-p then q' from 'p or q'. Our contrasting predictions are that people will sometimes judge P(if not-p then q) to be lower than P(p or q), and that they will find some instances of inferring 'if not-p then q' from 'p or q' weak inferences.

The experimental evidence on P(if not-p then q) and P(p or q)

We tested our hypothesis that people will sometimes estimate P(if not-p then q) to be less than P(p or q) in an experiment run by Eyvind Ohm at the University of Plymouth. In a variation on the method used in Evans et al. (2003), we presented 61 participants with information about distribution of a pack of cards bearing coloured shapes. For example:

A pack contains cards which are either blue or yellow and have either a triangle or a circle printed on them. In total there are:

10 blue triangles	(p & q)
40 blue circles	(p & not-q)
40 yellow triangles	(not-p & q)
10 yellow circles	(not-p & not-q)

How likely is the following claim to be true of a card drawn at random from the pack?

The card is either blue or has a triangle printed on it (p or q)
If the card is not blue, then it has a triangle printed on it (if not-p then q)

The rating scale ran from 1 (very unlikely) to 7 (very likely). Card frequencies for each truth table combination were set at either 10 or 40. We tested several linguistic forms, but will here only focus on results from the group of participants who evaluated the forms 'p or q' and 'if not-p then q' (n=30). The results are presented in Table 8.1. For every frequency distribution, estimates of P(p or q) were consistently higher than estimates of P(if not-p then q), supporting our hypothesis. Averaging across frequency distributions, we found that the mean estimate of P(p or q) was 5.1, considerably higher than the mean estimate of P(if not-p then q), which only amounted to 3.7 (t=11.6, p<.0001). Geiger, Oberauer, and Fischer (2006) presented similar results.

Tversky and Kahneman (1993) found that people sometimes commit the conjunction fallacy of judging P(p & q) to be greater than P(p), even though 'p & q' logically implies p. However, they also discovered that people tend not to commit this fallacy in transparent contexts in which they are given simple frequency distributions. (See Sloman & Over, 2003 and Stanovich & West, 1998 on the conjunction fallacy and transparent contexts.) The contexts we used in the above experiment were obviously transparent in this sense, and we see no reason at all to conclude that our participants are committing a fallacy in judging P(p or q) to be greater than P(if not-p then q). In fact, as the equations we gave above indicate, the conditional probability hypothesis implies that P(p or q) should be greater than or equal to P(if not-p then q).

An experimental test on inferring 'if not-p then q' from 'p or q'

We recently designed an experiment to test our prediction that inferring 'if not-p then q' from 'p or q' is a relatively strong inference when 'p or q' depends on non-constructive reasoning, and a relatively weak inference when 'p or q' is itself introduced by constructive reasoning. Recall our argument above that, when people are given 'p or q' as a premise on its own, they will assume pragmatically that it has a non-constructive justification and has not been inferred constructively from p. They will not make this assumption, of course, if they are shown that 'p or q' has itself been inferred from p. This experiment was run by Helen Neilens at the University of Plymouth. One group of participants (n = 33) were given the following problem:

CLAIM

There is an Ace in the hand or there is a King in the hand

Table 8.1 Mean probability estimates for P(p or q) vs. P(if not-p then q). SDs in parentheses

pq, p¬q, ¬pq, ¬p¬q	P(p or q)		P(if not-p then q)		t
10, 10, 10, 10	4.9	(1.2)	3.5	(1.0)	4.6*
40, 10, 10, 10	5.6	(1.0)	3.3	(1.3)	8.7*
10, 40, 10, 10	5.6	(1.2)	3.2	(1.2)	10.1*
10, 10, 40, 10	5.5	(1.2)	5.3	(1.0)	0.6
10, 10, 10, 40	3.4	(1.2)	2.5	(1.4)	2.8*
40, 40, 10, 10	5.6	(1.3)	3.4	(1.3)	6.7*
40, 10, 40, 10	5.8	(1.1)	5.1	(1.0)	2.7*
40, 10, 10, 40	4.5	(1.0)	2.4	(1.1)	7.2*
10, 40, 40, 10	5.4	(1.4)	5.0	(1.1)	1.1
10, 40, 10, 40	4.3	(1.1)	2.7	(1.2)	5.1*
10, 10, 40, 40	4.5	(1.1)	4.0	(0.9)	1.7
40, 40, 40, 10	6.1	(1.0)	4.9	(1.5)	4.9*
40, 40, 10, 40	4.9	(1.1)	2.4	(1.2)	7.7*
40, 10, 40, 40	5.4	(0.7)	4.1	(0.8)	5.8*
10, 40, 40, 40	4.6	(1.1)	4.0	(0.8)	2.2*
40, 40, 40, 40	5.1	(1.1)	4.0	(1.0)	5.7*
Mean across distributions	5.1	(0.6)	3.7	(0.4)	11.6*

Note: Starred comparisons are significant at p<.05 or higher, two-tail.

CONCLUSION

Therefore, if there is not an Ace in the hand then there is a King in the hand
How convincing is the conclusion (1 – 5)?

We take this to be the non-constructive case. Participants will assume there is a general reason to believe the disjunction that does not depend on a belief (denied by supposition in the Ramsey test) that there is an Ace in the hand. Hence we expected that people would rate the conclusion as highly convincing.

A second group (n = 30) were presented with the following version:

CLAIM

There is an Ace in the hand

ARGUMENT

There is an Ace in the hand or there is a King in the hand

CONCLUSION

Therefore, if there is not an Ace in the hand then there is a King in the hand
How convincing is the conclusion (1 – 5)?

In this constructive case, we have made it clear that the disjunction is a consequence of the belief that there is an Ace in the hand. This belief, and the disjunction that depends on it, should now be suspended by supposition that there is not an Ace in the hand, leading to much lower confidence in the conclusion. The results strongly supported our prediction. Mean ratings of convincingness were 4.04 (sd 1.35) for the first non-constructive case, but only 2.33 (sd 1.44) for the constructive case, a highly reliable difference (t = 4.80, p < .001). This very striking finding strongly supports our theory that people introduce ordinary conditionals using the Ramsey test. It also disconfirms the claim of Johnson-Laird and Byrne (2002, p. 650) that everyone accepts the 'validity' of inferring 'if not p then q' from 'p or q' for the ordinary conditional. People do not always accept this inference. Both this experiment and the previous one on judged probability imply that people will draw the inference in certain contexts, but only when it is pragmatically or probabilistically justified by their background beliefs.

Broader implications and conclusions

The questions discussed in this chapter do not concern some small technical points about logic, but rather matters of profound importance for the way in which we should view and attempt to understand human reasoning. Many researchers on human reasoning have long presupposed a deduction paradigm, in which the normative standard for inferences in natural language has often been elementary extensional logic. They have labelled 'illusory' inferences that do not conform to extensional logic (Johnson-Laird & Savary, 1999), and have endorsed inferences that do comply with it but which are logically invalid for the ordinary conditional (Johnson-Laird & Byrne, 2002). They have viewed conditional reasoning as a process of moving from conditionals to specific conclusions and tended to ignore introduction inferences. But not even logicians have restricted themselves to elimination inferences; they have also stated rules for introduction inferences. Still less should psychologists appear indifferent to where conditionals come from. We should now start to investigate the different justifications people can have for the premises that they assert or believe. These justifications can affect, as we hope to have demonstrated, what they will infer from the premises in conditional reasoning.

There has been an obsession with the conclusions that can be drawn once a conditional is assumed, and a near total disregard for the conditions under which conditional beliefs can be introduced. (There is a gap between early proposals on conditional introduction in Braine & O'Brien, 1991, Rips, 1994, and Rips & Marcus, 1977, and more recent work on the Ramsey test in Evans & Over, 2004 and Oaksford & Chater, 2007). One result of this attitude has been the failure until recently for most researchers to realize the significance of (or even be aware of the existence of) the 'paradoxes' of the material conditional. Because a material conditional means the same as 'not-p or q', it can be introduced whenever we know merely that 'not-p' holds or that q holds. Some psychologists have explicitly endorsed the 'validity' of these introduction inferences for the ordinary conditional (Johnson-Laird & Byrne, 2002, p. 651), which logically imply that this conditional is truth functional (Evans & Over, 2004, pp. 66-67). The result is that such inferences as the following are supposedly 'valid':

Jane does not smoke. So if she smokes, her health will improve.

Jack's cough will get worse. So if he gives up smoking, his cough will get worse.

The above inferences are intuitively absurd, and the Ramsey test explains why (Bennett, 2003; Evans & Over, 2004). We may believe that Jane is a healthy person who does not smoke, but under the supposition she does smoke, we are most definitely not confident that her health will improve. We may believe that Jack is a smoker whose cough will get worse, but supposing he gives up, we are confident that it will get better. The above inferences are logically valid for the material conditional, but are logically invalid for the ordinary conditional, as it is suppositional and introduced by the Ramsey test.

We like the term *suppositional* conditional because it suggests how closely this form is linked with our capacity for hypothetical thinking. We use hypothetical thought to introduce the ordinary conditional into our beliefs and our discourse. We commonly do this when engaged in decision making as in:

If we go out this evening, we will have to get up early to finish the work

If we work this evening, we can sleep late tomorrow morning

These are examples of suppositional conditionals that we quite naturally introduce into our belief system as a reflection of mental simulation and hypothetical thought. And of course, they facilitate our decision making. Is the pleasure of going out tonight, worth the pain of getting up early in the morning?

In this chapter, we have focussed on a very specific case: reasoning from 'p or q' to 'if not p then q'. However, it is an important test case and one to which some precise arguments can be applied. If this were a valid inference, as Johnson-Laird and Byrne (2002, p. 650) claim, then the ordinary conditional would be the material conditional. But of course it is not logically valid, and the ordinary conditional is suppositional. Our experimental evidence strongly supports our arguments. The first experiment above was on transparent contexts, and the judged probability of 'if not-p then q' there was consistently lower than the judged probability of 'p or q' (Table 8.1). This result in itself shows that the inference cannot be logically valid for the ordinary conditional, for the reasons we gave earlier. If we were obsessed by the deduction paradigm, that would be the end of our story. But logically invalid inferences can be probabilistically strong, and we have specified conditions under which inferring 'if not-p then q' from 'p or q' is probabilistically strong. The inference has this quality when 'p or q' is justified non-constructively but not when it is justified constructively. This prediction was confirmed in our second experiment above.

We have made much of the distinction between constructive or 'bottom-up' reasoning and non-constructive or 'top-down' reasoning. Non-constructive reasoning can lead to a disjunction 'p or q' that expresses genuine uncertainty: we are confident that 'p or q' holds but are not confident that p holds and not confident that q holds. The classic pattern associated with the difficulty of disjunctive reasoning (Evans, 2007; Shafir, 1994) critically depends on the disjunction being non-constructive. In the terminology of hypothetical thinking theory (Evans, 2006, 2007), it is mainly non-constructive disjunctions that violate the principle of singularity, as can be seen in the Toplak and Stanovich (2002) task described above. The same goes for a very wide range of disjunction effects, from Bruner's (Bruner, Goodnow, & Austin, 1956) findings that disjunctive concepts are more difficult to acquire, through Wason's THOG problem (Wason & Brooks, 1979), to Tversky and Shafir's (1992) Hawaii vacation and two-step gambles – all of these can be considered cases of non-constructive disjunctions.

In many ordinary contexts, people tend to interpret disjunctions non-constructively by default, due to Gricean considerations. We propose that participants in our second experiment made this default assumption in the non-constructive case, making the inference to 'if not-p then q' from 'p or q' pragmatically justified. But in the constructive case, where people believe 'p or q' only because they believe p, the inference is unjustified. Now in a Ramsey test on 'if not-p then q', people have to set aside the belief in p and with it the belief in 'p or q' when that depends only on p. Again, we have shown experimentally that when such a case is made fully explicit to the participants, their confidence in the inference drops markedly. To our knowledge, this is the first clear experimental demonstration of the psychological reality of the Ramsey test (as extended by Stalnaker, 1968). The result demonstrates that people will set aside a specified belief when they make a supposition to evaluate a conditional.

It should be a basic requirement of an account of the ordinary conditional that it explains how this conditional is introduced into beliefs and discourse. Mental model theory (Johnson-Laird & Byrne, 2002) has long failed to satisfy this requirement for every type of ordinary conditional, from the indicative to the deontic and counterfactual (Evans & Over, 2004). Theories of mental logic (beginning with Rips & Marcus, 1977) have done much better in this respect, but our position is that the requirement can only be fully met by a theory of hypothetical thinking and the Ramsey test. Engaging in a Ramsey test, we must sometimes hypothetically set aside some of our beliefs. When considering a conditional 'if not-p then q', and supposing 'not-p' in a Ramsey test, we must suspend a belief in 'p or q' that has been introduced on the basis of a belief in p. More generally, we propose the following as a principle that underlies the Ramsey test. When the only reason people have for a belief b2 is that they have inferred b2 from another belief b1, a supposition that requires them to set aside b1 also requires them to suspend b2. One implication of this proposal is that is it necessary to investigate sequences of inferences in the study of conditional reasoning. As we have illustrated in this chapter, we cannot profitably study when 'if not-p then q' is inferred from the premise 'p or q' without asking how 'p or q' has itself been inferred, whether constructively or non-constructively. We must study sequences of inferences more generally and in the Ramsey test to understand the nature of the ordinary conditional. We strongly recommend that researchers now shift their attention away from the study of if-elimination inferences (which have been done to death) and towards the study of how conditionals are inferred as a result of sequences of inferences. This should provide a rich new paradigm for study of belief-formation, hypothetical thinking, reasoning, and decision making.

Acknowledgements

The research reported in this chapter was partly supported by an ESRC Research Grant awarded to the authors, RES-000-22-1432. We should like to thank Nick Chater, Sonja Geiger, Simon Handley, Gernot Kleiter, Klaus Oberauer, David O'Brien, Niki Pfeifer, and Steven Sloman for helpful comment and discussion.

References

Adams, E. (1998). *A primer of probability logic*. Stanford: CLSI publications.

Bennett, J. (2003). *A philosophical guide to conditionals*. Oxford: Oxford University Press.

Braine, M. D. S. & O'Brien, D. P. (1991). A theory of If: A lexical entry, reasoning program, and pragmatic principles. *Psychological Review*, **98**, 182–203.

Braine, M. D. S. & O'Brien, D. P. (1998). (Eds). *Mental logic*. Mahwah, NJ: Lawrence Erlbaum Associates.

Braine, M. D. S., Reiser, B. J., & Rumain, B. (1984). Some empirical justification for a theory of natural propositional reasoning. *Psychology of Learning and Motivation*, **18**, 313–337.

Bruner, J. S., Goodnow, J. J., & Austin, G. A. (1956). *A Study of Thinking*. New York: Wiley.

Byrne, R. M. J. (1989). Suppressing valid inferences with conditionals. *Cognition*, **31**, 61–83.

Dummett, M. (1978). *Truth and other enigmas*. London: Duckworth.

Edgington, D. (2003). What if? Questions about conditionals *Mind and Language*, **18**, 380–401.

Evans, J. St.B. T. & Over, D. E. (1996). *Rationality and reasoning*. Hove: Psychology Press.

Evans, J. St.B. T. (2006). The heuristic-analytic theory of reasoning: Extension and evaluation. *Psychonomic Bulletin & Review*, **13**, 378–395.

Evans, J. St.B. T. (2007). *Hypothetical thinking: Dual process in reasoning and judgement*. Hove, UK: Psychology Press.

Evans, J. St.B. T. & Over, D. E. (2004). *If*. Oxford: Oxford University Press.

Evans, J. St.B. T., Handley, S. J., Hadjchristidis, C., Thompson, V. A. Over, D. E., & Bennett, S. (2007). On the basis of belief in causal and diagnostic conditionals. *Quarterly Journal of Experimental Psychology*, **60**, 635–643.

Evans, J. St.B. T., Handley, S. J., & Over, D. E. (2003). Conditionals and conditional probability. *Journal of Experimental Psychology: Learning, Memory and Cognition*, **29**, 321–355.

Evans, J. St.B. T., Handley, S. J., Neilens, H., & Over, D. E. (2007). Thinking about conditionals: A study of individual differences. *Memory and Cognition*, **35**, 1759–1771.

Evans, J. St.B. T., Over, D. E., & Handley, S. J. (2005). Supposition, extensionality and conditionals: A critique of Johnson-Laird & Byrne (2002). *Psychological Review*, **112**, 1040–1052.

Geiger, S. M., Oberauer, K., & Fischer, K. (2006). On the representation of conditionals and disjunctions: Are disjunctions represented truth functionally and conditionals not? Talk presented at the Cognitive Section Annual Conference, British Psychological Society, Lancaster University, 6–8 September 2006.

Girotto, V. & Johnson-Laird, P. N. (2004). The probability of conditionals. *Psychologia*, **47**, 207–225.

Grice, P. (1989). *Studies in the way of words*. Cambridge, MA: Harvard University Press.

Hadjichristidis, C., Stevenson, R. J., Over, D. E., Sloman, S. A., Evans, J. St.B. T., & Feeney, A. (2001). On the evaluation of *If p then q* conditionals. In *Proceedings of the 23rd Annual Meeting of the Cognitive Science Society*, Edinburgh.

Hahn, U. & Oaksford, M. (2007). The rationality of informal argumentation: A Bayesian approach to reasoning fallacies. *Psychological Review*, **114**, 704–732.

Handley, S., Evans, J. St.B. T., & Thompson, V. A. (2006). The negated conditional: A litmus test for the suppositional conditional? *Journal of Experimental Psychology: Learning, memory, and cognition*, **32**, 559–569.

Johnson-Laird, P. N. & Byrne, R. M. J. (2002). Conditionals: A theory of meaning, pragmatics and inference. *Psychological Review*, **109**, 646–678.

Johnson-Laird, P. N. & Savary, F. (1999). Illusory inference: A novel class of erroneous deductions. *Cognition*, **71**, 191–299.

Kahneman, D. & Tversky, A. (1982). The simulation heuristic. In D. Kaheman, P. Slovic, & A. Tversky (Eds.), *Judgment under uncertainty: Heuristics and biases* (pp. 201–210). Cambridge: Cambridge University Press.

Levesque, H. J. (1989). Logic and the complexity of reasoning. In R. H. Thomason (Ed.), *Philosophical logic and artificial intelligence* (pp. 73–107). Dordrecht, The Netherlands: Kluwer Academic Publishers.

Oaksford, M. (2006). Making connections in conditional inference. *American Journal of Psychology*, **119**, 161–167.

Oaksford, M. & Chater, N. (2001). The probabilistic approach to human reasoning. *Trends in Cognitive Sciences*, **5**, 349–357.

Oaksford, M., Chater, N. & Larkin, J. (2000). Probabilities and polarity biases in conditional inference. *Journal of Experimental Psychology: Learning, Memory and Cognition*, **26**, 883–889.

Oberauer, K. & Wilhelm, O. (2003). The meaning(s) of conditionals: Conditional probabilities, mental models and personal utilities. *Journal of Experimental Psychology: Learning, Memory and Cognition*, **29**, 688–693.

Ormerod, T. C. & Richardson, H. (2003). On the generation and evaluation of inferences from single premises. *Memory and Cognition*, **31**, 467–478.

Over, D. E. (2007a). The logic of natural sampling. *Behavioral and Brain Sciences*, **30**, 277.

Over, D. E. (2007b). Content-independent conditional inference. In M. J. Roberts (Ed.), *Integrating the mind*. Hove: Psychology Press.

Over, D. E. & Evans, J. St.B. T. (2003). The probability of conditionals: The psychological evidence. *Mind & Language*, **18**, 340–358.

Over, D. E., Hadjichristidis, C., Evans, J. St.B. T., Handley, S. J., & Sloman, S. A. (2007). The probability of causal conditionals. *Cognitive Psychology*, **54**, 62–97.

Pfeifer, N. & Kleiter, G. D. (2005). Coherence and nonmonotonicity in human reasoning. *Synthese*, **146**, 93–109.

Pfeifer, N. & Kleiter, G. D. (2006). Inference in conditional probability logic. *Kybernetika*, **42**, 391–404.

Politzer, G. & Baratgin, J. (2006). What is the chance of winning (or losing) a conditional bet? Brief Technical Report, Institut Jean-Nicod. http://jeannicod.ccsd.cnrs.fr/aut/Guy+Politzer/

Ramsey, F. P. (1990). General propositions and causality (original publication, 1931). In D. H. Mellor (Ed.), *Philosophical papers* (pp. 145–163). Cambridge: Cambridge University Press.

Rips, L. J. (1983). Cognitive Processes in Propositional Reasoning, *Psychological Review*, **90**, 38–71.

Rips, L. J. (1994). *Psychology of proof*. Cambridge, MA: MIT Press.

Rips, L. J. & Conrad, F. G. (1983). Individual differences in deduction. *Cognition and Brain Theory*, **6**, 259–85.

Rips, L. J. & Marcus, S. L. (1977). Suppositions and the analysis of conditional sentences. In M. A.Just & P. A. Carpenter (Eds.), *Cognitive Processes in Comprehension* (pp. 185–219). New York: Wiley.

Saunders, C. & Over, D. E. (2009). In two minds about rationality? In J. St.B. T. Evans & K. Frankish (Eds.), *In two minds*. Oxford: Oxford University Press.

Shafir, E. (1994). Uncertainty and the difficulty of thinking through disjunctions. *Cognition*, **50**, 403–430.

Sloman, S. A. (2005). *Causal models: How people think about the world and its alternatives*. New York: Oxford University Press.

Sloman, S. A. & Over, D. E. (2003). Probability judgment from the inside and out. In D. E. Over (Ed.), *Evolution and the psychology of thinking: The debate* (pp. 145–169). Hove, UK: Psychology Press.

Stalnaker, R. (1968). A theory of conditionals. *American Philosophical Quarterly Monograph Series*, **2**, 98–112.

Stalnaker, R. (1975). Indicative conditionals. *Philosophia*, **5**, 269–286.

Stanovich, K. E. & West, R. F. (1998). Individual differences in framing and conjunction effects. *Thinking and Reasoning*, **4**, 289–317.

Toplak, M. E. & Stanovich, K. E. (2002). The domain specificity and generality of disjunctive reasoning: Searching for a generalizable critical thinking skill. *Journal of Educational Psychology*, **94**, 197–209.

Tversky, A. & Kahneman, D. (1973). Availability: A heuristic for judging frequency and probability. *Cognitive Psychology*, **5**, 207–232.

Tversky, A. & Kahneman, D. (1983). Extensional versus. Intuitive reasoning: The conjunction fallacy in probability judgment. *Psychological Review*, **90**, 293–315.

Tversky, A. & Shafir, E. (1992). The disjunction effect in choice under uncertainty. *Psychological Science*, **3**, 305–309.

Wason, P. C. & Brooks, P. G. (1979). THOG: The anatomy of a problem. *Psychological Research*, **41**, 79–90.

Weidenfeld, A., Oberauer, K., & Horning, R. (2005). Causal and non-causal conditionals: An integrated model of interpretation and reasoning. *Quarterly Journal of Experimental Psychology*, **58**, 1479–1513.

Chapter 9

The conditional in mental probability logic

Niki Pfeifer and Gernot D. Kleiter

Introduction

Since Störring's (1908) pioneering experiments on syllogistic reasoning at the beginning of the last century, experimental psychology has investigated deductive reasoning in the framework of classical logic. The most prominent examples are the theories of mental models (Johnson-Laird, 1983) and mental rules (Braine, 1998; Rips, 1994). A fragment of the model theory of classical logic is central to mental models. Likewise, a fragment of the proof theory of classical logic is central to mental rules. In this tradition, classical logic is considered as the 'surest guide' towards a competence model for the psychology of reasoning (Macnamara, 1986). Classical logic did not only guide the psychological theories, it also determined the experimental methodology and the evaluation of human performance.

In the last decade the situation has changed. At present, approaches that extend or go beyond classical logic introduce new frameworks in the field. Examples are nonmonotonic reasoning, possibility theory (Benferhat, Bonnefon, & Da Silva Neves, 2005) logic programming (Stenning & van Lambalgen, 2004, 2010), probabilistic approaches (Chater & Oaksford, 1999; Evans, Handley, & Over, 2003; Liu, 2003; Lu, Lo, &Wu, 1996; Oaksford & Chater, 1991, 2002, 2007; Oberauer & Wilhelm, 2003; Over & Evans, 2003; Over, Hadjichristides, Evans, Handley, & Sloman, 2007).

The present chapter describes a probabilistic framework of human reasoning. It is based on probability logic. While there are several approaches to probability logic, we adopt the *coherence* based approach (Coletti & Scozzafava, 2002; Gilio, 2002). We assume that rules similar to the principles of probability logic are basic rules of the human inference engine. We therefore call our approach 'mental probability logic' (Pfeifer & Kleiter, 2005b, 2009). Conditionals are of special importance in the approach. Their interpretation is different from the interpretation in other approaches. We conceive conditionals as non-truth functional, as uncertain, and as nonmonotonic. They allow for exceptions. Below, we call such conditionals 'nonmonotonic conditionals'. We note that causal, counterfactual, deontic, or pragmatic conditionals (see Bonnefon & Politzer, 2010) are not in the scope of this chapter, because their logical forms require formalisms that go beyond the scope of the present framework. Causal conditionals require logical operators for intervention, counterfactuals and deontic conditionals require possible worlds semantics, and pragmatic conditionals require a theory of the context of their uttering.

Many investigations on cognitive processes report errors, fallacies, or biases. Well known are perceptual illusions, biases in judgment under uncertainty, or errors in deductive reasoning. While these phenomena may be startling and stimulating in the scientific process, they do not lead to theories that explain human performance in a *systematic* way. Collecting slips of the tongue does not lead to a theory of speaking. Such phenomena should be integrated in a systematic theory and not studied in isolation.

Psycholinguists distinguish performance and competence (Chomsky, 1965). Competence describes what functions a cognitive system can compute (Marr, 1982; Oaksford & Chater, 1991). Human reasoning can solve complex problems and perform sophisticated inferences. When developing a theory of reasoning, one should have an explanation of these processes in mind. Such an explanation requires a competence theory on the computational level. In the long run, we want to develop a psychological theory that accounts for both competence and performance. At the competence level, a systematic formal theory is required. The formal theory provides the rationality standards and provides tools for computational descriptions of the human reasoning competency. At the performance level, a specification of the cognitive representations and processes is required. The explanation of typical reasoning, good and bad inferences requires a theory of how representations are formed and manipulated.

On the competence level, classical logic provided a rich systematic framework. Nonmonotonic reasoning systems, like SYSTEM P, (Kraus, Lehmann, & Magidor, 1990; Adams, 1975; Gilio, 2002) provide a more promising framework. For several reasons classical logic alone is a Procrustean framework (Oaksford & Chater, 1991, 2007; Pfeifer & Kleiter, 2005a, 2006a). The two most important reasons are the monotonicity property (i) and the IF–THEN relation (ii).

(i) Monotonicity is a meta-property of classical logic. It states that adding premises to a valid argument can only increase the set of conclusions. Monotonicity does not allow to retract conclusions in the light of new evidence. In everyday life, however, we often retract conclusions when we face new evidence. Moreover, experiments on the suppression of conditional inferences show that human subjects withdraw conclusions when new evidence is presented (Bonnefon & Hilton, 2002, 2004; Byrne, 1989; Byrne, Espino, & Santamaria, 1999; Dieussaert, De Neys, & Schaeken, 2005; Politzer, 2005). Thus, the monotonicity principle is psychologically implausible. We discuss a coherence based semantic for non-monotonic reasoning and empirical results below.

(ii) The conditional in classical logic is the *material conditional*. Table 9.1 lists its truth conditions. The material conditional, $A \supset B$, is true if, and only if, it is not the case that the *antecedent*, A, is true and the *consequent*, B, is false.

While the material conditional is extremely useful in formal fields like mathematics (derivations, proofs), it has severe drawbacks in the formalization of common sense conditionals. In common sense reasoning, conditionals are inherently uncertain, as they hold only 'probably', 'normally', or 'usually'. A few exceptions do not invalidate the conditional. Nonmonotonic conditionals express uncertain relations between the IF and the THEN part of a conditional assertion. The nonmonotonic conditional is interpreted as a 'high' conditional probability assertion,

Table 9.1 Truth table of the material conditional, and the betting interpretation of the conditional event, $B|A$. "A" and "B" denote propositions. "t" and "f" denote "true" and "false", respectively

State of world		Material conditional	Betting interpretation
A	**B**	$A \supset B$	$B|A$
t	t	t	win
t	f	f	lose
f	t	t	money back
f	f	t	money back

If A normally B if, and only if,

the probability of B given A, P(B|A), is 'high'.

Here, the probability function, $P(\cdot)$, is a one-place function and the conditional event, $B|A$, is its argument. The conditional event, $B|A$, is distinct from the material conditional of logic, $A \supset B$. In the following paragraphs we argue why the core of the IF–THEN corresponds to the conditional event and why it does not correspond to the material conditional.

The material conditional leads to counterintuitive consequences, known as the paradoxes of the material conditional. Recent empirical data suggests, that people do not endorse the paradoxes of the material conditional (Pfeifer & Kleiter, in press). Below, we discuss an empirical study on one of these paradoxes (PREMISE STRENGTHENING[1]). We do not want to import the paradoxes of the material conditional into the mental probability logic. This is one reason why we interpret the non-probabilistic conditional as a conditional event, $B|A$ (Adams, 1975; Pfeifer & Kleiter, 2003, 2006a, 2009). The paradoxes arise because of the truth-functionality of the material conditional, which will be discussed in the next paragraph.

The truth value of the material conditional is determined for all four possible combinations of truth values of the antecedent and the consequent (see Table 9.1). Therefore, the material conditional is truth functional. In the long history of logic,[2] the truth functionality of the material conditional was criticized several times, especially for those cases in which the antecedent is false. It is counter to intuition to call a conditional true if its antecedent is false. PREMISE STRENGTHENING, for example, is logically valid because (per definition) the material conditional is true if its antecedent is false. Ramsey (Ramsey, 1926) and de Finetti (de Finetti 1937, 1974) pointed out that the truth value of the conditional event, $B|A$, is *indeterminate* if the conditioning event, A, is false. In a betting interpretation this corresponds to the case in which a bet is annulled if the conditioning event does not happen. If you bet, for example, that

team X wins

on the condition that

team X plays against team Y,

then the stakes are payed back in the case that the game is cancelled (*team X does not play against team Y*; see Table 9.1). If the conditioning event does not happen, the conditional event is not true. The conditional event is indeterminate if the conditioning event is false. Thus, the vertical stroke | in the conditional event is not truth functional. Therefore, the paradoxes of the material conditional do not arise.

The conditional event is a *genuine* conditional. It cannot be constructed by Boolean operators like negation ($\neg$, 'not'), disjunction ($\vee$, 'or'), or conjunction ($\wedge$, 'and'). The material conditional, however, is not a genuine conditional. The definition of the material conditional depends upon which Boolean operator is considered to be basic. $A \supset B$ can be defined, for example, by negation

---

[1] PREMISE STRENGTHENING is an argument with one premise and one conclusion: *from $A \supset B$ infer $(A \wedge C) \supset B$.* Can the conditional in the conclusion be false if the premise is true? If $A \wedge C$ is false, then the conditional is true (because false antecedents make the material conditional true). If $A \wedge C$ is true, the conditional is true (because of the premise). Thus, it cannot be the case that the premise is true and the conclusion is false at the same time. Therefore, PREMISE STRENGTHENING is logically valid.

[2] The roots of the material conditional go back to Philon of Megara. He lived around the 4th and 3rd century BC (Kneale, 1984).

and disjunction, negated conjunction, or by intuitively indigestible definientia.[3] None of these definientia are conditionals, but they are logically equivalent to the material conditional. A genuine conditional (like the nonmonotonic conditional) cannot be expressed by something that goes completely beyond IF–THEN formulations. Therefore, we prefer genuine conditionals to nongenuine conditionals.

We see that the conditional probability interpretation of nonmonotonic conditionals has at least three theoretical advantages compared with the material conditional interpretation: (i) *probability* accounts for uncertainty and nonmonotonicity, (ii) *conditional events* are genuine conditionals and (iii) conditional events are free of the paradoxes of the material conditional. What is the empirical status of the conditional probability interpretation? The next section gives a brief overview on recent probabilistic approaches to human conditional reasoning.

Probabilistic approaches to human conditional reasoning

There is a long tradition of probabilistic approaches to human judgment and decision making. The judgment/decision tasks were associated with inductive reasoning. Therefore their heavy use of probability theory. In the traditional psychology of reasoning, however, the tasks were associated with deductive reasoning. Therefore the heavy use of classical logic. Recently, both traditions began to merge (Johnson-Laird & Shafir, 1993). In the early nineties of the last century, Chater and Oaksford introduced probabilistic models to the field of deductive reasoning (Chater & Oaksford, 1999; Oaksford & Chater, 1991, 1994, 2007; Oaksford, Chater, & Larkin, 2002). The probabilistic approach to deductive reasoning claims that even 'purely logical' tasks are solved as if they were tasks belonging to probability theory. The Wason Selection Task, for example, is solved as if the human subjects would maximize information gain (Oaksford & Chater, 1994). Syllogisms are solved as if the subjects would process Bayesian probabilities (Chater & Oaksford, 1999). And argument forms like the MODUS PONENS or the MODUS TOLLENS are solved as if the subjects were experts in probability logic (Pfeifer & Kleiter, 2007, 2009). During the last five years, the interest in probabilistic approaches to human deductive reasoning increased rapidly. Recent probabilistic approaches to human deductive reasoning can roughly be classified by (i) the postulated interpretation of the IF–THEN and (ii) the postulated relation between the premise(s) and the conclusion (see Figure 9.1).

The truth conditions of the IF–THEN in the mental model theory coincide with the material conditional (left branch of Figure 9.1). If the subjects 'fully flesh out' all truth table cases of the IF–THEN, then $P($IF–THEN$)$ is equal to the probability of the material conditional (see Evans, Over, & Handley, 2005; Johnson-Laird & Byrne, 2002 for a discussion).

On the right hand side of Figure 9.1 is the conditional probability interpretation (the IF–THEN is interpreted as a conditional event). We note that the numerical probabilities of the material conditional, $P(A \supset B)$, and of the corresponding conditional probability, $P(B|A)$, can differ substantially. Dorn (1992) gives a compelling example. Consider a fair die with six sides. Let A be *the next throw of the die will come up a 5*, and let B be *the next throw of the die will come up an even number*. By the way, IF A, THEN B is here intuitively implausible. A denotes one out of the six possible outcomes, thus $P(A) = 1/6$. B denotes three out of the six possible outcomes, thus $P(B) = 1/2$. Summing up the probabilities of those truth table cases that make $A \supset B$ true (see Table 9.1), gives $P(A \supset B) = 5/6$. $P(B|A)$ is determined only if a 5 comes up (if a 5 does not comes up, A is false). If A is true, then B is false (because 5 is not an even number), hence $P(B|A) = 0$. $P(B|A) = 0$ reflects the fact that here IF A, THEN B is intuitively implausible.

---

[3] For example, $A \supset B$ is definable by negation and disjunction $\neg A \vee B$, by the negated conjunction $\neg(A \wedge \neg B)$, and by the intuitively indigestible definiens $((A \downarrow A) \downarrow B) \downarrow ((A \downarrow A) \downarrow B)$ as well, where "$A \downarrow B$" is read as "neither A, nor B" $(\neg(A \vee B))$.

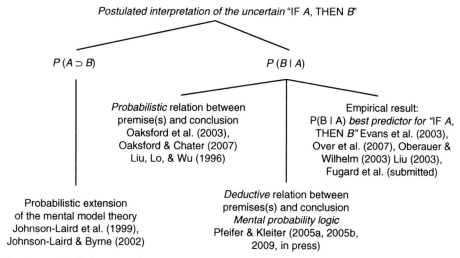

Fig. 9.1 Probabilistic approaches to human conditional reasoning and selected exemplar studies. P(A⊃B) denotes the probability of the material conditional. P(B|A) denotes the conditional probability.

As the values of $P(A \supset B)$ and of $P(B|A)$ can differ substantially, you might ask, which of both interpretations predicts the human understanding of IF–THEN better? Studies on human understanding of IF–THEN do not endorse the probability of the material conditional interpretation. Rather, conditional probability seems to be the best predictor for human understanding of IF–THEN (Evans, Handley, & Over, 2003; Fugard, Pfeifer, Mayerhofer, & Kleiter, submitted; Oberauer & Wilhelm, 2003; Over & Evans, 2003; Over et al., 2007; Liu, Lo, & Wu, 1996). We take this result as an important building block for a competence theory of human reasoning. In the following sections, we discuss human inference from conditional premises.

Coherence based probability logic

One of the best known principles in probability logic is Adams' concept of p-validity (1975, 1998). An argument is p-valid, if and only if, the uncertainty of the conclusion of the argument cannot exceed the sum of the uncertainties of its premises. The uncertainty $u(A)$ is defined by the 1-complement of the corresponding probability, $u(A) = 1 - P(A)$. If an argument is p-valid, then the corresponding non-probabilistic argument is logically valid. Logical validity, however, does not guarantee p-validity.

In terms of interval probability, the lower probability of a p-valid conclusion is not sensitive (i) to the specific logical form of the premises and (ii) to the order of the probabilities of the premises. The two properties hold for unconditional events only and reflect the fact that in this case the events are truth functional. Only the lower bounds of the conclusions of those arguments that contain conditional events can be sensitive to the structure of the premises and to the specific pattern of the probability assessment.

If human subjects interpret the IF–THEN as a material conditional, then their probability responses in p-valid arguments should be insensitive (i) to the logical form of the premises and (ii) to permutations of the probabilities of the premises. There is, however, strong evidence that *human subjects are sensitive to structure and assignment.*

We think that the investigation of lower and upper probabilities is important for the psychology of reasoning. We investigate structure, assignment, and inference in probabilistic argument forms. If the probability of the conclusion is constrained by the probabilities of the premise(s), the inference is called 'probabilistically informative'. If the assignment of the unit interval, [0,1] to the conclusion is coherent under *all* assessments of the premise(s), the inference is called 'probabilistically non-informative'. In this case the premises do not constrain the probability of the conclusion. As a trivial example, assume you know that $P(A) = .7$. Based on this premise, you can only infer that $P(B) \in [0,1]$. This is probabilistically non-informative.

While logical validity is a necessary condition for p-validity, logical validity is not a necessary condition for probabilistic informativeness. The non-probabilistic forms of the DENYING THE ANTECEDENT[4] and AFFIRMING THE CONSEQUENT[5] are not logically valid, but the probabilistic versions are probabilistically informative (but not p-valid). Moreover, PREMISE STRENGTHENING, HYPOTHETICAL SYLLOGISM,[6] and CONTRAPOSITION[7] are logically valid, but neither probabilistically informative nor p-valid.

If the premises of a probabilistically informative argument are certain (probabilities equal to 1), and if the argument is logically valid, then its conclusion is certain. If the premises of a probabilistically informative argument are certain, and if the argument is not logically valid, then the probability of its conclusion may be anywhere in the unit interval. If all premises are given for sure, then the logically invalid arguments make also probabilistically no sense. Classical logic is thus a 'limiting case' for probabilistically informative arguments.

This special role of classical logic is an important reason why we do not want to exclude classical logic from our approach. In everyday life, however, premises are usually not given for sure. In these cases classical logic does not provide an appropriate theoretical frame. Probabilistic versions of argument forms and the relationships between logical validity, probabilistic informativeness, and p-validity are investigated in Pfeifer and Kleiter (2006a, 2009).

In psychology, the most often investigated argument forms containing conditionals are the conditional syllogisms MODUS PONENS and MODUS TOLLENS, and the related logical fallacies DENYING THE ANTECEDENT and AFFIRMING THE CONSEQUENT. Each of the four argument forms consists of the conditional premise IF A, THEN B, one categorical premise, and a conclusion. In the original probabilistic approach of Oaksford, Chater, & Larkin (2002) the probability of the conclusion of a conditional syllogism is equal to the conditional probability of the conclusion given the categorical premise. As an example consider the MODUS PONENS,

$$\text{from } \underbrace{\overbrace{\text{IF } A, \text{ THEN } B}^{\text{Premises}} \text{ and } \underbrace{A}_{\text{categorical}}}_{\text{conditional}} \text{ infer } \overbrace{B}^{\text{Conclusion}}$$

$P(B|A)$ predicts the endorsement of the MODUS PONENS. The conditional premise, IF A, THEN B, is ignored in the model. The original model was modified (Liu, 2003; Oaksford & Chater, 1991) such that the conclusion is conditionalized on the categorical and on the conditional premise. In this approach, the inference-relation between the premise(s) and the conclusion is *uncertain* (see Figure 9.1).

---

[4] *from IF A THEN B and NOT-A infer NOT-B*
[5] *from IF A THEN B and B infer A*
[6] *from IF A THEN B and IF B THEN C infer IF A THEN C*
[7] *from IF A THEN B infer IF NOT-B THEN NOT-A*

Our approach follows a different intuition (see Figure 9.1). We assume a coherent probability assessment of the premise(s) and the inference problem consists in deriving *deductively* the (interval-)probability of the conclusion. Elementary probability theory provides rules how to deduce the probability of a target event (the conclusion) from the probabilities of a number of other events (the premise(s)). In general, we consider as *premises* a triple consisting of (i) a given set of arbitrary *conditional events*, $A_1 \mid B_1,..., A_n \mid B_n$, (ii) the associated probability assessment $p_1,...,p_n$, and (iii) a (possibly empty) set of logical relations between the events.[8] The *conclusion* is a further conditional event $A_{n+1}|B_{n+1}$. The inference problem is solved when $P(A_{n+1} \mid B_{n+1})$ is determined. Bayes' Theorem, for example, finds the probability of a conditional event, $A|B$, when the probabilities of three other events, A, $B|A$, and $B|\neg A$, are given. Bayes' Theorem may then be written as an inference rule

from $P(A) = x$ and $P(B|A) = y$ and $P(B|\neg A) = z$

infer $P(A|B) = xy/(xy+(1-x)z)$,

where the first row contains the premises (the assessment is assumed to be coherent) and the second row contains the conclusion.

To evaluate the rationality of human inferences, we investigate to what extent humans infer *coherent* probability assessments from a given set of premises. A probability assessment is *coherent* if it does not admit one or more bets with sure loss (often called a 'Dutch book'). Compared with the criterion of maximizing expected utility (traditionally used in the judgment and decision making literature), coherence is much weaker. Coherence is one of the key concepts in the theory of subjective probability. It was introduced by de Finetti (1937, 1974). More recent work includes Colletti and Scozzafava (2002); Gilio (2002); Lad (1996); Wally (1991). Coherence provides an adequate normative foundation for the mental probability logic and has many psychologically plausible advantages compared with classical concepts of probability:

◆ Coherence is in the tradition of subjective probability theory in which probabilities are conceived as *degrees of belief*. Degrees of belief are coherent descriptions of partial knowledge states. For the mental probability logic framework, the interpretation of probability as degrees of belief is naturally more appropriate than 'relative frequency' interpretations of probability (for example, Reichenbach, or von Mises). Relative frequency interpretations of probability are about 'objective entities' in the outside world. Mental probability logic, however, investigates epistemic states of uncertainty.

◆ The framework of coherence does not require to start from a *complete Boolean algebra*. Complete algebras are psychologically unrealistic since they can neither be unfolded in the working memory nor be stored in the long term memory. Humans try to keep the memory load as small as possible and try to process only relevant information. Only the information contained in the premises is relevant for drawing inferences. Additional probabilities constitute additional premises.

◆ *Conditional probability, P(B|A),* is a *primitive* notion. The probability value is assigned *directly* to the conditional event, $B|A$, as a *whole* (Coletti & Scozzafava, 2002). The conditioning event A must not be a logical contradiction, but $P(A)$ can be equal to zero. The method of assigning the probability values directly to the conditional event, $B|A$, contrasts with the classical approach

---

[8] *Unconditional events* are treated as special cases of conditional events. An unconditional event, A, is defined as the conditional event A *given logical truth, A|verum*. The according probabilities are identical, $P(A) =_{def} P(A|verum)$. '$P(A)$' is a shortcut for '$P(A|verum)$'.

to probability, where conditional probability is defined by the fraction of the 'joint', $P(A \wedge B)$, and the 'marginal', $P(A)$, probabilities, where $P(A) \neq 0$. It is psychologically plausible that subjects usually assign the uncertainty directly to the conditional (and not by building fractions).

◆ Because of lack of knowledge (time, effort), it may be impossible for a person to assign precise probabilities to an event. *Imprecise* probability assessments may be expressed by interval-valued probabilities or by second order probability distributions (Pfeifer & Kleiter, 2006c).

These advantages explain why we take coherence and not the classical concept of probability as the normative basis for the mental probability logic. The subsequent sections summarize selected empirical work, and we discuss to which extent coherence based probability logic describes actual human inferences. Studies on the conditional syllogisms are reported in Pfeifer and Kleiter (2007, 2009). Studies on the nonmonotonic SYSTEM P rules, and argument forms that are monotonic counterparts of the SYSTEM P rules (HYPOTHETICAL SYLLOGISM, PREMISE STRENGTHENING, and CONTRAPOSITION) are reported in Pfeifer and Kleiter (2003, 2005a, 2006b, in press).

Example 1: The nonmonotonic conditional in the modus ponens

Formal background

The logical form of the MODUS PONENS is

> *from $A \supset B$ and A infer B* ,

where A and B denote propositions and $\supset$ denotes the material conditional. The MODUS PONENS is logically valid. The conditional probability version of the MODUS PONENS is

> *from $P(B|A) = x$ and $P(A) = y$ infer $P(B) \in [z', z'']$* ,

where the probability value of the conditional premise is equal to x and the probability value of the categorical premise is equal to y. The probability of the conclusion (B) is in the probability interval from *at least z'* to *at most z''*, $[z', z'']$. The derivation of the coherent probability interval of the conclusion of the MODUS PONENS is explained in Figure 9.2. The lower bound z' is equal to the product xy and the upper bound z'' is equal to $xy + 1 - y$. Thus, the probability of the conclusion is constrained by the probabilities of the premises. This argument form is also p-valid.

The uncertainty of the premises may be expressed by interval-valued probabilities. A person may specify, for example, that an event A has at least probability x. The MODUS PONENS with interval probabilities in the premises has the form

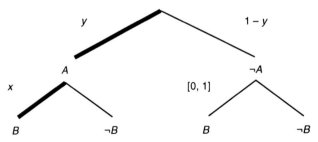

Fig. 9.2 Derivation of the probabilistic MODUS PONENS. The probabilities of the premises are given, $P(B|A) = x$ and $P(A) = y$ (the bold branches on the left). The lower and the upper probability bounds of the conclusion, $P(B)$, are derived by the theorem of total probability, $P(B) = P(A) P(B|A) + P(\neg A) P(B|\neg A)$. $P(B|\neg A)$ is unknown and can take any value in $[0,1]$. $P(B) = xy$ if $P(B|\neg A) = 0$, and $P(B) = xy + 1 - y$ if $P(B|\neg A) = 1$. Therefore, $xy \leq P(B) \leq xy + 1 - y$.

from $P(B|A) \in [x',x'']$ and $P(A) \in [y',y'']$

infer $P(B) \in [x'y', 1-y'+x''y'']$,

where x' and x'' are the lower and upper bounds of the conditional premise, and y' and y'' are the lower and upper bounds of the categorical premise, respectively. If a person knows a lot about the propositions in the premises, then she will assess tight intervals. If her knowledge is vague and ambiguous, then she will assess wide intervals.

Imprecise probabilities are sometimes criticized by the following argument. It is paradox to say that, if a person is not able to assess one precise point probability, she may overcome the difficulty by assessing now two precise probabilities. We only partially agree with this argument. In everyday life intervals are very often used to communicate imprecision. We would prefer to represent degrees of belief by distributions which are 'smeared' across the whole zero-one range. Statistics uses second order probability density functions to describe knowledge about uncertain quantities. This complicates the formal models considerably though. In the present context it seems reasonable to consider interval probabilities as approximations to confidence intervals. It is possible, however, to replace 'probability logic' by a 'statistical logic' which investigates logical argument forms with probability distributions. We described first steps in Pfeifer and Kleiter (2006c). An advantage of such an approach is the possibility to update the distributions in the light of observational data like frequencies or averages. Bayesian statistics offers a rich theoretical background.

Empirical investigation of the modus ponens

In our experiments, we try to construct cover-stories that have a neutral content, that is as independent as possible from the background knowledge of the subjects. Moreover, we take care that only the information explicitly contained in the argument enters the task. The MODUS PONENS, for example, involves only two premises. Accordingly, the probabilistic version of the MODUS PONENS contains only two probabilities, $P(B|A)$ and $P(A)$. We translated the probabilistic MODUS PONENS into several cover-stories, of the following kind (Pfeifer & Kleiter, 2007):

> Claudia works at the blood donation services. She investigates to which blood group the donated blood belongs and whether the donated blood is Rhesus-positive.
>
> Claudia is 60% certain: <u>If</u> the donated blood belongs to the blood group A, <u>then</u> the donated blood is Rhesus-positive.
>
> Claudia is 75% certain: A recent donated blood belongs to the blood group A.
>
> How certain should Claudia be that this recent donated blood is Rhesus-positive?

The cover-stories contained the probabilities of the premises. The task of the participants was to infer from the premises the probability(-interval) of the conclusion. In all experiments we paid special attention to encouraging the participants to engage in reasoning and to avoid quick guessing. The participants were students of the Salzburg University. They were tested individually in a quiet room in the department. They were asked to take enough time.

Introductory examples explained that the solution can be a point value, or an interval. The response modality was formulated accordingly. It was up to the participants to give point or interval value responses. In each experimental condition the content of the cover story remained constant, the percentages were varied.

In the MODUS PONENS tasks with certain premises (100% in both premises), all participants solved the task correctly and responded '100%' ($n = 45$, Pfeifer & Kleiter, 2007). In the tasks with uncertain premises we observed that the participants inferred probabilities that were close to the normative values. This result mirrors the endorsement rate of 89–100% reported for the classical form of the MODUS PONENS (Evans, Newstead, & Byrne, 1993). In one experiment the participants also evaluated the negated conclusion, ¬B, from the same premises (n = 30, Pfeifer & Kleiter, 2007). Again, in the tasks with certain premises all participants inferred correctly '0%'. These results indicate three things. First, the participants do not adopt a simple matching strategy. Second, the participants are perfect in the 'certain MODUS PONENS' and the respective task with the negated conclusion. Third, the reliability of our experimental conditions is high. The results agree with the literature. Human subjects are perfectly competent to make MODUS PONENS inferences if the premises are certain.

In the MODUS PONENS, tasks with uncertain premises about 70% of the responses were interval responses (averaged over different tasks). Figure 9.3 presents results of the MODUS PONENS (Pfeifer & Kleiter, 2007). Each interval response belongs to one of the following six categories: (i) the response is coherent (the lower and the upper probabilities are both in the coherent interval), (ii) only the lower bound response is coherent, (iii) only the upper bound response is coherent, (iv) the interval response is too low, (v) the interval response is too high, and (vi) too wide interval responses. The majority of the interval responses falls into the coherent category (i).

We evaluated the agreement of the responses and the normative values by χ^2-values. The χ^2-values were calculated with the help of (i) the actual number of responses falling into the normatively correct intervals and (ii) the expected number, which was determined by the size (range) of the normative intervals (guessing assumption). High χ^2-values in the predicted direction

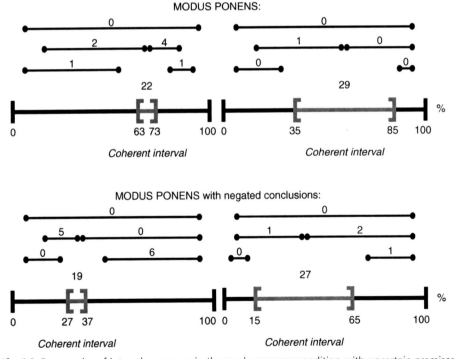

Fig. 9.3 Frequencies of interval responses in the modus ponens condition with uncertain premises (n = 30). In the left column the premises were P(B|A) = .7 and P(A) = .9, and in the right column the premises were P(B|A) = .7 and P(A) = .5. Each participant inferred P(B) (first row) and P(¬B) (second row) from the premises. The majority of the interval responses are coherent.

(a high value in the opposite direction did not occur) indicate more than expected coherent responses. Compared with MODUS TOLLENS, AFFIRMING THE CONSEQUENT, and DENYING THE ANTECEDENT, the by far best agreement with the coherent intervals is observed for the MODUS PONENS (Pfeifer & Kleiter, 2009).

To explain the difficulty of an inference task, Evans (1982) proposed two important properties of the tasks, directionality and negativity. A task is forward/backward directed if it requires inference from the antecedent/consequent to the consequent/antecedent. A task is positive/negative if it does/does not involve negation. Positive forward tasks are easy. Negative backward tasks are difficult. These are well known findings in the literature. In Pfeifer and Kleiter (2009), we propose first steps for a systematic explanation of these effects. Inferring the probability of the conclusion from the premises of the backward tasks requires to build fractions, which is difficult in general. The negative tasks require the building of complements, which means further steps in the reasoning processes. The MODUS PONENS is therefore easy, because it is the most elementary positive forward task.

A third property, that may contribute to the good agreement of the actual responses and the normative lower probabilities, is the fact that normatively the lower probabilities of the conclusions are just the product of the two probabilities in the premises. The conclusion must always be considerably less than the smaller one of the two premise probabilities. The participants may have a good understanding of this fact. For first steps towards a process model based on propositional graphs see Pfeifer and Kleiter (2009).

We next turn to a critical test of human probabilistic reasoning. If the probability of A is x, then the probability of its negation is the complement of the probability of A, $P(\neg A) = 1 - x$. What is the complement of a probability interval? It is given by the following equivalence

$$P(A) \in [x', x''] \text{ if, and only if } P(\neg A) \in [1 - x'', 1 - x'] .$$

This property is called *conjugacy*. Conjugacy is a necessary condition for coherence (Walley, 1991). Are humans able to infer the interval complements for negations? We observed that in the MODUS PONENS problems a surprisingly high number of lower and upper probabilities agreed perfectly with the conjugacy property (Pfeifer & Kleiter, 2007).

Coherence based semantic for nonmonotonic reasoning

Nonmonotonic reasoning is a branch of artificial intelligence that, among many other branches, investigates the formalization of common sense reasoning. It investigates inferences that allow to retract conclusions in the light of new evidence. There are many systems of nonmonotonic reasoning (see Gabbay & Hogger, 1994). SYSTEM P is a set of inference rules that satisfy basic rationality postulates of nonmonotonic reasoning (Adams, 1975; Kraus, Lehmann, & Magidor, 1990).[9] SYSTEM P is of particular significance, since it is broadly accepted in the nonmonotonic reasoning community. The principles of SYSTEM P are also discussed in several other systems, weaker ones (Hawthorne & Makinson, 2007) and stronger ones (Goldszmidt & Pearl, 1996; Lehmann & Magidor, 1992; Schurz, 1997).

The role of the conditional in SYSTEM P is of special interest in the present context. As explained above, nonmonotonic conditionals are conditionals that allow for exceptions. Nonmonotonic conditionals occur in phrases like 'birds can normally fly' or just 'birds can fly'. Their defeasibility

---

[9] The 'P' in 'SYSTEM P' stands for the preferential model semantics proposed in Kraus, Lehmann, & Magidor (1990).

is often not stated explicitly. Nonmonotonic conditionals play an essential role in each inference rule of SYSTEM P. SYSTEM P determines which inferences about nonmonotonic conditionals are acceptable and which ones are not acceptable. Only weakened versions of the monotonic inferences (PREMISE STRENGTHENING, HYPOTHETICAL SYLLOGISM, etc.) are acceptable. SYSTEM P satisfies two desirable properties: (i) SYSTEM P is 'weak' (or cautious) enough in the sense that the undesirable monotonicity principle does not hold, and (ii) SYSTEM P is 'strong' enough to draw default conclusions, with the possibility left to withdraw them in the light of new evidence. These two properties are violated in classical logic.

If conditionals are represented by conditional events with associated probabilities, then the principles of SYSTEM P allow an interpretation in probability theory. Gilio (2002) has developed a probability semantic for nonmonotonic reasoning, which is based on coherence. Coherent conditional probabilities represent nonmonotonic conditionals. The degree of normality is represented by the associated conditional probability. Gilio has shown for each rule of SYSTEM P how the (interval-)probability of the conclusion is constrained by the premises. All the rules of SYSTEM P are probabilistically informative. All the rules of SYSTEM P are p-valid (Adams, 1975). Furthermore, if all probabilities in the premises are equal to 1, then the probability of the conclusion is equal to 1. If the nonmonotonic conditional is replaced by the material conditional, then the rules of SYSTEM P are logically valid.

We explain how nonmonotonic inferences are cast into a probabilistic format by the standard example of nonmonotonic reasoning, namely the Tweety problem:

> Tweety is a bird, and as you know that birds can normally fly, you conclude by default that Tweety can fly. When you learn that Tweety is a penguin, common sense tells you to retract your default conclusion that Tweety can fly.

The probabilistic version of the Tweety example runs as follows:

Premise 1:	$P[\text{Fly }(x)\,|\,\text{Bird}(x)] = .95$.	*(Birds can normally fly.)*
Premise 2:	Bird(Tweety).	*(Tweety is a bird.)*
Conclusion 1:	$P[\text{Fly}(\text{Tweety})] = .95$.	*(Tweety can normally fly.)*

Premise 1 and 2 are the initial premises, Conclusion 1 is the default conclusion. This inference is justified by the probabilistic MODUS PONENS. Premise 3–5 introduce new evidence. Conclusion 2 is the new (default) conclusion, after the revision in the light of the new evidence:

Premise 3	Penguin(Tweety).	*(Tweety is a penguin.)*
Premise 4:	$P[\text{Fly }(x)\,|\,\text{Penguin}(x)] = .01$.	*(Penguins normally can't fly.)*
Premise 5:	$P[\text{Bird }(x)\,|\,\text{Penguin}(x)] = .99$.	*(Penguins are normally birds.)*
Conclusion 2:	$P[\text{Fly }(\text{Tweety})\,|\,\text{Bird}(\text{Tweety}) \wedge \text{Penguin }(\text{Tweety})] \in [0, .01]$.	*(If Tweety is a bird and a penguin, normally Tweety can't fly.)*

The inference from Premise 1–5 to Conclusion 2 is justified by the CAUTIOUS MONOTONICITY rule of SYSTEM P (from *A normally B* and *A normally C* infer *A∧B normally C*; see Gilio, 2002). Premise 4 and Premise 5 are instantiations of the premises and Conclusion 2 is an instance of the conclusion of the CAUTIOUS MONOTONICITY. CAUTIOUS MONOTONICITY is a cautious version of PREMISE STRENGTHENING. Both are discussed in the next section.

Example 2: Nonmonotonic conditionals and premise strengthening

Formal background

PREMISE STRENGTHENING is logically valid, since $A \supset C$ logically implies $(A \wedge B) \supset C$. For nonmonotonic (Kraus, Lehmann, & Magidor, 1990), counterfactual (Lewis, 1973), and causal conditionals, however, PREMISE STRENGTHENING is *not* valid. Consider the following inference involving nonmonotonic conditionals:

IF the bird Tweety is frightened, NORMALLY Tweety flies away.

Therefore: IF the bird Tweety is frightened and if Tweety is a penguin, NORMALLY Tweety flies away.

Replacing the nonmonotonic conditionals (IF–NORMALLY) by counterfactual conditionals (IF–WERE—THEN–WOULD BE), or by causal conditionals (–CAUSES THAT–), shows that PREMISE STRENGTHENING is counterintuitive. PREMISE STRENGTHENING is probabilistically non-informative,

from $P(C|A) = x$ infer $P(C|A \wedge B) \in [0,1]$.

SYSTEM P contains a cautious version of the PREMISE STRENGTHENING, namely the CAUTIOUS MONOTONICITY, which is probabilistically informative (Gilio, 2002).

from $P(C|A) = x$ and $P(B|A) = y$

infer $P(C|A \wedge B) \in [\max\{0,(x+y-1)/y\}, \min\{x/y,1\}]$.

Empirical investigation of monotonicity

In Pfeifer & Kleiter (2003), we divided forty participants into two groups. Twenty participants received fourteen CAUTIOUS MONOTONICITY tasks and twenty participants received fourteen PREMISE STRENGTHENING tasks. The premises and the conclusions of the tasks map the corresponding inference rule (see the previous section). The content of the cover-stories was the same in both conditions. We varied the percentages in the premises within both conditions. If the participants understand the probabilistic non-informativeness of the PREMISE STRENGTHENING, they should infer wide and non-informative intervals.

In the CAUTIOUS MONOTONICITY condition, about 63% of the responses were interval responses (averaged over different tasks). In the PREMISE STRENGTHENING condition, 69% of the responses were interval responses. Figure 9.4 presents the frequencies of the lower and of the upper bound responses. The interval responses are clearly larger in the PREMISE STRENGTHENING condition than in the CAUTIOUS MONOTONICITY condition. In both conditions the lower and the upper bound responses are quite close to the normative values.

In the PREMISE STRENGTHENING condition, more than half of the participants responded by lower bounds $\leq 1\%$. More than half of the participants responded by upper bounds that are equal to the values presented in the premises of the tasks. On the average, 27% of the participants responded by intervals with both lower bounds $\leq 1\%$ and upper bounds $\geq 91\%$ ($n_1 = 20$, 14 tasks). Most participants understood that the lower bound can be practically zero. Most participants used a matching heuristic for inferring the upper bound. Apparently, most participants correctly inferred the lower bound of the conclusion but did not continue to search the upper bound.

If the conditional were interpreted as a material conditional, then PREMISE STRENGTHENING would be probabilistically informative (Pfeifer & Kleiter, 2006a, in press). Psychologically, the following prediction follows: most subjects infer $P(A \wedge B \supset C) \in [x,1]$ from $P(A \supset C) = x$. Most participants, however, responded by lower bounds close to zero and by upper bounds close to x. Thus, most participants did not interpreted the conditional as a material conditional.

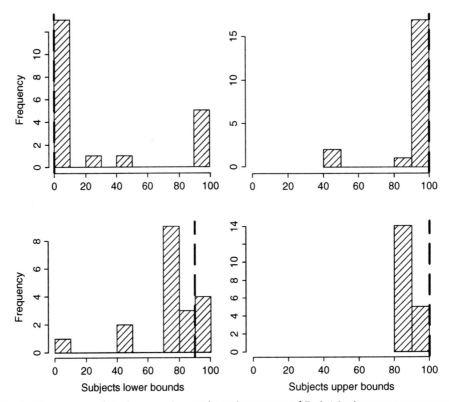

Fig. 9.4 Frequencies of the lower and upper bound responses of Task 1 in the PREMISE STRENGTHEN-ING condition (upper row; $n_1 = 20$) and in the CAUTIOUS MONOTONICITY condition (lower row; $n_2 = 19$) (Pfeifer & Kleiter, 2003). Most responses are close to the normative lower and upper bounds (dashed lines), respectively.

In the CAUTIOUS MONOTONICITY condition, the correlation between the mean lower bound responses and the normative lower bounds over all fourteen tasks was very high ($r = 0.92$). Subjects are sensitive to the probabilistic non-informativeness of PREMISE STRENGTHENING—at least concerning the lower bound. Subjects are cautious with monotonicity.

Example 3: Nonmonotonic conditionals and hypothetical syllogism

The HYPOTHETICAL SYLLOGISM is logically valid, since $A \supset B$ and $B \supset C$ logically imply $A \supset C$. Thus, the material conditional is transitive. The nonmonotonic conditional, however, is not transitive. The probabilistic version of the HYPOTHETICAL SYLLOGISM is probabilistically non-informative,

from $P(C|B) = x$ and $P(B|A) = y$ infer $P(C|A) \in [0,1]$.

The HYPOTHETICAL SYLLOGISM is not contained in the nonmonotonic SYSTEM P and adding it would make SYSTEM P monotonic. However, a weaker version of the HYPOTHETICAL SYLLOGISM is contained in SYSTEM P, namely the CUT rule ('cut' is a shortcut for 'cumulative transitivity'),

from $P(C|A \wedge B) = x$ and $P(B|A) = y$ infer $P(C|A) \in [xy , xy+1-y]$.

The CUT is a conditional version of the MODUS PONENS. The reason is clear by comparing the probability propagation rules of both argument forms and by dropping the conditioning event A.

We observed that the participants in the HYPOTHETICAL SYLLOGISM condition did not understand the probabilistic non-informativeness. They inferred informative intervals close to the coherent values of the CUT problems. We explain this result as follows (Pfeifer & Kleiter, 2006b). Adams (1975) stressed the probabilistic invalidity of the HYPOTHETICAL SYLLOGISM. He suggested to interpret its occurrence in common sense reasoning as an instantiation of CUT. Bennett (2003) justified Adams' suggestion in terms of conversational implicatures (see Grice, 1989). If a speaker first utters a premise of the form *A normally B* and then utters as the second premise *B normally C*, the speaker actually means by the second premise a sentence of the form (*A and B*) *normally C*. The speaker does not mention '*A and*' to the addressat because *A and* is already conversationally implied and 'clear' from the context. Suppose we speak (as we did in Pfeifer & Kleiter, 2006b) about cars on a *big parking lot* that are *blue*, and suppose we then add that

> You know with 91% certainty: if a car is *blue*, then the car has *grey tire-caps*,

you probably assume that we are speaking about the blue cars *that are on the big parking lot*, even if we do not mention this explicitly.

This interpretation explains why participants do not infer wide intervals. If the conversational implicature hypothesis is correct, then the participants actually interpret the HYPOTHETICAL SYLLOGISM tasks as instances of the CUT rule.

Another rule of SYSTEM P is the RIGHT WEAKENING rule, which is probabilistically informative and, like CUT, a cautious version of the HYPOTHETICAL SYLLOGISM,

> from $P(B|A) = x$ and $B \supset C$ is logically true infer $P(C|A) \in [x,1]$.

Practically all participants inferred correctly the lower bound in the RIGHT WEAKENING tasks (Pfeifer & Kleiter, 2006b). The percentage of participants that inferred correctly '100%' as the upper bound varied between 50% and 75%.

Example 4: Nonmonotonic conditionals and contraposition

Formal background

CONTRAPOSITION belongs to the class of inferences often called 'immediate' or 'direct' inferences. CONTRAPOSITION is an inference from one conditional premise to a conditional conclusion. CONTRAPOSITION denotes the logical equivalence of $A \supset B$ and $\neg B \supset \neg A$. Because of this equivalence we call the corresponding argument forms 'CONTRAPOSITION':

> from $A \supset B$ infer $\neg B \supset \neg A$,

and

> from $\neg B \supset \neg A$ infer $A \supset B$.

If the conditional is interpreted as a material conditional, then $P(A \supset B) = P(\neg B \supset \neg A)$. Thus, the corresponding probabilistic argument form assigns exactly the same probability value to the conclusion as given in the premise. If, however, the conditional is interpreted as a conditional probability, then $P(B|A)$ is not necessarily equal to $P(\neg A|\neg B)$. The corresponding probabilistic argument forms are

> from $P(B|A) = x$ infer $P(\neg A|\neg B) \in [0,1]$

and

> from $P(\neg A|\neg B) = x$ infer $P(B|A) \in [0,1]$,

for all probability values x. We see here a clear watershed between argument forms containing the material conditional and argument forms containing the conditional event. If the subjects interpret the conditional as a material conditional then a simple matching strategy is the best strategy for CONTRAPOSITION problems. If the subjects interpret the conditional as a conditional event, however, the argument is probabilistically non-informative and any assessment of the conclusion is coherent. Thus, the material conditional interpretation predicts matching, and the conditional probability interpretation predicts non-informative probability intervals.

The mental model theory (Johnson-Laird, et al., 1999 and Johnson-Laird & Byrne, 2002) postulates that the core meaning of a conditional corresponds to the material conditional. Usually, human subjects represent a conditional by an implicit mental model. An implicit mental model consists of a mental model of the conjunction of the antecedent and the consequent, plus a 'mental footnote' which represents the two truth table cases where the antecedent is false ($\neg A \wedge B$ and $\neg A \wedge \neg B$). All three truth table cases are just those in which $A \supset B$ is true (see Table 9.1). Thus, IF A, THEN B is represented by

$A \wedge B$

...

where "..." represents the mental footnote. Because of the mental footnote, the whole representation is called the 'implicit mental model' of the conditional. Under some circumstances, subjects 'flesh out' the implicit mental model by replacing the mental footnote by representations of $\neg A \wedge B$ and of $\neg A \wedge \neg B$. The resulting mental model is called 'fully explicit'. Fully explicit mental models require much more working memory load than implicit mental models. Therefore the mental model theory claims that conditionals are represented usually by implicit and not by explicit mental models.

In general, the probability of the implicit mental model of IF A, THEN B is equal to $P(A \wedge B) + P(\ldots)$. We assume that the probabilistic assessment of the truth table cases is coherent. The mental model theory assumes that the subjects focus on $P(A \wedge B)$. For simplicity, we assume that the probability of the 'mental footnote', $P(\ldots)$, is ignored by the subject. Thus, we make no special assumptions about $P(\ldots)$. If the subjects form implicit mental models, and if $P(\ldots)$ is ignored, then the CONTRAPOSITION inference consists of inferring $P(\neg A \wedge \neg B)$ from $P(A \wedge B)$. If $P(A \wedge B) = x$, then $P(\neg A \wedge \neg B) \in [0, 1-x]$, because the truth table cases must add up to one.

The probability of the fully explicit mental model is equal to $P(A \wedge B) + P(\neg A \wedge B) + P(\neg A \wedge \neg B)$. The probability of the fully explicit mental model corresponds to the probability of the material conditional. Table 9.2 presents the implicit and the fully explicit mental models of the CONTRAPOSITION.

Table 9.2 Probabilistic CONTRAPOSITION in the mental model theory and in the conditional probability interpretation. The first row corresponds to the premise and the second row corresponds to the conclusion. For simplicity, the 'mental footnote' is ignored. The probability of the premise is given (x), and the subject infers the probability of the conclusion. Mental model theory predicts that the premise constrains the probability of the conclusion. Mental probability logic predicts that contraposition is probabilistically non-informative.

Probabilistic CONTRAPOSITION	Mental models		Conditional probability
	fully explicit	implicit	
P(if A, then B) = x	P(A⊃B) = x	P(A∧B) = x	P(B|A) = x
P(if ¬B, then ¬A) = ?	P(¬B⊃¬A) = x	P(¬B∧¬A)∈ [0,1-x]	P(¬A|¬B)∈ [0,1]

CONTRAPOSITION is probabilistically informative in the mental model theory. CONTRAPOSITION is probabilistically non-informative in the mental probability logic (because of the conditional probability interpretation of the IF–THEN). The next section investigates these claims empirically.

Empirical results of the contraposition

We presented (among other tasks) both forms of CONTRAPOSITION to the participants (Pfeifer & Kleiter, 2006b). In the CONTRAPOSITION task with the negations in the premise, 58% of the participants inferred both lower bounds ≤7% and upper bounds ≥93% ($n_1 = 40$). These wide interval responses indicate understanding of the probabilistic non-informativeness of the argument. In the CONTRAPOSITION task with the negations in the conclusion, the respective percentage was 40% ($n_2 = 40$).

Practically all of the participants who did not infer such wide intervals responded either by point values close to zero, or by point values that are close to one hundred. We believe that these participants stop inferring probabilities as soon as they see one extreme bound of the interval of the conclusion and take this as the probability of the conclusion. Apparently, they understand that the one extreme pole of the unit interval is a coherent assessment of the conclusion and neglect to continue to search for the other one.

In the CONTRAPOSITION task with the negations in the premise, only three of the forty participants reproduced the value presented in the premise. In the CONTRAPOSITION task with the negations in the conclusion, ten of the forty participants reproduced the value presented in the premise. Over all conditions only thirteen of the eighty participants responded by reproducing the percentage contained in the premise. Thus only 16% of the participants conform with the probability of the material conditional interpretation (fully explicit mental model). As noted above, it is not clear whether these participants actually interpret the conditional as a material conditional or whether they simply apply a matching strategy. Nevertheless, this is strong evidence against the material conditional interpretation.

In the CONTRAPOSITION task with the negations in the premise, only four of the forty participants responded by the [0%,7%] interval, which corresponds to the implicit mental model. In the CONTRAPOSITION task with the negations in the conclusion, none of the responses corresponds to the implicit mental model. Overall, only 10% of the interval responses of the participants correspond to the implicit mental model.

The results challenge two predictions of the mental model theory. First, the broad majority of the interval responses should be explained by implicit and explicit mental models. Second, more implicit mental models should be observed than explicit mental models. Our data do not support these predictions.

Finally as a technical remark, CONTRAPOSITION implies the monotonicity property of classical logic. Since most participants understand that CONTRAPOSITION is probabilistically non-informative their reasoning can be interpreted as nonmonotonically and not as monotonic.

Concluding remarks

We described a probabilistic approach to human conditional reasoning. Nonmonotonic conditionals were investigated in the framework of probability logic. We selected a special probability logic which is based on coherence. It combines logic and subjective probability theory. Probability logic tells us how to infer deductively the coherent (lower and upper) probability of the conclusion from the premises. The structure of the inference task is analyzed in a rigorous way: everything known is made explicit in the premises. We make only one implicit assumption, namely that the assessment of the premises must be coherent. The cover-stories of our tasks were designed to map the structure of the probability logical arguments. We took special care that the content of the cover-stories is neutral and that they don't evoke uncontrolled background knowledge in the subjects.

In some recent studies on the conditional, the experimenter provided the subjects the probabilities of *all* possible states (rows in the truth table, elementary events, constituents) in the sample space. This corresponds to a complete knowledge of the joint probability distribution. Logical argument forms, though, contain only a few premises, and their probabilistic versions contain correspondingly only a few probabilities (marginal and conditional probabilities). When the probabilities of all possible states are known, the inference task is substantially different from its original logical argument form. As an example, assume the following assessment of all possible states in the sample space:

$$P(A \wedge B) = .5, \ P(A \wedge \neg B) = .1, \ P(\neg A \wedge B) = .2, \ P(\neg A \wedge \neg B) = .2$$

This assessment describes a situation of complete probabilistic knowledge. In this situation, the premises of the MODUS PONENS are $P(A) = .60$ and $P(B|A) = .83$, and the conclusion is $P(B) = .70$. If, however, the truth table cases are unknown, and all we know is that $P(A) = .60$ and that $P(B|A) = .83$, then we are in a situation of incomplete probabilistic knowledge. Then we get an interval in the conclusion, $P(B) \in [.50, .90]$ (see Figure 9.2). This example shows the necessity to work with interval probabilities. Since situations of complete probabilistic knowledge are seldom in everyday life, experimenters should also focus on reasoning from incomplete probabilistic knowledge. Interval probabilities are psychologically highly plausible and we presented empirical evidence that they are actually used when offered as a response mode. We observed that subjects are especially good in inferring the lower probability bound of the conclusion of the probabilistic MODUS PONENS.

The four conditional inferences (MODUS PONENS, etc.) are prominent in psychology and were investigated several times. We investigated argument forms that go beyond those four conditional inferences. PREMISE STRENGTHENING, CONTRAPOSITION, and HYPOTHETICAL SYLLOGISM and the rules of SYSTEM P are conditional argument forms. They involve more general properties of conditionals. The material conditional is transitive and monotonic. The nonmonotonic conditional is neither transitive nor monotonic.

We observed that many subjects understand the probabilistic non-informativeness of PREMISE STRENGTHENING and of CONTRAPOSITION. The interval responses in the corresponding SYSTEM P rules were close to the normative values. Subjects seem not to understand the probabilistic non-informativeness of HYPOTHETICAL SYLLOGISM. We explained this result by conversational implicatures. Subjects interpret the HYPOTHETICAL SYLLOGISM problems as instances of the CUT rule, which is a corresponding SYSTEM P rule. For some inference rules of SYSTEM P on may speculate that they are at the core of the human inference engine (especially the LEFT LOGICAL EQUIVALENCE and the RIGHT WEAKENING rules, see Pfeifer & Kleiter, 2005a, 2006b).

In our experiments, we presented the uncertainty of the premises in terms of percentages. We wanted to avoid verbal paraphrases. Phrases like 'probably' are ambiguous. The subject must infer the meaning of such phrases. Inferences to an interpretation of verbal paraphrases bias the experiment, since different participants may infer different meanings. By presenting percentages in the premises, the degree of uncertainty is controlled in the experiment. The investigation of reasoning *to an interpretation* is important for the understanding of how subjects form representations. In our studies, however, we were concerned with reasoning *from an interpretation*, which refers to how subjects manipulate representations from fixed interpretations. The importance of the distinction between reasoning to an interpretation and reasoning from an interpretation is stressed by Stenning and van Lambalgen (2004, 2010). Future work will investigate cognitive representations and processing of the probabilities.

While we were primarily concerned with reasoning from fixed premises, our studies also provide insight into how humans interpret the IF–THEN. The CONTRAPOSITION problem, for example, provides a clear watershed between the probability of the material conditional interpretation and the conditional probability interpretation. Our data clearly favor the conditional probability interpretation of the IF–THEN. This result adds to the results of Over, Evans, & Elqayam (2010). Moreover, we showed how predictions of the probabilistic extension of the mental model theory can be expressed in the language of probability logic. These predictions were not corroborated.

We investigated probabilistic inference problems that mirror central properties of nonmonotonic reasoning and properties of monotone logics. We have not yet investigated withdrawing conclusions in the light of new evidence, but our data corroborate broadly some basic rationality postulates of nonmonotonic reasoning. Future empirical work will be devoted to weaker and stronger systems than SYSTEM P. Moreover, we plan to use computer controlled experiments, take reaction times, and investigate the revision of default conclusions.

Acknowledgments

We thank David Over and the referee for helpful comments. This work is supported by the Austrian Science Fund, FWF (project P20209 "Mental probability logic") and by the European Science Foundation EUROCORES programme LogICCC (FWF project I141).

References

Adams, E. W. (1975). *The logic of conditionals.* Dordrecht: Reidel, Adams, E. W. (1998). *A Primer of Probability Logic.* Stanford: CSLI.

Benferhat, S., Bonnefon, J. F., & Da Silva Neves, R. (2005). An overview of possibilistic handling of default reasoning, with experimental studies. *Synthese,* **1**(2), 53–70.

Bennett, J. (2003). *A philosophical guide to conditionals.* Oxford: Oxford University Press.

Bonnefon, J.-F. & Politzer, (2010). *Pragmatic conditionals, Conditional pragmatics, and the pragmatic component of conditional reasoning.* Chapter 14, this book.

Bonnefon, J.-F. & Hilton, D. J. (2002). The suppression of modus ponens as a case of pragmatic preconditional reasoning. *Thinking & Reasoning,* **8**(1), 21–40.

Bonnefon, J.-F. & Hilton, D. J. (2004). Consequential conditionals: Invited and suppressed inferences from valid outcomes. *Journal of Experimental Psychology: Learning, Memory, and Cognition,* **30**(1), 28–37.

Braine, M. D. S. & O'Brien, D. P. (Eds.) (1998). *Mental logic.* Mahwah: Erlbaum.

Byrne, R. M. J. (1989). Suppressing valid inferences with conditionals. *Cognition,* **31**, 61–83.

Byrne, R. M. J., Espino, O., & Santamaría, O. (1999). Counterexamples and the suppression of inferences. *Journal of Memory and Language,* **40**, 347–373.

Chater, N. & Oaksford, M. (1999). The probability heuristics model of syllogistic reasoning. *Cognitive Psychology,* **38**, 191–258.

Chomsky, N. (1965). *Aspects of the theory of syntax.* Cambridge: MIT Press.

Coletti, G. & Scozzafava, R. (2002). *Probabilistic logic in a coherent setting.* Dordrecht: Kluwer.

De Finetti, B. Foresight: Its logical laws, its subjective sources (1937). In Kyburg, H. Jr. & Smokler, H. Jr. (Eds.) (1964). *Studies in subjective probability,* (pp. 55–118). New York: Wiley.

De Finetti, B. (1974). *Theory of probability,* volume 1, 2. Chichester: John Wiley & Sons, Original work published 1970.

Dieussaert, K., De Neys, W., & Schaeken, W. (2005). Suppression and belief revision, two sides of the same coin? *Psychologica Belgica,* **45**(1), 29–46.

Dorn, G. J. W. (1992). Popper's law of the excess of the probability of the conditional over the conditional probability. *Conceptus*, **26**(67), 6–61.

Evans, J. St.B. T. (1982). *The psychology of deductive reasoning*. London: Routledge.

Evans, J. St.B. T., Handley, S. H., & Over, D. E. (2003). Conditionals and conditional probability. *Journal of Experimental Psychology: Learning, Memory, and Cognition*, **29**, 321–355.

Evans, J. St.B. T., Newstead, S. E., & Byrne, R. M. J. (1993). *Human Reasoning*. Hove: Erlbaum.

Evans, J. St.B. T., Over, D. E., & Handley, S. J. (2005). Suppositions, extensionality, and conditionals: A critique of the mental model theory of Johnson-Laird and Byrne. *Psychological Review*, **112**(4), 1040–1052.

Fugard, A. J. B., Pfeifer, N., Mayerhofer, B. & Kleiter, G. D. (submitted). How people interpret conditionals: Shifts towards the conditional event.

Gabbay, D. M. & Hogger, C. J. (Eds.) (1994). *Handbook of logic in artificial intelligence and logic programming*, volume 3. Non-monotonic reasoning and uncertain reasoning. Oxford: Clarendon Press.

Gilio, A. (2002). Probabilistic reasoning under coherence in System P. *Annals of Mathematics and Artificial Intelligence*, **34**, 5–34.

Goldszmidt, M. & Pearl, J. (1996). Qualitative probabilities for default reasoning, belief revision, and causal modeling. *Artificial Intelligence*, **84**, 57–112.

Grice, H. P. (Ed.) (1989). *Studies in the way of words*. Cambridge: Harvard University Press.

Hawthorne, J. & Makinson, D. (2007). The quantitative/qualitative watershed for rules of uncertain inference. *Studia Logica*, **86**, 1–52.

Johnson-Laird, P. N. (1983). *Mental models: Towards a cognitive science of language, inference and consciousness*. Cambridge: Cambridge University Press.

Johnson-Laird, H. P. & Byrne, R. M. J. (2002). Conditionals: A theory of meaning, pragmatics, and inference. *Psychological Review*, **109**(4), 646–678.

Johnson-Laird, P. N., Girotto, V., Legrenzi, P., & Legrenzi, M. S. (1999). Naive probability: A mental model theory of extensional reasoning. *Psychological Review*, **106**(1), 62–88.

Johnson-Laird, P. N. & Shafir, E. (Eds.) (1993). Reasoning and Decision Making. *Cognition*, Special Issue, 49.

Kneale, W. & Kneale, M. (1984). *The development of logic*. Oxford: Clarendon Press.

Kraus, S., Lehmann, D. & Magidor, M. (1990). Nonmonotonic reasoning, preferential models and cumulative logics. *Artificial Intelligence*, **44**, 67–207.

Lad. F. (1996). *Operational subjective statistical methods: A mathematical, philosophical, and historical introduction*. New York: Wiley.

Lehmann, D. & Magidor, M. (1992). What does a conditional knowledgebase entail? *Artificial Intelligence*, **55**(1), 1–60.

Lewis, D. (1973). Counterfactuals and comparative possibility. In Harper, W. L., Stalnaker, R. and Pearce, G. (Eds.). *Ifs*, (pp. 57–85). Dordrecht: Reidel.

Liu, I.-M. (2003). Conditional reasoning and conditionalization. *Journal of Experimental Psychology: Learning, Memory, and Cognition*, **29**(4), 94–709.

Liu, I.-M., Lo, K.-C., & Wu, J.- T (1996). A probabilistic interpretation of 'If—Then'. *The Quarterly Journal of Experimental Psychology*, **49**(A), 828–844.

Macnamara, J. (1986). *The place of logic in psychology*. Cambridge: MIT Press.

Marr, D. (1982). *Vision. A computational investigation into the human representation and processing of visual information*. San Francisco: W. H. Freeman,

Oaksford, M. & Chater, N. (1991). Against logicist cognitive science. *Mind & Language*, **6**(1), 1–38.

Oaksford, M. & Chater, N. (1994). A rational analysis of the selection task as optimal data selection. *Psychological Review*, **101**, 608–631.

Oaksford, M. & Chater, N. (2007). *Bayesian rationality: The probabilistic approach to human reasoning*. Oxford: Oxford University Press.

Oaksford, M., Chater, N., & Larkin, J. (2002). Probabilities and polarity biases in conditional inference. *Journal of Experimental Psychology: Learning, Memory, and Cognition*, **26**, 883–899.

Oberauer, K. & Wilhelm, O. (2003). The meaning(s) of conditionals: Conditional probabilities, mental models and personal utilities. *Journal of Experimental Psychology: Learning, Memory, and Cognition*, **29**, 680–693.

Over, D., Evans, J. St.B. T., & Elqayam, S. (2010). Conditionals and non-constructive reasoning. Chapter 8, this book.

Over, D. E. & Evans, J. St.B. T. (2003). The probability of conditionals: The psychological evidence. *Mind & Language*, **18**, 340–358.

Over, D. E., Hadjichristidis, C. Evans, J. S., Handley, S. J., & Sloman, S. A. (2007). The probability of causal conditionals. *Cognitive Psychology*, **54**, 62–97.

Pfeifer, N. & Kleiter, G. D. (2003). Nonmonotonicity and human probabilistic reasoning. In *Proceedings of the 6th Workshop on Uncertainty Processing*, (pp. 221–234), Hejnice, 2003. September 24–27th.

Pfeifer, N. & Kleiter, G. D. (2005a). Coherence and nonmonotonicity in human reasoning. *Synthese*, **146**(1–2), 93–109.

Pfeifer, N. & Kleiter, G. D. (2005b). Towards a mental probability logic. *Psychologica Belgica*, **45**(1), 71–99. Updated version at: www.users.sbg.ac.at/~pfeifern/.

Pfeifer, N. & Kleiter, G. D. (2006a). Inference in conditional probability logic. *Kybernetika*, **42**, 391–404.

Pfeifer, N. & Kleiter, G. D. (2006b). Is human reasoning about nonmonotonic conditionals probabilistically coherent? In *Proceedings of the 7th Workshop on Uncertainty Processing*, Mikulov, September 16–20th, pp. 138–150.

Pfeifer, N. & Kleiter, G. D. (2006c). Towards a probability logic based on statistical reasoning. In *Proceedings of the 11th IPMU Conference (Information Processing and Management of Uncertainty in Knowledge-Based Systems)*, (pp. 2308–2315). Paris: Edition E. D. K.

Pfeifer, N. & Kleiter, G. D. (2007). Human reasoning with imprecise probabilities: Modus ponens and Denying the antecedent. In *5th International Symposium on Imprecise Probability: Theories and Applications*, (pp. 347–356). Prague, Czech Republic, 16–19th July.

Pfeifer, N. & Kleiter, G. D. (2009). Framing human inference by coherence based probability logic. *Journal of Applied Logic*, **7**(2), 206–217.

Pfeifer, N. & Kleiter, G. D. (in press). Uncertain deductive reasoning. In K. Manktelow, Over, D. E., and S. Elqayam (Eds.), *The science of reasoning: A Festschrift for Jonathan St. B. T. Evans*. Hove, UK: Psychology Press.

Politzer, G. (2005). Uncertainty and the suppression of inferences. *Thinking & Reasoning*, **11**(1), 5–33.

Ramsey, F. P. Truth and probability (1926). In D. H. Mellor, (Ed.) 1978. *Foundations. Essays in philosophy, logic, mathematics and economics*, (pp. 58–100). London: Routledge & Kegan Paul.

Rips, L. J. (1994). *The psychology of proof: Deductive reasoning in human thinking*. Cambridge: MIT Press.

Schurz, G. (1997). Probabilistic default reasoning based on relevance and irrelevance assumptions. In D. Gabbay et al., (Eds.). *Qualitative and Quantitative Practical Reasoning*, number 1244 in LNAI (pp. 536–553). Berlin: Springer.

Stenning, K. & van Lambalgen, M. (2004). A little logic goes a long way: Basing experiment on semantic theory in the cognitive science of conditional reasoning. *Cognitive Science*, **28**, 481–529.

Stenning, K. & van Lambalgen, M. (2010). The logical response to a noisy world. Chapter 5, this book.

Störring, G. (1908). Experimentelle Untersuchungen zu einfachen Schlußprozessen. *Archiv für die Gesamte Psychologie*, **11**, 1–127, 1908.

Walley, P. (1991). *Statistical Reasoning with Imprecise Probabilities*. London: Chapman and Hall.

Part 3

Long term memory: Function, representation, and process

Chapter 10

Semantic memory retrieval, mental models, and the development of conditional inferences in children

Henry Markovits

Deductive reasoning allows humans to make inferences that are valid without any recourse to how the 'real world' works. The ability to reason about situations that are hypothetical or abstract is a clear example of a uniquely human ability. The idea that one can sit down at a desk and 'discover' facts about the real world simply through deduction has always had a particular fascination, so much so that logic has become a field of study in itself. The question of how people make inferences has also been an important one in psychology, although the framing of the psychological question has varied in important ways. In the following, we will examine answers to this question in the specific case of conditional (if-then) reasoning.

Conditional reasoning requires making an inference from a given premise of the general form 'If P then Q'. There are good reasons for focussing on this kind of reasoning in the present context. First, if-then reasoning is probably the most common form of inferential reasoning encountered in everyday life. Even very young children use 'if' at a very early age (Scholnick & Wing, 1995). The importance of this kind of reasoning is reflected in the empirical literature since if-then reasoning is the most widely studied of any specific form of deductive reasoning. This has given researchers a much better idea of what kinds of factors might underlie both developmental patterns and adult variation, and allows a clearer comparison between predictions and empirical data than is the case with other forms of deductive reasoning.

Conditional reasoning in its most basic sense involves making inferences with a given major premise of the form 'p implies q' and one of four possible minor premises. Modus ponens (MP) is the logical principle that involves reasoning with the premises 'p implies q, p is true' and leads to the logically correct conclusion 'q is true'. Modus tollens (MT) involves reasoning with the premises 'p implies q, q is false' and leads to the logically correct conclusion 'p is false'. These two are valid logical forms, since they both lead to a single, logically correct conclusion. Affirmation of the consequent (AC) involves reasoning with the premises 'p implies q, q is true'. Denial of the antecedent (DA) involves reasoning with the premises 'p implies q, p is false'. In both cases the implied conclusions, 'p is true' for AC and 'q is false' for DA are not logically correct. Neither of these forms leads to a single, logically correct conclusion and the correct response would be to deny the implied (biconditional) conclusion in both cases. We will refer to them as the uncertain logical forms.

One of the most important general results to have come out of the many studies examining conditional reasoning in both children and adults is the fact that the kinds of inferences that are made are highly dependent on the nature and structure of the reasoner's knowledge about the conditional premises (Barrouillet & Lecas, 1998; Cummins, 1995; Cummins et al., 1991;

Janveau-Brennan & Markovits, 1999; Markovits, 2000; Markovits, 1985; Markovits & Vachon, 1990; Markovits, Fleury, Quinn, & Venet, 1998; Thompson, 1994). This basic fact is the cornerstone to our approach to reasoning. Empirical studies that have examined the effects of content on conditional reasoning in both children and adults allow the clear conclusion that reasoners actively use their knowledge about the premises in order to make inferences.

The studies that have looked at content-based variation in conditional reasoning provide some clear and consistent indications of the specific forms of knowledge about conditionals that are used when reasoning. The first kind concerns potential alternative antecedents to the consequent. When reasoning with an 'If P then Q' premise, an alternative antecedent is any case, A, such that 'If A then Q' is also considered to be true by the reasoner (note that this implies that the specific relation, i.e., causal, class inclusion, etc., between the two terms in the conditional is the same in both cases). Many studies have shown that reasoning with both the AC and DA forms is particularly sensitive to the relative number of such potential antecedents available to both children and adult reasoners (Cummins, 1995; Cummins, et al., 1991; Janveau-Brennan & Markovits, 1999; Markovits & Vachon, 1990; Thompson, 1994). A second important class of information concerns what Cummins (Cummins, 1995; Cummins et al., 1991) has called disabling conditions. These are conditions that can allow the antecedent to be true while the consequent is false. For example, take the premise 'If a rock hits a window, the window will break'. One potential disabling condition in this case, is having a window that is made of plexiglass, thus allowing the conclusion that if a rock hits a plexiglass window, the window will not break. Empirical studies have shown that reasoners will use potential disabling conditions in a way that promotes rejection of the basic if-then premise (Cummins, 1995; Cummins, et al., 1991; De Neys, Schaeken, & d'Ydewalle, 2003; Janveau-Brennan & Markovits, 1999; Markovits & Potvin, 2001). These studies have shown that use of disabling conditions is associated with tendencies to reject the invited conclusion for the MP and MT forms. A final class of information concerns what Markovits and Barrouillet (2002) have referred to as complementary cases, i.e., cases of (not-P and not-Q). While there has been little direct research on such cases, there are two sorts of evidence that indicates that such information may be accessed relatively easily. First, there is evidence from semantic analyses of the meaning of conditionals that correspond to promises and threats (Fillenbaum, 1975). These studies clearly show that when people interpret phrases such as 'If you eat your soup then you'll have dessert', they also understand that 'If you do not eat your soup, then you'll not have dessert'. Such an implicit inference appears to be acquired quite early, and its influence appears to increase developmentally (Cahan & Artmann, 1997). The relative ease of access to complements to the conditional is also consistent with developmental findings that clearly show that many young children tend to reason with if-then conditionals as if these were biconditionals (Knifong, 1974; O'Brien & Overton, 1980), something that would be done if complements to the conditional were easily available.

The model of conditional reasoning that I have recently presented (Markovits & Barrouillet, 2002) accounts for both developmental and content related variation in inferential performance by explicitly allowing for differential access to these three classes of information. In the following, I will present a multinomial process tree model of conditional reasoning that is based on this, and use it to simulate children's reasoning. Before presenting the simulation in detail, a brief summary of the basic model and its principle postulates will be given.

The basic framework of this model is that of mental model theory (Johnson-Laird, 1983; Johnson-Laird & Byrne, 1991). A key postulate supposes that the nature of the model sets that are actually used during reasoning is strongly determined by the way that information is structured in long-term memory. Access to information about the premises, i.e., alternatives to the antecedent, disabling conditions, and complements, will thus depend on a variety of factors which include both the way that this information is stored in memory and the processes required to extract it. Factors, such as the type of conditional relation between antecedent and consequent (Janveau-Brennan & Markovits, 1999; Markovits & Barrouillet, 2002), the strength of association between a given form of information and the premises (Quinn & Markovits, 1998), the necessity to generate additional retrieval cues in order to access information (Cummins, 1995; Markovits et al., 1998), and individual differences in retrieval efficiency (De Neys, Schaeken, & d'Ydewalle, 2002; Janveau-Brennan & Markovits, 1999; Markovits & Quinn, 2002) will affect the relative difficulty of accessing information about the premises that can be used in model construction. Second, we assume that when children make inferences with a given major and minor premise, they will use the minor premise as a retrieval cue which will partly determine the strength of activation of these three classes of information. Retrieval is done on-line during reasoning. Working memory constraints will affect this process in two important, but distinct, ways. First, limited working memory has been shown to have effects on the efficiency of information retrieval from long-term memory (Anderson, Reder, & Lebiere, 1996; Rosen & Engle, 1996). This has, in turn, been shown to affect conditional reasoning in a way that is independent of processing constraints (Markovits & Quinn, 2002). Second, limited working memory will constrain the quantity of information that can be retrieved. We do not assume that there is any constraint on the type of information that will be retrieved. Rather, we suppose that when a child is reasoning with a specific major and minor premise, this will result in some degree of activation of one or more of the three classes of information. For any given class of information, the probability that the reasoner can activate and retrieve at least one member of this class will depend on the way that this information is structured in long-term memory, the nature of the minor premise and the efficiency of the reasoner's retrieval processes. Finally, we assume that if at least one instance of a given class of information is retrieved during the reasoning process, then it will be incorporated into the mental model set that will be used in order to evaluate a given conclusion. If this is not the case, then the model set will not use the corresponding element.

A multinomial process tree model of conditional reasoning

For any given premise and for a given reasoner, one of the important factors that will determine which of the possible forms of information will be activated is (1) the way that this information is structured in long-term memory (De Neys, Schaeken, & d'Ydewalle, 2003; Markovits, 2000; Markovits, et al., 1998; Quinn & Markovits, 1998) and (2) the retrieval efficiency of a given reasoner (De Neys, Schaeken, & d'Ydewalle, 2003; Janveau-Brennan & Markovits, 1999; Markovits & Quinn, 2002). For any given major and minor premise, a specific reasoner can be characterized by the probability that he or she will retrieve at least one member of the alternatives class, which is indicated as A, and the probability that they will retrieve at least one member of the complementary class, which we will indicate as C (disabling cases will be considered later on). Thus, during the model construction phase, a reasoner can construct one of four possible model sets. These are composed of a model representing the major premise (the initial model in the classical formulation of mental model theory), with other models that represent one or both of the alternatives and complements class:

M1		p	q
M2		p	q
		Not-p	not-q

M3	p	q
	Not-p	q
M4	p	q
	Not-p	q
	Not-P	not-q

We can use a multinomial process tree (MPT) model, (Batchelder & Riefer, 1999; see also Markovits & Quinn, 2002) in order to simulate this process of model construction (see Figure 10. 1). This model allows calculating the probability of producing each of these four model sets; this is indicated in Table 10.1.

It is important to remark that the values of A and C will vary according to the particular minor premise. This is because the minor premise is used as a retrieval cue, along with the major premise. Alternatives refer to cases of [not-P is true and Q is true], while complements refer to cases of [not-P is true and not-Q is true]. Thus, the level of overlap of the minor premise with either alternatives or complements will determine the associative value of a given minor premise. The minor premise for the AC form is 'Q is true', which will make this a strong cue for alternatives and a less strong cue for complements. The minor premise for the DA form is 'P is false', which cues equally for alternatives and complements. Thus, it can be assumed that the DA minor premise will generate less activation of alternatives and more of complements than the AC minor premise (but see Barrouillet, Markovits, & Quinn (2001) for an example where this is not the case). The minor premise for the MT form is 'Q is false', which is a strong cue for complements. Thus, it can be assumed that the MT minor premise should generate less activation of alternatives and more of complements than the DA premise.

Now, given estimates of A and C, the probability of generating the four model sets specified above and, in turn the probability of accepting any given conclusion for the four logical forms, can be calculated. This model supposes that one of the key factors that determine both individual differences and developmental differences in reasoning relates to differences in the efficiency of retrieval of information from long term memory. When reasoners are attempting to derive a conclusion for a given set of premises, they must retain these premises in working memory and attempt to manipulate them. There are clearly documented effects of working memory load on information retrieval (Anderson, Reder, & Lebiere, 1996; Rosen & Engles, 1996), which show that a concurrent cognitive load does reduce the efficiency of retrieval. Incorporating this factor into the model will be done by variation in the A and C parameters.

While retrieval efficiency is an important factor in understanding developmental and individual factors in reasoning, another constraint concerns how children's processing capacity might affect the way that children reason. There are two related ways that limited working memory capacity constrains reasoning. The first is the possible limitation as to the maximum number of models that can be retained in memory. Halford (Andrews & Halford, 1998; Halford, Wilson, & Phillips, 1998) has presented evidence that younger children appear to be limited to processing two simultaneous

Table 10.1 Probability of generating each of the four possible model sets

Model set	Probability
M1	[1–A] [1–C]
M2	[1–A]C
M3	A[1–C]
M4	AC

relational schemata. The models that are used for reasoning resemble such schemata and it seems reasonable to suppose that younger children will have difficulty in manipulating more than two such models in the context of a given inference. In fact, a recent analysis of 6- and 7-year old children's justifications of conditional inferences has been found to be consistent with use of only two models (Markovits, 2000). However, by 8 or 9 years of age, children appear to be able to store 3 models simultaneously in working memory, although with some difficulty. Thus, we will assume that younger children, 6 to 7 years of age, will only be able to reason with model sets that contain no more than two elements. For these children, this leads to considering only model sets M1, M2, and M3 as possible outcomes of the initial activation and retrieval process. We will assume that children older than this can generate all four of the possible model sets.

One other way that limited working memory capacity can influence the reasoning process has to do with the necessity of applying a decision algorithm to the model set that has been constructed by the reasoner. Specifically, mental model theory assumes that a putative conclusion will be denied if there is at least one model in which this conclusion is false or if there is no model in which this conclusion is true. This procedure requires that reasoners must be able to scan their model sets and apply the algorithm to each one. Clearly, the more models there are to scan, the greater is the possibility of making an error. In order to simulate this process, a single parameter, P, will be used which represents the probability of correctly using the decision algorithm with a model set of sufficient complexity. A further assumption is made that younger children will have some degree of difficulty in applying this algorithm to 2-model sets, and that older children will have difficulty only with 3-model sets. Specifically, it is assumed that younger children will make no errors when using single-model sets, but that when they use 2-model sets, there will be a probability of (1−P) that they will make an error in applying the decision algorithm that will lead to a mistaken conclusion. Similarly, for older children, it is assumed that they will make no errors with 1- and 2-model sets, but that there will be a probability of (1−P) that they will make an error in applying the decision algorithm.

Given these parameters, the probability of a reasoner making any particular conclusion can then be calculated. The following calculations refer to the probability of a reasoner endorsing the "invited" inference for each of the four logical forms. Specifically, for MP, this is the conclusion that 'Q is true'; for MT, this is the conclusion that 'P is false'; for AC, this is the conclusion that 'P is true'; for DA, this is the conclusion that 'Q is false'. For each of the four logical forms, the probability that a reasoner will endorse the corresponding invited conclusion is calculated.

Equations for the MP inference

In the case of the MP inference, younger children, who are assumed to be limited to 1- or 2-model sets, M1, M2 and M3, are first considered. In this case, it is also assumed that when they reason with a 2-model set, the probability that they will correctly apply the decision algorithm is P. In this case, the baseline is the probability of producing only model sets M1, M2, and M3. The variable 'Total' is defined as the combined probability of producing M1 or M2 or M3. Specifically,

$$\text{Total} = [1 - A][1 - C] + [1 - A]C + A[1 - C] = 1 - AC$$

Now, examining Table 10.2 shows that all three of the model sets M1, and M2 allow the conclusion that 'Q is true'. However, model sets M2 and M3 contain 2-models, and in these cases the probability of the reasoner correctly making the conclusion that 'Q is true' is P. Thus, the relative probability of a young reasoner accepting the conclusion that 'P is true' is:

$$[\text{Prob}(M1) + \text{Prob}(M2)P + \text{Prob}(M3)P]/\text{Total}$$

Table 10.2 The conclusion allowed by each of the four possible model sets for each of the four logical forms of conditional reasoning

Set	Models	Probability	Inference made on each of the four logical forms			
			MP (p is true)	AC (q is true)	DA (p is false)	MT (q is false)
M1	p q	$(1 - A)(1 - C)$	q is true	p is true	Uncertain	Uncertain
M2	p q not-p not-q	$(1 - A) C$	q is true	p is true	q is false	p is false
M3	p q not-p q	$A (1 - C)$	q is true	Uncertain	q is true	Uncertain
M4	p q not-p q not-p not-q	$A C$	q is true	Uncertain	Uncertain	p is false

Substituting the values from Table 10.1 gives the following formula:

$$\text{Prob}(\text{``Q is true''}) = [[1 - A][1 - C] + [1 - A]CP + A[1 - C]P] / [1 - AC]$$

Older children are assumed to be capable of generating 3-model sets but will have problems applying the decision algorithm to 3-model sets but not to sets with fewer than 3 models. Using the same logic as previously, all four model sets lead to the conclusion that 'Q is true'. In addition, since M4 contains 3 models, children reasoning on the basis of M4 will correctly make this conclusion with a probability of P. Thus:

$$\text{Prob}(\text{``Q is true''}) = \text{Prob}(M1) + \text{Prob}(M2) + \text{Prob}(M3) + \text{Prob}(M4)P$$

Substituting the values from Table 10.1, gives the following formula:

$$\text{Prob}(\text{`P is true'}) = [1 - A][1 - C] + [1 - A]C + A[1 - C] + ACP$$

Equations for the AC inference

The probability of a reasoner accepting the 'P is true' conclusion for the AC inference is now examined, initially for younger children, who are assumed to be limited to 2-model sets. Examining Table 10.2 shows that both the model sets M1, and M2 allow the conclusion that 'P is true', while M3 does not. Model set M2 contains 2-models, and in this case the probability of the reasoner correctly making the conclusion that 'Q is true' is P. Similarly, the probability of the reasoner mistakenly accepting this conclusion with M3 is (1–P). Thus, the relative probability of a young reasoner accepting the conclusion that 'P is true' is:

$$[\text{Prob}(M1) + \text{Prob}(M2)P + \text{Prob}(M3)(1–P)]/\text{Total}$$

Substituting the values from Table 10.1 gives the following formula:

$$\text{Prob}(\text{`P is true'}) = [[1 - A][1 - C] + [1 - A]C \, P + A[1 - C][1 - P]] / [1 - AC]$$

For older children, only model sets M1 and M2 lead to the conclusion that 'P is true'. Since M4 contains 3 models, it is supposed that these children will mistakenly accept this conclusion with a probability of (1–P). Thus:

$$\text{Prob}(\text{`P is true'}) = \text{Prob}(M1) + \text{Prob}(M2) + \text{Prob}(M4)(1–P)$$

Substituting the values from Table 10.1, gives the following formula:

$$\text{Prob}(\text{`P is true'}) = [1 - A][1 - C] + [1 - A]C + AC[1 - P]$$

Equations for the DA inference

For the DA form, the probability of a reasoner accepting the conclusion that 'Q is false' is calculated, initially for younger children, who are assumed to be limited to 2-model sets. Examining Table 10.2 shows that only model set M2 allows the conclusion that 'Q is false', while M1 and M3 do not. Model sets M2 and M3 contain 2-models. The probability of a reasoner concluding that 'Q is false' with M2 is P, and the probability of making this conclusion when reasoning with M3 is (1–P). Thus, the relative probability of a young reasoner accepting the conclusion that 'P is true' is:

[Prob(M2)P + Prob(M3)(1 – P)]/Total

Substituting the values from Table 10.1 gives the following formula:

Prob('Q is false') = [[1 – A]C P + A[1 – C][1–P]] / [1 – AC]

For older children, only model set M2 leads to the conclusion that 'Q is false'. Since M4 contains 3 models, it is supposed that these children will mistakenly accept this conclusion with a probability of (1–P). Thus:

Prob('Q is false') = Prob(M2) + Prob(M4)(1 – P)

Substituting the values from Table 10.1, gives the following formula:

Prob('Q is false') = [1 – A]C + AC[1 – P]

Equations for the MT inference

For the MT form, the probability of a reasoner accepting the conclusion that 'P is false' is calculated, initially for younger children, who are assumed to be limited to 2-model sets. Examining Table 10.2 shows that only model set M2 allows the conclusion that 'P is false', while M1 and M3 do not. Model sets M2 and M3 contain 2-models. The probability of a reasoner concluding that 'Q is false' with M2 is P, and the probability of making this conclusion when reasoning with M3 is (1–P). Thus, the relative probability of a young reasoner accepting the conclusion that 'P is false' is:

[Prob(M2)P + Prob(M3)(1 – P)]/Total

Substituting the values from Table 10.1 gives the following formula:

Prob("P is false") = [[1 – A]C P + A[1 – C][1 – P]] / [1 – AC]

For older children, model sets M2 and M4 lead to the conclusion that 'P is false'. Since M4 contains 3 models, children using this model set will accept this conclusion with a probability of P. Thus:

Prob('P is false') = Prob(M2) + Prob(M4)P

Substituting the values from Table 10.1, gives the following formula:

Prob('P is false') = [1 – A]C + ACP

Introducing disabling conditions into the model

What these equations represent is the probability of a reasoner endorsing the invited conclusion to each of the four logical forms. These equations use three basic parameters, A, C, and P. Now, there is one further factor that must be also considered before generating a complete model of reasoning. Recent studies have examined the impact of what Cummins (Cummins, 1995; Cummins et al., 1991) has referred to as 'disabling conditions'. These are conditions, d, such that P and d are true and Q is false. For example, consider the premise 'If a rock is thrown through a window, the window will break'. A potential disabling condition in this case is having a window that is made of plexiglass. This allows for the following reasoning 'If a rock is thrown through a window that is made of plexiglass, the window will not break'. There is evidence that when reasoners are given conditional premises without explicit instructions to 'suppose that the premises are true', they will activate disabling conditions and that these will affect performance on the MP and MT forms, although to differing extents. Specifically, Cummins has found that the tendency to reject the invited inference for the MP and MT forms depends on the relative number of disabling conditions available in memory. There is also evidence that disabling conditions are retrieved from memory during reasoning, and that retrieval functions in a similar way to that observed with alternatives (De Neys, Schaeken, & d'Ydewalle, 2003; Janveau-Brennan & Markovits, 1999). These basic results are also consistent with the fact that only the minor premises for MP ('P is true') and MT ("Q is false") should directly cue for disabling conditions, with the cuing being less strong for the MT form since this also cues for complements. However, disabling conditions are somewhat more complex than either alternatives and complements, since there is also evidence that using the standard logical instructions 'suppose that the premises are true' has the effect of inhibiting retrieval of disabling conditions (Markovits & Potvin, 2001; Vadeboncoeur & Markovits, 1998). In order to model the effects of disabling conditions, the following assumptions are made. First, that there is no significant activation of disabling conditions for the AC and DA forms, and, second, that activation of a disabling condition when reasoning with either the MP or MT forms will result in the construction of a single model set that contains the disabling condition and some combination of other elements. This model set will produce a denial of the invited conclusion for both MP and MT forms if properly manipulated, and that the probability of this happening is equal to P.

Using these simplifying assumptions, the equations for MP and MT must be corrected in two ways. First, if D represents the probability of retrieving a disabling condition, then the probability of accepting the invited conclusion must be decreased by D. Also, since the model set containing a disabling condition is considered separately from the four basic model sets, the relative probability of accepting the invited conclusion must also adjust for the addition of this model set to the total number of model sets that can be produced. This gives the following equations:

For MP with young children who are limited to 2-model sets:

$$\text{Total} = [1-A][1-C] + [1-A]C + A[1-C] + D$$

$$\text{Prob('Q is true')} = [[1-A][1-C] + [1-A]CP + A[1-C]P - DP]/[[1-A][1-C] + [1-A]C + A[1-C] + D]$$

For MP with children who can manipulate 3-model sets:

$$\text{Total} = [1-A][1-C] + [1-A]C + A[1-C] + AC + D$$

$$\text{Prob('P is true')} = [[1-A][1-C] + [1-A]C + A[1-C] + ACP - DP]/[[1-A][1-C] + [1-A]C + A[1-C] + AC + D]$$

For MT with young children who are limited to 2-model sets:

$$\text{Prob('P is false')} = [[1-A]CP + A[1-C][1-P] - DP]/[[1-A][1-C] + [1-A]C + A[1-C] + D]$$

For MT with children who can manipulate 3-model sets:

$$\text{Prob('P is false')} = [[1-A]C + ACP - DP]/]/[[1-A][1-C] + [1-A]C + A[1-C] + AC + D]$$

At this point, there is a complete set of equations that allow prediction of performance on the four logical forms as a function of five basic parameters. These are N, the maximum number of models that a child can store in working memory; P, the probability of correctly applying the decision algorithm to any model set with N models; A, the probability of retrieving an alternative case during reasoning; C, the probability of retrieving a complementary case during reasoning; D, the probability of retrieving a disabling condition during reasoning.

Estimating model parameters

In order to simulate the developmental pattern in conditional reasoning, estimates of what these values might be are required. Following Halford, Wilson, & Phillips (1998), N = 2 for children who are less than about 8-years of age, and N = 3 for older children. Thus, for North American elementary school grades 1 and 2, N = 2 and for children in higher grade levels, N = 3. P is the probability of correctly applying the decision algorithm with a model set of N models. One estimate of P be can be derived from Markovits (2000). This suggests that when younger children are reasoning with 2-model sets, their efficiency is in the range of 80% or so. When older children are dealing with 3-model sets, their efficiency is in the range of 50%. These allow setting the following values to N and P as a function of grade level. These values are of course somewhat arbitrary, but they do reflect what appears to be a likely developmental pattern.

Grade level	N	P
1	2	.80
2	2	.90
3	3	.20
4	3	.30
5	3	.40
6	3	.50

The next problem is determining potential values for A, C, and D. These values are assumed to vary, with development, with specific content, and with the nature of the specific minor premise used in a given inference. One way of obtaining a realistic estimation of what these values might be relies on the supposition that when asked to justify their inferences, children will refer to salient information that is in the model set used to make the inference. The question then is how best to use these justifications to make a reasonable estimate of what the corresponding models are. In order to do this, two assumptions are made. The first one is that when a disabling condition is present in the model set, the reasoner will tend to use this preferentially as a justification. There are several reasons for this assumption, but the most direct is simply that a disabling condition will have the strongest effect on the inferential process and thus the greatest relevance, in the sense that has been used by Sperber & Wilson (1986). Second, it is assumed that if there is no disabling condition, reasoners will preferentially use alternate antecedents if these are present, for the same basic reason, followed by complements if neither disabling conditions or alternative antecedents are present.

Three existing data sets that have examined both responses and justifications to conditional reasoning problems will be used to estimate retrieval parameters. These are a study by Janveau-Brennan and Markovits (1999), which looked at conditional reasoning using causal conditionals (if cause P then effect Q), which had either few or many potential alternatives to the antecedent, a study by Markovits, Venet, Janveau-Brennan, Malfait, Pion, & Vadeboncoeur (1996), which looked at reasoning using class based conditionals (All P have characteristic Q), which were chosen to have many potential alternatives and were presented in either a realistic or a fantasy context, and a study by Markovits (2000), which used class based conditionals with either many or few potential alternatives. The data sets for these studies were re-analyzed in order to give a detailed analysis of justifications that were used by reasoners by grade level and premise type. These are given in Tables 10.3, 10.4, and 10.5. Note that these tables include the observed values for alternate antecedents and disabling conditions, and the adjusted values for complements. The algorithm for this latter is described below.

Before proceeding to the simulation, these combined data were examined to look at some patterns in the relative use of alternatives and disabling conditions. In order to do this, the class-based premises used in the Markovits et al. (1996) study in the realistic condition were considered to be equivalent to class-based premises with many potential alternatives, and premises presented in a fantasy context were discarded. The results of the three studies for grades 1, 2, and 5 were combined (these were the grades for which there was data for all four premise types). This gave a total of 462 children across these three grade levels, with the number of subjects per cell varying between 22 and 55.

The combined data was then examined, initially concentrating on use of alternatives to the antecedent as a justification. Table 10.6 gives the percentage of justifications that referred to potential alternative antecedents as a function of grade level, premise type and relative number of available alternative antecedents for this combined data set. Inspection of this table shows a clear pattern, one that is reflected in mean use of alternatives in justifications when collapsed across all other factors. Specifically, and as expected, the mean percentage of these justifications is greatest for the AC form (44.9%) than for the DA form (22.6%), which is greater in turn than the numbers observed for the MT form (7.4%) and for the MP form (4.7%). This basic pattern is relatively consistently found across all of the premise types and grade levels, and supports the idea that the minor premise in each of the four logical forms will differentially cue for alternative antecedents. Note that this model also predicts that a change in the formulation of the minor premise of the DA form can result in a much stronger cuing effects for antecedents (Barrouillet et al., 2001). One other factor that is particularly interesting is the effect of age. Overall, there is a clear increase in the use of alternative antecedents with age. A second analysis then looked at use of disabling conditions. Since the absolute numbers of disabling conditions used by children were relatively small, the combined totals for the four forms are given. The mean percentage of disabling conditions used was greatest for the MP form (8.2%), less for the MT form (3.1%), and close to zero for the AC form (0.4%) and for the DA form (0.3%). This pattern is also consistent with expectations. In this case there was also a general increase in use of disabling conditions with age.

Thus the way that children's justifications are distributed among the four logical forms is quite consistent with some key ideas that are the basis of this model. First, they clearly support the idea that children use the minor premise as a cue for retrieving information during reasoning. Second, they also support the idea that one of the key factors in the development of reasoning is the increasing efficiency with which children can retrieve information that is stored in long-term memory.

The basic pattern of the justifications that children use for the four logical forms is clearly consistent with the model. The next step will be to predict what kinds of inferences children will make based on the idea that their justifications are representative of information included in the mental model set that is used for reasoning. One key assumption here is that when children incorporate either disabling conditions or alternative antecedents into their model sets, they will use these as justifications (with priority given to disabling conditions). This allows an estimate the relative probability of retrieving one of these two classes of information by the relative frequency of their use as an explicit justification. One other general question remains in order to allow for a reasonable estimation of the relative probability of retrieving information corresponding to complements. Analysis of the three studies that have asked for children's justifications shows that children will often use other forms of information, such as simple repetition of premises, or empirically based justifications (with this being more common in younger children). In order to translate these, one further assumption must be made. Specifically, it is assumed that children will use these forms of justification when a conclusion seems obvious to them, and they feel constrained to formulate some reason. When will this happen? In the case of the MP and AC forms, this will be the case when reasoners use M1 to accept the invited conclusion (i.e., when they base their conclusion on the single model representing the major premise terms). Thus, for the MP and AC forms, justifications that mention disabling conditions, alternative antecedents, or complements will provide some direct estimation of the relative frequency with which these elements are generated by reasoners, since we assume that other responses, are generated when none of these three types of information is present. One exception to this concerns repetition of the premises. In some cases, reasoners will simply repeat the premises as shorthand for the complement, since 'if P then Q' statements imply the invited inference that 'if not-P then not-Q' (Fillenbaum, 1975). It can then be assumed that, for the MP and AC inferences, this will be the case about 50% of the time. In the case of the DA and MT forms, the situation is more complex. In these cases, the 'most obvious' response occurs when the reasoner has generated the complement, since this is the only model that allows immediate acceptance of the invited inference in both cases. This suggests that many of the other kinds of responses that are generated by children may well indicate the presence of the complement. Thus, in this case, it will simply be assumed that all responses other than specific references to disabling conditions, alternatives or complements actually indicate the existence of complements in the reasoner's model set.

In order to estimate the values of A and D, the relative frequency with which alternatives and disabling conditions are used as justifications will be used as the probability that these conditions can be retrieved, for each of the four logical forms. For example, if children at a given age, when making the MP inference for a specific type of premise, use a potential alternative to the antecedent as a justification, 25% of the time, the probability of retrieving a potential alternative, A, will be .25, for that minor premise, premise type and age level. The value of C for the MP and AC inferences is estimated by adding the rates of explicit references to the complement to 50% of the rate of repetition of premises. For the DA and MT inferences, C is determined by adding the relative frequency of explicit use of complements to that of any other justification that does not refer to alternatives or disabling conditions.

Simulating children's reasoning

This model can then be used to simulate the kinds of inferences that children make using the data sets for which children's justifications are available. The first set that is examined is taken from Markovits (2000), for which the pattern of justification used is given in Table 10.3. In this study, children at grades 1, 2, and 5 were given class-based premises. These were of two kinds, premises for which there were many potential alternative antecedents and one for which there were relatively few such antecedents. Table 10.7 gives both the estimated percentage of times the invited conclusion was accepted for the four logical forms according to the model and the observed values. This same procedure was done using data from the Janveau-Brennan & Markovits (1999) study. In this study, children at five grade levels were given causal conditional premises that had either relatively few or relatively many potential alternatives to the antecedent (see Table 10.4). Table 10.8 gives the observed and predicted responses to the four logical forms by premise type and grade level. Finally, another data set, taken from Markovits, et al. (1996) was also examined (see Table 10.6). In this study, the same premises (which were chosen to have many potential

Table 10.3 Percentage of justifications given for each logical form in the Markovits (2000) study adjusted for complements

Grade	Justification	Class-based premises with few alternatives				Class-based premises with many alternatives			
		AC	DA	MP	MT	AC	DA	MP	MT
1	Alternatives	25.0	0	0	2.3	45.5	18.2	9.1	6.8
	Complements	17.0	97.7	36.4	90.9	6.8	82	18.2	93.0
	Disabling	4.5	2.3	9.1	6.8	2.3	0	0	0
2	Alternatives	47.7	31.8	4.5	9.1	62.5	35.0	10.0	2.5
	Complements	20.5	65.9	50.0	86.4	18.8	65.0	50.0	95.0
	Disabling	0	2.3	13.6	4.5	0	0	0	2.5
5	Alternatives	84.1	65.9	9.1	27.3	93.8	68.8	0	10.4
	Complements	6.8	34.1	63.4	59.1	5.2	31.2	62.5	77.1
	Disabling	0	0	18.2	13.6	0	0	12.5	12.5

antecedents) were used, but these were embedded into either a realistic or a fantasy context (the context was shown to have had an affect on the relative degree of activation of information about the premises). Table 10.9 gives the observed and predicted responses to the four logical forms by context and grade level.

Table 10.4 Percentage of justifications given for each logical form in the Janveau-Brennan & Markovits (1999) study adjusted for complements

Grade	Justification	Causal premises with few alternatives				Causal premises with many alternatives			
		AC	DA	MP	MT	AC	DA	MP	MT
1	Alternatives	12.5	6.3	4.2	5.2	21.8	7.3	6.4	1.8
	Complements	14.1	93.8	10.9	94.8	10.5	92.7	10.0	97.3
	Disabling	1.0	0	11.5	0	0	0	0	0.9
2	Alternatives	21.0	11.0	1.0	5.0	40.4	16.4	8.7	2.9
	Complements	18.5	89.0	16.0	95.0	12.0	83.7	13.5	96.2
	Disabling	0	0	11.0	0	0	0	0	1.0
3	Alternatives	34.4	16.7	1.04	4.17	50.0	14.9	3.5	7.9
	Complements	15.1	83.3	3.6	94.8	12.7	85.1	12.7	91.2
	Disabling	0	0	16.7	1.0	0	0	0	0.9
5	Alternatives	57.3	31.3	1.0	15.6	81.1	50.9	4.7	11.3
	Complements	10.9	67.7	9.4	79.2	6.6	49.1	14.2	84.9
	Disabling	0	1.0	30.2	5.2	0	0	0.9	3.8
6	Alternatives	64.4	39.4	0	13.5	83.7	46.9	7.1	6.1
	Complements	3.8	60.6	3.4	76.9	3.6	53.1	15.3	87.8
	Disabling	0	0	41.3	9.6	1.0	0	4.1	6.1

Table 10.5 Percentage of justifications given for each logical form in the Markovits, et al. (1996) study with adjusted complements for all logical forms

Grade	Justification	Class-based premises in a realistic context				Class-based premises in a fantasy context			
		AC	DA	MP	MT	AC	DA	MP	MT
2	Alternatives	33.3	45.8	4.2	0	16.7	0	0	0
	Complements	4.2	54.2	6.3	100	18.8	100	20.8	100
	Disabling	0	0	0	0	0	0	0	0
4	Alternatives	63.2	47.4	0	7.9	25.0	32.5	0	2.5
	Complements	32.6	52.6	5.2	92.1	16.3	67.5	13.8	97.5
	Disabling	0	0	0	0	0	0	0	0
6	Alternatives	73.7	57.9	0	15.8	25.0	36.1	0	0
	Complements	3.9	42.1	2.6	84.2	18.1	63.9	18.1	100
	Disabling	0	0	0	0	0	0	0	0

There are thus a total of 22 separate data sets, involving several grade levels and a large variety of premise types. In order to get an idea of the fit of the model to these sets, the correlations between the observed values and the predicted values were calculated. The correlations for the MP, MT, AC and DA forms were .944, .866, .971, and .871, respectively. Thus, this model accounts for between 75% and 94% of the variance in responses to the four logical forms. It is useful to note that the lower correlations were not related to response variability, as shown by the very high correlation for the AC form, for which the observed variation in responses was very large.

Table 10.6 Percentage of justifications referring to potential alternative antecedents for each of the four logical forms as a function of grade level, premise type and relative number of available antecedents for combined data set

Grade level	Premise type	Number of alternatives	Logical form			
			MP	MT	AC	DA
1	Causal	Few	4.2	5.2	12.5	6.3
		Many	6.4	1.8	21.8	7.3
	Class	Few	0.0	2.3	25.0	0.0
		Many	9.1	6.8	45.5	18.2
2	Causal	Few	1.0	5.0	21.0	11.0
		Many	8.7	2.9	40.4	16.3
	Class	Few	4.5	9.1	47.7	31.8
		Many	6.8	1.1	46.6	40.9
5	Causal	Few	1.0	15.6	57.3	31.3
		Many	4.7	11.3	81.1	50.9
	Class	Few	9.1	27.3	84.1	65.9
		Many	0.0	10.4	93.8	68.8

Table 10.7 Responses to the four logical forms predicted and real (Markovits, 2000)

Grade		Premises with few alternatives				Premises with many alternatives			
		MP	MT	AC	DA	MP	MT	AC	DA
1	Real	77	66	68	77	86	66	55	48
	Predicted	78	63	73	74	95	74	61	64
2	Real	77	70	43	52	90	70	38	28
	Predicted	72	69	61	49	95	81	47	51
5	Real	77	43	14	21	73	44	10	10
	Predicted	76	39	19	25	84	60	9	23

Instead, the lower correlations were for the two forms for which the estimate of the probability of retrieval of complements was possibly the least accurate.

These data provide quite convincing evidence that the multinomial process tree model is able to accurately predict the relative distribution of responses across the four logical forms for children within the age levels examined in these studies. One of the major factors in the model concerns relative access to stored information. In particular, the model is very sensitive to the extent to which alternative antecedents are retrieved. The model predicts that increasing access to alternatives results in decreases in the acceptance of the invited conclusion to all four of the logical forms. Since access to alternatives generally increases quite rapidly with age for the AC and DA forms, this would explain the large age-related decreases observed in the rate at which these conclusions are accepted. The same basic phenomena is observed with the MT form, although to a lesser extent, since the overall probability of activating an alternative is much lower than for the AC and DA forms. Developmentally, this results in very young children accepting the MT inference at a very high rate, with a decrease in such responding with increasing age. Given that the 'logically correct' response to the MT form is accepting the invited conclusion, this leads to a pattern of responding where younger children will appear to perform more logically than older ones on MT, a pattern that has indeed been found (O'Brien & Overton, 1980; 1982). Although the MP

Table 10.8 Responses to the four logical forms predicted and real in the Janveau-Brennan & Markovits (1999) study

Grade		Premises with few alternatives				Premises with many alternatives			
		MP	MT	AC	DA	MP	MT	AC	DA
1	Real	78	82	90	84	97	88	83	95
	Predicted	79	76	87	75	100	76	82	74
2	Real	76	88	81	90	99	93	60	84
	Predicted	80	85	82	79	98	85	65	73
3	Real	69	89	66	85	100	94	51	87
	Predicted	83	91	70	81	100	84	55	83
5	Real	57	75	41	71	98	85	18	49
	Predicted	67	66	46	58	98	75	22	39
6	Real	51	70	36	58	95	88	7	55
	Predicted	56	61	37	49	94	77	17	41

Table 10.9 Responses to the four logical forms predicted and real in the Markovits, et al. (1996) study

Grade		Realistic context				Fantasy context			
		MP	MT	AC	DA	MP	MT	AC	DA
2	Real	100	100	50	25	100	92	63	63
	Predicted	99	90	71	38	98	90	86	90
4	Real	100	87	29	37	98	95	65	50
	Predicted	100	87	51	45	100	96	78	61
6	Real	97	97	18	18	92	100	64	50
	Predicted	100	77	28	30	100	100	77	52

form does not activate alternatives very highly, the same basic prediction as for MT would be made. There is also some evidence that children will respond by refusing the MP inference more frequently when there is increased activation of an alternative (Markovits & Vachon, 1990; Rumain, Connell, & Braine, 1983).

Conclusion

In this chapter, we have presented a multinomial process tree model for conditional reasoning, based on Markovits and Barrouillet's (2002) developmental theory of conditional reasoning. This model assumes that reasoners produce inferences from a set of mental models, in which the basic elements are determined directly by the kind of information about the premises that are retrieved from long term memory during the inferential process. The nature of this representation is strongly determined by the way the relevant information is structured in long-term memory, the relative efficiency of the retrieval process, and the capacity of the working memory in which mental models are held and processed. Specifically, the theory assumes that when presented with a conditional premise of the form 'if P then Q', reasoners construct a first P–Q model the content of which is directly provided by the conditional premise. It is also assumed that reasoners attempt to access knowledge that is relevant for the relation between P and Q from their long-term memory, and that this knowledge is used to construct additional mental models. This knowledge belongs to one of three classes of information. The first corresponds to the complementary class because it contains cases of the form [not P and not Q]. The second class contains those cases in which alternatives differing from P result in the same consequent Q [not-P and Q]. Finally, the third class corresponds to what Cummins (1995) has called disabling conditions, i.e., conditions that can allow the antecedent to be true while the consequent is false [P and not-Q]. The model set that is used for making a given inference will be determined by which of these three possible classes of information is retrieved during the reasoning process. Thus, the nature of the model sets used to make a given inference can be characterized by the probability of retrieving each of the three classes of inference.

This model specifies two main constraints on conditional reasoning. The first corresponds to the nature of the mental model set constructed, which depends both on the structure of the available knowledge in long-term memory and on the efficiency of its retrieval, a process that is probabilistic in nature. The second constraint results from working memory limitations that determine the maximum number of mental models that can be processed as well as the efficiency of this processing. As far as the nature of the model set constructed is concerned, it depends on three parameters, A, C, and D, that refer to the probability of retrieving at least one member of the alternative, complementary, and disabling condition classes respectively. These probabilities depend in turn on the nature of the minor premise from which a conclusion is to be drawn. For example, knowing that the consequent Q is satisfied will obviously increase the probability of retrieving an alternative case and decrease the probability of accessing a member of the complementary class or a disabling condition. As far as working memory limitations are concerned, it is assumed that young children are limited to a maximum of two models (see Halford, et al., 1998), whereas older children can process three-model sets. When these maximum numbers are reached, a parameter P determines the probability for a correct processing, a probability that increases with age.

This model proved to be highly predictive of the performances of various groups of children of different ages. It is thus able to account for developmental processes. Moreover, it gives a simple account of the ubiquitous content effects in conditional reasoning. Indeed, the model assumes that inference production depends strongly and directly on the availability of knowledge in long-term memory. Thus, even if it is supposed that the maximum complexity of the mental model set a given individual can process is fixed, performance can greatly vary from one content to another depending on the availability of the relevant knowledge to construct the adequate representation. Thus, this model satisfies the agenda that Evans (1991) fixed for any theory of reasoning, because it accounts for the human reasoning competence, for the errors produced, as well as for developmental and content effects.

Finally, it should be noted that the good fit observed between computational and empirical data results from an evaluation of the A, C, and D parameters that are based on verbal reports and justifications given by children. This point suggests that, contrary to what it has been sometimes argued (e.g., Evans, 1989), justifications and verbal reports of reasoning activities are not just post hoc rationalizations of reasoning processes, which remain at least in part unconscious. In contrast, this suggests that, in line with mental model theory, reasoning is achieved through an explicit process of manipulating representations that are held in the focus of attention in working memory. There is thus no reason to cast in doubt the verbal report individuals can give of their lines of reasoning. Even if the retrieval processes that underpin the construction of the models remain largely automatic and unconscious, the content of the models on which reasoning is based can be explicitly reported and used as justifications for a given conclusion.

However, the model presented here departs from the standard mental models theory that assumes that there exists some core meaning for 'If' that corresponds to the three possible states of affairs (p . q, not p . q, and not p . not q), a core meaning that can be modulated by content and context (Johnson-Laird & Byrne, 2002). Instead, the basic claim used here is far simpler. The mental models used to make a specific conditional inference result from a simple process of retrieval from long-term memory. This is made possible by the fact that this process does not provide reasoners with isolated tokens that might be organized in a predefined way, but with meaningful relations between specific events that are related to the relation and the events involved in the conditional premise. Thus, though the computational model and the equations that are presented here might seem rather complex, the cognitive processes they mimic are very simple and general. This is the reason for which there is no need to hypothesize specialized cognitive rules, algorithms, or representational schemas devoted to deduction in order to account for developmental and content effects in conditional reasoning.

Author note

Preparation of this manuscript was supported by grants from the National Sciences and Engineering Council of Canada (NSERC) and from the Fonds pour la Formation de Chercheurs et l'Aide a la Recherche (FCAR) to the first author.

Correspondence concerning this article should be addressed to Henry Markovits, Psychology Department, University of Plymouth, Drake Circus, Plymouth, Devon PL4 8AA, United Kingdom. E-mail: hmarkovits@plymouth.ac.uk

References

Anderson, J. R. (1993). *Rules of the mind.* Hillsdale, NJ: Lawrence Erlbaum Assoc.

*Anderson, J. R., Reder, L. M., & Lebiere, C. (1996). Working memory: Activation limitations on retrieval, *Cognitive Psychology*, **30**, 221–256.

*Andrews, G. & Halford, G. S. (1998). Children's ability to make transitive inferences: The importance of premise integration and structural complexity, *Cognitive Development*, **13**, 479–513.

*Barrouillet, P. & Lecas, J. F. (1998). How can mental models account for content effects in conditional reasoning: A developmental perspective. *Cognition*, **67**, 209–253.

Barrouillet, P. & Lecas, J. F. (1999). Mental models in conditional reasoning and working memory. *Thinking and Reasoning*, **5**(4), 289–302.

Barrouillet & Lecas (2002). Content and context effects in children's and adult's conditional reasoning. *Quarterly Journal of Experimental Psychology*, **55A**(3), 839–854.

Barrouillet, P., Grosset, N., & Lecas, J. F. (2000). Conditional reasoning by mental models: Chronometric and developmental evidences. *Cognition*, **75**, 237–266.

*Barrouillet, P., Markovits, H., & Quinn, S. (2001). Developmental and content effects in reasoning with causal conditionals. *Journal of Experimental Child Psychology*, **81**, 235–248.

*Batchelder, W. H. & Riefer, D. M. (1999). Theoretical and empirical review of multinomial process tree modeling. *Psychonomic Bulletin and Review*, **6**(1), 57–86.

Braine, M. D. S. (1978). On the relation between the natural logic of reasoning and standard logic. *Psychological Review*, **85**, 1–21.

Braine, M. D. S. (1990). The "natural logic" approach to reasoning. In W. F. Overton (Ed.), *Reasoning, necessity and logic: Developmental perspectives.* Hillsdale, NJ: Lawrence Erlbaum Assoc.

Braine, M. D. S. & O'Brien, D. P. (1991). A theory of if: Lexical entry, reasoning program, and pragmatic principles. *Psychological Review*, **98**, 182–203.

Bucci, W. (1978). The interpretation of universal affirmative propositions. *Cognition*, **6**, 55–77.

Byrnes, J. P. & Overton, W. F. (1986). Reasoning about certainty and uncertainty in concrete, causal, and propositional contexts. *Developmental Psychology*, **22**, 793–799.

*Cahan, S. & Artman, L. (1997). Is everyday experience dysfunctional for the development of conditional reasoning. *Cognitive Development*, **12**(2), 261–279.

Chater, N. & Oaksford, M. (1999). The probability heuristics model of syllogistic reasoning. *Cognitive Psychology*, **38**, 191–258.

Cheng, P. W. & Holyoak, K. J. (1985). Pragmatic reasoning schemas. *Cognitive Psychology*, **17**, 391–416.

*Cummins, D. D. (1995). Naive theories and causal deduction, *Memory and Cognition*, **23**(5), 646–658.

*Cummins, D. D., Lubart, T., Alksnis, O., & Rist, R. (1991). Conditional reasoning and causation. *Memory and Cognition*, **19**(3), 274–282.

*De Neys, W., Schaeken, W., & d'Ydewalle, G. (2002). Inference suppression and semantic memory retrieval: Every counterexample counts. *Memory and Cognition*, **31**, 581–595.

Dias, M. G. & Harris, P. L. (1988). The effect of make-believe play on deductive reasoning. *British Journal of Developmental Psychology*, **6**, 207–221.

Dias, M. G. & Harris, P. L. (1990). The influence of the imagination on reasoning. *British Journal of Developmental Psychology*, **8**, 305–318.

*Evans, J. St.B. T. (1989). *Biases in human reasoning: Causes and consequences.* Hove: Lawrence Erlbaum.

*Evans, J. St.B. T. (1991). Theories of human reasoning: The fragmented state of the art. *Theory and Psychology*, **1**, 83–105.

*Fillenbaum, S. (1975). If: some uses. *Psychological Research*, **37**, 245–260.

Goel, V., Buchel, C., Frith, C., & Dolan, R. J. (2000). Dissociation of mechanisms underlying syllogistic reasoning. *NeuroImage*, **12**, 504–514.

Halford, G. S., Bain, J. D., Maybery, M. T., & Andrews, G. (1998). Induction of relational schemas: Common processes in reasoning and complex learning. *Cognitive Psychology*, **35**(3), 201–245.

*Halford, G. S., Wilson, W. H., & Phillips, S. (1998). Processing capacity defined by relational complexity: Implications for comparative, developmental, and cognitive psychology. *Behavorial and Brain Sciences*, **21**(6), 803–864.

Hawkins, J., Pea, R. D., Glick, J., & Scribner, S. (1984). 'Merds that laugh don't like mushrooms': Evidence for deductive reasoning by preschoolers. *Developmental Psychology*, **20**(4), 584–594.

Inhelder, B. & Piaget, J. (1958). *The growth of logical thinking from childhood to adolescence*. New York: Basic Books.

*Janveau-Brennan, G. & Markovits, H. (1999). The development of reasoning with causal conditionals. *Developmental Psychology*, **35**(4), 904–911.

*Johnson-Laird, P. N. (1983). *Mental Models*. Cambridge: Harvard University Press.

*Johnson-Laird, P. N. & Byrne, R. M. J. (1991). *Deduction*. Hillsdale, NJ: Laurence Erlbaum Assoc.

*Johnson-Laird, P. N. & Byrne, R. M. J. (2002). Conditionals: a theory of meaning, pragmatics, and inference. *Psychological Review*, **109**, 646–678.

Johnson-Laird, P. N., Byrne, R. M. J., & Schaeken, W. (1992). Propositional reasoning by model. *Psychological Review*, **99**, 418–439.

Johnson-Laird, P. N & Steedman, M. (1978). The psychology of syllogisms. *Cognitive Psychology*, **10**, 64–99.

Karmiloff-Smith, A. (1995). *Beyond modularity: A developmental perspective on cognitive science*. Cambridge, MA: Bradford Books, MIT Press.

Klaczynski, P. A. & Narashimham, G. (1998). Representations as mediators of adolescent deductive reasoning. *Developmental Psychology*, **5**, 865–881.

*Knifong, J. O. (1974). Logical abilities of children - two styles of approach. *Child Development*, **45**, 78–83.

Kuhn, D. (1977). Conditional reasoning in children. *Developmental Psychology*, **13**, 342–353.

Lecas, J.F. & Barrouillet, P. (1999). Understanding of conditional rules in childhood and adolescence: A mental models approach. *Current Psychology of Cognition*, **18**(3), 363–396.

Marcus, S. L, & Rips, L. J. (1979). Conditional reasoning. *Journal of Verbal Learning and Verbal Behavior*, **18**, 199–223.

*Markovits, H. (1985). Incorrect conditional reasoning among adults: Competence or performance? *British Journal of Psychology*, **76**, 241–247.

*Markovits, H. (2000). A mental model analysis of young children's conditional reasoning with meaningful premises. *Thinking and Reasoning*, **6**(4), 335–348.

Markovits, H. (2002). *Is inferential reasoning probabilistic?* Manuscript submitted for publication.

Markovits, H. & Barrouillet, P. (2002). The development of conditional reasoning: A mental model account. *Developmental Review*, **22**(1), 5–36.

Markovits, H., Doyon, C. & Simoneau, M. (2002). Individual differences in working memory and conditional reasoning with concrete and abstract content. *Thinking and Reasoning*, **8**(2), 97–107.

Markovits, H. & Potvin, F. (2001). Suppression of valid inferences and knowledge structures: The curious effect of producing alternative antecedents on reasoning with causal conditionals. *Memory and Cognition*, **29**(5), 736–744.

*Markovits, H. & Quinn, S. (2002). Efficiency of retrieval correlates with 'logical' reasoning from causal conditional premises. *Memory and Cognition*, **30**(5), 696–706.

Markovits, H. & Vachon, R. (1989). Reasoning with contrary-to-fact propositions. *Journal of Experimental Child Psychology*, **47**, 398–412.

*Markovits, H. & Vachon, R. (1990). Conditional reasoning, representation, and level of abstraction. *Developmental Psychology*, **26**(6), 942–951.

*Markovits, H., Fleury, M.-L., Quinn, S., & Venet, M. (1998). Conditional reasoning and the structure of semantic memory. *Child Development*, **64**(3), 742–755.

Markovits, H., Venet, M., Janveau-Brennan, G., Malfait, N., Pion, N., & Vadeboncoeur, I. (1996). Reasoning in young children: Fantasy and information retrieval. *Child Development*, **67**, 2857–2872.

Oaksford, M. & Chater, N. (2001). The probabilistic approach to human reasoning. *Trends in Cognitive Sciences*, **5**(8), 349–357.

Oaksford, M., Chater, N., & Larkin, J. (2000). Probabilities and polarity biases in conditional inference. *Journal of Experimental Psychology: Learning, Memory, and Cognition*, **26**(4), 883–899.

O'Brien, D. P., Costa, G., & Overton, W. F. (1986). Evaluations of causal and conditional hypotheses. *Quarterly Journal of Experimental Psychology*, **38A**, 493–512.

*O'Brien, D. P. & Overton, W. F. (1980). Conditional reasoning following contradictory evidence: A developmental analysis. Journal of Experimental Child Psychology, 30, 44–61.

O'Brien, D. P. & Overton, W. F. (1982). Conditional reasoning and the competence-performance issue: A developmental analysis of a training task. *Journal of Experimental Child Psychology*, **34**, 274–290.

Overton, W. F., Ward, S. L., Black, J., Noveck, I. A., & O'Brien, D. P. (1987). Form and content in the development of deductive reasoning. *Developmental Psychology*, **23**(1), 22–30.

*Quinn, S. & Markovits, H. (1998). Conditional Reasoning, Causality, and the Structure of Semantic Memory: Strength of Association as a Predictive Factor for Content Effects. *Cognition*, **68**, B93-B101.

Quinn, S. & Markovits, H. (2002). Conditional reasoning with causal premises: Evidence for a retrieval model. *Thinking and Reasoning*, **8**(3), 179–191.

Rips, L. J. (1983). Cognitive processes in propositional reasoning. *Psychological Review*, **90**, 38–71.

Rips, L. J. (1994). *The psychology of proof: Deductive reasoning in human thinking*. Cambridge, MA: MIT Press.

Roberge, J. J. & Flexer, B. K (1979). Further examinations of formal operational reasoning abilities, *Child Development*, **50**(2), 478–484.

*Rosen, V. M. & Engle, R. W. (1996). The role of working memory capacity in retrieval. *Journal of Experimental Psychology: General*, **126**(3), 211–227.

Rumain, B., Connell, J., & Braine, M.D.S. (1983). Conversational comprehension processes are responsible for reasoning fallacies in children as well as adults. *Developmental Psychology*, **19**, 471–481.

*Scholnick, E. K. & Wing, C. S. (1995). Logic in conversation: Comparative studies of deduction in children and adults. *Cognitive Development*, **10**(3), 319–345.

Sigel, I. E. (Ed.). (1999). *Development of mental representation: Theories and applications*. Mawah, NJ: Lawrence Erlbaum Assoc.

*Sperber, D. & Wilson, D. (1986). *Relevance: Communication and cognition*. Oxford: Basil Blackwell.

*Thompson, V. A. (1994). Interpretational factors in conditional reasoning. *Memory and Cognition*, **22**(6), 742–758.

Vadeboncoeur, I. & Markovits, H. (1999). The effect of instructions and information retrieval on accepting the premises in a conditional reasoning task. *Thinking and Reasoning*, **5**(2), 97–113.

Venet, M. & Markovits, H. (2001). Understanding uncertainty with abstract conditional premises. *Merrill-Palmer Quarterly*, **47**(1), 74–99.

Ward, S. L. & Overton, W. F. (1990). Semantic familiarity, relevance, and the development of deductive reasoning. *Developmental Psychology*, **26**, 488–493.

Wildman, T. M. & Fletcher, H. J. (1977). Developmental increases and decreases in solutions of conditional syllogism problems. *Developmental Psychology*, **13**, 630–636.

Chapter 11

Counterexample retrieval and inhibition during conditional reasoning: Direct evidence from memory probing

Wim De Neys

In one of Bill Waterson's hilarious 'Calvin and Hobbes' cartoons, Calvin is standing in the garden with a big can of water. The plants in the garden are on the verge of wilting and with an evil grin on his face, Calvin proudly exclaims that it is up to him to decide if they get water or not. He keeps on shouting that their very lives are in *his* hands and that *he* controls their fate. Calvin's aspirations of absolute power are short-lived, however. In the next frame, we can see a very disappointed Calvin standing in the middle of a sudden rain shower that is providing the victorious plants with all the water they could ever dream of.

This cartoon is decorating my office door. It is a superb illustration of a classic reasoning fallacy. Calvin knows that if you water plants, they stay healthy. Based on this conditional (e.g., 'if, then') knowledge he infers that if he doesn't water the plants, it follows that they will die. In logic, this inference is known as the Denial of the Antecedent fallacy (DA). A conditional links a specific precondition or cause (e.g., you water the plants) with a specific consequence or effect (e.g., the plants stay healthy). Logically speaking, a conditional utterance implies that if the precondition is met, the effect should always follow. However, this does not mean that if the precondition is not met, the effect cannot occur. There might be other conditions that can result in the occurrence of the effect (e.g., 'it might rain'). Most adults will spontaneously think of such alternative causes and this will help them to avoid Calvin's fallacious reasoning (and utter disappointment).

Over the last two decades it has been argued that the search for such alternatives (or 'counterexamples') lies at the core of the conditional reasoning process. It is assumed that when faced with a conditional, people will spontaneously search their semantic memory for stored alternative causes. Retrieval of such alternatives helps people to reject invalid inferences such as the above illustrated DA or related Affirmation of the Consequent (AC) fallacy.

Numerous studies showed that the easier it is for people to think of possible alternatives, the less they accept the invalid AC and DA inferences. In one of the classic studies Cummins, Lubart, Alksnis, and Rist (1991) measured in a pretest how many alternative causes people could generate for a set of conditionals. When Cummins used these conditionals in a reasoning task with different participants, she found that the invalid inferences were less frequently accepted when a conditional had many vs. few possible alternatives. Likewise, Markovits and Quinn (2002) measured individual differences in people's memory retrieval capacity (i.e., how easily they could come up with alternatives for a set of conditionals) in a pretest. A subsequent reasoning test showed that participants with a better retrieval capacity were less likely to commit the AC or DA fallacy.

Retrieving stored alternatives from memory makes people better logical reasoners: It helps us to reject *invalid* inferences. Unfortunately, people's tendency to take stored background knowledge about the conditional relation into account can also bias their reasoning. During reasoning people will not only spontaneously think of alternative causes of the conditional but also of so-called disabling conditions. These are possible conditions that prevent the effect from occurring even though the proper cause was present. When people take such disabling conditions into account they will also start rejecting *valid* inferences. For example, standard logic tells us that whenever the antecedent of a conditional occurs, we should conclude that the consequent will follow. This is the famous Modus Ponens (MP) inference, one of the most basic rules in classic logic. A dramatic illustration of people's failure to draw a simple MP inference is the disaster at the nuclear power plant in Chernobyl. The well-trained Russian operators clearly knew that if a specific safety test turned out positive, this implied that the reactor was overheated and should be shut down. Nevertheless, when that ill-fated day in 1986 the crucial safety test indeed turned out positive the operators did not draw the simple MP conclusion. What happened was that, just as many people in standard reasoning studies, they spontaneously thought of possible disablers such as 'the test is wrong' or 'maybe it's just an exercise'. Taking these disabling conditions into account resulted in a failure to draw the valid conclusion (and one of the biggest disasters in modern history).

Fortunately, the situation is not as dramatic as the Chernobyl example would suggest. Although the pervasive impact of disabler retrieval on people's willingness to draw the MP or related Modus Tollens (MT) inference is well-documented (e.g., Byrne, 1989; De Neys, Schaeken, & d'Ydewalle, 2002, 2003a) there is evidence that indicates that people manage to selectively block the impact of disablers. For example, stressing the logical nature of a reasoning task typically results in better performance on the valid problems, and this performance boost has been attributed to a selective inhibition of disablers (Vadeboncoeur & Markovits, 1999). A number of recent studies also argued that people's inhibitory capacity (i.e., the ability to resist interference from inappropriate memory activations) contributes to sound reasoning on the valid MP problems (e.g., De Neys, Schaeken, & d'Ydewalle, 2005; Handley, Capon, Beveridge, Dennis, & Evans, 2004; Markovits & Doyon, 2004; Simoneau & Markovits, 2003). Markovits and Doyon, for example, measured people's susceptibility to interference with a task based on a test where people had to refrain from the automatic tendency to complete a sentence with a strongly associated word. Such tests have been used as a measure of inhibition in patients with cerebral lesions (Burgess & Shallice, 1996). Participants also solved a conditional reasoning task with problems that had very salient disablers. Markovits and Doyon observed that people who performed well on the interference resistance measure did manage to reason correctly with the valid problems. As the authors noted, these people's inhibitory capacity apparently also helped them to discard the disabling information in the reasoning task.

As a result of the above findings, it has become very popular in the reasoning literature to characterize conditional reasoning as an interplay of a counterexample retrieval and inhibition process (e.g., De Neys et al., 2005; Markovits & Barrouillet, 2002; Quinn & Markovits, 2002; Simoneau & Markovits, 2003). Despite the popularity of this characterization, however, it is clear that the framework has moved a lot of the explanatory burden to memory mechanisms (e.g., search for alternatives and inhibition of disablers). If a memory researcher were to look at the studies, she would notice that the evidence for the postulated memory processes is typically quite indirect. Indeed, most reasoning studies focus on the output of the reasoning task. We tend to infer characteristics of the memory mechanism based on people's reasoning performance. For example, we typically measure the counterexample availability in a pilot study and test how people reason with the conditionals afterwards. When people reject invalid inferences for which the pretest showed that there were alternatives available, we attribute the rejection to successful retrieval of an alternative. Of course, the fact that the pilot work shows that people can easily think of an alternative or that the participant in question is very good at memory retrieval does not in itself imply that the alternative was also accessed and used while the participant was solving the reasoning task. Likewise, the fact that someone who tends to accept valid inferences also tends to score 'very good' on an inhibition test does not prove that disablers were actively discarded during the reasoning process. These assumptions are not unreasonable, but the problem is that they make strong postulations about memory activations during the reasoning process that are not unequivocally validated.

Validating the popular assumptions about the background knowledge retrieval and blocking calls for a more direct memory probing. The present study introduces a classic procedure from the memory literature to accomplish this goal. In the study participants solved a standard conditional reasoning task where they had to evaluate a set of valid and invalid arguments. After each reasoning problem participants were presented with a lexical decision task. In this task participants have to determine whether a string of presented letters is a word or not. Since the work of Meyer and Schvaneveldt (1971), the task has become one of the most popular methods to probe semantic memory activations. Half of the strings that were presented were non-words (e.g., 'golfrixnt'). When participants had just been presented with an invalid conditional argument (e.g., 'If you water the plants, they stay healthy. You do not water the plants. Therefore, they do not stay healthy') half of the words that were presented in the lexical decision task were possible alternatives (i.e., target words, e.g., 'rain') whereas the other half were completely unrelated words (e.g., 'letter'). If people think of possible alternatives while solving the reasoning problem, this should result in a classic facilitation effect in the lexical decision task. The remaining activation following the retrieval of the alternatives during reasoning should result in faster lexical decision times (i.e., the time people need to decide whether the letter string is a word) for the target than for the unrelated words.

When participants had just solved a valid conditional argument (e.g., 'If the test is positive, then the reactor is overheated. The test is positive. Therefore, the reactor is overheated) the target words in the subsequent lexical decision task were words that were closely associated with possible disablers (e.g., 'exercise') whereas the other half of the words were completely unrelated to the disablers. It is well established in memory studies that when people have to temporarily neglect information or avoid using it, recall of this information will be distorted (e.g., MacLeod, Dodd, Sheard, Wilson, & Bibi, 2003; Neil, 1997; Tipper, 1985). Hence, temporarily putting your knowledge about possible disablers aside during reasoning should also hinder subsequent recall of these disablers and associated knowledge. Hence, if people really attempt to discard possible disablers that pop-up in mind during reasoning one would expect to see longer lexical decision times for target words than for unrelated words after people solved valid arguments.

In sum, the crucial prediction based on the counterexample retrieval and inhibition framework is that the lexical decision times should show an interaction between the type of reasoning problem and word type. If people retrieve alternatives while solving invalid problems, they should be faster to recognize the target vs. unrelated words. If people inhibit disablers while solving valid problems, this pattern should reverse and target words should take longer to recognize than unrelated words.

With respect to the validation, it is important to note that despite the popularity of the retrieval and inhibition framework there are possible alternative accounts. At the start of the psychological reasoning research era in the 1950s, for example, the reasoning community was convinced that the human reasoning engine did not care about the content of a problem and focused exclusively on the structure of a problem. According to this traditional, logistic view, reasoning is considered to be nothing more than applying a set of stored logical rules. Hence, people would accept or reject inferences based on whether the structure of the problem would (mis)match with their logical knowledge without any need to postulate an additional counterexample retrieval and blocking mechanism. The fact that people who score better on more general cognitive ability measures, such as retrieval efficiency or interference resistance, also reason better could be explained by assuming that these more gifted people also have a better, more precise logical database. Such a traditional logistic view faces it own problems but it underscores the point that the postulated activation of stored alternatives and blocking of disablers needs some direct validation.

In addition, recent studies have explicitly argued against the role of counterexample retrieval (e.g., Geiger & Oberauer, 2007; Verschueren, Schaeken, & d'Ydewalle, 2005). Geiger and Oberauer argued that people's willingness to draw conditional conclusions would be estimated from the frequency of exceptions regardless of what causes them. In this view, people would not be retrieving specific stored counterexamples from memory but would rather go through a quick and less demanding probabilistic estimation process to compute the frequency with which exceptions to the rule occur. For example, when deciding to conclude whether or not the light inside the fridge will go on if they open the fridge, people would roughly estimate the number of times that the light inside the fridge did not go on in the past without searching for specific 'reasons' or counterexamples (e.g., the light bulb might be broken). The present study will allow us to test these alternative accounts. If the frequency or logistic views are right and people do not retrieve counterexamples during reasoning, then we should not observe any facilitation or distortion effects in the subsequent lexical decision task.

Experiment

Method

Participants

Twenty undergraduates studying at York University (Toronto, Canada) participated voluntarily. All participants were native English speakers or had lived more than 10 years in Canada or the United States.

Material

Reasoning task Participants were presented with a standard conditional reasoning task where they were asked to evaluate the validity of eight conditional inferences (four valid and four invalid problems). The four valid problems had a logically valid argument structure (either a Modus Ponens or the related Modus Tollens inference). We specifically selected conditionals for the valid problems for which previous pilot generation work (e.g., Cummins, 1995; De Neys et al., 2002, 2003b) had showed that people readily thought of many salient disabling conditions. It is assumed that taking these disablers into account normally results in the rejection of the valid inference (e.g., the introductory Chernobyl example) and will need to be avoided. The four invalid problems had a logically invalid argument structure (either an Affirmation of the Consequent or the related Denial of the Antecedent inference). For these invalid problems we specifically selected conditionals for which the pilot work showed that people could generate many possible alternative causes. It is assumed that taking these alternatives into account during reasoning will help rejecting the invalid inferences. Bellow is an example of the format of the reasoning task:

If Bart's food goes down the wrong way, then he has to cough.
Bart has to cough

Therefore, Bart's food went down the wrong way.
1. The conclusion is valid
2. The conclusion is invalid

A complete overview of all eight problems can be found in the Appendix.

Note that we selected conditionals with many disablers for the valid problems to make sure that disablers would be activated during the reasoning task. If people cannot think of a possible disabler there would not be a conflict between semantic knowledge and logic and no need for an inhibition process. Likewise, for the invalid problems we selected conditionals with many possible alternatives.

In theory, it is possible that when a conditional has very salient disablers, people will also think of these when solving an invalid problem. Although it has been shown that this has only a limited impact on people's judgment, we wanted to exclude any possible bias on the recall measure. Therefore, we made sure that the selected conditionals for the invalid problems had only a small number of disablers so that successful disabler retrieval was unlikely. Likewise, the selected conditionals for the valid problems had only a small number of possible alternatives.

To make sure that the reasoning task was not too repetitive we presented two subtypes of valid problems (MP and MT) and two subtypes of invalid problems (AC or DA). Since lexical decision data were similar for these respective subtypes, they were collapsed in the valid and invalid category.

Lexical decision task After each problem a total of 20 letter strings was presented. Participants indicated whether the string was a word or not by pressing one of two response keys. Half of the letter strings were non-words, the other half were English words. Five of the presented words were target words that were closely related to the possible counterexamples (i.e., disabling conditions for valid problems and alternative causes for invalid problems) of the conditional in the reasoning task. The other five words were unrelated to these counterexamples.

All target words were selected from the pilot generation material of De Neys et al. (2002; 2003b) where participants generated possible alternatives and disablers for the set of conditionals. Targets for valid problems were single words associated with frequently generated disabling conditions (e.g., 'exercise' or 'error' in the Chernobyl example) whereas target words for invalid problems were associated with frequently generated alternative causes (e.g., 'rain' or 'shower' in the Calvin example). Unrelated words were selected with the help of the online version of the Edinburgh Word Association Thesaurus (Kiss, Armstrong, Milroy, and Piper, 1973). After we had constructed an initial list of target and unrelated words, two raters were asked to validate the classifications. In the few cases that judgments diverged the specific word was replaced with an alternative that all parties could agree on. A complete overview of the selected words can be found in the Appendix.

The length and word frequency of presented targets and unrelated words was matched on each problem. The word strings were presented in random order with the restriction that targets could not be presented on consecutive trials.

Procedure

All participants were tested individually. Participants were first familiarized with the task format. They were shown an example of a reasoning problem and practiced the lexical decision task. It was clarified that in the actual experiment both tasks would always alternate. Instructions for the reasoning task were taken from Vadeboncoeur and Markovits (1999) and explicitly stressed the logical nature of the reasoning task. The eight reasoning problems were presented in random order. Each reasoning trial began with the appearance of a fixation point for 0.5 s, which was replaced by a problem to solve. The problem remained on the screen for a maximum of 15 s or until participants responded 'valid' or 'invalid' by pressing one of two response keys (previous work showed that people needed no longer than about 12 s to solve similar problems, e.g., De Neys et al., 2002). The lexical decision trials (with the 20 words specifically selected for that problem) started immediately after the key press. Words were presented in the centre of the screen and participants were instructed to respond as quickly as possible, while avoiding errors.

After the lexical decision trials, the experiment was briefly paused until the participant was ready to continue with the next reasoning problem.

Results and discussion

Reasoning task

The reasoning task was properly solved. Overall, 85% of the valid problems and 69% of the invalid problems were correctly evaluated with only small inter-individual performance variation (SD valid problems = .22, SD invalid problems = .26). These numbers are close to what Vadeboncoeur and Markovits (1999) obtained with a similar reasoning task and indicate that the lexical decision trials did not bias reasoning performance.

Lexical decision task

The central question concerns participants' performance on the lexical decision task. The dependent measure was the mean time (ms) taken by subjects to characterize each letter string as a word or non-word. As in the classic lexical decision studies, incorrect classifications of the letter strings were infrequent (less than 6% error rate across all trials) and where they did occur they were excluded from the analysis. Lexical decision times were submitted to a 2 (reasoning problem: valid or invalid) x 2 (word type: target or unrelated) repeated measures ANOVA. Figure 11.1 shows the results.

There was a main effect of problem type, $F(1, 19) = 8.72$, $p < .01$, $\eta^2_p = .31$, whereas the effect of word type was not significant, $F(1, 19) < 1$. As predicted, the two factors also interacted, $F(1, 19) = 5.42$, $p < .05$, $\eta^2_p = .22$. As Figure 11.1 shows, after solving an invalid problem lexical decision times for target words were faster than for unrelated words. When participants had just solved a valid problem, lexical decision times showed the opposite pattern with slower responses for target words than for unrelated words. Planned contrasts showed that lexical decision times on the target words were significantly longer after solving a valid problem than after solving an invalid problem $F(1, 19) = 14$, $p < .005$, $\eta^2_p = .42$. Lexical decision times did not differ for the unrelated words, $F(1, 19) < 1$.

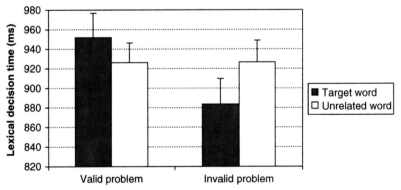

Fig. 11.1 Lexical decision times (ms) for target and unrelated words after participants solved valid and invalid conditional inference problems. Error bars are standard errors.

Conclusion

The present results nicely fit with the counterexample retrieval and inhibition view. When participants had solved an invalid problem, target words that were related to possible alternatives were recognized faster than unrelated words. This facilitation effects provides direct evidence for the claim that the alternatives had already been accessed during the reasoning task. On the other hand, when participants had solved valid problems the target words that were related to possible disablers were recognized slower than unrelated words. The finding that the memory access for disabling information was temporarily impaired is prima facie evidence for the claim that this information was inhibited during the reasoning process. Note that the observed facilitation and distortion was specifically tied to the target words. Unrelated words that were not associated with possible counterexamples were not affected. Hence, it is not the case that conditional reasoning generally facilitated or impaired memory access. Results indicate that only semantic knowledge that was specifically associated with possible counterexamples had been activated. These findings are hard to reconcile with any framework that would deny the role of counterexample retrieval and inhibition in conditional reasoning. The memory probing approach indicates that the search for counterexamples lies at the very heart of the conditional reasoning process.

Acknowledgements

I would like to thank Vinod Goel, Ratna Pardal, and Angela Badulescu for their help running this study.

References

Burgess, P. W. & Shallice, T. (1996). Response suppression, initiation and strategy use following frontal lobe lesions. *Neuropsychologia*, **34**, 263–273.

Byrne, R. M. J. (1989). Suppressing valid inferences with conditionals. *Cognition*, **31**, 61–83.

Cummins, D. D. (1995). Naive theories and causal deduction. *Memory and Cognition*, **23**, 646–658.

Cummins, D. D., Lubart, T., Alksnis, O., & Rist, R. (1991). Conditional reasoning and causation. *Memory and Cognition*, **19**, 274–282.

De Neys, W., Schaeken, W., & d'Ydewalle, G. (2002). Causal conditional reasoning and semantic memory retrieval: A test of the semantic memory framework. *Memory and Cognition*, **30**, 908–920.

De Neys, W., Schaeken, W., & d'Ydewalle, G. (2003a). Causal conditional reasoning and strength of association: The disabling condition case. *European Journal of Cognitive Psychology*, **42**, 177–190.

De Neys, W., Schaeken, W., & d'Ydewalle, G. (2003b). Inference suppression and semantic memory retrieval: Every counterexample counts. *Memory and Cognition*, **31**, 581–595.

De Neys, W., Schaeken, W., & d'Ydewalle, G. (2005). Working memory and everyday conditional reasoning: Retrieval and inhibition of stored counterexamples. *Thinking & Reasoning*, **11**, 349–381.

Geiger, S. & Oberauer, K. (2007). Reasoning with conditionals: Does every counterexample count? It's frequency that counts. *Memory and Cognition*, **35**, 2060–2073.

Handley, S. J., Capon, A., Beveridge, M., Dennis, I., & Evans, J. St. B. T. (2004). Working memory, inhibitory control, and the development of children's reasoning. *Thinking and Reasoning*, **10**, 175–195.

Kiss, G. R., Armstrong, C., Milroy, R., & Piper, J. (1973). An associative thesaurus of English and its computer analysis. In A. J. Aitkin, R. W. Bailey, & N. Hamilton-Smith (Eds.), *The computer and literary studies.* Edinburgh, UK: University Press.

MacLeod, C. M., Dodd, M. D., Sheard, E. D., Wilson, D. E., & Bibi, U. (2003). In opposition to inhibition. In B. H. Ross (Ed.), *The Psychology of Learning and Motivation, Vol. 43* (pp. 163–206). San Diego, CA: Academic Press.

Markovits, H. & Barrouillet, P. (2002). The development of conditional reasoning: A mental model account. *Developmental Review*, **22**, 5–36.

Markovits, H. & Doyon, C. (2004). Information processing and reasoning with premises that are empirically false: Interference, working memory, and processing speed. *Memory and Cognition*, **32**, 592–601.

Markovits, H. & Quinn, S. (2002). Efficiency of retrieval correlates with 'logical' reasoning from causal conditional premises. *Memory and Cognition*, **30**, 696–706.

Meyer, D. E. & Schvaneveldt, R. W. (1971). Facilitation in recognizing pairs of words: Evidence of a dependence upon retrieval operations. *Journal of Experimental Psychology*, **90**, 227–234.

Neill, W. T. (1997). Episodic retrieval in negative priming and repetition priming. *Journal of Experimental Psychology: Learning, Memory, and Cognition*, **23**, 1291–1305.

Quinn, S. & Markovits, H. (2002). Conditional reasoning with causal premises: Evidence for a retrieval model. *Thinking and Reasoning*, **8**, 179–191.

Simoneau, M. & Markovits, H. (2003). Reasoning with premises that are not empirically true: Evidence for the role of inhibition and retrieval. *Developmental Psychology*, **39**, 964–975.

Tipper, S. P. (1985). The negative priming effect: Inhibitory priming by ignored objects. *Quarterly Journal of Experimental Psychology*, **37A**, 571–590.

Vadeboncoeur, I. & Markovits, H. (1999). The effect of instruction and information retrieval on accepting the premises in a conditional reasoning task. *Thinking and Reasoning*, **5**, 97–113.

Verschueren, N., Schaeken, W., & d'Ydewalle, G. (2005). Everyday conditional reasoning: A working memory–dependent tradeoff between counterexample and likelihood use. *Memory and Cognition*, **33**, 107–119.

Appendix

Table A1 List of conditionals for the reasoning task

Valid problems:

1. If the trigger is pulled, then the gun fires. (MP)

2. If the correct switch is flipped, then the porch light goes on. (MT)

3. If the ignition key is turned, then the car starts. (MP)

4. If the match is struck, then it lights. (MT)

Invalid problems:

5. If Bart's food goes down the wrong way, the he has to cough. (DA)

6. If Mary jumps in the swimming pool, the she gets wet. (AC)

7. If the apples are ripe, then they fall from the tree. (DA)

8. If the water is poured on the campfire, then the fire goes out.(AC)

Table A2 List of selected target and unrelated words in the lexical decision task for each of the eight reasoning problems

	Target	**Unrelated**
Conditional 1	unloaded	waitress
	blank	onion
	broken	forest
	safety	author
	jammed	monkey
Conditional 2	failure	manager
	blackout	overcoat
	old	amp
	burnedout	arrowhead
	removed	leagues
Conditional 3	damaged	invites
	busted	floral
	empty	guest
	wrong	shore
	refill	beaver

Conditional 4	wet	tar
	damp	lion
	worn	cady
	used	face
	softly	spring
Conditional 5	cold	data
	sick	wave
	dry	paw
	asthma	lentil
	smoke	smirk
Conditional 6	rain	rice
	shower	writer
	hosed	zebra
	bath	fare
	splashed	gangster
Conditional 7	storm	ivory
	wind	wall
	birds	paint
	shaken	stream
	dropped	surgeon
Conditional 8	died	mark
	smother	pigment
	sand	card
	extinguish	politician
	blanket	article

Chapter 12

How semantic memory processes temper causal inferences

Denise Cummins

Philosopher John Mackie (1974) called causation 'the cement of the universe'. Causation constitutes the structural foundation of the physical and social worlds, binding events together in predictable and interpretable ways. It should come as no surprise, then, that causal reasoning is a fundamental component of higher cognition. We use it to make sense of events in our everyday lives as wide-ranging as why our car didn't start to why wars exist.

The majority of research on causal inference in psychology has focused on how humans (and non-human animals) determine which factors produced a given event, a process called *causal attribution* (e.g., Anderson & Scheu, 1995; Cheng & Novick, 1992; Fuselgang, Thompson, & Dunbar, 2006; Kelly, 1973; Schustack & Sternberg, 1981; Sloman & Hagmayer, 2006; Waldemann, Hagmayer, & Blaisdell, 2006). This is by no means, however, the only type of causal inference that we are required to make in our daily lives. Frequently, we must decide how to bring about desired events or prevent undesired ones from occurring.

Cummins (1995, 1997, 1998) proposed a framework for causal inference which made explicit how reasoners use certain types of knowledge to guide the inference process. This framework has received support from a number of studies (e.g., Chan & Chua, 1994; Cummins, Lubart, Alksnis, & Rist, 1991; de Neys, Schaeken, & d'Ydewalle, 2002, 2003a, 2003b, 2005a, 2005b; Elio, 1998; Janvau-Brennan & Makovits, 1999; Markovits, 2000; Markovits, Fleury, Quinn, & Venet, 1998; Markovis & Quinn, 2002; Quinn & Markovits, 1998, 2002; Verschueren, Schaeken, de Neys & d'Ydewalle, 2004; Verschueren, Schaeken, & d'Ydewalle, 2005). The unique aspect of this framework is its analysis of how memory activation processes interact with reasoning processes to produce sound judgements. The work presented here formalizes this framework in terms of a model that makes explicit how memory activation processes and hypothesis plausibility influence causal judgement. This cognitive phenomenon is common in everyday life. We often find ourselves with events to be explained (e.g., why our car didn't start) and little more than our prior knowledge and beliefs to guide our inferences and actions (e.g., 'I left the car lights on. The battery's probably dead'.) The main claim of the proposed model is that this interactive process does not necessarily result in fallacious reasoning. Instead, memory activation tempers the inference process, leading to sound and reasonable judgements.

Why truth-functional logic is an insufficient model of causal reasoning

Consider the following questions:

(1) Does the presence of the cause guarantee the effect? (Are abused children doomed to repeat the patterns of their abusive parents?)

(2) Does the absence of the cause guarantee the absence of the effect? (Does the absence of child abuse during childhood guarantee non-abusive parenting practices?)

(3) Does the absence of the effect necessarily imply that the cause was absent? (Can we safely infer that a person was not abused as a child given that the person is a non-abusive parent?)

(4) Does the presence of the effect necessarily imply the occurrence of the cause? (Does abusive parenting necessarily imply a history of abuse during childhood?)

At first glance, it might seem that these inferences could be analyzed as instances of simple conditional reasoning. The hypothesis

Abuse during childhood is a cause of abusive parenting

could be represented as a universally quantified conditional statement of the form

If a person suffered abuse during childhood, then the person will abuse his children.

Question 1 concerns causal sufficiency: We want to know whether the cause is sufficient to bring about the effect. In our example, we want to know whether we can safely infer that a particular person will become an abusive parent because he or she was abused as a child. After instantiation, this corresponds to a Modus Ponens (MP) inference:

If John suffered abuse during childhood, then John will abuse his children.

John suffered abuse as a child.

Therefore, John will abuse his children.

Question 2 concerns causal necessity: We want to know whether the absence of the abuse guarantees the absence of abusive parenting practices corresponds. This corresponds to a Deny the Antecedent (DA) inference:

If John suffered abuse during childhood, then John will abuse his children.

John did NOT suffer abuse as a child.

Therefore, John will NOT abuse his children.

Like question 1, question 3 concerns causal sufficiency: We want to know whether the absence of abusive parenting implies a childhood free of abuse. This corresponds to a Modus Tollens (MT) inference:

If John suffered abuse during childhood, then John will abuse his children.

John does NOT abuse his children.

Therefore, John did NOT suffer abuse as a child.

Finally, like question 2, question 4 also concerns causal necessity: We want to know whether we can infer that someone was abused as a child because we witness him or her abusing a child. This corresponds to an Affirming the Consequent (AC) inference:

If John suffered abuse during childhood, then John will abuse his children.

John abuses his children.

Therefore, John suffered abuse as a child.

As reasonable as this analysis seems, truth-functional arguments, do not capture everyday causal reasoning—and this is not because people are poor reasoners. Rather, it is because standard truth-conditional logic is not powerful enough to model causal inference. Causal conditionals are not truth-functional, that is, their semantics are not captured by the truth functions of first order logic. As philosophers since David Hume (1739) have pointed out, causal necessity and sufficiency are distinct from logical necessity and sufficiency. This means that one cannot simply map causal conditionals onto truth-functional conditionals.

The inadequacies of truth-functional construals of causal judgement become readily apparent in everyday causal reasoning. Consider the MP argument shown above. Should a rational reasoner conclude that John is guaranteed to become an abusive parent given that he was abused as a child? In other words, is childhood abuse a sufficient cause for abusive parenting later? If this argument were treated as a simple truth-functional argument, the answer would be yes. The entailment relations are fixed by the truth-function for the material conditional. But this flies in the face of common sense and good research: Although childhood abuse is a true cause of abusive parenting, the relationship is far from perfect. This means that, although the general law 'Abuse during childhood is a cause of abusive parenting' is true, its conditional counterpart 'If a person suffers abuse during childhood, then the person will abuse his children' expresses a non-deterministic relationship that is not captured by the truth function for the material conditional.

Consider now the AC argument presented above. Is a rational reasoner justified in concluding that John suffered abuse as a child because John has been shown to be an abusive parent? In other words, is it necessary to have been abused as a child in order to become an abusive parent? If the conditional were treated as a material conditional, then the answer would be no because the truth-function for the material conditional makes this argument invalid. Is this rational? Suppose there were other reasons why someone would become an abusive parent other than having suffered abuse during childhood. If the weight of evidence showed that, among likely causal candidates, suffering abuse during childhood was far and away the cause most reliably associated with abusive parenting, then one could argue that accepting this conclusion would be justified even though the antecedent is neither causally nor logically necessary for the consequent.

Models of causal inference

How, then, do we make causal inferences such as these? A number of models have been proposed which analyze causal reasoning in terms of probabilistic decision-making (Cheng & Novick, 1992; Fuselgang, Thompson, & Dunbar, 2006; Kelly, 1973; Over, Hadjichristidis, Evans, Handley, & Sloman, 2007; Schustack & Sternberg, 1981; Sloman & Hagmayer, 2006; Waldemann, Hagmayer, & Blaisdell, 2006). Over et al. (2007) specifically compared response patterns predicted by material truth-functions and the Ramsey test—a proposal by philosopher William Ramsey which states that the subjective probability of a natural language conditional $P(p{\rightarrow}q)$ is the conditional subjective probability $P(q|p)$. The latter better fit the data than the former.

Probabilistic models of causal reasoning, however, typically do not provide a complete explanation of the phenomenon, leaving considerable unexplained variance. Characteristically missing is a process model which describes how knowledge activation and can temper or even overshadow probabilistic decision-making processes. For example, by using verbal protocols, Verschueren (2005) and colleagues found that participants with low working memory capacity more often use probabilistic information, whereas participants with higher working memory capacity were more likely to use counterexample information. They concluded that memory processes can change the nature of the reasoning.

There is considerable evidence now that a core process in causal reasoning is activation of knowledge in semantic memory concerning *alternative causes* and disablers (Cummins, Lubart, Alksnis, & Rist, 1991; Cummins, 1995, 1997, and 1998; Markovits & Quinn, 2002; deNeys, et al., 2002, 2003a, 2003b, 2005a, 2005b; Quinn & Markovits, 2002.) Alternative causes are factors (other than the one under current consideration) that can bring about the event in question. Disablers are factors that can prevent an effect from occurring even though a viable cause is present (Cummins et al., 1991). For example, research indicates that the presence of a non-abusive role-model during childhood constitutes a disabler that can mitigate against someone becoming an abusive parent despite a history of abuse (Kaufman & Zigler, 1988; Martin & Elmer, 1992). Such a factor is referred to as a disabler because it 'disables' a true cause-effect relationship rather than invalidating or disproving it.

Abuse during childhood is indeed a true cause of abusive parenting, but the cause-effect relationship is *not deterministic*. It can be suppressed or 'disabled' by mitigating factors, such as the presence of a non-abusive role model. (This is the reverse of *enabling conditions*, which are factors that must be present for a true cause to produce an effect, although they themselves are not causes. An example is oxygen, which enables combustion when combined with a true cause, such as striking a match.) Note that the presence of disablers cast doubt on the *sufficiency* of the cause to yield the effect.

Cummins and colleagues found that reasoners' willingness to endorse an inference was inversely proportional to the number of disabling conditions or alternative causes that characterized the conditional (Cummins et al., 1991; Cummins, 1995). They found that conclusion ratings for MP and MT were significantly higher for arguments based on conditionals that were characterized by *few* disabling conditions than for arguments based on conditionals that were characterized by many. For example, contrast the MP argument above with the following MP argument:

> *If this twelve ton weight is dropped onto this crystal wineglass, the wineglass will shatter.*
> *The twelve ton weight was dropped onto the crystal wineglass.*
> *Therefore, the wineglass shattered.*

This conditional is characterized by few (if any) disablers. Everyday reasoners are more inclined to accept conclusions based on causal conditionals that admit of few disablers than those that admit of many. This effect has been replicated in a variety of studies with both adults (de Neys et al., 2002a, 2002b; Chan & Chua, 1994; Elio, 1998; Quinn & Markovits, 1998) and children (Janveau-Brennan & Markovits, 1999; Markovits, 2000; Markovits, et al., 1998).

Cummins and colleagues also found that acceptance ratings were significantly higher for causal necessity arguments when they were based on conditionals that were characterized by few alternative causes than those that were characterized by many alternative causes, and, again, this effect has been replicated many times with both adults (de Neys et al., 2002a, 2002b; Chan & Chua, 1994; Elio, 1998; Markovits & Potvin, 2001; Quinn & Markovits, 1998) and children (Janveau-Brennan & Markovits, 1999; Markovits, 2000; Markovits et al., 1998). For example, everyday reasoners are less likely to accept the above AC argument than the following argument which is based on a causal conditional that admits of few alternative causes:

> *If John touched the wall with his bare fingertips, his fingerprints will be on it.*
> *John's fingerprints were found on the wall.*
> *Therefore, John touched the wall with his bare fingertips.*

Despite the fact that AC is truth-functionally invalid, a juror who refused to accept this argument would constitute a prosecutor's nightmare; the acceptance of such forensic evidence in our justice system stems precisely from this sort of reasoning. It constitutes good judgement, not reasoning error. Aside from John having touched the wall (and by further inference, having been in the room), it is difficult to imagine any alternative cause that would result in his fingerprints ending up there. Note that the presence or possibility of alternative causes casts doubt on the *necessity* of the purported cause for yielding the effect.

A number of studies have confirmed that retrieval of disablers and alternative causes occurs spontaneously during causal inference and greatly influences the judgement process. Using verbal protocol analysis, Vershueren et al. (2004) found that people spontaneously retrieve information concerning disablers when evaluating causal sufficiency arguments, and alternative causes when evaluating causal necessity arguments. Furthermore, consistent with Cummins' framework, the number of counterexamples retrieved was negatively correlated with argument acceptance ratings. Also consistent with this model of memory activation processes, De Neys et al. (2002) found that response latencies for causal judgements were positively correlated with the number of alternatives/disablers associated with the content of the conditional. Causal necessity judgements were positively correlated with number of alternative causes that characterized a conditional and causal sufficiency judgements were correlated with number of disablers. They also found that individual differences in retrieval efficiency influence judgements: Reasoners who were capable of retrieving a large number of items from memory under time constraints gave lower acceptance ratings to causal sufficiency arguments than did reasoners who evidence less efficient retrieval processes.

Expanding on this research, Markovits (2000) proposed an account which described the inference process in terms of mental models. On this account, reasoners construct a model of the conditional's antecedent and consequent propositions (e.g., 'A person is abused during childhood', 'The person becomes an abusive parent'), and then search memory for counterexamples to the model. In contrast to Cummins' framework, however, Markovits and colleagues proposed that reasoners maintain a *principle of reasoning economy* (Markovits et al., 1998; Quinn & Markovits, 2000). According to this principle, the retrieval of a single counterexample is sufficient to halt the memory search process and cause rejection of the argument conclusion under consideration. The number of counterexamples impacts only the likelihood that a counterexample will be found.

Recent research, however, casts some doubt on the reasoning economy principle. De Neys (2003b) presented reasoners with arguments in which the number of explicitly mentioned disablers or alternative causes ranged from 0 to 4. They found a significant negative linear trend on acceptance ratings. deNeys et al. (2003) also reported that while 'thinking aloud', reasoners did not halt the retrieval process upon retrieving a single counterexample. Instead, they continued to retrieve disablers or alternatives until a final judgement was made.

While these results constitute strong evidence that memory processes influence the judgement process in predictable ways, a number of unresolved issues remain. The first is the precise nature of the retrieval-judgement function. Although de Neys et al. reported a significant linear component to this function, their results suggest that the function may be better described as a non-linear function. When plotting the acceptance ratings within the set of 0-4 disablers/alternatives, the trend between 3 and 4 was less steep than the trend between 0 and 3. Further, when analyzing the functions within subject, they found what appeared to be a threshold at about 3 retrieved items, after which ratings changed very little.

Semantic memory activation function

The hypothesis proposed here is that activation spreads throughout the network of associated counterexamples (disablers and alternative causes), and the judgement value assigned to the conclusion drops off significantly the farther it spreads. This is for two reasons. First, strongly associated items are presumed to be activated earlier than weakly associated items and are presumed to have greater impact on judgement values due to this difference in associative strength. Second, it is assumed that being able to retrieve even one or two counterexamples is sufficient to cast doubt on the conclusion relative to being able to retrieve none at all, but that subsequent retrievals have diminished impact. In other words, the psychological difference between 0 and (e.g.,) 3 items is greater than the psychological difference between (e.g.,) 4 and 8. These contingencies are captured quantitatively in the function depicted in Figure 12.1.

Non-linear functions are common among other cognitive and perceptual phenomena (e.g., sensory thresholds, serial position curves). Negatively decelerating ones like this one are typical of spreading activation functions in associative memory models. The likelihood of retrieval of any particular counterexample depends on how strongly it is associated with the content of the conditional. Consequently, the first few retrieved items have the largest impact on the judgement

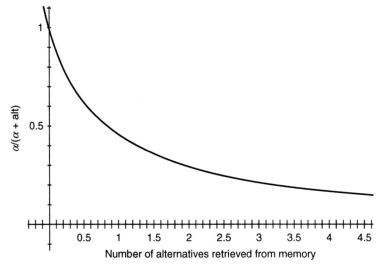

Fig. 12.1 The relationship between number of alternatives and the function $\alpha/(\alpha + \text{alt})$. In this graph, alt can refer to either alternative causes or disablers.

process, with subsequent items contributing significantly less. Mathematically, this function can be expressed as

$$\alpha/(\text{alt} + \alpha)$$

or

$$\alpha/(\text{disab} + \alpha)$$

depending on whether the counterexamples in question are alternative causes (alt) or disabling conditions (disab). α is a parameter whose value ranges from 0 to 1; it simply expresses the steepness of the curve, and its value is determined empirically.

The role of plausibility

Judgements are also influenced by the perceived plausibility of the causal conditional. For example, reasoners may find '*If John touched the wall with his bare fingertips, his fingerprints will be on the it*' more plausible than '*If Susan has her ears pierced, she will have a car accident*'. A number of studies have shown that plausibility contributes strongly to causal attribution judgements (e.g., Ahn & Kalish, 2000; Ahn, Kalish, Medin, & Gelman, 1995; White, 2000). The impact of a conditional's plausibility on causal inferences has not yet been investigated. Instead, researchers have investigated the impact of disabler or alternative cause plausibility and found that that the degree to which these factors impact argument acceptance ratings does indeed vary systematically with their perceived plausibility (Chan & Chua, 1994; de Neys et al., 2002b).

This is an important issue because it speaks directly to the nature of the reasoning process. Mental model theories describe human reasoning as a deliberate search for counterexamples. This implies that memory search processes are engaged regardless of the plausibility of the model constructed by the reasoner. In contrast, it is assumed here that memory activation processes are automatic in a manner similar to the Swinney (1979) effect in lexical access. Swinney found that when processing words in sentences, all possible word meanings are initially activated, and sentence context determines which meanings remain activated. Similarly, upon reading (or hearing) a causal conditional, information associated with the semantic content of the conditional is automatically activated regardless of the plausibility of the conditional.

The model

When judgements are belief-based, plausibility determines the degree to which this activated information is actually used to guide the inference process. The lower the plausibility, the less impact activated information is posited to have on the judgement process. This state of affairs can be captured by a parameter **B**. (B—for 'believability'—was chosen in order to avoid P—for 'plausibility'—which could be confused with probability.) The strength of **B** can be determined by a number of factors, such as the reasoner's understanding of a plausible causal mechanism by which the cause can produce the effect in question (as in the physics underlying short circuits causing fires), the confidence the reasoner places in an authority who asserts the causal claim (as in an electrician asserting that short circuits are a primary cause of house fires), or the strength of empirical evidence the reasoner believes supports the causal claim. This parameter can range from a value of -1 (completely implausible) to $+1$ (completely plausible) with 0 representing uncertainty.

Consider first reasoning scenarios that require one to judge whether an effect will occur in the presence of a viable cause. These inferences are constrained by beliefs concerning disablers by Cummins (Cummins et al., 1991; Cummins, 1995, 1998) (also referred to as *preventive causes* by Cheng and colleagues—Cheng, 1997; Cheng & Novick, 1992). Note that disablers have the effect of preserving belief in the putative causal law while simultaneously reducing confidence in inferences based on it. Consider the examples shown above for causal sufficiency. When these arguments are based on truth-functional conditionals, they can be evaluated simply on the basis of the truth-function for the material conditional. When based on causal conditionals, the reasoning process can captured by the following, where C_S stands for 'causal', B stands for believability (plausibility) of the causal connection, *disab* stands for number of disabling conditions, and α is a constant that ranges from 0 to 1:

Causal Conditional: If a person is abused in childhood, that person will abuse his children.

Causal$_{sufficiency}$: John was abused as a child. Will he abuse his children?

$$C_S = B[\alpha/(alt + \alpha)]$$

Causal$_S$: John does NOT abuse his children. Was he NOT abused as a child?

$$C_S = B[\alpha/(alt + \alpha)]$$

Using our example, having non-abusive role models was found to prevent abused children from becoming abusive parents. This means that even if we knew that someone was abused as a child, we would be less likely to infer that he or she would go on to become an abusive parent *if we also knew about this disablers*. Similarly, given that we know someone is not an abusive parent, we would be hesitant to conclude that he or she had not been abused as a child if we also knew that non-abusive role-models can prevent someone from becoming abusive themselves. *Disablers*, therefore, do not undermine our belief in a causal generalization (e.g., we may still believe that child abuse begets child abuse), although they do diminish the likelihood of drawing inferences based on it. If exception cases are noted and no disabling conditions can be identified, however, then confidence in the causal law is seriously undermined. If researchers in our abuse example had <u>not</u> been able to find preventive factors to explain the exception cases, the existence of those cases would have seriously undermined the plausibility of the causal law.

Now consider scenarios that require the reasoner to judge whether a particular cause produced an observed effect, such as the examples of Affirming the Consequent and Denying the Antecedent shown above. These judgements will be tempered by beliefs concerning possible alternative causes for the effect in question. Using our child abuse example, imagine that researchers observe a case of abusive parenting, and are asked how likely they think it is that this person is an abusive parent because he or she was abused as a child. Again, if these arguments were based on truth-functional conditionals, they would constitute invalid arguments and no conclusion could be drawn. But they are instead based on causal conditionals. The impact of beliefs concerning plausibility and alternative causes on causal necessity judgements can be expressed by the following rules, where B is a value representing the plausibility of the cause-effect relationship, *alt* is the number of plausible alternative causes, and α is a constant whose value lies between 0 and 1:

Causal Conditional: If a person is abused in childhood, that person will abuse his children.

Causal$_N$: John abuses his children. Was he abused as a child?

$$\text{Causal}_N = B[\alpha/(alt + \alpha)]$$

Causal$_N$: John does NOT abuse his children. Was he NOT abused as a child?

$$\text{Causal}_N = B[\alpha/(alt + \alpha)]$$

The exception terms, $[\alpha/alt + \alpha]$ and $[\alpha/disab + \alpha]$, state that the impact of alternative causes or disablers on a causal judgement is not linear. Instead, if even a single plausible alternative or disabler is deemed possible in the circumstances, the likelihood of making a causal judgement is significantly diminished. If multiple causes or disablers are deemed possible, the likelihood decreases further, but the contribution of each subsequent alternative cause is diminished. When graphed (with $alt > 0$ or $disab > 0$ and $\alpha \cong .8$), the judgement function looks like the illustration in Figure 1. Alternative causes and disablers are part of the reasoner's semantic memory. The retrieval process is assumed to obey standard activation parameters, that is, it can be controlled or automatic, and activation spreads from one node to another, dropping exponentially with distance. *When reasoning is solely belief-based*, this activation process is presumed to impact the judgement process only when the candidate cause surpasses some critical level of plausibility. In this model, this means B has a value greater than zero.

Table 12.1 illustrates the predictions made at three levels of plausibility (1, .7, .5, .2 and 0) and three levels of alternative causes or disablers (0, 1, 4, and 9). α is set to .8. Notice that the judgement values drops off precipitously between 0 and 1 alternatives, with the impact of subsequently retrieved alternative having a diminished effect. The values indicate that when no alternative causes or disablers can be retrieved, the reasoner's willingness to accept the conclusion of the causal argument is equal to his or her belief in the plausibility of the cause-effect relationship stated in the casual premise. Retrieval of alternative causes or disablers reduces that willingness considerably.

Table 12.1 The Value of Causal Judgements as a Function of the Plausibility of the Causal Premise (B) and Number of Alternative Causes (or Disablers)

Alt Causes (Disab)	Plausibility				
	B = 1	B = .7	B = .5	B = .2	B = 0
0	1.00	.70	.50	.20	0
1	.44	.31	.10	.09	0
4	.17	.12	.15	.03	0
9	.08	.06	.02	.02	0

Note:
$\alpha = .8$
B can range from 0 (Highly Implausible) to 1 (Highly Plausible)
Values in table = $B[\alpha/(alt + \alpha)]$

Quality of alternatives and disablers

It should also be noted that *disab* and *alt* in the above equations refer to *quality* counterexamples. When asked to generate counterexamples, subjects will often include in their lists items that they themselves believe to be implausible, but because they are associated with the cause-effect relationship in memory, they are retrieved along with other, higher quality items. Using verbal protocol methodology, Elio (1998) proposed a taxonomy of disablers which was extended to alternative causes by Vershueren et al. (under review). This taxonomy distinguishes among seven classes of disablers, but three of these classes accounted for the majority (~90%) of protocol data. These three, in order of proportion of the data accounted for, were as follows:

(1) Missing enabler (39%). The reasoner stated that the cause was insufficient to produce the effect, either because it required a co-factor (e.g., oxygen in the case of igniting gasoline to produce fire), or because the cause was incomplete in some way (e.g., a cut not being deep enough to produce bleeding).

(2) Demoting the conditional to default (30%). The reasoner 'demotes' the conditional to expressing a default—but not exclusive—outcome (e.g., the cause *usually* produces the effect, but not always; the cause *increases the likelihood* of the effect occurring.) In other words, the reasoner represents the causal conditional in probabilistic rather than deterministic terms.

(3) Disabler or alternative cause present (21%). Here, the reasoner explicitly mentions a disabler or alternative cause that precludes accepting the standard conclusion (e.g., If John were abused as a child *but his grandmother was a non-abusive role model*, then John would not become an abusive parent.)

The remaining four categories of items are automatically retrieved, but they have very little impact on the judgement process: rejecting the conditional entirely as false (~1%), claiming that the event of interest was highly exceptional (~5%), making reference simply to 'passage of time' (~2%), and generalizing the situation (0% for causal conditionals; these were observed for other types of conditionals, such as promises).

To summarize, causal inference can be made on the basis of beliefs alone. These beliefs express causal mechanisms that imbue one event with the power to produce another. Beliefs concerning alternative causes diminish the likelihood of making causal generalizations and causal attributions, and beliefs concerning disabling conditions diminish the likelihood of drawing inferences on the basis of a causal generalization.

Future directions

An important question currently under investigation is how ruling out disablers and alternative causes impacts the judgement process. Presumably, explicitly ruling out disablers or alternative causes that are strongly associated with the causal conditional under consideration should raise acceptance ratings for plausible conditionals. But because this model predicts that plausibility plays a significant role in determining causal judgements, ruling out disablers and alternative causes for implausible conditionals should have little affect on acceptance ratings.

References

Ahn, W. & Kalish, C. W. (2000). The role of mechanism beliefs in causal reasoning. In Keil, F. C. & Wilson, R. A. (Eds.), *Explanation and cognition.* (pp. 199–225). Cambridge, MA: MIT Press.

Ahn, W., Kalish, C. W., Medin, D. L., & Gelman, S. A. (1995). The role of covariation versus mechanism information in causal attribution. *Cognition*, **54**, 299–352.

Anderson, J. R. & Scheu, C. F. (1995). Causal inferences as perceptual judgments. *Memory & Cognition*, **23**, 510–524.

Chan, D. & Chua, F. (1994). Suppression of valid inferences: Syntactic views, mental models, and relative salience. *Cognition*, **53**, 217–238.

Cheng, P. W. (1997). From covariation to causation: A causal power theory. *Psychological Review*, **104**, 367–405.

Cheng, P. W. & Novick, L. R. (1992). Covariation in natural causal induction. *Psychological Review*, **99**, 365–382.

Cummins, D. D. (1995). Naive theories and causal deduction. *Memory & Cognition*, **23**, 646–658.

Cummins, D. D. (1997). Reply to Fairley and Manktelow's comment on 'Naïve theories and causal deduction'. *Memory & Cognition*, **25**, 415–416.

Cummins, D. D. (1998). The pragmatics of causal inference. *Proceedings of the Twentieth Annual Meeting of the Cognitive Science Society.*

Cummins, D. D., Lubart, T., Alksnis, O., & Rist, R. (1991). Conditional reasoning and causation. *Memory and Cognition*, **19**, 274–282.

de Neys, W., Schaeken, W., & d'Ydewalle, G. (2002b). Causal conditional reasoning and semantic memory retrieval: A test of the 'semantic memory framework'. *Memory & Cognition*, **30**, 908–920.

de Neys, W., Schaeken, W., & d'Ydewalle, G. (2003a). Causal conditional reasoning and strength of association: The disabling condition case. *European Journal of Cognitive Psychology*, **15**, 161–176.

de Neys, W., Schaeken, W., & d'Ydewalle, G. (2003b). Inference suppression and semantic memory retrieval: Every counterexample counts. *Memory & Cognition*, **31**, 581–595.

de Neys, W., Schaeken, W., & d'Ydewalle, G. (2005a). Working memory and everyday conditional reasoning: Retrieval and inhibition of stored counterexamples. *Thinking & Reasoning*, **11**, 349–381.

deNeys, W., Schaeken, W., & d'Ydewalle, G. (2005b). Working memory and counterexample retrieval for causal conditionals. *Thinking & Reasoning*, **11**, 123–150.

Elio, R. (1998). How to disbelieve p-> q: Resolving contradictions. *Proceedings of the Twentieth Meeting of the Cognitive Science Society*, 315–320.

Fugelsang, J. A., Thompson, V. A., & Dunbar, K. N. (2006). Examining the representation of causal knowledge. *Thinking & Reasoning*, **12**, 1–30.

Hume, D. (1739). *A treatise of human nature.* Oxford: Oxford University Press.

Janveau-Brennan, G. & Markovits, H. (1999). The development of reasoning with causal conditionals. *Developmental Psychology*, **35**, 904–911.

Kaufman, J. & Zigler, E. F. (1988). Do abused children become abusive parents? *Annual Progress in Child Psychiatry and Child Development*, **29**, 591–600.

Kelley, H. H. (1973). The processes of causal attribution. *American Psychologist*, **28**, 107–128.

Mackie, J. L. (1974). *The cement of the universe: A study in causation.* Oxford: Clarendon Press.

Markovits, H. (2000). A mental model analysis of young children's conditional reasoning with meaningful premises. *Thinking & Reasoning*, **6**, 335–347.

Markovits, H., Fleury, M., Quinn, S., & Venet, M. (1998). The development of conditional reasoning and the structure of semantic memory. *Child Development*, **69**, 742–755.

Markovits, H. & Quinn, S. (2002). Efficiency of retrieval correlates with "logical" reasoning from causal conditional premises. *Memory & Cognition*, **30**, 696–706.

Martin, J. A. & Elmer, E. (1992). Battered children grown up: A follow-up study of individuals severely maltreated as children. *Child Abuse and Neglect*, **16**, 75–88.

Over, D. E. Hadjichristidis, C., Evans, J. St.B. T., Handley, S. J., & Sloman, S. A. (2007). The probability of causal conditionals. *Cognitive Psychology*, **54**, 62–97.

Quinn, S. & Markovits, H. (1998). Conditional reasoning, causality, and the structure of semantic memory: Strength of association as a predictive factor for content effects. *Cognition*, **68**, B93-B101.

Quinn, S. & Markovits, H. (2002). Conditional reasoning with causal premises: Evidence for a retrieval model. *Thinking & Reasoning, 8*, 179–191.

Schustack, M. W. & Sternberg, R. J. (1981). Evaluation of evidence in causal inference. *Journal of Experimental Psychology: General, 110*, 101–120.

Sloman, S. A. & Hagmayer, Y. (2006). The causal psycho-logic of choice. *Trends in Cognitive Sciences, 10*, 407–412.

Swinney, D. (1979). Lexical access during sentence comprehension: (Re)consideration of context effects. *Journal of Verbal Learning and Verbal Behavior, 5*, 219–227.

Vershueren, N., Schaeken, W., & d'Ydewalle, G. (2005). Everyday conditional reasoning: A working memory-dependent tradeoff between counterexample and likelihood use. *Memory & Cognition, 33*, 107–119.

Vershueren, N., Schaeken, W., de Neys, W., & d'Ydewalle, G. (2004). The difference between generating counterexamples and using them during reasoning. *The Quarterly Journal of Experimental Psychology, 57A*, 1285–1308.

Waldmann, M. R., Hagmayer, Y., & Blaisdell, A. P. (2006). Beyond the Information Given: Causal Models in Learning and Reasoning. *Current Directions in Psychological Science, 15*, 307–311.

White, P. A. (2000). Causal judgment from contingency information: The interpretation of factors common to all instances. *Journal of Experimental Psychology: Learning, Memory, & Cognition, 26*, 1083–1102.

Chapter 13

A successive-conditionalization approach to conditional reasoning

In-mao Liu

A successive-conditionalization approach to conditional reasoning

A distinction has often been made between occasions when people reason in accord with formal logical procedures and occasions when people reason pragmatically or plausibly. Recently, Rips (2001) presented evidence that people can evaluate arguments in at least two qualitatively different ways: in terms of their deductive correctness and in terms of their inductive strength.

In this chapter, I introduce the successive-conditionalization approach (Liu, 2003; Liu, Lo, & Wu, 1996) to conditional reasoning and attempt to show that this approach measures the knowledge-based component, which essentially represents the inductive strength involved in conditional reasoning, separately from the assumption-based component, which essentially represents the deductive correctness involved in conditional reasoning. Next, this successive-conditionalization approach will be contrasted to the mental models approach. Finally, the successive-conditionalization approach will be contrasted to an approach based on interpreting a conditional statement to represent the conditional probability of the consequent given the antecedent.

Deductive correctness vs. inductive strength

Rips (2001) used four types of arguments to test whether people can evaluate arguments in terms of their deductive correctness and in terms of inductive strength. In the following are two types of example arguments.

> (A) Deductively correct, inductively strong (valid-strong):
>
> If car X11 runs into a brick wall, it will stop. (13.1)
>
> Car X11 runs into a brick wall.
> _____
> Car X11 will strop.

> (B) Deductively incorrect, inductively strong (invalid-strong):
>
> Car X11 runs into a brick wall. (13.2)
> _____
> Car X11 will stop.

Argument 13.1 is in the form known as Modus Ponens (MP), which is valid and deductively correct. Argument 13.2 has the same form as Argument 13.1, except that the major premise (If car X11 runs into a brick wall, it will stop) is missing. Argument 13.2 is called the reduced MP problem (Liu et al., 1996). This argument is deductively invalid, because the conclusion does not necessarily follow from the premise. However, it is causally consistent and inductively strong.

Rips (2001) used two more types of argument, i.e., one that is deductively correct and causally inconsistent and another that is deductively inconsistent and causally inconsistent. He tested a one-dimensional view of argument evaluation that assessments of both correctness and strength are a function of an argument's position on a single psychological continuum. For this purpose, in the deduction and induction conditions, he had participants give the probabilities of responding 'valid' or 'not valid' or responding 'strong' or 'not strong'. He found that participants judged the valid-weak arguments deductively correct more often than the invalid-strong arguments, but judged the latter inductively strong more often than the former. Based on this finding, he claimed to support the view that people have distinct ways to evaluate arguments.

Closely connected to the issue of how Argument 13.1 is related to Argument 13.2 is the fact that the inference involved in Argument 13.2 can rigorously be shown to be a component process of the inference involved in Argument 13.1 (Liu, 2003 for details). This can easily be seen by comparing Argument 13.2 to Argument 13.1. In Argument 13.2, people draw the conclusion that *car X11 will stop*, given the premise that *car X11 runs into a brick wall*. In Argument 13.1, people draw the same conclusion given the same premise, under the assumption that *if car X11 runs into a brick wall it will stop*. Thus, Argument 13.1 involves a higher-order reasoning process over and beyond the component process involved in reasoning Argument 13.2.

It is understandable why Rips (2001) called Argument 13.2 'inductively strong'. This type of inference is apparently based on people's world knowledge, and referred to as the knowledge-based component (Liu, 2003; Liu et al., 1996). The additional process involved in Argument 13.1 reasoning over and above the knowledge-based component is referred to as the assumption-based component.

The successive-conditionalization approach

Consider the following MP argument:

> If it is a dog, then it is an animal.   13.3
> It is a dog.
>
> _____
>
> Therefore, it is an animal.

In this argument, given the major premise (if it is a dog, then it is an animal) and the minor premise (it is a dog), the conclusion certainly follows. There is one more valid argument known as Modus Tollens (MT), which consists of the same major premise, a different minor premise (It is not an animal), and a different conclusion (Therefore, it is not a dog). On the other hand, consider the following argument known as Affirmation of the Consequent (AC):

> If it is a dog, then it is an animal.   (13.4)
> It is an animal.
>
> _____
>
> Therefore, it is a dog.

In this argument, given the major premise and the minor premise, the conclusion does not necessarily follow (invalid argument), because an animal could be, and couldn't be, a dog. Early investigators used the 'sometimes true, sometimes not true' option as a correct choice, although more recent investigators frequently use the 'can't tell' option as a correct choice. There is also one more invalid argument known as Denial of the Antecedent (DA), which consists of the same major premise, a different minor premise (It is not a dog), and a different conclusion (Therefore, it is not an animal). The correct choice for DA is also 'can't tell', because something that is not a dog couldn't be, and could be, an animal.

It may be more convenient, if various options such as 'can't tell', 'it is true', and 'it isn't true' could be arranged in the same continuum of 'certainty-uncertainty' or 'probability'. If the reasoner is asked to rate how probable the conclusion (it is a dog) is true, then only one question for asking the reasoner is necessary, instead of preparing many options for the reasoner to answer. In the sequel, a probabilistic approach is used to refer to such a way of asking the reasoner to rate how probable the conclusion is true.

One important advantage of adopting such probabilistic approach is that it is compatible with everyday reasoning. Unlike the dog-animal analytic problem, very few people endorse everyday MP reasoning problems with perfect certainty (e.g., George, 1995; Stevenson & Over, 1995).

For example, let us consider the following argument form used in everyday reasoning:

If p, then q. (If the glass is heated, it will break.) $\qquad$ (13.5)

p. (The glass is heated.)

Therefore, q. (It will break.)

Since it is always uncertain whether the heated glass will break or not, the probabilistic approach can be seen to be especially suitable for such everyday reasoning.

The most important advantage of adopting the probabilistic approach lies, however, in its applicability of the rule of successive conditionalization (Jeffrey, 1981). It should first be noted that 'conditionalizing C on B' is equivalent to computing the probability of C given B. According to this rule, the result of successive conditionalization on two statements (premises) is the same as that of conditionalizing once on the conjunction of those two premises. The conditionalization rule may be applied for making MP, MT, DA, and AC inferences as follows.

MP/MT inferences

In the probabilistic approach for computing MP inferences, the reasoner is supposed to compute the probability of the conclusion q given the two premises: (a) $p \rightarrow q$, a notation for 'if p then q', and (b) p. There are three options in attempting this computation. The first option is to attempt to integrate $p \rightarrow q$ (first premise) and p (second premise) to arrive at q, which is found to be the conclusion itself. It is assumed that most reasoners do not use this option unless they are logically trained. The second option is to compute the probability of the conclusion (q) given the first premise ($p \rightarrow q$). There is no way to compute this probability, because $p \rightarrow q$ refers to a hypothetical situation. It is difficult to see how q could be conditionalized on $p \rightarrow q$. The third option is to compute the probability of the conclusion (q) given the second premise (p), i.e., the probability of q given p. This computation is feasible, because p refers to an event, e.g., an event that the glass is heated, and q refers to an event that it will break. Given that the glass is heated, reasoners are capable of computing the probability that it will break, based on their world knowledge. The process of computing the probability of q given p will be referred to as the first-step conditionalization.

After selecting the third option, reasoners then attempt to compute the probability of q given p under the assumption of $p \rightarrow q$. The process of computing the probability of q given p, conditionalized on $p \rightarrow q$, will be referred to as the second-step conditionalization. This successive conditionalization which underlies the process of executing the third option can be described by the following first two equations as follows:

First-step conditionalization: P (q given p) = P ($q \mid p$) (13.6)

Second-step conditionalization: P ((q given p)given $p{\to}q$) = P (q given $p \mid p{\to}q$) (13.7)

Conditionalizing once on the two premises: P ($q \mid p{\to}q, p$) (13.8)

In Equation 13.6 is shown the first-step conditionalization, which computes the probability of the conclusion given the second premise. The result of the first-step conditionalization is conditionalized again on the major premise in Equation 13.7. The successive-conditionalization rule states that the result of this successive conditionalization on the categorical premise first and then on the major premise is the same as that of conditionalizing once on the conjunction of these two premises. The result of conditionalizing once on the conjunction of the two premises is shown in Formula 13.8, which is generally given as an MP problem to reasoners.

The case of MT inferences is similar to the MP case. Thus, analogous to Equations 13.6–7 and Formula 8, there are Equations 13.9–10 and Formula 13.11 as follows:

First-step conditionalization: P (not-p given not-q) = P (not-$p \mid$ not-q) (13.9)

Second-step conditionalization: P ((not-p given not-q) given $p{\to}q$)

= P (not-p given not-$q \mid p{\to}q$) (13.10)

Conditionalizing once on the two premises: P (not-$p \mid p{\to}q$, not-q) (13.11)

The conditionalization rule states that the result of the successive conditionalization on the categorical premise first in Equation 13.9 and then on the major premise in Equation 13.10 is the same as that of conditionalizing once on the conjunction of these two premises (Formula 13.11).

Translating validity into probability, the results obtained for MP and MT are compatible with material implication of conditional inferences. The converse that probability be translated into validity is not correct (e.g., Rips, 2001). Rips cited the following example to demonstrate that P (conclusion | premise) = 1 but the argument is not deductively correct:

Calvin randomly chooses a real number between 3 and 4. (13.12)

Calvin does not choose π.

If it is assumed, however, that the probability space consists of a finite number of elements, then the converse that probability be translated into validity could be correct. In everyday reasoning, however, this finiteness condition is generally satisfied.

Knowledge-based components

The result of the first-step conditionalization gives the knowledge-based component for MT as well as for MP. This component corresponds to Rips' (2001) inductive strength, and is estimated empirically in the present approach.

The experimental procedure for estimating the knowledge-based component is to use the reduced problem, which poses a question, 'Given the categorical premise, what is the probability of the conclusion', for collecting probability ratings. In previous studies, Liu and associates (e.g., Liu, 2003; Liu et al., 1996) used three types of conditional relationship through a preliminary study: high percieved sufficiency, medium perceived sufficiency, and low percieved sufficiency.

These three types of conditional relationship may be exemplified by the following three conditional statements: (a) 'If a substance is a diamond, then it is very hard', (b) 'If John moves to a new house, then he adds some furniture', and (c) 'If Mary has long hair, then she is a quiet woman'.

It is easy to see why 'the probability of q given p' represents the knowledge-based component of MP inferences. Given that a substance is a diamond, it is highly probable that it is very hard, based on people's world knowledge. High school and college students generally give a mean rating of about .95 (e.g., Liu, 2003; Liu et al., 1996). They also judge the probability to be about .75 that a person adds some furniture, given that he or she moves to a new house. However, the probability of an unknown woman to be quiet on the base of her having long hair would be judged to be nearly by chance of .50 to .60.

It is also not difficult to see why 'the probability of not–p given not–q' represents the knowledge-based component of MT inferences. Given that a substance is not very hard, it is highly probable that this substance is not a diamond. Adults generally give a mean rating in the range from .80 to .90 (e.g., Liu, 2003; Liu et al., 1996). This probability rating is lower than the probability rating involved in inferring that the substance is hard given that it is a diamond. This is apparently because people are asked to infer an event's complement from an event's complement. People also tend to infer that a person does not move to a new house from an observation that he or she does not add some furniture. This probability rating is about .65. Finally, in the low-sufficiency condition people give about a .50 probability rating in inferring that a woman does not have long hair from the fact that she is not quiet.

In conclusion, the results of the first-step conditionalization give the conditional probability of the conclusion given the categorical premise for MP/MT, which represents the knowledge-based component. For the knowledge-based component of MP, it represents the ability to infer from an event to another event. For the knowledge-based component of MT, on the other hand, it represent the ability of inferring from the complement of an event to the complement of another event. The effect of perceived sufficiency on MP/MT has been known (e.g., Byrne, 1989; Cummins, Lubart, Alksnis, & Rist, 1991; Rumain, Cornell, & Braine, 1983; Staudenmayer, 1975; Thompson, 1994). With the introduction of the reduced MP/MT problems, however, it is clear that perceived sufficiency affects MP/MT responses by affecting their knowledge-based component (e.g., Liu, 2003; Liu et al., 1996).

Assumption-based components

The second-step conditionalization for MP refers to the process of computing the probability of q given p, conditionalized on $p{\rightarrow}q$ (see Equation 13.7). In this computation, if reasoners are able to detect 'q given p' to be related to $p{\rightarrow}q$, then the probability of 'q given p' given '$p{\rightarrow}q$' is adjusted upwards. The amount reasoners adjusted upwards is referred to as the assumption-based component of MP. Similarly, the assumption-based component of MT is defined from Equations 13.9 and 13.11, as follows:

Assumption-based component of MP: $P\ (q \mid p{\rightarrow}q, p) - P\ (q \mid p)$ (13.13)

Assumption-based component of MT: $P\ (\text{not-}p \mid p{\rightarrow}q, \text{not-}q) - P\ (\text{not-}p \mid \text{not-}q)$ (13.14)

Thus, the assumption-based component refers to the ability of reasoners to reason beyond the knowledge-based component by taking into account the conditional-statement premise. It is assumed that reasoners' ability to perform the second-step conditionalization depends on the following two factors. First, reasoners are able to hold 'p therefore q' and '$p{\rightarrow}q$' simultaneously in their working memory to detect their relationship. Second, reasoners have an ability to detach '$p{\rightarrow}q$' from reality. Otherwise, reasoners would be unable to see the hypothetical nature of '$p{\rightarrow}q$', and tend to see '$p{\rightarrow}q$' to reflect 'p therefore q', i.e., reality. When reasoners are able to perform the second-step as well as the first-step conditionalization, it can be shown through the successive-conditionalization procedure that

$$\text{MP: } P\,(q\mid p{\rightarrow}q, p) = 1 \tag{13.15}$$

$$\text{MT: } P\,(\text{not-}p\mid p{\rightarrow}q, \text{not-}q) = 1 \tag{13.16}$$

Let us then consider a situation in which reasoners are unable to perform the second-step conditionalization in making MP or MT inferences, i.e., reasoners stop at the first-step conditionalization, because they are unable to detect how the result of the first-step conditionalization is related to the conditional-statement premise. In this situation, we observe

$$\text{MP: } P\,(q\mid p{\rightarrow}q, p) = P\,(q\mid p) \tag{13.17}$$

$$\text{MT: } P\,(\text{not-}p\mid p{\rightarrow}q, \text{not-}q) = P\,(\text{not-}p\mid \text{not-}q) \tag{13.18}$$

In actuality, reasoners tend not to manifest the extremes of performing the second-step conditionalization in full (Equations 13.15–16) or not performing at all (Equations 13.17–18). Reasoners tend to detect the result of the first-step conditionalization to be somewhat related to the conditional-statement premise. Therefore, MP/MT responses tend to be in between the extremes, as follows.

$$\text{MP: } P\,(q\mid p) \le P\,(q\mid p{\rightarrow}q, p) \le 1 \tag{13.19}$$

$$\text{MT: } P\,(\text{not-}p\mid \text{not-}q) \le P\,(\text{not-}p\mid p{\rightarrow}q, \text{not-}q) \le 1 \tag{13.20}$$

In manipulating perceived sufficiency, it was pointed out that perceived sufficiency affects MP responses by affecting only the first-step conditionalization. In fact, the result of the first-step conditionalization is defined to stand for perceived sufficiency in the case of MP. In the condition of high perceived sufficiency, $P\,(q\mid p)$ is quite high. Therefore, although there could be an upward adjustment through the second-step conditionalization, as Iniqualities 20 show, MP responses have an upper bound. There would be no room available for this upward adjustment to become significant. In the medium and low sufficiency conditions, on the other hand, significant assumption-based components have often been observed for adult participants in MP inferences.

With respect to the assumption-based component of MT inferences, it has been consistently observed in the medium sufficiency condition but not in the low and high sufficiency conditions for high-school students (Liu, 2003; Liu et al., 1996). Although the observed MT responses reflected both the assumption-based and knowledge-based components in the medium sufficiency condition, the presence of the assumption-based component in this condition may be explained as follows. For the complete MT problems, participants are to judge the probability of '*Given not−q, how probable not−p is*' under the assumption that *If p then q*. However, in the medium sufficiency condition, the presence of *If p then q* in the complete problems could help the participants retrieve *If not−q, then not−p*, because *not−q* is fairly sufficient for *not−p*. With retrieval of *If not−q, then not−p*, the participants are now responding to '*If not−q, then not−p. Given not−q, how probable is not−p?*' This explains the presence of the assumption-based component, because the participants are now making MP responses. In the low sufficiency condition, the assumption-based component is absent because *If p, then q* will not remind participants of *If not−q, then not−p* by the definition of low sufficiency.

In making MT inferences, reasoners have to compute the probability of '*not−p* given *not−q*', conditionalizing on 'if p then q', in the second-step conditionalization. In this case, '*not−p* given *not−q*' appears quite different from 'if p then q'. This is the reason why high school students generally fail to find a relationship between the conditional-statement premise and the conclusion given the categorical premise, and do not proceed to compute the second-step conditionalization in MT inferences.

When the antecedent and consequent clauses of the normal conditionals in Experiment 1 are reversed in Experiment 2 (Liu, 2003), the conditional arguments appear to refer to imaginary objects or persons (e.g., *If a substance is very hard, then it is a diamond*). It was found in this case that there was some observable assumption-based component of MT. It was reasoned that these MT problems could remind participants as if they were mathematics problems. High school students had generally acquired rules such as contrapositive arguments (inferring '*not–q* implies *not–p*' from '*p* implies *q*') in their mathematics courses. By converting 'if *p* then *q*' into 'if *not–q* then *not–p*', students could see how the outcome of the first-step conditionalization is related to a new conditional-statement premise ('if *not–q* then *not–p*'), enabling them to compute the second-step conditionalization.

Although the assumption-based component was consistently found to be absent in making MT inferences in everyday problems, these findings were all observed from high school participants (Liu, 2003; Liu et al., 1996). Recent studies (e.g., Chou, 2007; Wang, 1999) using college students as participants found, however, that the assumption-based component is usually observable in making MT inferences under the low sufficiency condition.

DA/AC responses

As in the case of MP/MT inferences, reasoners proceed to compute the first-step and and second-step conditionalization in making DA/AC inferences (Equations 13.21–22 and Formula 13.23 for DA, Equations 13.24–25 and Formula 13.26 for AC), as follows:

First-step conditionalization: $P \text{ (not-}q \text{ given not-}p) = P \text{ (not-}q \mid \text{not-}p)$ (13.21)

Second-step conditionalization: $P \text{ ((not-}q \text{ given not-}p) \text{ given } p {\rightarrow} q)$

$= P \text{ (not-}q \text{ given not-}p \mid p {\rightarrow} q)$ (13.22)

Conditionalizing once on the two premises: $P \text{ (not-}q \mid p {\rightarrow} q, \text{not-}p)$ (13.23)

First-step conditionalization: $P \text{ (}p \text{ given } q) = P \text{ (}p \mid q)$ (13.24)

Second-step conditionalization: $P \text{ ((}p \text{ given } q \text{) given } p {\rightarrow} q)$

$= P \text{ (}p \text{ given } q \mid p {\rightarrow} q)$ (13.25)

Conditionalizing once on the two premises: $P \text{ (}p \mid p {\rightarrow} q, q)$ (13.26)

In the case of DA/AC, it can be shown mathematically that the result of the second-step conditionalization is the same as that of the first-step conditionalization. In other words, the conclusion given the categorical premise is not probabilistically related to the conditional-statement premise for DA/AC, as follows:

DA: $P \text{ (not-}q \mid p {\rightarrow} q, \text{not-}p) = P \text{ (not-}q \mid \text{not-}p)$ (13.27)

AC: $P \text{ (}p \mid p {\rightarrow} q, q) = P \text{ (}p \mid q)$ (13.28)

Knowledge-based components

As in the case of MP/MT, the knowledge-based component is defined by the probability of the conclusion given the categorical premise for DA/AC. In this sense, there should be no additional principles necessary to describe the knowledge-based component for DA/AC. It was noted that there are two principles for describing the knowledge-based component for MP/MT.

First, knowledge-based components are entirely determined by the magnitude of the probability of the conclusion given the categorical premise, which represents a summary statistic acquired through an individual's past life (Oaksford & Chater, 1998). Second, the probability of the conclusion given the categorical premise is lower for MT than for MP, because the former involves inferring from the complement of an event to the complement of another event. Thus, the knowledge-based component is generally lower for DA than for AC, because the former also involves inferring from the complement of an event to the complement of another event.

Assumption-based components

The rule of successive conditionalization yields no assumption-based component in making DA/AC responses, which generally accords with experimental findings (e.g., Liu, 2003). In other words, DA/AC responses are affected by perceived necessity in exactly the same way as their knowledge-based components are. In spite of the fact that previous invesgitators did not use probability measures in their experiment, it is striking to note that they generally found DA/AC responses to be affected by perceived necessity (e.g., Bucci, 1978, Experiment 2; Byrne, 1989; Cummins et al., 1991; Rumain et al., 1983; Markovits, 1984; Staudenmayer, 1975; Thompson, 1994, 1995).

Remarks

In the successive-conditionalization framework, it should be noted that the probabilistic approach is especially illuminating and appropriate in interpreting the result of the first-step conditionalization, which does not generally give the values of 0 or 1, but does give a value between 0 and 1. This is because the first-step conditionalization involves inferring from an event to another event, which represents a person's world knowledge acquired through his or her own life.

In performing the second-step conditionalization, it is generally assumed that reasoners take the conditional premise to be true, as being instructed. It is only with this assumption that it is understandable to observe 100% endorsement of MP by Evans (1977). In this study the major premises are phrased in abstract terms, such as 'If the letter is G then the number is 9'. The conditional probability of finding the number being 9 given the letter being G would be nearly 0. Therefore, if the reasoner comprehend the conditional-statement premise through its conditional probability of the consequent given the antecedent, then the result of 100% endorsement of MP would be impossible.

Working with the conditionals phrased in terms of thematic materials, such as 'If Mary has an essay to write, she will stay late in the library', Byrne, Espino, and Santamaria (1999) also observed a mean of 95% endorsement of simple MP inferences in their experiment. Again, the conditional probability of Mary to stay late in the library given that she has an essay to write would be generally small. Therefore, unless reasoners are assumed to comprehend the literal meaning of if-then by taking the conditional to mean that Mary will certainly stay late in the library if she has an essay to write, such nearly complete endorsement of simple MP inferences would be difficult to understand.

The assumption of taking the conditional premise by its literal meaning in conditional reasoning seems to be contradictory with a long tradition in philosophy of assuming that belief in the conditional premise is measured by the conditional probability of the consequent given the antecedent (e.g., Adams, 1965, 1966; Edginton, 1995; Lewis, 1986; Ramsey, 1931). There is no contradiction in the two assumptions, because belief in the conditional premise reflects a conscious appraisal while comprehending its literal meaning represents an unconscious process (i.e., taking it for granted without assessing its probability).

The mental models approach

The rule of successive conditionalization (Jeffrey, 1981) is essentially deductive and compatible with the material-implication approach. One difference between the successive-conditionalization approach and the material-implication approach is that the second-step conditionalization is always implemented for MP and MT in the latter approach. Another important difference is that the present approach does not consider logic as a model of thought, so that logically equivalent statements need not necessarily have the same meaning.

According to the material-implication approach, the antecedent of conditionals is sufficient for the consequent. Thus, when p happens, q is certain to happen, and P (conditional statement premise) = 1. The mental-models approach, which essentially abides by material implication, has two versions: one probabilistic and another nonprobabilistic. Let us consider the nonprobabilistic version first and the probabilistic version next as follows.

Nonprobabilistic version

Johnson-Laird and his collaborators (e.g., Johnson-Laird & Byrne, 1991; Johnson-Laird, Byrne, & Schaeken, 1992; Johnson-Laird, Byrne, & Tabossi, 1989) hypothesized that given the 'if-then' premise reasoners start to construct an initial representation of the major premise, in which p becomes associated with q. Mental model theory also claims that reasoners can, in principle, flesh out the initial representation, leading to a biconditional or a conditional interpretation.

In a biconditional interpretation, two representations are constructed: (a) p becomes associated with q, and (b) *not–p* becomes associated with *not–q*. In a conditional interpretation, on the other hand, three representations are constructed: (a) p becomes associated with q, (b) *not–p* becomes associated with *not–q*, and (c) *not–p* becomes associated with q.

Original formulation

Based on these assumptions, mental model theory then claims that MP and AC are easier than MT and DC. This is because MP and AC inferences could be made solely on the basis of the initial representation, in which the occurrence of p makes it possible for the occurrence of q (MP) and the occurrence of q makes it possible for the occurrence of p (AC), because p is associated with q. MT and DC are more difficult than MP and AC, because the former require reasoners to construct two (biconditional interpretation) or more than two representations (conditional interpretation).

Markovits and Barroulillet's variant of mental model theory

Markovits and Barroulillet (2002) incorporated the alternatives factor and the disabling conditions factor into mental model theory to account for the development of conditional reasoning. In the following, only their account of conditional reasoning in older children and adolescents is briefly presented.

In making the MP inference, Markovits and Barroulillet (2002) claimed that reasoners will start with the initial model and will use 'p is true' as a retrieval cue. They assumed that there are two strategies for freshing out this model, depending on whether disabling cases are readily activated in memory. If this is not the case, then the initial model will be used and the MP inference will be made. On the other hand, if a disabling case is activated at a sufficiently high level, then retrieval of this information will be incorporated into the model of the premises. In this case, the reasoner will conclude that if p is true then q is not necessarily true. It is also claimed that some reasoners will rely on the consequent of the major premise as a retrieval cue to activate alternative cases. In this case, the model of 'b' (alternative cases) as associated with q will be constructed in addition to the initial model, leading to an 'uncertain' conclusion sometimes.

For MT Markovits and Barroulillet (2002) contend that older children could construct three models characteristic of the conditional interpretation, using the major premise as a retrieval cue. In this case, the overall cognitive load is much higher, since both amount of information retrieved and number of models are greater. When reasoners are capable of processing such a relatively large quantity of information, they would tend to make the logically correct conclusion ('p is false') more often in this case.

For the AC inference, the minor premise ('q is true') will tend to strongly activate possible alternatives, if they are available. Reasoners will thus use either the initial model and make the biconditional inference to AC or will produce the two models that include a possible alternative. In this case, they will respond with uncertainty to the inference.

For the DA inference, Markovits and Barroulillet (2002) assumed that the minor premise ('p is false') will tend to activate the complementary class and the alternative class. If only the complementary class is strongly activated, then the two models corresponding to the biconditional inference will be produced, which will tend to the inference that 'q is false'. If the alternative class is also activated, then the three models corresponding to the conditional inference will be produced, which will lead to the conclusion that q may or may not be true.

Remarks

Although Markovits and Barroulillet (2002) incorporated the disabling conditions factor and the alternatives factor into mental model theory to account for MP/MT and DA/AC inferences, these two factors would be difficult to calibrate to give some precise predictions. For instance, it is difficult to compare alternatives involved in one type of conditional relationship to alternatives involved in another type of conditional relationship.

Probabilistic version

The mental-models approach is not consistent in its probability assignment to conditionals. In its mental model of extensional reasoning, Johnson-Laird, Legrenzi, Girotto, Legrenzi, and Carverni (1999) maintained that individuals who are unfamiliar with the probability calculus can infer the probabilities of events in an extensional way. In other words, they construct mental models of what is true in the various possibilities. The probability of an event depends on the proportion of models in which it occurs. It is based on this interpretation that the probability of the material conditional is estimated as follows:

$$P \text{ (material conditional)} = P \text{ (TT)} + P \text{ (FT)} + P \text{ (FF)} \tag{13.29}$$

On the other hand, Johnson-Laird and Byrne (2002) stated that the three possibilities of this interpretation of the conditional meaning are described completely by the following conjunction of conditionals: *If A then C, and if not A then either C or not C* (p. 649). In other words, the conditional, *If A then C*, seems to refer only to the TT case in which p is true and q is true. Thus, it is not known whether Johnson-Laird and Byrne actually mean that

$$P \text{ (material conditional)} = 1 \tag{13.30}$$

The experimental results obtained from Johnson-Laird et al. (1999) seem to support Equation 13.30, although these investigators interpreted their finding differently. In their Experiment 2, they had the connective If A then B (There is a box in which if there is a yellow card then there is a brown card) among other connectives. For each connective, 22 participants were asked the following questions:

(1) *At least A*: In the box there is at least a yellow card.

(2) *A and B*: In the box there is a yellow card and a brown card.

(3) *A and not B*: In the box there is a yellow card and there is not a brown card.

(4) *B and not A*: In the box there is a brown card and there is not a yellow card.

(5) *Neither A nor B*: In the box there is neither a yellow card nor a brown card.

Their important finding in the present connection is that '8 participants inferred the probability of A and B as 100%, which is predicted from the omission of the implicit model of the conditional' (p. 73). However, if nearly 40% of participants responded in that way, it may not be dismissed as due to the omission of the implicit model of the conditional. Thus, the mental models theory is flexible in choosing P (material conditional) = P (TT) + P (FT) + P (FF) or P (material conditional) = 1.

Conclusion

It is still not known how the probability of conditionals affects actual reasoning processes. As an advantage of the successive-conditionalization approach, it is clear, however, that it is possible to determine whether MP and MT responses arise from the knowledge-based or/and assumption-based components, which has been a source of confusion in other approaches, including mental models theory. With Markovits and Barroulillet's (2002) reformulation by taking into account the alternatives factor, this approach does not differ significantly from the successive-condition-alization approach with respect to DA and AC responses.

The conditional-probabilistic approach

Many investigators reasoned that conditionals are uncertain or probabilistic (e.g., George, 1995; Liu et al., 1996; Oaksford, Chater, & Larkin, 2000; Politzer & Braine, 1991; Stevenson & Over, 1995). Let us specifically consider George's study, more recent studies (e.g., Evans, Handley, & Over, 2003; Oberauer & Wilhelm, 2003), and Oaksford et al.'s study separately as follows.

George's study

George (1995) measured essentially the conditional probability of the consequent given the antecedent of conditionals by what he called the entailment task. To take the conditional 'If exports decrease, then unemployment rises' as an example, participants were instructed to assume absolutely that the premise (exports decrease) is true in order to decide whether it entails the suggested conclusion (unemployment rises) or not. Participants answered by checking one of the seven options (true, probably true, rather true, uncertain, rather false, probably false, false). In the confidence task, George attempted to measure participants' confidence of the truth of each conditional. He asked participants to evaluate the truth of each of the conditional statements by checking one of the same seven options used for the entailment task. The results showed that in these two tasks the frequency of choice of the various response options was highly comparable for each conditional statement.

If the truth of an event can be equated with its occurrence, whether an event is true may be interpreted to mean whether the event certainly occurs. Then, the confidence task essentially measures the probability of a conditional statement. George's (1995) results showed that observed probability of a conditional statement is comparable to the conditional probability of the consequent given the antecedent. For those participants who received both entailment task and confidence task, he further observed that the correlation coefficients between these two tasks were about .80. Therefore, George's results seem to anticipate the studies by Evans et al. (2003) and Oberauer and Wilhelm (2003). This is because both studies all claim that the psychological meaning of conditionals is characterized by conditional probability or conjunctive probability, but not by material implication.

The literal meaning of 'if-then' is that in the hypothetical state described by the antecedent the state described by the consequent certainly occurs. In other words, the antecedent of a conditional is known to be sufficient for the consequent. In the confidence task, when participants are instructed to evaluate their degree of confidence in the truth of a conditional statement, they are likely to abandon the literal meaning of conditionals. They could likely scrutinize their long term memory for assessing whether the consequent could be true given the antecedent, because they are asked to evaluate the degree of confidence in the truth of a conditional statement. In a conditional-reasoning task, it is not likely for reasoners to stop at the conditional-statement premise to evaluate its probability.

More recent studies

Based on their experimental results, Evans et al. (2003) and Oberauer and Wilhelm (2003) claim that the psychological meaning of conditionals is characterized by conditional probability or conjunctive probability, but not by material implication. More specifically, Evans et al.'s method consists of making explicit the composition of a pack of cards. Participants are then asked to rate whether a conditional statement, such as 'If the card is yellow then it has a circle printed on it', is true of a card drawn at random from the pack. Oberauer and Wilhelm used a similar procedure and observed essentially the same results.

Under the experimental condition as described by Evans et al. (2003) and Oberauer and Wilhelm (2003), participants would consider the composition of the pack of cards as one of the givens, and take the question involving 'If the card is yellow then it has a circle printed on it' to mean 'Given that the card is yellow it has a circle printed on it'. Most participants are then to give an answer in terms of conditional probabilities or conjunctive probabilities. Girotto and Johnson-Laird (2004) expressed a similar view that, in responding to the question, 'What is the probability that if p then q?', participants easily confuse the question as a direct request for the conditional probability by applying the probability operator to the main clause (i.e., q) rather than to the whole conditional.

These two studies by Evans et al. (2003) and Oberauer and Wilhelm (2003) only concern conditionals about frequency distributions that are assumed to be understood by the participants. More recently, using causal conditionals of a sort that are ubiquitous in real-world reasoning and decision, Over, Hadjichristidis, Evans, Handly, and Sloman (2007) support the conditional probability hypothesis that subjective probability of a natural language conditional is the subjective conditional probability. It may be concluded that the conditional probability hypothesis holds if participants are to explicitly evaluate the probability of natural language conditionals.

Oaksford, Chater, and Larkin's study

Oaksford et al. (2000) proposed that people endorse a conditional argument in direct proportion to the conditional probability of the conclusion given the second premise, as follows:

$$\text{MP: } P (q \mid p) \tag{13.31}$$

$$\text{MT: } P (\text{not-}p \mid \text{not-}q) \tag{13.32}$$

$$\text{DA: } P (\text{not-}q \mid \text{not-}p) \tag{13.33}$$

$$\text{AC: } P (p \mid q) \tag{13.34}$$

They then derived expressions for the conditional probabilities for each inference on the basis of a contingency table for a conditional rule. Therefore, their approach differs significantly from the successive-conditionalization approach.

Oaksford and Chater (2007) considered that the conditional premise is not disregarded in Formulations 13.31–34, but reasoners are assumed to conditionalize on it. They also assume that the probability of conditionals is equal to the conditional probability of q given p.

At the present, there are many formulations with respect to the probability of conditionals. Their impact on reasoning processes, however, still remains to be seen.

Conclusions

In a conditional reasoning task, as in any deductive reasoning task, reasoners are instructed to estimate the probability of the conclusion on the assumption that the premises are true. Many investigators (e.g., George, 1995) noted that some reasoners could assume the premises to be true while others could not. There are also studies (e.g., Politzer & Braine, 1991; Stevenson & Over, 1995) that presented evidence that reasoners tend to comprehend the conditional premise as uncertain. More recent investigators (e.g., Evans et al., 2003; Oberauer & Wilhelm, 2003; Over et al., 2007) directly measured the probability of conditionals in support of the conditional probability hypothesis.

To some extent, the successive-conditionalization approach could handle this series of observations as follows. There is no dispute about the first-step conditionalization, because it measures only the probability of the conclusion given the second premise in the reduced problems, which represents the knowledge-based component. To take MP for instance, reasoners then attempt to compute the probability of q given p under the assumption of 'if p then q', which is referred to as the second-step conditionalization. If reasoners are able to assume the conditional premise to be true, following the instructions, then there could be a substantial assumption-based component. On the other hand, if reasoners take the conditional premise to stand for the conditional probability of q given p, then an observed assumption-based component could be nearly absent. In conclusion, the successive-conditionalization procedure could be a viable alternative for studying any type of deductive reasoning in the future.

Acknowledgements

This study was supported by National Science Grant 94–2413-H-194–003-. I am grateful to Guy Politzer for his comments on an earlier version of this chapter.

References

Adams, E. W. (1965). A logic of conditionals. *Inquiry*, **8**, 166–197.

Adams, E. W. (1966). Probability and the logic of conditionals. In Hintikka, J. and Suppes, P. (Eds.), *Aspects of Inductive Logic* (pp. 256–316). Amsterdam: North-Holland.

Bucci, W. (1978). The interpretation of universal affirmative propositions. *Cognition*, **6**, 55–77.

Byrne, R. M. J. (1989). Suppressing valid inferences with conditionals. *Cognition*, **31**, 61–83.

Byrne, R. M. J., Espino, O., & Santamaria, C. (1999). Counterexamples and the suppression of inferences. *Journal of Memory and Language*, **40**, 347–373.

Chou, T.-h. (2007). The mechanism of suppression effects in conditional reasoning. Unpublished PhD thesis, National Chung-Cheng University, Chia-Yi, Taiwan.

Cummins, D. D. (1995). Naive theories and causal deduction. *Memory & Cognition*, **23**, 646–658.

Cummins, D. D., Lubart, T., Alksnis, O., & Rist, R. (1991). Conditional reasoning and causation. *Memory & Cognition*, **19**, 274–282.

Edgington, D. (1995). On conditionals. *Mind*, **104**, 235–329.

Evans, J. St.B. T. (1977). Linguistic factors in reasoning. *Quarterly Journal of Experimental Psychology*, **29A**, 297–306.

Evans, J. St.B. T., Handley, S. J., & Over, D. E. (2003). Conditionals and conditional probabilities. *Journal of Experimental Psychology: Learning, Memory, and Cognition*, **29**, 321–325.

George, C. (1995). The endorsement of the premises: Assumption-based or belief-based reasoning. *British Journal of Psychology*, **86**, 93–111.

Girotto, V. & Johnson-Laird, P. N. (2004). The probability of conditionals. *Psychologia*, **47**, 207–225.

Jeffrey, R. C. (1981). Formal logic, its scope and limits (2nd ed.). New York: McGraw-Hill.

Johnson-Laird, P. N. & Byrne, R. M. J. (1991). *Deduction*. Hove, U.K.: Erlbaum.

Johnson-Laird, P. N. & Byrne, R. M. J. (2002). Conditionals: A theory of meaning, pragmatics, and inference. *Psychological Review*, **109**, 211–228.

Johnson-Laird, P. N., Byrne, R. M. J., & Tabossi, P. (1989). Reasoning by model: The case of multiple quantification. *Psychological Review*, **96**, 658–673.

Johnson-Laird, P. N., Byrne, R. M. J., & Schaeken, W. (1992). Propositional reasoning by model. *Psychological Review*, **99**, 418–439.

Johnson-Laird, P. N., Legrenzi, P., Girotto, P., Legrenzi, M.S., & Caverni, J-P. (1999). Naïve probability: A mental model theory of extensional reasoning. *Psychological Review*, **106**, 62–88.

Lewis, D. (1986). *Philosophical Papers*. Volume 2. Oxford: Oxford University Press.

Liu, I.-m. (2003). Conditional reasoning and conditionalization. *Journal of Experimental Psychology: Learning, Memory, and Cognition*, **29**, 694–709.

Liu, I.-m., Lo, K.-c., & Wu, J.-t. (1996). A probabilistic interpretation of "if-then". *Quarterly Journal of Experimental Psychology*, **49A**, 828–844.

Markovits, H. (1984). Awareness of the 'possibles' as a mediator of formal thinking in conditional reasoning problems. *British Journal of Psychology*, **75**, 367–376.

Markovits, H., & Barrouillet, P. (2002). The development of conditional reasoning: A mental model account. *Developmental Review*, **22**, 5–36.

Oaksford, M. & Chater, N. (1998). *Rationality in an uncertain world*. Hove, UK: Psychology Press.

Oaksford, M. & Chater, N. (2007). *Bayesian rationality: The probabilistic approach to human reasoning*. Oxford, UK: Oxford University Press.

Oaksford, M., Chater, N., & Larkin, J. (2000). Probabilities and polarity biases in conditional inference. *Journal of Experimental Psychology: Learning, Memory and Cognition*, **26**, 883–899.

Oberauer, K. & Wilhelm, O. (2003). *Journal of Experimental Psychology: Learning, Memory, and Cognition*, **29**, 680–693.

Over, D. E., Hadjichristidis, C., Evans, J. St.B. T., Handlely, S. J., & Sloman, S. A. (2007). The probability of causal conditionals. *Cognitive Psychology*, **54**, 62–97.

Politzer, G. & Braine, M. D. S. (1991). Responses to inconsistent premises cannot count as suppression of valid inferences. *Cognition*, **38**, 103–108.

Ramsey, F. P. (1931). *The foundations of mathematics and other logical essays*. London: Routledge & Kegan Paul.

Rips, L. J. (2001). Two kinds of reasoning. *Psychological Science*, **12**, 129–134.

Rumain, B., Connell, J., & Braine, M. D. S. (1983). Conversational comprehension processes are responsible for reasoning fallacies in children as well as adults. *Developmental Psychology*, **19**, 471–481.

Staudenmayer, H. (1975). Understanding conditional reasoning with meaningful propositions. In R. J. Falmagne (Ed.), *Reasoning: Representation and process* (pp. 55–79). New York: Wiley.

Stevenson, R. J. & Over, D. E. (1995). Deduction from uncertain premises. *Quarterly Journal of Experimental Psychology*, **48A**, 613–645.

Thompson, V. A. (1994). Interpretational factors in conditional reasoning. *Memory & Cognition*, **22**, 742–758.

Thompson, V. A. (1995). Conditional reasoning: The necessary and sufficient conditions. *Canadian Journal of Experimental Psychology*, **49**, 1–58.

Wang, Z. J. (1999). *A two-component model of conditional reasoning*. Unpublished master's thesis, National Chung-Cheng University, Chia-Yi, Taiwan.

Chapter 14

Pragmatic conditionals, conditional pragmatics, and the pragmatic component of conditional reasoning

Jean-François Bonnefon and Guy Politzer

Introduction

Although there is not yet a single, dominant theory of the psychological processes underlying conditional reasoning (i.e., the cognitive manipulation of 'If *p*, then *q*' statements), an agreement exists that the theory requires a pragmatic component—that is, an account of how the linguistic *content* of a conditional statement and the *context* of its enunciation affect reasoners' interpretation and inferences.

An impressive amount of empirical data has been collected to date on the pragmatics of conditional reasoning. To get a crude idea of the importance of the topic, consider that of all papers on the psychology of conditional reasoning indexed in the *Web of Science*, about 1 in 6 includes the word 'pragmatic' in its title, abstract, or keywords. For comparison purpose, the same is true of only 1 paper in 10 about the word 'probability'.

This intense research activity is in stark contrast with the slow theoretical progress that has been made with respect to the pragmatic component of theories of conditional reasoning. Indeed, this component is often the least developed of past and current theories, and the temptation is strong to use pragmatics largely as a theoretical convenience—that is, as a means to explain away phenomena that other components of the theory cannot account for.

In order to accelerate the development of the pragmatic component of the future, grand theory of conditional reasoning, it is necessary to better circumscribe its domain of explanation. That the component is meant to address the pragmatic dimension of conditional reasoning does not mean it has to address everything pragmatic that can happen when reasoning conditionally. Our objective in this chapter is to arrive at some simple, preliminary criteria to define what the pragmatic component of the theory should explain (the pragmatics of conditional reasoning) and what is off its explanatory limits (things pragmatic that incidentally affect conditional reasoning).

Research on the pragmatics of conditional reasoning can be organized in two sets. The first set deals with non-standard, 'pragmatic' conditionals. Very crudely, these conditionals have a social function that goes beyond informing someone of a relation between the antecedent and the consequent, and invite inferences of their own, without the need for a minor premise. We will see that almost all such conditionals (that have been studied so far) involve some utility considerations, in the sense of decision theory. The second set deals with conditional pragmatics, that is, the basic pragmatic implicatures that are generally triggered by conditional sentences—most notoriously obversion. We suggest that these two sets define the domain of explanation of the pragmatic component of a theory of conditional reasoning. Their intersection (of which we give several detailed examples below) is of prime interest to such a component, but their exclusion might for now be considered off the limits of its explanatory mission—although we will consider at the end of this chapter some possibilities for future extensions of the two basic sets.

Our agenda in this chapter is to review research on pragmatic conditionals and research on conditional pragmatics, in order to define their intersection and their exclusion. This agenda implies that we will not provide the reader with an exhaustive review of the literature on pragmatics and reasoning. Such reviews are already available, for early (Hilton, 1995) as well as more recent research (Politzer, 2004). Neither will we provide the reader with a detailed discussion of existing theories of conditional reasoning and their current pragmatic component (Braine & O'Brien, 1991, Evans & Over, 2004, Johnson-Laird & Byrne, 2002). The interested reader may nevertheless refer to Politzer (2007) for a critical review of these theories and to Bonnefon (2004) and Evans, Over, and Handley (2005) for some considerations on the pragmatic component of Mental Model theory (Johnson-Laird & Byrne, 2002).

Lastly, we will not consider in this chapter how the pragmatic component should be articulated with the other components of a theory of conditional reasoning. We will limit ourselves to the following essential remark. There is a subtle two-way influence between pragmatic and reasoning processes. On the one hand, before the reasoning processes proper leading from premises to conclusion are executed, the elaboration of their actual logical form that results from various enrichment, implicatures and access to long term memory must take place. But on the other hand, these latter pragmatic processes themselves crucially depend on fast, partly unconscious, deductive and abductive inferences. We view the explanation of this mutual determination as the major aim of future research for both the psychology of reasoning (beyond conditional reasoning) and the investigation of utterance comprehension.

Pragmatic conditionals

In everyday life, conditional statements are used purposively. Often, this purpose is simply to inform listeners of a relation between the antecedent and the consequent, for example a causal [1a] or temporal [1b] relation:

(1)   a. If Queen Elizabeth dies, then Prince Charles will become King;
           b. If this is the plane to Brussels, then the next one is to Berlin.

But conditionals can do much more than just convey information about some causal or temporal relation. Let us call *pragmatic conditionals* all conditional statements that serve some social function other than, or beyond that of communicating a relation between their antecedent and consequent. It will often be the case that this social function aims at influencing in some way the behaviour of others, and that the analysis of the conditional statement involves considerations of utility, in the decision-theoretic sense. This is the reason why we will refer to them as *utility conditionals*. Most importantly, and in contrast with standard conditional, pragmatic conditionals invite inferences without the need for any additional, minor premise.[1] In the rest of this section, we review the various forms of utility conditionals that have been studied to date (i.e., consequentials, persuasion conditionals, inducements, obligations and permissions, directives), and we detail the inferences they invite. We then briefly mention two pragmatic yet non-utility conditionals (i.e., preconditionals and biscuit conditionals).

---

[1]   It can be useful to think of regular 'if *p*, then *q*' conditionals as having the illocutionary force (Austin, 1962) of *informing* other individuals of a relation between *p* and *q*. Pragmatic conditionals can have another illocutionary force, such as committing to some course of action, or directing the actions of other individuals. They can also inform of something that is unrelated to the relation between *p* and *q*.

Consequential conditionals

Consequential conditionals (Bonnefon & Hilton, 2004) provide us with a gentle introduction to other utility conditionals. Although they are based on utility considerations, consequential conditionals are still aimed at affecting the beliefs of listeners, rather than their behaviour. Furthermore, the five defining features of consequential conditionals (Bonnefon & Hilton, 2004, p. 29) can easily be adapted to define other sorts of utility conditionals. 'If p, then q' is a consequential conditional if and only if:

(2)   a. p is an action of a third party, the agent. The agent is neither the speaker nor the listener;
      b. q is a consequence of taking action p;
      c. q is valued: It is either a good (positive, desirable) or a bad (negative, undesirable) outcome to the agent;
      d. p is an action under the control of the agent;
      e. q is known by the agent to be a consequence of p.

Consider these two statements as an illustration:

(3)   a. If the CEO admits the fraud, he'll serve time in jail;
      b. If Sophie takes this drug, she'll make a good recovery.

In statement [3a], the antecedent is an action (admitting the fraud) that is under the control of the agent (the CEO), who is neither the speaker nor the listener. The consequent is a valued outcome of this action, in that case the undesirable consequence of serving time in jail, and that consequence is foreseeable by the agent. Statement [3a] is thus a negative-outcome consequential conditional, or a 'negative consequential' for short. The analysis of statement [3b] is very similar except that the consequence there (making a good recovery) is desirable. Statement [3b] is thus a positive-outcome consequential conditional, or a 'positive consequential' for short.

Positive consequentials invite the pragmatic inference that the agent is going to take action p (Sophie will take the drug), while negative consequentials invite the pragmatic inference that the agent is not going to take action p (the CEO will not admit the fraud). Furthermore, the strength with which these implicatures are invited is proportional to the extremity of the consequential outcome. Very desirable or undesirable outcomes strongly invite the implicature about the antecedent action—more so than do moderately desirable or undesirable outcomes. We will have more to say later on about the way these implicatures can complicate reasoning. As for now, we continue our journey through utility conditionals.

Persuasion conditionals

Persuasion conditionals (Thompson, Evans, & Handley, 2005) have a lot in common with consequentials, but their goal is to persuade the listener that a course of action should be undertaken, rather than to suggest to the listener that a third-party is going to undertake a course of action. 'If p, then q' is a persuasion conditional if and only if (adapted from Thompson et al., 2005, p.240):

(4)   a. p refers to a hypothetical action of a third party who is neither the speaker nor the listener and whose agency may be implied rather than stated explicitly;
      b. q is a consequence of taking action p;
      c. q is either a desirable or an undesirable outcome;
      d. p is an action under the control of the third party;
      e. The consequences q do not accrue specifically to the listener, the speaker, or the third party.

The critical difference between a consequential and a persuasion conditional is to be found by comparing [3c] and [4e]. In a consequential conditional, the consequences q accrue to the agent in p; but the consequences of a persuasion conditional are directed more globally, and can accrue to entire societies [5a] or non-human entities [5b]:

(5) a. If the Kyoto accord is ratified, there will be a severe downturn in the economy;
     b. If the Kyoto accord is ratified, greenhouse gas emissions will be reduced.

As shown in example [5], persuasion conditionals of opposite valence are often used together to argue the merits and drawbacks of a course of action, or (in a more partisan way) to argue the merits of a course of action and the drawbacks of failing to undertake this same course of action. Indeed, persuasion conditionals invite the pragmatic inference that their action antecedent should (or should not) be undertaken, as a function of the valence of its consequences. More precisely, persuasion conditionals invite the pragmatic inference that *their speaker* believes their antecedent should or should not be undertaken—again, we will have more to say later on about how this perspective issue impacts inferences on a conditional reasoning task.

Conditional inducements

The illocutionary goal of conditional inducements is no longer to predict the behaviour of a third party (consequential conditionals) or to argue that the third party should undertake some course of action (persuasion conditionals), but rather to bribe (by promise or by tip) or to coerce (by threat or by warning) the listener into some course of action. Conditional promises and threats can be defined along the same lines as consequential and persuasion conditionals (see also Amgoud, Bonnefon, & Prade, 2007, Beller, Bender, & Kuhnmünch, 2005, Evans, 2005, López-Rousseau & Ketelaar, 2004, 2006):

(6) a. p is an action under the control of the listener;
     b. q is a consequence of taking action p;
     c. q is an action under the control of the speaker;
     d. q is either a desirable or an undesirable outcome to the listener;
     e. p has the same valence to the speaker as q has to the listener.

The valence of p and q is positive for promises [7a], negative for threats [7b]:

(7) a. If you buy this computer, I'll throw in a box of free CDs;
     b. If you throw a tantrum, I'll ground you.

Tips and warnings are very similar to promises and threats, respectively, except that q is no longer within the control of the speaker (Evans & Twyman-Musgrove, 1998, Newstead, Ellis, Evans, & Dennis, 1997), and that the speaker has no longer any particular stake in p (Ohm & Thompson, 2004).

Conditional inducements invite the pragmatic inference that the listener will (or will not, for threats and warnings) take action p, as a function of their efficiency (Ohm & Thompson, 2006, Verbrugge, Dieussaert, Schaeken, & Van Belle, 2004; for a pioneering study, see Fillenbaum, 1976). Efficient inducements virtually guarantee that the listener will or will not take action p; inefficient inducements offer no such guarantee. The efficiency of tips and warnings critically depends on the perceived predictive accuracy of the speaker, just as the efficiency of promises and threats critically depends on the degree of control the speaker exerts on q.

A remarkable asymmetry has been observed with respect to the efficiency of threats and warnings (Verbrugge et al., 2004). An efficient threat should not be disproportionate, i.e., the punishment should be balanced to the offense. A proportionate threat such as [8a] is much more efficient than its disproportionate version [8b]:

(8) a. If you tell your brother that Santa does not exist, I'll ground you;
     b. If you tell your brother that Santa does not exist, we will return all your presents to the store.

Remarkably, this result does not hold for promises. Promises do not have to be proportionate, because unlike threats, they engage the speaker (Beller et al., 2005, Verbrugge et al., 2004). The promise [9a] is just as credible as the promise [9b]:

(9)   a. If you behave, I'll give you $100;
      b. If you behave, I'll let you watch a cartoon tonight.

While one may think that [9a] is not very good parenting, one will not question the fact that the parent will stay true to her promise and deliver the $100 if the child does behave.

Deontic conditionals and conditional directives

While conditional inducements attempt to *influence* the behaviour of others, deontic conditional (and conditional directives) attempt to *rule* the behaviour of others (or the self) by stating which behaviour is permitted [10a] or mandatory [10b], conditional on certain circumstances:

(10) a. If I finish this chapter tonight then I can take the weekend off;
      b. If workers are repairing a road, then a policeman must be directing the traffic.

The distinction between deontic conditionals and conditional directives is a subtle matter of attitude. All conditional directives are deontic conditionals, but not all deontic conditionals are conditional directives (Hilton, Kemmelmeier, & Bonnefon, 2005). Indeed, one can have an indicative attitude to deontic conditionals, that is, one can use them as an indicative description of a rule issued by another authority. For example, statement [10b] could be the answer of a police superintendent to another's question of 'what is the jurisdiction about traffic works in this county?' By answering [10b], the superintendent is not using her authority to issue a new jurisdiction: she is merely describing an existing one. In contrast, conditional directives always consist of issuing a new regulation to be followed by the listener, such as:

(11) a. If workers are repairing a road, then assign a policeman to direct the traffic;
      b. If a customer isn't touching any clothes, don't offer your help.

Deontic conditionals and conditional directives invite inferences about the preferences of those who accept or issue them. For example, individuals who accept an obligation rule of the form 'If p, then must q' are those who have a strict preference for pq over $p\neg q$. Likewise, people who accept a permission rule of the form 'If p, then may q' are those who have a loose preference for pq over $p\neg q$ (Over, Manktelow, & Hadjichristidis, 2004).

(12) a. If one eats sweet foods, then one must brush one's teeth;
      b. If one cleans the house, then one may have a drink.

One who accepts the obligation [12a] is one who has a strict preference for eating sweet foods and brushing teeth, rather than eating sweet foods and not brushing teeth. One who accepts [12b] is one who has a loose preference for cleaning the house and having a drink, rather than cleaning the house and not having a drink; that is, they may also be indifferent between the two situations.

Note that permission rules often invite an additional pragmatic inference about preferences. One who accepts a permission rule 'If p, then may q' is likely to be one who has a strict preference for pq over $\neg pq$. For example, one who accepts the permission rule [12b] is likely to be one who finds it preferable to have a drink after cleaning the house, rather than to have a drink without cleaning the house. This reading of the permission rule assumes that it serves either as an inducement or as a deterrent; either one hates cleaning the house, and the drink is an inducement to do so, or one has a tendency to drink too much, and cleaning the house is a deterrent against doing so.

Conditional directives also invite specific inferences about the preferences of the authority who issued them (Hilton et al., 2005). Different formulations of the conditional directive point to different preferences. For example, the formulation 'If p, then do q' is a cue that the authority wishes to avoid errors of omission rather than errors of commission: that is, the authority has a preference for $\neg pq$ over $p\neg q$. Interestingly, two logically equivalent formulations do not necessarily point to the same preferences. The formulations 'If $\neg p$ then don't do q' and 'do q only if p' are logically equivalent, and both signal a wish to avoid errors of omission $\neg pq$; but only the latter also signals a wish to avoid errors of commission $p\neg q$. Consider the three following directives, given by a navy officer to the crew:

(13) a. If you see an unusual 'blip,' then launch the depth charges;
      b. If you don't see an unusual 'blip,' then don't launch the depth charges;
      c. Launch the depth charges only if you see an unusual 'blip.'

The directive [13a] signals a wish to avoid errors of omission rather than errors of commission. The officer prefers bombing a few whales rather than letting a single enemy submarine creep in. With the directive [13b], the officer seems more concerned with not wasting the depth charges on any false alarm. Finally, although the directive [13c] is logically equivalent to [13b], it manages to convey concern for both types of errors: not bombing an unusual blip, and bombing what was not after all an unusual blip.

Non-utility pragmatic conditionals

Some non-standard conditionals have been considered that do not seem to have any strong connection with notions of decision-theoretic utility. One among them is worth mentioning because it has not prompted (yet) any empirical work, and is rather used as a traditional example of how strange some conditionals can be:

(14) a. There are biscuits on the sideboard if you want some;
      b. If you are thirsty, then there is beer in the fridge.

Statement [14a] is the classic example given by Austin (1970), p. 212, after which these conditionals are sometimes called 'biscuit' conditionals (DeRose & Grandy, 1999). Example [14b] is more commonly used outside the British world. Biscuit conditionals are intriguing because none of their obverse, their converse or their contrapositive sounds felicitous:

(15) a. ?If there is beer in the fridge then you are thirsty;
      b. ?If you are not thirsty then there is no beer in the fridge;
      c. ?If there is no beer in the fridge then you are not thirsty.

This oddity is due to the fact that biscuit conditionals invite the inference that their consequent is true no matter what. Thus, [15a] and [15c] sound strange because they treat the presence or absence of beer as an hypothesis rather than a certainty; likewise, [15b] sounds strange because it implies that the absence of beer is a true possibility, which it is not in [14b].

But then why use a conditional structure in the first place if the consequent is true no matter what? The peculiarity of a biscuit conditional is that what is conditionalized on its antecedent is not its consequent per se, but rather the conversational relevance of asserting its consequent: The speaker would have no point in mentioning there is beer in the fridge if the listener was not thirsty. One natural sequence would be to ask first whether the listener is thirsty, and then (if the answer is affirmative) mention that there is beer in the fridge. The biscuit conditional offers a shortcut through this exchange, by allowing the speaker to acknowledge the fact that she is assuming the answer to her unspoken question to be affirmative.

Another non-utility pragmatic conditional is worth mentioning here, because it will play an important role in the suppression effects we will address in section 4.2. A 'preconditional'

(Bonnefon & Hilton, 2002) is a conditional 'if *p* then *q*' where *p* is not, from common knowledge, a sufficient condition of *q*, but rather a pre-requisite for *q*:

(16) a. If I have some money left on Monday, I'll invite you to lunch;
    b. If the shops are open, I'll buy mixers on my way to the party.

Preconditionals invite the inference that their antecedent is quite possibly not satisfied (Bonnefon & Hilton, 2002, Politzer, 2005). Pulling a pre-requisite from the background and putting it in the position usually reserved to sufficient conditions is a way for the speaker to suggest that there is a problem with its satisfaction, which cannot be taken for granted. The speaker in [16a] likely hints that there is a fair chance she will be broke by Monday, and the speaker in [16b] likely suggests that the shops could be closed at the time he will leave to the party.

Summary

The pragmatics of conditional reasoning is partly a matter of *pragmatic conditionals*—conditionals whose function goes beyond the mere communication of a relation such as a causal or temporal relation. These pragmatic conditionals invite inferences of their own, without the need for a minor premise. These inferences often involve preferences, or decision-theoretic considerations of utility—and we introduced the term *utility conditionals* to refer to this subclass of pragmatic conditionals. We reviewed various types of utility and non-utility conditionals, as well as the inferences they invite. We now turn to the second aspect of the pragmatics of conditional reasoning—that is, the basic implicatures triggered by the conditional construction.

Conditional pragmatics

The investigation of the pragmatics of conditional reasoning does not stop at exotic conditionals. It also involves, and actually started with, the basic pragmatic inferences triggered by most conditional sentences. We first consider the phenomenon of invited inferences: Does a conditional invite its obverse, and why? And does the invitation extend to the converse? We then consider the conditional field hypothesis, according to which a conditional sentence is just the pragmatic tip of a conjunctive/disjunctive iceberg.

The invited inferences

In a seminal paper, Geis and Zwicky (1971) pointed out that many conditional statements, such as [17a], are routinely understood as implying their obverse [17b]:

(17) a. If David gets a raise, then he will buy a new car;
    b. If David does not get a raise, then he will not buy a new car.

This observation has been extremely influential among students of conditional reasoning, and is sometimes taken as the very basis of the pragmatic component to conditional reasoning (e.g., Braine & O'Brien, 1991, Evans & Over, 2004). Psychologists and linguists, however, have gradually departed in their analysis of this phenomenon.

    The invitation of the obverse [17b] from the conditional [17a] is generally considered by linguists as part of the larger question of *conditional perfection*, that is, the interpretation of 'if' as 'if and only if' (see for reviews and theoretical positions van der Auwera, 1997; Horn, 2000). From this perspective, [17a] is claimed to invite the conveyed meaning :

(18) If and only if David gets a raise, he will buy a new car.

To explain the inference from [17a] to [18], van der Auwera (1997) appeals to the pragmatic notion of a scalar implicature: One ought not make a logically weaker claim when one is in a position to make a stronger claim—therefore, making the lesser claim pragmatically implies that the stronger claim is incorrect, or at least unwarranted (Grice, 1989; Horn, 1984; Strawson, 1952). Armed with this notion, van der Auwera (1997) considers the following scale:

(19) a. (If p then q) and (if r then q) and (if s then q);
 b. (If p then q) and (if r then q);
 c. If p then q.

Within this scale, [19a] entails [19b] and [19c], and [19b] entails [19c]. Thus, making the weaker claim [19c] invites the inference that the stronger claims [19a] and [19b] would be incorrect; that is, that q *only if* p, hence the interpretation [18]. Now, one might point out the existence of another simple ordered scale of logical propositions:

(20) a. If and only if p then q;
 b. If p then q.

Since [20a] logically entails [20b], one might argue that the assertion of the weaker claim [20b] invites the pragmatic inference that the stronger claim [20a] is incorrect—that is, that the assertion of the conditional pragmatically implies that the biconditional is false!

Horn (2000) provides a solution to this paradox through considerations of lexicalization and economy of speech that we will not summarize here. Horn's conclusion is that the proper informativeness scale for generating scalar implicatures from conditionals is neither [19] nor [20], but rather [21]:

(21) a. Whether or not p, q;
 b. If p then q.

The assertion of [21b] would invite the pragmatic inference that [21a] is unwarranted, which would in turn transform the conditional [21b] into its biconditional form [22a], which finally implies the obverse form [22b]:

(22) a. If and only if p then q;
 b. If $\neg p$, then $\neg q$.

Horn further argues that the implicature is not based on Grice's first (upper-bounding) maxim of quantity, but rather on the second maxim of quantity, which produces lower-bounding implicata such as understatements (e.g., 'drink' for 'drink alcohol'): That way, uttering 'if p then q' becomes a way to mean the stronger 'if and only if p then q.'

It is worth insisting that the phenomenon linguists are interested in is that of conditional perfection, not that of invited inferences per se. Likewise, psychologists have rarely been interested in invited inferences for their own sake, but rather as a means to explain the endorsement of the conditional fallacies of Affirming the Consequent [23a] and Denying the Antecedent [23b]:

(23) a. If p then q, q, therefore p;
 b. If p then q, $\neg p$, therefore $\neg q$.

One explanation for the endorsement of these two arguments is to consider, just as linguists do, that reasoners pragmatically 'perfect' the conditional into its biconditional form. This is essentially the position of Mental Model theory (Johnson-Laird & Byrne, 2002). But if such was the case, we would expect reasoners to endorse [23a] and [23b] with the same frequency, since they both result from the same process of conditional perfection. However, as pointed out by Evans and Over (2004, chapters three and six), behavioural data rather suggest that reasoners primarily accept [23a] when reasoning with abstract conditionals, and [23b] when reasoning with everyday, realistic conditionals.

The solution put forward by Evans and Over (2004), chapter nine, as well as Bonnefon, Eid, Vautier, and Jmel (2008) consists of assuming that the fallacy of Affirming the Consequent occurs when reasoners pragmatically derive the inference from 'if p then q' to its converse 'if q then p'; that the fallacy of Denying the Antecedent occurs when reasoners pragmatically derive the inference from 'if p then q' to its obverse 'if $\neg p$ then $\neg q$'; and that there is no strong association between the invited inference to the obverse and the invited inference to the converse. Realistic conditionals primarily invite the former, and abstract conditionals primarily invite the latter. Most importantly, none of these invited inferences is assumed to perfect a conditional into a biconditional.

Note how this solution departs in two critical ways from traditional linguistic analyses of invited inferences. First, the issue of invited inferences is explicitly decoupled from the issue of conditional perfection, that is, the hypothesis is made that invited inferences can occur without conditional perfection. Second, an assumption is made that not only the obverse can be pragmatically invited (which is uncontroversial), but also the converse. The invitation of the converse 'if q then p' is never explicitly considered in analyses of conditional perfection, which rather focus on the invitation of the obverse, in its traditional form 'if $\neg p$ then $\neg q$,' or in its alternate form 'q only if p.'

Now, the issue of whether conditionals may pragmatically invite their converse in addition to their obverse is a moot point from the perspective of conditional perfection—because a biconditional reading of the conditional licenses both its obverse and its converse. It is actually quite remarkable, then, that the obverse is always mentioned as the invited inference resulting from conditional perfection, and that the converse is always left unmentioned.

The issue gets more difficult when invited inferences are considered outside the phenomenon of conditional perfection. What is needed then is a pragmatic explanation of each of the invited inferences,[2] together with an explanation of why they are not always invited together. Although it is not our purpose to review or to offer such explanations in this chapter, we do consider them a necessary ingredient of the future, grand theory of conditional reasoning. Note also that the problem is further compounded by the possibility that the reasoner may (unknown to the experimenter) engage in plausible reasoning rather than follow the often vague instructions to execute a deductive argument, in which case there is no fallacy.

The conditional field

There is much more to a conditional than just two propositions and a connective. Even before the modern tools of pragmatic analysis became available, philosophers such as Ramsey (1931) had the intuition that the conditional was the compact form of a larger, unspoken logical structure:

> In general we can say with Mill that 'If P then Q means that Q is inferrable from P, that is, of course, from P together with certain facts and laws not stated but in some way indicated by the context.

Kindred to this intuition are two ideas found in Mackie's (1974) theory of causation. First, causal statements assume the satisfaction of a number of implicit conditions that are not mentioned in the statement because they are usually satisfied in the normal state of the world. Although the

---

[2] That is, provided that both inferences are indeed the result of a pragmatic process. A case could be made, which we will not make here, that although the fallacy of Denying the Antecedent does result from the pragmatic invitation of the obverse, the fallacy of Affirming the Consequent results from a matching process that does not reflect any pragmatic phenomenon—especially in the case of abstract materials, where this fallacy is known to occur especially frequently.

effect would not have occurred if these conditions had not been satisfied, they are not usually thought of as a cause. When looking for the cause of an explosion, individuals assume, rather than focus on, the presence of oxygen in the air. Second, the cause of an event is often just one of many possible causes, each of them with its own set of additional conditions.

Capitalizing on these notions, and generalizing them from causal to other conditional statements, Politzer (Politzer, 2001, 2003, Politzer & Bourmeau, 2002) suggests that a conditional statement such as 'If A, then ϕ' really refers to the fine-grained logical structure [24]:

$$(24) \quad (A \wedge A_1 \wedge \ldots \wedge A_\alpha) \vee (B \wedge B_1 \wedge \ldots \wedge B_\beta) \vee \ldots \vee (N \wedge N_1 \wedge \ldots \wedge N_\nu) \rightarrow \Phi;$$

where each of $A, B, \ldots, N$ would warrant the inference to ϕ, as long as certain background conditions are satisfied. The fact that A is explicitly mentioned as the antecedent of ϕ in the conditional pragmatically triggers, as discussed in the previous section, an invited inference to the falsity of [25a], which can be understood either as [25b] or [25c], both of which entail that all $B, \ldots, N$ are false, or that at least one proposition is false in each of the sets $\{B_1, \ldots, B_\beta\}, \ldots, \{N_1 \ldots N_\gamma\}$.

(25)   A. Whether or not A, ϕ;

    B. If $\neg A$ then $\neg\phi$;

    c. ϕ only if A.

The set $\{A_1, \ldots, A_\alpha\}$ in [24] is the set of background conditions without which ϕ could not be inferred from A. This set is referred to as the 'conditional field' of A, or, alternatively, as the set of the Complementary Necessary Conditions (CNCs) of A. Note that B has its own conditional field $\{B_1, \ldots, B_\beta\}$, and that the same is true all the way down to N, which has its own conditional field $\{N_1, \ldots, N_\gamma\}$. These conditional fields may overlap to some extent.

Not all cncs have the same degree of necessity for the consequent of the conditional to be true—some merely render the consequent more or less likely to be true, others are such that their non-satisfaction makes it definitely impossible for the consequent to be true. Note also that the non-satisfaction of a CNC may mean either that some proposition is false, or that it is true—in the domain of causality, these two sorts of CNCs are known as enablers and disablers, respectively. Finally, note that not all CNCs are equally available. Consider conditional [26]:

(26) If Jenny turns on the air conditioner, then she feels cool.

De Neys, Schaeken, and d'Ydewalle (2002) report that when prompted to find several explanations to the fact that Jenny did not feel cool although she had turned on the air conditioner, 95% of participants mentioned [27a], and 50% mentioned [27b]. This is a demonstration that the CNC [27a] is more available than the CNC [27b]. And yet the CNC [27b] is itself more available than a virtually unlimited number of low-availability CNCs such as [27c], which can only be delivered after a special abductive effort.

(27)   a. The air conditioner is broken;
    b. Jenny has a fever;
    c. Jenny had previously set the house on fire.

Independently of a CNC's importance, polarity, or availability, it is implicitly assumed to be satisfied from the assertion of a statement such as 'if A, then ϕ'. The reason for this assumption is to be found in conversational pragmatics. According to expectations of cooperativeness or relevance (Sperber & Wilson, 1986, 1995), in uttering the conditional sentence, the speaker guarantees that the utterance is worth paying attention to. In the frame of a deductive argument, this amounts to a guarantee that one is licensed to infer ϕ as soon as A is reasonably likely (Sperber, Cara, & Girotto, 1995).

Therefore, the speaker uttering 'If A then ϕ' must believe that the CNCs of A are satisfied—if not, her statement would violate elementary expectations of cooperativeness and relevance.

In sum, a conditional statement 'If A, then ϕ' is only the compact, conversational form of a complex logical entailment whose antecedent is a disjunction of conjunctive components. Each conjunctive component is on its own sufficient to make ϕ true, but all conjunctive components except one (the one that includes A) are pragmatically ruled out by an invited inference. Thence, the truth of all conjuncts but A in the conjunctive component that includes A is pragmatically inferred from expectations of cooperativeness and relevance. Of course, as any other pragmatic inference, the inferences we have just discussed are cancellable as a function of context. As it will appear in the next section, this defeasible character is the source of a number of pragmatic effects on conditional reasoning.

Intersection

We have organized research on the pragmatics of conditional reasoning as falling in either one of two sets: research on pragmatic conditionals, on the one hand, and research on conditional pragmatics, on the other hand. These two sets are not and should not be disjoint—indeed, research at their intersection is especially relevant to all theories that attempt to account for the pragmatics of conditional reasoning. In this section, we consider in turn whether pragmatic conditionals invite the same inferences as other conditionals, and how pragmatic conditionals can communicate indirect information about the conditional field of other conditionals, yielding the well-known 'suppression effects.'

Invited inferences from pragmatic conditionals

Interestingly, Geis and Zwicky (1971) illustrated their seminal point about invited inferences with a pragmatic conditional, namely, a promise [28]:

(28) If you mow the lawn, I'll give you five dollars.

Promises do indeed strongly invite their obverse [29]:

(29) If you don't mow the lawn, I won't give you five dollars.

Remarkably, this invited inference appears to be linked to the specific illocutionary goal of a promise, rather than to the general mechanism of scalar implicature discussed on p. 241–43. The illocutionary goal of [28] is to induce the listener into mowing the lawn, through the prospect of a reward for doing so. For the inducement to be efficient, the speaker must be assumed not to mean [30], because it would defeat the whole point of using the five dollars as an inducement:

(30) Whether or not you mow the lawn, I'll give you five dollars.

Note the difference with the traditional (scalar) invited inferences on p. 241: We believe that [31] is false because it would be a self-defeating meaning for the speaker of [28]—not because [30] is a logically stronger claim than [28], and that asserting [30] means that one is not in the epistemic position to assert [28].

Even more remarkably, while threats also strongly invite their obverse, they appear do so for different reasons again. Consider the threat [31], from a parent to a teenager who is driving to a party:

(31) If you come home later than midnight, I'll take back your car.

Now imagine that the teenager comes back home before midnight, and that no remarkable event took place. We have a strong intuition that the parent will not take back the car in that case, and indeed that it would be unfair and unjustified to do so. That is, we believe that the parent asserting [31] has a *moral obligation* (Beller et al., 2005) to mean [32a], or alternatively not to mean [32b]:

(32) a. If you come home before midnight, I won't take back your car.
      b. Whatever hour you come home, I'll take back your car.

Note how this is different from a scalar implicature: We do not believe that the parent asserted (31) because she was not in an epistemic position to assert [32b]. Note also that the invited inference from a threat is slightly more complicated than the invited inference from a promise. While it is the case that, just as for promises, meaning [32b] would be self-defeating for the parent attempting to deter her child from coming home late, there is a moral dimension to the invited inference from threats that is absent from the invited inference from promises.

Not much attention has been given yet to the extent to which other pragmatic conditionals invite their obverse and/or converse, and most importantly why they do so. This issue is likely to prove especially important for directives. Indeed, as we already mentioned, using a directive such as [33a] conveys that the authority is especially concerned about errors of omission, whilst using a directive such as [33b] conveys that the authority is especially concerned about errors of commission.

(33) a. If you see an unusual 'blip,' then launch the depth charges;
      b. If you don't see an unusual 'blip,' then don't launch the depth charges.

Now, if the assertion of [33a] invites the inference to its obverse [33b], how does that translate in terms of the perceived preferences of the authority regarding errors of omission or commission? Could it be that while [33a] does invite [33b], the invitation does not extend to the conveyed meaning of [33b] about the preferences of the authority? Although this suggestion seems intuitively plausible, its empirical test is left to future research.

We finally need to mention the very specific case of invited implicatures from biscuit conditionals. As we already explained, biscuit conditionals do not license the invited inference to their obverse, their converse, or even to their contrapositive—see p. 240.

Suppression effects

We emphasized earlier that pragmatic conditionals invite inferences of their own, without the need for a minor premise. In 'The conditional field' on p. 244 we saw that conditionals come with the ceteris paribus assumption that the CNCs in their conditional field are satisfied. In this section, we consider how reasoners can doubt this ceteris paribus assumption because of the presence of a pragmatic conditional, and the inferences it triggers.

Consider the seminal library example from Byrne (1989):

(34) a. If Ruth has an essay to write, she will study late in the library;
      b. If the library stays open, she will study late in the library;
      c. Ruth has an essay to write.

From premises [34ac], most reasoners conclude that 'She will study late in the library'. But when premise [34b] is added to the problem, the endorsement of that conclusion drops dramatically—it is 'suppressed' (Bonnefon & Hilton, 2002, Chan & Chua, 1994, Manktelow & Fairley, 2000, Oaksford & Chater, 2003, Politzer, 2005, Politzer & Bourmeau, 2002, Stevenson & Over, 1995). What is remarkable in this problem is that while [34a] is a standard conditional,[3] [34b] is not. It is what we

---

[3] See Politzer and Bonnefon (2006) and Verbrugge, Dieussaert, Schaeken, Smessaert, and Van Belle (2007) for an extension of this effect to non-standard causal conditionals where the cause and the effect switch

have identified on p. 240 as a 'preconditional' pragmatic conditional, which invites the inference that something is wrong with its antecedent—that its antecedent is likely not to be satisfied.

How does that inference impact the conditional field of [34a]? Remember that [34a] is just the compact form of a complex conditional whose antecedent is a disjunction of conjunctions. To simplify matters, let us consider that [34a] is the compacted form of [35], which only includes two disjuncts of two conjuncts each:

(35) (*Essay* ∧ *Open*) ∨ (*Textbooks* ∧ *Available*) ⊃ *Late*;

where Essay stands for 'Ruth has an essay to write,' Open stands for 'the library stays open,' Textbooks stands for 'Ruth has textbooks to read,' Available stands for 'the textbooks are available,' and Late stands for 'she will study late in the library.'

The assertion of [34a] invites the inference that Ruth has no reason to study late other than having an essay to write. Furthermore, the assertion of [34a] comes with the ceteris paribus assumption that the conditional field of Essay is satisfied, that is, that Open is true. Now, the pragmatic effect of asserting the preconditional [34b] is precisely to raise doubt about the satisfaction of Open, and this doubt is transferred to the certainty of [34a]. As a result, the conclusion 'Ruth will study late in the library' cannot any longer be derived with certainty from the premises in (34) (Bonnefon & Hilton, 2002, Politzer, 2005).

Preconditionals are not the sole pragmatic conditionals that can have such an impact on the CNCs of other conditionals. Consequential conditionals in particular give rise to another kind of suppression effect:

(36) a. If Emma goes to the party then she buys a new dress;
     b. If Emma buys a new dress, she can't pay the rent next week.
     c. Emma goes to the party.

Most reasoners draw the conclusion 'Emma buys a new dress' when presented with premises [36ac], but they no longer do when premise [36b] is added to the problem (Bonnefon & Hilton, 2004). Here again, the conditional in [36a] is a standard causal conditional which comes with the ceteris paribus assumption that background CNCs are satisfied. One of these is the generic assumption that people do not undertake actions whose consequences would be undesirable. That is, [36a] can be reformulated as [37]:

(37) PARTY ∧ NOTHING BAD ⊃ DRESS;

where Party stands for 'Emma goes to the party,' Nothing Bad stands for 'There is no foreseeable undesirable consequence of buying a new dress,' and Dress stands for 'Emma buys a new dress.' Now, the consequential conditional [36b] precisely emphasizes a foreseeable undesirable consequence of buying a new dress, and thus raises doubts about the certainty of [36a]. Even more directly, we saw on p. 237 that consequential conditionals with a negative outcome, such as [36b], pragmatically invite the inference that their antecedent is false—in that example, that Mary is not going to buy a new dress. This pragmatic inference conflicts with the conclusion of Modus Ponens applied to [36ac], and makes reasoners reluctant to conclude that Mary is going to buy a new dress from the three premises in [36].

In sum, pragmatic conditionals trigger inferences, and these inferences may concern the propositions that are unspoken in the compact, asserted version of another conditional. What happens as a result is often a striking deviation from logical expectations, as in the suppression effects we have reported in this section.

---

positions—yielding a conditional that is indifferently called epistemic, inferential, or evidential (Dancygier, 1998, Declerck & Reed, 2001, Pearl, 1988, Sweetser, 1990).

Exclusion and extensions

The purpose of this chapter was to delimit the contour of what the pragmatic component of conditional reasoning should account for, as opposed to things pragmatic that happen when reasoning conditionally, but that ought not constrain the psychological theory of conditional reasoning. We have argued that the pragmatic component to conditional reasoning should account for at least two sets of results. First, the results obtained in the study of pragmatic conditionals; second, the results obtained in the study of conditional pragmatics. The intersection of these two sets (e.g., the suppression effects) is especially relevant and would benefit from a more systematic programme of research.

Having considered these two sets and their intersection, we are left now with the delicate task of considering their exclusion. There is indeed research that appeals to pragmatic notions to predict conditional reasoning effects, but that does not deal with pragmatic conditionals nor with conditional pragmatics. We suggest that this type of research, while it contributes to the understanding of reasoning in the wide sense, need not constrain the pragmatic component of psychological theories of conditional reasoning. Consider for example the 'Modus Shmollens' inference of Bonnefon and Villejoubert (2007):

> (38) Carol and Didier are eating a soup;
> a. If the soup tastes like garlic, then there is garlic in the soup;
> b. Carol tells Didier: 'there is no garlic in this soup';
> c. Therefore, the soup tastes like garlic.

Although [38c] is quite an intuitively compelling conclusion, it is also a horrible logical fallacy. The fact that there is no garlic in the soup, combined with the conditional [38a], yields the conclusion that the soup does not taste like garlic. However, the mere fact that the absence of garlic was asserted by one character to another triggers the pragmatic expectation that the presence of garlic was highly plausible in that context—for example, because the soup tasted like garlic.

This is undoubtedly a study of conditional reasoning, and it is undoubtedly based on pragmatic concepts—namely, the pragmatic analysis of negation as the denial of a belief the listener is implicitly assumed to hold. But does it have to constrain theories of conditional reasoning? Probably not. That is not to say that this result does not constrain theories of reasoning, in the wide sense, as it raises questions about the way the theory should handle negation. But the Bonnefon and Villejoubert (2007) study is a perfect example of an investigation of something pragmatic that impacts conditional reasoning, as opposed to an investigation of the specific pragmatics of conditional reasoning.

We certainly do not have the final say on what ought and what ought not be considered relevant to the specific pragmatics of conditional reasoning. The two sets we have defined are only meant to serve as preliminary criteria to help delimitate the explanatory domain of the pragmatic component of the future grand theory of conditional reasoning. Future research is likely to extend these two sets or to augment them with brand new bodies of results. As an example of such an augmentation, and as a conclusion to this chapter, we wish to suggest that research on the pragmatics of reasoning would benefit from considering a robust pragmatic framework that it has completely neglected thus far, namely, considerations of politeness.

The traditional application of pragmatics to conditional reasoning has been to explain the unexpected conclusions that pragmatic reasoners draw when they are being Gricean. However, psychologists have been almost exclusively concerned with the type of conversational implicature which, in Gricean theory, is linked with the first maxim of quantity. Other implicatures exist, however, which enable one *to say less in order to mean more*, which is the basis of a whole range of politeness effects. These effects may reflect R-based implicatures (Horn, 1989), I-based implicatures

(Levinson, 2000), the revised principle of relevance (Sperber & Wilson, 1986, 1995, postface to the 1995 edition), or the principles of Politeness Theory (Brown & Levinson, 1978/1987).

The possible tension between the demands of exhaustive information and the demands of politeness, which may constitute opposite poles in social interaction, could prove to shed specific insights into the interpretation of conditional statements. Integrating politeness considerations to the more traditional Gricean or post-Gricean approaches which have so far been focussed on informativeness is one of the many tasks necessary to further develop the pragmatic component of the psychological theory of conditional reasoning.

References

Amgoud, L., Bonnefon, J. F., & Prade, H. (2007). The logical handling of threats, rewards, tips, and warnings. *Lecture Notes in Artificial Intelligence*, **4724**, 235–246.

Austin, J. L. (1962). *How to do things with word*. Oxford: Clarendon Press.

Austin, J. L. (1970). Ifs and cans. In *Philosophical papers* (2nd ed., pp. 205–232). Oxford: Clarendon Press.

Beller, S., Bender, A., & Kuhnmünch, G. (2005). Understanding conditional promises and threats. *Thinking and Reasoning*, **11**, 209–238.

Bonnefon, J. F. (2004). Reinstatement, floating conclusions, and the credulity of mental model reasoning. *Cognitive Science*, **28**, 621–631.

Bonnefon, J. F., Eid, M., Vautier, S., & Jmel, S. (2008). A mixed Rasch model of dual-process conditional reasoning. *Quarterly Journal of Experimental Psychology*, **61**, 809–824.

Bonnefon, J. F. & Hilton, D. J. (2002). The suppression of modus ponens as a case of pragmatic preconditional reasoning. *Thinking and Reasoning*, **8**, 21–40.

Bonnefon, J. F. & Hilton, D. J. (2004). Consequential conditionals: Invited and suppressed inferences from valued outcomes. *Journal of Experimental Psychology: Learning, Memory, and Cognition*, **30**, 28–37.

Bonnefon, J. F. & Villejoubert, G. (2007). Modus Tollens, Modus Shmollens: Contrapositive reasoning and the pragmatics of negation. *Thinking and Reasoning*, **13**, 207–222.

Braine, M. D. S. & O'Brien, D. P. (1991). A theory of *if*: Lexical entry, reasoning program, and pragmatic principles. *Psychological Review*, **98**, 182–203.

Brown, P. & Levinson, S. C. (1987). *Politeness: Some universals in language usage*. Cambridge: Cambridge University Press. (Original work published 1978)

Byrne, R. M. J. (1989). Suppressing valid inferences with conditionals. *Cognition*, **31**, 61–83.

Chan, D. & Chua, F. (1994). Suppression of valid inferences: syntactic views, mental models, and relative salience. *Cognition*, **23**, 646–658.

Dancygier, B. (1998). *Conditionals and prediction. Time, knowledge, and causation in conditional constructions*. Cambridge: Cambridge University Press.

De Neys, W., Schaeken, W., & d'Ydewalle, G. (2002). Causal conditional reasoning and semantic memory retrieval: A test of the semantic memory framework. *Memory and Cognition*, **30**, 908–920.

Declerck, R. & Reed, S. (2001). *Conditionals. A comprehensive empirical analysis*. Berlin and New York: Mouton de Gruyter.

DeRose, K. & Grandy, R. E. (1999). Conditional assertions and "biscuit" conditionals. *Noûs*, **33**, 405–420.

Evans, J. St.B. T. (2005). The social and communicative function of conditional statements. *Mind & Society*, **4**, 97–113.

Evans, J. St.B. T. & Over, D. E. (2004). *If*. Oxford: Oxford University Press.

Evans, J. St.B. T., Over, D. E., & Handley, S. J. (2005). Suppositions, extensionality, and conditionals: A critique of the mental model theory of Johnson-Laird and Byrne (2002). *Psychological Review*, **112**, 1040–1052.

Evans, J. St.B. T. & Twyman-Musgrove, J. (1998). Conditional reasoning with inducements and advice. *Cognition*, **69**, B11–B16.

Fillenbaum, S. (1976). Inducements: On the phrasing and logic of conditional promises, threats, and warnings. *Psychological Research*, **38**, 231–250.

Geis, M. L. & Zwicky, A. (1971). On invited inferences. *Linguistic Inquiry*, **2**, 561–566.

Grice, H. P. (1989). *Studies in the way of words*. Cambridge, MA: MIT Press.

Hilton, D. J. (1995). The social context of reasoning: Conversational inference and rational judgement. *Psychological Bulletin*, **118**, 248–271.

Hilton, D. J., Kemmelmeier, M., & Bonnefon, J. F. (2005). Putting ifs to work: Goal-based relevance in conditional directives. *Journal of Experimental Psychology: General*, **135**, 388–405.

Horn, L. R. (1984). Toward a new taxonomy for pragmatic inference: Q-based and R-based implicature. In D. Schiffrin (Ed.), *Meaning, form, and use in context* (pp.11–42). Washington, DC: Georgetown University Press.

Horn, L. R. (1989). *A natural history of negation*. Chicago: University of Chicago Press.

Horn, L. R. (2000). From if to iff: Conditional perfection as pragmatic strengthening. *Journal of Pragmatics*, **32**, 289–326.

Johnson-Laird, P. N. & Byrne, R. M. J. (2002). Conditionals: A theory of meaning, pragmatics, and inference. *Psychological Review*, **109**, 646–678.

Levinson, S. C. (2000). *Presumptive meanings: The theory of generalized conversational implicature*. Cambridge, MA: MIT Press.

López-Rousseau, A. & Ketelaar, T. (2004). "If...": Satisficing algorithms for mapping conditional statements onto social domains. *European Journal of Cognitive Psychology*, **16**, 807–823.

López-Rousseau, A. & Ketelaar, T. (2006). Juliet: If they do see thee, they will murder thee: A satisficing algorithm for pragmatic conditionals. *Mind & Society*, **5**, 71–77.

Mackie, J. L. (1974). *The cement of the universe*. Oxford: Oxford University Press.

Manktelow, K. I. & Fairley, N. (2000). Superordinate principles in reasoning with causal and deontic conditionals. *Thinking and Reasoning*, **6**, 41–65.

Newstead, S. E., Ellis, C., Evans, J. St.B. T., & Dennis, I. (1997). Conditional reasoning with realistic material. *Thinking and Reasoning*, **3**, 49–76.

Oaksford, M. & Chater, N. (2003). Conditional probability and the cognitive science of conditional reasoning. *Mind and Language*, **18**, 359–379.

Ohm, E. & Thompson, V. (2004). Everyday reasoning with inducements and advice. *Thinking and Reasoning*, **10**, 241–272.

Ohm, E. & Thompson, V. (2006). Conditional probability and pragmatic conditionals: Dissociating truth and effectiveness. *Thinking and Reasoning*, **12**, 257–280.

Over, D. E., Manktelow, K. I. & Hadjichristidis, C. (2004). Conditions for the acceptance of deontic conditionals. *Canadian Journal of Experimental Psychology*, **58**, 96–105.

Pearl, J. (1988). *Probabilistic reasoning in intelligent systems*. San Mateo, CA: Morgan Kaufmann.

Politzer, G. (2001). How to doubt about a conditional. In S. Benferhat & P. Besnard (Eds.), *Lecture notes in artificial intelligence, ECSQARU 2001* (pp. 659–667). Berlin: Springer.

Politzer, G. (2003). Premise interpretation in conditional reasoning. In D. Hardman & L. Macchi (Eds.), *Thinking: Psychological perspectives on reasoning, judgment and decision making* (pp. 79–93). Chichester: Wiley.

Politzer, G. (2004). Reasoning, judgement, and pragmatics. In I. Noveck & D. Sperber (Eds.), *Experimental pragmatics* (pp. 94–115). London: Palgrave.

Politzer, G. (2005). Uncertainty and the suppression of inferences. *Thinking and Reasoning*, **11**, 5–33.

Politzer, G. (2007). Reasoning with conditionals. *Topoï*, **26**(1), 79–95.

Politzer, G. & Bonnefon, J. F. (2006). Two varieties of conditionals and two kinds of defeaters help reveal two fundamental types of reasoning. *Mind and Language*, **21**, 484–503.

Politzer, G. & Bourmeau, G. (2002). Deductive reasoning from uncertain conditional. *British Journal of Psychology*, **93**, 345–381.

Ramsey, F. P. (1931). *The foundations of mathematics and other logical essays* (R. B. Braithwaite, Ed.). London: Routledge and Kegan Paul.

Sperber, D., Cara, F., & Girotto, V. (1995). Relevance theory explains the selection task. *Cognition*, **57**, 31–95.

Sperber, D. & Wilson, D. (1995). *Relevance, communication and cognition*. Oxford: Blackwell. (Original work published 1986).

Stevenson, R. J. & Over, D. E. (1995). Deduction from uncertain premises. *Quarterly Journal of Experimental Psychology*, **48A**, 613–643.

Strawson, P. F. (1952). *Introduction to logical theory*. London: Methuen.

Sweetser, E. E. (1990). *From etymology to pragmatics*. Cambridge: Cambridge University Press.

Thompson, V. A., Evans, J. St.B. T., & Handley, S. J. (2005). Persuading and dissuading by conditional argument. *Journal of Memory and Language*, **53**, 238–257.

van der Auwera, J. (1997). Pragmatics in the last quarter century: The case of conditional perfection. *Journal of Pragmatics*, **27**, 261–274.

Verbrugge, S., Dieussaert, K., Schaeken, W., Smessaert, H., & Van Belle, W. (2007). Pronounced inferences: A study on inferential conditionals. *Thinking and Reasoning*, **13**, 105–133.

Verbrugge, S., Dieussaert, K., Schaeken, W., & Van Belle, W. (2004). Promise is debt, threat another matter: The effect of credibility on the interpretation of conditional promises and threats. *Canadian Journal of Experimental Psychology*, **58**, 106–112.

Part 4

Integrative approaches

Chapter 15

Reasoning with conditionals in artificial intelligence

Robert Kowalski

Introduction

Conditionals of one kind or another are the dominant form of knowledge representation in Artificial Intelligence. However, despite the fact that they play a key role in such different formalisms as production systems and logic programming, there has been little effort made to study the relationships between these different kinds of conditionals. In this paper I present a framework that attempts to unify the two kinds of conditionals and discuss its potential application to the modelling of human reasoning.

Among the symbolic approaches developed in Artificial Intelligence, production systems have had the most application to the modelling of human thinking. Production systems became prominent in the late 1960s as a technology for implementing expert systems in Artificial Intelligence, and then in the 1970s as a cognitive architecture in Cognitive Psychology. However, although they have been used extensively to study human skills, they seem to have had little impact on studies of human reasoning. This lack of interaction between cognitive architectures based on production systems and studies of human reasoning is especially surprising because both emphasize the central role of conditionals.

Conditionals in production systems (called production rules) have the form *if conditions then actions* and look like logical implications. Indeed, some authors, such as Russell and Norvig (2003), take the view that production rules are just logical implications used to reason forward to derive candidate *actions* from *conditions* (*modus ponens*). However, other authors, such as Thagard (2005) deny any relationship between logic and production rules at all.

In some characterisations of production rules, they are described as expressing procedural knowledge about what to do when. In this paper, I will argue that production rules can be given a logical semantics, and this semantics can help to clarify their relevance for modelling human reasoning.

Conditionals are also a distinctive feature of logic programming, which has been used widely, also since the 1970s, both to implement practical applications and to formalize knowledge representation in Artificial Intelligence. Conditionals in logic programming have both a logical interpretation as conditionals of the form *conclusion if conditions* and an interpretation as procedures that reduce the goal of establishing the *conclusion* to the sub-goals of establishing the *conditions*. Goal-reduction is a form of *backward reasoning*. Although forward reasoning has been studied extensively in psychology, backward reasoning seems to have received little attention in studies of human reasoning.

Instead, studies of reasoning in Psychology emphasize the use of classical negation, including its use in such classically valid inferences as *modus tollens* and in such classical fallacies as denial of the antecedent. In contrast, classical negation has had relatively few applications in Artificial Intelligence, where negation as failure and the closed world assumption (*not P* holds if and only if *P* does not hold) have been more widely used in practice.

Studies of reasoning in Psychology treat affirmation of the consequent as a fallacy. In Artificial Intelligence, however, it is treated as abductive inference. Both abduction and negation as failure are forms of non-monotonic reasoning.

In this paper, I will outline an abductive logic programming (ALP) approach that aims to reconcile production rules and logic within a unifying agent-based framework. In this framework, logic programs are conditionals used to represent an agent's beliefs, and have a descriptive character. Production rules are conditionals in logical form, used to represent the agent's goals, and have deontic force. Abduction is used both to represent hypotheses that explain the agent's observations and actions that might achieve the agent's goals. Abductive hypotheses can have associated probabilities.

The ALP agent framework embeds goals and beliefs in an observation-thought-decision-action cycle, similar to the production system cycle, and similar to other agent cycles developed in Artificial Intelligence. In the ALP agent framework, the thinking component of the cycle is a combination of forwards reasoning, as in production systems, and backwards reasoning, as in logic programming. Negation is represented both by means of negation as failure and by means of integrity constraints.

Because this book is directed primarily towards a psychological audience and because my own expertize lies in Artificial Intelligence, I will focus on the potential contribution of Artificial Intelligence to studies of human reasoning. However, I anticipate that there is much to be gained from applying results about human reasoning to Artificial Intelligence. In particular, it seems likely that results about the psychology of reasoning with negation can suggest useful directions in which to extend AI reasoning techniques.

The remainder of the paper has four main parts, dealing with production systems, logic programs, the relationship between production systems and logic programs, and the ALP agent model. In addition, there is a section on integrity constraints, to help motivate the interpretation in ALP of stimulus-response production rules as a species of integrity constraint, and a section on the agent language AgentSpeak, which can be regarded as an extension of production systems in which actions are generalized to plans of action.

The semantics and proof procedures of logic programming and ALP are based on classical logic, but are sufficiently different to be a potential source of difficulty for some readers. For this reason, I have put details about the minimal model semantics in an appendix. I have also included an appendix about the interpretation of natural language conditionals in logic programming terms, because it interrupts the main flow of the paper.

Before settling down to the main part of the paper, I first present a motivating example, discuss the Wason selection task, and present some historical background.

A motivating example

Consider the following real world example of a sign posted in carriages on the London underground:

> *Emergencies:*
> *Press the alarm signal button to alert the driver.*
> *The driver will stop if any part of the train is in a station.*
> *If not, the train will continue to the next station, where help can more easily be given.*
> *There is a 50 pound penalty for improper use.*

The sign is intended to be read and for its contents to be assimilated by passengers travelling on the underground. For this purpose, a passenger needs to translate the English text from natural language into a mental representation. In AI, such mental representations include logic, logic programs, production rules and other procedural representations. Here is the main part of a translation of the London underground sign into the ALP agent representation that I will describe later in the paper:

> You alert the driver that there is an emergency
> if you are on the underground and there is an emergency
> and you press the alarm signal button.
> The driver will stop the train immediately
> if you press the alarm signal button and any part of the train is in a station.
> The driver will stop the train (and help can more easily be given) at the next station
> if you press the alarm signal button
> and not any part of the train is in a station.
> You will be liable to a 50 pound penalty
> if you press the alarm signal button improperly.

The first sentence of the translation shows how procedures are represented in logic programming form as conditionals that are used backwards to reduce goals that match the conclusion of the conditional to sub-goals that correspond to the conditions. The first, second, and third sentences show that the conditional form of natural language sentences should not to be taken literally, but may need to include extra conditions (such as *you press the alarm signal button*) and extra qualifications (such as the driver will stop *the train*) implicit in the context. The fourth sentence shows that the meaning of a natural language sentence may be a conditional whether or not the surface structure of the sentence contains an explicit mark of a conditional.

However, the translation of the sign does not represent its full import, which depends upon the reader's additional background goals and beliefs. These might include such goals and beliefs as[1]:

> If there is an emergency then you get help.
> You get help if you are on the underground and you alert the driver.

I will argue later that the first sentence is a maintenance goal, which is a special case of an integrity constraint of the kind used to maintain integrity in active database systems. Maintenance goals are similar to plans in the intelligent agent programming language AgentSpeak. I will also argue that they generalize production rules in production systems.

In the ALP agent framework, goals, and beliefs are embedded in an observation-thought-decision-action cycle. Given an observation of an emergency, the maintenance goal would be used to reason forward, to derive the achievement goal of getting help. The logic program would be used to reason backward, to reduce the goal of getting help to the action sub-goal of pressing the alarm signal button. Assuming that there are no other candidate actions to consider, the agent would commit to the action and attempt to solve it by executing it in the environment.

The selection task

I will not attempt to analyze the Wason selection task and its variants (Wason, 1968) in detail, but will outline instead how the ALP agent framework addresses some of the problems that have been observed with human performance in psychological experiments.

---

[1] These two sentences also help to explain the significance of the phrase *where help can more easily be given.* The passenger's background knowledge may also contain other ways of getting help. Arguably, the phrase is intended to help the passenger to evaluate alternative candidate actions, in deciding what to.

Consider the following simplified abstraction of the selection task presented to a subject in natural language:

> *Given some incomplete information/observations,*
> *what conclusions can be derived using the conditional if P then Q?*

The task is given with a concrete instance of the conditional, such as *if there is a vowel on one side of a card then there is an even number on the other side* and *if a person is drinking alcohol in a bar then the person is over eighteen years old.* To solve the task, the subject first needs to translate the conditional into a mental representation. The subject then needs to use the mental representation of the conditional, possibly together with other background goals and beliefs, to derive conclusions from the observations. I will argue that many of the reasons for the variation in subjects' performance on the selection task can be demonstrated using the ALP agent model with this simplified formulation of the task.

In the ALP agent model, the subject needs first to decide whether the English language conditional should be understood as a belief or as a goal. If it is understood as a belief, then it is represented as a clause in a logic program. If it is understood as a goal, then it is represented as an integrity constraint, to monitor updates. These two alternatives, understanding the conditional as a belief or as a goal, correspond roughly to the descriptive and deontic interpretations of the conditional respectively. In concrete instances of the task, the syntactic form of the conditional, its semantic content, and the way in which the task is formulated can all influence the interpretation.

Suppose the subject interprets the conditional as a belief, which is then represented as a logic programming clause:

> *Q if P*

Assuming that there are no other clauses, including background clauses, that have the same conclusion Q, the clause is then interpreted as the *only* way of concluding Q. In the completion semantics (Clark, 1978) of logic programming, this can be expressed explicitly in the form:

> *Q if and only if P*

The equivalence here is asymmetric in the sense that the formula on the right hand side is taken to be the definition of the predicate on the left hand side of the equivalence, and not the other way around.

In the ALP agent model described in this paper, given an observation O, the agent can reason both forwards from O, to derive consequences of the observation, and backwards from O, to derive explanations of the observation. In the selection task, therefore, forward reasoning can be used to derive Q from an observation of P, and backward reasoning can be used to derive P as an explanation of an observation of Q. These are the classic responses to Wason's original card version of the selection task.

The modus tollens derivation of *not P* from *not Q* is also possible, but more difficult, because it is first necessary to derive *not Q* from some initial positive observation Q'. This is because, in general, an agent's observations are represented only by atomic sentences. Negations of atomic sentences need to be derived from positive observations. In card versions of the selection task, for example, the conclusion that a card does not have a vowel on one of its sides needs to be derived by a chain of reasoning, say from an observation that it has the letter B on that side, to the conclusion that it has a consonant on that side, to the conclusion that it does not have a vowel on that side. As Sperber, Cara, and Girotto (1995) argue, the longer the derivation, and the greater the number of irrelevant, alternative derivations, the less likely it is that a subject will be able to perform the derivation.

In the ALP agent model, the relationship between positive and negative concepts, needed to derive a negative conclusion from a positive observation, is expressed in the form of integrity constraints, such as:

if mortal and immortal then false	i.e.	*not(mortal and immortal)*
if odd and even then false	i.e.	*not(odd and even)*
if vowel and consonant then false	i.e.	*not(vowel and consonant)*
if adult and minor then false	i.e.	*not(adult and minor)*
etc.		

and more generally as:

if Q' and Q then false	i.e.	*not(Q' and Q)*

where Q' is the positive observation or some generalization of the observation (such as the card has a consonant on the face) and *if Q then false* is an alternative syntax for the negation *not Q*.

In the ALP agent model, given a concrete observation that leads by a chain of forward reasoning to the conclusion Q', a further step of forward reasoning with the integrity constraint is needed to derive *not Q*. Backward reasoning with the conditional (replacing Q by its definition P) then derives *not P*.

Thus in card versions of the Wason selection task, when the conditional is interpreted as a belief, the derivations of P from Q and of Q from P are straight-forward, the derivation of *not P* from some contrary positive observation that implies *not Q* is difficult, but possible. But the derivation of *not Q* from *not P* is not possible at all, because of the asymmetry of the equivalence Q *if and only if* P.

Suppose instead that the subject interprets the conditional as a goal. In the ALP agent model, this is represented by an integrity constraint of the form:

if P then Q.

Such integrity constraints are used to reason forwards, like production rules, in this case to derive Q from P. They are not used backwards to derive P from Q, which is consistent with experimental data for deontic versions of the selection task.

As in the case where the conditional is interpreted as a belief, negative premises, such as *not P* and *not Q*, need to be derived by forward reasoning from positive atomic observations, using integrity constraints of such form as:

if Q' and Q then false
if P' and P then false

and the same considerations of computational complexity apply.

Assuming that the positive observations imply both Q' and P' and that both:

if Q then false
if P then false

have been derived, then the only further inference that is possible is:

From *if P then Q*
and   *if Q then false*
derive *if P then false*
i.e.   *not P.*

However, this inference step, which is both easy and natural for human subjects, is not possible in some existing ALP proof procedures. I will argue later that this is because these proof procedures implement the wrong semantics for integrity constraints. The semantics needed to justify this inference step is the *consistency view of integrity constraint satisfaction*. I will discuss this problem and its solution later in the paper. In the meanwhile, it is interesting to note that the selection task may suggest a direction for solving technical problems associated with proof procedures developed for practical applications in AI.

A personal view of the history of logic in AI

To put the issues dealt with in this paper into context, it may be helpful to consider their historical background.

Heuristic versus formal approaches

It is widely agreed that the most important work concerning logic in the early days of AI was the Logic Theorist (Newell et al., 1957), which managed to prove 38 of the first 52 theorems in Chapter 2 of Principia Mathematica. The Logic Theorist pioneered the heuristic approach, employing three inference rules, 'backward reasoning', 'forward chaining' and 'backward chaining', without traditional logical concerns about semantics and completeness. In contrast with formal theorem-proving techniques, these heuristic inference rules behaved naturally and efficiently.

Logic Theorist led to GPS, a general problem solver, not directly associated with logic, and later to production systems. Production rules in production systems resembled conditionals in traditional logic, but did not suffer from the inscrutability and inefficiencies associated with formal theorem-proving.

In the meanwhile, McCarthy (1958) advocated a formal approach, developing the Advice Taker, using formal logic for knowledge representation and using theorem-proving for problem-solving. In the Advice-Taker approach, the theorem-prover was a 'black box', and there was no attempt to relate the behaviour of the theorem-prover to common sense techniques of human problem-solving. The theorem-proving approach led to the development of question-answering systems, using complete and correct theorem-provers, based on mathematical logic.

Resolution (Robinson, 1965) was developed within the formal logic tradition, with mainly mathematical applications in mind. Its great virtue was its simplicity and uniformity, compressing the rules and logical axioms of symbolic logic into a single inference rule. It could not be easily understood in human-oriented terms, but was presented as a machine-oriented logic. Its early versions were very inefficient, partly because the resolution rule did not have an intuitive interpretation.

Towards the end of the 60s, there were two main trends among symbolic approaches to AI: the heuristic (sometimes called 'scruffy' or 'strong') approach, mainly associated with production systems, which behaved in human-intelligible terms, uninhibited by mathematical concerns about semantics, but emphasizing the importance of domain-specific knowledge; and the formal ('neat' or 'weak') approach, exemplified by resolution-based systems, emphasizing domain-independent, general-purpose problem-solving. Production systems were beginning to have applications in expert systems, and resolution was beginning to have applications in mathematics and question-answering.

Procedural representations of knowledge and logic programming

In the meanwhile, critics of the formal approach, based mainly at MIT, began to advocate procedural representations of knowledge, as superior to declarative, logic-based representations. This led to the development of the knowledge representation and problem-solving languages Planner and micro-Planner. Winograd's PhD thesis (1971), using micro-Planner to implement a natural language dialogue for a simple blocks world, was a major milestone of this approach. Research in automated theorem-proving, mainly based on resolution, went into sharp decline.

The battlefield between the logic-based and procedural approaches moved briefly to Edinburgh during the summer of 1970 at one of the Machine Intelligence Workshops organized by Donald Michie (van Emden, 2006). At the workshop, Pappert and Sussman from MIT gave talks vigorously attacking the use logic in AI, but did not present a paper for the proceedings. This created turmoil among researchers in Edinburgh working in resolution theorem-proving. However, I was not convinced that the procedural approach was so different from the SL-resolution system I had been developing with Donald Kuehner (1971).

During the next couple of years, I tried to reimplement Winograd's system in resolution logic and collaborated on this with Alain Colmerauer in Marseille. This led to the procedural interpretation of Horn clauses (Kowalski 1973/1974) and to Colmerauer's development of the programming language Prolog. I also investigated other interpretations of resolution logic in problem solving terms (Kowalski 1974/1979), exploiting in particular the fact that all sentences in resolution logic can be expressed in conditional form.

However, at the time, I was not aware of the significance of production systems, and I did not understand their relationship with logic and logic programming. Nor did I appreciate that logic programming would become associated with general-purpose problem-solving, and that this would be misunderstood as meaning that logic programming was suitable only for representing 'weak' general-purpose knowledge. I will come back to this problem later in the paper.

Non-monotonic reasoning, abduction, and argumentation

In the mid-1970s, Marvin Minsky (1974) launched another attack against logic from MIT, proposing frames as a representation of stereotypes. In contrast with formal logic, frames focussed on the representation of default knowledge, without the need to specify exceptions strictly and precisely. This time the logic community in AI fought back with the development of various non-monotonic logics, including circumscription (McCarthy, 1980), default logic (Reiter, 1980), modal non-monotonic logic (McDermott & Doyle, 1980), autoepistemic logic (Moore, 1985) and negation as failure in logic programming (Clark, 1978).

(Poole et al., 1987) argued that default reasoning can be understood as a form of abductive reasoning. Building upon their results, Eshghi, and I (1989) showed that negation as failure in logic programming can also be understood in abductive terms. More recently, Dung and his collaborators (Bondarenko et al., 1997; Dung et al., 2006) have shown that most non-monotonic logics can be interpreted in terms of arguments and counter-arguments supported by abductive hypotheses. Moreover, Poole (1993, 1997) has shown that Baysian networks can be understood as abductive logic programs with assumptions that have associated probabilities.

Intelligent agents

Starting in the late 1980s and early 1990s, researchers working in the formal logic tradition began to embed logic-based representations and problem-solving systems in intelligent agent frameworks. The intelligent agent approach was given momentum by the textbook of Russell and Norvig (2003), whose first edition was published in 1995. In their book, Russell and Norvig credit Newell, Laird, and Rosenblum (Laird et al., 1987; Newell, 1990) with developing SOAR as the 'best-known example of a complete agent architecture in AI'.

However, SOAR was based on production systems and did not have a logical basis. Among the earliest attempts to develop formal, logic-based agent architectures were those of Rao and Georgeff

(1991) and Shoham (1991), both of which were formulated in BDI (Belief, Desire, Intention) terms (Bratman, Israel, & Pollack, 1988). Although their formal specifications were partly formulated in modal logics, their implementations were in procedural languages that looked like extensions of production systems. The ALP agent model (Kowalski 2001, 2006; Kowalski & Sadri, 1999) was developed to reconcile the use of logic for agent specification with its use for implementation. Instead of using modalities to distinguish between beliefs and desires, it uses an extension of the database distinction between data and integrity constraints, treating beliefs like data and desires (or goals) like integrity constraints.

Production systems

Production systems were originally developed by the logician Emil Post as a mathematical model of computation, and later championed by Alan Newell as a model of human problem solving (Anderson & Bower, 1973; Newell, 1973). Production systems restrict knowledge representation to a combination of *facts*, which are atomic sentences, and *condition-action rules*, which have the syntax of conditionals, but arguably do not have a logical semantics. They also restrict reasoning to a kind of modus ponens, called *forward chaining*.

A typical *production system* (Simon, 1999) involves a 'declarative' memory consisting of atomic sentences, and a collection of procedures, which are *condition-action rules* of the form:

> *If conditions C, then actions A.*

Condition-action rules are also called *production rules*, just plain *rules*, or *if-then rules*. The most typical use of production rules is to implement stimulus-response associations. For example:

> *If it is raining and you have an umbrella, then cover yourself with the umbrella.*
> *If you have an essay to write, then study late in the library.*

The action part of a rule is often expressed as a command, or sometimes as a recommendation, to perform an action.

Production rules are executed by means of a cycle, which reads an input fact, uses *forward chaining* (from conditions to actions) to match the fact with one of the conditions of a production rule, verifies the remaining conditions of the rule, and then derives the actions of the rule as candidates to be executed. If more than one rule is 'triggered' in this way, then *conflict-resolution* is performed to decide which actions should be executed. Inputs and actions can be internal operations or can come from and be performed upon an external environment.

Conflict resolution can be performed in many ways, depending upon the particular production system language. At one extreme, actions can be chosen purely at random. Or they can be determined by the order in which the rules are written, so that the first rule to be triggered is executed first. At the opposite extreme, actions can be chosen by means of a full scale decision-theoretic analysis, analyzing the expected outcomes of actions, evaluating their utility and probability, and selecting one or more actions with highest expected utility.

Compared with classical logic, which has both a declarative, model-theoretic semantics and diverse proof procedures, production systems arguably have no declarative semantics at all. Production rules look like logical implications, without the semantics of implications. Moreover, forward chaining looks like *modus ponens*, but it is not truth-preserving, because there is no notion of what it means for a condition-action rule to be true.

The similarity of production rules to implications is a major source of confusion. Some authors (Thagard, 2005) maintain that production systems enable *backward reasoning*, from actions that are goals to conditions that are sub-goals. MYCIN (Shortliffe, 1976), for example, one of the earliest expert systems, used backward reasoning for medical diagnosis. MYCIN was and still is described as a production system, but might be better understood as using an informal kind of logic.

When production rules are used to implement stimulus-response associations, they normally achieve unstated goals implicitly. Such implicit goals and the resulting goal-oriented behaviour are said to be *emergent*. For example, the emergent goal of covering yourself with an umbrella if it is raining is *to stay dry*. And the emergent goal of studying late in the library if you have an essay to write is *to complete the essay*, which is a sub-goal of *passing the course*, which is a sub-goal of *getting a degree*, which is a sub-goal of the top-level goal of *becoming a success in life*.

In contrast with systems that explicitly reduce goals to sub-goals, systems that implement stimulus-response associations are an attractive model of evolutionary theory. Their ultimate goal, which is to enable an agent to survive and prosper in competition with other agents, is emergent, rather than explicit.

Although the natural use of production systems is to implement stimulus-response associations, they are also used to simulate backward reasoning, not by executing production rules backwards, but by treating goals as facts and by forward chaining with rules of the form:

> *If goal G and conditions C then add H as a sub-goal.*

Indeed, in ACT-R (Anderson & Bower, 1973), this is the typical form of production rules used to simulate human problem solving in such tasks as the Tower of Hanoi.

Thagard (2005) also draws attention to this use of production rules and claims that such rules cannot be represented in logical form. He gives the following example of such a rule:

> *If you want to go home for the weekend, and you have the bus fare,*
> *then you can catch a bus.*

Here the 'action' *you can catch a bus* is a recommendation. The action can also be expressed as a command:

> *If you want to go home for the weekend, and you have the bus fare,*
> *then catch a bus.*

The use of the imperative voice to express actions motivates the terminology 'conflict resolution' to describe the process of reconciling conflicting commands.

The differences between production systems and logic programming are of two kinds. There are technical differences, such as the fact that production rules are executed in the forward direction, the fact that conclusions of production rules are actions or recommendations for actions, and the fact that production rules are embedded in a cycle in which conflict resolution is performed to choose between candidate actions. And there are cultural differences, reflecting a more casual attitude to issues of correctness and completeness, as well as a greater emphasis on 'strong', domain-specific knowledge in contrast to 'weak' general-purpose problem-solving methods.

The technical differences are significant and need to be treated seriously. In the ALP agent model, in particular, we take account of forward chaining by using logic programs and integrity constraints to reason forwards; we take account of the imperative nature of production rules by treating them as goals rather than as beliefs; and we take account of the production system cycle by generalizing it to an agent cycle, in which thinking involves the use of both goals and beliefs.

However, the cultural differences are not technically significant and are based upon a failure to distinguish between *knowledge representation* and *problem-solving*. Knowledge can be weak or strong, depending on whether it is general knowledge that applies to a wide class of problems in a given domain, like axioms of a mathematical theory, or whether it is specialized knowledge that is tuned to typical problems that arise in the domain, like theorems of a mathematical theory.

However, some strong knowledge may not be derivable from general-purpose knowledge in the way that theorems are derivable from axioms. Strong knowledge might be more like a mathematical conjecture or a rule of thumb, which is incomplete and only approximately correct. Strong knowledge can exist in domains, such as expert systems, where there exists no weak knowledge that can serve as a general axiomatization.

Logic is normally associated with weak knowledge, like mathematical axioms; and production systems are associated with strong knowledge, as in expert systems. But there is no reason, other than a cultural one, why logic can not also be used to represent strong knowledge, as in the case of mathematical theorems or conjectures.

In contrast with knowledge, which can be weak or strong, problem-solving methods are generally weak and general-purpose. Even production systems, with their focus on strong knowledge, employ a weak and general-purpose problem-solving method, in their use of forward chaining. Logic programs similarly employ a weak and general-purpose method, namely backward reasoning.

Logic programming

A short introduction to logic programming

Logic programming has three main classes of application: as a general-purpose programming language, a database language, and a knowledge representation language in AI. As a programming language, it can represent and compute any computable function. As a database language, it generalizes relational databases, to include general clauses in addition to facts. And as a knowledge representation language it is a non-monotonic logic, which can be used for default reasoning. Its most well-known implementation is the programming language Prolog, which combines pure logic programming with a number of impure features.

In addition to the use of logic programming as a normative model of problem solving (Kowalski, 1974/79), Stenning and van Lambalgen (2004, 2005, 2008) have investigated its use as a descriptive model of human reasoning.

Logic programs (also called *normal logic programs*) are sets of conditionals of the form:

If B_1 and... and B_n then H

where the *conclusion H* is an atomic formula and the *conditions B_i* are *literals*, which are either atomic formulas or the negations of atomic formulas. All variables are implicitly universally quantified in front of the conditional. Conditionals in logic programs are also called *clauses*. *Horn clauses*[2] are the special case where all of the conditions are atomic formulae. *Facts* are the special case where $n = 0$ (there are no conditions) and there are no variables. Sometimes clauses that are not facts are also called *rules,* inviting confusion with production rules.

Goals (or *queries*) are conjunctions of literals, syntactically just like the conditions of clauses. However, all variables are implicitly existentially quantified, and the intention of the goal is to find an instantiation of the variables that makes the goal hold.

For example, the three sentences:

If you have the bus fare and you catch a bus
and not something goes wrong with the bus journey,
then you will go home for the weekend.

---

[2] Horn clauses are named after the logician Alfred Horn, who studied some of their model-theoretic properties.

If you have the bus fare and you catch a bus,
then you will go home for the weekend.
You have the bus fare.

are a clause, a Horn clause and a fact respectively. Notice that the second sentence can be regarded as an imprecise version of the first sentence. Notice too that the first two clauses both express 'strong' domain-specific knowledge, rather than the kind of weak knowledge that would be necessary for general-purpose planning.

The sentence *you will go home for the weekend* is a simple, atomic goal.

Backward reasoning (from conclusions to conditions) treats conditionals as goal-reduction procedures:

to show/solve H, show/solve B_1 and... and B_n.

For example, backward reasoning turns the conditionals:

If you study late in the library then you will complete the essay.
If you have the bus fare and you catch a bus,
then you will go home for the weekend.

into the procedures:

To complete the essay, study late in the library.
To go home for the weekend, check that you have the bus fare, and catch a bus.

Because conditionals in normal logic programming are used only backwards, they are normally written backwards:

H if B_1 and... and B_n.

so that backward reasoning is equivalent to 'forward chaining' in the direction in which the conditional is written. The Prolog syntax for clauses:

$H :- B_1,..., B_n$.

is deliberately ambiguous, so that clauses can be read either declaratively as conditionals written backwards or procedurally as goal-reduction procedures executed forwards.

Whereas positive, atomic goals and sub-goals are solved by backward reasoning, negative goals and sub-goals of the form *not G*, where *G* is an atomic sentence, are solved by *negation as failure: not G* succeeds if and only if backward reasoning with the sub-goal *G* does not succeed.

Negation as failure makes logic programming a non-monotonic logic. For example, given only the clauses:

An object is red if the object looks red and not the object is illuminated by a red light.
The apple looks red.

then the consequence:

The apple is red.

follows as a goal, because there is no clause whose conclusion matches the sub-goal *the apple is illuminated by a red light,* and therefore the two conditions for the only clause that can be used in solving the goal both hold. However, given the additional clause *the apple is illuminated by a red light,* the sub-goal now succeeds and the top-level goal now fails, non-monotonically withdrawing the consequence *The apple is red.* However, the consequence *not the apple is red* now succeeds instead.

Goals and conditions of clauses can be generalized from conjunctions of literals to arbitrary formulae of first-order logic. The simplest way to do so is to use auxiliary predicates and clauses (Lloyd & Topor, 1984). For example, the goal:

> *Show that for all exams,*
> *if the exam is a final exam, then you can study for the exam in the library.*

can be transformed into the normal logic programming form:

> *Show that not the library is useless.*
> *the library is useless if the exam is a final exam and*
> *not you can study for the exam in the library.*

This is similar to the transformation[3] noted by Sperber, Cara, and Girotto (1995) needed to obtain classically correct reasoning with conditionals in variants of the Wason Selection Task. It is important to note, however, that the transformation applies in logic programming only when the conditional is interpreted as a goal, and not when it is interpreted as a clause.

The computational advantage of the transformation is that it reduces the problem of determining whether an arbitrary sentence of first-order logic holds with respect to a given logic program to the two simple inference rules of backward reasoning and negation as failure alone.

Strong versus weak methods in logic programming

In practice, expert logic programmers use both the declarative reading of clauses as conditionals, so that programs correctly achieve their goals, and the procedural reading, so that programs behave efficiently. However, it seems that few programmers achieve this level of expertize. Many programmers focus primarily on the declarative reading and are disappointed when their programs fail to run efficiently. Other programmers focus instead on the procedural reading and loose the benefits of the declarative reading.

Part of the problem is purely technical, because many declarative programs, like the clause:

> *Mary likes a person if the person likes Mary.*

reduce goals to similar sub-goals repeatedly without termination. This problem can be solved at least in part by employing more sophisticated ('stronger'), but still general-purpose problem-solvers that never try to solve similar sub-goals more than once (Sagonas et al., 1994).

However, part of the problem is also psychological and cultural, because many programmers use logic only to specify problem domains, and not to represent useful knowledge for efficient problem-solving in those domains.

The planning problem in AI is a typical example. In classical planning, the problem is specified by describing both an initial state and a goal state, and by specifying the preconditions and post-conditions of atomic actions. To solve the problem, it is then necessary to find a sequence of atomic actions that transforms the initial state into the goal state. This is sometimes called *planning from first principles*, or by *brute force*. In many domains it is computationally explosive.

The alternative is to use a collection of precompiled plan schemata that apply to a wide class of commonly occurring problems in the given domain. These plan schemata typically reduce a top-

---

[3] The use of the auxiliary predicate is merely a technical device, which is useful for maintaining the simple syntax of goals and clauses. However, it is also possible to employ a more natural syntax in which the conditional is written directly in the form of a denial: *Show that not there is an exam, such that (the exam is a final exam and not you can study for the exam in the library).*

level goal to high-level actions, rather than to atomic actions, in a hierarchy of reductions from higher-level to lower-level actions. This is sometimes called *planning from second principles*, and it can be very efficient, although it may not be as complete as planning from first principles.

Algorithms and their specifications are another example. For instance, the top-level specification of the problem of sorting a list can be expressed as:

> *list L' is a sorted version of list L if L' is a permutation of L and L' is ordered.*

No 'weak' general-purpose problem-solving method can execute this specification efficiently.

The Prolog implementation of backward reasoning, in particular, treats the specification as a procedure:

> *To sort list L obtaining list L', generate permutations L' of L,*
> *until you find a permuation L' that is ordered.*

However, there exist a great variety of efficient sorting algorithms, which can also be expressed in logic programming form. For example, the top-level of the recursive part of quicksort:

> *To quicksort a list L into L', split L into two smaller lists L_1 & L_2 and*
> *quicksort L_1 into L'_1 and quicksort L_2 into L'_2 and shuffle L_1 & L_2 together into L'.*

I leave the Horn clause representation of the procedure to the reader. Suffice it to say that quicksort is a sufficiently 'strong' problem-solving method that it behaves efficiently even when executed by a weak problem-solving method, such as backward reasoning. Stronger, but still general-purpose methods, such as parallelism, can improve efficiency even more.

Two kinds of semantics

There are two main kinds of semantics for logic programs, with two main ways of understanding what it means for a goal to hold. Both of these semantics interpret the clauses of a program as the *only* clauses that can be used to establish the conclusions of clauses. This interpretation is a form of the *closed world assumption* (Reiter, 1978).

In the *minimal model semantics*, a logic program defines a set of minimal models, and a goal holds if it is *true* in one or more of these models. The minimal model semantics comes in a *credulous* version, in which a goal holds if it is true in *some* minimal model; and a *sceptical* version, in which a goal holds if it is true in *all* minimal models.

The notion of minimal model is very simple in the case of Horn clause programs, because every Horn clause program has a unique minimal model, in which an atomic sentence is true if and only if it is true in all models. However, it is more complicated for normal logic programs with negative conditions. For this reason, a more detailed discussion of the minimal model semantics is given in the appendix.

The main (and arguably simpler) alternative to the minimal model semantics is the *completion semantics*, in which clauses are understood elliptically as the if-halves of definitions in if-and-only-if form (Clark, 1978). If a predicate does not occur as the conclusion of a clause, then it is deemed to be *false*. This interpretation is called the *predicate (or Clark) completion*. A goal holds in the completion semantics if it is a *theorem*, logically entailed by the completion of the logic program.

Consider, for example, the logic program:

> *you get help if you press the alarm signal button.*
> *you get help if you shout loudly.*

The completion[4] of the program is:

> *you get help if and only if you press the alarm signal button or you shout loudly.*
> *you press the alarm signal button if and only if false. (i.e. not you press the alarm signal button.)*
> *you shout loudly if and only if false. (i.e. not you shout loudly.)*

which logically entails the conclusion: *not you get help.*

Negation as *finite* failure is *sound* with respect to the completion semantics:

> *not G* is logically entailed by the completion
> if *G fails finitely.*

It is also complete in many cases.

The completion and minimal model semantics have different notions of what it means for a goal, which in both cases can be any formula of first-order logic, to hold with respect to a given logic program. In both semantics, the same proof procedures of backward reasoning and negation as failure can be used. However, in the minimal model semantics, negation as failure includes possibly infinite failure, whereas in the completion semantics, negation as failure is finite.

Given a program and goal, in most cases these two semantics give the same results. In some cases, these results differ from those sanctioned by classical logic, but are similar to those observed in psychological studies of human reasoning. However, as we have seen at the beginning of the paper, the selection task presents a challenge, which we will discuss again later in the paper.

Two kinds of proof procedures

The standard proof procedure for logic programming, used in Prolog for example, generates a *search tree*, whose *nodes* are labelled by goals. The *root* of the tree is labelled by the initial goal. Given any node in the tree, labelled by a goal, say:

> *B & B1 &… & Bn*

backward reasoning proceeds by first selecting a sub-goal for solution, say *B* for simplicity.

If there is more than one sub-goal that can be selected, then, as with conflict-resolution in production systems, a decision needs to be made, selecting only one. Any selection strategy can be used. Prolog selects sub-goals in the order in which they are written. However, more intelligent, but still 'weak', problem-solving strategies, such as choosing the most constrained sub-goal first (the one that has fewest candidate solutions), can also be used (Kowalski, 1974/79).

If the selected sub-goal *B* is a positive, atomic goal, then backward reasoning continues by looking for a clause whose conclusion matches *B*. In the propositional case, if *B* is identical to the conclusion of a clause *B if B′$_1$ &… & B′$_m$* then *backward reasoning* replaces the selected sub-goal by the conditions of the clause, obtaining a *child* of the node labelled by the new goal:

> *B′$_1$ &… & B′$_m$ & B$_1$ &… & B$_n$*

In the more general case, the selected sub-goal needs to be unified with the conclusion of a clause, and the unifying substitution is applied to the new goal. A node has as many children as there are such clauses whose conclusion matches the selected sub-goal.

If the selected sub-goal *B* is the negation *not B′* of an atomic formula *B′* containing no variables, then *negation as failure* is applied, generating a subsidiary search tree with the same program, but

---

[4] The use of *if and only if* here does not make the two sides of the 'equivalence' symmetric. The left-hand side is a predicate defined by the formula on the right-hand side.

with the initial goal B'. The selected sub-goal *not B'* succeeds if and only if the subsidiary search tree contains no solution, and the *only child* of the node is labelled by the new goal:

B_1 &... & B_n

A *solution* is a finite branch of the search tree that starts from the initial node and ends with a node labelled by the empty conjunction of sub-goals (where $n = 0$). Because the search tree may contain infinite branches, the proof procedure is semi-decidable.

Given a program and an initial goal, the search tree is generated and explored, to find a solution. Prolog uses a depth-first search strategy, exploring branches in the order in which clauses are written. Depth-first search is risky, because it can get lost down an infinite branch, when there are solutions lying around on alternative finite branches. However, when it works, it works very efficiently. But other search strategies, such as breadth-first, best-first and parallel search strategies, which are guaranteed to find a solution if one exists, are also possible.

If a search tree is too big, no search strategy can search it efficiently. Sometimes the problem is inherently difficult, and there is no alternative but to search the space as patiently as possible. But in many domains, as we have seen, the problem can be reformulated, using 'stronger' knowledge, which results in a smaller, more manageable search tree.

The alternative to generating a search tree is to reason explicitly with the program completion, representing the current state of the search by a single formula, which corresponds to the expanding frontier of the search tree. Reasoning with the completion was introduced as a proof procedure for abductive logic programming by (Console et al., 1991) and extended by (Fung & Kowalski, 1997).

Backward reasoning is performed by replacing predicates with their definitions, resulting in a logically equivalent formula. For example:

Goal: *you get help and you study late in the library*
Program: *you get help if and only if*
                you press the alarm signal button or you shout loudly.
New goal: *[you press the alarm signal button and you study late in the library] or*
                [you shout loudly and you study late in the library].

Reasoning with the completion represents the current state of the search to solve a goal as a disjunction of conjunctions of literals, say:

$(A \ \& \ A_1 \ \& ...\& \ A_\alpha) \ or \ (B \ \& \ B_1 \ \& ... \ \& \ B_\beta) \ or...or \ (C \ \& \ C_1 \ \& ... \ \& \ C_v).$

Each disjunct corresponds to the goal at the end of an unextended branch in a search tree. The entire disjunction corresponds to the set of all goals at the current frontier of the search tree. The initial goal is represented by an initial disjunction with only one disjunct. Replacing an atom by its definition, called *unfolding*, corresponds to *replacing* a node at the tip of a branch by *all* of its children.

In the propositional case, unfolding a selected positive goal atom, say B, replaces it with its definition:

B *if and only if* D_1 *or...or* D_n

and distributes conjunction over disjunction, so that the new state of the search is represented by a new, logically equivalent formula of the form:

$(A \ \& \ A_1 \ \& ...\& \ A_\alpha) \ or \ (D_1 \ \& \ B_1 \ \& ... \ \& \ B_\beta) \ or...or \ (D_n \ \& \ B_1 \ \& ... \ \& \ B_\beta) \ or...or \ (C \ \& \ C_1 \ \& ... \ \& \ C_v).$

In the special case where the definition has the form:

B *if and only if true*

then the new formula is simplified to:

$(A \& A_1 \& ... \& A_\alpha)$ or $(B_1 \& ... \& B_\beta)$ or...or $(C \& C_1 \& ... \& C_\nu)$.

In the special case where the definition has the form:

B if and only if false

then the new formula is simplified to:

$(A \& A_1 \& ... \& A_\alpha)$ or...or $(C \& C_1 \& ... \& C_\nu)$.

In the propositional case, the initial goal *succeeds* if and only if the formula *true* is derived by means of a finite number of such equivalence-preserving inference steps. The goal *fails finitely* if and only if the formula *false* is derived.[5]

If the selected atom is a negative literal, say *not B'*, then a subsidiary derivation is initiated with the initial goal *B'* (viewed as a disjunction with only one disjunct, which is a conjunct with only one conjunct). If the new initial goal fails finitely, then the selected atom is replaced by *true* and the new formula is simplified to:

$(A \& A_1 \& ... \& A_\alpha)$ or $(B_1 \& ... \& B_\beta)$ or...or $(C \& C_1 \& ... \& C_\nu)$.

If the initial goal succeeds, then the selected atom is replaced by *false* and the new formula is simplified to:

$(A \& A_1 \& ... \& A_\alpha)$ or...or $(C \& C_1 \& ... \& C_\nu)$.

For example, consider the problem of determining whether:

The apple is red.

follows from the program:

An object is red if the object looks red and not the object is illuminated by a red light.
The apple looks red.

In the completion semantics this can be represented in the form[6]:

Goal₁:	*The apple is red.*
Program:	*An object is red if and only if*
	the object looks red and not the object is illuminated by a red light.
	The apple looks red if and only if true
	The apple is illuminated by a red light if and only if false

Using the completion, it is possible to derive the following sequence of formulae:

Goal₂:	*The apple looks red and not the apple is illuminated by a red light.*	
Goal₃:	*not the apple is illuminated by a red light.*	
	Subsidiary goal₁:	*the apple is illuminated by a red light.*
	Subsidiary goal₂:	*false*
Goal₄:	*true*	

---

[5] In the general case, the process of matching goals with conclusions of definitions introduces equalities, which represent the instantiations of variables need to solve those goals. The initial goal succeeds if and only if a consistent set of equalities is derived.

[6] This is not the real completion, which makes the stronger closed world assumption that nothing is illuminated by a red light. In fact, it would be more appropriate to represent the predicate *is illuminated by a red light* by an abducible predicate, to which the closed world assumption does not apply. The form of the completion used in this example has been chosen as a compromise, to simplify the example.

The example shows that reasoning with the if-halves of clauses and generating a search tree simulates reasoning explicitly with the completion. Indeed, reasoning informally it can be hard to tell the two proof procedures apart.

The relationship between logic programs and production rules

Viewing logic programs and production rules informally, it can also be hard to tell them apart, because in many cases they generate the same goal-reduction behaviour. Indeed, Simon (1999) includes Prolog, along with ACT-R, 'among the production systems widely used in cognitive simulation'. Stenning and van Lambalgen (2004, 2005, 2008) also observe that forward chaining with production rules of the form:

If goal G and conditions C then add H as a sub-goal.

behaves like backward reasoning with clauses of the form:

G if C and H.

The production rule and the clause both behave as the goal-reduction procedure:

To achieve G, show C, and achieve H as sub-goal.

The production rule can be understood as representing the procedure *subjectively* (or *intentionally*), in terms of the causal effect of the goal *G* on the agent's state of mind. The clause, on the other hand, views it *objectively* (or *extensionally*), in terms of causal effects in the agent's environment. However, in both cases, the direction of the conditional is from conditions that are causes to conclusions that are effects. This switching of the direction of the conditional is related to the switching associated with *evidential conditionals, epistemic,* and *inferencial conditionals* as noted by Pearl (1988), Dancygier (1998) and Politzer and Bonnefon (2006). In Appendix B, I argue that the completion semantics helps to explain the switching and truncation of conditionals observed in many psychological studies, as discussed by Politzer and Bonnefon (2006)

Thagard's example of the production rule:

If you want to go home for the weekend, and you have the bus fare,
then you can catch a bus.

can be understood as a subjective representation of the goal-reduction procedure:

To go home, check that you have the bus fare, and catch a bus.

which can be represented objectively by the logic programming clause:

you will go home for the weekend if
you have the bus fare and you catch a bus.

Notice that the causal relationship in both formulations of the procedure has as an implicit associated degree of uncertainty. In the case of the production rule, the uncertainty is associated with whether or not the agent's conflict resolution strategy will chose the action of the rule if other rules with other incompatible actions are triggered at the same time.

In the case of the clause, the uncertainty is associated with whether or not other implicit and unstated conditions also hold. This implicit condition can be stated explicitly using negation as failure:

you will go home for the weekend if
you have the bus fare and you catch a bus and
not something goes wrong with the bus journey.

The formulation without this extra condition can be regarded as an approximation to the fully specified clause. It is an approximation, not only because it is missing the condition, but also because it is not sufficient to take any old bus to get home, but it is necessary to take a bus that is on a route that goes home.

This representation with an extra condition, using negation as failure, does not attempt to quantify or even to qualify the associated degree of uncertainty. However, as we will see later, in abductive logic programming (ALP) it can be quantified by using instead an abducible predicate, say *the bus journey is successful*, and by associating a probability with the abducible predicate. For example:

> *you will go home for the weekend if*
> *you have the bus fare and you catch a bus and*
>
> *line the bus journey is successful.*
> *the bus journey is successful (with probability .95).*
> *something goes wrong with the bus journey (with probability .05).*

In the meanwhile, it is worth noting that the ALP formulation provides a link with Bayesian networks (Pearl, 1988). David Poole (1993, 1997) has shown, in general, that assigning a probability p to a conditional *A if B* is equivalent to assigning the same probability p to an abducible predicate, say *normal*, in the clause *A if B and normal*. In particular, he has shown that abductive logic programs with such probabilistic abducible predicates have the expressive power of discreet Bayesian networks. A similar result, but with a focus on using statistical learning techniques to induce logic programs from examples, has also been obtained by Taisuke Satoh (1995). In recent years this has given rise to a booming research area combining probability, learning, and logic programming (De Raedt & Kersting, 2003).

The relationship between logic programs that are used to reason backwards and production rules that are used to represent goal-reduction procedures does not solve the problem of the relationship between logic programs and production systems in general. In particular, it does not address the problem of understanding the relationship when production rules are used instead to represent stimulus-response associations. For example, it is unnatural to interpret the condition-action rule:

> *If it is raining and you have an umbrella, then cover yourself with the umbrella.*

as a goal-reduction procedure, to solve the goal of covering yourself with an umbrella by getting an umbrella when it rains.

I will argue that stimulus-response production rules are better understood as *maintenance goals*, which are treated as integrity constraints in abductive logic programming.

Integrity constraints

In conventional databases, integrity constraints are used passively to prevent prohibited updates. But in abductive logic programming, they are like integrity constraints in active databases, where they both prevent prohibited updates and perform corrective actions to ensure that integrity is maintained. Production rules, used as stimulus-response associations, can be understood as integrity constraints of this kind.

Thus the condition-action rule for covering oneself when it rains can be understood as an active integrity constraint:

> *If it is raining and you have an umbrella, then you cover yourself with the umbrella.*

This is identical in syntax to the condition-action rule, except that the action part is not expressed as a command or recommendation, but as a statement in declarative form. Unlike the original condition-action rule, the integrity constraint has the syntax of a logical implication.

In fact, integrity constraints are just a particular species of goal; and, like other kinds of goals, they can be sentences of first-order logic. They also have the same semantics as goals in logic programs (Godfrey et al., 1998). This includes both the credulous and sceptical versions of the minimal model semantics, in which integrity constraints are sentences that are true in minimal models of a logic program. It also includes the completion semantics, in which they are sentences logically entailed by the if-and-only-if completion of the program.

However, it is also natural to understand the semantics of integrity constraints in consistency terms: An integrity constraint holds if and only if it is *consistent* with respect to the program. The consistency view comes in two flavours: In the minimal model semantics, the consistency view is equivalent to the credulous semantics: An integrity constraint is consistent with respect to the minimal model semantics of a logic program if and only if it is true in some minimal model of the program. In the completion semantics, an integrity constraint is satisfied if and only if it is consistent with the completion of the program relative to classical model theory. We will see later that the consistency view of constraint satisfaction seems to be necessary in the selection task.

The difference between integrity constraints and conventional goals is partly terminological and partly pragmatic. In problem-solving, a conventional goal is typically an *achievement goal*, which is a one-off problem to be solved, including the problem of achieving some desired state of the world. In contrast, a typical integrity constraint is a *maintenance goal* that persists over all states of the world. In the context of intelligent agents, the term *goal* generally includes both *maintenance goals* and *achievement goals*.

Maintenance goals typically have the form of conditionals and can be hard to distinguish from clauses.[7] The distinction between clauses and maintenance goals can be better understood by viewing them in terms of the data base distinction between data and integrity constraints (Nicolas & Gallaire, 1978).

In conventional relational databases, data is defined by relationships, which can be viewed in logical terms as facts (variable-free atomic sentences). For example:

The bus leaves at time 9:00.
The bus leaves at time 10:00. etc.

However, in deductive databases, relationships can also be defined by more general clauses. For example:

The bus leaves at time X:00 if X is an integer and $9 \leq X \leq 18$.

Given appropriate definitions for the predicates in its conditions, the clause replaces the 10 separate facts that would be needed in a conventional relational database.

Compare this clause with the conditional:

If the bus leaves at time X:00,
then for some integer Y, the bus arrives at its destination at time X:Y and $20 \leq Y \leq 30$.

The existential quantifier in the conclusion of the sentence means that the sentence cannot be used to define data, but can only be used to constrain it. In a passive database, it would be used to reject any update that records an arrival time earlier than 20 minutes or later than 30 minutes after departure. However, in an active database, it could attempt to make its conclusion true and self-update the database with a record of the arrival, generating an appropriate value for *Y*.

---

[7] In this respect, they resemble the conditionals in the selection task, which can be interpreted descriptively or deontically.

Obviously, the capability to make such an update lies outside the powers of even an active database. However, it is a feature of many intelligent agent systems, such as Agent0 (Shoham, 1991). Whereas actions in production systems can be executed as soon as all of their conditions are satisfied, actions in Agent0 have associated times, and they can be executed when their associated times equal the actual time.

An intelligent agent might use integrity constraints to maintain the integrity of its 'knowledge base', in much the same way that an active database system uses integrity constraints to maintain the integrity of its data. However, whereas backward reasoning is adequate for solving achievement goals, maintaining integrity is more naturally performed by combining backward and forward reasoning (Kowalski, Sadri, & Soper, 1987):

> Integrity checking is triggered by an observation that updates the agent's knowledge base. Forward reasoning is used to match the observation either with a condition of an integrity constraint *I* or with a condition of a clause *C*. It proceeds by using backward reasoning to verify any remaining conditions of the integrity constraint *I* or clause *C*; and then, if these condtions are satisfied, it derives the conclusion. If the derived conclusion is the conclusion of an integrity constraint *I*, then the conclusion is a new goal, typically an achievement goal. However, if it is the conclusion of a clause *C*, then it is treated as a derived update and processed by further forward reasoning.

An achievement goal can be solved by backward reasoning, as in normal logic programming. But, instead of failing if a sub-goal cannot be reduced to further sub-goals, if the sub-goal is an action, then an attempt can be made to make it true by executing it successfully.[8] The result of the attempt is added as a new update to the knowledge base.

This informal description of forward and backward reasoning with clauses and forward reasoning with integrity constraints is compatible with different semantics and can be formalized both in terms of search trees and in terms of reasoning with the completion. In both cases, it gives a logical semantics to production rules of the stimulus-response variety and it facilitates combining them with logic programs. It also facilitates the modelling of agents that combine the ability to plan pro-actively with the ability to behave reactively.

Intelligent agents and agentspeak

The ability to combine planning for a future state of the world with reacting to the present state is a characteristic of both human and artificial agents. In the next section, we will see how these abilities are combined in ALP agents. ALP agents can be viewed in BDI (Belief, Desire, Intention) (Bratman, Israel, & Pollack, 1988) terms, as agents whose beliefs are represented by clauses, whose desires (or goals) are represented by integrity constraints, and whose intentions are collections of actions to be performed in the future.

Arguably, the most influential of the BDI agent models is that of Rao and Georgeff (1991), its successor dMARS (d'Inverno, 1998), and their abstraction and simplification AgentSpeak (Rao, 1996). Although the earliest of these systems were specified in multi-modal logics, their procedural implementations bore little resemblance to their logical specifications. AgentSpeak abandoned the attempt to relate the modal logic specifications with their procedural implementations, observing instead that '...one can view agent programs as multi-threaded interruptible logic programming clauses'.

---

[8] If the abducible sub-goal is an observable predicate, then the agent can actively attempt to observe whether it is true or false. Active observations turn the simplified formulation of the selection task discussed at the beginning of the paper into one that more closely resembles standard formulations, in which the subject is asked to perform an action.

However, this view of AgentSpeak in logic programming terms is restricted to the procedural interpretation of clauses. In fact, procedures in AgentSpeak are much closer to production rules than they are to clauses in logic programming. Like production systems, AgentSpeak programs have both a declarative and a procedural component. The declarative component contains both *belief literals* (atoms and negations of atoms) and *goal atoms*, whereas the procedural component consists of *plans*, which are an extension of production rules. Plans are embedded in a cycle similar to the production system cycle, and have the syntactic form:

Event E: conditions C ⇐ goals G and actions A.

Here the event *E* can be the addition or the deletion of a belief or the addition of a goal. Like production rules, plans are executed in the direction in which they are written, by a kind of forward chaining. Production systems are the special case where the set of goals *G* is empty.

Here are some typical AgentSpeak plans:

+!quench_thirst: have_glass ⇐
        !have_soft_drink;
        fill_glass; drink.

+!have_soft_drink: soft_drink_in_fridge ⇐
        open_fridge;
        get_soft_drink.

+rock_seen(R): not battery_low ⇐
        ?location(R,L);
        !move_to(L);
        pick_up(R).

+ there is a fire: true ⇐ +there is an emergency.

Observations and actions do not have associated times, and the declarative memory provides only a snapshot of the current state of the world. To compensate for this lack of a temporal representation, the prefixes $+, -, !,$ and? are used to stand for *add, delete, achieve,* and *test* respectively.

Notice that the first two plans are goal-reduction rules, the third plan is a stimulus-response rule, and the fourth plan behaves like a logical implication used to reason forwards.

Like rules in production systems, plans in AgentSpeak do not have a declarative reading. However, in the special case where the triggering event *E* is the addition of a goal, and the plan has the form:

Goal E: conditions C ⇐ goals G and actions A.

the plan can be reformulated as a corresponding logic programming clause:

E' if C' and G' and A' and temporal constraints.

where the prefixed predicates of AgentSpeak are replaced by predicates with explicit associated times. The corresponding clause is identical in behaviour to the plan, but also has a declarative reading. Using an (overly) simple, explicit representation of time,[9] the clauses corresponding to the first two plans illustrated above are:

quench_thirst at time T_5 if have_glass at time T_1 and
        have_soft_drink at time T_2 and
        fill_glass at time T_3 and drink at time T_4 and $T_1< T_2< T_3< T_4 <T_5$.
have_soft_drink at time T_4 if soft_drink_in_fridge at time T_1 and
        open_fridge at time T_2 and
        get_soft_drink at time T_3 and $T_1< T_2< T_3< T_4$.

---

[9] Notice that the explicit representation of time draws attention to implicit assumptions of persistence, for example the assumption that *have_glass at time T_1* persists until time T_5 .

As in the case of stimulus-response production rules, plans in which the triggering event is the addition or deletion of a belief can be represented by means of an integrity constraint. For example, the integrity constraint corresponding to the third plan above is:

> If rock_seen(R) at time T and not battery_low at time T and location(R,L) at time T
> then move_to(L) at time T +1 and pick_up(R) at time T+2.

In addition to goal-reduction rules and stimulus-response associations, there is a third kind of production rule and AgentSpeak plan, illustrated by the fourth plan above, in which the event *E* is an observation and the goals and actions are simply the addition of beliefs. The fourth plan corresponds to a logic programming clause:

> there is an emergency if there is a fire.

that is used to reason forwards in abductive logic programming, rather than backwards in normal logic programming, as we shall see again below.

Abductive logic programming (ALP)

Abductive logic programming (Kakas et al., 1998) extends normal logic programming by combining closed predicates that are defined in the conclusions of clauses with abducible (open or undefined) predicates that occur in the conditions, but not in the conclusions of clauses. Abducible predicates are instead constrained, directly or indirectly, by integrity constraints.

A brief introduction to ALP

In general, given a logic program *P* and integrity constraints *I*, the *abductive task* is given by a problem *G*, which is either an achievement goal or an observation to be explained. The task is solved by finding a set Δ of atomic sentences in the abducible predicates, such that:

> Both *I* and *G* hold with respect to the extended, normal logic program P ∪ Δ.

Δ is called an *abductive explanation* of *G*.

This characterisation of abductive logic programming is compatible with different semantics[10] defining what it means for a goal or integrity constraint to hold with respect to a normal logic program. It is compatible, in particular, with the minimal model semantics, the completion semantics and the consistency view of constraint satisfaction. It is also compatible with different proof procedures, including both search tree proof procedures and proof procedures that reason explicitly with the completion.

Consider the following abductive logic program (with a much simplified representation of time), in which the integrity constraint is a denial:

Program:	*Grass is wet if it rained.*
	Grass is wet if the sprinkler was on.
Abducible predicates:	*it rained, the sprinkler was on, the sun was shining.*
Integrity constraint:	*not (it rained and the sun was shining)*
or equivalently	*if it rained and the sun was shining then false.*
Observation:	*Grass is wet.*

---

[10] Sometimes the set Δ is allowed to contain the negations of atomic sentences in the abducible predicates, in which case there is an additional requirement that Δ be consistent.

In abductive logic programming, reasoning backwards from the observation (treated as a goal), it is possible to derive two alternative explanations of the observation:

> *it rained.*
> *the sprinkler was on.*

Depending on the proof procedure, the two explanations are derived either on different branches of a search tree or as a single formula with an explicit disjunction.

Suppose that we are now given the additional observation:

> Observation: *the sun was shining.*

Backward reasoning with the new observation is not possible. But, depending on the proof procedure, as we will see in the next section, the new observation and the integrity constraint reject the hypothesis *it rained*, leaving *the sprinkler was on* as the only acceptable explanation of the observation that the *Grass is wet*.

Proof procedures for ALP

The standard proof procedure for ALP augments the search tree proof procedure for normal logic programming in two ways. First, it includes all integrity constraints in the initial goal, expressed in the form of denials. Second it accumulates abductive hypotheses as they are needed to solve the initial goal, and it adds these to the program as the search to find a solution continues.

For example, the initial goal, at the root of the search tree, needed to explain the observation that the *Grass is wet* in the previous section, would be expressed in the form[11]:

> *Grass is wet and not (it rained and the sun was shining)*

Selecting the first sub-goal *Grass is wet*, backward reasoning generates two alternative branches in the search tree, with two children of the root node:

> *it rained and not (it rained and the sun was shining)*
> *the sprinkler was on and not (it rained and the sun was shining)*

On each branch, the proof procedure solves the abducible sub-goal by adding it to the set of hypotheses Δ:

> *not (it rained and the sun was shining)* Δ = *{it rained}*
> *not (it rained and the sun was shining)* Δ = *{the sprinkler was on}*

On both branches, negation as failure is applied to the remaining negative sub-goal, generating subsidiary search trees with new initial goals, and with the program augmented by the hypotheses generated so far:

> *it rained and the sun was shining* Δ = *{it rained}*
> *it rained and the sun was shining* Δ = *{the sprinkler was on}*

Given no additional information, both subsidiary search trees fail to contain a solution (in both cases *the sun was shining* fails). So the negative goals on the two branches of the original search tree succeed, resulting in two alternative solutions of the initial goal:

> Δ = *{it rained}* Δ = *{the sprinkler was on}*

---

[11] Strictly speaking, the denial should be formulated as a negative literal, by introducing an auxiliary predicate, but this is just a technical requirement, which can be avoided by slightly complicating the syntax of conditions of clauses, as in this example.

However, given the additional observation *the sun was shining* added to the program, the first subsidiary search tree, with the goal *it rained and the sun was shining*, now contains a solution, because both sub-goals now succeed, and the corresponding negative goal now fails, leaving only the one solution to the initial goal:

Δ = {*the sprinkler was on*}

Although the search tree proof procedure can be extended to include forward reasoning with clauses and integrity constraints, it is easier to illustrate forward reasoning with completion proof procedures instead. There are different proof procedures that use the completion explicitly.

For example, the proof procedure of Console et al. (1991) represents integrity constraints as denials and uses the consistency view of constraint satisfaction, whereas the IFF proof procedure of Fung and Kowalski (1997) and the SLP proof procedure of Kowalski, R., Toni, F. and Wetzel, G. (1998) represent integrity constraints as implications. The IFF and SLP proof procedures differ mainly in their implementation of constraint satisfaction. IFF implements the theorem-hood view, and SLP implements the consistency view.

Given the problem of explaining the observation that the *Grass is wet*, the IFF and SLP proof procedures behave identically. The initial goal and program are expressed in the form:

Goal₁: *Grass is wet and (if it rained and the sun was shining then false)*
Program: *Grass is wet if and only if it rained or the sprinkler was on.*

Unfolding the first sub-goal, replacing it by its definition and distributing conjunction over disjunction, we obtain the equivalent new goal:

Goal₂: *[it rained and (if it rained and the sun was shining then false)] or*
[the sprinkler was on and (if it rained and the sun was shining then false)]

Forward reasoning within the first disjunct of the new goal adds the conclusion *if the sun was shining then false* to the disjunct:

Goal₃: *[it rained and (if it rained and the sun was shining then false) and*
(if the sun was shining then false)] or
[the sprinkler was on and (if it rained and the sun was shining then false)]

The proof procedure now terminates, because there are no further inferences that can be performed. It is a property of the IFF and SLP proof procedures that both of the hypotheses *it rained* and *the sprinkler was on* entail the observation, and the integrity constraint is both entailed by and consistent with the completion of the program extended with the completion of the hypotheses.

If the new observation *the sun was shining* is now added to both disjuncts of the current state of the goal, we obtain:

Goal₄: *[it rained and (if it rained and the sun was shining then false) and*
(if the sun was shining then false) and the sun was shining] or
[the sprinkler was on and (if it rained and the sun was shining then false) and
the sun was shining]

Forward reasoning with the new observation in both disjuncts, adds *false* to the first disjunct and *if it rained then false* to the second disjunct. Simplifying the first disjunct to *false* leaves only the second disjunct in the form:

Goal₅: *[the sprinkler was on and (if it rained and the sun was shining then false) and*
the sun was shining and (if it rained then false)]

The proof procedure terminates again. This time, the hypothesis that *the sprinkler was on* is now the only hypothesis that entails the observation and satisfies the integrity constraint. In this example, the same proof procedure implements both the theorem-hood and the consistency views of constraint satisfaction.

The IFF and SLP proof procedures differ, however, on the deontic version of the selection task. Because IFF implements the theoremhood view of constraint satisfaction and uses integrity constraints only for forward reasoning, it cannot derive *if P then false* (i.e. *not P*) from *if Q then false* (i.e. *not Q*) and the integrity constraint *if P then Q*. But SLP can perform this inference, because it implements a general-purpose resolution method to check consistency.

The IFF proof procedure is sound and, with certain modest restrictions on the form of clauses and integrity constraints, complete with respect to the completion of the program in the Kunen (1987) three-valued semantics. SLP is sound, but not complete, because consistency is not semi-decidable. However, this is not an argument against the consistency view – any more than the fact that there is no proof procedure for proving all truths of arithmetic is an argument against the notion of truth in arithmetic. (See, in particular, the Horn clause program for arithmetic in Appendix A.)

ALP agents

The notion of ALP agent, in which abductive logic programming is embedded as the thinking component of an observation-thought-decision-action cycle, was introduced in (Kowalski, 1995) and was developed further in (Kowalski 2001, 2006; Kowalski & Sadri, 1999). It is also the basis of the KGP (Knowledge, Goals, and Plans) agent model of (Kakas el al, 2004). The ALP proof procedure of (Kowalski & Sadri, 1999) is the IFF proof procedure, whereas the informal proof procedure described in this paper and in (Kowalski 2001, 2006) extends IFF by incorporating forward reasoning with clauses, as in the integrity checking method of (Kowalski, Sadri, & Soper, 1987). The proof procedure of KGP extends IFF with constraint handling procedures.

The observation-thought-decision-action cycle of an ALP agent is similar to the production system and AgentSpeak cycles. The agent's beliefs are represented by clauses. Achievement and maintenance goals, as well as prohibitions, are represented by integrity constraints. Observations (or hypotheses that explain observations) and actions are represented by abducible predicates.

In the ALP agent cycle, reasoning can be interrupted, as in AgentSpeak, both by incoming observations and by outgoing actions. An incoming observation, for example, might trigger an integrity constraint and derive an action that needs to be performed immediately, interrupting the derivation of plans and the execution of actions that need to be performed only later in the future.

Consider the English sentences in the following example:

If you have an essay to write, then you study late in the library.
If there is an emergency, then you get help.
If you press the alarm signal button, then you get help.
If there is a fire, then there is an emergency.

The four sentences all have conditional form. Moreover, the second and third sentences have the same conclusion *you get help*. However, despite their similar syntax, the first two sentences would function as *maintenance goals* and would be represented by integrity constraints in the ALP agent model. The last two sentences would function as beliefs and would be represented by clauses. The predicates *there is a fire* and *you press the alarm signal button* are abducible predicates, representing possible observations and actions respectively. The predicate *you study late in the library* would be defined by other clauses.

To be precise, all of the predicates would need to include associated times. These times would reflect the fact that getting help in an emergency is more urgent than studying late in the library.

Given an update recording an observation that *you have an essay to write*, forward reasoning with the first sentence would derive the achievement goal *you study late in the library* and set in train a process of backward reasoning and action execution to solve the achievement goal.

A second update recording an observation that *there is a fire* would interrupt this process and initiate a chain of forward reasoning to determine the consequences of the new update. Forward reasoning with the fourth sentence derives the consequence *there is an emergency*. Forward reasoning with the second sentence derives the new achievement goal *you get help*. Backward reasoning with the third sentence reduces this goal to the abducible sub-goal, *you press the alarm signal button*. Because the sub-goal is an action abducible, it can be solved only by making it true, executing it successfully in the environment. Because the action is urgent, it interrupts the process of studying late in the library, which can be returned to later.

In production systems and AgentSpeak, all four sentences would be represented uniformly as production rules or plans, and they would all be executed by forward chaining. Different uses of a belief would be represented by different rules or plans. For example, in AgentSpeak, the four sentences above would be represented by such plans as:

> + you have an essay to write: true ⇐! you study late in the library
> + there is an emergency: true ⇐! get help.
> +! get help: true ⇐ press the alarm signal button.
> +? there is a fire: there is an emergency ⇐ true.
> + there is a fire: true ⇐ + there is an emergency.
> +! there is an emergency: true ⇐! there is a fire.

Because AgentSpeak plans do not have a uniform logical reading, they can not easily be used to represent weak domain-general knowledge, as is possible in logic programming. On the one hand, this is a limitation, but on the other hand it probably encourages programmers to write more efficient domain-specific problem-solving methods.

Decision-making in ALP agents – another role for probability

The ALP agent observation-thought-decision-action cycle includes a decision-making component to choose between alternatives courses of action, including alternative ways of solving the same goal. Different alternatives may solve an initial goal with different degrees of utility, as well as have other desirable or undesirable consequences as side effects.

This decision-making process is further complicated by the uncertainty of the consequences of an agent's candidate actions, due to the uncertain behaviour of other agents and the uncertainty of the environment. Thus the problem of deciding between different courses of actions requires consideration of both utility and uncertainty. According to the norms of classical decision theory, a rational agent should choose a course of actions that optimizes overall expected utility, including the utility of any side effects, and taking into account any associated uncertainties.

Decision theory is a normative ideal, which requires a large body of knowledge and huge computational resources. As a consequence, it is often more practical for an agent to employ heuristic strategies that approximate the normative ideal. One of the simplest of these strategies is to use a fixed priority ordering of goals and beliefs, to give preference to one set of actions over another.

Consider, for example, the following two ways of going home for the weekend:

you will go home for the weekend if you have the bus fare and you catch a bus home.
you will go home for the weekend if you have a car and you drive the car home.

Both alternatives can be used to solve the goal of going home, but with different utilities and probabilities. Taking into account the state of the car and the reliability of the bus service, it may be possible to associate explicit probabilities with the two clauses. For example:

you will go home for the weekend if you have the bus fare and you catch a bus home. (with probability .95)
you will go home for the weekend if you have a car and you drive home. (with probability .80)

However, as Poole (1993, 1997) has shown, the same effect can be achieved by associating probabilities with abducible predicates:

you will go home for the weekend if you have the bus fare and you catch a bus home
and the bus journey is successful.
you will go home for the weekend if you have a car and you drive the car home
and the car journey is successful.
the bus journey is successful. (with probability .95)
the car journey is successful. (with probability .80)

To do a full-scale decision-theoretic analysis, in addition to determining the probabilities, it would also be necessary to determine the degree to which the alternatives accomplish their intended goal, as well as to the quantify the costs and benefits of other possible consequences.[12] For example, driving the car may be more comfortable than taking the bus, and the bus schedule may be inconvenient. But taking the bus may cost less money, and, by contributing to the reduction of global carbon emissions, help to save the planet.

You could do a PhD calculating the probabilities and utilities and combining them to find the optimal solution. But, the result might be equivalent to just giving preference to the use of one alternative over the other. This could be done, for example, just using normal logic programming clauses, Prolog-fashion in a fixed order. For example, in the order:

you will go home for the weekend if you have the bus fare and you catch a bus home
and not something goes wrong with the bus journey.
you will go home for the weekend if you have a car and you drive the car home
and not something goes wrong with the car journey.

Conclusions

I have argued that the two main kinds of conditionals used in AI, namely production rules and logic programming clauses, can be combined naturally in the ALP agent model and can simulate human performance on some reasoning tasks. Because production systems have been used widely as a cognitive architecture, but have not been much used to model human reasoning, there are grounds for believing that the ALP agent model may have value as a general cognitive architecture.

---

[12] In classical Decision Theory, the possible outcomes of candidate actions are given in advance. The extension of the IFF proof procedure to include forward reasoning with clauses makes it possible to derive consequences of candidate actions to help in deciding between them (Kowalski, 2006), using clauses of the form *effect if cause*. The same clauses can also be used backwards to generate plans to achieve desired *effects* by reducing them to possible *causes*.

Psychological studies of human reasoning are a test and a challenge for agent models developed in Artificial Intelligence. Although the ALP agent model performs well on some of these tests, the basic model needs to be extended, to include forward reasoning with clauses and to implement the consistency semantics of integrity constraints. I believe that these extensions, and possibly others that might be needed to simulate human reasoning in other psychological experiments, will also be useful for computer applications in AI.

Acknowledgements

Many thanks to Fariba Sadri, Michiel van Lambalgen and Keith Stenning for helpful discussions, and to Keith Clark, Luis Pereira, Keith Stenning and Guy Politzer for useful comments on an earlier draft of this paper. Thanks too to Mike Oaksford for the invitation to contribute to this volume.

References

Anderson, J. & Bower, G. (1973). *Human Associative Memory*. Washington, D.C.: Winston.

Bondarenko, A., Dung, P. M., Kowalski, R., & Toni, F. (1997). An abstract argumentation-theoretic approach to default reasoning. *Journal of Artificial Intelligence*, **93**(1–2), 63–101.

Bonnefon, J.-F. & Politzer, G. (2007). Pragmatic conditionals, conditional pragmatics, and the pragmatic component of conditional reasoning. (This volume).

Bratman, M. E., Israel, D. J., & Pollack, M. E. (1988). Plans and resource-bounded practical reasoning. *Computational Intelligence*, **4**, 349–355.

Clark, K.L. (1978). Negation by failure. In Gallaire, H. and Minker, J. (Eds.), *Logic and Databases* (pp. 293–322). Plenum Press.

Colmerauer, A., Kanoui, H., Pasero, R., & Roussel, P. (1973). *Un systeme de communication homme*-machine *en Francais*. Research report, Groupe d'Intelligence Artificielle, Universite d'Aix-Marseille II, Luminy.

Console, L., Theseider Dupre, D., & Torasso, P. (1991). On the relationship between abduction and deduction. *Journal of Logic and Computation*, **1**(5), 661–690.

d'Inverno, Luck, M. M., Georgeff, M. P., Kinny, D., & Wooldridge, M. (1998). A formal specification of dMARS. In: *Intelligent Agents IV: Proceedings of the Fourth International Workshop on Agent Theories, Architectures and Languages. Lecture Notes in Artificial Intelligence*, **1365**. Springer-Verlag, 155–176.

Dancygier, B. (1998). *Conditionals and Prediction. Time, Knowledge, and Causation in Conditional Constructions*. Cambridge: Cambridge University Press.

De Raedt, L. & Kersting, K. (2003). Probabilistic logic learning. In: SIGKDD. *Explorations*, **5/1**, 31–48.

Dung, P. M., Kowalski, R., & Toni, F. (2006). Dialectic proof procedures for assumption-based, admissible argumentation. *Journal of Artificial Intelligence*, **170**(2), 114–159.

van Emden, M. (2006). The early days of logic programming: A personal perspective. *The Association of Logic Programming Newsletter*, Vol. 19 n. 3, August 2006. http://www.cs.kuleuven.ac.be/~dtai/projects/ALP/newsletter/aug06/

van Emden, M. & Kowalski, R. (1976). The semantics of predicate logic as a programming language. *JACM*. **23**(4), 733–742.

Fung, T.H. & Kowalski, R. (1997). The IFF proof procedure for abductive logic programming. *Journal of Logic Programming*.

Gelfond, M. & Lifschitz, V. (1990). Logic programs with classical negation. *Proceedings of the Seventh International Conference on Logic Programming* (pp. 579–597). MIT Press.

Godfrey, P., Grant, J., Gryz, J., & Minker, J. (1998). Integrity constraints: semantics and applications. In *Logics for databases and information systems* (pp. 265–306). Kluwer, Norwell, MA, USA.

Kakas, A., Kowalski, R., & Toni, F. (1998). The role of logic programming in abduction. In D. Gabbay, C.J. Hogger, J.A. Robinson (Eds.), *Handbook of Logic in Artificial Intelligence and Programming 5*. (pp. 235–324). Oxford University Press.

Kakas, A., Mancarella, P., Sadri, S., Stathis, K., & Toni, F. (2004). *The KGP model of agency,* ECAI04, General European conference on artificial intelligence, (pp. 33–37). Valencia, Spain.

Kowalski, R. (1973). Predicate logic as programming language. Memo 70, department of artificial intelligence, Edinburgh University. Also in *Proceedings IFIP Congress,* Stockholm, North Holland Publishing Co., 1974, 569–574. Reprinted In *Computers for Artificial Intelligence Applications,* (eds. B. Wah, and G.-J. Li), IEEE Computer Society Press, Los Angeles, 1986, 68–73.

Kowalski, R. (1974). *Logic for Problem Solving.* DCL Memo 75, department of artificial intelligence, U. of Edinburgh. Expanded edition published by North Holland Elsevier 1979. Also at http://www.doc.ic.ac.uk/~rak/.

Kowalski, R. (1995). Using metalogic to reconcile reactive with rational agents. In K. Apt and F. Turini (Eds.) *Meta-Logics and Logic Programming,* MIT Press.

Kowalski, R. (2001). Artificial intelligence and the natural world. *Cognitive Processing,* **4**, 547–573.

Kowalski, R. (2006). The logical way to be artificially Intelligent. *Proceedings of CLIMA VI.* F. Toni and P. Torroni (Eds.), (pp. 1–22). Springer Verlag, LNAI.

Kowalski, R. & Kuehner, D. (1971). Linear resolution with selection function. *Artificial Intelligence,* Vol. **2**, 227–260. Reprinted in *Anthology of Automated Theorem-Proving Papers,* Vol. 2, Springer-Verlag, 1983, 542–577.

Kowalski, R. & Sadri, F. (1999). From logic programming towards multi-agent systems. *Annals of Mathematics and Artificial Intelligence,* **25**, 391–419.

Kowalski, R. & Sergot, M. (1986). A logic-based calculus of events. In *New Generation Computing,* **4**(1), 67–95. Also in the language of time: A Reader (eds. Inderjeet Mani, J. Pustejovsky, and R. Gaizauskas) Oxford University Press. 2005.

Kowalski, R., Sadri, F., & Soper, P. (1987). Integrity checking in deductive databases. In: *Proceedings of VLDB,* (pp. 61–69). Morgan Kaufmann, Los Altos, Ca.

Kowalski, R., Toni, F., & Wetzel, G. (1998). Executing suspended logic programs. *Fundamenta Informatica,* **34**(3), 1–22.

Kunen, K. (1987). Negation in logic programming. *Journal of Logic Programming,* **4**(4), 289–308.

Laird, J. E., Newell, A., & Rosenblum, P. S. (1987). SOAR: an architecture for general intelligence. *Artificial Intelligence,* **33**(1), 1–64.

Lloyd, J. W. & Topor, R. W. (1984). Making PROLOG more expressive. *Journal of Logic Programming,* **1**(3), 225–240.

McCarthy, J. (1958). Programs with common sense, *Symposium on Mechanization of Thought Processes.* Teddington, England: National Physical Laboratory.

McCarthy, J. (1980). Circumscription – A form of non-monotonic reasoning. *Artificial Intelligence,* **13**, 27–39.

McDermott, D. & Doyle. (1980). Nonmonotonic logic I. *Artificial Intelligence,* **13**, 41–72.

Minsky, M. (1974). A framework for representing knowledge. Technical report: AIM-306, Cambridge, MA: Massachusetts Institute of Technology.

Moore, R. C. (1985). Semantical considerations on nonmonotonic logic. *Artificial Intelligence,* **25**, 75–94.

Newell, A. (1973). Production systems: Models of control structure. In W. Chase (Ed.), *Visual Information Processing* (pp. 463–526). New York: Academic Press.

Newell, A. (1990). *Unified theories of cognition.* MA, USA: Harvard University Press Cambridge.

Newell, A., Shaw, J. C., & Simon, H.A. (1957). Empirical explorations of the logic theory machine. Proc. Western Joint Comp. Conf, 218–239.

Nicolas, J. M. & Gallaire, H. (1978). Database: Theory vs. interpretation. In H. Gallaire and J. Minker (Eds.), *Logic and Databases.* New York: Plenum.

Pearl, J. (1988). *Probabilistic Reasoning in Intelligent Systems.* San Mateo, CA: Morgan Kaufmann.

Politzer G. & Bonnefon J-F. (2006). Two varieties of conditionals and two kinds of defeaters help reveal two fundamental types of reasoning. *Mind and Language,* **21**, 484–503.

Politzer G. & Bonnefon J-F. Two aspects of reasoning competence: A challenge for current accounts and a call for new conceptual tools. In M. Oaksford and N. Chater (Eds.), *Cognition and conditionals: Probability and logic in human thinking* (pp. 371–386). Oxford: Oxford University Press.

Poole, D., Goebel, R., & Aleliunas R. (1987). Theorist: a logical reasoning system for defaults and diagnosis. In N. Cercone and G. McCalla (Eds.), *The Knowledge Frontier: Essays in the Representation of Knowledge* (pp. 331–352). Springer Verlag, New York.

Poole, D. (1993). Probabilistic horn abduction and Bayesian networks. *Artificial Intelligence*, **64**(1), 81–129.

Poole, D. (1997). The independent choice logic for modeling multiple agents under uncertainty. *Artificial Intelligence*, **94**, 7–56.

Rao, A. S. (1996). Agents breaking away. In Walter Van de Velde and John W. Perrame (Eds.), *Lecture Notes in Artificial Intelligence, Volume 1038,* Amsterdam, Netherlands: Springer Verlag.

Rao, A. S. & Georgeff, M. P. (1991). *Modeling rational agents with a BDI*-architecture. Second international conference on principles of knowledge representation and reasoning. 473–484.

Reiter, R. (1978). On closed world data bases. In H. Gallaire and J. Minker (Eds.), *Logic and Data Bases* (pp. 119–140). New York: Plenum.

Reiter, R. (1980). A logic for default reasoning. *Artificial Intelligence*, **13**, 81–132.

Robinson, J. A. (1965). A machine-oriented logic based on the resolution principle. *Journal of the ACM*, **12**(1), 23–41.

Russell, S. J. & Norvig, P. (2003). *Artificial Intelligence: A Modern Approach* (2nd ed.), Upper saddle river, NJ: Prentice Hall.

Sagonas, K., Swift, T., & Warren, D. (1994). XSB as an efficient deductive database engine. In *ACM SIGMOD, ACM SIGMOD Record archive*, **23**(2), 442–453.

Sato, T. (1995). A statistical learning method for logic programs with distribution semantics. In *Proceedings of the 12th International Conference on Logic Programming*. MIT Press. 715–729.

Shoham, Y. (1991). AGENT0: A simple agent language and its interpreter. In *Proceedings of the Ninth National Conference on Artificial Intelligence*, (AAAI-91), AAAI Press/MIT Press, Anaheim, California, USA, 704–709.

Shortliffe, E. (1976). *Computer-based Medical Consultations: MYCIN*. North Holland: Elsevier.

Simon, H. (1999). Production systems. In R. Wilson and F. Keil (Eds.), *The MIT Encyclopedia of the Cognitive Sciences* (pp. 676–677). MIT Press.

Sperber, D., Cara, F., & Girotto, V. (1995). Relevance theory explains the selection task. *Cognition*, **52**, 3–39.

Stenning, K. & van Lambalgen, M. (2004). A little logic goes a long way: basing experiment on semantic theory in the cognitive science of conditional reasoning. *Cognitive Science*, **28**(4), 481–529.

Stenning, K. & van Lambalgen, M. (2005). Semantic interpretation as computation in nonmonotonic logic: the real meaning of the suppression task. *Cognitive Science*, **29**(6), 919–996.

Stenning, K. & van Lambalgen M. (2008). *Human reasoning and cognitive science.* MIT Press.

Thagard, P. (2005). *Mind: Introduction to Cognitive Science.* Second Edition. MIT Press.

Wason, P. C. (1964). Reasoning. In B. Foss (Ed.), *New Horizons in Psychology*. Harmondsworth: Penguin Books.

Wason, P. C. (1968). Reasoning about a rule. *The Quarterly Journal of Experimental Psychology*, **20**(3), 273–281.

Winograd, T. (1971). *Procedures as a Representation for Data in a Computer Program for Understanding Natural Language* MIT AI Technical Report 235, February 1971. Also published as a full issue of the journal *Cognitive Psychology* **3**(1), 1972, and as a book, *Understanding Natural Language* (Academic Press, 1972).

Appendix A

The minimal model semantics of logic programming

Horn clause programs

The minimal model semantics is consistent with the declarative reading of clauses as implications in classical logic. However, in programming and database contexts and with Horn clause programs **P**, the semantics is also much simpler than in classical logic. In such cases, because clauses always have positive conclusions, it is natural to regard the set of clauses **P** as defining the set of positive, atomic sentences **A** that are logically implied by **P**.

This relationship between **P** and an atomic sentence **A** can be understood purely in terms of classical, logical consequence:

A is true in every model of **P**.

However, sets of Horn clauses **P** have the special property (van Emden & Kowalski, 1976) that there exists a *unique minimal model* **M** of **P** such that:

For every atomic sentence **A**,

A is true in every model of **P** if and only if **A** is true in **M**.

This minimal model **M** can be represented syntactically as the set of all atomic sentences **A** that are true in **M**. The model **M** is *minimal* in the sense that it is the smallest set of atomic sentences that is a model of **P**.

For example, the Horn clauses, which define equality and addition and multiplication for the natural numbers:

$X + 0 = X$
$X + (Y + 1) = (Z + 1) \; if \, X + Y = Z$
$X \cdot 1 = X$
$X \cdot (Y + 1) = W \; if \, X \cdot Y = Z \; and \; Z + X = W$

have a unique minimal model, which is the standard model of arithmetic. In contrast, the completion of the Horn clause program is equivalent to the Peano axioms of arithmetic, without the axioms of induction.

The minimal model can be constructed in the limit, simply by repeatedly applying *modus ponens* and universal instantiation in all possible ways to all the clauses in **P**. This model construction property can also be interpreted as the completeness property of forward reasoning for atomic consequences. Backward reasoning, in the form of SLD-resolution (Kowalski, 1973/1974), which is equivalent to the search tree proof procedure, is also sound and complete for atomic consequences of Horn clauses.

The minimal model semantics of negation

The simplest case is that of a Horn clause program **P** and the negation *not G* of a positive atomic sentence G. According to the minimal model semantics:

not G holds if and only if *not G* is *true* in the minimal model **M** of **P**.

More generally, for any sentence *G*, including any sentence of first-order logic:

> *G holds* if and only if *G* is *true* in **M**.

Backward reasoning and negation as infinite failure are sound and complete inference rules for this semantics. In other words:

> *G succeeds* if and only if *G* is *true* in **M**.

This property depends upon the rewriting of first-order formulae into goals that are conjunctions of literals augmented with auxiliary clauses, as mentioned earlier.

The minimal model semantics can be extended in a number of different ways to the more general case of normal logic programs *P*, which contain negative literals in the conditions of clauses. One of the simplest and most natural of these extensions interprets *not G* literally as *G does not hold* and expands *P* with a set Δ of true sentences of the form *not G*. The phrase *does not hold* can be treated as a positive auto-epistemic predicate, so that the expansion *P* ∪ Δ can be treated as a Horn clause program, which has a unique minimal model **M**:

> **M** is a *model* of *P* if all the sentences in Δ are true in **M**.[13]

It is common to restrict auto-epistemic expansions Δ to ones that are total or maximal.[14] For simplicity, in this paper, I refer to this semantics and its variants simply and collectively as the *minimal model semantics* of negation as failure.

A program with negation as failure can have several such minimal models. According to the *credulous* version of this semantics,

> *a goal holds if and only if it is true in some minimal model.*

According to the *sceptical* version of the same semantics,

> *a goal holds if and only if it is true in all minimal models.*

In both cases, the goal can be any sentence of first-order logic, and backward reasoning and negation as infinite failure can be used to determine whether or not a goal holds.

---

[13] In other words, there is no *not G* in Δ such that *G* belongs to **M**.

[14] If Δ consists of *all* such true sentences, then the resulting model is called a *stable model* (Gelfond and Lifschitz, 1990). A program can have many or no stable models. For example, the program {*p if not q, q if not p*} has two stable models {*p, not q*} and {*q, not p*}, but the program {*p if not p*} has no stable models.

Appendix B

Conditionals in natural language

Part of the problem with understanding natural language conditionals is the problem of translating them into logical form. We saw an example of this in the motivating example at the beginning of the paper. However, the completion semantics suggests that there can be an added difficulty with choosing between different logical forms, corresponding to the two directions of the completion of a definition.

Switching the direction of conditionals

Consider, for example, the two clauses:

> *A if B.*
> *A if C.*

whose completion is

> *A if and only if B or C.*

The only-if-half of the completion is implicit in the original set of two clauses. But it is also possible to write the two clauses in the *switched form,* in which the only-if half is explicit and the if-half is implicit:

> *B or C if A.*

The disjunction in the conclusion of the switched form can be eliminated by using negative conditions, yielding the switched clauses:

> *B if A and not C.*
> *C if A and not B.*

For example, the two clauses for getting help can be transformed into the following switched forms:

> *you have pressed the alarm signal button or you shouted loudly if you get help.*
> *you have pressed the alarm signal button if you get help and you have not shouted loudly.*
> *you shouted loudly if you get help and you have not pressed the alarm signal button.*

The completion semantics, therefore, justifies four ways of representing the same conditional relationship: the if-form, the if-and-only-if form, the only-if form and the only-if form with negative conditions. Both the first and the fourth representation can be represented as logic programming clauses, and it can be difficult for a programmer to know which representation to use.

In applications such as fault diagnosis in AI, different kinds of representation are common. The first representation is common because it models causality in the form *effect if cause.* But this representation requires the use of abduction to explain observations. The fourth representation, which models causality in the switched form *cause if effect and not other-causes,* is also common because it requires only the use of deduction.

Truncated conditionals

Bonnefon and Politzer (2007) observe that many conditionals in natural language have a truncated form $A \rightarrow \Phi$ that, to be understood fully, needs to be put into a wider context of the form:

$(A \& A1 \& \ldots \& A_\alpha) \text{ or } (B \& B1 \& \ldots \& B_\beta) \text{ or} \ldots \text{or } (C \& C1 \& \ldots \& C_\nu) \rightarrow \Phi$

In this wider context, there may be both additional, unstated conditions $(A_1 \& \ldots \& A_\alpha)$ and additional, unstated, alternative ways $(B \& B_1 \& \ldots \& B_\beta) \text{ or} \ldots \text{or } (C \& C_1 \& \ldots \& C_\nu)$ of establishing the conclusion Φ.

But, as we have seen, this wider context is exactly a logic program, which can also be expressed in the completion form:

$(A \& A_1 \& \ldots \& A_\alpha) \text{ or } (B \& B_1 \& \ldots \& B_\beta) \text{ or} \ldots \text{or } (C \& C_1 \& \ldots \& C_\nu)) \leftrightarrow \Phi$

The completion suggests the alternative possibility that a conditional might, instead, be a truncated form of the switched, only-if half $\Phi \rightarrow A$ of the wider context. I will come back to this possibility in the next section.

But, first, consider the following example of a simple truncated conditional, in logic programming form:

X flies if X is a bird.

The wider context is a more precise statement that includes extra conditions and alternative ways of flying. In most AI knowledge representation languages, it is common to express the conditional more precisely (although not as completely as in Bonnefon and Politzer's wider context) by lumping all of the extra conditions into a single condition, which is assumed to hold by default. For example:

X flies if X is a bird and not X is unable to fly.

Here the predicate *X is unable to fly* can be defined by other clauses, such as:

X is unable to fly if X is crippled.
X is unable to fly if X has not left its nest. etc.

which is equivalent to specifying other conditions for the clause. The minimal model and completion semantics both incorporate the closed world assumption that, unless there is evidence that a bird is unable to fly, then the bird is assumed to fly by default.

In general, the full alternative:

$(A \& A_1 \& \ldots \& A_\alpha) \rightarrow \Phi$

which spells out all the missing conditions of a truncated conditional $A \rightarrow \Phi$ can be expressed in logic programming style with a default condition, which can be defined separately. For example in the form:

Φ if A & not exceptional
exceptional if not A_1….
exceptional if not A_α

Typically, the condition A of a truncated conditional $A \rightarrow \Phi$ is the most significant of the conditions $A \& A_1 \& \ldots \& A_\alpha$, and the truncated conditional can be regarded as an *approximation* of the full alternative $(A \& A_1 \& \ldots \& A_\alpha) \rightarrow \Phi$.

The precise form, say $A \& \text{not exceptional} \rightarrow \Phi$, of a truncated conditional can be viewed as a solution of the *qualification problem*: How to suitably qualify a conclusion to adequately account for all its conditions, without specifying them all in advance and in detail. This precise form of the truncated conditional has the advantage that the conclusion can be qualified precisely from the outset by means of a single default condition, and exceptions to that condition can be spelled out separately in successively more precise formulations. The qualification problem is one aspect of the notorious *frame problem* in Artificial Intelligence, which has a similar solution.[15]

Truncated and switched conditionals

I argued in the previous section that the completion semantics explains why it may be difficult to determine the right direction for a conditional. This difficulty is compounded when a conditional is a truncated conditional $A \to \Phi$, which is part of a wider context

$$(A \& A_1 \& ... \& A_\alpha) \text{ or } (B \& B_1 \& ... \& B_\beta) \text{ or...or } (C \& C_1 \& ... \& C_v) \to \Phi$$

because the converse of the truncated conditional $\Phi \to A$ is itself a truncation of the switched form:

$$\Phi \to (A \& A_1 \& ... \& A_\alpha) \text{ or } (B \& B_1 \& ... \& B_\beta) \text{ or...or } (C \& C_1 \& ... \& C_v)$$

Understanding these two different ways in which a natural language conditional relates to its wider context might help to explain how people reason with conditionals. Consider the following example from (Politzer & Bonnefon, 2006).

Given the two sentences:

If an object looks red, then it is red.
This object looks red.

it is natural to draw the conclusion:

This object is red.

However, given the additional sentence:

If an object is illuminated by red light, then it looks red.

it is natural to withdraw the conclusion. But it is not natural to combine the two conditionals and draw the obviously false conclusion:

If an object is illuminated by red light, then it is red.

This way of reasoning can be explained if the two conditionals both refer to the same wider context, but the first one is switched. In logic programming, this wider context can be expressed in the clausal form:

An object looks red if it is red and not abnormal.
An object looks red if it is illuminated by a red light and not abnormal'.

In this analysis, the first inference that *this object is red* is explained by interpreting the first clause as the *only* clause that can be used in establishing that *an object looks red* and interpreting the first conditional as the switched, only-if half of the completion of the clause.

The withdrawal of the inference is explained by interpreting the new conditional as indicating that there is an additional alternative way of establishing that *an object looks red*, as represented by

---

[15] For example, in the event calculus (Kowalski and Sergot, 1986), the fact that a property is assumed to hold from the time it is initiated until it has been terminated is expressed in the form:

P holds at time T_2 if an event E initiates P at time T_1 and $T_1 < T_2$

and not (an event E' terminates P at time T and $T_1 < T < T_2$)

the second clause of the logic program. The only-if half of the two clause program no longer implies the withdrawn inference.

The failure to draw the obviously false conclusion is explained by the fact that in the wider context, the meaning of the two conditionals is actually the two clauses, which express alternative ways of establishing the same conclusion, and which do not combine to imply the false conclusion.

In summary, the example illustrates that a pair of natural language conditionals whose surface structure has the form:

$$\Phi \rightarrow A$$
$$B \rightarrow \Phi$$

Might actually have a very different deep structure, say:

(A & not abnormal) or (B & not abnormal') $\leftrightarrow \Phi$

or in clausal form:

Φ *if A & not abnormal*
Φ *if B & not abnormal'*

Chapter 16

Towards a reconciliation of mental model theory and probabilistic theories of conditionals

Sonja M. Geiger and Klaus Oberauer

Conditional sentences and thoughts are ubiquitous in everyday life. For example, we might have an idea of the whereabouts of our friend depending on current weather conditions, and could express this as:

> Example 1: 'If the weather is sunny, then Emma will be at the beach'.

Knowing that Emma is a surfer on the Australian west coast, this conditional would seem highly likely. Looking out of the window on a beautiful day we will therefore happily conclude that we could find Emma on the beach.

In other circumstances it might not be sufficient to be fairly confident in a conditional. Consider a judge who has to decide whether a piece of evidence should be allowed in court. The prosecutor has presented the following assumption:

> Example 2: 'If John has touched the weapon, then his fingerprints are on it'.

Should the judge allow the jurors to conclude that John did not touch the weapon (and thus is likely to be innocent) from the presented evidence that his fingerprints are not on the weapon? Whereas for the former conditional, a judgement based on a degree of belief might do the circumstances justice, the latter example calls for an infallible judgement that ideally should not allow any degree of uncertainty. One recurrent theme of this chapter will be the ways in which people treat uncertainty in their thinking with conditionals, and the ways in which competing theories of conditionals treat uncertainty.

The psychological investigation of how people think about conditional sentences is concerned with two main questions:

1. How do people *interpret* conditional sentences?
2. How do people *reason from* conditional sentences?

The two questions are linked because people's *interpretation* of a conditional is likely to influence the way they *reason from* it. We will discuss theoretical assumptions and evidence regarding both questions.

Two theories of conditionals

Two major theoretical approaches currently compete in explaining human reasoning about and with conditionals, the mental model theory (MMT) and the family of probabilistic theories. The theory of mental models (Johnson-Laird, 1983; 2001; Johnson-Laird & Byrne, 1991; 2002) assumes that people represent the meaning of a conditional sentence by models of the possibilities compatible with the sentence. The original model theory was a theory of deductive inference with no place for uncertainty: Given a set of premises, a situation was regarded as either possible or impossible, and thus, a conclusion was logically valid or invalid, with no degrees in between. Two later augmentations enable the MMT to incorporate uncertainty. One is the assumption that people draw on domain knowledge to build models of counterexamples; the other is the possibility to assign numerical values reflecting the probability of each of the possibility the models represent. Both augmentations will be discussed in the next section.

Over the last decade, alternatives to MMT have been put forward. These theories have in common the assumption that people represent conditionals not in terms of models of possibilities, but in terms of subjective probabilities; therefore we call them probabilistic theories (Evans & Over, 2004; Oaksford & Chater, 1995; 2001). Uncertainty lies at the heart of probabilistic theories; people are assumed to endorse propositions, and to draw inferences, with varying degrees of belief expressed as subjective probabilities. The 'suppositional theory' of Evans and Over (2004) focuses on the interpretation of conditionals. The probabilistic account of Oaksford and Chater (2001, Oaksford, Chater, & Larkin, 2000) focuses on the four basic inferences from conditionals in which a conditional premise 'if p then q' is combined with one of the four possible minor premises (p, not-p, q, or not-q). A third theory that will be discussed in the reasoning section is the dual process account by Verschueren, Schaeken, and d'Ydevalle (2005). Although it is not a pure probabilistic theory, but rather a theory that combines assumptions of both major approaches mentioned above, it also relies to a great extent on subjective probabilities (or 'likelihoods', as the authors call them).

In what follows we will discuss evidence concerning the two main research questions on conditionals in the light of the two theoretical approaches, the MMT and the probabilistic theories. We will show that probabilistic theories (in particular the suppositional theory) account well for people's interpretations of conditionals, but are much less successful in explaining inferences from conditionals. Conversely, MMT fails to capture people's interpretations of conditionals, but accounts well for how they draw conclusions from conditionals.

Interpretation of conditionals

The mental model theory

According to the MMT, conditional sentences are represented by mental models of possibilities that are compatible with this sentence. A fully fleshed out set of models of a statement of the form 'if p then q' comprises all possible combinations of p or $\neg p$ with q or $\neg q$ that are compatible with the conditional (the hook symbol '$\neg$' stands for 'not'). These are the pq conjunction and the two conjunctions involving $\neg p$. For our Example 2, the mental models would be:

Touched the weapon	fingerprints on it (pq case)
Didn't touch the weapon	fingerprints on it ($\neg pq$ case)
Didn't touch the weapon	no fingerprints on it ($\neg p \neg q$ case)

Depending on a person's capacity to hold multiple models in working memory simultaneously, all three or only the first (initial) model will be represented. A core principle of MMT is the *principle of truth*: Models represent only situations compatible with the premises, not situations ruled out by the premise (i.e., the $p \neg q$ *case*).

Unlike a basic conditional, for content-rich conditionals the principle of pragmatic or semantic modulation, introduced by Johnson-Laird and Byrne (2002), allows this basic set of models to be modified by people's knowledge of the subject matter of a conditional and by the pragmatic

Table 16.1 Truth table cases for the conditional 'If the weather is sunny, Emma is at the beach'

Situation	Example	No of days
pq	Sunny weather days on which Emma is at the beach	15
p¬q	Sunny weather days on which Emma is *not* at the beach	5
¬pq	Bad weather days on which Emma is at the beach.	2
¬p¬q	Bad weather days on which Emma is *not* at the beach.	8

context of its utterance. For instance, knowing about ways in which a person can touch a weapon without leaving fingerprints would modulate the mental models a seasoned criminalist builds for Example 2, such that a model of 'John touched the weapons, and his fingerprints are not on it' would be included as well.

An early technique for investigating people's interpretation of conditionals is the classic truth-table tasks. Participants are asked to evaluate the truth or falseness of a conditional sentence 'if p then q' for the four cases of a truth table, that is, the four possible combinations of p and not-p with q and not-q (cf. Table 16.1). Johnson-Laird and Tagart (1969) found that people judge the *pq* case as rendering the conditional true, the *p¬q* case as rendering it false, and the two *¬p* cases as irrelevant. This pattern, called the *defective truth- table* pattern, has been widely replicated since (e.g., Evans, Handley, Neilens, & Over, 2007; Oberauer, Geiger, Fischer, & Weidenfeld, 2007).

The MMT in its current formulation[1] has problems with explaining the truth-table data. According to the principle of truth only true cases should be represented. If a conditional is initially represented with a single explicit model of *pq* there is no mechanism to enable people to distinguish between the three remaining cases, which are simply not represented. Likewise, if people flesh out all three models, there is no mechanism to distinguish between the *pq* and the two *¬p* cases, they are all represented in the same way. In either case, there is no way the theory can predict that people will judge the *pq* case as rendering the conditional true, the *p¬q* cases as rendering the conditional false, but the two *¬p* cases as irrelevant.

The probabilistic view

The defective truth-table pattern is readily explained under a probabilistic view of the conditional. The main assumption of the suppositional account of Evans & Over (2004) is that people assign a conditional 'if p then q' a probability corresponding to P(q|p). One way to attain this probability is to run a 'Ramsey test', in which people focus on the true antecedent cases and compute the ratio of true

---

[1] In the original version of the MMT of conditionals, Johnson-Laird and Byrne (1991) offer an explanation for the defective truth-table pattern along the following lines. They assume that people initially represent the conditional by a single explicit model of the *pq* conjunction, together with an implicit model of other possibilities, noted by three dots:

[p] q
...

The brackets around p signify that p is represented exhaustively, implying that the implicit model (symbolized by the three dots) cannot include *p*-models. With this representation, people could judge that the *pq* conjunction is compatible with the conditional, and they can determine that the *p¬q* conjunction is incompatible with it, because it cannot be included in the implicit models. As long as the implicit models are not fleshed out, however, people cannot make any judgements about the two cases involving ¬p, and hence, they judge them as irrelevant. In their later version of the MMT, Johnson-Laird and Byrne (2002) abandon the brackets, and with it the model based explanation for the defective truth table.

Imagine a deck of 2000 cards, each card having an A or B printed on it in either red or blue. There are:

900 cards with an A printed in red

100 cards with an A printed in blue

500 cards with a B printed in red

500 cards with a B printed in blue

A random sample of 10 cards is drawn from this deck.

How likely is it that the following sentence is true for this sample of 10 cards:

'If the card has an A, then it is printed in red'

Please give an answer ranging from 0 (absolutely impossible) to 100 (absolutely certain).

Fig. 16.1 Example for a probabilistic truth table task (Oberauer & Wilhelm, 2003).

consequent to false consequent cases within this mental simulation. Considering Example 1, 'If it is sunny, then Emma will be at the beach', this means that people focus on sunny days and try to estimate the proportion of those days Emma spent at the beach compared to days she spent somewhere else. Regarding Emma's whereabouts during the last month as summarized in Table 16.1, we can calculate the probability of the Emma-conditional as 15/20. To compute this probability, the two $\neg p$ cases (i.e., bad weather days), are irrelevant, and therefore judged as such in the classic truth table task.

More support for this view comes from studies with the probabilistic variant of the truth-table task (Evans et al., 2003, Oberauer & Wilhelm, 2003). In this task, researchers manipulate the objective $P(q|p)$ by assigning different frequencies to the truth-table cases. Participants are asked to what extent they are willing to believe a conditional under varying probability conditions. The design used in one such study (Oberauer & Wilhelm, 2003) is illustrated in Figure 16.1. This design orthogonally varies two probabilities, $P(q|p)$ and $P(pq)$. Several experiments with this design consistently yielded two findings. First, the majority of participants gave estimates of the probability of the conditional that closely covaried with $P(q|p)$, and often the estimates were even numerically close to the objective values of $P(q|p)$. Second, a substantial minority of participants gave $P(pq)$ as their estimate of the probability of the conditional. The same two findings were obtained with a slightly different design by Evans et al. (2003). Whereas the original experiments were conducted with conditionals with as little context and associations to world knowledge as possible, the two findings were meanwhile replicated with pseudonaturalistic conditionals embedded in fictitious context stories (Oberauer, Weidenfeld, & Fischer, 2007) and with everyday causal conditionals (Over, Hadjichristidis, Evans, Handley, & Sloman, 2007). Even when the task makes no mention of 'probability', but rather asks people simply to judge whether a given conditional is true or false, their judgements depend on the conditional probability of the consequent, given the antecedent (Oberauer & Wilhelm, 2003).

The probabilistic theories fare very well in light of these data. They predict the modal pattern in the classical truth-table task, and the believability judgements of the majority groups in studies using the probabilistic truth-table task. The judgements of the minority group can be explained by assuming sloppy execution of the Ramsey test (Evans et al., 2003; Oberauer, Geiger, et al., 2007). In support, Evans, Handley, Neilens, and Over (2007) found that the minority group had lower scores on an intelligence test.

The MMT on the other hand is challenged to explain the majority response in the probabilistic truth-table task. Johnson-Laird, Legrenzi, Girotto, Legrenzi, and Caverni (1999) extended the MMT to judgements about the probability of statements. They assumed that models can be assigned numerical values reflecting their probability or frequency, so that a possible situation, represented by a model, can be represented as being more or less likely to occur. The probability of a statement is computed as the proportion of cases that match one of the statement's models, which equals the sum of the probabilities assigned to its models. We thus can also calculate the probability of the Emma-conditional as the proportion of days matching models compatible with the conditional. As long as we treat the conditional as a basic conditional, these would be three models corresponding to three of the four cases in Table 16.1 (excluding the combination of 'sunny' and 'not on the beach'), and the probability of the conditional would be $1-P(p\neg q) = 25/30$. This value contrasts with $P(q|p) = 15/20$, which was the majority answer in all the studies with the probabilistic truth-table task summarized above. Alternatively, the MMT can assume that people work with an initial representation in which only the pq conjunction is represented explicitly. In that case they should give $P(pq) = 15/30$ for our example as their estimate. This was only a minority response in the numerous studies. Virtually nobody based their belief on $1-P(p\neg q)$.

Girotto and Johnson-Laird (2004) claim that the majority response also arises from model based reasoning. To arrive at $P(q|p)$ as an estimate of the probability of the conditional, people are said to judge the $p\neg q$ case as false and the two $\neg p$ cases as irrelevant, because the $\neg p$ cases are not explicitly represented. This explanation runs into the same problems as encountered above with the defective truth-table pattern: According to the *principle of truth* in the MMT, false cases (here: the $p\neg q$ case) shouldn't be represented at all and thus have the same status as the $\neg p$ cases that are not explicitly represented. There is no way within the MMT to distinguish between irrelevant and false cases in its current formulation. Without this distinction, a computation of $P(q|p)$ cannot be explained.

This brief overview of studies on how people interpret conditionals led to a fairly encouraging evaluation of probabilistic theories, and a very unfavourable evaluation of MMT. We will now turn to findings from the literature on inferences from conditionals and show that that evidence suggests largely the reverse conclusion.

Reasoning from conditionals

The mental model theory

Researchers interested in inferences from conditionals have mostly studied the four basic inference forms summarized in Table 16.2. According to the MMT, the ideally rational reasoning process involves three steps: in a first step reasoners represent the premises by a set of mental models

Table 16.2 Overview of the four conditional inference forms

	Major premise (conditional): If John touched the weapon, then his fingerprints are on it (If p, then q).	
	Minor premise	Default conclusion (inference acceptance)
MP	John has touched the weapon (p).	His fingerprints are on it (q).
MT	John's fingerprints are not on the weapon (¬q).	He has not touched it (¬p).
AC	John fingerprints are on the weapon (q).	He has touched it (p).
DA	John hasn't touched the weapon (¬p).	His fingerprints are not on it (¬q).

compatible with both premises, next they draw a conclusion that is novel and true in all models, and in the third step they test whether there are additional models that are compatible with the premises but not with the conclusion (so called 'counterexamples').

Actual reasoners deviate from this ideal process model because they may fail to include all possibilities compatible with the premises in their models. This explains why people often endorse the inferences that are not licensed by propositional logic (AC and DA) – they fail to represent the $\neg pq$ conjunction as a counterexample – and why they sometimes reject the logically valid MT inference – they fail to represent the $\neg p \neg q$ conjunction. A meta-analysis by Schroyens, Schaeken, and d'Ydewalle (2001) shows that the MMT gives a good account of the average endorsement frequencies of the four basic inference forms.

The MMT of conditional reasoning makes a number of specific predictions that were successfully tested. One of the assumptions of MMT is that people are more likely to flesh out all three models of a conditional with increasing mental capacity. Barouillet, Grosset, and Lecas (2000) could show that, as they grow older, children move from an inference pattern based on a single model of the pq conjunction (accept MP and AC, reject DA and MT) to a pattern based on two models (pq and $\neg p \neg q$, leading to acceptance of all four inferences) and finally to a pattern based on all three models (accept MP and MT, reject AC and DA). Further evidence for the operation of mental models comes from investigations of illusory (i.e., logically not licensed) inferences. Applying the principle of truth to certain combinations of premises, Johnson-Laird and Savary (1999) could show that people indeed make illusory inferences, sometimes even inferring as necessary what is actually impossible.

Although designed as a theory of deductive reasoning, MMT has been applied early on to reasoning in contexts of uncertainty. Byrne (1989) was the first to demonstrate that counterexamples based on domain knowledge suppress the acceptance of logically warranted inferences. For example, if presented with the following information:

(1) 'If John has touched the weapon, then his fingerprints are on it'.

(2) 'If the weapon has not been wiped, then the fingerprints are on it'.

(3) 'John has touched the weapon',

people tend to reject the conclusion 'John's fingerprints are on the weapon' more often than when (2) is omitted. Thus, reminding people of a potential counterexample (i.e., a way of causing a $p \neg q$ combination) leads people to suppress the logically valid MP inference. Other experiments have shown that activating knowledge of alternative causes (e.g., reminding people that fingerprints could be transferred to a weapon using sticky tape) serve to suppress the inferences AC and DA. The suppression effect of counterexamples has been widely replicated since (Byrne, Espino, & Santamaria, 1999; Cummins, 1995; Cummins, Lubart, Alksnis, & Rist, 1991; DeNeys, Schaeken, & D'Ydewalle, 2003; Markovits & Potvin, 2001; Thompson, 1995). In the context of MMT, suppression effects are explained by assuming that activating counterexamples in one's knowledge base makes it more likely that people include a mental model of the counterexample in their models of the premises. Adding a model of the $p \neg q$ conjunction blocks MP and MT; adding a model of $\neg pq$ blocks AC and DA.

We next discuss how the three theories in the probabilistic camp explain reasoning with conditional premises.

The conditional probability model

Oaksford and Chater (2001, Oaksford et al., 2000) were the first to propose a probabilistic theory of drawing inferences from conditionals. Their main assumption is that people endorse a conclusion to the degree that their subjective conditional probability of that conclusion, given the minor premise, is high. Oaksford et al. (2000) presented a mathematical model with three parameters, P(p), P(q), and an exception parameter ε that is equal to P(¬q|p). From these parameters they derive the probabilities of the conclusion, given the minor premise, for each of the four basic inferences (see Table 16.3). For our example sentence, these conditional probabilities correspond to the following:

MP: P(q|p) = P(fingerprints | touched)

MT: P(¬p|¬q) = P (not touched | no fingerprints)

AC: P(p|q) = P (touched | fingerprints)

DA: P(¬q|¬p) = P (no fingerprints | not touched).

Oaksford et al. (2000) present data consistent with the model from three experiments in which P(p) and P(q) were manipulated. In the first two experiments, the probabilities were manipulated through explicit information about the frequency of cases given in the instructions; in the third experiment they were manipulated indirectly through the content material. Oberauer, Weidenfeld, and Hörnig (2004) tested the predictions of the probabilistic model of Oaksford et al. (2000), manipulating P(p) and P(q) through a probability learning procedure in which participants observed a series of exemplars, the features of which occurred with different frequencies. This study did not find the predicted effects of P(p) and P(q) on the endorsement of the basic inferences. There are two methodological differences between the Oaksford et al. (2000) experiments and those by Oberauer et al. (2004) that could explain the discrepant results. Oaksford et al. (2000) asked participants to rate the acceptability of the conclusions of the four basic inference forms on a six-point scale, whereas Oberauer et al., asked for a binary judgement whether or not the conclusion follows from the premises. Moreover, whereas Oberauer et al. (2004) gave the usual deductive-inference instruction, asking participants to evaluate whether the conclusion followed with logical necessity from the premises, Oaksford et al., gave no such instruction.

The suppositional theory

Evans and Over (2004) propose a dual-process theory of reasoning. One process (attributed to System 1) directly makes MP inferences, assigning a degree of belief in the conclusion that varies as a function of the probability of the conditional premise, which equals P(q|p). A second process (attributed to System 2) engages in more elaborate thought processes, among them a suppositional argument deriving the MT inference. This multi-step derivation starts from a hypothetical supposition of p, from which it derives q through an MP inference, and then notices a contradiction of that putative

Table 16.3 Conditional inferences and their respective probabilities according to different authors

	Evans and Over (2004)	Oaksford et al. (2000)	Verschueren et al. (2005) Thompson (1995)
MP	P(q|p)	P(q|p)	P(q|p) = sufficiency
MT	P(suppos) × P(q|p)	P(¬p|¬q)	P(q|p) = sufficiency
AC	P(converse) × P(p|q)	P(p|q)	P(p|q) = necessity
DA	P(Inverse) × P(¬q|¬p)	P(¬q|¬p)	P(p|q) = necessity

p = antecedent of the conditional, q = consequent. P(suppos) = probability of successfully carrying out the suppositional argument towards MT. P(converse) and P(inverse) are the probabilities of adding the converse or the inverse, respectively, to the set of premises.

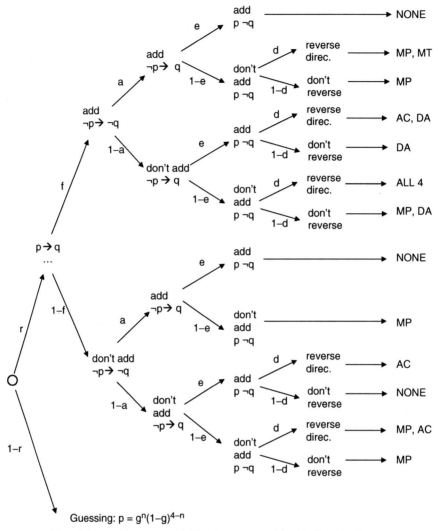

Fig. 16.2 Multinomial processing-tree model for the MMT model with directionality. Parameters: r = probability of engaging in reasoning, f = probability of fleshing out initial model (adding ¬p¬q model), a = probability of considering alternative causes (adding ¬pq model), e = probability of considering exceptional circumstances (adding p¬q model), d = probability of reversing direction of reasoning; g = probability of accepting any inference by guessing. At the end of each branch of the tree the predicted pattern of inferences accepted is shown. The probability of traversing each path is the product of the parameters along the path. From Oberauer (2006), with permission of Elsevier.

conclusion with the minor premise. The strength of the inference from the supposition of *p* to the supposition of *q* again depends on the believability of the conditional. Thus, to the degree that the suppositional argument is even attempted, the degree of belief assigned to the MT conclusion should also depend on P(*q*|*p*). Regarding AC and DA, Evans and Over (2004) assume that people might pragmatically add the converse (If *q* then *p*) and/or the inverse (If not *p* then not *q*) of the original conditional to the set of premises. If they do, they draw AC (converse) and DA (inverse), respectively, using the MP inference schema afforded by the first process.

The only direct test of the suppositional theory of reasoning we are aware of was conducted by one of us in the context of a study that formalized and competitively fitted several theories (Oberauer, 2006), which will be described below. In that study, the suppositional theory did not fare well.

A dual-process theory integrating probabilistic and model-based reasoning

Verschueren, Schaeken, and d'Ydewalle (2005) proposed a version of a dual-process theory that combines a probabilistic inference process with a model-based process. Their System-1 process is similar to that of the suppositional theory. It computes a degree of belief in the conclusion of all four inferences, depending on subjective conditional probabilities (called 'likelihoods' by Verschueren et al.). For MP and MT the relevant conditional probability is $P(q|p)$, reflecting the perceived sufficiency of the conditional. Unlike in the suppositional theory, the conditional probability determining endorsement of both AC and DA is $P(p|q)$, reflecting the perceived necessity of the conditional. That is, the more necessary the antecedent p (eg. for Example 2, touching the weapon) is thought to be for the consequent (fingerprints are on it), the higher a person's subjective $P(p|q)$, and the more belief is conferred on AC and DA through the probabilistic process. In Example 2, the antecedent is highly necessary for the consequent (it is hard to think of ways getting fingerprints on items without touching them) which predicts a high acceptance of AC and DA for this conditional, whereas it is only moderately sufficient (it is much easier to think of ways getting fingerprints off) which should lead to relatively low acceptance of MP and MT.

Sufficiency and necessity of a conditional are assumed to be derived by a quick, heuristic estimation process based on knowledge of relevant frequencies. A second process consists of searching for counterexamples that potentially falsify the putative conclusions derived by the fast heuristic process. This System-2 process is assumed to be based on mental models, and to yield categorical judgements. Thus, people reject the conclusion generated by System 1 whenever they can think of a counterexample to that conclusion, otherwise they accept the conclusion with the degree of belief provided by System 1.

As can be seen from Table 16.2, the theories of Oaksford et al. (2000), Evans and Over (2004), and Verschueren et al. (2005) agree in predicting that subjective conditional probabilities should affect the degree to which people endorse the basic inference forms. All three theories agree that endorsement of MP depends on $P(q|p)$, and endorsement of AC depends on $P(p|q)$. The theories differ in which probability they assume determines DA and MT.

A comparative test of reasoning theories

One of us tested the four theories of reasoning from conditionals discussed here, using two large data sets from web-based experiments in which participants evaluated the four basic inference forms (Oberauer, 2006). The theories were expressed as mathematical models. Three of them were formalized as multinomial processing-tree models (MMT, suppositional theory, and Verschueren's dual-process theory); the Oaksford et al. (2000) model was adapted to categorical evaluations by assuming a threshold on the probability of the conclusions that could vary between participants and was estimated as a free parameter. The models were evaluated by fitting them to the relative frequencies of the 16 possible evaluation patterns. By accepting or rejecting each of the four inference forms, each participant generated one pattern of decisions over MP, AC, DA, and MT (for instance, a participant who accepted MP and MT but rejected AC and DA produced pattern 1001).

Two models provided an acceptable fit to both data sets. One was a version of MMT augmented by a directional bias: Inferences in forward direction, from the antecedent to the consequent

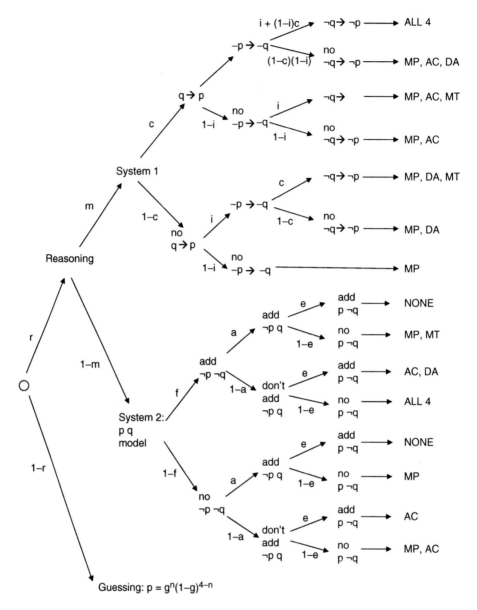

Fig. 16.3 Multinomial processing-tree model for the dual-process model. Parameters: r = probability of engaging in reasoning; m = probability of using System 1 (probabilistic system) for evaluating the inferences; c = probability of adding the converse as pragmatic implicature; i = probability of adding the inverse as pragmatic implicature; f = probability of adding the $\neg p \& \neg q$ mental model; a = probability of adding the, $\neg p \& \neg q$ mental model; e = probability of adding the exception model $p \& \neg q$; g = probability of accepting an inference through guessing. From Oberauer (2006), with permission of Elsevier.

(i.e., MP and DA) were assumed to be accepted more readily than inferences in backward direction. The other model providing a good fit was a dual-process model capturing the assumption of Verschueren et al. (2005). These two models are illustrated in Figure 16.2 and

Figure 16.3, respectively. Neither the Oaksford et al. (2000) model nor two versions of the suppositional theory could account for the data. The dual-process model includes a parameter governing the probability of basing conclusions on the probabilistic System 1 or on the model-based System 2. The parameter estimates obtained in Oberauer (2006) imply that in the majority of cases participants base their conclusions on 'System 2'.

The reason why only models that at least included MMT as a component were successful lies with the correlations between acceptance decisions on the four inference forms. People who accepted AC were more likely to also accept DA, and people who accepted DA were more likely to also accept MT. The first of these correlations points to the role of the $\neg pq$ contingency which, if added as a mental model, blocks both AC and DA. The second correlation can be explained by variability in whether or not people construct a model for the $\neg p \neg q$ contingency; only if they do they can make the DA and MT inferences. The correlations between inference acceptance decisions support the assumption of MMT that people reason about possible situations characterized by a conjunction of true or false antecedent with true or false consequent. The probabilistic models have no place for these conjunctions, but rather assigns probabilities to separate representations of antecedent and consequent. Therefore, they tend to predict more independence between acceptance decisions than there is in the data.

Conclusion

Purely probabilistic theories of reasoning from conditionals have met with mixed empirical success at best. The MMT, in contrast, has gained support from several experiments testing its predictions. When several formal models of reasoning were tested directly against each other, the two models fairing best were a version of MMT, and a dual-process model in which MMT described one of the processes.

Two questions and two theories: Steps toward integration

We find ourselves in the challenging situation of having two theoritical perspectives, both of which are supported by a substantial body of findings from one line of research each. Probabilistic theories are strongly supported by experiments asking about how people interpret conditionals, but they fail to account well for people's reasoning with conditional premises. MMT is strongly supported by data from reasoning experiments, but fails to account for people's interpretation of conditionals.

One reason for this puzzling picture could be that the two questions – the one about the meaning of conditionals and the one about reasoning – were addressed not only with different experimental paradigms but also with different methods. Experiments investigating people's interpretation of conditionals have gained much insight from the direct manipulation of frequencies or probabilities in the (often artificial) content domains of the conditionals in question. This method is likely to reveal the sensitivity of cognitive processes to probabilistic information, thus supporting a probabilistic view of the interpretation of conditionals. The literature on reasoning with conditionals, in contrast, has predominantly used the deduction paradigm, in which people are asked to take the premises as true, are not given any information about the task's content domain (and discouraged from drawing on any knowledge they may have about it), and are instructed to decide whether a conclusion follows with logical necessity. When the tasks are framed in this way, they are likely to reveal people's ability to represent what is possible, given a set of premises, and to manipulate these representations.

There is, of course, a strand of research on reasoning with conditionals that has addressed the role of domain knowledge and of uncertainty, starting with the study of Byrne (1989) on inference suppression mentioned above, and continued by others who more directly measured and manipulated people's domain-specific beliefs (Cummins et al., 1991, Cummins, 1995, Thompson, 1995, De Neys et al., 2002, 2003, Verschueren et al., 2005). The common approach of these studies is to ask a group of participants to rate a number of everyday causal conditionals such as, for instance, 'If John touched the weapon then his fingerprints are on it'. Some studies asked whether, and how many, counterexamples participants can think of to the conditional. There are two kinds of counterexamples: Cases in which the consequent is true but the antecedent is false, called 'alternative causes' (e.g., John did not touch the weapon but his fingerprints are on it nonetheless), and cases where the antecedent is true but the consequent is not, called 'disabling conditions' (e.g., John touched the weapon but his fingerprints are not on it). An alternative rating task is to ask people to what degree the antecedent is *sufficient* for the consequent, and to what degree it is a *necessary* condition for the consequent. The studies cited above, and others following them, have firmly established that these variables have a strong impact on how much people endorse the conclusions of the four standard inference forms with everyday causal conditionals as premises. In general, many disabling conditions, as well as low sufficiency, lead to lower acceptance rates of MP and MT; many alternative causes, and low necessity, lead to lower acceptance rates of AC and DA.

The theoretical interpretation of these findings is ambiguous. In the context of MMT, the standard interpretation follows Byrne (1989). Conditionals with many alternative causes are likely to remind reasoners of the possibility of cases in which the antecedent is false and the consequent true. Therefore, reasoners are likely to build a model of the $\neg pq$ conjunction, which blocks AC and DA. Conditionals with many disabling conditions are likely to activate knowledge of cases with true antecedent but false consequent, thereby encouraging the construction of a $p\neg q$ model, which blocks MP and MT. In the context of probabilistic theories, conditionals with a large number of disabling conditions are also characterized by low sufficiency or low subjective $P(q|p)$, and typically also by low $P(\neg p|\neg q)$. Likewise, conditionals with a large number of alternative causes, are characterized by a low necessity, or low $P(p|q)$, and usually also by low $P(\neg q|\neg p)$. Thus, both theoretical approaches can account for the existing findings on the impact of domain knowledge on reasoning with everyday causal conditionals.

There is a subtle distinction between the theoretical interpretations offered for these knowledge effects by MMT and by probabilistic theories. According to MMT, what matters is whether people consider a counterexample as a possibility. If they do, they build a model of it, and refrain from drawing the conclusion. Many variables could influence whether a counterexample is considered as possibility, among them the availability of counterexample cases in memory, the number of different counterexamples (the more there are, the more likely it is that reasoners think of at least one of them), and their subjective probability of occurrence. According to probabilistic theories, all that matters should be the relative frequency of occurrence of counterexamples. The proportion of $p\neg q$ counterexamples among all cases of p determines $P(q|p)$, and the proportion of $\neg pq$ counterexamples among all cases of q determines $P(p|q)$.

Two recent studies attempted to exploit these differences to distinguish between the MMT account and the probabilistic account of knowledge on reasoning with causal (and noncausal) conditionals. Both studies also obtained measures of people's degree of belief in the conditional, thereby enabling a direct comparison of the variables investigated on people's interpretation of conditionals, and their reasoning from these conditionals. Weidenfeld, Oberauer, and Hörnig (2005) constructed a set of pseudonaturalistic conditionals, that is, conditionals with fictitious content but set in a realistic context story, for example: 'If a dog suffers from the disease Midosis, then one finds the substance Xathylen in its blood' (both the disease and the substance were made up). For these conditionals the authors obtained ratings of how many disabling conditions and how many alternative causes participants could think of, ratings of the subjective conditional probability $P(q|p)$, ratings of the probability of the conditional itself, and judgements of acceptance or rejection of MP and MT inferences.

The different ratings were correlated with each other and with the acceptance rates for MP and MT, across conditionals, in a way consistent with previous research. For instance, conditionals with many disabling conditions received ratings of low $P(q|p)$ and ratings of low probability of the conditional, and their acceptance rates for MP and MT were relatively low. These correlations were used to test a path model (see Figure 16.4.) that included two paths through which the availability of counterexamples (here: $p\neg q$ cases) affected reasoning. The indirect path, mediated through subjective $P(q|p)$ and the subjective probability of the conditional, reflects the assumptions of the probabilistic view that the acceptance of MP and MT is a direct consequence of these probabilities, which in turn depend on knowledge about the possibility and likelihood of counterexamples. The direct path from counterexamples to inference acceptance rates reflects the assumption of MMT that being able to think of one or more counterexamples immediately gives rise to a mental model of that counterexample, which blocks acceptance of MP and MT. Weidenfeld et al. (2005) found that both paths had significant weights, but the weights of the direct path was stronger than that of the indirect path.

In our own study (Geiger and Oberauer, in press) we went one step further and separated two features of counterexamples, the number of different counterexamples people can think of for a particular conditional, and their expected frequency or probability of occurrence. Consider again the conditional in Example 1: One could think of many different disabling conditions that might prevent Emma from being on the beach on a sunny day (Emma might be sick, a Tsunami might have washed away the beach, a kidnapper might have snatched Emma, and so on). Yet, none of them might be thought of as very likely, so reasoners might still be inclined to infer with a high degree of confidence that, given the sun shines, Emma will be found on the beach. In contrast, consider the conditional of Example 2: There might be only two disabling conditions that come to mind for 'If John touched the weapon, his fingerprints are on it' (John could have wiped the weapon, and John could have worn gloves). Knowing that John is a smart and experienced criminal, however, would motivate reasoners to regard both possibilities as highly likely. Thinking of just one of them could therefore be sufficient to block the MT inference from 'John's fingerprints are not on the weapon' to 'John has not touched it'.

We conducted two experiments with fictional conditionals that bore no relation to participants' domain knowledge (e.g., conditionals about the features of animals on a newly discovered planet), in which we independently manipulated how many different disabling conditions were offered in the context stories, and the probability of all these disabling conditions taken together. In a third experiment, we drew on everyday conditionals that were rated by separate groups of participants; one group estimated how often disabling conditions (i.e., $p\neg q$ cases) are expected to occur for each conditional, and the other group was asked to list as many different disabling conditions as possible for each conditional. Based on these ratings we selected four sets of conditionals for the four design cells (crossing number of disabling conditions with frequency of disabling conditions) as premises in the inference tasks.

The consistent result from all three experiments was that the expected relative frequency of counterexamples had a large effect on the degree of endorsement of MP and MT inferences; the number of different counterexamples people could think of had only a minor effect. This result is in line with what should be expected from the probabilistic view, on which only the probability of counterexamples is relevant for the degree of belief in a conclusion. The MMT, in contrast, should predict that many different counterexamples make it more likely that at least one of them comes to mind and thereby triggers the construction of a model of that counterexample, independent of how frequent this case is expected to occur.

To summarize, the studies of Weidenfeld et al. (2005) and of Geiger and Oberauer (2007) yielded somewhat contradictory conclusions on the relative merits of MMT and the probabilistic view in explaining how people incorporate domain knowledge, and the uncertainty arising from it, in their reasoning processes. Whereas the path model of Weidenfeld et al. (2005) suggested a relatively minor role for probabilistic information in determining inference acceptance rates, the results of Geiger and Oberauer (2007) indicate that probabilistic (or frequency) information is the main determinant of inference endorsement. One potentially important difference between these studies is that Weidenfeld et al. (2005) asked people to make a binary decision to accept or reject the conclusions of MP and MT. In the Geiger and Oberauer (2007) experiments, we measured inference acceptance with a gradual answer scale reflecting the level of confidence with which a conclusion is drawn, ranging over six levels from 'I am very sure that I can draw this conclusion' to 'very sure I cannot draw this conclusion'. We speculate that the answer scale provided for the inference task affected how people reasoned toward an inference. When a categorical yes/no judgement is required, it seems appropriate to base this judgement on whether or not a counterexample is regarded as possible. When a graded rating of subjective confidence or degree of belief is asked for, people might be more willing to take into account not only the possibility of a counterexample but also its probability of occurrence.

To conclude, reasoning from conditionals is sensitive to probabilistic information, although the degree to which it affects reasoning, over and above knowledge about possibilities, seems to depend on contextual features such as the answer scale provided. A viable theory of reasoning therefore should not be limited to using representations of what is possible, but should also allow for representing information about the probability of each possibility, and specify algorithms for how this information is used. In the final section of this chapter we will sketch the outline of a modification of MMT that meets this requirement.

A probabilistic revision of mental model theory

We start by reviewing the fundamental differences between MMT and the probabilistic view. They concern two assumptions. First, the MMT assumes that the meaning of conditionals is represented by a set of mental models that are compatible with it, and thus, its probability is the sum of the probabilities across these models. This assumption is at odds with the data, and also with recent developments in the philosophy of logic (cf. Bennett, 2003). It seems appropriate to give it up, and endorse the probabilistic interpretation of conditionals instead. The second difference between the two theoretical viewpoints is that the reasoning processes specified in MMT works with representations of what is possible; they don't take into account the probability of these possibilities. Probabilistic approaches, in contrast, assume that inferences are based on the probabilities of certain possibilities. Given that proponents of MMT already introduced the notion of numerical annotations to models to represent their probabilities, it would not require a fundamental revision of MMT to make its reasoning processes sensitive to probabilities.

We therefore propose as a first theoretical step to revise MMT's assumption about the meaning of conditionals. Conditionals are not represented by a set of mental models, but by a production rule, that is, an element of procedural knowledge (Anderson, 1983). The production is to add a representation of the consequent q to every model of the antecedent p in working memory. This production can be regarded as the core meaning of 'if p then q' and is used in two procedures. One of them is a model-construction procedure. Whenever a model of the antecedent p is held in working memory, the construction procedure adds a model of q to it, thereby constructing a model of the pq conjunction.

The second procedure utilizing the core production is the Ramsey test for evaluating the degree of belief in a conditional in light of evidence, as first proposed by Evans et al. (2003) and Evans and Over (2004). When considering a conditional 'if p then q', this procedure starts by building a mental model of the antecedent p as a possibility (i.e., it represents the supposition that p is true). The core production expands this model by adding a representation of the consequent q to it. The Ramsey test proceeds by searching for information (in memory or the environment) on the frequency or probability of the situation represented by the initial supposition p, and on the frequency or probability of the expanded model pq. The subjective probability of the conditional is estimated as the ratio of $P(pq)$ to $P(p)$. The Ramsey test as described here differs slightly from the procedure described by Evans and colleagues, who proposed that $P(pq)$ is set in relation to $P(p\neg q)$. Estimating the frequency or probability of the $p\neg q$ conjunction would require building a model of this conjunction, that is, a model of a situation that is not possible under the conditional. This goes against the principle of truth in MMT, which is important for the theory's success in predicting, among other things, illusory inferences (Johnson-Laird & Savary, 1999). The Ramsey test as described here (following Oberauer, Geiger, et al., 2007) does not violate the principle of truth.

Reasoning with conditional premises is based on the construction of mental models of possibilities that consist of conjunctions of the truth or falsity of p with the truth or falsity of q, much as described in the original MMT. One difference from the original MMT is that the conditional premise is not represented by a set of models. Rather, models are constructed to represent the possibilities that are compatible with the *minor* premise. The conditional premise serves to constrain this set of models.

Thus, reasoning begins with placing a model of the minor premise in working memory. In the next step, this model is expanded by adding a component representing the other term mentioned in the conditional – that is, if the minor premise specifies the truth value of p, then the model is expanded by adding q or $\neg q$, and if the minor premise specifies the truth value of q, the initial model is expanded by adding p or $\neg p$. Because the minor premise does not say anything about the truth value of the second component, there are always two possibilities of expanding the initial model, leading to two models. For example, if the minor premise is 'p', the two models would be pq and $p\neg q$. At this point, the conditional premise exerts its constraining effect: The procedure that adds q to every representation of p produces a conflict with the $\neg q$ component in the $p\neg q$ model, and therefore that model is eliminated. Finally, reasoners evaluate whether the proposed conclusion holds in all models, or generate a conclusion that is true in all models.

Let's see how this basic mechanism of reasoning operates on the four basic inference forms, before expanding it by assumptions on the effect of domain knowledge and the representation of probabilities.

MP: First a model of minor premise p is built. The minor premise is compatible with two ways of expanding this model, adding q as well as adding $\neg q$. The addition of q is assisted by the production rule representing of the conditional, whereas the addition of $\neg q$ is blocked by it. Thus, only the pq model is established in working memory. Based on this model, the inference 'q' can be drawn.

AC: A model of minor premise q is built. It can be expanded by adding p or by adding $\neg p$. The conditional does not constrain this expansion, so both models, pq *and* $\neg pq$, are built. On the basis of both models, no firm conclusion can be drawn about p. There are, however, two ways in which reasoners can arrive at the typical AC conclusion, the affirmation of p. First, they can endorse the converse of the given conditional, 'if q then p', as a pragmatic implicature (Evans & Over, 2004). This converse conditional would generate a production rule that adds a p component to every q. Hence, the pq model would be generated but the $\neg pq$ model would be blocked. Second, limitations of working memory capacity could allow only one model to be held. In that case, there could be various causes for preferring the pq model over the $\neg pq$ model, among them a preference for modelling cases that match the terms mentioned in the conditional (Evans & Lynch, 1972), or a tendency to avoid negations (in cases where antecedent and consequent of the conditional are formulated without negations). If reasoners end up with a single model of the pq conjunction, they would endorse the conclusion 'p'.

DA: Initially, a model of minor premise ¬p is built. Because the given conditional does not place constraints on q in the presence of ¬p, the initial model is expanded into two models, ¬pq and ¬p¬q. If the reasoner added the inverse, 'if not p then not q', to the given conditional, the corresponding constraining procedure would block the ¬pq model. It should be noted here that, if the reasoner added the converse, 'if q then p', this would also lead to elimination of the ¬pq model in the context of a DA argument, and likewise, assuming the inverse would eliminate the ¬pq model in the context of an AC argument. Thus, whereas the converse and the inverse are pragmatic implicatures that can be endorsed independently, as assumed by Evans and Over (2004), each of them has the same consequence for both AC and DA, namely, blocking the construction of the ¬pq model, thereby contributing to a positive correlation between acceptance of these two inferences.

MT: The process starts with a model of ¬q, which could be expanded into the p¬q model and the ¬p¬q model. The former is blocked by the production that enforces a q accompanying each p, leaving ¬p¬q as the only model, which licenses the conclusion 'not p'.

The basic processes of constructing mental models for the four inference forms outlined above lead to largely the same sets of models as specified in the original MMT, and thus, results in similar predictions for the endorsement of conclusions. One important difference is that we drop the MMT assumption that model construction always starts with the pq model as the initial model of the conditional. In our scheme, the ¬p¬q model is as likely to be constructed (in the context of DA and MT) as the pq model (in the context of MP and AC).[2] This raises a question: Why are MP inferences endorsed much more often than MT inferences? The reason for this asymmetry is that there is a further route to MP (but not to MT) that bypasses the model construction and elimination process as outlined above: Given an initial model of the minor premise p, the production incorporating the meaning of the conditional immediately adds a model of q. Rather than using this procedure to construct a pq model for further analysis, reasoners can use it to generate the conclusion 'q' directly. This direct route to the MP conclusion corresponds to the 'System-1' process in the dual-process model shown in Figure 16.4 whereas the model-based procedure described above corresponds to the 'System 2' process. When the person interprets the given conditional as implying the converse or the inverse, the direct route can use them to also derive AC or DA, respectively. Thus, our revised model theory as developed so far maps onto the dual-process model that has been successfully fit to two large data sets (Oberauer, 2006), without having to assume two separate systems of reasoning. The two processes just reflect two ways of using the same representations and procedures.

As outlined so far, the revised model theory specifies a purely deductive reasoning procedure. How is knowledge of the content domain of reasoning incorporated into the process? There are at least two ways in which knowledge affects the reasoning process. First, the cognitive availability of instances or categories matching each of the possible situations affects the probability that that situation is represented as a mental model. For instance, in the context of an AC argument such as

---

[2] In practice, the difficulties with representing negations could make it harder to generate and reason from the ¬p¬q model compared to the pq model, but that effect should be eliminated by using negations in the conditional itself (for instance, a conditional of the form 'if not p then not q' would lead to model ¬p¬q for MP and AC, and of model pq for DA and MT).

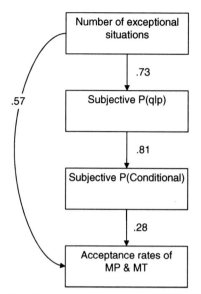

Fig. 16.4 Path model for conditional reasoning, redrawn from Weidenfeld et al. (2005), with permission of Taylor and Francis. Results are shown only for the subgroup receiving deductive instructions in the inference. Printed with permission of Taylor and Francis in Weidenfeld, A., Oberauer, K., & Hörnig, R. (2005). Causal and noncausal conditionals - an integrated model of interpretation and reasoning. *Quarterly Journal of Experimental Psychology*, 58(8), pp. 1479–1513(1435).

'If John has touched the weapon, his fingerprints are on it. John's fingerprints are on the weapon', reasoners start with a model of the weapon with John's fingerprints on it, representing the minor premise. This model is potentially expanded in two ways, by adding a model of John touching the weapon, and by adding a model of John not touching the weapon. The second of these models, however, is unlikely to be built because it represents an extremely implausible state of affairs: John's fingerprints on an object he never touched. If reasoners can think of an alternative cause for how John's fingerprints came to be on the weapon (e.g., being transmitted by sticky tape from another object John touched with the purpose of framing him), they are more likely to construct a model of the false-antecedent, true-consequent conjunction, and thus to reject the AC conclusion.

A second way in which domain knowledge enters the reasoning process is through numerical annotations to the models that represent their frequencies or probabilities. When asked to decide whether a conclusion follows or does not follow, reasoners should try to eliminate one of the two possibilities modelled in the context of each inference form, and infer that nothing follows if they cannot eliminate one, as described above. When they are asked to estimate the probability or believability of a conclusion, in contrast, they will try to assign probabilities to the two alternative models and compute their ratio for an estimate of the conditional probability of the conclusion, given the minor premise. The role of the conditional premise in this case is not to eliminate the model of the $p\neg q$ conjunction but rather to reduce its probability. The degree to which that happens depends itself on the degree of belief people have in the conditional premise.

Conclusion

We have argued that the currently available evidence on how people interpret conditionals favours the probabilistic view, whereas evidence on how people reason with conditional premises supports the mental-model view. This motivated our search for a way to integrate the best parts of both approaches. The interpretation of conditionals in terms of conditional probabilities is incompatible with a truth-functional interpretation of conditionals (Lewis, 1976, Evans & Over, 2004). Therefore, we propose to give up the idea that the meaning of conditionals can be represented by the set of mental models that meet their truth conditions, or which are compatible with the conditional. Conditionals are not truth-functional, that is, they don't have truth conditions by which we can determine whether a given conditional is true or false simply from what is the case in a world. We believe that the core meaning of 'if p then q' is best expressed by a production that adds a representation of q to every representation of p in working memory. This production can be used in two ways when it comes to reason from conditionals. When the minor premise matches the conditions of application of the production (i.e., the antecedent of the conditional it represents), the conditional's consequent can be generated as a conclusion directly. Alternatively, reasoners can build mental models of situations compatible with the minor premise and use the production that incorporates the conditional to constrain these models. The two inference routes map onto the two processes in the dual-process model as outlined in Figure 16.3. They reflect not two separate systems of information processing but simply two ways of using the same system.

References

Adams, E. W. (1965). On the logic of conditionals. *Inquiry*, **8**, 166–197.

Adams, E. W. (1981). Truth, proof, and conditionals. *Pacific Philosophical Quarterly*, **62**, 323–339.

Anderson, J. R. (1983). *The architecture of cognition*. Cambridge: Harvard University Press.

Anderson, J. R. (1995). *Cognitive psychology and its implications*. New York: W. H. Freeman.

Barrrouillet, P., Grosset, N., & Lecas, J. -F. (2000). Conditional reasoning by mental models: Chronometric and developmental evidence. *Cognition*, **74**, 1–30.

Byrne, R. M. (1989). Suppressing valid inferences with conditionals. *Cognition*, **31**, 61–83.

Byrne, R. M., Espino, O., & Santamaria, C. (1999). Counterexamples and the suppression of interferences. *Journal of Memory and Language*, **40**, 347–373.

Byrne, R. M. & Tasso, A. (1999). Deductive reasoning with factual, possible, and counterfactual conditionals. *Memory & Cognition*, **27**, 726–740.

Cummins, D. (1995). Naive theories and causal deduction. *Memory & Cognition*, **23**, 646–658.

Cummins, D., Lubart, T., Alksnis, O., & Rist, R. (1991). Conditional reasoning and causation. *Memory and Cognition*, **19**, 274–282.

DeNeys, W., Schaeken, W., & D'Ydewalle, G. (2003). Inference suppression and semantic memory retrieval: Every counterexample counts. *Memory & Cognition*, **31**(4), 581–595.

Evans, J. St.B. T. (2003). In two minds: dual process accounts of reasoning. *Trends in Cognitive Sciences*, **7**(10), 454–459.

Evans, J. St.B. T. (2006). The heuristic-analytic theory of reasoning. Extension and evaluation. *Psychonomic Bulletin & Review*, **13**(3), 378–395.

Evans, J. St.B. T., Handley, S., Neilens, H., & Over, D. E. (2007). Thinking about conditionals: A study of individual differences. *Memory & Cognition*, **35**, 1772–1784.

Evans, J. St.B. T., Handley, S. J., & Over, D. E. (2003). Conditionals and conditional probability. *Journal of Experimental Psychology: Learning, Memory and Cognition*, **29**, 321–335.

Evans, J. St.B. T. & Over, D. E. (2004). *If*. Oxford: Oxford University Press.

Geiger, S. M. & Oberauer, K. (2007). Reasoning with conditionals: Does every counterexample count? It's frequency that counts. *Memory & Cognition*, **35**, 2060–2074.

Girotto, V. & Johnson-Laird, P. N. (2004). The probability of conditionals. *Psychologia*, **47**, 207–225.

Johnson-Laird, P. N. (1983). *Mental models*. Cambridge: Cambridge University Press.

Johnson-Laird, P. N. (2001). Mental models and deduction. *Trends in Cognitive Sciences*, **5**, 434–442.

Johnson-Laird, P. N. & Byrne, R. M. (1991). *Deduction*. Hove & London: Earlbaum.

Johnson-Laird, P. N. & Byrne, R. M. (2002). Conditionals: A theory of meaning, pragmatics, and inference. *Psychological Review*, **109**, 646–678.

Johnson-Laird, P. N. & Savary, F. (1996). Illusory Inferences about Probabilities. *Acta Psychologica*, **93**, 69–90.

Johnson-Laird, P. N., Legrenzi, P., Girotto, V., Legrenzi, M. S., & Caverni, J. -P. (1999). Naive probability: A mental model theory of extensional reasoning. *Psychological Review*, **106**, 62–88.

Lewis, D. (1976). Probabilities of conditionals and conditional probabilities. *The Philosophical Review*, **85**, 297–315.

Markovits, H. & Potvin, F. (2001). Suppression of valid inferences and knowledge structures: the curious effect of producing alternative antecedents on reasoning with causal conditionals. *Memory & Cognition*, **29**(5), 736–744.

Oaksford, M. & Chater, N. (1994). A rational analysis of the selection task as optimal data selection. *Psychological Review*, **101**, 608–631.

Oaksford, M. & Chater, N. (1995). Theories of Reasoning and the Computational Explanation of Everyday Inference. *Thinking and Reasoning*, **1**, 121–152.

Oaksford, M. & Chater, N. (2001). The probabilistic approach to human reasoning. *Trends in Cognitive Sciences*, **5**, 349–357.

Oaksford, M., Chater, N., & Larkin, J. (2000). Probabilities and polarity biases in conditional inference. *Journal of Experimental Psychology: Learning, Memory, and Cognition*, **26**, 883–899.

Oberauer, K. (2006). Reasoning with conditionals: A test of formal models of four theories. *Cognitive Psychology*, **53**, 238–283.

Oberauer, K., Geiger, S. M., Fischer, K., & Weidenfeld, A. (2007). Two meanings of 'if'? Individual differences in the interpretation of conditionals. *Quarterly Journal of Experimental Psychology*, **60**(6), 790–819.

Oberauer. K, Weidenfeld, A., & Hörnig, R (2004). Logical reasoning and probabilities: A comprehensive test of Oaksford and Chater (2001). *Psychonomic Bulletin & Review*, **11**(3), 521–527.

Oberauer, K., Weidenfeld, A., & Fischer, K. (2007). What makes us believe a conditional? The roles of covariation and causality. *Thinking & Reasoning*, **13**, 340–369.

Oberauer, K. & Wilhelm, O. (2003). The meaning(s) of conditionals: Conditional probabilities, mental models, and personal utilities. *Journal of Experimental Psychology: Learning, Memory, & Cognition*, **29**, 680–693.

Over, D. E. & Evans, J. St.B. T. (2003). The probability of conditionals: The psychological evidence. *Mind & Language*, **18**, 340–358.

Over, D. E., Hadjichristidis, C., Evans, J. St.B. T., Handley, S., & Sloman, S. A. (2007). The probability of causal conditionals. *Cognitive Psychology*, **54**, 62–97.

Ramsey, F. P. (1990 (originally published in 1929)). General propositions and causality. In H. D. Meller (Ed.), *Foundations: Essays in Philosophy, logic, mathematics and economics* (pp. 145–193). London: Humanities Press.

Schroyens, W., Schaeken, W., & d'Ydewalle, G. (2002). The processing of negations in conditional reasoning: A meta-analytic case-study in mental model and/or mental logic theory. *Thinking and Reasoning*, **7**(7), 121–172.

Schroyens, W., Walter, & Handley, S. (2003). In search of counter-examples: Deductive rationality in human reasoning. *The Quarterly Journal of Experimental Psychology*, **56A**(7), 1129–1145.

Thompson, V. A. (1995). Conditional reasoning: the necessary and sufficient conditions. *Canadian Journal of Experimental Psychology*, **40**(1), 1–60.

Thompson, V. A. (2000). Task specific nature of domain general reasoning. *Cognition*, **76**, 209–268.

Verschueren, N., Schaeken, W., & d'Ydewalle, G. (2005). A dual process theory on everyday conditional reasoning. *Thinking and Reasoning*, **11**(3), 239–278.

Weidenfeld, A., Oberauer, K., & Hörnig, R. (2005). Causal and noncausal conditionals - an integrated model of interpretation and reasoning. *Quarterly Journal of Experimental Psychology*, **58**(A), pp. 1479–1513.

Chapter 17

Conditional inference and constraint satisfaction: Reconciling mental models and the probabilistic approach

Mike Oaksford and Nick Chater

Introduction

The conditional construction, 'if p then q' in English, is the probably the most important term in human language. It occurs in all human languages (Comrie, 1986) and allows people to express their knowledge of the causal or law-like structure of the world and of others' behaviour, e.g., if you turn the key the car starts, if John walks the dog he stops for a pint of beer; to make promises, e.g., if you cook tonight, I'll wash up all week; to regulate behaviour, e.g., if you are drinking beer, you must be over 18 years of age; to suggest what would have happened had things been different, e.g., if the match had been dry it would have lit, among many other possible uses. The conditional also provides the core of all logical systems and one of the main procedures for controlling the flow of most computer programmes. Unsurprisingly, it is also the most researched expression in the psychology of reasoning.

The psychology of reasoning has from its inception followed a two pronged approach. First, it seeks to establish empirical results on how people reason. Second, it seeks to evaluate people's reasoning according to some normative standard, usually provided by standard logic. Recently it has become clear that standard logic may not be the correct standard by which to judge most human reasoning. Some researchers have pointed out that behaviour that appears irrational from the perspective of one normative theory seems perfectly rational from the perspective of another. This is perhaps less surprising in the context of the standard framework for computational explanation in cognitive science which is multi-levelled (e.g., Anderson, 1990; Marr, 1982; Newell & Simon, 1972; Pylyshyn, 1984). The computational (Marr, 1982) or rational level (Anderson, 1990) specifies what the cognitive system is trying to compute when tackling a particular cognitive task. The algorithmic level specifies how the cognitive system computes the function specified at the computational level. Finally, the implementational level specifies the physical hardware on which the computation is performed. In this framework, the normative theories used to judge human reasoning are computational level theories, i.e., they define the function the system is trying to compute. For all levels of computational explanation, it is an empirical question as to which provides the better theory. For a long time in the psychology of reasoning, standard logic was assumed to provide the normative standard and the main goal was to explain away deviations from this standard at the algorithmic level.

However, there are always exceptions to the rule. For example, some psychological theories have proposed accounts of the conditional that were not compatible with standard logic (Braine & O'Brian, 1991). As with more recent work suggesting a probabilistic standard for human reasoning, such accounts raise the issue that there may be more than one computational level theory for the conditional. In fact, treating the normative literature on conditionals as a potential source of computational level theories, there is a plethora of possibilities, only very few of which have ever been explored empirically in the psychology of reasoning. Each account attempts to capture some of our intuitions about how we interpret and reason with conditionals.

The plethora of possible computational level theories of the conditional is mirrored at least in part by the current plurality of psychological theories in this area (Braine & O'Brian, 1991; Evans & Over, 2004; Johnson-Laird, & Byrne, 2002; Oaksford, Chater, & Larkin, 2000; Rips, 1994; Verschueren, Schaeken, & d'Ydewalle, 2005). However, the relationships between these theories, and with computational level theories , is never as clear cut as the model of computational explanation we have outlined would require. This is for a couple of reasons. At a relatively trivial level, there has simply been inattention to these theoretical distinctions. Perhaps more deeply, there is a strategic choice as to which level of computational explanation will allow more progress to be made. Chater, Oaksford, Nakisa, and Reddington (2003) have argued that there can be slippage in both directions between normative computational level theories and algorithmic level theories. So normative theories may be developed or applied without specifying how they are implemented at the algorithmic level. Moreover, algorithmic level theories may be developed without specifying exactly what it is they are computing. Chater et al. (2003) cite many examples of both strategies and both are in evidence in the psychology of reasoning. For example, recent probabilistic approaches concentrate on the computational level. This approach proposes a probabilistic computational level standard against which to evaluate human reasoning. Judged against this standard, human reasoning behaviour is seen in a much more favourable light, i.e., more of people's reasoning behaviour conforms to what they should be doing. Mental models theory, on the other hand, concentrates on the algorithmic level. Mental representations and processes are proposed to explain the observed reasoning behaviour but with no indication as to whether people are behaving as they should or in a way that will lead to successful action.

It is this feature of mental models theory that is responsible for its enviable breadth. Without having to pursue the computational level question, rapid progress may be made articulating the mental representations and processes that might account for the experimental results. For example, Johnson-Laird and Byrne (2002), while discussing many normative theories of conditionals, never compare the results of their experiments with these theories nor do they suggest what inferences people should make in the context of the experimental tasks they discuss. However, this leaves the question, 'why do people reason like this?' unanswered. The very breadth of the theory then becomes problematic. For example, is there one normative theory which is supposed to answer this question for all the domains covered by mental models theorists, or is a different normative theory required in each domain? If the former, then there is little evidence of progress in developing what would amount to the 'super logic' of human reasoning. If the latter, again there is little evidence of mental models theorists comparing people's behaviour and their algorithmic level theories to existing normative theories in these domains. However, in the complete absence of a normative computational level theory, it is perhaps legitimate simply to rely on intuitions about what is and what is not a good inference (although again, attempts to identify appropriate normative theories have been far from exhaustive).

Inferential intuitions form the core evidence base for deriving normative theories. Logicians and mathematicians test their theories against their own and others intuitions. It is the job of the normative theories to systematize these intuitions and so develop theories that can tell whether more complex inferences conform to our basic level intuitions. This contrasts with the psychology of reasoning which deals with experimental results. However, as Cohen (1981) has observed, experimental results are also based on naïve participants' inferential intuitions. Consequently, any observed deviations from existing normative theories could prompt changes to the normative theories as these intuitions are the final arbiter of good and bad inferences. On this view, irrational behaviour is impossible as experimental findings prompt the development of new normative theories. However, there has always been a debate in the rationality literature over whose intuitions should count (Goodman, 1983/1954; Thagard, 1988). Should we be aiming at broad 'reflective equilibrium' where all people's intuitions are put in to the picture or a narrow 'reflective equilibrium' where only the intuitions of an expert minority are in the frame? These are important philosophical issues that we cannot resolve here. However, for what follows, we need at least to make our position clear.

Our position is dictated by the following observations. First, as a practical issue, it is simply a fact that all extant normative theories have been formulated by experts using their own intuitions. Practically these theories, e.g., logic, probability theory, decision theory have served us well and revising them does not seem desirable. Secondly, in the psychology of human reasoning the case for a revisionary strategy is unproven. Typically there is little or no consideration of alternative normative theories for a particular task, let alone an exhaustive consideration of such theories (for exceptions see, Birnbaum, 1983; Oaksford & Chater, 1994; and more recently, Evans & Over, 2004; Pfeifer & Kleiter, 2005). Third, recent ecological and rational analysis approaches to cognition show that while people's behaviour may not be perfectly rational, it can be shown to conform to existing normative standards when combined with reasonable assumptions about the environment (e.g., Oaksford & Chater, 1994). Fourth, because we are dealing with a computational device there is bound to be some slippage between competence and performance, i.e., between the computational and the algorithmic levels. Inferential behaviour reflects both levels and hence cannot provide sufficient evidence to pursue a revisionary strategy. However, we would argue that a computational level theory should at least account for the majority of the inferential behaviour observed. If it does not,[1] then it is rather like proposing a theory of aerodynamics that does not apply to most flying objects.[2] That is, this situation provides exactly the conditions under which revision or a different normative theory (if they exist) *is* required, at pain of providing an empirically inadequate computational level theory.

These observations point to the conclusion that existing normative theories probably provide an adequate starting point from which to select normative theories of reasoning. Which theory is normative for which task is an empirical issue, i.e., which normative theory accounts for most of the data. Finally, some behaviour in inference tasks will be explained at the algorithmic level but only a minority of behaviour. These points articulate the general framework within which we have been constructing probabilistic theories of human reasoning. Adopting this framework may point the way out of a current log jam in our progress in understanding conditional reasoning.

Recently Schroyens and Schaeken (2003) have argued that an extended mental models theory could account for more data—92% of the variance—than our conditional probability model

---

[1] For example some logic based accounts of Wason's selection task account for as little of 4% of the observed responses, with the slack being taken up by the performance level.

[2] Note that it does not have to apply to them all. For example, our current theories of aerodynamics cannot explain ground effect flight where, for example, an inverted delta wing allows massively reduced fuel consumption when flying close to the ground. This also provides a good analogy for the slippage between computational levels of explanation. We can build ground effect aircraft (algorithmic level) even if we don't understand why they work (computational level). Of course, it then becomes a desiderata to revise aerodynamic theory to explain why we can build these machines, just as we have suggested mental modellers should be interested in finding out why people draw the conclusions predicted by mental models theory. However, because we are dealing with computational explanation, some, but not the majority, of the slippage can be taken up in the performance theory.

(Oaksford, Chater, & Larkin, 2000)—84% of the variance. Oaksford and Chater (2003) replied that their purely computational level theory accounted for more of the data than the computational level theory on which mental models is based, i.e., standard logic—56% of the variance. More recently, Oberauer (2006) has argued that various implementations of mental models theory provide better fits to the data than the probabilistic approach. Oberauer's (2006) model claims to incorporate the algorithmic level only by making some assumptions concerning distributions of the parameters considered as random variables and by including a threshold. It also does not take account of recent revisions of the model (Oaksford & Chater, 2008). This does not constitute a serious algorithmic implementation of the probabilistic approach. Consequently, in Oberauer (2006) like is not being compared with like.

Following Marr (1982), we would argue that an empirically adequate computational level theory of the function the cognitive system is trying to compute is the most appropriate starting place for constructing a computational explanation of human reasoning (Oaksford & Chater, 1995, 1996, 1998). In this respect, model comparison exercises apparently showing better fits for algorithmic level theories are largely beside the point. As we have just observed, there can be slippage between the computational and algorithmic levels (Chater et al., 2003). So in a particular scientific domain, it may be more productive to pursue one theoretical level at the expense of another, although both are essential to a complete explanation. Consequently, the probabilistic account will eventually have to address the algorithmic level and mental models theory will eventually have to address the computational level (see Oberauer & Oaksford, 2008). It could be that when the computational level is addressed in mental models theory, it can be shown to provide better fits to the data than probability theory, i.e., it provides a descriptively more adequate and a normatively justified computational level theory (Oaksford & Chater, 1996). On the other hand, when the algorithmic level is addressed in the probabilistic approach it may be shown that it provides better fits to the data than mental models (Oaksford & Chater, 2003). That is, not only does it provide better fits than logic at the computational level when appropriately implemented, it is also more empirically adequate at the algorithmic level.

The purpose of this chapter is to take the first tentative steps towards an algorithmic level account of the probabilistic approach and to demonstrate its face-validity by comparing it to a variety of data on conditional inference. The algorithmic approach we adopt will show why the cognitive system needs something like mental models. We first briefly introduce our account of the probabilistic approach. We then introduce the algorithmic level model. We then apply the model to the data.

The probabilistic approach to conditional inference

We have proposed a computational level account of conditional inference as dynamic belief update (Oaksford & Chater, 2007; Oaksford, Chater, and Larkin, 2000). So if a high probability is assigned to *if x is a bird, x flys*, then on acquiring the new information that *Tweety is a bird*, one's degree of belief in *Tweety flys* should be revised to one's degree of belief in *Tweety flys given Tweety is a bird*, i.e., one's degree of belief in the conditional. So using P_0 to indicate *prior* degree of belief and P_1 to indicate *posterior* degree of belief, then:

$$P_1(q) = P_0(q|p), \text{ when } P_1(p) = 1. \tag{17.1}$$

Thus according to this account, the probability with which someone should endorse the MP inference is the conditional probability. This is the approach taken in Oaksford et al. (2000).

However, as Oaksford and Chater (2007) point out, there is a problem with extending this account to MT, DA and AC (Sober, 2002). The appropriate conditional probabilities for the categorical premise of these inferences to conditionalize on are $P(\neg p|\neg q)$, $P(\neg q|\neg p)$, and $P(p|q)$ respectively. However, the premises of MT and the fallacies do not entail values for these conditional probabilities (Sobel, 2004; Sober, 2002; Wagner, 2004). Oaksford et al. (2000) suggested that people had prior knowledge of the marginals, $P(p)$ and $P(q)$, which together with $P(q|p)$ do entail appropriate values (see, Wagner [2004] for a similar approach) $(P_0(q|p) = a, P_0(p) = b, P_0(q) = c)$:

$$\text{MP} \quad P_1(q) = P_0(q|p) = a \tag{17.2}$$

$$\text{DA} \quad P_1(\neg q) = P_0(\neg q|\neg p) = (1 - c - (1 - a)b)/(1 - b) \tag{17.3}$$

$$\text{AC} \quad P_1(p) = P_0(p|q) = ab/c, \tag{17.4}$$

$$\text{MT} \quad P_1(\neg p) = P_0(\neg p|\neg q) = (1 - c - (1 - a)b)/(1 - c) \tag{17.5}$$

Equations (17.2) to (17.5) show the posterior probabilities of the conclusion of each inference assuming the posterior probability of the categorical premise is 1. By using Jeffrey conditionalization (Jeffrey, 1983), these cases can be readily generalized to when the probability of the categorical premise is less than 1 (Oaksford & Chater, 2007).

In the subjective approach that we adopt, conditional probability is defined by the Ramsey test. As Bennett (2003, p. 53) says:

> The best definition we have [of conditional probability] is the one provided by the Ramsey test: your conditional probability for q given p is the probability for q that results from adding $P(p) = 1$ to your belief system and conservatively adjusting to make room for it.

The Ramsey test means that the definition of conditional probability invokes a currently unarticulated mental process. Moreover, it means that any assessment of the conditional probability involves one's prior beliefs, B, held in LTM memory. So, for say MP, people assess the consequent probability given the conjunction of the antecedent and their prior beliefs, i.e., $P_0(q|p, B)$. In proposing an implementation of the probabilistic approach, we hope to more fully articulate the mental processes that may underlie the Ramsey test and so show how other prior beliefs may therefore influence the judgement of the relevant conditional probabilities.

Conditionals and constraint satisfaction: model presentation

We recently suggested that more theoretical effort should be directed at specifying the mental processes underlying the Ramsey test (Oaksford & Chater, 2007). We attempt to go some of the way towards this goal by using a very simplified constraint satisfaction neural network model. The key idea is that people can interrogate their prior beliefs by clamping on or clamping off the units corresponding to the categorical premise and conclusion of a conditional inference. However, people also need control processes to record and store the outcomes of these interrogations especially as inferences may trigger an exploration of more than one possibility. We propose that annotated mental model representations stored in working memory are one way to do this. Moreover, if several possibilities are explored, then these may be integrated in working memory to derive a response. We first consider the nature of the conditional knowledge captured in LTM that provides constraints on human reasoning.

The nature of conditional knowledge in LTM

We assume that people's cognitive representations of conditionals have evolved to deal with the uncertain context sensitive dependencies that we experience in the everyday world. For example, we all know that the best way to start a car is to turn the key, i.e., *if you turn the key (p) the car starts* (*q*), but we also know that this only happens in contexts where there are no *defeaters*, i.e., conditions which if untrue could defeat the conclusion, e.g., the petrol tank is not empty (*d1*) or the battery is not flat (*d2*). So we know that the general form of a conditional is:

$$If\ p\ then\ q|C \tag{17.6}$$

That is, *q* follows *p* but only in the right context *C*, where $C = d1, d2...dn$. However, we can never fully specify the context *C*, i.e., people can never know all of the defeaters or know whether they hold on a particular occasion (Oaksford & Chater, 1991). So they must make closed world assumptions, i.e., they can only represent the defeaters they know about. Moreover because the real world is an open system the cognitive system must treat the relationship between *p* and *q* probabilistically. There is also inevitably more than one dependency that leads to the same outcome, e.g., you can jump start your car if it doesn't start because the battery is flat. So there will always be other dependencies:

$$if\ r\ then\ q|C \tag{17.7}$$

Notice that in (17.7) the context changes subtly from (17.6), because one would only invoke (17.7) in a context in which *d1* is known to be false. That is, alternative dependencies and defeaters can be intimately linked.

We continue to use *causal* conditionals as examples because causal conditional reasoning has been most investigated empirically. As we have discussed before (Oaksford, 1989; Oaksford & Chater, 2007), one approach to conditionals is to treat them as denoting real causal relations in the world (Barwise & Perry, 1983). This would mark off the causal case as special because other conditional sentences, e.g., deontic conditionals and promises, do not obviously denote real dependencies in the world that are independent of human agency. Our view is that people do represent conditionals in a very similar way to the causal case, although perhaps supplemented with utilities. Consequently, although we find it expedient to present the model through lens of causal conditionals, we intend the underlying representations and processes to be of broader applicability. We now present an overview of the model.

A dual process constraint satisfaction model

In Figure 17.1, we have implemented this simple system of two alternative conditionals and their defeaters as a constraint satisfaction neural network. In this instantiation of the model, we consider this simple neural network to be the pre-potent representations in long term memory (LTM) that are most active on encountering a conditional sentence. That is, the network is embedded in the far larger network which encodes world knowledge. Note that we consider this to be a very preliminary model and we discuss alternative ways of construing it and additional work that may improve on it and make it more realistic in the sequel. The connections with arrowheads indicate facilitatory connections and those with circular ends indicate inhibitory connections. Thus both *p* and *r* will activate the *q* unit, whereas *d1* and *d2* will inhibit it. There are also connections between *p* and *r* and *d1* and *d2*. These simply encode the weak co-occurrence relations between antecedent conditions and defeaters, e.g., sometimes, but rarely, when you turn the key the battery is flat. The inhibitory link between *p* and *r* is related to our observation above about the relationship between alternative dependencies and defeaters. You would only bump start a car (*r*) if you had tried starting it by turning the key (*p*) and failed. Therefore the alternative cause is usually only invoked when the primary cause (the normal mode of achieving the effect described in the consequent) is absent.

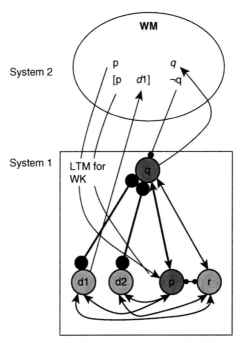

Fig. 17.1 A Dual Process implementation of the probabilistic model.

People can interrogate this network and store the results as annotated mental models in working memory (WM). So on encountering the MP inference for (17.6), they may clamp on the p-unit, corresponding to the categorical premise, e.g., the key is turned. The network is allowed to settle into a new equilibrium state and the activation of the q-unit is read off. We argue that this process in the model corresponds to performing a Ramsey test. The activation level of the q-unit corresponds to the probability of q given that p is true and our other prior beliefs, B, embodied in the connection weights in the network. The result of performing this Ramsey test can be stored in WM as an annotated mental model. In Figure 17.1, clamped units are represented as normal text in a mental model in WM. The target of the inference, q, is in italics.

People may also interrogate LTM to see under what conditions the opposite of the conclusion is possible. This involves clamping the p-unit on and the q-unit off (in the second row of the mental model in WM both p and q are in normal text). In the model, because of the weak co-occurrence relation between p (turning the key) and the defeaters, one of $d1$ or $d2$ will become active because they are no longer inhibited by the q-unit. So $d1$ is added to the mental model. The activation level of the activated (as opposed to clamped) unit is represented as an annotation to the model that relates to the unclamped unit represented in the mental model.

Figure 17.1 also shows that we can construe the model in terms of dual process theory (Evans & Over, 2004). The operations over world knowledge in LTM can be considered as System 1 processes. These processes are heuristic, fast, automatic, and largely unconscious. Notice, however, that would not prevent these processes from being normatively justified if they can be seen to implement a probabilistic account of reasoning (even if only to an approximation). In contrast, the storage and manipulation in WM of the results of interrogating LTM about various possibilities can be considered a System 2 process. These processes are analytic, slow, controlled and may be conscious.

This model suggests that mental models (or a similar representational format) are required to store the results of interrogating world knowledge in LTM about various possibilities. Consequently, the emergence of the ability to consider possibilities by interrogating LTM and Working Memory capacity must be intimately linked in evolutionary history. Moreover, the cognitive system would require this function to be performed regardless of whether there was a demand for explicit verbal reasoning with conditional sentences. That is, this ability is perhaps the pre-adaptation (Bickerton, 2000), that has allowed the development of our explicit reasoning abilities.

We now show that the activation levels of an unclamped unit can be interpreted as a real posterior probability given the activations of the clamped units, i.e., in the first model, $P(q|p,B)$, and the second, $P(d1|p,\neg q,B)$, thereby establishing the link between the probabilistic approach and mental models theory.

Model operation and probabilistic interpretation

The probabilistic interpretation relies on setting the weights and the bias terms into units to particular values (McClelland, 1998). Figure 17.2 shows the LTM component of the model including the bias terms which are represented as additional weights between each unit and a bias unit. We have also subdivided the units into *context* units, i.e., representations of the context, C, in which the antecedents of a conditional lead to their consequent. As we described above these correspond to the defeaters that if present could prevent the consequent from occurring.

There are three components to understanding how a network like this can be interpreted as computing real posteriors (McClelland, 1998). First, the activation function must take the following logistic form:

$$a_i(t) = 1/(1 + e^{-G \sum w_{ij} a_i(t-1) - Bias}) \qquad (17.8)$$

(17.8) relates the activation level of unit i at time t, $a_i(t)$, to its activation level at time $t-1$, $a_i(t-1)$, the weights from units j into unit i, w_{ij}, the bias term, $Bias$, and a *gain* parameter, G (we discuss G

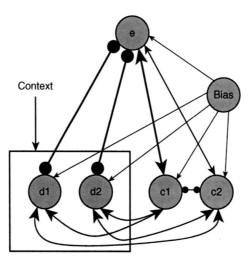

Fig. 17.2 The LTM constraint satisfaction network showing the bias term and context units.

in more detail in the section on *schizotypy and conditional inference*). Second, the weights must be set to a quantity referred to as consistency:

$$w_{ij} = \ln((P(x_i, x_j)\, P(\neg x_i, \neg x_j))/(P(x_i, \neg x_j)\, P(\neg x_i, x_j))) \tag{17.9}$$

That is, the weights between unit x_i and unit x_j depend on their co-occurrence statistics. Finally, the bias term for unit x_i should be set to the log of the prior odds:

$$Bias(x_i) = \ln(P(x_i)/(1 - P(x_i))) \tag{17.10}$$

Setting the weights in this way has the consequence that the network will compute the real posterior probability given the values of the clamped units and other prior knowledge (McClelland, 1998). However, this is not strictly the case for the LTM component of the network presented in Figure 17.1. This is because one other condition that must be met is that in a feed-forward network, units at lower levels must be conditionally independent of the units they are connected to at the next level up. So formally, for example, $P(p|q,d1,B) = P(p|q,B)$. However, the weak connections, for example, between $d1$ and p prevent this condition being properly met. Moreover, we will allow the network to operate in either direction, i.e., not just as a feed-forward network. We finally observe that given the connectivity of the network used for the LTM component, it is not guaranteed to settle in to a stable configuration. However, for now it is sufficient to comment that in using the network to model reasoning data, we encountered few problems. For the moment we ignore the possible consequences of the other choices we have made here, but we will return to them in the *general discussion*.

Drawing inferences in the model

How do people draw inferences in this model? There are a few observations to make. Firstly, in this framework all inference involves accessing world knowledge in LTM, even when abstract materials are used (see Oaksford & Chater, 2007). This is because even for such material, we assume that a representation, like the network in Figure 17.1, is constructed and the parameters of the model (weights and biases) fixed by analogy to prior conditional knowledge (either all prior conditional knowledge or the most recently accessed [see e.g., Stewart, Chater, & Brown, 2006)]. This proposal is based simply on the analogy with the causal case discussed above. Most conditionals will allow the defeater/alternatives structure embodied in the model and derived primarily from causal examples. Second, the nature and quality of the inferences made will be determined by the number of possibilities that one explores by interrogating LTM. Clearly, WM limitations will place tight constraints on the number of possibilities considered (a point wholly familiar from mental models theory). Third, WM limitations also put serious constraints on the nature of the operations that can be performed on the stored representations and their annotations (see Stewart, Chater, & Brown (2006) for a similar point in a cognate area). We assume that only very simple operations are performed on the annotations, like addition, subtraction, and averaging.

One principle behind drawing inferences in the model is to encode the most probable conclusion in WM:

Encode the most probable of x and $\neg x$ where x is the target of the inference.

So if the p unit is clamped on and the q unit activity is greater than .5 when the network settles, then q is represented in WM annotated with the units activity, a_x (given the choices made above, unit activations are constrained in the 0–1 probability interval). However, if after settling, the q unit activity is less than .5, then $\neg q$ is represented in WM with the annotation $1 - a_x$. The situation in which the key is turned (p unit clamped on) but the q unit is not very active (i.e., a reasoner thinks the car may not start), would be when, say, someone also thinks the petrol tank is empty, i.e., *d1* is active. That is, the situation looks more like the second case we considered above.[3] The linguistic form of the rule identifies what is the target of the inference, i.e., it is the opposite clause, *p* or *q*, to that stated or denied in the categorical premise. To implement this principle requires symbolic representations of some form in WM (Oaksford, 2008).

To see the force of this last point let us consider what a non-linguistic organism without WM would be capable of. First, units in LTM could only become active contingent on the presence in its immediate environment of the objects or events described in the antecedent and consequent of a conditional rule. Second, the premises of the denial inferences, DA and MT could not be presented to such an organism. This is simply because most things are not occurring in the world. But it would be counterproductive to therefore clamp off all units representing non-occurring events as this would prevent them coming on when the situation changes. Third, such an organism could only make 'untargeted' predictions about what may happen next. All the units which become active consequent on clamping on a unit (representing the object or event which is the current focus of attention) would provide predictions for what happens next. If the organism has successfully encoded the dependencies that are important to it then the most active unit should correspond to the consequent of an *assertable* conditional sentence, one for which $P(q|p)$ is high (Adams, 1998). In sum, an organism with just the LTM component of the model is incapable of drawing the range of inferences that attach to a conditional. Some form of WM is required together with symbolic representations that can encode negation. These are very similar to the pre-requisites for rationality described by Bennett (1964).[4]

However, the behaviour of an organism without these pre-requisites could still be described as adaptively rational. That is, if it has successfully encoded the dependencies that are important to it, it will be able to adapt its behaviour successfully to its environment. Moreover, if its world knowledge is encoded in LTM in the way we have proposed, then it should be able to make pretty good assessments of many conditional probabilities (although this ability would have to be interrogated non-linguistically).

We have recently argued that there is an underlying tension between the inductive strength ($P(C|P)$) of an inference from premises (P) to a conclusion (C) and its deductive validity ($P \models C$) but that inductive strength usually dominates (Oaksford & Hahn, 2007). We argued that 'while people may well be capable of assessing deductive correctness when explicitly asked to, this is rarely, if ever, their focus of interest in evaluating an argument', (Oaksford & Hahn, 2007, p. 274) and that, 'deductive correctness and inductive strength should generally be seen as working together rather than as independent systems' (Oaksford & Hahn, 2007, p. 298). The current model goes some way to showing how the processes underlying both abilities are interdependent: assessing inductive strength requires at least proto-logical/linguistic ability to identify inferential targets and to assess denial inferences.

----

[3] In cases where contrast sets arise for a category the most likely constrast class member could be activated (Oaksford, 2002; Oaksford & Chater, 1994; Oaksford & Stenning, 1992). For example, take a conditional like *if a bird is a swan it is white*, and the situation we have just described. Because there are only two colours of swans, white and black, the inhibition of the white unit, should allow activation of the black unit (these would be connected by a mutually inhibitory link, encoding their mutual exclusivity). In these cases, rather than representing ¬*q*, i.e., '*not* white', 'black' would be explicitly represented in WM, i.e., as the more specific information.

[4] In a discussion redolent of Mandeville's (1714) *Fable of the Bees*, Bennett (1964) considers the additional cognitive equipment bees would require before we would describe their behaviour as rational. Linguistic capability and the ability to make and challenge denials are identified as central.

The first of three possibilities for interrogating the network that we now consider is where just the categorical premise of an inference is clamped on, the network is allowed to settle, i.e., a Ramsey test is performed, and the target activation is then read off. Figure 17.3 shows the behaviour of the model when the p-unit in clamped on or the q-unit is clamped off corresponding to MP and MT respectively (Panels A and B) and when they are both clamped on (Panel C) and both clamped off (Panel D).

Possibility 1

If all people do is clamp on or off the unit corresponding to the categorical premise, then the inductive strength of each of the argument forms and their corresponding annotated mental models are shown below:

$$
\begin{array}{lll}
\text{MP} & (p\ \text{ON})\ P(\text{MP}) = a(q) & \mathbf{p}\ \ q \\
\text{DA} & (p\ \text{OFF})\ P(\text{DA}) = 1 - a(q) & \mathbf{\neg p}\ \ \neg q \\
\text{AC} & (q\ \text{ON})\ P(\text{AC}) = a(p) & p\ \ \mathbf{q} \\
\text{MT} & (p\ \text{OFF})\ P(\text{MT}) = 1 - a(p) & \neg p\ \ \mathbf{\neg q}
\end{array}
$$

These WM representations are inherently directional, i.e., they go from the clamped unit (bold) *to* the unclamped target (italic) of the inference. They therefore amount to representing the obverse (DA), the converse (AC), and the contrapositive (MT) of the original conditional premise.

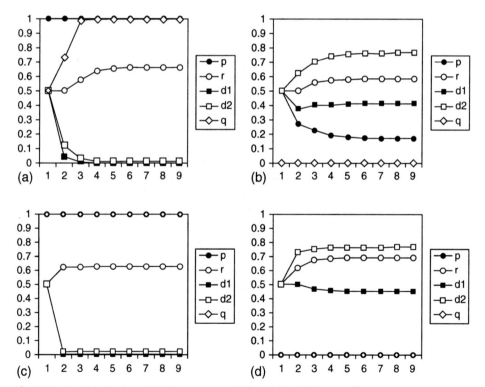

Fig. 17.3 Model behaviour: MP/Clamp on p-unit (Panel A), MT/Clamp off q-unit (Panel B), MP & AC/Clamp on p- and q-units (Panel C), DA & MT/Clamp off p- and q-units (Panel D).

The annotation is the activation of the unit corresponding to the inferential target, e.g., for MP the activation of the q unit, $a(q)$, with the p unit clamped on which is taken as the estimate of $P(q|p,B)$.

Evans and Over (2004) proposed exactly such directional representations of these relations as a prerequisite for drawing DA, AC or MT. Their theoretical proposal emerges as a consequence of our implementation of the probabilistic approach which requires a way of recording the results of interrogating probabilistic world knowledge. It also relates directly to having an *active* representation like the constraint satisfaction network on which a cognitive agent can *intervene* by clamping on units, like using the 'do' operator in a Causal Bayes Net (Chater & Oaksford, 2006; Pearl, 2000; Sloman, 2005). Evans and Over (2004) propose that these directional representations are formed only if pragmatic world knowledge indicates that they hold. This is precisely the information that is captured by the 'encode the most probable' principle. The probability of say $\neg q$ given that the p unit is clamped off is $1-P(q|\neg p, B)$. So the obverse will only be represented if prior world knowledge, B, and the supposition that p is not present leads to $P(q|\neg p, B) < .5$ in our implementation of the Ramsey test.

One could argue that the operations performed over world knowledge in LTM are not required to establish directional representations. This is because this information can also be obtained from the linguistically presented premises: the target is always the opposite conditional clause to the categorical premise, and has the same polarity. But such a proposal misses the point made by both the probabilistic approach and by Evans and Over (2004): the premises of DA, AC, and MT do not provide sufficient information to *warrant* representing the obverse, converse, or contrapositive. Moreover, participants seem sensitive to this fact because if representing these relations was simply triggered by the surface form of the inference, then presumably participants would always draw all four inferences. The current proposal is that people consult prior probabilistic world knowledge in LTM to see whether these relationships can be represented. Of course there is always a certain chance that the opposite of these relations is represented, e.g., $\neg p\ q$ for DA. This will happen if $P(q|\neg p, B) > .5$. As we suggest next, this will only happen under certain circumstances (familiar from suppression experiments [Byrne, 1989; Cummins, Lubarts, Alksnis, & Rist, 1991]). The proposal that whether these relations are represented is a probabilistic decision also suggests that the opposite conclusion should be endorsed at 1 minus the probability of endorsing the standard conclusion. So for DA, people should endorse the $\neg q$ conclusion with say probability $P(DA)$ and they should endorse the opposite conclusion with probability $1 - P(DA)$. In experiments where the opposite conclusion is presented, this is exactly what people do (Oaksford et al., 2000; Oaksford & Chater, 2007; although see Marcus & Rips, 1979).

Another aspect of this proposed implementation is that a natural order over which possibilities are assessed emerges. The level we have just considered is clearly the most basic. Shorn of the ability to characterize denial inferences and to record the results of interrogating world knowledge, the current level provides the bare requirement for an organism to be able to predict and anticipate the environment based on learned knowledge. Another way of representing this knowledge could be production rules, which operate in a purely MP way, i.e., if the antecedent is satisfied expect the consequent. The current proposal builds on this base the minimum that is required to perform the other inferences and justifiably represent them in WM.

Possibility 2

However, humans, with more extended WM capacity, may consider other possibilities, as we suggested above. Although, there is accumulated evidence that seems to show that people rarely assess more than an initial model of the premises of an inference (e.g., Newstead, Handley, & Buck, 1999). Nonetheless, if people do consider more than one possibility, we suggest that the next one they consider is clamping on/off both units corresponding to the categorical premise and the target of the inference. So for MP and AC, they clamp on both the p unit and the q unit; whereas for MT and DA, they clamp off both these units. Why would people do this? The principle grounds are pragmatic. People are interrogating their world knowledge in LTM to see if other conditions need to be satisfied for the inference to go through given the pre-potent model. This process will lead to building representations in WM that encodes more about defeaters ($d1$ and $d2$) and alternative causes ($c1$), in a manner similar to that proposed by Byrne et al. (1999). In our current account this will require people to appropriately annotate these models. We argue that these processes may lead to apparently non-normative errors. The reason for this is that retrieving this additional information involves considering more fine grained partitions of the probability space than participants are explicitly asked to do in the premises.

Let us look first at MP and AC. When both the p unit and the q unit are clamped on, the $d1$ and $d2$ units will be hard off (as they are strongly inhibited by q; see Figure 17.3, Panel C). The r unit will be activated by q being clamped on (this will only be partially balanced by the inhibitory connection between p and r). The raises the possibility of an alternative cause, e.g., the car was bump started.[5] Conceptually, this possibility bears little on the question of whether the car started (q) given the key was turned (p). That is, in accordance with the normative theory provided by Causal Bayes Nets, the second cause (r) should be 'explained away' once it is known the first cause (p) and the effect (q) occurred (see Ali, Schlottman, Shaw, Chater, & Oaksford, this volume). So once people know the car started and the key was turned, they discount the possibility that the car was bump started. In contrast, in our constraint satisfaction network, where key turning (p) and bump starting (r) are weakly negatively correlated, the activation of the r unit shows that there is a certain probability, $P(r|p, q, B)$, that an alternative cause was also present. However, such causal over-determination will not *reduce* the probability that the car starts, and so for MP participants still assign a probability of 1 that the car starts.

However, while having little effect on MP, we explore what we think participants may do if they further inquire into the possible effect of r. Since they are inquiring in to the probability that q occurs given p, they should now explore the probability that q occurs given p and r, $P(q|p, r, B)$. To do this they could re-interrogate the model by clamping on the p and r units and read off $a(q)$ as an estimate of $P(q|p, r, B)$. Alternatively, they could use Bayes' theorem on $P(r|p, q, B)$ to *calculate* $P(q|p, r, B)$:

$$P(q|p, r, B) = P(r|p, q, B)P(q|p, B)/P(r|p,B)$$

Error may enter in here because participants may ignore the priors in the calculation or assume they are equal ($P(q|p, B) = P(r|p,B)$) and so use the likelihood $P(r|p, q, B)$ as the estimate of the posterior $P(q|p, r, B)$. This could distort participants' assessment of the MP inference. However, for MP, as we have said, causal over-determination suggests that participants never contemplate this possibility.

In contrast, for AC the situation is different because p is the target of the inference. According to the normative account (see Ali, Schlottman, Shaw, Chater, & Oaksford, this volume) the causes (p and r) are *conditionally* independent given the effect (q). However, when q is known,

---

[5] Note that the r unit will become active to similar levels when just the p unit is clamped on as in the first case we considered (see, Figure 17.3, Panels A and C). However, to see the difference between the two cases it helps to view the clamped units as retrieval cues. The active unclamped units are the retrieved items. In the first case—clamp p—q is the most active retrieved item. In the second case—clamp p and q—r is the most active retrieved item.

then they become dependent so that if one cause is known to occur (i.e., p) the possibility of the other cause occurring (r) is discounted. However, following the above strategy in the current model, the activity of r provides an estimate of $P(r|p, q, B)$. The possibility of r should lead participants to inquire into the probability of p given q and r, $P(p|r, q, B)$, by clamping on r and q. But again if reasoners attempted to calculate this probability, ignoring the priors would lead them to use their estimate of $P(r|p, q, B)$, $a(r)$, as an estimate of $P(p|r, q, B)$. We suggest that given the limited operations they are likely to perform in WM, when participants consider this possibility (p ON, q ON) they simply moderate the probability of p, $a(p) = 1$, by averaging with $a(r)$ as an estimate of $P(p|r, q, B)$. So retrieving r by clamping in the p- and the q-units, leads them to reduce their estimate of the probability that p from $a(p) = 1$ to $(a(p) + a(r))/2$.

Another way of looking at this line of reasoning is to consider the significance of clamping units on or off. Clamping the p unit on just represents the supposition that p is present with probability 1. This does not mean that p was responsible for q, especially now as the activation of the r unit indicates that there is another possibility. So although we have supposed p to be present, the probability that it was responsible for q requires revision given the other possibility, r, that has been discovered by interrogating the model. Our assumption is that people simply average the two activation levels to provide a revised assessment that it was p that led to q on this occasion.

A similar argument applies for the denial inferences MT and DA when both the p unit and the q unit are clamped off (see Figure 17.3, Panel D). Take MT. The target is p and the fact that this is clamped off licenses $\neg p$ to be represented. In this model, the r representation will also become active. Should this affect the annotation, as for AC? In this case the answer is no. This is because r is also an instance of something that is $\neg p$ and so shouldn't affect one's assessment of this conclusion. On the other hand, when assessing the DA inference the target is q. The active representations will include the alternative cause r and the defeaters $d1$ and $d2$. They suggest that even if r is present, it too could not cause q because $d1$ and $d2$ are present. One can see why this situation should affect the assessment of the probability of q by considering a real world instantiation of this representation. In the LTM representation we can intervene on both p and q, considered as cause and effect respectively, simultaneously. In the real world we cannot do this, we can only intervene at earlier points in the causal order and see whether the effects occur. So all we can do is not turn the key ($\neg p$). The only way in which we can intervene such that even if we attempted to bump start the car (r), it still wouldn't start is to make sure the petrol tank is empty ($d1$) or the points are welded ($d2$). So it is when we re-interpret our interventions on our model back into the world that we see the relevance of $d1$ and $d2$ to the DA conclusion. We assume participants take the average of $a(d1)$ and $a(d2)$ as the estimate of the probability that q is inactive (even though r is active).

The probabilities of each inference given these interventions on the representation and their corresponding annotated mental models are shown below:

MP	(p ON, q ON)	$P(MP) = a(q) = 1$	[**p** r] *q*
DA	(p OFF, q OFF)	$P(DA) = (a(d1)+a(d2))/2$	[**¬p** r] *¬q* | d1, d2
AC	(p ON, q ON)	$P(AC) = (a(p)+a(r))/2$	[**p** r] *q*
MT	(p OFF, q OFF)	$P(MT) = 1 - a(p) = 1$	[**¬p** r] *¬q* | d1, d2

In these models, the clamped units are again represented in bold, the target of the inference is in italics, and the activated unclamped units are in normal text. The annotated mental models draw a clear distinction between antecedent conditions (p and r), consequent conditions (q), context ($d1, d2$), and target (italic), clearly identify the relevance of the factors affecting the probability of an inference. For example, for DA given the antecedent conditions, $\neg p$ and r, $\neg q$ is only possible given $d1$ and/or $d2$ are present.

Possibility 3

We also examined a third case, where for MP and MT, the p unit is on but the q unit is off and for AC and DA, the p unit is off but the q unit is on. The last case corresponds to exploring the possibility where the corresponding inferences cannot be drawn. The probabilities of each inference given this intervention on the representation and their corresponding annotated mental models are shown below:

MP	(p ON, q OFF)	$P(\text{MP}) = 1 - ((a(d1) + a(d2))/2)$	**p** ¬**q** | d1, d2
DA	(p OFF, q ON)	$P(\text{DA}) = 1 - a(r)$	[¬**p** r] **q**
AC	(p OFF, q ON)	$P(\text{AC}) = 1 - a(r)$	[¬**p** r] **q**
MT	(p ON, q OFF)	$P(\text{MT}) = 1 - ((a(d1) + a(d2))/2)$	**p** ¬**q** | d1, d2

This last case shows how people might retrieve possible defeaters and alternative causes from LTM and how they influence the assessment of the probability of the relevant inference. As for Possibility 2, when we are looking at the annotation required for, say the MP inference, i.e., to q, the answer seems obvious because the reasoner has clamped p on and q off and so the annotation must be 0. But again this misinterprets the significance of clamping units on or off. Clamping the q unit off just represents that q is not present. This does not mean that p was what was responsible for q's absence on this occasion, especially now as the activation of the d units indicates that there is another possibility. So although we have supposed p to be present, the probability that it was responsible for q requires revision given the other possibilities that have been discovered by interrogating the model. As before, we assume that people simply average the two activation levels to provide a revised assessment that it was p that led to q on this occasion.

Conditionals and constraint satisfaction: model testing

There are a variety of possible ways in which we could go about evaluating this model and we have only explored a few so far. In particular, it would be interesting to speculate on whether the stored representations in WM are used independently of their annotations to draw inferences in a way similar to that recommended by mental models theory. In the current account, the way in which people build up a representation of the results of interrogating their models is much more like Evans and Over (2004) than mental models theory (Johnson-Laird & Byrne, 2002). Pragmatic modulation by world knowledge will affect the contents of WM on an inference by inference basis. That is, there is no single representation built up of the conditional premise that serves to identify all the inferences someone will and will not draw. If this is something people do, it happens at a later evolutionary or developmental stage than the model we present, when people become able to further abstract from these records of interrogating world knowledge to perhaps perform something like deductive inference.

Another important function of storing this information in WM is that the processes of interrogating the model are *suppositional*, as Evans and Over (2004) have argued, based on the Ramsey Test. Consequently, it is crucial to retain a record of what one has supposed to be the case, i.e., which units one has clamped on or off, so that the right units can be unclamped to allow the system to resume its normal mode of operation.

Exploiting these connections raises the possibility of seeing, for example, how well this implementation of a dual process theory maps on to some of the accounts recently assessed by Oberauer (2006). To the extent that a close correspondence could be established, this model would inherit whatever support was found in Oberauer's model fitting exercise. However, such explorations are for the future. As a first attempt to examine the face validity of our model, we have simply used a very rough and ready way of using the annotations to predict inference endorsement rates on the assumption that different individuals may generate different combinations of the three possibilities for interrogating the network that we have just introduced. Consequently, there are level 1 predictions, where people use either Possibility 1, or Possibility 2, or Possibility 3 but no combinations. There are level 2 predictions, where people adopt one of the three binary combinations of these Possibilities. Finally there are level 3 predictions, where people consider all three Possibilities. To compute a predicted rate of endorsement for an inference we simply average over these seven cases. This is equivalent to the claim that the distribution of people who adopt various combinations of Possibilities is flat or equiprobable. It also amounts to the claim that people examine the same Possibilities for all inferences, whereas of course they may, for example, only look at Possibility 1 for MP but go deeper, i.e., look at more Possibilities, for MT, DA and AC. This crude way of combining the information blurs the natural ordering over cases, where Case 1 is the most shallow level and Case 3 the deepest. Our approach is no different to mental models theory, which requires different proportions of participants to adopt the different interpretations they propose (ten in Johnson-Laird & Byrne, 2002). These proportions are free parameters that must be determined from the data. One reason we keep to the simplest assumptions possible is that the complexity of the theory already far outweighs the complexity of the data. That is, with such a large number of parameters potentially free to vary, we are bound to capture the data. Consequently, our main goal is simply to use minimal assumptions in order to demonstrate some level of conformity to reality.

One key feature of the model is that it is reasonably clear as to which manipulations should have the desired effect on our predictions when trying to captures various experimental data sets. For example, if one wants to model the effect of many additional antecedents or defeaters (Cummins et al., 1991), then one will want to increase the strength of the connections between $d1$, $d2$, and q. No doubt some combination of other adjustments to the model *may* produce a similar effect. But because this *algorithmic level* model is a *representation* of how a reasoner thinks the world to be, one only need be concerned with *relevant* manipulations. Indeed this is one advantage of an algorithmic level model that is supposed to represent the world. The fact that it has many parameters one could vary to emulate the data is besides the point (as it would not be in fitting a computational level model, in which achieving a good fit by varying the wrong parameters is a bad thing).

We now examine a range of manipulations: task presentation, explicit and implicit suppression effects, negative conclusion bias, and the effects of schizotypy on conditional reasoning. We show that manipulations of the relevant aspects of the model, qua representation of the meaning of the premises provided (including pragmatic world knowledge), produce something close to the observed behavioural effects. The importance of moving to an algorithmic level implementation is particularly brought out in modelling the effects of schizotypy (Sellen, Oaksford, & Gray, 2005). This is because the relevant parameter that we manipulate is the Gain parameter, i.e., a systems level parameter, varying which simulates the effect of dopamine deficiency. Without moving to the current algorithmic implementation one could not possibly model these effects. We begin with task presentation.

Task presentation

'Task presentation' refers to the response mode people are given (Evans, Clibbens, & Rood, 1995; Evans & Handley, 1999; Schroyens, Schaeken, & d'Ydewalle, 2001). So participants might not be given an actual conclusion to consider at all. Rather they are given the conditional and categorical premises and are asked to write down what they think follows. This is called the *production* task. Alternatively, they will be given the single valid conclusion (and sometimes its negation

[Marcus & Rips, 1979; Oaksford, Chater, & Larkin, 2000]), which they must evaluate as either following from the premises or not. This is called the *evaluation* task. Finally, they may be given the antecedent, the consequent and their negations, which they must choose between in order to make a response. This is called the *selection* task.

We do not have the space to review other possible explanations of the effects of these manipulations. Our goal is primarily to provide a first pass assessment of the model rather than provide detailed model comparisons. Within the model, there does seem to be a relatively straightforward interpretation of these kinds of between task differences in terms of the *depth of processing* that they encourage. By 'depth of processing', we mean in ascending depth, whether they consider just Possibility 1, or Possibility 1 and Possibility 2, or whether they consider all the possibilities including Possibility 3. In the production task, without an explicitly stated target conclusion, only Possibility 1 may be considered. In the evaluation task, where the appropriate target conclusion is presented, participants might be more likely to consider Possibility 2. The evaluation task is the only task variant in which the negation of the target conclusion is specifically presented as a possibility. Consequently, one would expect deeper levels of processing, i.e., participants consider Possibilities 1, 2 and 3 or perhaps just Possibilities 2 and 3.

Figure 17.4 shows 'eye-ball' fits of the model to the data. The way we have gone about this is to come up with a range of parameter values for the model that made intuitive sense and which seemed to provide reasonable fits to baseline data from Schroyens and Schaeken's (2003) meta-analysis of conditional inference tasks using simple alphanumeric stimuli. These baseline fits are shown in Panel A of Figure 17.4. There is no point in assessing the actual fits as the number of free parameters precludes doing this in a meaningful way. Our approach was to set the parameters to capture the baseline, and then to see if reasonable fits to the data using different behavioural manipulations could be achieved by manipulating only the relevant parameters of the model. So to model the task presentation effects, all we did was sum the annotations for the different Possibilities to generate the predictions thereby simulating different levels of processing. Again simple un-weighted averages where calculated over the different possibilities. Panel B of Figure 17.3 show the data generated from a series of studies using the production and evaluation task (Evans et al., 1995; Evans & Handley, 1999; Schroyens et al., 2001). This Panel also shows the result of summing only over Possibilities 1 and 2 for each inference. Panel C of Figure 17.4 shows

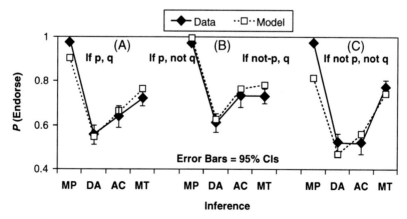

Fig. 17.4 The fit of the model to the data varying task presentation: baseline (Panel A), production and evaluation tasks (Panel B), selection tasks (Panel C).

data from selection tasks from the same sources and the results of summing over Possibilities 2 and 3 and Possibilities, 1, 2, and 3. As Figure 17.4 shows, these eye ball fits are reasonable.

The major discrepancy is the lack of fit for MP in Panel C. Oaksford and Chater (2007) suggested that people may revise down $P(q|p)$ for inferences other than MP, which is the only inference for which the appropriate conditional probability is asserted to be high (the appropriate conditional probability has to be inferred for the remaining inferences). This might be one of the circumstances in which people do not investigate all inferences to the same depth. Given the statement of the premises, participant may only ever investigate Possibility 1 for MP and only go deeper for the remaining inferences. As we said at the beginning of this section, this is not a possibility we directly explore in providing these eye-ball only fits. However, this is clearly an option for future work on this or related models.

Suppression effects

Suppression effects have been investigated using two different paradigms: the explicit suppression task (e.g., Byrne, 1989) and the implicit suppression task (e.g., Cummins, Lubarts, Alksnis, & Rist, 1991). While these two paradigms actually produce markedly different results, theoretical approaches tend not to differentiate the mental processes responsible for these effects. We first briefly outline the contrasting paradigms.

Suppression effects[6] arise when the presence—explicit or implicit—of defeaters ($d1$, $d2$) or alternative causes (r) are manipulated. In an explicit manipulation (Byrne, 1989) people are given an explicit further conditional sentence:

If you turn the key the car starts   (Rule)

If there is petrol in the tank the car starts   (d1)

If the car is bump started, it starts   (r)

When the Rule is presented together with $d1$, MP and MT are endorsed at a lot lower rates but DA and AC are unaffected. When the Rule is presented together with r, DA and AC are endorsed at a lot lower rates but MP and MT are unaffected. These effects are shown in Figure 17.5.

Similar effects can be observed using an implicit suppression paradigm (Cummins et al., 1991). In this task, a series of rules are pre-tested for whether people think they have many defeaters or alternative causes. A fully crossed factorial design can then be employed using rules that have many or few alternative causes and defeaters. We describe each cell by an ordered pair <r, d>, i.e., MM, FF, MF and FM. The results of a replication of Cummins (1995), which was used as a control condition in Sellen, Oaksford, and Gray (2005), is shown in Figure 17.6.

As Figures 17.5 and 17.6 reveal, the effects in the explicit task are very large, whereas the effects in the implicit task, while in the same direction, are far smaller. With one exception, we know of no attempt in the literature to explain this discrepancy. The exception is Byrne, Espino, and Santamaria (1999) who suggested that suppression effects only really occur when people are given the information about defeaters and alternative causes explicitly, thereby dismissing the implicit effects. However, in recent years the number of replications of implicit effects has been legion and so they cannot be dismissed so lightly.

---

6 'Suppression effects' is really a misnomer because it implies that 'valid' inferences are suppressed, whereas of course according to a probabilistic account, nothing is being suppressed. Rather people are endorsing inferences to a degree commensurate with their prior beliefs.

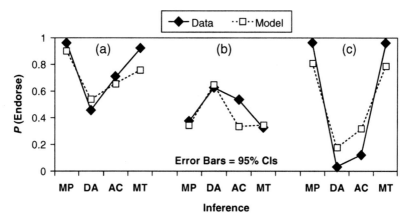

Fig. 17.5 The fit of the model to the data on explicit suppression effects (Byrne, 1989): baseline (Panel A), defeaters (Panel B), alternative causes (Panel C).

Capturing these effects in the current model is relatively straightforward. In the explicit paradigm, a further conditional is stated relating the consequent (q) to either an alternative cause (r) or a defeater (say, $d1$) acting as the antecedent. The explicit statement of the conditional should have two effects. First, it should lead participants to interpret the probability of q given r, $P(q|r)$ as high or the probability of q given $d1$, $P(q|d1)$ as low (Adams, 1998; Evans & Over, 2004). Second, it should lead them to consider directly the possibility that these conditions are present and so to interrogate the model by clamping on either the $d1$ or r units. We modelled these effects by increasing the weights between these units and the q unit. Moreover, we clamped on the unit corresponding either to $d1$ or to r as well as the unit corresponding to the categorical premise for the four inferences. The results are also shown in Figure 17.5. We adjusted these weights from the

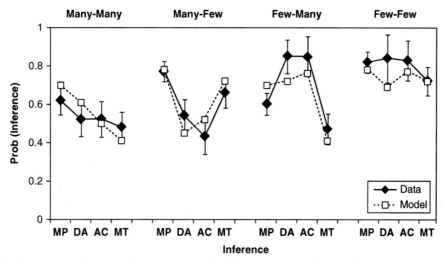

Fig. 17.6 The fit of the model to the data on implicit suppression effects (Sellen, Oaksford, & Gray, 2005, Control: Low-Schizotypy Condition) for the four conditions.

baseline (Figure 17.5, Panel A, same model as shown in Figure 17.4, Panel A). As can be seen, the effects are very marked and get very close to the magnitude of the effects seen in the data.

In contrast, in the implicit paradigm, without the explicit rule statement there is no hint provided that either *r* or *d1* are present. Consequently, people will not explicitly consider these possibilities by clamping on the *d1*- or the *r*-units as in the explicit task. There are a variety of possibilities to model the effects of many or few defeaters or alternative causes. Units could be added corresponding to these extra alternative causes and defeaters. However, in the model their joint effect will depend on how associated they are with *p*. That is, simply adding more *d*- or *r*-units without considering the probability of their joint occurrence with *p* will not have the predicted effect. There is evidence that this is the critical factor in accounting for these effects. For example, there has been research showing that the strength of association between the *p* and either *r* or *d1*, varies suppression effects (e.g., De Neys, Schaeken, & d'Ydewalle, 2003). Moreover, recent research by Geiger and Oberauer (2007) has shown that, as this model would predict, it is the frequency of the occurrence of defeaters and alternative causes that produce suppression effects and not the number of different types of defeater or alternative cause. To model these effects, we therefore increased or decreased the connection weights from baseline for the connections between the *p*-unit and either the *r*- or *d1*-units and averaged across cases for each inference as before.[7] The results are also shown in Figure 17.6. As can be seen, the effects are smaller than in the explicit task and get very close to the magnitude of the effects seen in the data.

Negative conclusion bias

Negative conclusion bias arises when negated constituents are included in the conditional rules used in the conditional inference task (Evans, 1977, 1983). Negations ('¬') are varied in the antecedent and consequent to produce four rule forms: *if p then q*; *if p then ¬q*; *if ¬p then q*; *if ¬p then ¬q*. Negative conclusion bias refers to the phenomenon where people are more willing to endorse the conclusion if it is negated. For example, consider DA. For the *if p then q* rule the conclusion is ¬q and this is endorsed more highly than the conclusion of the same inference on the *if p then ¬q* rule for which the conclusion is *q*.

According to Oaksford et al. (2000), this phenomenon is caused by people interpreting negated categories as being more probable. This is because the contrast sets defined by negated categories are larger than their affirmative counterparts. For example, the set of Martini drinks is far smaller than the set of drinks that are not Martinis. This argument suggests that the prior probabilities of *p* and *q* are the relevant parameters to vary in order to capture the effects of introducing negations. This was exactly the way these effects were modelled in Oaksford et al. (2000) and in the current model this manipulation is achieved by varying the bias terms into the *p*- and/or the *q*-units. For the low probability, i.e., the un-negated, clause a prior probability of .2 (log prior odds = -2) was used and for the high probability case, i.e., the negated, clause a prior probability of .8 (log prior odds = 2) was used.

Figure 17.7 shows the overall fits of the model to the data. Again, no attempt has been made to optimize the fit to the data. The central point is that the main qualitative patterns in the results emerge simply from adjusting the appropriate parameters of the model.

Schizotypy, context, and conditional inference

Sellen, Oaksford, and Gray (2005) investigated the effects of schizotypy on conditional inference using Cummins' (1995) implicit suppression paradigm. The results of the control, low schizotypy

---

[7] In the model, these are the connections that violate the conditional independence assumption.

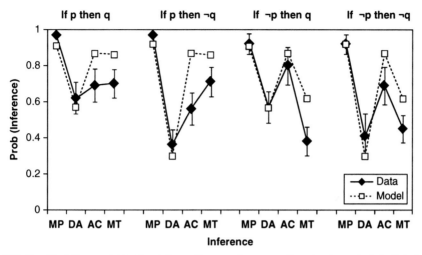

Fig 17.7 The fit of the model to the data on the negations paradigm (meta-analysis in Oaksford, Chater, & Larkin, 2000) for the four conditional statements.

group in Sellen et al. (2005) are shown in Figure 17.6, clearly revealing effects of both alternative (r) and additional ($d1$ and $d2$) antecedents, i.e., of alternative causes and defeaters. Figure 17.8 shows the results for the high schizotypy group. The most striking feature of these results is that while there are effects for alternative causes, no effects of defeaters were observed. That is, DA and AC are clearly endorsed much less frequently when there are many alternatives (Many-Many, Many-Few) than when there are few (Few-Many, Few-Few). However, there were no differences for MP and MT between the conditions where there were many defeaters (Many-Many, Few-Many) and where there were few (Many-Few, Few-Few). Thus the effects of high schizotypy seem to be specific to defeaters. As we have already argued in outlining the general structure of

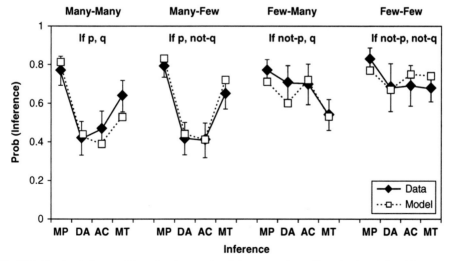

Fig 17.8 The fit of the model to the data on implicit suppression effects in the High Schizotypy Condition of Sellen, Oaksford, and Gray (2005) for the four conditions.

conditional world knowledge, defeaters are part of the context that has to be right for a conditional rule to be predictively useful. So if you know the battery is flat turning the key is pointless.

Schizotypy is generally thought to define a dimension of individual variation which at one extreme is closely linked to schizophrenia. Consequently models of abnormal cognitive processing in schizophrenia should be relevant to explaining effects in the high schizotypy group. One, by now quite old, account of abnormal cognitive processing in schizophrenia is Cohen and Servan-Schreiber's (1992) neural network model. There are two important elements of this model. First, they assume that many problems in cognitive processing in schizophrenia are due to the processing of context in pre-frontal cortex. Second, these problems are created by a reduction in levels of dopamine, which Cohen and Servan-Schreiber argue affects the Gain parameter, G (see Equation 8), of the appropriate context units in their neural network models. Higher gain, i.e., higher dopamine levels, 'potentiates' the response of these units so that less input is required for a given level of activation. In simulating schizophrenic performance, Cohen and Servan-Schreiber reduced the gain in the context units from 1.0 to a lower value, thereby simulating the lower levels of dopamine found in the pre-frontal cortex of schizophrenics.

In simulating the effects of schizotypy on conditional inference, we carried out a similar procedure. We began with exactly the same parameter settings as we used to model the data shown in Figure 17.5, using a gain parameter value of 1.0. We then reduced the gain parameter in the context units, $d1$ and $d2$, to 0.2. Figure 17.8 show the results of this manipulation, showing quite close fits to the data. In sum, one benefit of moving to an algorithmic level model, specifically a model with some, albeit very limited, neurological plausibility, is the ability to simulate effects on reasoning that couldn't be captured by any other existing model.

Discussion

In this paper, we have presented a very preliminary algorithmic implementation of the probabilistic approach using a constraint satisfaction neural network. In this implementation, inference involves interrogating LTM for probabilistic world knowledge and there are a variety of possible ways of doing this. This process therefore demands a way of storing the results of each interrogation while other possibilities are considered. This simple fact implicates the need for dual systems in reasoning. A Working Memory control system is required to record, store and subsequently integrate the results of interrogating LTM to produce a conclusion. These latter processes may develop into a system capable of independent operation, which could underpin our logical abilities. After all, what needs to be stored are precisely the representations of the possibilities ruled in or out by a conditional. Hence, by considering an implementation of a probabilistic account in neural networks, we perhaps get a glimpse of why a reasoning system like mental models may have evolved or develop over the lifespan.

In discussing this model, we have considered the limited constraint satisfaction model as the pre-potent units in a much larger network. Another way of viewing this network is as an explicit local 'mental mechanism' (Chater & Oaksford, 2006) constructed in WM that has its parameter values set by prior knowledge in LTM (see also, Oaksford & Chater, 2009a,b). Such a mechanism contrasts with a mental model in that it can be dynamically manipulated in order to consider different possibilities, it is not just a static representation of those possibilities. Nonetheless, mental model like representations would still be needed to record the results of exploring different possibilities within the mechanism. A mental mechanism view would also relate these models much more closely to current applications of Bayes' Nets to high level cognition, as we discuss in Chater and Oaksford (2006) and Ali et al. (this volume).

An important element of this implementation concerns the rationality debate. A full probabilistic interpretation of the operation of a constraint satisfaction neural network imposes constraints not incorporated into this model. Thus, for example, causes (p and r) and defeaters ($d1$ and $d2$) are not conditionally independent of the effect (q) in this implementation. This issue also arose in Ali et al.'s (this volume) work on how causal Bayes nets may provide a source of prediction in conditional inference. There, while many predictions were significantly confirmed, deviations also arose that were attributable to a similar possible source, i.e., correlated causes. Consequently, the degree to which the current model approximates probabilistic rationality is also up for debate. However, the current implementation would appear to capture people's intuitions about correlated causes. Although we have not investigated the possibility that effects might be independent (due to unique defeaters, see Ali et al., this volume). The explanatory strategy of explaining deviations from normative rationality by appeal to the algorithmic implementation is also wholly familiar in reasoning research. It is exactly the way that mental models theory accounts for deviations from logical reasoning.

Future research using this and related models would provide learning opportunities about more complex causal set ups. The idea would be to also train up an artificial neural network using similar training sets and compare human and network performance on subsequent inference tasks. This would provide much more constrained predictions in which the model parameters are fixed by learning rather than adjusted by hand to fit the results on inference.

References

Adams, E. W. (1998). *A primer of probability logic.* Stanford: CLSI Publications.

Anderson, J. R. (1990). *The adaptive character of thought.* Hillsdale, NJ: Lawrence Erlbaum Associates.

Barwise, J. & Perry, J. (1983). *Situations and attitudes.* Cambridge MA: MIT Press.

Bennett, J. (1964). *Rationality.* London: Routledge & Kegan Paul.

Bennett, J. (2003). *A philosophical guide to conditionals.* Oxford England: Oxford University Press.

Bickerton, D. (2000). Biomusicology and language evolution studies. In N. L. Wallin, B. Merker, & S. Brown (Eds.), *The Origins of Music* (pp. 153–164). Cambridge MA: MIT Press.

Braine, M. D. S. & O'Brien, D. P. (1991). A theory of if: A lexical entry, reasoning program, and pragmatic principles. *Psychological Review*, **98**, 182–203.

Byrne, R. M. J. (1989). Suppressing valid inferences with conditionals. *Cognition*, **31**, 1–21.

Byrne, R. M. J., Espino, O., & Santamaria, C. (1999). Counterexamples and the suppression of inferences. *Journal of Memory and Language*, **40**, 347–373.

Chater, N. & Oaksford, M. (2006). Mental mechanisms: Speculations on human causal learning and reasoning. In K. Fiedler, & P. Juslin (Eds.), *Information sampling and adaptive cognition* (pp. 210–238). Cambridge: Cambridge University Press.

Chater, N., Oaksford, M., Nakisa, R., & Redington, M. (2003). Fast, frugal and rational: How rational norms explain behavior. *Organizational Behavior and Human Decision Processes*, **90**, 63–86.

Cohen, L. J. (1981). Can human irrationality be experimentally demonstrated? *Behavioral and Brain Sciences*, **4**, 317–370.

Cohen, J. D. & Servan-Schreiber, D. (1992). Context, cortex, and dopamine: A connectionist approach to behavior and biology in schizophrenia. *Psychological Review*, **99**, 45–77.

Cummins, D. D. (1995). Naïve theories and causal deduction. *Memory & Cognition*, **23**, 646–658.

Cummins, D. D., Lubart, T., Alksnis, O., & Rist, R. (1991). Conditional reasoning and causation. *Memory & Cognition*, **19**, 274–282.

De Neys, W. D., Schaeken W., & d'Ydewalle G. (2003). Causal conditional reasoning and strength of association: The disabling condition case. *The European Journal of Cognitive Psychology*, **15**, 161–176.

Evans, J. St.B. T. (1977). Toward a statistical theory of reasoning. *Quarterly Journal of Experimental Psychology*, **29**, 621–635.

Evans, J. St.B. T. (1983) Linguistic determinants of bias in conditional reasoning. *Quarterly Journal of Experimental Psychology*, **35A**, 635–644.

Evans, J. St.B. T., Clibbens, J., & Rood, B. (1995). Bias in conditional inference: implications for mental models and mental logic. *Quarterly Journal of Experimental Psychology*, **48A**, 644–670.

Evans, J. St.B. T. & Handley, S. J. (1999). The role of negation in conditional inference. *Quarterly Journal of Experimental Psychology*, **52A**, 739–769.

Evans, J. St.B.T. & Over, D. E. (2004). *If*. Oxford, England: Oxford University Press.

Geiger, S. M. & Oberauer, K. (2007). Reasoning with conditionals: Does every counterexample count? It's frequency that counts. *Memory & Cognition*, **35**, 2060–2074.

Goodman, N. (1983). *Fact, fiction and forecast*. 4th Edition, Cambridge, Mass: Harvard University Press. (Originally 1954).

Jeffrey, R. (1983). *The Logic of decision*. 2nd Edition, Chicago, University of Chicago Press

Johnson-Laird, P. N. & Byrne, R. M. J. (2002). Conditionals: A theory of meaning, pragmatics, and inference. *Psychological Review*, **109**, 646–678.

Marr, D. (1982). *Vision*. San Francisco: W. H. Freeman

Marcus, S. L. & Rips, L.J.(1979). Conditional reasoning. *Journal of Verbal Learning and Verbal Behavior*, **18**, 199–223.

McClelland, J. L. (1998).Connectionist models and Bayesian inference. In M. Oaksford & N. Chater, (Eds.), *Rational models of cognition* (pp. 21–53). Oxford: Oxford University Press.

Newell, A. & H. A. Simon. (1972). *Human problem solving*. Englewood Cliffs, NJ: Prentice-Hall.

Oaksford, M. (1989). *Cognition and inquiry: The pragmatics of conditional reasoning*. Unpublished doctoral dissertation, Centre for Cognitive Science, University of Edinburgh.

Oaksford, M. (2002). Contrast classes and matching bias as explanations of the effects of negation on conditional reasoning. *Thinking & Reasoning*, **8**, 135–151.

Oaksford, M. (2008). Stimulus equivalence and the origins of reasoning, language, and working memory. *Cognitive Studies*, **15**, 392–407.

Oaksford, M. & Chater, N. (1991). Against logicist cognitive science. *Mind and Language*, **6**, 1–38.

Oaksford, M. & Chater, N. (1994). A rational analysis of the selection task as optimal data selection. *Psychological Review*, **101**, 608–631.

Oaksford, M. & Chater, N. (1995). Theories of reasoning and the computational explanation of everyday inference. *Thinking & Reasoning*, **1**, 121–152.

Oaksford, M. & Chater, N. (1996). Rational explanation of the selection task. *Psychological Review*, **103**, 381–391.

Oaksford, M. & Chater, N. (1998). *Rationality in an uncertain world*. Hove, England: Psychology Press.

Oaksford, M. & Chater, N. (2003). Computational levels and conditional reasoning: Reply to Schroyens and Schaeken (2003). *Journal of Experimental Psychology: Learning, Memory & Cognition*, **29**, 150–156.

Oaksford, M. & Chater, N. (2007). *Bayesian rationality: The probabilistic approach to human reasoning*. Oxford: Oxford University Press.

Oaksford, M. & Chater, N. (2008). Probability logic and the *Modus Ponens-Modus Tollens* asymmetry in conditional inference. In N. Chater, & M. Oaksford (Eds.), *The probabilistic mind: Prospects for Bayesian cognitive science* (pp. 97–120). Oxford: Oxford University Press.

Oaksford, M. & Chater, N. (2009a). Precis of 'Bayesian rationality: The probabilistic approach to human reasoning.' *Behavioral and Brain Sciences*, **32**, 69–84.

Oaksford, M. & Chater, N. (2009b). The uncertain reasoner: Bayes, logic and rationality. *Behavioral and Brain Sciences*, **32**, 105–120.

Oaksford, M., Chater, N., & Larkin, J. (2000). Probabilities and polarity biases in conditional inference. *Journal of Experimental Psychology: Learning, Memory and Cognition*, **26**, 883–889.

Oaksford, M. & Hahn, U. (2007). Induction, deduction and argument strength in human reasoning and argumentation. In A. Feeney, & E. Heit (Eds.), *Inductive reasoning* (pp. 269–301). Cambridge: Cambridge University Press.

Oaksford, M. & Stenning, K. (1992). Reasoning with conditionals containing negated constituents. *Journal of Experimental Psychology: Learning, Memory and Cognition*, **18**, 835–854.

Oberauer, K. (2006). Reasoning with conditionals: A test of formal models of four theories. *Cognitive Psychology*, **53**, 238–283.

Oberauer, K. & Oaksford, M. (2008). What must a psychological theory of reasoning explain? Comment on Barrioullet, Gauffroy, and Lecas (2008). *Psychological Review*, **115**, 773–778.

Newstead, S. E., Handley, S. J., & Buck, E. (1999). Falsifying mental models: Testing the predictions of theories of syllogistic reasoning. *Memory & Cognition*, **27**, 344–354.

Pearl, J. (2000). *Causality: Models, reasoning and inference*. Cambridge: Cambridge University Press.

Pfeifer, N. & Kleiter, G. D. (2005). Towards a mental probability logic. *Psychologica Belgica*, **45**, 71–99.

Pylyshyn, Z. W. (1984). *Computation and cognition: Toward a foundation for cognitive science*. Montgomery, Vermont: Bradford.

Rips, L. J. (1994*). The Psychology of proof*. Cambridge, MA: MIT Press.

Schroyens, W. & Schaeken, W. (2003). A critique of Oaksford, Chater and Larkin's (2000) conditional probability model of conditional reasoning. *Journal of Experimental Psychology: Learning, Memory and Cognition*, **29**, 140–149.

Schroyens, W., Schaeken, W., & d'Ydewalle, G. (2001). The processing of negations in conditional reasoning: A meta-analytic study in mental models and/or mental logic theory. *Thinking and Reasoning*, **7**, 121–172.

Sellen, J., Oaksford, M., & Gray, N. (2005). Schizotypy and conditional inference. *Schizophrenia Bulletin*, **31**, 1–12.

Sloman, S.A. (2005). *Causal models*. Oxford: Oxford University Press.

Sobel, J. H. (2004). *Probable* modus ponens *and* modus tollens *and updating on uncertain evidence*. Unpublished manuscript, Department of Philosophy, University of Toronto, Scarborough. (www.scar.toronto.ca/~sobel/ConfDisconf.pdf).

Sober, E. (2002). Intelligent design and probability reasoning. *International Journal for Philosophy of Religion*, **52**, 65–80.

Stewart, N., Chater, N., & Brown, G. D. A. (2006). Decision by sampling. *Cognitive Psychology*, **53**, 1–26.

Thagard, P. (1988). *Computational philosophy of science*. Cambridge, MA: MIT Press.

Verschueren, N., Schaeken, W., & d'Ydewalle, G. (2005). A dual-process specification of causal conditional reasoning. Thinking & Reasoning, **11**, 278–293.

Wagner, C. G. (2004). *Modus tollens* probabilized. *British Journal for Philosophy of Science*, **55**, 747–753.

Chapter 18

Towards a metacognitive dual process theory of conditional reasoning

Valerie A. Thompson

Dual-Process Theories (DPT) have emerged as the dominant theoretical framework for human reasoning and decision making (e.g., Evans, 2007; Kahneman, 2003; Klaczynski & Robinson, 2000; Sloman, 2002; Stanovich, 2004). These theories commonly assume that reasoning and decision making are accomplished by the joint action of two types of processes: Automatic System 1 (S1) processes give rise to a highly contextualized representation of the problem and produce rapid, heuristic answers. System 2 (S2) implements more deliberate, decontextualized analytic processes. S1 processes are assumed to dominate reasoning, producing judgements that are based on intuitive beliefs, stereotypes, emotions, or readily available instances. S2 intervention is necessary to produce judgements based on the quality of the evidence, the application of relevant normative principles, or hypothetical thinking, but is rarely engaged. Together with the assumption that System 2 processes may, themselves, be prone to error (i.e., because of limited working memory resources, absence of good normative models, and a tendency to 'satisfice'), DPT potentially explain so-called biases and errors in a broad range of reasoning tasks.

Although these theories have been successful on many levels, they still lack the specification necessary to 'define more precisely the nature of the interaction between the two processes (S1 and S2) and to assist the generation of experimental predictions about particular reasoning tasks', (Evans, 2006, p. 379). In terms of predicting the outcome of any given reasoning attempt, the crucial questions for DPT are 1) What is the nature of the S1 output? 2) When and in what way does S2 intervene? And 3) How does this intervention produce the final answer?

The purpose of this chapter is move towards this goal and to outline a DPT of conditional reasoning. To do so, I will attempt to answer each of the three questions posed above on the basis of current data. Where data are insufficient or contradictory, I will suggest means of resolution. In the course of this analysis, I will argue that current formulations of DPT are fundamentally incomplete without a model of metacognitve processes.

A dual process theory framework

The basic assumptions of DPT are represented in Figure 18.1. Although the extant models differ somewhat in emphasis, this Figure represents their common underlying assumptions. S1 processes produce a default response (A1) that is generated as the final answer unless something triggers S2 processes. Because S1 processes are thought to be those routinely involved in the comprehension of discourse, pattern recognition, etc., this S1 output incorporates background knowledge, pre-existing beliefs, and categorical relations (Evans, 2006; Kahneman, 2003; Stanovich, 2007). S1 processes are also thought to be elicited readily and rapidly, and without effort or deliberation on the part of the reasoner.

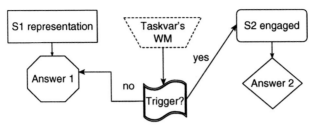

Fig. 18.1 Common assumptions of dual process theories.

In contrast, deductive reasoning requires one to work out the entailments of a set of premises, regardless of whether the conclusions or premises concur with one's belief system. This requires the reasoner to set aside the initial response and generate an alternative (Evans, 2007; Stanovich, 2007). To do so, one must inhibit A1 (Handley, Capon, Beveridge, Dennis, & Evans, 2004; Markovits & Doyon, 2004), and construct an alternative model or representation (Evans, 2007; Stanovich 2007); this in turn requires sufficient cognitive capacity to be successful (e.g., de Neys, 2006a, b; Stanovich, 2007). In most cases, evidence of S2 intervention is measured by the number of responses that accord with a normative model of performance, such as deductive logic.

The available evidence has corroborated these basic assumptions. Normatively correct responses are produced more often by high- than low-capacity reasoners (see Stanovich, 1999 for review) and by those who show better skills at inhibition (Handley et al., 2004; Markovits & Doyon, 2004). In keeping with the assumption that the highly contextualized A1 is produced unless there is a trigger, normatively correct responses are more prevalent under strict logic instructions than under instructions that do not make reference to logical principles (Schroyens, Schaeken, & Handley, 2003). Indeed, when asked to indicate, from their own perspective, which inferences followed from a conditional, participants accepted only about 50% of the inferences and did not discriminate valid from invalid inferences (Thompson, Evans, & Handley, 2005). In contrast, when asked which inferences followed from the point of view of the person who wrote the conditional, reasoners endorsed more inferences, and clearly differentiated valid from invalid inferences. In sum, therefore, the evidence supports the assumption that S2 engagement is an effortful, resource-demanding process, and that it is not usually engaged unless there is a trigger.

The framework outlined above, while tenable at a general level, is nonetheless under-specified at several points. First, the nature of the S1 processes that are engaged is not clear, nor is the nature of the output produced by those processes. For example, it is commonly assumed that when reasoners have given an answer that accords with their prior beliefs, they have made a response based largely on S1 output (Evans & Curtis-Holmes, 2005; Klaczynski & Robinson, 2000; Stanovich, 1999). However, a belief-based response can come about by two different processes, one that is likely to be classified as S1, and the other that is likely to be an S2 process (Versheuren, Schaeken, & D'Ydewalle, 2005a). The first is a rapid assessment of the likelihood or truth of a conditional statement, whereas the second entails a deliberate search for counter-examples. Although both processes produce belief-based responses, the latter is clearly an S2 process, as evidenced by the role of WM (de Neys, Schaeken, & d'Ydewalle, 2005). Moreover, as argued below, there is evidence to suggest that S1 processes might also make use of pragmatic implicatures and other comprehension strategies, such that A1 may be based on structural or linguistic variables that are not belief-based. Thus, the starting point for a DPT of conditional inference requires specification of the S1 processes and output.

In the same way that relying on belief-based responses may not be a good measure of S1 involvement, relying on normatively correct responses may likewise provide an inaccurate estimate of the probability of S2 engagement. That is, for a variety of reasons, S2 may produce a normatively incorrect response, either because of capacity limitations, misapprehension of the task, absence of the relevant logical principles, etc. Consequently, relying on normatively correct responses as an indicator of S2 conflates two dimensions, namely the probability and success of S2 engagement.

Finally, current models of DPT have not done an adequate job of specifying the conditions that trigger S2 engagement (Thompson, 2007). To date, most models rely on external triggers, such as the time allotted for the task (Evans & Curtis-Holmes, 2005; Roberts & Newton, 2001), instructions (Schroyens et al., 2003), and perspective (Thompson et al., 2005). But, even in the control conditions of these studies, some reasoners produce normative responses; this variance is typically ascribed to individual differences in capacity (Stanovich, 1999). Nonetheless, the correlation with capacity is not perfect; among those of low capacity, there are some who produce normative responses and among those of high capacity, there are those that do not.

Elsewhere (Thompson, 2007), I have argued that the metacognitive experiences associated with generating A1 are important, but neglected factors in triggering S2. The importance of metacognitive experiences is illustrated in the following problem (Fredricks, 2005):

Example 1:

> If it takes 5 machines 5 minutes to make 5 widgets, how long would it take 100 machines to make 100 widgets? _____ minutes.

A large majority of people answer this simple problem incorrectly, presumably because they do not take the time to work out the rate of production. Instead, the initial response (100) generated by S1 processes is accepted with little S2 analysis. Why? I propose that this occurs because the initial S1 analysis is accompanied by a feeling of certainty that A1 is correct; in cases where that certainty is lower, the probability of S2 should be higher. I have termed this initial metacognitive judgement the Feeling of Rightness (FOR) and develop a model of the FOR in conditional reasoning below. In addition, I address another neglected metacognitive process in deductive reasoning, namely the confidence associated with the final answer produced.

A dual process model of conditional inference

In the sections below, I develop a DPT model of the conditional inference task. For this task, participants are provided with the conditional statement (if p then q) and a minor premise ($p, \sim p$, q, or $\sim q$) and are asked to either evaluate or generate a conclusion. For the evaluation task, participants are typically asked to evaluate four inferences: two are normatively correct on principles of logical necessity (MP: $p \therefore q$ and MT:$\sim q \therefore \sim p$) and two are technically fallacies (AC: $q \therefore p$ and DA: $\sim p \therefore \sim q$).

S1 output

What is the nature of the S1 output? The goal of this first section is to consider possibilities for the outcome of early, automatic processes. In doing so, I make the following assumptions: That S1 processes are fast, and so deliver their output early in the reasoning process. This initial output I will refer to as A1. Measuring this output requires that reasoners be induced to produce the first answer that occurs to them under time pressure. In keeping with others (e.g., Stanovich, 2004), it is acknowledged that S1 is not a unitary set of processes, but includes a diverse set of operations. Thus, I will also consider the possibility that more than one output may be made available by S1 and that these outputs may be in conflict. The output that follows S2 intervention will be termed A2, even if it remains the same as A1.

Belief

As above, the most popular candidate for S1 processes is the recruitment of pre-existing beliefs. Indeed, there is a wealth of data to confirm that beliefs play an important role in conditional inference (e.g., Cummins et al., 1991; Markovits & Barrouillet, 2002; Thompson, 2000). However, because these studies typically allow reasoners ample time to make a response, it is not clear whether the belief-effects are S1 or S2 processes. Clearly, from a DPT perspective, we need to delineate the contributions of S1 and S2 processes to generating belief-consistent output. Even if we assumed that the observed effects originated in S1, there still remain a number of unanswered questions. Specifically, we need to be able to differentiate between the two elements of the task that may give rise to belief effects: the conditional statement itself and the conclusion that is evaluated/ generated. Finally, reasoners may make two sorts of belief assessments, one concerning the probability that a conditional or inference is true, and a second by another by evaluating automatically primed counter-examples. The goal for DPT's is to determine which, if any, of these processes contribute to A1.

Belief in the conditional statement

A conditional statement is judged to be true to the extent that the probability of q/p approaches one (Evans, Handley, & Over, 2003; Oberauer & Wilhelm, 2003; Ohm & Thompson, 2004, 2006; Over & Evans, 2003). In other words, when q is likely given the occurrence of p, the conditional is judged true; when q is unlikely given p, the conditional is judged false. We know that reasoners make this judgement; from the point of view of DPT, the question arises as to whether it is an early and automatic process or one that requires deliberation. If it is early and automatic, what effect does this assessment of belief have on subsequent reasoning outcomes?

By analogy to syllogistic reasoning, it is possible that doubt in the premises might cast doubt on the conclusions (Thompson, 1996); that is, reasoners might apply a principle of *soundness* as well as *validity*. However, in the case of conditional inference, the data suggest that belief in the conditional premise has a selective effect on the inferences that are endorsed. Thompson (1994; 2000) demonstrated that one measure of belief in the conditional, namely the degree to which p is considered sufficient for q, selectively mediated responses to MP and MT, but had no effect on AC, DA. Instead, these latter inferences were mediated by the degree to which p was considered to be necessary for q. These data suggest that belief in the conditional per se is not relevant to evaluating the AC and DA inferences; moreover, because belief in the MP and MT inferences themselves was confounded with belief in the conditional, it is not clear what role, if any, belief in the conditional played in evaluating those inferences either.

Markovits and Schroyens (2007) recently provided a more direct test of the hypothesis that belief in the conditional premise affects subsequent inferences. These researchers compared inferences based on premises that were clearly false (if an animal is a mammal, then it has wheels) to those that were plausible, but not always true (if an animal is a mammal, then it has legs). MP inferences were endorsed more often for the former than the latter, presumably because the obvious untruth of the statements cued reasoners to the need to inhibit their world knowledge. That they were less successful in the latter case suggests that information about the believability of the premises is available early on and carries over to later stages of reasoning. In this study, the MP inferences were always unbelievable, such that belief in them was not perfectly correlated with belief in the conditional, as was the case in Thompson's studies. However, because different inferences were evaluated in the implausible and plausible conditions (i.e., whales have wheels vs.

whales have legs), it is still possible that the observed differences could be attributed to differences in believability of the conclusions, rather than in the conditional premise. Thus, although suggestive, the available evidence does not answer the question regarding when, or if, information about belief in the conditional is available at an early stage of processing.

Even less is known about how other interpretive dimensions of the conditional statement might be relevant to the generation of A1. There are numerous dimensions along which conditional statements can be interpreted, e.g., they can express several types of indicative and deontic relationships (Thompson, 2000) and can even invite deontic conclusions (Thompson et al., 2005). Interpretations may be guided by principles of relevance (Sperber et al., 2005), by assertability conditions (Ohm & Thompson, 2007), subjective utility (Ohm & Thompson, 2007; Over, Manktelow, & Hadjichristidis, 2004), etc. At this point however, it is not clear what role, if any, these factors play in the generation of A1, nor the extent to which they contribute to later, S2 processes.

Belief in the inference

By analogy to syllogistic conclusions, we would expect conditional inferences to be accepted or rejected on the basis of the degree to which they were perceived to be true or false, even when the believability of the premises is held constant (Thompson, 1996; Thompson et al., 2003). Consistent with that expectation, participants' endorsement of conditional inferences varies with their degree of belief in the conclusion given the minor premise (Oaksford, Chater, & Larkin, 2000; Ohm & Thompson, 2006).

There is some debate, however, regarding the basis of this belief. One possibility is that conclusion believability is determined by the availability of counter examples (Cummins et al., 1991; Markovits & Barrouillet, 2002, Thompson, 1995; 2000). Consistent with this view, instances of 'p & $\sim q$' tend to block the acceptance of the MP and MT inferences whereas instances of '$\sim p$ & q' block the acceptance of AC and DA inferences. Alternatively, conclusion believability may be determined by estimating the probability that the conclusion is true, given that the premises are true (Geiger & Oberauer, 2007; Thompson, 1995; 2000). For example, to make the MP inference, reasoners may assess the probability that q will happen given the occurrence of p, perhaps by estimating the likelihood that p occurs without q.

Clearly, probability estimates and the availability of counter-examples are confounded: When many counter-examples are available, the probability that the conclusion is true is low. Nonetheless, these are distinct constructs: It is possible for there to be only one counter-example available, but if that counter-example is very likely to occur, then the probability of the conclusion is low. Conversely, if there are many counter-examples available, but none are likely, then the probability is high. Although few attempts have been made to disentangle these variables experimentally, the available evidence suggests that the assessed likelihood or probability, rather than the number of counter-examples per se, mediates conditional inferences (Geiger & Oberauer, 2007; Thompson, 2000).

Another issue concerns the extent to which inferences are mediated by belief in the conclusion as opposed to belief in the conditional premise. As described above, these variables are often confounded, at least in the case of the MP and MT inferences. In the case of the DA and AC inferences however, the evidence indicates that belief in the conclusion determines inference acceptability regardless of premise. For example, Thompson (1994; 2000) found that the acceptability of the AC and DA inference varied as a function of degree of belief in the conclusions even when belief in the conditional was held constant; Cummins et al. (1991) made a similar observations based on the availability of counter-examples. To my knowledge, there are no comparable data for the MP and MT inferences because, if the materials are realistic, then belief in the conditional is completely confounded with belief in the conclusions, as the following two examples illustrate:

Example 2:

> If the butter is heated, then it melts.
> The butter is heated. Therefore, it will melt.

Example 3:

> If the t.v. is plugged in, then it works.
> The t.v. is plugged in. Therefore, it will work.

Example 2 illustrates the case where the conditional statement and the MP inference are both believable; Example 3 illustrates the case where the conditional statement and the MP inference are both unbelievable. To disentangle these variables, one needs to structure the questions differently and introduce nonsense syllables, as per the method used in syllogistic reasoning to control belief in the premises (e.g., Thompson et al., 2003):

Example 4:

> If an animal is a dog, then it is an argonnel.
> Argonnels have three legs.
> Therefore dogs have three legs.

In this case, the conditional statement is neither believable nor unbelievable; in this way, it will be possible to manipulate degree of belief in the conclusions while controlling for degree of belief in the premises.

S1 vs S2 as the source of belief effects

Regardless of the source of the belief effects, the next question to be answered concerns the degree to which belief in either the conclusion or the conditional premise contributes to the generation of A1, or is an explicit process that contributes to A2. The evidence suggests that both possibilities may be true. For example, Vershueren et al. (2005a) argued that there are both fast, automatic belief effects and slow, deliberate ones (see also Thompson, 1995; 2000). Reasoners were asked to indicate if counter-examples were possible for MP and AC inferences and to rate the probability of q/p and p/q. Reasoners were also timed reasoning with same premises, and trials were divided by median split into slow and fast trials. Using multiple regression analyses, they found that fast inferences were better predicted by likelihood ratings than counter-example availability, and that the reverse was true for slow trials. They concluded that an appraisal of likelihood is available quickly, but that generating counter-examples is a longer, more deliberate process. Consistent with this conclusion, high WM-capacity reasoners are more likely than low-capacity reasoners to rely on counter-examples (Vershueren, Schaeken, & d'Ydewalle, 2005b), and retrieving counter-examples requires WM capacity (de Neys, 2003, Schaeken, & d'Ydewalle, 2005).

On this basis, one might conclude that a global evaluation of belief forms part of the A1 response. This assessment of belief appears to be based on an assessment of likelihood rather than the availability of counter-examples. On the other hand, it is also possible that some counter-examples are primed automatically (Markovits & Barrouillet, 2002), but that others require deliberate retrieval (Grosset, Barrouillet, & Markovits, 2005). Consider the following two problems:

Example 5:

> If someone eats too much, then they will put on weight.
> Someone puts on weight. Do they eat too much?

Example 6:

> If someone quits smoking, then they will put on weight.
> Someone puts on weight. Have they quit smoking?

A counter-example for the second problem is strongly associated with the premise, and consequently, reasoners solve this problem quickly; counter-examples are less strongly cued by the first problem and reasoners take longer to make this inference (Grosset et al., 2005). In addition, when asked to retrieve counter-examples under dual-task conditions, retrieval of weakly associated, but not strongly associated counter-examples was reduced relative to no-load conditions (De Neys et al., 2005). These data indicate that some counter-examples, such as those cued by the second premise, may be available automatically and thus contribute to the generation of A1.

In sum, on the basis of the data presented above, it seems reasonable to advance a provisional hypothesis that both degree of belief in a conditional inference, as indexed by the perceived likelihood of the conclusion given the premise, as well as automatically cued counter-examples may be available quickly and automatically. However, even if they are available automatically, it is possible that evaluating counter-examples may take longer than evaluating likelihood information. That is, for this to happen, S2 needs to be involved, if only to resolve the contradiction between stated inference and the counter-example. This would explain why counter-example based reasoning took longer than likelihood reasoning in the Vershueren et al. (2005a) study.

Structural inferences

There is also evidence that inferences may be primed or triggered by the conditional statement by means other than belief (Rader & Sloutsky, 2002). According to mental models theory (Johnson-Laird & Byrne 2002), reasoners comprehend a conditional by formulating a model that represents the concepts denoted by p and q. Although the various formulations of mental models theory differ with respect to how much other information is proposed to be represented at this initial stage (Markovits & Barrouillet, 2002; Thompson, 2000; Thompson & Mann, 1995;), most formulations of the theory propose that the initial model of a conditional minimally represents p and q:

p q

.....

The ellipse denotes other possibilities that might be represented at a subsequent stage.

Under these assumptions, inferences that are easily available are those supported by the initial model: MP ($p \therefore q$) and AC ($q \therefore p$). To test this hypothesis, Rader and Sloutsky (2002) embedded a conditional statement and the minor premise to either the MP and AC arguments in a story context. On a later recognition task, participants were faster to recognize the words that would form part of the conclusions to those arguments than they were to recognize control words, even though there was no need for them to draw the inference in order to comprehend the text. These data suggest that the MP and AC inferences are generated automatically, making them candidates for A1.

Interestingly, however, other data shows that DA and MT inferences might also be made quickly and may also be candidates for A1 answers (Schroyens, et al., 2003). Participants were either asked to make their inferences as quickly as possible or allowed as much time as necessary to do so. In the speeded condition, participants made more inferences of all types than in the free time condition. As the conditionals described arbitrary relations between letters and numbers, this difference in inference patterns could not have been cause by belief. However, because this was a paper and pencil task and not timed, it is not clear how quickly these inferences were generated, nor if they were the first response available. Thus, the evidence to support DA and MT as automatically generated inferences is less compelling than for MP and AC.

Triggering Conditions

DPT's assume that automatic, S1 processes produce an answer, A1, that is kept unless S2 is triggered. As above, triggering conditions include characteristics of task (instructions, perspective, time allotted) and the individual (WM capacity, thinking dispositions) that increase the probability of S2 intervention, at least as measured by the probability of producing normatively correct responses. However, relatively little attention has been paid to the property of the stimuli themselves, and in particular, to reasoners' interpretations of the experience of processing those stimuli in mediating S2 interventions. That is, all other things being equal, why does one A1 receive relatively little subsequent analysis, whilst another is subject to scrutiny? Elsewhere (Thompson, 2007), I have argued that the answer to this question lies with the same type of metacognitive monitoring processes that are known to influence memory retrievals, problem solving, reading comprehension, and other cognitive functions.

Feeling of Rightness

Metacognitive judgements are routinely used to assess the workings of our cognitive processes, and in particular, the degree to which such processes have functioned or will function correctly. Critically, from the point of view of the current argument, these judgements determine whether the current output suffices or whether further effort is required (e.g., Mazzoni & Cornoldi, 1993; Nelson, 1993; Son, 2004; Son & Metcalfe, 2000). If the name of the person you have just met comes confidently to mind, you will address that person by name; if not, you may choose an alternative form of greeting. Similarly, if you are not confident that you will remember all the items you need at the store, you will make a list to remind yourself. In other words, one's behaviour is determined not only by the content of the memory, but by one's subjective appraisal of the accuracy of that memory (Koriat & Levy-Sadot, 1999).

Surprisingly, the role of metacognitive processes in reasoning have been relatively neglected. However, it is almost certain that they play the same kind of role as they do in other judgements; namely, to provide a means to assess the output of one's cognitive processes and determine whether further action should be taken. Under this view, the metacognitive experience that accompanies A1 is the signal that this answer suffices or that further analysis is required. I will call this experience the Feeling of Rightness (FOR).

What determines the strength of the FOR? Similar processes (e.g., Feeling of Familiarity (FOF), Judgement of Learning (JOL), and Feeling of Knowing (FOK)) have been studied extensively in the context of memory. This family of metacognitive experiences provides a good basis for theorizing about the FOR because, as above, it is seems reasonable to assume that the determinants of A1 are largely retrieved from memory.

The central point made by theorists in the domain of memory is that the origins of metacognitive judgements lie in properties of retrieval processes rather than in the properties of the item retrieved (e.g., Benjamin, Bjork, & Schwartz, 1998; Busey, Tunnicliff, Loftus, & Loftus, 2000; Jacoby, Kelley, & Dywan, 1989; Koriat, 1995; 1997; Koriat & Levy- Sadot, 1999; Schwartz, Benjamin & Bjork, 1997). Thus, judgements such as the FOK and FOF are determined by the familiarity of the retrieval cues (Reder & Ritter, 1992; Schunn, Reder, Nhouyvanisvong, Richards, & Stroffolino, 1997; Vernon & Usher, 2003), the amount of ancillary information that is brought to mind during the retrieval attempt (Koriat, 1993; 1995; Koriat, Levy-Sadot, Edry, & de Marcas, 2003), and the fluency with which an item is brought to mind (e.g., Benjamin, Bjork, & Schwartz, 1998; Jacoby et al., 1989; Kelly & Jacoby, 1993; 1996; Matvey, Dunlosky, & Guttentag, 2001; Whittlesea & Leboe, 2003). Indeed, fluency of processing is such a compelling basis for memory attributions that easy or efficient processing of an item gives rise to the attribution that the item has been previously experienced, *even when it has not* (e.g., Jacoby et al., 1989; Whittlesea, Jacoby, & Girard, 1990).

FOR and conditional inference

On this basis, it is hypothesized that the FOR that accompanies A1 plays a role in triggering S2 intervention. A strong FOR should act as a signal that further analysis is not required. A weak FOR should signal the need for further thought. As an illustration, give the first answer that comes to mind to each of the following problems:

Example 7:

> (Valerie to Jamie) If our paper is accepted, I will treat you to dinner.
> Valerie treated Jamie to dinner. Was the paper accepted?

Example 8:

> If an animal is a bird, then it can fly.
> Robins can fly. Are robins birds?

Even if you answered 'yes' to both questions, the first answer was likely produced with a sense of uncertainty, whereas the second was not. This uncertainty also likely triggered S2 analysis for the first problem: What do we know about Valerie and Jamie? Is there some other reason for why Valerie might treat Jamie? Are they good at getting papers accepted? In contrast, the second problem likely receives little subsequent analysis (except by expert reasoners!), and as much research has shown, is answered in the affirmative despite being fallacious. It is important to note that certainty and belief are not confounded: One can be definitely uncertain (i.e., be convinced that the correct answer is 'maybe') and one can disbelieve with certainty as the next examples show:

Example 9:

> If an animal is a German Shepherd, then it is a dog.
> Fido is a dog. Is Fido a German Shepherd?
> (Definitely) MAYBE

Example 10:

> If a figure is a square, then it has four sides of equal length.
> This figure does not have four sides of equal length. Is it a square?
> (Definitely) NO

Determinants of FOR in conditional inference

As described above, fluency of retrieval, as defined as speed or probability with which an answer comes to mind (Benjamin et al., 1998) is a major determinant of metamemorial experiences. By extension, it seems likely that the FOR in conditional inference should be mediated by the accessibility of the various attributes of A1, such as the ease with which a judgement of likelihood is made or the speed with which a counterexample comes to mind.

FOR and S2 intervention

The strength of the FOR should predict the type and degree of S2 intervention. At the extremes, very strong FOR's should be correlated with the inclination to accept A1, and weak FOR's with the inclination to rethink it. That is, strong FOR's should signal that further analysis is not required, and be associated with shallow S2 processing, such as acknowledging that the answer feels right or seems plausible (Kahneman, 2003). More elaborate S2 involvement is predicted for weak FOR's, although as described below, engagement of S2 does not necessarily mean that the initial answer will change.

Epistemic self-regulation

Scores on measures such as the Actively Open-minded Thinking Scale (AOT; Sa, Stanovich, & West, 1999; Stanovich & West, 2007; Stanovich & West, 1997) predict the probability of normatively correct responses over and above the effect of IQ (Stanovich, 1999). The AOT measures reasoners' self-reported tendency to engage active, flexible, hypothetical thinking (e.g., 'No one can talk me out of something I know is right' and 'If I think longer about a problem I will be more likely to solve it'). One explanation for the relationship between performance and AOT scores is that high-AOT reasoners are more likely to inhibit S1 (Stanovich, 2007), perhaps by ignoring or downplaying the input provided by the FOR. In other words, measures of thinking dispositions may tap a predisposition to monitor one's cognitive processes to ensure that their outputs are consistent with higher-order epistemic values (Stanovich, 2007).

Whereas the AOT relies on self-reported behaviour, Fredrick's Cognitive Reflections Test (CRT; 2005) offers a behavioural measure of self-monitoring skill. This test consists of three items, including the 'widget' problem presented in Example 1. These items do not require sophisticated analysis to solve, but all require reasoners to put aside a compelling A1 in order to achieve the correct solution.

Regardless of how such monitoring skills are measured, they are likely to play a role in triggering S2 intervention. Indeed, individual differences in monitoring skills have been linked to successful performance in a number of domains, such as reading (e.g., Lin, Moore, & Zabrucky, 2001; Pressley, 2003), acquiring optical principles (Prins, Veenman, & Elshout, 2006), and mathematical problem solving (Desoete & Roeyers, 2006; Lucangeli, Tressoldi, & Centron, 1998).

Other triggering conditions

Lack of belief in a putative inference may trigger S2 analysis (e.g., Klaczynski & Robinson, 2000; Newstead, Pollard, & Evans, 1992). On this view, reasoners who are presented with an unbelievable conclusion will engage S2 processes in an attempt to discover a more palatable one (but see Thompson et al., 2003 for an alternative view). In the context of conditional reasoning, for example, reasoners presented with an unbelievable conclusion may attempt a deliberate search for a counter-example to refute it. A similar process may mediate generated inferences, when the invited inference conflicts with belief, as the following example illustrates:

Example 11:

> If you go out in the rain without a coat, you will catch a cold.
> Valerie is out in the rain without a coat. Therefore...

In this case, the putatively automatic inference, 'she will catch cold' is not believable and may trigger S2 analysis to resolve the contradiction between the inference and the knowledge that cold are spread by viruses and not rain showers.

Conversely, it is possible that believability of a conclusion contributes to the FOR. That is, lack of plausibility or the ready availability of a counterexample may lower the FOR associated with an inference. In the case above, for example, the MP inference may be cued quickly and automatically in response to the minor premise, but with little confidence.

Finally, it is possible that S1 cues several responses. As described previously, S1 is assumed to represent not one, but a multiplicity of systems that potentially operate in parallel. For example, S1 may be cued to make both a structural inference and to generate a belief-consistent response; evaluation of the believability of the conditional and believability of the putative inference may be triggered simultaneously, etc. In cases where S1 cues different responses, S2 may be needed to determine which one is produced as the final answer.

Type of S2 intervention

Traditionally, the standard by which S2 intervention is measured is the proportion of normatively correct responses generated for an inference. Many researchers agree that this standard provides a narrow and often inappropriate measure of human rationality (e.g., Evans & Over, 2004; Oaksford & Chater, 2007); nonetheless, the practice continues, presumably because it is an easy and convenient measure. Perhaps the most compelling reason to doubt the utility of normative responses as indicators of S2 engagement is the fact that many processes that would definitely be classified as analytic process produce non-normative responses. Indeed, there are at least three ways for S2 to be engaged, only one of which results in a change of answer (Thompson, 2007): 1) A1 is endorsed with little analysis, perhaps by verifying its plausibility; 2) A1 is rationalized or justified; 3) an alternative representation of the problem is created. Moreover, even if an alternative representation is produced, there is no guarantee that the outcome will accord with normative standards.

A1 endorsed with little S2 analysis

Kahnmen (2003) argued that all inference require at least some S2 involvement because an explicit response is generated. However, he argues, the degree of involvement may be minimal, such that A1 is accepted with little scrutiny. This entails the most minimal commitment of analytic resources, and amounts to little more than an explicit acceptance of the answer generated by implicit processes. A related option that entails a minimally larger degree of S2 involvement is an explicit attempt to consider whether the solution seems reasonable. Assuming that it satisfies the current goal state and is otherwise plausible, again, it is likely to be accepted without further analysis (Evans, 2006; Roberts, 2004). If it is not, it may be rejected with little further analysis, or may be subject to re-evaluation (see option three below).

Such a process would explain why the normatively fallacious inference 'Robins are birds' is drawn for Example 8. This inference is likely produced (or endorsed) fluently, producing a high FOR, so that there is nothing to trigger S2 intervention. If S2 processes were monitoring this output, as described above, the inference would still likely pass muster because it is plausible: 'Of course robins are birds. What else can they be?'. Conversely, an unbelievable conclusion could be rejected without further involvement by S2 processes.

A1 is rationalized or justified

A second model for S2 engagement is that analytic processes may be engaged to justify A1. In other words, there might be an explicit attempt to explain why A1 is correct. Such processes are well documented in a variety of domains. For example, Shynkaruk and Thompson (2006) found that when given time to rethink an answer given under time pressure, fewer than 30% of answers changed. This suggests that, for many, the answer that would be given when allowed extra time to think is the same answer that would be given under time pressure, regardless of the validity of the initial answer.

If reasoners are not generating an alternative response, what are they doing? One possibility is that they are justifying their initial responses (Evans, 1996). In support of this hypothesis, Evans

(1996; see also Ball, Lucas, Miles, & Gale, 2003; Lucas & Ball, 2005) found that on Wason's four-card selection task, people spent more time deliberating about the cards they were going to select than the cards they were going to reject, presumably to rationalize their initial choice. Indeed, there is evidence to suggest that many choices, judgements, and attitudes are generated by implicit processes and are therefore not easily available to conscious introspection; consequently, the role of analytic processes might be limited to trying to construct explanations for why such choices, judgements, and attitudes have been made (see Stanovich, 2004, Chapter 2; Wilson & Dunn, 2004 for review).

In the context of conditional reasoning, this would involve a set of processes that are relatively unstudied. That is, as described in the next section, the processes by which reasoners change their answers are relatively well documented, but the conditions and methods used to rationalize an initial answer are not well understood. Some speculation is possible, however. For example, one way to rationalize a conclusion is to construct a plausible explanation for it (see Brem & Rips, 2000; Kuhn, 1991 for summaries). In the case of conditional reasoning, this might be an explanation for how the conclusion might happen, how the p and q terms of the conditional are linked, etc. In Example 7, for instance, one might construct the explanation that the paper was accepted because the purpose of the dinner was to celebrate an achievement, and getting a paper published is an achievement.

Alternatively, reasoners might recruit additional knowledge that lends support to A1 (Baron, 1995). In the case of Example 7, one might know that Valerie and Jamie are successful at publishing papers, so that the conclusion is highly probable. A related mechanism would be to bring to mind other instances in which they had gone out to celebrate a publication.

S2 engaged to reformulate the problem

Finally, the reasoner may attempt to reformulate the initial model or representation of the premises, with the goal of deriving a different solution (Evans, 2006; Johnson-Laird & Byrne, 1991; Stanovich, 2007; Torrens, Thompson, & Cramer, 1999). This option requires the most cognitive effort and success at this stage is tied to traditional measures of cognitive capacity such as IQ (see Stanovich, 1999 for review) and WM (e.g., de Neys, 2006 a, b; Gilhooly, Logie, & Quinn, 1999; Markovits & Doyon, 2004). In order to reformulate an answer, the initial A1 must be inhibited (de Neys, Schaeken, & d'Ydewalle, 2005a; Handley et al., 2004; Markovits & Doyon, 2004), and then an alternative representation formulated. Moreover, as described above, this effort is not guaranteed to produce normatively correct responses *even granted sufficient capacity*, because reasoners may not have sufficient understanding of the task or necessary logical principles to produce a normative response (Evans, 2006; Markovits & Barrouillet, 2002; Stanovich, 2007). For example, a reasoner might deliberately invoke a biconditional interpretation of the statement or a conjunctive understanding of the rule (Evans et al., 2003; Thompson & Byrne, 2002) that produces a non-normative response.

Indeed, the most widely investigated means of producing an alternative response to A1 entails a knowledge-based, as opposed to rule-based search. In particular, reasoners may explicitly search for counter-examples to the conclusion. This is a WM demanding process and evidence suggests that this process is more likely for high than low capacity reasoners (Versheuren et al., 2005b).

In summary, although there are a variety of processes associated with S2 engagement, only a small proportion of them produce normatively correct responses. Consequently, there is a need to adopt alternative measures of S2 engagement that better diagnose the range of possible S2 options. For example, given that S2 processes are, by nature, conscious and explicit, think aloud protocols (e.g., Evans et al., 1983; Vershueren et al., 2005b), strategy choice paradigms (Campbell & Xue, 2001), answer justifications (e.g., Klaczynksi & Robinson, 2000), or even response time analyses (de Neys, 2006a; Thompson et al., 2003) should be used in addition to the analysis of conclusions endorsed.

Final judgements of confidence (FJC)

Finally, I consider a second issue raised by a metacognitive analysis of DPT, namely, how reasoners evaluate confidence in the inferences they have made. Whereas the FOR is posited to reflect confidence in a fast, intuitive answer with little or no S2 intervention, the FJC reflects judgements of confidence in answers made following S2 engagement, however limited it might have been. This is an important issue: Presumably, as in other domains, reasoners make inferences with more or less certainty and take actions that reflect that certainty. Surprisingly, however, there is relatively little known about reasoner's confidence in their deductive inferences. In the sections that follow, I develop some hypotheses based on the preceding analysis.

Relationship between FOR and FJC

All other things being equal, FJC should be highly correlated with FOR. However, this relationship should change as a function of the type and probability of S2 intervention. Thus, when A1 is given as the final answer, FOR and FJC should be strongly correlated. When it is not, the relationship may even be negative, as the prepotent A1 continues to suggest its rightness (Sloman, 2002). Thus, conditions that encourage changing A1, such as low FOR's, strong logic instructions, or instructions to reason from another's perspective should weaken the relationship between FOR's and FJC's. Finally, interventions that promote rationalization as opposed to reconsideration, should increase FCJ's but not weaken the relationship between FOR and FJC.

Metacognitive beliefs and FJC's

By analogy to other metacognitive judgements, such as the FOK and JOL (e.g., Brewer & Sampaio, 2006; Kelley & Jacoby, 1996; Koriat & Levy -Sadot, 1999; Koriat, et al., 2004; Matvey, et al., 2001; Schwarz, 2004;), it is proposed that FJC's reflect two sources of information (Thompson, 2007). The first is implicit; this is the experiential basis that underlies the FOR. That is, the FOR is posited to reflect an implicit, affective response that carries little cognitive content and whose origins are not available to introspection (e.g., Brewer & Sampaio, 2006, Koriat, et al., 2004; Koriat & Levy-Sadot, 1999; Matvey, et al., 2001; Schwartz, 2004). The experiential component of the FOR produces a feeling of confidence without corresponding knowledge concerning the basis of that confidence.

The second source is explicit, and comes in the form of reasoners' metacognitive beliefs (Thompson, 2007). Although these can be accessed explicitly, the reasoner may not be aware of their contribution to a particular judgement. For example, people understand how memory deteriorates over time and this understanding can moderate their confidence in the accuracy of their memory (Koriat et al., 2004), although such beliefs may have a limited effect on a given occasion because they may not be easily accessible in that context.

An initial study by Shynkaruk and Thompson (2006) supported the role of metacognitive beliefs in a syllogistic reasoning paradigm. For each problem they solved, reasoners were asked to evaluate conclusions and give confidence ratings twice: The first time was an initial, fast assessment of the conclusion and the second response was made after deliberation. Confidence was higher on the first than the second response, regardless of whether accuracy increased, decreased or the answer did not change. The authors argued that the increase in confidence was a function of reasoners' metacognitive beliefs that decisions considered over time are superior to those made under pressure.

Other source of metacognitive beliefs may be reasoners' global assessment of their reasoning ability or thinking style as indexed by measures such as the Rational Experiential Inventory

(REI; Pacini & Epstein, 1999). Consistent with this hypothesis, Prowse-Turner and Thompson (2007) observed that those who scored high on the rationality portion of the REI expressed a high degree of confidence in their evaluation of syllogistic arguments, even though they were no more accurate than those who scored low in rationality (see also Dunning, Johnson, Ehrlinger, & Kruger, 2003; Jonsson & Allwood, 2003).

Metacognitive beliefs may also reflect the extent of one's domain-specific knowledge in a domain. That is, if people believe themselves to be knowledgeable about a particular topic, this may engender confidence in judgements associated with that domain (Costermans, Lories, & Ansay, 1992; Cowley, 2004; Gill, Swann, & Sivera, 1998; Morgan & Cleave-Hogg, 2002). Shynkaruk and Thompson (2006) found evidence to suggest that these beliefs contribute to confidence in reasoning judgements: reasoners were more confident when evaluating conclusions to which they could apply pre-existing knowledge (i.e., that were believable or unbelievable) than neutral conclusions, although they were no more accurate with the believable than the neutral conclusions.

Summary and conclusions

In this chapter, I have attempted to apply the basic DPT assumptions to developing a model of conditional inference. In keeping with the basic assumptions of DPT, it was assumed that automatic S1 processes generate an initial representation of the problem that enables an early response, A1. This response is assumed to be given as the final answer unless S2 is triggered to reformulate the representation and provide an alternative.

Although the basic assumptions of the theory are well-substantiated, I have argued that there remain numerous unanswered questions about the nature of the processes executed at each of these stages. For example, S1 processes may generate a representation based on the believability of the conditional statement, the believability of the inference, an initial mental model of the statement, readily available counter-examples, or a combination of these (and other, as yet unknown) factors. It is important to note that even though many of these factors are known to determine the final inferences reasoners draw, it is not clear which, if any, of these outputs arise from automatic S1 processes.

S2 processes are likewise eclectic. Although the production of normative responses is normally assumed index to S2 engagement, I have argued that this is an inadequate measure given the diversity of potential S2 processes. Specifically, S2 may be engaged at a very superficial level, doing little more than endorsing or acknowledging the S1 output. S2 may also be engaged in a more meaningful way to rationalize or justify the initial response. In neither of these cases will S2 engagement result in a change to A1, nor will the engagement result in a normatively correct response unless, by chance, A1 was normatively correct. Conversely, the reasoner may attempt to reformulate A1 in a way that does not produce normatively correct answers by a) searching for counter-examples (i.e., counter-examples to MP and MT produce non-logical answers) or b) applying a non-normative rule of inference. In sum, S2 may be engaged to fulfil a variety of goals, many of which cannot be measured by normative responses.

In addition to raising questions concerning the operations of key processes depicted in Figure 18.1, I have argued that additional processes need to be added to the current formulations of DPT. In particular, the conditions that trigger or initiate S2 responses are not well-documented. I have proposed that integrating the reasoning literature with the literature on metacognition provides a fruitful basis for theorizing about these triggering conditions.

A Metacognitive DPT model is presented in Figure 18.2. In this view, A1 incorporates two elements: the content of the inference and a metacognitive judgement called the FOR. This FOR is assumed to be based on the experiences associated with generating A1, for example, the fluency or ease with which A1 is produced. The FOR is predicted to mediate the probability and degree of

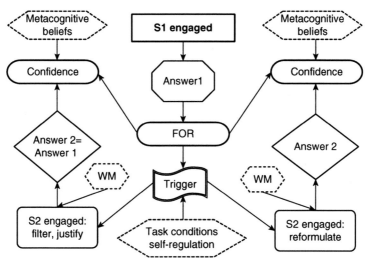

Fig. 18.2 A metacognitive dual process theory.

S2 engagement, such that strong FOR's are associated with minimal engagement and weak FOR's with more elaborate forms of engagement.

Finally, A2, like A1, is assumed to be generated with two components: the inference per se and a judgement of confidence. This final judgement of confidence is predicted to reflect contributions from the FOR, as well as from reasoners' metacognitive beliefs about their ability, knowledge in the domain, conditions that engender good reasoning, etc. This FJC is assumed to play the same role in reasoning that it does in other domains: that is, to mediate behaviour. FJC's that are delivered with high confidence may be argued vociferously, used as a basis of decision-making, and otherwise acted upon. FJC's that are weak may signal the need to search for more information, seek advice, rethink the problem, etc.

Of course, Figure 18.2 is not meant to be definitive. It is offered as a preliminary set of hypotheses about how the various processes might interact, rather than as the definitive version of a theory. For example, although WM capacity is depicted in the model as contributing primarily to the execution of S2 processes, it is possible that the inclination to trigger those processes may also be capacity-dependent (Evans, 2007). Thus, the Figure is intended to organize the issues and questions, and to serve as a platform for generating testable research questions.

Author Notes

Portions of this chapter were presented at the 2nd London Reasoning Workshop in September, 2007 at Birkbeck College, University of London. I would like to acknowledge Birkbeck College and the National Sciences and Engineering Research Council of Canada for their financial support. Many thanks also to Jamie Campbell and Wim de Neys for helpful comments and suggestions on an earlier draft of this manuscript.

References

Baron, J. (1995). Myside bias in thinking about abortion. *Thinking & Reasoning*, **1**, 201–220.

Ball, L. J., Lucas, E. J., Miles, J. N. V., & Gale, A. G. (2003). Inspection times and the selection task: What do eye-movements reveal about relevance effects? *The Quarterly Journal of Experimental Psychology A: Human Experimental Psychology*, **56**, 1053–1077.

Baron, J. (1995). Myside bias in thinking about abortion. *Thinking and Reasoning*, 1, 221–235.

Benjamin, A. S., Bjork, R. A., & Schwartz, B. L. (1998). The mismeasure of memory: When retrieval fluency is misleading as a metamnemonic index. *Journal of Experimental Psychology: General*, 127, 55–68.

Brem, S. K. & Rips, L. J. (2000). Explanation and evidence in informal argument. *Cognitive Science*, 24, 573–604.

Brewer, W. F. & Sampaio, C. (2006). Processes leading to confidence and accuracy in sentence recognition: A metamemory approach. *Memory*, 14, 540–552.

Busey, T. A., Tunnicliff, J., Loftus, G. R., & Loftus, E. F. (2000). Accounts of the confidence-accuracy relation in recognition memory. *Psychonomic Bulletin & Review*, 7, 26–48.

Campbell, J. I. D. & Xue, Q. (2001). Cognitive arithmetic across cultures. *Journal of Experimental Psychology: General*, 130, 299–315.

Costermans, J., Lories, G., & Ansay, C. (1992). Confidence level and feeling of knowing in question answering: The weight of inferential processes. *Journal of Experimental Psychology: Learning, Memory, and Cognition*, 18, 142–150.

Cowley, E. (2004). Recognition confidence, recognition accuracy and choice. *Journal of Business Research*, 57, 641–646.

Cummins, D. D, Lubart, T., Alksnis, O., & Rist, R. (1991). Conditional reasoning and causation. *Memory and Cognition*, 19, 274–282.

De Neys, W. (2006a). Automatic-heuristic and executive-analytic processing during reasoning: Chronometric and dual-task considerations. *Quarterly Journal of Experimental Psychology*, 59, 1070–1100.

De Neys, W. (2006b). Dual processing in reasoning: Two systems but one reasoner. *Psychological Science*, 17, 428–433.

De Neys, W., Schaeken, W., & d'Ydewalle, G. (2005). Working memory and counterexample retrieval for causal conditionals. *Thinking & Reasoning*, 11, 123–150.

Desoete, A. & Roeyers, H. (2006). Metacognitive macroevaluations in mathematical problem solving. *Learning and Instruction*, 16, 12–25.

Dunning, D., Johnson, K., Ehrlinger, J., & Kruger, J. (2003). Why people fail to recognize their own incompetence. *Current Directions in Psychological Science*, 12, 83–87.

Evans, J. St.B. T. (2007). On the resolution of conflict in dual process theories of reasoning. *Thinking & Reasoning*, 321–339.

Evans, J. St.B. T. (2007). *Hypothetical thinking: Dual processes in reasoning and judgement*. New York: Psychology Press.

Evans, J. St.B. T. (2006). The heuristic-analytic theory of reasoning: Extension and evaluation. *Psychonomic Bulletin and Review*, 13, 378–395.

Evans, J. St.B. T. (1996). Deciding before you think: Relevance and reasoning in the selection task. *British Journal of Psychology*, 87, 223–240.

Evans, J. St.B. T., Barston, J. L., & Pollard, P. (1983). On the conflict between logic and belief in syllogistic reasoning. *Memory and Cognition*, 11, 295–306.

Evans, J. St.B. T. & Curtis-Holmes, J. (2005). Rapid responding increases belief bias: Evidence for the dual-process theory of reasoning. *Thinking & Reasoning*, 11, 382–389.

Evans, J. St.B. T., Handley, S. J., & Over, D. E. (2003). Conditionals and conditional probability. *Journal of Experimental Psychology: Learning, Memory, and Cognition*, 29, 321–335.

Evans, J. St.B. T. & Over, D. E. (2004). *If*. New York: Oxford University Press.

Frederick, S. (2005). Cognitive reflection and decision making. *Journal of Economic Perspectives*, 19, 25–42.

Geiger, S. M & Oberauer, K. (2007). Reasoning with conditionals: Does every counterexample count? It's frequency that counts. *Memory & Cognition*, 35(8), 2060–2074.

Gilhooly, K; Logic, R. H., & Wynn, V. (1999). Syllogistic reasoning tasks, working memory, and skill. *The European Journal of Cognitive Psychology*, 11, 473–498.

Gill, M. J., Swann, W. B. Jr., & Sivera, D. H. (1998). On the genesis of confidence. *Journal of Personality and Social Psychology*, **75**, 1101–1114.

Grosset, N., Barrouillet, P., & Markovits, H. (2005). Chronometric evidence for memory retrieval in causal conditional reasoning: The case of the association strength effect. *Memory & Cognition*, **33**, 734–741.

Handley, S. J., Capon, A., Beveridge, M., Dennis, I., & Evans, J. St.B. T. (2004). Working memory, inhibitory control and the development of children's reasoning. *Thinking & Reasoning*, **10**, 175–195.

Jacoby, L. L., Kelley, C. M., & Dywan, J. (1989). Memory attributions. In H. L. Roediger III & F. I. M. Craik (Eds.), *Varieties of Memory and Consciousness: Essays in Honour of Endel Tulving*. (pp. 391–422). Hillsdale, NJ: Lawrence Erlbaum Associates, Inc.

Johnson-Laird, P. N. & Byrne, R. M. J. (2002). Conditionals: A theory of meaning, pragmatics, and inference. *Psychological Review*, **109**, 1–33.

Johnson-Laird, P. N. & Byrne, R. M. J. (1991). *Deduction*. Hillsdale, NJ: Lawrence Erlbaum Associates, Inc.

Jonsson, A. C. & Allwood, C. M. (2003). Stability and variability in the realism of confidence judgements over time, content domain, and gender. *Personality and Individual Differences*, **34**, 559–574.

Kahneman, D. (2003). A perspective on judgment and choice: Mapping bounded rationality. *American Psychologist*, **58**, 697–720.

Kelley, C. M. & Jacoby, L. L. (1996). Adult egocentrism: Subjective experience versus analytic bases for judgment. *Journal of Memory and Language*, **35**, 157–175.

Kelley, C. M. & Jacoby, L. L. (1993). The construction of subjective experience: Memory attributions. In M. Davies & G. W. Humphreys (Eds.), *Consciousness: Psychological and Philosophical Essays*. (pp. 74–89). Malden, MA: Blackwell Publishing.

Klaczynski, P. A. & Robinson, B. (2000). Personal theories, intellectual ability, and epistemological beliefs: Adult age differences in everyday reasoning biases. *Psychology and Aging*, **15**, 400–416.

Koriat, A. (1997). Monitoring one's own knowledge during study: A cue-utilization approach to judgments of learning. *Journal of Experimental Psychology: General*, **126**, 349–370.

Koriat, A. (1995). Dissociating knowing and the feeling of knowing: Further evidence for the accessibility model. *Journal of Experimental Psychology: General*, **124**, 311–333.

Koriat, A. (1993). How Do We Know That We Know? The Accessibility Model of the Feeling of Knowing. *Psychological Review*, **100**, 609–639.

Koriat, A., Levy-Sadot, R. (1999) Processes underlying metacognitive judgments: Information-based and experience-based monitoring of one's own knowledge. In S. Chaiken, & Y. Trope (Eds.), *Dual-Process Theories in Social Psychology* (pp. 483–502). New York, NY: Guilford Press.

Koriat, A., Bjork, R. A., Sheffer, L., & Bar, S. K. (2004). Predicting one's own forgetting: The role of experience-based and theory-based processes. *Journal of Experimental Psychology: General*, **133**, 643–656.

Koriat, A., Levy-Sadot, R., Edry, E., & de Marcas, S. (2003). What do we know about what we cannot remember? Accessing the semantic attributes of words that cannot be recalled. *Journal of Experimental Psychology: Learning, Memory, and Cognition*, **29**, 1095–1105.

Kuhn, D. (1990). *The skills of argument*. New York: Cambridge University Press.

Lin, L. M., Moore, D., & Zabrucky, K. M. (2001). An assessment of students' calibration of comprehension and calibration of performance using multiple measures. *Reading Psychology*, **22**, 111–128.

Lucangeli, D., Tressoldi, P. E., & Cendron, M. (1998). Cognitive and metacognitive abilities involved in the solution of mathematical word problems: Validation of a comprehensive model. *Contemporary Educational Psychology*, **23**, 2557–275.

Lucas, E. J. & Ball, L. J. (2005). Think-aloud protocols and the selection task: Evidence for relevance effects and rationalisation processes. *Thinking & Reasoning*, **11**, 35–66.

Markovits, H. & Barrouillet, P. (2002). The development of conditional reasoning: A mental model account. *Developmental Review*, **22**, 5–36.

Markovits, H. & Doyon, C. (2004). Information processing and reasoning with premises that are empirically false: Interference, working memory, and processing speed. *Memory & Cognition*, **32**, 592–601.

Markovits, H. & Schroyens, W. (2007). A curious belief-bias effect. *Experimental Psychology*, **54**, 38–43.

Matvey, G., Dunlosky, J., & Guttentag, R. (2001). Fluency of retrieval at study affects judgements of learning (JOLs): An analytic or nonanalytic basis for JOLs? *Memory and Cognition*, **29**, 222–233.

Mazzoni, G. & Cornoldi, C. (1993). Strategies in study time allocation: Why is study time sometimes not effective? *Journal of Experimental Psychology: General*, **122**, 47–60.

Morgan, P. J. & Cleave-Hogg, D. (2002). Comparison between medical students' experience, confidence and competence. *Medical Education*, **36**, 534–539.

Nelson, T. O. (1993). Judgments of learning and the allocation of study time. *Journal of Experimental Psychology: General*, **122**, 269–273.

Newstead, S. E., Pollard, P., & Evans, J. S. (1992). The source of belief bias effects in syllogistic reasoning. *Cognition*, **45**, 257–284.

Oaksford, M. & Chater, N. (2007). *Bayesian rationality the probabilistic approach to human reasoning.* New York: Oxford University Press.

Oaksford, M., Chater, N., & Joanne, L. (2000). Probabilities and polarity biases in conditional inference. *Journal of Experimental Psychology: Learning, Memory, and Cognition*, **26**, 883–899.

Oberauer, K. & Wilhelm, O. (2003). The meaning(s) of conditionals: Conditional probabilities, mental models, and personal utilities. *Journal of Experimental Psychology: Learning, Memory, and Cognition*, **29**, 680–693.

Ohm, E. & Thompson, V. A. (2007). Conditional persuasion: Truth, effectiveness and subjective utility. Manuscript under review.

Ohm, E. & Thompson, V. A. (2006). Conditional probability and pragmatic conditionals: Dissociating truth and effectiveness. *Thinking and Reasoning*, **12**, 257–280.

Ohm, E. & Thompson, V. A. (2004). Everyday reasoning with inducements and advice. *Thinking and Reasoning*, **10**, 241–272.

Over, D. E. & Evans, J. St.B. T. (2003). The probability of conditionals: The psychological evidence. *Mind and Language*, **18**, 340–358.

Over, D. E., Manktelow, K. I., & Hadjichristidis, C. (2004). Conditions for the acceptance of deontic conditionals. *Canadian Journal of Experimental Psychology*, **58**, 96–105.

Pacini, R. & Epstein, S. (1999). The relation of rational and experiential information processing sytles to personality, basic beliefs, and the ratio-bias phenomenon. *Journal of Personality and Social Psychology*, **76**, 972–987.

Pressley, M. (2003). Metacognition and self-regulated comprehension. In A. Farstrup & J. Samuels (Eds.), *What Research has to say about Reading Instructions* (pp. 291–309). Newark, DE: International Reading Association.

Prowse-Turner, J. & Thompson, V. A. (2007). Factors affecting the confidence-accuracy relationship in deductive reasoning. Manuscript under review.

Prins, F. J., Veenman, M. J., & Elshout, J. J. (2006). The impact of intellectual ability and metacognition on learning: New support for the threshold of problematicity theory. *Learning and Instruction*, **16**, 374–387.

Rader, A. E. & Sloutsky, V. M. (2002). Processing of logically valid and logically invalid conditional inferences in discourse comprehension. *Journal of Experimental Psychology: Learning, Memory, and Cognition*, **28**, 59–68.

Reder, L. M. & Ritter, F. E. (1992). What determines initial feeling of knowing? Familiarity with question terms, not with the answer. *Journal of Experimental Psychology: Learning, Memory, and Cognition*, **18**, 435–451.

Roberts, M. J. (2004). Heuristics and reasoning I: Making deduction simple. In J. P. Leighton & R. J. Sternberg (Eds.), *The Nature of Reasoning* (pp. 234–272). Cambridge, UK: Cambridge University Press.

Roberts, M. J. & Newton, E. J. (2001). Inspection times, the change task, and the rapid-response selection task. *Quarterly Journal of Experimental Psychology*, **54A**, 1031–1048.

Sá, W. C., West, R. F., & Stanovich, K. E. (1999). The domain specificity and generality of belief bias: Searching for a generalizable critical thinking skill. *Journal of Educational Psychology*, **91**, 497–510.

Schroyens, W., Schaeken, W., & Handley, S. (2003). In search of counter-examples: Deductive rationality in human reasoning. *The Quarterly Journal of Experimental Psychology*, **56A**, 1129–1145.

Schunn, C. D., Reder, L. M., Nhouyvanisvong, A., Richards, D. R., & Stroffolino, P. J. (1997). To calculate or not to calculate: A source activation confusion model of problem familiarity's role in strategy selection. *Journal of Experimental Psychology: Learning, Memory, and Cognition*, **23**, 3–29.

Schwartz, B. L., Benjamin, A. S., & Bkork, R. A. (1997). The inferential and experiential bases of metamemory. *Current Directions in Psychological Science*, **6**(5), 132–137.

Schwarz, N. (2004). Metacognitive experiences in consumer judgment and decision making. *Journal of Consumer Psychology*, **14**, 332–348.

Shynkaruk, J. M. & Thompson, V. A. (2006). Confidence and accuracy in deductive reasoning. *Memory & Cognition*, **34**, 619–632.

Sloman, S. A. (2002). Two systems of reasoning. In G. D. Griffin & D. Kahneman (Eds.), *Heuristics and Biases: The Psychology of Intuitive Judgment* (pp. 379–396). New York, NY: Cambridge University Press.

Son, L. K. (2004). Spacing one's study: Evidence for a metacognitive control strategy. *Journal of Experimental Psychology: Learning, Memory, and Cognition*, **3**, 601–604.

Son, L. K. & Metcalfe, J. (2000). Metacognitive and control strategies in study-time allocation. *Journal of Experimental Psychology: Learning, Memory, and Cognition*, **26**, 204–221.

Sperber, D., Cara, F., & Girotto, V. (1995). Relevance theory explains the selection task. *Cognition*, **57**, 31–95.

Stanovich, K. E. (2007). Distinguishing the reflective, algorithmic, and autonomous minds: Is it time for a Tri-process theory? In J. Evans & K. Frankish (Eds.), *In Two Minds: Dual Processes and Beyond*. Oxford: Oxford University Press.

Stanovich, K. E. (2004). *The Robot's Rebellion: Finding Meaning in the Age of Darwin*. Chicago, ILL: The University of Chicago Press.

Stanovich, K. E. (1999). *Who is rational?: Studies of individual differences in reasoning*. Mahwah, NJ, US: Lawrence Erlbaum Associates Publishers.

Stanovich, K. E. & West, R. F. (2007). Natural my side bias is independent of cognitive ability. Thinking & Reasoning, **13**, 225–247.

Stanovich, K. E. & West, R. F. (1997). Reasoning independently of prior belief and individual differences in actively open-minded thinking. *Journal of Educational Psychology*, **89**, 342–357.

Thompson, V. A. (2007). Dual-process theories: A metacognitive perspective. To appear in J. St.B. T. Evans & K. Frankish (Eds). *In two minds: Dual processes and beyond*. Oxford: Oxford University Press.

Thompson, V. A. (2000). The task-specific nature of domain-general reasoning. *Cognition*, **76**, 209–268.

Thompson, V. A. (1996). Reasoning from false premises: The role of soundness in making logical deductions. *Canadian Journal of Experimental Psychology*, **50**, 315–319.

Thompson, V. A. (1995). Conditional reasoning: The necessary and sufficient conditions. *Canadian Journal of Experimental Psychology*, **49**, 1–60.

Thompson, V. A. (1994). Interpretational factors in conditional reasoning. *Memory and Cognition*, **22**, 742–758.

Thompson, V. A. & Byrne, R. M. J. (2002). Reasoning counterfactually: Making inferences about things that didn't happen. *Journal of Experimental Psychology: Learning, Memory, and Cognition*, **28**, 1154–1170.

Thompson, V. A., Evans, J. St.B. T., & Handley, S. J. (2005). Persuading and dissuading by conditional argument. *Journal of Memory and Language*, **53**, 238–257.

Thompson, V. A. & Mann, J. (1995). Perceived necessity explains the dissociation between logic and meaning: The case of 'only if.' *Journal of Experimental Psychology: Learning, Memory, and Cognition*, **21**, 1–14

Thompson, V. A., Striemer, C. L., Reikoff, R., Gunter, R. W., & Campbell, J. I. D. (2003). Syllogistic reasoning time: Disconfirmation disconfirmed. *Psychonomic Bulletic & Review*, **10**, 184–189.

Torrens, D., Thompson, V. A., & Cramer, K. M.(1999). Individual differences and the belief bias effect: Mental models, logical necessity, and abstract reasoning. *Thinking & Reasoning, 5*, 1–28.

Vernon, D. & Usher, M. (2003). Dynamics of metacognitive judgments: Pre- and post retrieval mechanisms. *Journal of Experimental Psychology: Learning, Memory, and Cognition, 29*, 339–346.

Verschueren, N., Schaeken, W., & D'Ydewalle, G. (2005a). A dual-process specification of causal conditional reasoning. *Thinking & Reasoning, 11*, 239–278.

Verschueren, N., Schaeken, W., & D'Ydewalle, G. (2005b). Everyday conditional reasoning: A working memory-dependent tradeoff between counterexample and likelihood use. *Memory & Cognition, 33*, 107–119.

Whittlesea, B. W., Jacoby, L. L., & Girard, K. (1990). Illusions of immediate memory: Evidence of an attributional basis for feelings of familiarity and perceptual quality. *Journal of Memory and Language, 29*, 716–732.

Whittlesea, B. W. A. & Leboe, J. P. (2003). Two fluency heuristics (and how to tell them apart). *Journal of Memory and Language, 49*, 62–79.

Wilson, T. D. & Dunn, E. W. (2004). Self-knowledge: Its limits, value, and potential for improvement. *Annual Review of Psychology, 55*, 493–518.

Chapter 19

A multi-layered dual-process approach to conditional reasoning

Niki Verschueren and Walter Schaeken

Introduction: a dual-process account of causal conditional reasoning

During the past decade the dual-process idea has gained substantial ground in the area of cognitive science. Stanovich and West (2000) brought a range of dual-process accounts together and concluded that when these theories are compared at a general level, you cannot but observe a striking family resemblance. The following table provides an overview of some general dual-process theories (based on Stanovich & West, 2000; 2003).

Stanovich and West (2000) labelled one process (System 1) as heuristic or associative: It operates in a fast and frugal way, results in pragmatic conclusions and is low in cognitive cost. The second process (System 2) is called analytic or rule-based and operates in a slow, meditative and conscious way, aiming at rather valid and normative conclusions.

In the dual-process accounts of Stanovich and West (2000) and Evans and Over (1996, 1997) each system is defined by a range of process characteristics (implicit/explicit, fast/slow, etc.) and a resulting conclusion (pragmatic/normative, personal/impersonal, etc.). However, when the two processes are decoupled from the products they produce, the scope of the dual-process idea widens (see Klaczynski, 2001a, 2001b). The dualism can then be traced back to the contrast between automatic processing and controlled processing (Schneider & Schiffrin, 1977) and linked to other research domains (see Chaiken & Trope, 1999 for a review on dual-process accounts in social psychology). The properties that can be ascribed to these two more general processes remain

Table 19.1 Overview of general dual process theories

Dual process Theories	System 1	System 2
Johnson-Laird (1983)	Implicit inferences	Explicit inferences
Evans (1984; 1989)	Heuristic processing	Analytic processing
Pollock (1991)	Quick and inflexible modules	Intellection
Reber (1993)	Implicit cognition	Explicit learning
Epstein (1994)	Experiential system	Rational System
Levinson (1995)	Interactional Intelligence	Analytic Intelligence
Evans and Over (1996)	Tacit thought processes	Explicit thought processes
Hammond (1996)	Intuitive Cognition	Analytical cognition
Sloman (1996)	Associative system	Rule-based system
Klein (1998)	Recognition Primed Decision	Rational Choice Strategy

roughly similar. The first system (heuristic process) is considered as holistic, implicit, relatively undemanding of cognitive capacity and relatively fast. The second system (analytic process) is considered to be an analytic and controlled mechanism. Therefore, it is demanding in cognitive capacity and relatively slow. The analytical process operates in a conscious and often deliberate way, whereas the heuristic process occurs automatically and at the periphery of awareness. It is thereby generally assumed that the heuristic process starts by default and can be amended or overridden by the analytical process (see e.g., Evans & Over, 1996, 1997; see Klaczynski 2001a, 2001b; Sloman, 1996 for more nuanced approaches).

To our opinion, the dual-process account provides a *framework for looking at facts and observations* rather than being a fully specified theory on human cognition. Saying that a dual-process theory can capture human reasoning by defining two reasoning processes would be plain naïve. Part of the misconception is that the word 'dual' is often understood as referring to 'two'. The culprit of the problem is nicely put in the following paragraph:

> *Surely, a herd of philosophers could spend the happier part of eternity debating and never deciding whether a wink and a nod constitute one or two events for a blind horse. Because there are generally no tangible referents for the 'processes' specified by dry psychology's talk of dual-processes, there is generally no proper way to count them, and hence no way to know whether they have been counted properly. Not to fear, because dry psychologists who champion dual-process models are usually not stuck on two. Few would come undone if their models were recast in terms of three processes, or four, or even five. Indeed, the only number they would not happily accept is one, because claims about dual-processes in dry psychology are not so much claims about how many processes there are, but claims about how many processes there aren't.*

> *(Gilbert, 1999, p. 4)*

Recent own research (Verschueren, Schaeken, & d'Ydewalle, 2004, 2005, 2006; Verschueren, Schaeken, De Neys, & d'Ydewalle, 2004) has made clear that there is more than one process involved in everyday conditional reasoning. We believe that the two main theories which explain how background knowledge affects reasoning performance – the probabilistic and the mental models account – both explain an important part of conditional reasoning and can be labelled heuristic and analytic, respectively. Other reasoning mechanisms may however account for some additional variance and even other dual-process accounts may be defended (see also George, 1997; Stevenson, 1997).

In this chapter we argue that the dual-process framework can be used for describing different aspects of conditional reasoning. When focussing on whether and how background information is taken into account, we believe there are at least three levels at which the heuristic/analytic bipolarity can be distinguished. Figure 19.1 gives an overview of these different levels and components. Boxes containing a city-tag are considered as heuristic parts of the inference process. Boxes containing a brain-tag are considered as rather analytic parts of the inference process. The highest level at which a dual-process perspective can be located concerns the decision whether to incorporate background information (Level 3: contextualization versus decontextualization). If we decide to integrate background information, we arrive at a second layer specifying two ways of taking background knowledge into account (Level 2: probabilities versus counterexamples). A final layer concerns how counterexample information is retrieved (Level 1: associative versus strategic).

The different aspects of the inference process can be illustrated with some open-ended answers to the following inference question:

Inference problem (AC):
    If there are advertisements for a product, then the sales records will rise.
    The sales records rose.

Were there advertisements for this product?

Different kinds of answers to this problem are for instance:

Level 1

Automatic retrieval of counterexamples: 'There have been extra advertisements or it could be that it is just a really good product'.

Strategic search for counterexamples: 'There have been extra advertisements unless the increase was setup by accountants'.

Level 2

Use of likelihood information: 'Given that the sales records rose, it is highly probable that there have been advertisements'.

Use of counterexample information: 'I guess there have been extra advertisements unless the sales records increased because of some other reason'.

Level 3

Contextualization tendency: 'Based on my present knowledge about sales records, I would say that it is possible that there have been extra advertisements, but it is also possible that there were no extra advertisements'.

Decontextualization tendency: 'There must have been advertisements, because if there were no advertisements, the sales records would not have risen, and they did, so there must have been advertisements'.

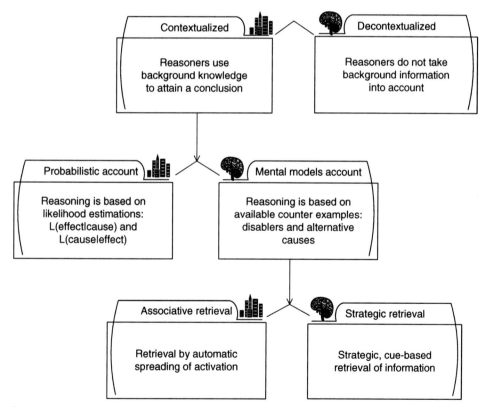

Fig. 19.1 Schematic overview of the three-layered dual-process theory on everyday conditional reasoning that can be recognized in this dissertation.

Note: A city-tag refers to a heuristic process; a brain-tag refers to an analytical process.

These answers illustrate that there are different answers that reasoners can provide to answer the inference question, and as many different ways in which researchers can interpret these given answers. The three levels of the heuristic/analytic polarities will now be discussed in more detail. We start at the deepest level: the difference in counterexample retrieval (Level 1), followed by the difference in type of knowledge that is used (Level 2), we end with the contrast of using versus not-using background information (Level 3).

Level 1

Information Retrieval

The pervasive impact of available background knowledge on the inference acceptance rates has brought research on counterexample retrieval to a central role in the literature on conditional reasoning (see e.g., Barrouillet, Markovits, & Quin, 2001; De Neys, Schaeken, & d'Ydewalle, 2005a, 2005b; Dieussaert, De Neys, & Schaeken, 2005; Markovits & Barrouillet, 2002; Markovits, Fleury, Quinn, & Venet, 1998). The research on information retrieval relates findings on general long-term memory retrieval processes to reasoning research. In most theories on conditional reasoning automatic associative retrieval is considered as the basic retrieval principle. It was only recently pointed out that this automatic search principle can be complemented with a strategic retrieval component (De Neys, 2006; Rosen & Engle, 1997). Both retrieval principles will be briefly discussed.

The *automatic retrieval principle* is mainly driven by semantic association (Moscovitch, 1995). Semantic activation works as follows: The active consideration of the currently attended elements leads to an automatic concurrent activation of strongly associated knowledge structures (Anderson, 1993; Cowan, 1999). For a conditional sentence (*if p, then q*), these structures are the complementary class (*not p & not q*), alternatives (*not p & q*) and disablers (*p & not q*). When processing a conditional inference, the categorical premise functions as a supplementary retrieval cue. It is assumed that counterexamples that automatically reach their critical activation threshold will enter consciousness and will be available for further processing. This retrieval principle operates fast, automatically and requires minimal processing resources.

Strategic counterexample retrieval is guided by active cue generation (Moscovitch, 1995; Rosen & Engle, 1997). In this case, the premises do not automatically lead to a target counterexample, but provide a starting point for a more deliberate, strategic, effort-demanding memory search. This cue-generated search allows a more efficient retrieval, yet it operates at the cost of allocating cognitive resources.

When both retrieval mechanisms are compared, we can consider the automatic retrieval mechanism as a more heuristic process and the strategic counterexample retrieval as a rather analytical process. As such, a first dual-process can be situated at the level of counterexample retrieval.

Counterexample retrieval is the first aspect of causal conditional reasoning which we will describe using the dual-process framework. Verschueren, Schaeken, De Neys and d'Ydewalle (2004) distinguished different types of counterexamples and examined whether different types of counterexamples are made available by different retrieval processes. The three types of counterexamples are illustrated with the following causal conditional inference 'If you drink a lot of coke, then you will gain weight. Anna drinks a lot of coke. Will she gain weight? (MP)'

Type 1 counterexamples are the prototypical counterexamples. They are semantically closely related to the content of the premises. They can be linked to the concept of causal scheme (Mackie, 1985), focal set (Cheng, 1997), and causal set (Chan & Chua, 1994). For the example above, Type 1 counterexamples are *'the person is working out'*, or *'the person is exposed to stress'*.

Type 2 counterexamples are semantically more remotely related. They refer to exceptions to the normal situation or to deferred conversational implicatures. A conversational implicature is an inference that the speaker intends and expects the hearer to draw in order to arrive at a relevant interpretation of the communicated assertion (Grice, 1975; Levinson, 2000, Sperber & Wilson, 1986). For the example above, Type 2 counterexamples are *'after she gained some weight, she immediately went on a diet'* or *'she only drinks diet coke'*.

Type 3 counterexamples are answers of low quality. They can be generated without assessing the underlying causal scheme that the conditional refers to. They include answers referring to some magical interference, plain luck, a non-literal reading or invalid responses. For the example above, a Type 3 counterexample is *'Harry Potter removed the fat'*.

Verschueren, Schaeken and Verbrugge (2006) assumed that Type 1 counterexamples can be retrieved along the semantic association principle by Markovits and Barrouillet (2002), although this does not necessarily imply that all Type 1 counterexamples are retrieved automatically. Based on insights from pragmalinguistic literature and psychological research on conversational implicatures, it was predicted that Type 2 counterexamples require a strategic retrieval process. Indeed, the process of producing conversational implicatures demands effort (De Neys & Schaeken, 2007; Noveck, 2001; Noveck & Posada, 2003). In case of Type 2 counterexamples, reasoners first recognize the implicature and subsequently suspend it.

Verschueren et al. (2006) found explicit support for the idea that there are indeed two distinct counterexample retrieval modes. One retrieval mechanism is considered as more difficult and relates to working memory capacity, whereas the other reasoning mechanism is unrelated to perceived difficulty and working memory capacity. In a first experiment participants were asked to generate counterexamples that are easy to generate and counterexamples that are difficult to generate. The results on the difference in subjective ease of retrieval were in line with the assumption that Type 2 counterexamples require an active effortful search. It was found that Type 2 counterexamples are generally considered hard to retrieve. In two additional experiments (a counterexample generation task and a reasoning task), it was found that differences in working memory capacity correspond to differences in the types of available counterexamples. The counterexamples that participants with a low working memory capacity retrieve are mainly Type 1 counterexamples, whereas participants with a high working memory capacity use an additional and considerable proportion of Type 2 counterexamples. In other words, the perceived difficulty in the first experiment may reside in the higher working memory demands of Type 2 counterexample retrieval.

What is then the strategy for analytic retrieval? Verschueren et al. (2006) distinguish two retrieval cues that can be used for guiding strategic retrieval. First, the active cue generation can be directed towards relevant elements that are part of the causal scheme but only weakly associated with the content of the premises (weakly associated Type 1 counterexamples). Second, the strategic retrieval cues can also result from scrutinizing underlying assumptions or conversational implicatures (Type 2 counterexamples). While it is still unclear on what basis strongly and weakly associated Type 1 counterexamples can be distinguished and how they can be retrieved, linguistic research on conversational implicatures and felicity conditions can form an important source of information for specifying the strategic retrieval process for Type 2 counterexamples.

So on Level 1 we distinguish counterexamples that are retrieved spontaneously through semantic association, from counterexamples that are the result of an active, strategic search process. This bipolarity concedes with the first heuristic-analytic contrast.

Level 2

Processing background information in everyday reasoning

The second bipolarity we will discuss refers to two different reasoning mechanisms, one using likelihood estimations, the second using counterexamples. When reasoners base their inference on a probability or likelihood estimate, the reasoning process places little demand on working memory, yields fast results and proceeds implicitly. These features point towards a heuristic process and can be described by the probabilistic account on human reasoning (Oaksford & Chater, 1998; 2001). When counterexamples are taken into account for deriving a conclusion, the reasoning process is slower, more explicit, and requires more processing resources. This process is labelled analytic and is best described by the mental models theory adapted for causal reasoning (see e.g., Markovits & Barrouillet, 2002).

Our dual-process specification is indebted to the generic dual-process theory of Evans and Over (1996). There are three objectives that are needed to substantiate a generic dual-process account so that it enables researchers to predict and explain performance in a specific task setting (from Evans, 2003):

1. The vague heuristic and analytic processes have to be specified

2. It has to be examined how both processes interact

3. The role of working memory for both processes has to be investigated.

The research reported in Verschueren, Schaeken and d'Ydewalle (2005a, 2005b) aims to answer to these requirements of a successful dual-process specification.

Specification

The first requirement, the procedural specification of the heuristic and analytic process, was attained by referring to, respectively, the probabilistic account and the mental models account. More specific, the reasoning principle described by the mental models theory – especially the adaptation of Markovits and his colleagues – provides an adequate specification of the analytic reasoning process. The heuristic reasoning process can be described by a probabilistic account in which the conclusions are drawn proportionally to L(effect | cause) and the L(cause | effect). These two accounts on conditional reasoning proved already valid in accounting for conditional reasoning performance (Markovits & Barrouillet, 2002; Oaksford, Chater, & Larkin, 2000). Based on Verschueren et al. (2005a, 2005b) we describe in the following paragraphs how these two processes match the heuristic (hence implicit, fast and relatively undemanding) versus analytic (explicit, fast and demanding) distinction.

First, the implicit/explicit characteristic of the heuristic/analytic polarity can be explained as follows. In the generic dual-process idea it is stated that a heuristic process occurs at the periphery of awareness, while the analytical process operates on a conscious level. Indeed, reasoners have no recollection of the situations they accessed for inferring a likelihood estimation, but they are conscious of each counterexample they retrieve.

Second, Verschueren et al. (2005a) tested whether the process based on likelihood information can be considered as a fast, heuristic process whereas the process based on counterexample information can be considered as a slower, analytical process. In a first experiment, there were three groups of participants. One group of participants had to rate both L(effect | cause) and the L(cause | effect) for the 20 sentences. A second group rated both counterexample-predictors (disablers and alternatives) for the same 20 sentences. A third group were given 20 reasoning problems; next to their answers, we registered their the problem solving time. The four inference types were randomly combined with the 20 sentences. Verschueren et al. (2005a) calculated, the mean L(effect | cause) and the L(cause | effect) ratings, the counterexample rating for disablers and alternatives, and the mean inference acceptance rates. By use of a multiple regression analysis they found that conclusions that are attained relatively fast draw on probability estimates, where-as counterexample information becomes more important when it takes more time to produce a conclusion.

The observed difference in beta-weights between the slow and fast responses sustain the idea that the process specification related to likelihood information can be considered as heuristic while the process relying on counterexample information can be labelled as analytic. This observation sustains the first requirement of Evans (2003).

Interaction

The second requirement refers to the interaction of both processes. The interaction between the generic heuristic and analytic processes centres on the override principle: A default, heuristic conclusion gets overwritten when an analytical conclusion can be produced. This override principle led to the following prediction for the specified dual-process account: The analytical conclusion will override the heuristic conclusion when counterexamples are retrieved relatively fast. Our test of this principle is based on the insight that the associative strength of the counterexample determines the speed and probability of retrieval. Hence, the override effect should be larger on sentences with strongly associated counterexamples. This prediction was validated by a multiple regression analysis in a new study, with more sentences and other participants. When the analytical conclusion can be given in time (that is, when counterexamples are highly associated and can be retrieved fast), the variation in answer patterns is mainly explained by variation in counterexample information. When it is hard to retrieve counterexamples fast (no highly associated counterexamples), the variation in inference patterns rather corresponds to variation in likelihood estimates. These results can be read as follows: Reasoners rely by default on likelihood information but if possible (i.e., when counterexamples can be found in time) they overwrite or amend this conclusion with analytic counterexample information. If this analytical process fails to produce a conclusion, reasoners can fall back on the heuristic conclusion referring to likelihood information.

The idea of analytical override implicates that there should be an additional advantage of relying on counterexample information rather than on likelihood information. We can list two possible advantages.

First, the frequency estimates based on natural sampling may be biased. The sample on which the frequency estimate is based may be non-representative. And even when the sample is representative, the estimation is still guided by fallible heuristics such as availability and representativeness (Over, 2003; Sloman & Over, 2003). Some of these biases can be overcome by analytical reflection on counterexample information.

A second reason for relying on counterexample information rather than on frequency information is that in everyday reasoning inferences are drawn in order to make a decision. Probabilistic conclusions inform you about a level of uncertainty. Although this level of uncertainty is informative, it is less suited to 'make up your mind' than a conclusion referring to a relevant counterexample. In the latter case, you get detailed information about why the default conclusion does not follow. For instance, 'If the light switch is flipped, the light goes on. I flip the light switch. Does the light go on?' (MP). A probabilistic conclusion could for instance be: 'In 9 out of 10 cases the light goes on', a mental models conclusion could be: 'The light goes on, unless the lamp is broken'. Now, suppose you flip the switch and the light doesn't come on. In this case a probabilistic forecast informs you that there was indeed a 1/10 chance of the light not going on. That is all information that you have. However, the counterexample provides a possible explanation for *why* the light did not go on, namely: '*The lamp is broken*'. You can now go and check whether the lamp is intact, if necessary replace the lamp and try again to switch on the light. In the goal-directed thinking and conversation process of everyday life, counterexample information gives detailed information about why a certain prediction or explanation might not hold. This level of informativeness can be preferred in everyday situations, and might explain why – although it is harder – participants prefer to reason analytically when they have enough time and processing resources available.

In a recent study (Verschueren, Peeters, & Schaeken, 2006) we got direct evidence supporting the assumption that a conclusion containing a specific counterexample is considered as a 'better' conclusion than a conclusion based on a likelihood estimate. In this study participants were asked to rank a range of possible conclusions according to their quality (give the answer that you consider the best one score 1, the next to best one score 2, and so on). Among the conclusions there was a conclusion with a frequency adverb and another with one specific counterexample (the frequency adverb was proportional to the obtained likelihood estimates; the counterexample was the most strongly associated one). Although the answer with the counterexample listed only one possible counterexample, the counterexample answer was by far preferred over the answer referring to a likelihood estimation.

In the regression studies we just described, it was found that the variation in counterexample ratings predicted the variation in inference acceptance for sentences with strongly associated counterexamples, whereas the variation in likelihood estimates predicted the variation in inference acceptance for sentences with only weakly associated counterexamples. In order to substantiate this mere relational observation, Verschueren et al. (2005a) asked participants in a third study to think aloud while solving causal inference problems. The concurrent verbalisations inform on the relative occurrence of the two processes. When participants use frequency adverbs (always, mostly, seldom) or refer to a likelihood (very likely, low, probable) this manifests the output of a heuristic process: When participants refer to counterexamples, they used an analytical reasoning process to attain a conclusion. The free production answers were recorded and it was verified whether participants used frequency adverbs and/or mention counterexamples. In this verbal protocol study, similar results were observed as in the two previous studies: Both counterexample and likelihood information are used in conditional reasoning and the relative importance of both reasoning mechanisms is mediated by the presence of strongly associated counterexamples. The combination of both methodologies (multiple regression and verbal protocol) provides converging evidence for the involvement of the two processes.

The verbal protocol study also validated the override *sequence:* A tentative heuristic conclusion can be overwritten when a more analytical conclusion based on counterexample information can be formulated. This concurs with the generic principle of analytic override proved thus valid for our current specification. Some examples of this heuristic-analytic override (from Verschueren 2004, literal translations from Dutch):

If you go on a diet, then you will lose weight. A person has lost weight. Did this person go on a diet?

Answer: *Probably he did, but it can also be that the person has been ill and ate less because of that [his illness] or so.*

If there are advertisements for a product, then the sales records rise. There are advertisements for a product. Will the sale records rise?

Answer: *Most of the time the sale records will rise, but if a product is bad then the story goes round under people that it is bad and then it will not sell.*

If someone is nearsighted, then he will wear glasses. Someone is near-sighted. Does this person wear glasses?

Answer: *Then he probably wears glasses but he can also wear contacts.*

Note that this 'override'-principle does not necessarily imply that the likelihood information is totally blocked or cancelled. The conclusion based on likelihood information is rather revised or amended with counterexample information. This subsequent amendment of counterexample information leads participants to a more informative conclusion.

Additionally, Verschueren et al. (2005a, 2005b) have focussed on answers where likelihood and counterexample information are combined and we provided some explicit text examples of how these two information types are combined in various ways. These combination answers exhibit information on how both information types interact. Aside from the heuristic/analytical override, we observed that likelihood information can be used to put the retrieved counterexamples into perspective. It should be emphasized that not all likelihood information relates to L(effect | cause) and L(cause | effect). Reasoners use likelihood information in a reasoning process that is far more complex than the heuristic reasoning process where inferences are drawn in direct proportion to the derived $L(q \mid p)$ or $L(p \mid q)$.

Working memory demands

The third requirement relates to working-memory involvement. It is generally assumed that the heuristic process imposes fewer demands on working memory than the analytical process. This assumption is corroborated by a correlational study as well by a preload study. Verschueren et al. (2005a) observed that the reasoning process based on likelihood information is mainly used by participants with a lower working memory capacity, and that counterexample use increases when working memory capacity increases. Verschueren, Schaeken, and d'Ydewalle (2004) asked participants to solve a secondary task loading working memory, concurrently to the reasoning task. Counterexample use decreased under secondary task loads, while this decrease was not observed for pure likelihood answers.

These results support the idea that the working memory demands are higher for the reasoning process based on counterexample retrieval than for the reasoning process based on likelihood information and hence corroborate the use of the labels heuristic and analytic.

In sum, one can conclude that with respect to Level 2 both theories on conditional reasoning – the probabilistic and the mental models account – are valid accounts and that they are best considered from a dual-process perspective. Both theories describe a different yet complementary aspect of common-sense reasoning. On a more general and combining level this dual-process investigation ratifies the pervasive impact of background knowledge on the reasoning performance and provides a comprehensive way of accounting for the diverging use of counterexamples and likelihood estimations.

Level 3

Deciding whether to use background information

A third level for using the dual-process idea in conditional reasoning concerns the polarity between contextualization and decontextualization. When people contextualize the reasoning problem, they consider elements of the context and relevant background knowledge as co-essential for deriving a sensible conclusion. On the other hand, when they decontextualize the problem, they do not take contextual or background information into account but reason solely on the basis of the information provided in the premises. Decontextualization involves separating task content and beliefs associated with that content from the underlying task structure. There are two distinct reasoning processes that do not rely on relevant background information for deriving a conclusion. Both will be briefly discussed.

Low Competence

First, reasoners may opt for decontextualization because they do not possess the cognitive resources that are needed to retrieve and integrate background knowledge. This 'matching'-tendency was specifically referred to in Verschueren et al. (2005b). They found that when working memory is preloaded some participants start to almost blindly accept the MP and AC inferences. Even when they are reasoning on sentences that have strongly associated counterexamples and $L(q \mid p)$-$L(p \mid q)$ likelihood estimations well below 1 (low sufficiency and necessity), the inferences are still accepted. This answer tendency can be linked to a decontextualized 'matching' strategy. With their working memory preloaded, participants have fewer resources available to retrieve and integrate the relevant background knowledge and fall back upon a decontextualized, yet computationally low demanding reasoning process.

This reasoning process can be understood as reasoning based on only the initial model representation of the conditional (Johnson-Laird & Byrne, 1991). Following the classic mental models theory this should lead to MP and AC acceptance and to an 'I don't know' answer to MT and DA. This can also be related to the computationally undemanding conjunctive interpretation of 'if-then' (Markovits & Barrouillet, 2002). It has to be noted that this initial model representation can contain a probabilistic tag linking the antecedent and consequent proposition (see Verschueren et al., 2005a and Schroyens & Schaeken, 2004 for an explicit account on probabilistic initial models). This probabilistic tag may then be motivated by some sort of epistemic uncertainty or inspired by an implicit and automatic guidance of background information.

High Competence

The second decontextualization tendency is especially observed with highly skilled participants. When they consider background knowledge as irrelevant for the task at hand, they will base their reasoning process solely on the given premises and reason by applying formal reasoning principles. Although we focussed on everyday reasoning, which is mainly contextualized, we observed a minor, yet stable formal decontextualization tendency in highly skilled participants. In Verschueren et al. (2006) and Verschueren et al. (2005b) reported that participants with a high working memory capacity selectively inhibit disabler retrieval. De Neys; Schaeken & d'Ydewalle (2003) relate this inhibition process to the idea that disablers conflict with the logical standard of MP acceptance. The selective inhibition of disablers can be seen as a manifestation of formal decontextualization within the domain of the everyday reasoning process.

The formal decontextualization can be linked to the generic dual-process account of Evans and Over (1996) and Stanovich and West (2000). Research on individual differences in reasoning showed that highly skilled participants are more likely to comply with logical standards (De Neys, et al., 2003; Klaczynski, 2001a; Stanovich & West, 2000): They strategically block the impact of available background knowledge when this information conflicts with normative standards. When reasoners are asked to make a deduction as in an everyday setting this decontextualization tendency is small and elusive, yet it has been observed and validated in several studies and adds to a full comprehension of the everyday reasoning process.

In a mood of wishful thinking, we could argue that the first decontextualized reasoning process can be considered as a heuristic process and the latter as an analytical process. However, because both reasoning processes differ in many aspects, any attempt to specify this dual-process idea could not but suffer from too many procrustean adjustments. There are however some findings that might substantiate such an attempt.

Many studies revealed that cognitive capacity is an important determinant of the formal decontextualization tendency (De Neys et al., 2003; Klaczynski, 2001a; Stanovich & West, 2000; Markovits & Barrouillet, 2002). Another important line of research concerns a specification of the *conditions* of formal decontextualization. Are there certain problem contents, contextual cues or instructions that trigger the formal decontextualization tendency? Can this more analytical reasoning mechanism be trained? Some of these factors have already been examined within the area of abstract conditional reasoning. Schroyens, Schaeken, and Handley (2003) showed that when participants are placed under a timing constraint, the effect of logical validity decreased. When they used instructions that stressed the logical constraint the validity effect increased (see also Vadeboncoeur & Markovits, 1999). Meiser, Klauer, and Naumer (2001) used a specific training procedure (mental models truth table task) to elevate the use of analytic reasoning processes leading to normatively (i.e., logically) correct responses in conditional reasoning. They found that the disruptive effects of secondary task loads increased after training. This increase in disruption was attributed to a more prevalent use of the trained, working memory demanding reasoning strategy.

It would be interesting to see whether the effects of logically stressed instructions and analytical training are also observed when everyday conditionals are used. Both manipulations (timing constraint and stressed logic) could lead to an increase in the otherwise rather exceptionally observed formal decontextualization tendency. Because computational competence limits analytical performance, the effect of this manipulation should mainly show on participants with medium to high intellectual capacities.

The three levels we come to describe illustrate the many faces of causal conditional reasoning and the attempts to describe one or more facets with theoretical models. Theorizing is classically a work in-depth, within each of the well-detailed theories of conditional reasoning there are still stones left unturned. This chapter provides an humble attempt to bring together most current theories and findings on causal 'if-then'-inference making. The result is intriguing by itself, yet it generates new directions, questions and possibilities.

We focussed on causal conditionals alone, while this book addresses conditional reasoning in general. We therefore briefly outline some possible research avenues on everyday conditional reasoning in general (causal and non-causal).

Everyday conditional reasoning

Causal conditionals are only one type of conditional sentences. Some other pragmatic types of conditional sentences include (from Dieussaert, Schaeken, & d'Ydewalle, 2002; Newstead, Ellis, Evans, & Dennis, 1997; and Thompson, 2000):

Promises: If you mow the lawn, then I will pay you 5 Euro.
Threats: If you do that one more time, then I will hit you.
Warnings: If you pull the dog's tail, then he will bite you.
Tips: If you stand on the right side of the cue, then it goes faster.
Obligation: If the traffic light turns red, then you have to stop.
Permission: If you are over 18, then you can drink alcohol.
Prohibition: If you are not a staff member, then you cannot enter this door.
Precaution: If you are driving a motorcycle, then you must wear a helmet.
Hypothesis: If the exhaust of the car is replaced, then the noise will disappear.
Counterfactuals: If I were a boy, then I would not wear earrings.
Intention: If the weather is fine, then I will go fishing.
Category/Definition: If an animal is a mammal, then it is warm-blooded.
Temporal: If this train goes to Leuven, then the next train goes to Gent.

Contingency: If the rooster crows, then it is dawn.
Contingent universals: If a truck is red, then it belongs to the Exxon Company.

It has already been shown that changing the pragmatic type of the conditional results in dramatic changes in the inference acceptance patterns (Dieussaert, et al., 2002; Newstead et al., 1997; Thompson, 2000). Investigating the relative importance of different heuristic and analytic processes can provide additional insight in the effects of pragmatic types. The relevance for conditional reasoning in general will be discussed for the three dual-process perspectives that we discussed earlier.

Types of counterexample retrieval

The taxonomy presented in Verschueren et al. (2004) can be applied to other types of conditionals. Especially for sentences of different pragmatic types but with an equal number of available alternatives and disablers it may be interesting to see whether we find differences in the taxonomic distribution. The occurrence of Type 2 counterexamples may be more important for threats, warnings, tips and promises, where the degree of speaker control is decisive for inference acceptance (Evans & Twyman-Musgrove, 1998). One could check whether the felicity conditions that are characteristic for different speech acts, can be recognized in the results from generation and thinking-aloud reasoning tasks and check whether they indeed provide some readily available retrieval cues, enhancing the probability of counterexample retrieval.

Types of background knowledge

When applying the dual-process theory to other types of conditionals, we may find that the effects of pragmatic types can be (partially) attributed to differences in the relative importance of the two reasoning processes. For example, the inferences that people accept are different for tips, 'If you perform well at work, then you will get a promotion', than for warnings, 'If you pull this dogs tail, then he will bite you'. (see Newstead, et al., 1997; Dieussaert et al., 2002). Based on Lewicka (1989, 1992) we expect that for sentences that have a consequent with a negative valence (warnings/threats) people will be more inclined to retrieve disablers – hence a more important role of the analytical process – than for sentences with a neutral or positive consequent (tips/promises; see also Verschueren, Schaeken, & d'Ydewalle, 2006). The findings of Verschueren, Peeters, and Schaeken (2006) provide already some initial support for this idea. If we replicate these differences in the relative importance of both processes, there might be an alternative explanation for the effects of pragmatic content on the inference acceptance rates. The difference in process use can be investigated by a verbal protocol study, next it can be explicitly tested by use of a regression analysis as used by Verschueren et al. (2003; 2006).

De/Contextualization

There are no specific hypotheses concerning the decontextualization of different pragmatic types. Because the levels of perceived sufficiency (and necessity) of the antecedent condition for the consequent covary with pragmatic type (see e.g., Newstead et al., 1997) we have to equate the sentences of different pragmatic types on a similar level of sufficiency if we want to investigate the decontextualization tendency independent from the perceived sufficiency. We can formulate two testable hypotheses on why the formal decontextualization tendency could differ among pragmatic types.

First, it is possible that various pragmatic types differ in the working memory demands for reasoning. For instance, it can be argued that reasoning with counterfactual conditionals demands more working memory than reasoning with other conditionals – the main reason is that in order to understand a counterfactual you have to represent both the factual and the counterfactual state of affairs (see e.g., Byrne & Tasso, 1999). Because of the higher load on working memory, we can expect that there will be fewer resources left to formally decontextualize the problem.

Second, it can be argued that conditional sentences that are uttered in a social context, such as promises, threats, obligations, permissions, and intentions presuppose a social contract. This enriched context could increase the difficulty of a formal decontextualization.

In sum, the framework we lined out can be translated to reasoning from different types conditionals. It can form a valuable perspective for framing known effects of pragmatic types and for developing new lines of research.

Final Thought

The research reported in this chapter forwards our understanding of how counterexample information is used in reasoning. We described a semantic counterexample classification system and revealed that a specific type of counterexamples (Type 2) has to be distinguished from the semantically related (Type 1) counterexamples. This second type requires a strategic retrieval process and the retrieval cues used for strategic retrieval relate to the conversational implicatures governing efficient communication. Aside of grasping some of the fundaments of counterexample *retrieval*, pinpointing different types of counterexamples has also led to a deeper and more differentiated comprehension of counterexample *use*.

We also brought two rival theories (a mental models account of reasoning and a probabilistic/likelihood account of reasoning) together in a dual-process perspective. It was found that reasoning based on likelihood information operates at the periphery of awareness, yields fast conclusions, and poses only minor demands on working memory. In contrast, reasoning based on counterexample information takes more time to attain a conclusion, taps heavier on working memory resources, and operates at a more conscious level. The first process is labelled heuristic, the latter is labelled analytic. Both existing theories – the probabilistic and the mental models account – describe important parts of the reasoning process, but when both theories are brought together in a dual-process perspective our comprehension of the everyday contextualization process reaches further depth and discernment.

We pointed to three levels at which a dual-process polarity can be distinguished. The bipartite heuristic/analytic theory is hereby considered as a guiding tool for classifying cognitive processes. Instead of using the generic and vague description of what constitutes a heuristic and an analytic reasoning process, we managed by use of this two-horse team to characterize the different processes akin to the distinct aspects of the human reasoning mechanism. The current chapter hopefully led to a substantial progress in describing what lies according to us at the heart of everyday reasoning: Contextualization.

References

Anderson, J. R. (1993). *The architecture of cognition*. Cambridge, MA: Harvard University Press.

Barrouillet, P., Markovits, H., & Quinn, S. (2001). Developmental and content effects in reasoning with causal conditionals. *Journal of Experimental Child Psychology*, **81**, 235–248.

Byrne, R. M. J. & Tasso, A. (1999). Deductive reasoning with factual, possible, and counterfactual conditionals. *Memory & Cognition*, **27**, 726–740.

Chan, D. & Chua, F. (1994). Suppression of valid inferences: Syntactic views, mental models and relative salience. *Cognition*, **53**, 217–238.

Chaiken, S. & Trope, Y. (1999). *Dual-process theories in social psychology*. New York: Guilford Press.

Cheng, P. W. (1997). From covariation to causation: A causal power theory. *Psychological Review*, **104**, 367–405.

Cowan, N. (1999). An embedded-process model of working memory. In A. Miyake & P. Shah (Eds.), *Models of working memory: Mechanisms of active maintenance and executive control* (pp. 62–101). Cambridge: University Press.

De Neys, W. (2006). Dual processing in reasoning: Two systems but one reasoner. *Psychological Science*, **17**, 428–433.

De Neys, W. & Schaeken, W. (2007). When people are more logical under cognitive load: Dual task impact on scalar implicature. *Experimental Psychology*, **54**, 128–133.

De Neys, W., Schaeken, W., & d'Ydewalle, G. (2005). Working memory and everyday conditional reasoning: Retrieval and inhibition of stored counterexamples. *Thinking & Reasoning*, **11**, 349–381.

De Neys, W., Schaeken, W., & d'Ydewalle, G. (2005). Working memory and counterexample retrieval for causal conditionals. *Thinking & Reasoning*, **11**, 123–150.

Dieussaert, K., De Neys, W., & Schaeken, W. (2005). Suppression and belief revision, two sides of the same coin?. *Psychologica Belgica*, **45**, 29–46.

Dieussaert, K., Schaeken, W., & d'Ydewalle, G. (2002a). The relative contribution of content and context factors on the interpretation of conditionals. *Journal of Experimental Psychology*, **49**(3), 181–195.

Epstein, S. (1994). Integration of the cognitive and psychodynamic unconscious. *American Psychologist*, **49**, 709–724.

Evans, J. St.B. T. (1984). Heuristic and analytic processes in reasoning. *British Journal of Psychology*, **75**, 451–468.

Evans, J. St.B. T. (1989). *Bias in human reasoning: Causes and consequences*. London: Erlbaum Associates.

Evans, J. St.B. T. (2003). In two minds: Dual-process accounts on reasoning. *Trends in Cognitive Sciences*, **7**, 454–459.

Evans, J. St.B. T. & Over, D. E. (1996). *Rationality and reasoning*. Hove, UK: Psychology Press.

Evans, J. St.B. T. & Over, D. E. (1997a). Rationality in reasoning: The problem of deductive competence. *Current Psychology of Cognition*, **16**, 3–38.

Evans, J. St.B. T. & Twyman-Musgrove, J. (1998). Conditional reasoning with inducements and advice. *Cognition*, **69**, B11–B16.

George, C. (1997). Limited or extended pluralism? Commentary on 'Rationality in Reasoning'. *Current Psychology of Cognition*, **16**, 87–92.

Gilbert, D. T. (1999). What the mind's not. In S. Chaiken & Y. Trope (Eds.), *Dual-process theories in social psychology* (pp. 3–12). New York: Guilford Press.

Grice, H. P. (1975). Logic and conversation. In P. Cole & J. L. Morgan (Eds.), *Studies in syntax: Speech acts 3*, (pp. 41–58). New York: Academic Press.

Hammond, K. R. (1996). *Human judgment and social policy*. New York: Oxford University Press.

Johnson-Laird, P. N. (1983). *Mental Models: Towards a cognitive science of language, inference and consciousness*. Cambridge, MA: Cambridge University Press.

Johnson-Laird, P. N. & Byrne, R. M. J. (1991). *Deduction*. Hove, UK: Lawrence Erlbaum Associates.

Klaczynski, P. A. (2001a). Analytic and heuristic processing influences on adolescent reasoning and decision making. *Child development*, **72**, 844–861.

Klaczynski, P. A. (2001b). Faming effects on adolescent tasks representations, analytic and heuristic processing, and decision making. Implications for the normative/descriptive gap. *Applied Developmental Psychology*, **22**, 289–309.

Klein, G. (1999). *Sources of power*. Cambridge, MA: MIT Press.

Levinson, S. C. (2000). *Presumptive meanings. The theory of generalized conversational implicature.*.London, UK: MIT Press.

Lewicka, M. (1989). Toward a pragmatic perspective on cognition: Does evaluative meaning influence rationality of lay inferences? *Polish Psychological Bulletin*, **20**, 267–285.

Lewicka, M. (1992). Pragmatic reasoning schemata with differing affective value of a consequent of logical implication. *Polish Psychological Bulletin*, **23**, 237–252.

Mackie, J. L. (1965). Causes and Conditions. *American Philosophical Quarterly*, **2**, 245–264.

Markovits, H. & Barouillet, P. (2002). The development of conditional reasoning: A mental model account. *Developmental Review*, **22**, 5–36.

Markovits, H., Fleury, M. L., Quinn. S., & Venet, M. (1998). The development of conditional reasoning and the structure of semantic memory. *Child development*, **69**, 742–755.

Meiser, T., Klauer, K. C., & Naumer, B. (2001). Propositional reasoning and working memory: The role of prior training and pragmatic content. *Acta Psychologica*, **106**, 303–327.

Moscovitch, M. (1995). Models of consciousnes and memory. In M. S. Gazzaniga (Ed.), *The cognitive neurosciences* (pp. 1341–1356). Cambridge, MA: MIT Press.

Newstead, S. E., Ellis, M. C., Evans, J. St.B. T., & Dennis, I. (1997). Conditional reasoning with realistic material. *Thinking and Reasoning*, **3**, 49–76.

Noveck, I. (2001). When children are more logical than adults: experimental investigations of scalar implicature. *Cognition*, **78**, 165–188.

Noveck, I. A. & Posada, A. (2003). Characterizing the time course of an implicature: An evoked potentials study. *Brain and Language*, **85**, 203–210.

Oaksford, M. & Chater, N. (1998). *Rationality in an uncertain world: Essays on the cognitive science of human reasoning.* Hove, UK: Psychology Press.

Oaksford, M. & Chater, N. (2001). The probabilistic approach to human reasoning. *Trends in Cognitive Sciences*, **5**, 349–357.

Oaksford, M., Chater, N., & Larkin, J. (2000). Probabilities and polarity biases in conditional inference. *Journal of Experimental Psychology: Learning, Memory and Cognition*, **26**, 883–899.

Over, D. E. (2003). From massive modularity to metarepresentation: The evolution of higher cognition. In D. E. Over (Ed.), *Evolution and the psychology of thinking: The debate* (pp. 121–144). Hove, UK: Psychology Press.

Pollock, J. L. (1991). OSCAR: A general theory of rationality. In J. Cummins & J. L. Pollock (Eds.), *Philosophy and AI: Essays at the interface* (pp. 189–213). Cambridge, MA: MIT Press.

Reber, A. S. (1993). *Implicit learning and tacit knowledge.* Oxford, UK: Oxford University Press.

Rosen, V. M. & Engle, R. W. (1997). The role of working memory capacity in retrieval. *Journal of Experimental Psychology: General*, **126**, 211–227.

Schneider, W. & Shiffrin, R. M. (1977). Controlled and automatic human information processing I: Detection, search and attention. *Psychological Review*, **84**, 1–66.

Schroyens, W. & Schaeken, W. (2004). Guilt by Association: On iffy propositions and the proper treatment of mental-models theory. *Current Psychology Letters*, **12**, Vol. 1. http://cpl.revues.org/document404.html.

Schroyens, W. Schaeken, W., & Handley, S. (2003). In search of counterexamples: Deductive rationality in human reasoning. *Quarterly Journal of Experimental Psychology*, **56**, 1129–1145.

Sloman, S. A. (1996). The empirical case for two systems of reasoning. *Psychological Bulletin*, **119**, 3–22.

Sloman, S. A. & Over, D. E. (2003). Probability judgment from the inside and out. In D. E. Over (Ed.), *Evolution and the psychology of thinking: The debate* (pp. 145–169). Hove, UK: Psychology Press.

Sperber, D. & Wilson, D. (1986/1995). *Relevance: Communication and cognition.* Harvard University Press and Blackwell.

Stanovich, K. E. & West, R. F. (2000). Individual differences in reasoning: Implications for the rationality debate? *Behavioural and Brain Sciences*, **23**, 645–726.

Stanovich, K. E. & West, R. F. (2003). Evlutionary versus instrumental goals: How evolutionary psychology misconceives human rationality. In D. E. Over (Ed.), *Evolution and the psychology of thinking: The debate* (pp. 171–230). Hove, UK: Psychology Press.

Stevenson, R. J. (1997). Deductive reasoning and the distinction between implicit and explicit processes. *Current Psychology of Cognition*, **16**, 222–229.

Thompson, V. (2000). The task-specific nature of domain-general reasoning. *Cognition*, **76**, 209–268.

Vadeboncoeur, I. & Markovits, H. (1999). The effect of instructions and information retrieval on accepting the premises in a conditional reasoning task. *Thinking and Reasoning*, **5**, 97–113.

Verschueren, N. (2004). *Contextualising conditional inferences*. Unpublished Phd-thesis, University of Leuven.

Verschueren, N., Peeters, G., & Schaeken, W. (2006). Don't let anything bad happen: The effect of consequence valence on conditional reasoning. *Current Psychology Letters*, 20.

Verschueren, N., Schaeken, W., De Neys, W., & d'Ydewalle, G. (2004). The difference between generating counterexamples and using them during reasoning. *Quarterly Journal of Experimental Psychology*, **57**, 1285–1308.

Verschueren, N., Schaeken, W., & d'Ydewalle, G. (2005a). A dual process theory on causal conditional reasoning. *Thinking and Reasoning*, **11**(3), 239–278.

Verschueren, N., Schaeken, W., & d'Ydewalle, G. (2005b). Everyday conditional reasoning: A working-memory dependent trade-off between counterexample and likelihood use. *Memory and Cognition*, **33**, 107–119.

Verschueren, N., Schaeken, W., & Verbrugge, S. (2006) Conversational Implicatures in Counterexample Retrieval: Working Memory and Crystallized Pragmatics. *Proceedings of the 28th Annual Conference of the Cognitive Science Society* (pp. 2311–2316). Mahwah, NJ: Erlbaum.

Chapter 20

Two aspects of reasoning competence: A challenge for current accounts and a call for new conceptual tools

Guy Politzer and Jean-François Bonnefon

Introduction: Taking stock of one century of research on deductive reasoning

The year 2008 coincides with the centenary of what is likely to be the first experimental work ever published on reasoning (Störring, 1908). It seems that for this author, as for the 'founding fathers' of scientific psychology, Aristotelian syllogistic was the only normative model of reference. For example, Binet (1898), in an essay titled 'the psychology of reasoning,' used as his unique logical reference the 'scholastic syllogism' (all men are mortal, etc.), on the basis of which he developed a common explanation of perception and reasoning. James (1908) took exactly the same syllogism as a foundation of all reasoning. Overall, it seems that those among the great psychologists of the past who investigated reasoning were content with integrating whatever logic they knew into their conception of thinking. This applies also to Piaget who, contrary to his predecessors, was in a position to exploit modern logic, in which he was knowledgeable. Indeed, Piaget claimed that at the ultimate stage of development of the individual, 'reasoning is nothing else than the very calculus involved by propositional operations, and, while this calculus remains linked to ordinary language in the individuals' thought, it can be symbolically expressed by way of the algebra of propositional logic' (Inhelder & Piaget, 1955, our translation).

For half a century, the psychology of reasoning focused on the individuals' *formal* reasoning competence, in the wake of a philosophical tradition focused on the question of human rationality—of which deductive competence was regarded as quintessential. From this perspective, it seemed natural enough to aim experimental work at comparing actual performance with the prescriptions derived from the then prevalent logical system, namely, standard logic. In sum, until the late 1960s or early 1970s, investigators of reasoning limited their investigations to the observation and classification of performance. They did not feel it necessary to put hypotheses to the test because there was just no *original* model of reasoning to test: The standard logical system of the time was assumed to provide both the way people ought to reason and, applying a form of psychologism, to reflect the way people did reason. Consequently, the only question left to investigate was the extent to which people might, after all, depart from the prescriptions of logic.

A new era started with the publication of the Wason and Johnson-Laird (1972) book, in which the authors examined participants' performance on a variety of tasks in propositional, relational and syllogistic reasoning. They concluded that 'there was no *existing* [emphasis added] formal calculus which correctly modelled our subjects' inferences' (p. 245). This and subsequent work established two facts regarding formal reasoning: (i) by and large, people possess some formal competence, but (ii) they nevertheless often commit errors. In particular, they fall prey to various biases, especially linked with the treatment of negation (see Evans, Newstead, & Byrne, 1993, for a later review). Conditional reasoning offers well-known examples of these results: Even with abstract propositional symbols, people solve Modus Ponens without difficulty, whereas they fail to solve Modus Tollens about one third of the time, whatever the material.

From the late 1970s onwards, the path was open to work out original theories for modelling human deductive performance, which manifested itself in Johnson-Laird's (1983; Johnson-Laird & Bara, 1978) first version of mental model theory and Braine's (1978) early version of mental logic. (The departure from standard logic is manifest in subsequent versions of these theories: Significantly, mental logic has its own semantics for connectives and does not claim completeness or soundness with respect to propositional logic, see Braine & O'Brien, 1998. Also, in the mental model theory of Johnson-Laird & Byrne, 2002, it is claimed that the conditional is not truth-functional.) The emphasis was still on formal reasoning, though. To fulfill the old agenda, experimenters used to choose arguments that were as decontextualized as possible, because world knowledge was considered parasitic. The old paradigm required that the participants produce or evaluate the conclusion of an argument whose premises were assumed to be true in a world or a micro-world as impoverished as possible. Indeed, another result of importance regarding deductive reasoning in general became evident: Performance changes altogether if formal material is replaced with meaningful material, which came as a puzzle for the narrow view which reduces deduction to its formal variety.

In the 1980s, the focus of deduction research shifted from formal competence to daily life abilities. This paradigm shift required to adapt to several critical aspects of everyday reasoning:

◆ In real life, people exploit huge knowledge bases kept in long term memory;
◆ Premises generally are uncertain because (a) the information is often probabilistic in nature, or (b) may be conveyed by general statements that have exceptions or imprecise quantification, and (c) because our sources of information (verbal communication, memory, perception and inference) are not fully reliable;
◆ Conclusions are defeasible (a new piece of information in the form of an additional premise may oblige one to retract a previously drawn conclusion);
◆ And finally, everyday reasoning as a whole is goal-oriented: It normally takes place within an individually or socially determined activity or schema in the course of which individuals use reasoning to a specific purpose (argue, give a proof, give an explanation, apply a law, a procedure, solve a problem, deliberate, derive a prediction, detect a contradiction, etc.).

When these specificities are taken into account, earlier approaches to deduction are no more appropriate without deep alteration, as they were designed to address formal reasoning, where premises are sure, conclusions are not defeasible, where all information is explicitly available, and where the conclusion is purely contemplative. In particular, relying on logic alone for modelling real life deduction is in principle inadequate because factual information must be integrated and, as just mentioned, this information generally is probabilistic.

The last period of reasoning research started in the early 1990s, after Oaksford and Chater (1991, 2001, 2007) had pleaded in favour of a probabilistic approach to the study of deduction, while inviting to reject the 'logicist' view. This marked a decisive break away from the presupposition that logic (in fact, standard logic) is the only possible source for modelling human deduction.

In summary, the initial enquiry into human formal deductive abilities has been more or less fulfilled, yielding a moderately positive answer (people do have some degree of formal competence), together with two main elaborate theoretical approaches (mental logic, mental models) specifically developed to explain performance on the artificial laboratory tasks. The new enquiry into ecologically valid deductive abilities started relatively recently. The present chapter, which is essentially theoretical and programmatic, is devoted to this question. After summarizing the knowledge available to date, we will be concerned with the question of the kind of formalism that could inspire the modelling of human performance in this domain. Because so many researchers in the fields of judgement and decision making have chosen the probability calculus as a model, it is tempting for investigators of reasoning to follow suit. So, we will pay special attention to the concept of probability and examine its adequacy to represent people's uncertainty in the domain of reasoning. We will argue that the probability calculus may not be any more appropriate than classical logic as a model. Finally, we will consider a few alternative formalisms that are possible candidates for modelling reasoning with uncertain premises.

Deduction from uncertain premises: a compendium of the main results

In this section, we organize the current knowledge about conditional reasoning with uncertain premises around three main observations. (In principle, we are interested in any deductive argument in which at least one premise is uncertain; but it turns out that most experimental data concern conditional arguments.)

In arguments whose form is deductive, but whose premises are uncertain, people have a tendency to draw an uncertain conclusion

Before we review the two types of evidence in support of this claim, we need to eliminate a possible misunderstanding: A deductive argument that yields an uncertain conclusion sounds like an oxymoron. Indeed, textbook definitions of deduction insist that the essential characteristic of a deductive argument lies in the certainty of its conclusion, that is, its conclusion cannot be false if its premises are true. We are concerned here with the use of arguments that, according to this definition, are formally categorized as deductive and such that one or several premises are uncertain, resulting in an uncertain conclusion. The question of whether these arguments may still be called 'deductive' is moot—we choose to answer affirmatively because the deductive form of the argument is descriptively invariant, even though the reasoner attributes levels of credibility to the premises or the conclusion.

Direct evidence in support of claim 2.1 has been obtained by overt manipulation of the credibility of the premises. George (1995) asked participants to estimate their confidence in controversial conditional assertions (e.g., 'if a painter is talented, then his/her works are expensive') or just in the entailment of the consequent by the antecedent ('a painter is talented'; does this entail: 'his/her works are expensive'?). Participants gave their estimate on a 7-point scale from *true* to *uncertain* (the mid-point) to *false*. Then, they rated their confidence in the conclusion of the associated Modus Ponens (MP), with strong emphasis on the instructions to assume the major premise to be true. About one half of the participants declared the conclusion true, indicating that they adopted a 'trustful mode' in which they abode by the instructions to assume the truth of the premises, and then engage in a standard deduction. But the other participants did not accept the conclusion as true and declared it uncertain to various degrees. So, in spite of the strength of the instructions, as many as one half of the participants adopted a 'distrustful mode' in which the uncertainty of the premises overpowered the instructions. The levels of confidence in the conclusion and the premise were highly correlated, suggesting that the confidence in the premise propagates to the conclusion and that the confidence in the latter is an increasing function of the confidence in the former.

This was confirmed using verbal expressions of certainty: George (1997) presented MP arguments in which the premise was an arbitrary conditional modified by either one of two probability expressions (e.g., 'if Pierre is in the kitchen, then it is very [probable/ improbable] that Marie is in the garden'). This time there were no specific instructions regarding the truth of the conditional premise. Participants had to evaluate the conclusion on a 9-point scale (*certainly true, almost certainly true, very probable, probable, not very probable*, etc., until *certainly false*). Most responses were uncertain: One half repeated the probability expression used in the premise; in the other cases, the responses generally consisted of the next degree (higher or lower) on the scale.

In another experiment, George (1997) examined the way people combine the uncertainty in case both premises are uncertain. He qualified both the major premise (an arbitrary conditional) and the minor premise of MP arguments with the same probability expressions (*certain, very probable, not very probable*). By crossing them, he obtained $3 \times 3 = 9$ types of arguments whose conclusion had to be evaluated on the 9-option scale of confidence already described. For all types of arguments, the most frequent response was a confidence rating equal to that of the premise with the lower probability (in particular when the two premises were uncertain to the same degree, the conclusion generally inherited this degree). The next most frequent response was a confidence rating lower than the smaller probability of the two premises.

Premises may also be conflicting, for instance one premise might favour a conclusion and another premise its negation. George (1999) used a four-premise argument combining two MP. Both conditional premises were uncertain and both minor premises were categorical as in 'if she meets Nicolas, it is very probable that she will go to the swimming-pool; if she meets Sophie, it is very improbable that she will go to the swimming-pool; she meets Nicolas; she meets Sophie'. Various combinations of confidence levels were considered, yielding different sets of premises among which some were conflicting, as in the example. The conclusion was evaluated on a 9-point scale (whose mid-point was *the odds are the same*). In the conflicting case, the mid-point of the scale was chosen two-thirds of the time, (and even 80% of the time if one aggregates points 4, 5, and 6 of the scale), showing that most people react with maximum uncertainty to such cases (a reaction called 'preservation of ambiguity').

This observation was confirmed and refined by Benferhat et al. (2005), using an elementary artificial knowledge base (referring to fictitious animal species) with subject-predicate assertions such as 'Hermaphrodite Glacyceae generally live in a solid environment' and 'Necrophagous Glacyceae generally do not live in a solid environment'. Given a hermaphrodite, necrophagous Glacycea, 80% of the participants declared that they could not conclude anything about its living or not in a solid environment. However, given the supplementary assertion 'Bulging Glacyceae generally live in a solid environment' and a hermaphrodite, necrophagous, bulging Glacycea, only one third declared that they could not conclude, the majority now opting for the Glacycea living in a solid environment, which suggests that their choice is determined by considering the predicate that has the greater number of reasons in its favour.

Performance on more complex sets of premises was investigated by Ford & Billington (2000) using syllogisms that had from three to six premises, in several of which the quantifier 'all' was replaced with 'usually'. With more than three premises the material seems to have been too difficult for participants, who resorted to a number of heuristics that we will not describe. However, performance on the three-premise arguments is suggestive. These were made of one of the following pairs of premises:

- 'Xs are usually Ys; all Ys are Zs';
- 'all Xs are Ys; Ys are usually Zs';
- 'Xs are usually Ys; Ys are usually Zs',

together with the singular premise 'x is an X', the conclusion to evaluate being 'x is a Z'. The conclusion 'it is likely that x is a Z' was nearly unanimously chosen, showing again propagation of the uncertainty. But notice that this answer is correct only for the first argument, the other two being entirely undetermined.

There is also indirect evidence of the propagation of uncertainty that has been obtained by covert manipulation of the credibility of the premises. We are referring to well-known results obtained with MP and MT arguments that will be very briefly recalled. In these tasks, instead of overtly manipulating confidence in arbitrary sentences, one exploits the levels of credibility offered by world knowledge. Thompson (1994, 1995) showed that for conditionals that conveyed definition, deontic or causal relations, the rate of endorsement of the conclusion was an increasing function of the 'perceived sufficiency' of the conditional sentences estimated by judges, defined as 'the degree to which the occurrence of the consequent is perceived as warranted when the antecedent occurs'. Liu et al. (1996) obtained similar results, defining the levels of credibility of the conditional sentence in terms of the conditional probability of the consequent given the antecedent (again, assessed by judges). Finally, in the causal domain, Cummins (1995; Cummins et al., 1991) observed that the credibility of the conclusion (whether measured by the rate of endorsement or by way of certainty scales) was a decreasing function of the number of disabling conditions (factors that can prevent an effect from occurring)—a number which arguably reflects the lack of confidence one can have in the causal relation. Disabling conditions are special cases, in the domain of causality, of complementary necessary conditions (or CNCs) whose fulfilment (or lack thereof) may defeat a conditional statement by breaking its credibility (Beller & Kuhnmünch, 2007; Politzer, 2001, 2003; Bonnefon & Politzer, this volume). The effect of these variables—number of CNCs produced by participants, probability of the consequent given the antecedent estimated by participants, and also their degree of belief in the conditional premise has been confirmed by Weidenfeld, Oberauer and Hörnig (2005) who observed that they were correlated with the rate of endorsement of the conclusion of MP and MT arguments; this obtained with forward and backward conditionals and, to a lesser extent, with arbitrary conditionals.

The addition of a premise may result in the reasoner's doubting or retracting the conclusion

Consider an argument whose form is deductive, whose premises are certain, and for which there exists a conclusion that people usually draw correctly and with confidence. It is often the case that after the introduction of an additional premise people may become reluctant to maintain this initial conclusion. They may even retract it altogether, a situation referred to as *nonmonotonic* reasoning. Experimentally, this phenomenon can be demonstrated in various ways.

A first way consists of adding a premise that directly and *overtly* casts doubt on an initial premise. For instance, Hilton, Jaspars and Clarke (1990) compared the conclusion given to standard MP (or MT) arguments such as 'if he works hard then he will pass; he works hard; therefore he will pass' and to the same argument supplemented with a categorical premise such as 'the exam is difficult'. This resulted in a shift in frequency from *true* answers to the non-committal *sometimes true and sometimes false,* a clear nonmonotonic effect (demonstrated here in a between-participant design).

This effect was refined in several subsequent studies by defining a gradation in the additional premise, in order to manipulate the extent to which the satisfaction of a CNC was compromised. For example, Stevenson and Over (1995) presented a major premise such as 'if John goes fishing, he will have a fish supper' with the appropriate minor premise (for MP or MT) and a second categorical premise in which frequency terms were used to establish degrees of confidence in the conditional ('John always catches a fish when he goes fishing'; 'almost always...'; 'sometimes...'; 'almost never...'; 'never...'). It was observed that the rate of endorsement of the conclusion was a decreasing function of the uncertainty introduced by the additional premise. Similar results were obtained by Manktelow and Fairley (2000) and by Politzer and Bourmaud (2002) who used a variety of conditionals (means-end, causal, remedial, decision rule) and manipulated also the strength, or degree of necessity, of the CNC (the latter manipulation resulting in a lack of confidence in the conclusion that was increasing with the strength of the CNC).

A second kind of experimental task that exhibits the revocation of a conclusion is characterized by the addition of a premise that directly and *covertly* casts doubt on an initial premise. This is known as the 'suppression effect' (Byrne, 1989; see Bonnefon and Politzer, this volume, for a brief description and a pragmatic analysis, and Bonnefon and Hilton, 2004, for a variant of the effect). We reproduce here the set of premises for convenience: (i) 'if she has an essay to write then she will study late in the library'; (ii) 'if the library stays open then she will study late in the library'; (iii) 'she has an essay to write'. The conclusion 'she will study late in the library' is drawn by most people who are presented only with premises (i) and (iii), but the rate of endorsement usually collapses to about 50% when premise (ii) is added.

Interestingly, this task was not presented by its author as an investigation of reasoning under uncertainty, and indeed it has none of the specific features of the tasks reviewed so far: The major conditional premise is not modified by a probability or a frequency term; in the impoverished context that is provided and when it is considered in isolation, there is no reason to question the credibility of the major conditional premise; and as far as the additional premise is concerned, it does not express a *categorical* denial or doubt about a CNC. The role of uncertainty is subtle and concealed but can be disclosed by a pragmatic analysis (Bonnefon & Hilton, 2002; Politzer, 2005), which shows that an adequate formalism for deduction with uncertain premises should have an interface with interpretive processes.

A last kind of experimental task leading to the revocation of a conclusion is characterized by the addition of a premise that *indirectly* casts doubt on an initial premise. This has been observed (Politzer & Bonnefon, 2006) when the major premise is an *inferential* conditional (Dancyger, 1993, also called *epistemic* by Sweetser, 1990, or *evidential* by Pearl, 1988, in the domain of causality). Inferential conditionals express that knowledge of the truth of the propositional content of the antecedent allows the speaker to infer the truth of the propositional content of the consequent, with an appropriate degree of confidence. They often convey causal relations in the effect-to-cause direction, such as 'if there is snow on the TV screen then there is a storm nearby'. (A useful test to identify this variety is the rephrasing with an epistemic *must*, as in 'if there is snow on the TV screen there must be a storm nearby'). Given the conditional and the minor premise 'there is snow on the TV set', people draw MP as usual; but with a third premise such as 'if the aerial is unplugged then there is snow on the screen', the rate of endorsement of the conclusion drops.

People tend to revise belief by expressing uncertainty rather than mere denial

Knowledge bases in real life are dynamic: New incoming information may be consistent or not with the information that is already in the base. In case it is not, the content of the base has to be modified in order to accommodate the new information in a consistent manner: People have to give up some part of this content and *revise* their knowledge base. The belief revision problem has been extensively investigated in artificial intelligence (Gärdenfors, 1988) and in philosophy (e.g., Harman, 1986). Is it possible to define some normative principles to follow when carrying out the revision of the knowledge base? Two different approaches have been put forward. One, called the *foundationalist* approach, is based on the notion that the propositions to give up are those that have the least support or justification. The other, called the *coherentist* approach, posits that some propositions are less important that others and should be abandoned first if the change is to be minimal; this leads to the notion of *epistemic entrenchment* which is a relation of order (technically a total pre-order) that obeys a small set of postulates. (e.g., if A logically entails B, A is less entrenched than B).

It can be seen that the coherentist view has two characteristics that are important for our purpose: It is basically formal (that is, entrenchment is not a matter of content) and relies on the notion of acceptance, that is, it deals with *accepted* propositions, without considering belief by degree. Elio and Pelletier (1997) considered the first characteristic in a series of experiments, where they examined whether the logical form of the propositions affects the entrenchment of belief. This was tested by considering the premises of simple arguments such as MP. After receiving a statement which contradicted the conclusion, participants were asked to choose among several belief sets the one they thought was the best way to reconcile all the knowledge. With both thematic and formal materials participants were more prone to give up the conditional than the categorical statement. The same authors investigated the principle of minimal change; they compared several algorithms that operationalize this concept and found that participants complied with none of them. They noticed that participants chose 'revisions that were not minimal with respect to what was changed, but were instead minimal with respect to what they believed to hold true without doubt'.

An interesting feature of these results is that in case participants were given an opportunity to select revision options that expressed uncertainty about a proposition, they preferred to select them rather than negating the proposition. This observation was to be generalized, notably by Politzer and Carles (2001), who used four arguments: a MP, a MT, a disjunctive syllogism (*A or B; not A; therefore B*), and a 'conjunctive syllogism' (*not both A and B; A; therefore not-B*). Each full argument was followed by the negation of the conclusion (the new piece of information) and five revision options which consisted of the negation of the major premise or of the minor premise, or of a doubt about each of these, or of a free response. The results indicated that the uncertain options were chosen about four times as often as the sure options, and this obtained for all four argument types and for most participants, considered individually. In sum, participants showed a strong tendency to revise the set of premises by characterizing one (or more) premise as doubtful rather than by denying them. A similar observation was made by Dieussaert et al. (2000).

In these tasks, people were presented with sure premises, so that the possible role of the initial degree of belief in the revision process was not considered. The second experiment of Politzer and Carles (2001) addressed this question. Paired MP arguments referring to everyday life events were used, such that the conditional premise was judged to be initially highly credible for the first one and little credible for the other one. The same kind of task as in the first experiment was used; while the low credibility premise was revised about 90% of the time, the paired high credibility premise was revised less than half the time. Not so surprisingly, one can conclude that, *ceteris paribus,* a less credible premise is less entrenched than a more credible one. This is confirmed by the observations made by Markovits and Schmeltzer (2007) in a quite different domain. They used a mechanical device and manipulated credibility by two intermediate variables: duration of experience with the device (the rate of revision of a causal conditional was higher with the shorter experience) and degree of randomness of the device (the rate was higher in the random case than in the deterministic case). As far as the issue of the effect of formal properties vs. content on entrenchment is concerned, it should be noticed that in the second experiment of Politzer and Carles (2001) judgments of plausibility crucially depended on world knowledge, and that the logical form of the premises as well as of the arguments were kept constant, so that only content varied: The notion that entrenchment is based only on formal properties is clearly not supported.

In sum, there is not much support for the coherentist view. People crucially take into account the credibility of the propositions in their knowledge base and their treatment of these does not seem to be compatible with the notion of bi-valued propositions. Moreover, even if there is evidence of a formal effect (not reviewed here) in the sense of a relative entrenchment of conditional statements (and, more generally, of compound statements) against categorical statements, this seems to interact with factors such as argument form, content, and testing procedure.

Finally, one difference between the revocation tasks and the belief revision task is noteworthy. As Elio and Pelletier (1998) put it, these can be viewed as 'opposite sides of the same coin: the coin of default reasoning'. In both cases, there is propagation of uncertainty—only the direction of this propagation is different. In the revocation tasks, the loss of credibility of a premise following an additional *conditional* information results in a doubt about the conclusion, showing a forward propagation of uncertainty (from premises to conclusion). In contrast, in the revision task, the *categorical* denial of a previously derived conclusion results in doubt about a premise, showing a backward propagation of uncertainty.

The lesson to draw

This short review of the processing of credibility within deductive arguments shows that reasoners are sensitive to a whole range of confidence levels from full belief to full disbelief through complete uncertainty—and that full belief, which formerly was the unique focus of interest, is only the extremity of a spectrum, suggesting that classical deduction could be modelled as the limit case of a general inferential system, with confidence as a parameter set to its maximal value.

The studies reviewed are basically descriptive. The mechanisms of propagation of credibility levels are yet to be discovered. We take it as evident that the two major approaches to deduction, mental rules (Braine & O'Brien, 1998; Rips, 1994) and mental models (Johnson-Laird & Byrne, 1991; Johnson-Laird, 2001), cannot be applied to uncertain reasoning *in their current state* because they were developed to treat the formal (and therefore, the certain) case and lack the means of representing the credibility of the propositions, as well as the propagation of the levels of credibility. In the rest of this chapter, we will consider the main alternative to logic, namely the probabilistic approach.

Moving from logic to probability

In view of the pervasive presence of uncertain premises in deductive reasoning, it may be tempting to reject all kind of logic, at least binary. Then, a natural candidate is the probability calculus. This choice is understandable. Probability calculus is highly useful and successfully applied in various areas of psychology and the cognitive sciences, not to mention other disciplines. Moreover, in its standard Bayesian version, the simplicity and apparent naturalness with which its axioms can be derived from Dutch book arguments in gambling situations (see e.g., Skyrms, 1986) is very appealing, and even fascinating. Indeed, one may be tempted to believe that such a derivation reveals to some extent the 'laws of thought'—which, after our experience with standard logic, gives an unmistakable impression of *déjà vu*. There are two kinds of reasons why we should exercise caution before we give such a role to probability calculus, and we are going to consider them in turn.

A fundamental ability: Proof generation

The ability to administer a proof is an essential component of human deductive abilities. In numerous situations, people plan and develop the administration of proofs. They do so in the course of daily argumentation, but also in their internal deliberations (when they mentally simulate a possible course of action), or in more specific settings, such as in school mathematics (e.g., demonstrating the solution of an elementary geometry problem). Even if explicit verbal proofs were the trace of a *post hoc* reorganisation or rationalisation of highly rapid and unconscious mechanisms, such a capability of displaying a rational proof would have to be explained—probably in identical terms.

In this perspective, the question that arises is 'can a model based solely on the probability calculus account for proof generation?' The answer seems to be negative. To illustrate the difficulty with an example, consider an easy argument of the type used by Braine et al. (1984): 'It is not true that there is both a J and a Q; there is an X and a J; conclusion: is there a Q?' Before considering the *production* of the conclusion, notice that even for an evaluation task the problem is computationally difficult. With premises A and B and conclusion C, one can apply Bayes' rule to the conjunction of the premises:

$$\Pr(C \mid A \wedge B) = \Pr(C \mid A) \frac{\Pr(B \mid A \wedge C)}{\Pr(B \mid A)}$$

but this computation has little psychological plausibility, because of its complexity, which increases sharply with the number of premises. Alternatively, one can think of applying the elementary theorems of the calculus, which provide bounds in the form of inequalites for conjunctions and disjunctions. We can consider first the easiest case where both premises are certain (an adequate theory must account for the sure case too): From $\Pr(X\&J) = 1$ and $\Pr(X\&J) \leq \Pr(J)$, there follows $\Pr(J) = 1$, which together with $\Pr(J\&Q) = 0$ yields $\Pr(Q) = 0$. The case where the premises are not certain is more difficult as inequalities are needed. But whatever the case, the important point is the following: Where does this algebraic demonstration come from? Obviously, in addition to the use of the probability calculus, one has to be able to administer a demonstration, which is a deductive activity that lies *outside* the calculus. More crucially, assuming now the conclusion to be no longer given, the daunting question of the origin of the conclusion in the production paradigm is left unresolved. In brief, something essential that is part of people's deductive competence, namely the ability to plan and develop a proof, is missing in a purely probabilistic approach. By contrast, logic-based theories of reasoning, especially rule-based theories, have no difficulty in accounting for this, as they assume the existence of a routine especially devoted to the step-by-step derivation of the conclusion.

The nature of uncertainty

The meta-cognitive ability to become aware of one's uncertainty with respect to a conjecture, resulting in the attribution of levels of credibility (or judgements of plausibility), is a fundamental characteristic of the human mind. Quite independently, the probability calculus as a mathematical theory of the measure of uncertainty has gained universal adoption. The relations between the mathematical concept of probability (together with its formal properties expressed, e.g., by Kolmogorov's axioms) and the psychological primitive notion of uncertainty should be considered with great care.

For one thing, its adoption as a normative framework may be inappropriate. For instance, the notorious difficulty to deal with ignorance using the probability calculus removes much of its interest in many psychological settings. Even when its use is technically justified, it should be kept in mind that a technical concept can provide a normative framework at the computational level, if while failing to capture people's intuitive notion at the descriptive level, which is the object of the psychological investigation. It might very well be the case that the use of probability (assumed to be a real number on the [0, 1] interval) results from learning and education, while in general individuals resort to a different notion to appraise the credibility of a conjecture (even though this may result in a number or a percentage because of social practice). Of course, this will not be the case in environments so organized as to lend themselves to numerical calculation. For instance, it as been shown that individuals can solve elementary problems of probability in situations where there is a sample space transparent enough to enable them to compute numbers of favourable cases, yielding real numbers (e.g., Gigerenzer & Hoffrage, 1995; Girotto & Gonzales, 2001; these authors hold different views regarding what information format counts as frequency versus probability information, which need not concern us here: see Sloman *et al.*, 2003, and Yamagishi, 2003 for an explanation in term of nested-set relations). This occurs even without formal training in probability, for example with young children (Fishbein, 1975; Girotto & Gonzales, 2007). The point is that there are various factors that can jointly or separately determine the credibility of a conjecture (such as, depending on their origin and their nature: witness or authority, perception, memory retrieval, inference, supporting principle, material evidence, etc.) and evidence based on a calculation that results in a numerical value is just one among these. In an impoverished context, such as in laboratory tasks, people may use their capabilities to carry out such calculations. In brief, probability might not capture the psychological notion of confidence in a conjecture, except in special circumstances.

More technically, the psychological format of representation of credibility (which we will denote cr) is unknown as long as the following questions are not answered, some of which being clearly empirically testable:

♦ Can all conjectures be compared to each other, whatever their domain? That is, do we always have either $cr(A) > cr(B)$ or $cr(A) = cr(B)$ or $cr(A) < cr(B)$?

♦ Does credibility have the property of compacity? That is, given $cr(A) > cr(B)$, is it always possible to find Z such that $cr(A) > cr(Z) > cr(B)$?

Keynes (1921) answered negatively to these two questions, and argued against the possibility to attribute a numerical value to every proposition. This led him to envisage a lattice structure, which in turn leads to the next question:

• Does credibility have the property of transitivity?
• If there exists a scale of measurement for credibility, what is its mathematical structure?
• Assuming credibility can be represented by real numbers, does the measure yield a degree (a point on a scale) or an interval? In other words, can credibility be captured by a single measure or quantity?
• Can credibility be represented by a non-numerical scale, in particular a verbal scale?
• Is there a simple relation between the credibility of a conjecture and the credibility of its negation?

As is well known, after choosing a specific answer to some of these questions (stated in more rigorous terms), the axioms of the probability calculus can be derived by Cox's (1961) theorem (see also Jaynes, 2002). Different answers lead to different formalisms. Halpern (2005) lists the following main formalisms to represent uncertainty that differ from probability measures: Lower and upper probability (Walley, 1991), belief functions (Shafer, 1976), possibility measures (Zadeh, 1978), ranking functions (Spohn, 1988), and for the nonnumeric case, relative likelihood (or partial preorder, Halpern, 1997) and "plausibility measures" of Friedman and Halpern (1995). For psychological theory, it is essential to not only justify the reasonableness of the choices (e.g., why take it as axiomatic that credibility in a conjecture decreases as credibility in its negation increases?) but also to put them to the test. We claim that in spite of six or seven decades of research on probability judgement there is no *decisive* argument, theoretical or empirical, to justify the prerequisites (that is, the decisions about the answers to give to the foregoing questions) to the adoption of the probability calculus for the psychological modelling of uncertainty.

The reason seems to be that, unlike Keynes and a few other notable exceptions, the majority of the theorists have taken the answers leading to the probability formalism as intuitively self-evident, so that the question of interest has been that of the extent to which individuals perform in agreement with the probability calculus. (In particular, are people 'well calibrated,' and do they revise in agreement with Bayes' rule?)

This has given rise to huge research programmes, in particular to the 'heuristics and biases' school (Kahneman et al., 1982; Gilovich et al., 2002). In brief, this stream of research was developed *within* probability theory taken as a norm of reference. Interestingly, those working in the field of decision making have been more critical with regard to the axioms of expected utility theory, and marginally, probability theory. (We have not considered the specific debate about Bayesianism, but see Baratgin and Politzer, 2006, for a thorough discussion of, and a negative answer to, the question of the *testability* of the hypothesis that the *subjective* Bayesian interpretation of probability is psychologically adequate to represent degrees of belief).

All this is reminiscent of what happened with classical logic. The relevance of our historical sketch of the fate of standard logic in modelling human deduction should now be clear: The fact that a formalism is well-known and highly successful in various cognate fields or disciplines does not warrant its adequacy for psychological modelling, and this, in principle, carries over from logic to probability. We do not claim that the probability calculus should be rejected, rather we claim that one should be cautious before adopting it as a model, be it normative or descriptive, because the nature of an individual's belief in a proposition is, for the time being, too poorly understood psychologically. In the same manner as theorists of the past were guilty of logicism, we should, in present days, be wary of the risk of 'probabilism'. After this exposition of our cautionary—if not skeptical—view, we turn to a more positive exercise, namely, the suggestion of possible directions for future research.

A more positive view

Of course, our reservations with regard to probability could fail to be substantiated by future research. Assuming probability passes the test which we have suggested, a few proposals exist which are highly interesting because they blend a deductive component (which we have shown to be indispensable) together with probability. These are probabilistic logics which, in a nutshell, identify the arguments whose conclusion is not entirely indeterminate, and in such cases provide bounds for the conclusion as a function of the probability of the premises. We mention Adam's (1996) logic and the probabilistic logic developed by Pfeifer and Kleiter (2005a, and this volume).

If, on the contrary, our reservations are supported, the main alternative to probability to capture the psychological notion of credibility is *plausibility* defined as an indication of the credibility that can be attached to a conjecture in virtue of the reliability of its source (Rescher, 1976). It is basically ordinal (but can be indexed on a numerical scale for practical convenience). Contrary to probability which is linked to an internal or content-related likelihood, plausibility depends on the external status of the supporting sources. Also, contrary to probability, plausibility is independent of alternative conjectures, so that there is no law of negation and a conjecture and its negation can have a high plausibility together.

With respect to entailment, given premises P_i and conclusion C, $Pl(C) \geq \min(Pl(P_i))$ that is, the conclusion cannot be less plausible than the least plausible premise, which is informative. This 'consequence principle' of plausibility (Rescher, 1976) contrasts with a consequence of the 'logical consequence principle' (Skyrms, 1986): $Pr(C) \geq Pr(\wedge_i P_i)$: The conclusion cannot be less probable than the probability of the conjunction of the premises, which may leave the conclusion indeterminate.

With respect to conjunction, plausibility is 'conservating': $Pl(A \wedge B) = min(Pl(A), Pl(B))$, whereas probability is 'degrading', that is we have only $Pr(A \wedge B) \leq Pr(A)$, which can reach zero even if the conjuncts' probabilities are not very low.

If future research supports the hypothesis that the psychological notion of confidence is adequately captured by the concept of plausibility, one may turn to the kind of formalisms that have adopted this view of uncertainty. Such is the case of the Dempster-Shafer theory of evidence (Shafer, 1976; see Gordon & Shortliffe, 1984, for an elementary introduction, Curley and Golden, 1994 for an exploratory study of their psychological adequacy, and Shafer and Tversky, 1985, for a systematic comparison of Bayesian probability and Shafer's belief functions) and of the theory of possibility (Dubois & Prade, 1988). We describe the latter because it provides an interesting normative framework and, with some complementation, a candidate for the elaboration of a descriptive model. Possibilistic logic is a weighted logic that was introduced in Artificial Intelligence in the 1980s, in order to handle uncertain and incomplete information. At the core of this enterprise is the old idea of reasoning from classical logical formulas, arranging them into stratified layers corresponding to different levels of confidence. Accordingly, the basic concept of possibilistic logic is that of an ordinal confidence measure on classical logical formulas. (Interestingly, but independently of our present purpose, possibility measures are also used to model preferences in decision-making, just as they are used to model confidence in reasoning.)

The possibility Π of an event A encodes the degree to which it is plausible, normal, expected. $\Pi(A)$ takes its value on an ordinal scale bounded by a top and a bottom element. It is customary to give the role of that scale to the unit interval $[0,1]$. The lower $\Pi(A)$, the less normal is A. In particular, $\Pi(A) = 0$ means that A is strictly impossible and the logical contradiction has a possibility of zero. $\Pi(A) = 1$ does not mean that A is certain, only that it would be entirely normal, not surprising to the least. Tautologies have a possibility of one. The possibility measure Π derives from a possibility distribution π over possible worlds Wi; π encodes a complete transitive pre-order, and it only provides ordinal information. The possibility $\Pi(A)$ is that of the most plausible world in which A holds, that is, $\Pi(A)$ is the greatest $\pi(Wi)$ such that Wi is a model of A. The characteristic property of a possibility measure Π is the max-decomposability of disjunction: $\Pi(A \vee B) = max(\Pi(A), \Pi(B))$.

Note that this decomposability forces at least one of $\Pi(A)$ or $\Pi(not\text{-}A)$ to be equal to 1. Indeed the possibility of any tautological formula must be equal to 1 (what is necessarily true cannot be abnormal to any degree); thus, the possibility of 'A or not-A' must be equal to 1, which imposes that the greater of $\Pi(A)$ and $\Pi(not\text{-}A)$ is equal to 1. Thus, either a proposition or its negation must be entirely possible. That is, however, the only constraint these two possibility degrees must satisfy. In particular, $\Pi(A)$ and $\Pi(not\text{-}A)$ can be simultaneously equal to 1. This corresponds to total ignorance about whether A is true, i.e., both A and not-A are entirely possible. Note the contrast with probability calculus, where $Pr(not\text{-}A)$ is entirely determined by $Pr(A)$.

Π has a dual measure N, called 'necessity', which encodes the degree to which A is necessarily true: $N(A) = 1 - \Pi(not\text{-}A)$. Using Π or N in computations is only a matter of formal taste. Every property of Π has its dual with respect to N, for example: $N(A \wedge B) = min(N(A), N(B))$.

A default rule such as 'If A then (generally) B' translates into the following constraint on the possibility distribution (Benferhat et al., 1997): $\Pi(A \wedge B) > \Pi(A \wedge not\text{-}B)$. This is equivalent to considering that in all the most possible worlds where A is true, B is also true, or, in other terms, that not-B can only be found in non-preferred models of A. In order to assess a putative conclusion Z, one needs to arrive at a possibility distribution that is consistent with the considered constraints (premises), then to read both $\Pi(Z)$ and $\Pi(not\text{-}Z)$ from the distribution.

It is not uncommon that several possibility distributions can accommodate the constraints. There are different solutions for choosing among these different distributions, which corresponds to several variants of possibilistic inference with various degrees of psychological plausibility (Benferhat et al., 2005).

Most interestingly, the most cautious of these methods yields exactly the same conclusions as System P, a well accepted set of axioms for nonmonotonic reasoning (Kraus et al., 1990; see also Pfeifer and Kleiter, 2005b and this volume). System P defines the rules for using the everyday, nonmonotonic conditional 'if E then normally (probably, usually) F' in syntactic proof derivations. In addition to the postulate that the everyday conditional is reflexive (if E, then normally E), System P allows the following inferences:

- From 'if E then normally F' and 'if F then G' (material implication), conclude that 'if E, then normally G';
- From 'E is equivalent to F' and 'if E then normally G', conclude that 'if F then normally G';
- From 'if E then normally F' and 'if E then normally G', conclude that 'if E, then normally (F and G)';
- From 'if E then normally G' and 'if F then normally G', conclude that 'if (E or F), then normally G';
- From 'if E then normally F' and 'if E then normally G', conclude that 'if (E and F), then normally G';
- From 'if E then normally F' and 'if (E and F) then normally G', conclude that 'if E, then normally G'.

Possibilistic logic thus offers both a representation of uncertainty (which differs in important respects from the probabilistic representation), and a method for constructing simple proofs, even when these proofs involve everyday, uncertain conditionals. Note, however, that proof derivation will only be simple when formulas other than conditional ones are themselves certain. Another one of the advantages of possibilistic logic is that it can handle ordinal measures of uncertainty; indeed, this seems to be one of the desiderata of any adequate psychological formalism, in view of the availability in language of qualitative expressions. The descriptive validity of possibility theory has been supported by the results of several experiments by Raufaste *et al.* (2003). They have shown that participants' (students and experienced professionals) ratings of possibility and necessity observe the main relations (duality, etc.) mentioned above. Of course, more research is needed.

That concludes our presentation of possibilistic logic, which we have offered as an illustration of the formal choices that are wide opened to psychologists willing to model human deduction. Indeed, for modelling human deduction, we need to address the two sides of human deductive competence. That is, we need both a formalism of uncertainty (to represent degrees of belief), for which logics derived from classical bi-valued logic are inadequate; and a logic to construct proofs, which the probability calculus does not offer. In addition, whether probability calculus captures a psychologically appropriate notion of uncertainty has yet to be established. Thus, we should be careful not to escape logicism only to fall prey to probabilism; and to give a chance to other uncertainty formalisms, which may offer a more plausible representation of uncertainty as well as a simple logic for proof derivation, especially in the limit case of sure premises.

Acknowledgement

The authors thank Jean Baratgin for his comments on a first draft of this chapter.

References

Adams, E. (1998). *A primer of probability logic*. Stanford: CSLI Publications.

Baratgin, J. & Politzer, G. (2006). Is the mind Bayesian? The case for agnosticism. *Mind and Society*, **5**, 1–38.

Binet, A. (1898). *La psychologie du raisonnement*. Paris: Alcan.

Benferhat, S., Bonnefon, J. F., & Da Silva Neves, R.M. (2005). An overview of possibilistic handling of default reasoning, with experimental studies. *Synthese*, **146**, 53–70.

Benferhat, S., Dubois, D., & Prade, H. (1997). Nonmonotonic reasoning, conditional objects and possibility theory. *Artificial Intelligence*, **92**, 259–276.

Bonnefon, J. F. & Hilton, D. J. (2002). The suppression of Modus Ponens as a case of pragmatic preconditional reasoning. *Thinking and Reasoning*, **8**, 21–40.

Bonnefon, J. F. & Hilton, D. J. (2004). Consequential conditionals: Invited and suppressed inferences from valued outcomes. *Journal of Experimental Psychology: Learning, Memory and Cognition*, **30**, 28–37.

Braine, M. D. S. (1978). On the relation between the natural logic of reasoning and standard logic. *Psychological Review*, **85**, 1–21.

Braine, M. D. S. & O'Brien, D. P. (1998). *Mental logic*. Mahwah, NJ: Lawrence Erlbaum.

Braine, M. D. S., Reiser B. J., & Rumain, B. (1984). Some empirical justification for a theory of natural propositional logic. In G. H. Bower, (Ed.), *The psychology of learning and motivation*, pp. 313–371. **18**, New York : Academic Press.

Byrne, R. M. J. (1989). Suppressing valid inferences with conditionals. *Cognition*, **31**, 61–83.

Cox, R. T. (1961). *The algebra of probable inference*. Baltimore: Johns Hopkins Press.

Cummins, D. D. (1995). Naive theories and causal deduction. *Memory and Cognition*, **23**, 646–658.

Cummins, D. D., Lubart, T., Alksnis, O., & Rist, R. (1991). Conditional reasoning and causation. *Memory and Cognition*, **19**, 274–282.

Curley, S. & Golden, J.I. (1994). Using belief functions to represent degrees of belief. *Organizational Behavior and Human Decision Processes*, **58**, 271–303.

Dancygier, B. (1993). Interpreting conditionals: Time, knowledge, and causation. *Journal of Pragmatics*, **19**, 403–434.

Dieussaert, K., Schaeken, W., De Neys, W., & d'Ydewalle, G. (2000). Initial belief state as a predictor of belief revision. *Current Psychology of Cognition*, **19**, 277–288.

Dubois, D. & Prade, H. (1988). *Possibility theory*. New York: Plenum Press.

Elio, R. (1997). What to believe when inferences are contradicted: The impact of knowledge type and inference rule. *Proceedings of the Nineteenth Annual Conference of the Cognitive Science Society*, (pp. 211–216). Mahwah NJ: Lawrence Erlbaum.

Elio, R. & Pelletier, F. J. (1997). Belief change as propositional update. *Cognitive Science*, **21**, 419–460.

Evans, J. St.B. T., Newstead, S. E., & Byrne, R. M. J. (1993). *Human reasoning. The psychology of deduction*. Hove: Lawrence Erlbaum.

Fischbein, E. (1975). *The intuitive sources of probabilistic thinking in children*. Dordrecht: Reidel.

Ford, M. & Billington, D. (2000). Strategies in human nonmonotonic reasoning. *Computational Intelligence*, **16**, 446–468.

Friedman, N. & Halpern, J.Y. (1995). Plausibility measures: a user's guide. In *Proceedings of the 11th Conference on Uncertainty in Artificial Intelligence* (pp. 175–184). San Francisco: Morgan Kaufmann.

Gärdenfors, P. (1988). *Knowledge in flux*. Cambridge: MIT Press.

George, C. (1995). The endorsement of the premises: Assumption-based or belief-based reasoning. *British Journal of Psychology*, **86**, 93–111.

George, C. (1997). Reasoning from uncertain premises. *Thinking and Reasoning*, **3**, 161–189.

George, C. (1999). Evaluation of the plausibility of a conclusion derivable from several arguments with uncertain premises. *Thinking and Reasoning*, **5**, 245–281.

Gilovich, T. Griffin, D., & Kahneman, D. (Eds.) (2002). *Heuristics and biases: The psychology of intuitive judgment*. Cambridge: Cambridge University Press.

Girotto, V. , & Gonzalez, M. (2001). Solving probabilistic and statistical problems: A matter of information and question form. *Cognition, 78*, 247–276.

Girotto, V. , & Gonzalez, M. (2007). Children's understanding of posterior probability. *Cognition, 106*(1), 325–344.

Gordon, J. & Shortliffe, E. H. (1984). The Dempster-Shafer theory of evidence. In B. G. Buchanan & E. H. Shortliffe (Eds.), *Rule-based expert systems*, (pp. 272–292). Reading, Mass: Addison-Wesley.

Halpern, J.Y. (1997). Defining relative likelihood in partially-ordered preferential structures. *Journal of A.I. Research, 7*, 1–24.

Harman, G. (1986). *Change in view. Principles of reasoning*. Cambridge: MIT Press.

Hilton, D. J., Jaspars, J. M. F., & Clarke, D. D. (1990). Pragmatic conditional reasoning: Context and content effects on the interpretation of causal assertions. *Journal of Pragmatics, 14*, 791–812.

Inhelder, B. & Piaget, J. (1968). *The growth of logical thinking from childhood to adolescence : an essay on the construction of formal operational structures*. London: Routledge. [Original French ed. 1955]

James, W. (1908). *Text-book of psychology, briefer course*. London: Macmillan.

Jaynes, E. T. (2002). *Probability theory: the logic of science*. Cambridge: Cambridge University Press.

Johnson-Laird, P. N. (1983). *Mental models*. Cambridge: Cambridge University Press.

Johnson-Laird, P. N. (2001). Mental models and deduction. *Trends in Cognitive Sciences, 5*, 434–442.

Johnson-Laird, P. N., & Byrne, R.M.J. (1991). *Deduction*. Hove: Lawrence Erlbaum, Kahneman, D., Slovic, P. & Tversky, A., (Eds.) (1982). *Judgment under uncertainty: Heuristics and biases*. Cambridge: Cambridge University Press.

Keynes, J. M. (1921). *A treatise on probability*. Cambridge: Macmillan.

Kraft, C. H., Pratt, J. W., & Seidenberg, A. (1959). Intuitive probability on finite sets. *Annals of Mathematical Statistics, 30*, 408–419.

Kraus, S., Lehmann, D., & Magidor, M. (1990). Nonmonotonic reasoning, preferential models and cumulative logics. *Artificial Intelligence, 44*, 167–207.

Manktelow, K. & Fairley, N. (2000). Superordinate principles in reasoning with causal and deontic conditionals. *Thinking and Reasoning, 6*, 41–65.

Markovits, H. & Schmeltzer, C. (2007). What makes people revise their beliefs following contradictory anecdotal evidence? The role of systemic variability and direct experience. *Cognitive Science, 31*, 535–543.

Oaksford, M. & Chater, N. (1991). Against logicist cognitive science. *Mind and Language, 6*, 1–38.

Oaksford, M. & Chater, N. (2001). The probabilistic approach to human resoning. *Trends in Cognitive Sciences, 5*, 349–357.

Oaksford, M. & Chater, N. (2007). *Bayesian rationality*. Oxford: Oxford University Press.

Pearl, J. (1988). *Probabilistic reasoning in intelligent systems: Networks of plausible inference*. San Francisco: Morgan Kaufmann.

Pfeifer, N. & Kleiter, G. D. (2005a). Towards a mental probability logic. *Psychologica Belgica, 45*, 71–99.

Pfeifer, N., & Kleiter, G. D. (2005b). Coherence and nonmonotonicity in human reasoning. *Synthese, 146*, 93–109.

Politzer, G. (2001). How to doubt about a conditional. In S. Benferhat & P. Besnard, (Eds.). *Symbolic and quantitative approaches to reasoning with uncertainty*, (pp. 659–667. LNAI 2143). Berlin: Springer.

Politzer, G. (2003). Premise interpretation in conditional reasoning. In D. Hardman & L. Macchi, (Eds.). *Thinking: Psychological perspectives on reasoning, judgment, and decision making* (pp. 79–93). London: Wiley.

Politzer, G. (2005). Uncertainty and the suppression of inferences. *Thinking and Reasoning, 11*, 5–33.

Politzer, G. & Bonnefon, J. F. (2006). Two varieties of conditionals and two kinds of defeaters help reveal two fundamental types of reasoning. *Mind and Language*, **21**, 484–503.

Politzer, G. & Bourmaud, G. (2002). Deductive reasoning from uncertain conditionals. *British Journal of Psychology*, **93**, 345–381.

Politzer, G. & Carles, L. (2001). Belief revision and uncertain reasoning. *Thinking and Reasoning*, **7**, 217–234.

Raufaste, E., da Silva Neves, R. & Mariné, C. (2003). Testing the descriptive validity of possibility theory in human judgments of uncertainty. *Artificial Intelligence*, **148**, 197–218.

Rescher, N. (1976). *Plausible reasoning*. Amsterdam: Van Gorcum.

Rips, L. J. (1994). *The psychology of proof*. Cambridge MA: MIT Press.

Shafer, G. (1976). *A mathematical theory of evidence*. Princeton: Princeton University Press.

Shafer, G. & Tversky, A. (1985). Languages and designs for probability judgments. *Cognitive Science*, **9**, 309–339.

Skyrms, B. (1986). *Choice and chance. An introduction to inductive logic*. Belmont CA: Wadsworth.

Sloman, S. A. , Over, D. E. , Slovak, L. & Stibel, M. (2003). Frequency illusions and other fallacies. *Organizational Behavior and Human Decision Processes*, **91**, 296–309.

Spohn, W (1988). Ordinal conditional functions: A dynamic theory of epistemic states. In W. Harper and B. Skyrms (Eds.), *Causation in decision, belief change and statistics* (pp. 105–134). Vol. 2. Dordrecht: Reidel.

Stevenson, R. J. & Over, D. E. (1995). Deduction from uncertain premises. *Quarterly Journal of Experimental Psychology*, **48A**, 613–643.

Störring, G. (1908). Experimentelle untersuchungen über einfache Schlussprozesse. *Archiv für die Gesante Psychologie*, **11**, 1–127.

Sweetser, E. (1990). *From etymology to pragmatics*. Cambridge MA: Cambridge University Press.

Thompson, V. A. (1994). Interpretational factors in conditional reasoning. *Memory and Cognition*, **22**, 742–758.

Thompson, V. A. (1995). Conditional reasoning: The necessary and sufficient conditions. *Canadian Journal of Experimental Psychology*, **49**, 1–60.

Wason, P. C. & Johnson-Laird, P. N. (1972). *Psychology of reasoning. Structure and content*. London: Batsford.

Walley, P. (1991). *Statistical reasoning with imprecise probabilities*. London: Chapman and Hall.

Weinfeld, A., Oberauer, K. & Hörnig, R. (2005). Causal and noncausal conditionals: An integrated model of interpretation and reasoning. *Quarterly Journal of Experimental Psychology*, **58A**, 1479–1513.

Yamagishi, K (2003). Facilitating normative judgments of conditional probability: Frequency or nested sets? *Experimental Psychology*, **50**, 97–106.

Zadeh, L.A. (1978). Fuzzy sets as a basis for a theory of possibility. *Fuzzy Sets and Systems*, **1**, 3–28.

Part 5

Epilogue

Chapter 21

Open issues in the cognitive science of conditionals

Nick Chater and Mike Oaksford

The chapters in this book have provided an overview of the state-of-the-art in the study of how people reason with conditionals. And outlining theories of conditionals has led to immediate contact with core debates concerning theories of human thought, and, indeed, the nature of rationality itself. Three issues arising across the volume seem to be of particularly broad significance:

(1) *Probability vs. logic?* What is the role of probability and or logic in explaining human thought? Are they in competition or are they complementary?

(2) *Single vs. multiple systems?* Is reasoning carried out by a single cognitive system, or by two or more reasoning systems?

(3) *Background knowledge and the frame problem.* How thought is influenced by, potentially arbitrarily large, amounts of background knowledge.

Regarding issue (1), *Probabiltity vs. logic*, twenty years ago there was little sign of the probabilistic ideas that play a large role in the present volume (e.g., the chapters by Ali, Schlottman, Shaw, Chater, & Oaksford; Geiger & Oberauer; Girotto & Johnson-Laird; Liu; Oaksford & Chater; Over, Evans & Elqayam; Pfeifer & Kleiter). Since then, however, probabilistic ideas have reverberated across the cognitive sciences (for surveys see Chater & Oaksford, 2008; Chater, Tenenbaum, & Yuille, 2007; Knill & Richards, 1996; Manning & Schütze, 1999; Pearl, 1988, 2000), and the neurosciences (Rao, Olshausen, & Lewicki, 2002). As is clear in this volume, probabilistic ideas have connected with prior philosophical work applying probability to conditionals (Adams, 1975; Edgington, 1995), as well as foundational discussions of the meaning of conditional statements (Evans & Over, 2004; Over, Evans & Elqayam, this volume; Ramsey, 1990/1931).

Turning to issue (2), *Single vs. multiple systems?*, we note that multiple-system theories of cognition have become increasingly prominent over the past decades (Evans, 2008; Evans & Frankish, in press; see the chapters by, e.g., Thompson, Verschueren, & Schaeken). Evans and Over (1996) have influentially advocated a distinction between rationality1, subserved by deliberative serial reasoning processes, and rationality2, presumed to arise from evolutionarily old, parallel, and perhaps associative cognitive mechanisms. Indeed, Stanovich (2009) argues that three distinct mechanism for reasoning may be required. Moreover, a wide range of related, though distinct, viewpoints have been outlined in cognitive science (Sloman, 1996), social psychology (e.g., Chaiken & Trope, 1999), and decision making (Kahneman & Frederick, 2005). Similarly, neuroscientists have also argued that behaviour may be the outcome of competition between a range of cognitive systems, at minimum distinguishing habit-based decision making and goal-directed behaviour (Daw, O'Doherty, Dayan, Seymour, & Dolan, 2006; McClure, Laibson, Loewenstein, & Cohen, 2004).

A complementary, though distinct, line of thought, concerning the possible multiplicity of reasoning processes, stems from the explosion of work tackling some of the core domains over which conditional reasoning occurs, including causal learning and reasoning (Gopnik & Schultz, 2007) and reasoning about norms (Cosmides, 1989). One theoretical thread has been the specialized mechanisms underpin different types of reasoning (Barkow, Tooby, & Cosmides, 1992; Hirschfeld & Gelman, 1994). Is such a viewpoint correct? And if it is, does this conclusion imply that the study of conditional reasoning itself should break into a million fragments? Or can a uniform account of reasoning apply uniformly across a wide variety of domains?

By contrast, there has perhaps been a decline in attention paid to the issue (3), *The problem of background knowledge*, highlighted above, concerning the integration of large amounts of background knowledge, to specific reasoning processes. Twenty years ago, the 'frame problem' (McCarthy & Hayes, 1969; Pylyshyn, 1987) stalked the cognitive sciences—indeed, it was seen as raising fundamental and potentially fatal problems for computational approaches to symbolic, logic-based approaches to cognitive science (Dreyfus, 1972; Fodor, 1983). The frame problem, as we discuss below, raises serious concerns about any cognitive or computational account that draws on background knowledge—and yet the influence of background knowledge seems to be pervasive through the study of reasoning, and in particular in the study of conditionals.

In this final chapter, we briefly review what we see as the state of play in these three key areas, and highlight directions for future research, both in the study of reasoning with conditionals, and in cognitive science more generally.

Probability vs. logic

Normative theories, i.e., accounts of how people *should* reason, play a key role in discussions of how people actually do reason, in a number of ways. First, they define standards of 'correct' reasoning, against which the quality of actual human reasoning can be assessed. (This role is analogous to the theory of arithmetic providing a standard against which the accuracy of mental arithmetic can be measured). Second, some degree of conformity to normative standards of reasoning is required to determine that people are *reasoning* at all, rather than, for example, responding purely at random, using rote memory, or putative associative mechanisms (although see the next section for further discussion of this possibility). Analogously, some degree of conformity with the principles of the arithmetic allows us to say that a person is performing mental addition rather than, say multiplication, or mere random number generation. Third, normative standards provide potential starting points for *descriptive theories* of reasoning—just as it would be hard to imagine formulating a successful cognitive account of mental arithmetic, in the absence of any understanding of the mathematical theory of arithmetic.

So what is the right normative theory for human reasoning? And, in particular, what is the right normative theory of reasoning with conditionals? Throughout the chapters of this book, two, apparently competing, normative frameworks have been considered: logic and probability—and within each of these, a range of specific proposals can be formulated.

The machinery of modern logic, from Frege onwards, has been developed to provide a rigorous foundation for mathematical reasoning; and, more recently, has been applied to a wide range of applications in computer science, including formulating a formal model of the meaning of computer programs and related projects (Winskel, 1993). These are typically domains in which certainty is possible—and indeed, such certainty is typically a motivating objective. A logical machinery underpinning mathematical proof may, for example, provide certainty in the conclusions drawn in mathematical reasoning; a logic-based semantics for a computer program provide certainty that it will compute the intended function (i.e., the program may be provably 'correct').

How, though, does logic fare, when used to provide an account of everyday inference—including conditionals about the everyday world? Outside mathematics, inference appears almost ubiquitously a matter of uncertain inference, rather than deduction. In everyday life, we are forced to work with fragments of information, whether derived from partial and noisy sensory input, linguistic input of dubious provenance, or uncertain background theories or assumptions. Thus, we might suggest that everyday reasoning, and real-world cognition more generally, primarily involves tentative conjecture, rather than water-tight argument. And this conclusion appears to apply at the very heart of conditional reasoning. Suppose I believe the conditional *if I turn the key, the car starts. I turn the key.* I *expect* the car to start—but I do not know this for certain. Indeed, there is an indefinitely large range of factors that might stop the car from starting: the battery might be flat, a crucial electrical cable might be severed, the engine might have been removed, and so on. My conclusions that the car will start is merely *tentative*—the premises do not seem to lend the certainty to my conclusion that might be expected from a logical analysis. Now, of course, it remains possible that the inference *is* certain, but that the failure of the conclusion to hold simply implies that one of the premises is false. Thus, if I am confident that I really did turn the key, perhaps I should conclude that my conditional is false. This viewpoint is implicit in many logic-based approaches; but it has its dangers. Given that all, or almost all, everyday regularities are uncertain, I might, by the same token, be forced to reject all, or almost all, conditionals; and from false premises nothing, of course, follows. So there is a danger of inferential paralysis—if I reject all everyday conditionals, then it is difficult to see how I can generate tentative conjectures about the world.

In an important series of papers, Stenning and van Lambalgen (this volume, 2004, 2005, see also 2007) have argued for understanding the process of uncertain default inference in logical terms, but shifting to non-monotonic logics (logics in which adding new premises may overturn previously drawn conclusions, as, for example, my expectation that the car will start is overturned when I realize that the battery has been removed).

Pfeifer and Kleiter (2005, 2006, this volume) suggest a different role for logic—as providing a mechanism for reasoning *about* probabilities. Thus, while an inference may be uncertain, there are mathematical relationships which hold with certainty. Regarding conditional inferences, this type of approach allows inferences from confidence intervals on the probability of P and *If P then Q*, to a confidence interval on the conclusion Q (this approach promises to provide a cleaner formulation of similar interval-based arguments in the context of syllogistic reasoning, Chater & Oaksford, 1999).

Another option is to view everyday reasoning is intrinsically probabilistic: and to attempt to use the machinery of Bayesian probability theory to provide a framework for inference. This approach presupposes that background knowledge specifies a *probabilistic model*—i.e., it specifies, either directly or indirectly, the joint distribution $Pr(X_1,...X_i,..., X_n)$ over the variables or states over which the reasoner is operating. New knowledge is then represented as providing a constraint, C, on these states; and inference involves determining $Pr(X_1,...X_i,..., X_n|C)$ (or more restricted claims, e.g., about a single state or a subset of states)—by conditioning on the fact that the constraint is true. There is a natural link to conditional reasoning here—the antecedent of the conditional can be viewed as the constraint; and the consequent is some claim about some subset of the $X_1,...X_i,..., X_n$, the probability of which may potentially be influenced by knowing that C holds. A possible extension of this view of conditional reasoning is that the conditional should be assigned a probability, based on the corresponding conditional probability: the probability of the consequent given the antecedent (e.g., Edgington, 1995; Evans & Over, 2004; Oaksford, Chater, & Larkin, 2000).

Yet the probabilistic approach also faces a range of challenges—perhaps the most fundamental is the assumption that background knowledge specifies a model, i.e., specifies the joint probabilities of all states of interest? The assumption that background knowledge specifies a probabilistic model may seem relatively innocuous in the context of, e.g., reasoning about coin flips or dice—because here, natural assumptions about, e.g., independence, and fairness', do straightforwardly specify the joint probabilities of the states of interest (although actually calculating these probabilities may not be computationally costly). But even moderately complex domains, where there are ill-defined causal or evidential relations between different variables, rapidly lead to considerable complexity, where the full power of graphical and causal models (Pearl, 1988, 2000), the theory of random processes (Grimmett & Stirzaker, 2001), and recent Bayesian developments in machine learning (e.g., Jordan, 1998) are rapidly invoked. As soon as we consider the broader problem of representing general knowledge, the bounds of current techniques are immediately exceeded (e.g., Paris, 1992). Indeed, whether we focus on logical or probabilistic methods, the problem of building a theory which will take account of background knowledge represents a daunting challenge for further research, both in cognitive science and artificial intelligence, as we shall now discuss.

Background knowledge and the frame problem

Both logical and probabilistic approaches to conditional reasoning, and indeed to reasoning in general, raise the spectre of the influence of background knowledge on reasoning. Thus, we argued that an apparent advantage of the probabilistic framework is that it provides a natural way of capturing non-monotonic reasoning, such that adding additional information can overturn a conclusion. But nonmonotonicity has the corollary that, in general, no conclusion is 'safe' until all relevant background knowledge has been considered. And, as we have seen, the influence of background knowledge on reasoning appears to pose problems for a straightforward separation of a knowledge-rich System 1, and rule-based System 2, processes of reasoning. But the influence of background knowledge raises alarming challenges for any theory of reasoning, whether based on probability or logic; whether invoking one or many systems of reasoning. This is because understanding the influence of background knowledge on reasoning involves solving the notorious *frame problem* (McCarthy & Hayes, 1969; Pylyshyn, 1987), which has haunted artificial intelligence and cognitive science for the last forty years.

The frame problem is, in a nutshell, the problem of knowing, in the light of a piece of new information, which pieces of background information should be revised—its name is taken from the problem of cartoon animation—in moving from frame to frame in a cartoon, in which, say an animated character makes some movement, which aspects of the background can be left invariant, and which need to be updated (e.g., because they are now thrown into shadow; or otherwise causally influenced by the animated character).

At first sight, the problem is straightforward—it seems that almost all background knowledge should be carried forward: putting the point in terms of conditionals, we might say, *if* proposition P is true before the new information, N, is learned, *then* it is still true after N is learned. This strategy is embodied in so-called 'frame axioms' in artificial intelligence systems—but how then is it possible to deal with the cases in which P *does* need to be updated, without landing the system in contradiction (i.e., inferring that P should change, but at the same time that background information should remain the same). The problem cannot be solved by enumerating the implications of new information, and treating these as special cases—because each adjustment to knowledge corresponds to a fresh change in belief, which raises the frame problem all over again. Moreover, in general, the problem of adjusting one's existing beliefs to a piece of new information is a matter of optimizing the 'global' fit with background knowledge—and such global adjustments can lead arbitrarily far in the 'web of belief' (Quine & Ullian, 1978).

But how is this assumption to be encoded? In terms of conditional reasoning, a natural strategy is to attempt to encode some kind of default rule: that knowledge should not be revised in the light of new evidence, unless there is some reason to do so. Thus, the claim that *if* P *then* Q may be viewed as holding only *other things being equal*. Thus, given a belief that birds fly (in terms of conditionals: for all x, if x is a bird, then x flies), we may conclude that Tweety, who is a bird, therefore flies. But on learning that Tweety is two days old, or has clipped wings, or is a penguin, we have a reason to belief that Tweety will not be able to fly—over-riding the conclusion of the default rule.

Analogous problems arise very generally (Fodor, 1983; Pylyshyn, 1987). Given knowledge K, adding a new fact F can typically reverse many of the previous consequences of K, in highly idiosyncratic ways. Crucially, it proves to be impossible to establish the inferential consequences of learning a new fact in advance. So, for example, learning a new fact about astronomy can, for example, readily modify my beliefs about chess. For example, suppose a reasoner has been told number-theoretic and astronomical 'facts' by the same source, a person of uncertain trustworthiness. Then learning that the number-theoretic 'fact' is wildly incorrect will typically cause the reasoner to doubt the putative astronomy-related fact. Thus, nonmonotonicty may apply to arbitrarily remote pieces of knowledge.

A despairing conclusion from such observations would be that the web of knowledge is desparately entangled: that there is no way of specifying 'local' inferential connections between pieces of knowledge—because any such local connections themselves rest on arbitrarily large amount of background knowledge. That is, the significance of each individual connection only holds in the light of arbitrarily large amounts of background knowledge: even the connection between switch-flipping and lights turning on is not a 'brute association', but an inference that holds good only in some contexts, yet not in others. To the degree that reasoning, and perhaps knowledge itself, cannot be readily broken into components, the task of building a computational account of the resulting 'jelly' seems far beyond our reach.

The depth of these problems is starkly evident in artificial intelligence. Any practical computational challenge which turns out to depend on general world knowledge turns out to be infeasible. Indeed, artificial intelligence has succeeded precisely for problems for which good performance can be achieved independent of general world knowledge. Thus, artificial intelligence has generated systems that achieve impressive levels of performance have been achieved in formal domains, sealed off from general world knowledge, such as chess, backgammon (Fürnkranz & Kubat, 2001), or aspects of logical theorem-proving (Fitting, 1996; Kowalski, this volume). And there has been substantial progress in image processing, voice recognition, and aspects of robotic control, where it has proved possible to make headway without presupposing any understanding of the world that is being seen, talked about, or manipulated (Russell & Norvig, 2003). Moreover, there have been useful models which exploit statistical properties of linguistic input, or aspects of a knowledge-base, yielding promising results, e.g., in analysis and classification of words, sentences or texts (e.g., Griffiths & Steyvers, 2004; Johnson & Riezler, 2002; Redington, Chater, & Finch, 1998) or in information retrieval (Blei, Jordan & Ng, 2003)—but these methods also resolutely avoid drawing on world knowledge (and frequently apply sophisticated probabilistic models). But attempting to build computational models of representation and reasoning with everyday, common-sense knowledge has proved an almost entirely fruitless task (McDermott, 1987).

Note that the frame problem relates very directly to theories of conditional inference based on the Ramsey Test (e.g., Ramsey, 1931/1990; Evans & Over, 2004, see Over, Evans, & Elaqayam, this volume). The Ramsey test proposes that people determine the probability they will associate with a conditional, if p then q, by supposing that p be added to their entire stock of background beliefs, B, and assessing the degree of belief in q in the light of p and B. Thus, in logic-based accounts, whether the conditional should be asserted depends on whether p, B validly implies that q. In the probabilistic accounts, the strength of the conditional can be associated with the probability of $\Pr(q|p, B)$. But assessing this probability, at least in the general case, requires precisely to solve the frame problem: to work out the implications of adding a new belief, p, to one's entire stock of beliefs.

How far can the cognitive science of reasoning progress, given that it seeks to understand the very knowledge-rich processes of inference that artificial intelligence has run into the sand? Multiple process theories, as discussed above, provide one source of hope—by separating off certain kinds of formal, conscious reasoning processes from the morass of general world knowledge, it may be hoped that a knowledge-free theory of reasoning might be constructed (in, for example, the frameworks on mental models [Johnson-Laird, 1983] or mental logics [Rips, 1994]), albeit of a theory which may need to be inflected by all manner of additional semantic and pragmatic factors (i.e., the influence of world knowledge), which stand outside the theory proper. Picking up on the discussion in the previous section, this strategy is always vulnerable to the concern that the influences of world knowledge may be so thorough-going that there is little explanatory work for the formal theory to do. Nonetheless, this approach is one viable, and currently very active, theoretical move for avoiding the problem of world knowledge.

Another strategy is to aim to focus on a limited domain: and to allow that background knowledge is relevant to specifying the probability in that domain (i.e., background knowledge may be sufficient to specify a probabilistic model of that domain). So, in the case of conditional inference, it may be that indefinitely large amounts of background knowledge may be involved in determining the conditional probability that a reasoner assigns to the car starting, given that the key is turned; and this knowledge may also be required to determine relevant priors, such as the (low) prior probabilities that, at any particular moment, the key turns or the car starts. But, *given* these probabilities, we can specify the joint probability distribution over the antecedent and consequent; and hence we can determine the 'correct' probabilistic inferences that should be drawn, given various conditional reasoning problems; and we can compare such reasoning with observed behaviour—and this is the strategy adopted by advocates of probabilistic approaches to conditionals. We might aim to extend this type of approach by defining a slightly richer probabilistic model: e.g., we might want to capture putative causal relationships between variables (e.g., Ali, Schlottman, Shaw, Oaksford, & Chater, this volume; Over, Hadjichristidis, Evans, Handley, & Sloman, 2007); or we might want to adopt a richer account of the relationship between the premises in conditional reasoning (e.g., Liu, 2003, this volume); or we might attempt to provide an algorithmic model of the relevant computations involved in resolving between conflicting conditionals, using a connectionist model (e.g., Oaksford & Chater, this volume).

This type of approach, then, does not confront the frame problem directly. Rather, background knowledge is used by the theorist to help specify increasingly complex probabilistic models of the reasoner's knowledge. Thus, different aspects of background knowledge may be assimilated piecemeal into a probabilistic account; but there is no attempt to confront the problem of representing the entire network of knowledge in its entirety—the frame problem is side-stepped, but the approach still yields non-trivial empirical predictions about how people reason.

The interconnected nature of everyday knowledge suggests that it may not be possible to build a *complete* model, probabilistic or otherwise, in the context of everyday reasoning—because to do so would require formalizing the 'web of knowledge' in its entirety. The probabilistic approach offers the hope that, nonetheless, progress is possible by formalizing knowledge piecemeal—e.g., understanding how people reason about the specific conditional, if the key turns, the car starts, based on relevant probabilities (which may perhaps be directly elicited or implicitly measured by experiment) that the reasoner holds, about the probability associated with the conditional, the antecedent, and so on, even though no account is given concerning the origin of these probabilities. On the other hand, we can, if we choose, trace further along the inferential web. Perhaps we might attempt to understand the origin of the high conditional probability that the car starts if the key is turned, using a theory of learning based on prior experience (Cheng, 1997; Shanks, 1995), and/or from the reasoner's 'theory' of the operation of mechanical devices (Gentner & Stevens, 1983).

Thus, according to this approach, any piece of reasoning may be analyzed in relation to related pieces of information, or inferences; but this process takes into account the nature of the entire web of background knowledge.

According to this viewpoint, theories of reasoning may be viewed as concerned with processes by which people changes their beliefs (Harman, 1986). And explaining the operation of the conditional, then, requires understand the relationship between pairs of beliefs (according to Ramsey's formulation, concerning how much reasoners should modify their belief in the consequent, on the supposition that the antecedent is true). And relations between beliefs typically, and perhaps almost always, hold only against the backdrop of other beliefs. Normative theories, including probability and logic, attempt to codify local relations between beliefs. They do not attempt to encompass the entire body of background knowledge—this would require solving the frame problem. One desideratum for local theories of reasoning is that they should, nonetheless, be able to extend naturally where additional pieces of local information are taken into account, perhaps overturning prior inferences. One appeal of the probabilistic framework is that it appears to provide a natural framework in which this can be done; but non-monotonic logical methods, as advocated by Stenning and van Lambalgen (this volume, 2007) provide another possible route.

Single vs. multiple systems

Faced with the complexity, variety, and flexibility of human thought and behaviour, and with the frame problem looming close by, two entirely contrary research strategies have a certain appeal. The first aims to divide what appears to be a single system into a two, many, or perhaps even a hierarchy, of separate systems. The goal of this dual, or multiple, systems perspective is to carve a complex system into smaller and more readily comprehensible subsystems, each of which may be have its own principles of operation. And, in particular, the study of reasoning may, on this strategy, be separated from the recruitment and application of background knowledge, which seem so intractable to analysis. The second strategy takes the opposite approach. It seeks to find general principles that unify cognitive phenomena; and viewing, as far as possible, the psychological variety as arising from different aspects of a single underlying system. The hope is that general principles and architectural hypotheses may help clarify, and be constrained by, experimental data and theoretical analysis, across a wide range of cognitive domains.

The first strategy has been, we suggest, in the ascendant throughout the cognitive and brain sciences (see also Epstein, 1994; Evans & Frankish, 2009; Evans & Over, 1996; Sloman 1996; Stanovich & West, 2000). For example, Evans and Over (2004) distinguish between System 1 cognitive processes, which are assumed to be primarily unconscious associative, fast, automatic, and not to draw on central computational resources. By contrast, System 2 processes are conscious, rule-governed, and logical. Systems 1 and 2 continually battle for control: only with significant cognitive effort is it possible for System 2 processes to override the rapid and intuitively appealing outputs of System 1 reasoning.

A similar picture of multiple systems fighting over the cognitive steering wheel arises in the study of learning and decision making. A cognitively basic reinforcement learning system, that has formed habits on the basis of the success or failure of past actions, is often attributed to the dopaminergic system in the basal ganglia (Daw, O'Doherty, Seymour, Dayan, & Dolan, 2006); and many paradoxical aspects of human behaviour are explained as resulting from the battle for control between these processes and high-level cognition, engaging, for example, pre-frontal cortex. Putative clashes between such mechanisms provide a natural starting point for explaining a variety of aspects of human and animal behavior, both in the laboratory, and in the study of addiction, depression and phobias (Epstein, 1994; Kahneman & Frederick, 2002; McClure, Laibson, Loewenstein, & Cohen, 2004).

The idea of a clash of internal cognitive mechanisms, embodying different styles of reasoning, is an intuitively appealing one. But does it really stand up to analysis? How far is there evidence for distinct, competitive, processes underpinning human cognition? We suspect that these questions will be crucially important in determining the future direction of reasoning research and cognitive science more generally (see, De Neys, this volume).

Accounts of reasoning that invoke multiple competing processes face two important challenges, one theoretical and one empirical: and both concern the nature of the interaction (or non-interaction) between the two systems.

The theoretical challenge is to understand how the putative System 1 and System 2 reasoning systems could operate independently; and if they cannot, how far can they usefully be viewed as distinct systems at all. Consider, for example, suppression effects in conditional reasoning (Byrne, 1989; see also Cummins, 1995), such as:

> If the switch is flipped, the light comes on
> The switch is flipped

Which appears, by modus ponens, to lead to the conclusion: *The light comes on*. Now suppose that the reasoner is given an extra piece of information:

> There is a power cut

What does the reasoner conclude? Intuitively, it seems obvious that, by drawing on background knowledge, the reasoner immediately concludes that the light does *not* come on. But such background knowledge is presumed to be the domain of System 1; a logic-based System 2 would seem to be compelled to drive through the conclusion that follows logically from the premises, i.e., that follows by Modus Ponens from the first two premises: that the light does come on.

So, if System 1 and System 2 worked independently, we would expect a clash between the two systems. In reality, theorists typically assume, instead, that System 2 is actually richly influenced by background knowledge, so that the conscious rule-governed System 2 does not reach this conclusion. But this theoretical move just gives up the idea that System 2 is a logic-based system at all— because a rule-based logical reasoning system is one that follows the rules of logic—and blocking a Modus Ponens inference is directly to flout one of the most fundamental rules of logic.

Indeed, more generally, conscious, effortful verbal reasoning—the paradigm task that System 2 is presumed to perform—is most naturally modeled as *argument*—i.e., as attempting to persuade oneself or others of a controversial proposition(Hahn & Oaksford, 2007). While theories of argument are numerous, and subject to much controversy, it is uniformly agreed that argument is not a matter of formal logic (Walton 1989); and, moreover, it is agreed that informal argument is richly dependent on vast quantities of background knowledge, on which the credibility of the argument rests (in line with natural language understanding more generally, e.g, Clark, 1975; Minsky, 1977). Hence, the business of the presumed System 2, providing verbal arguments for and against propositions or actions under consideration (Pennington & Hastie, 2000), involves rich engagement with general knowledge (presumed to be the business of System 1); and has little role for purely rule-based reasoning based on the *form* of the information available. Thus, there seem to be little role for a rule-based System 2, consciously reasoning according to logical rules (see, Hahn & Oaksford, 2007).

Now, people can, of course, learn to apply logical inference to linguistic input: they can learn to ignore some aspects of language, and concentrate on others—e.g., in the extreme, they can learn to translate natural language into predicate logic (ignoring non-logical content), and apply the rules of logic to determine what follows. But, for cognitive science, this fact seems no more important than that people can learn the rules of chess, and ignore irrelevant visual features of the pieces, the board, and block out their surroundings. Conscious application of logic is a highly effortful complex learned skill grounded in a hugely complex non-logical machinery, designed to deal with knowledge-rich, rather than formal, inference; it does not involve, we suggest, employing a dedicated cognitive system for rule-based, logical reasoning.

Conversely, System 1 seems, equally, to be difficult to characterize. It is typically assumed to be associative in character, and to be fast and automatic—and crucially to be independent of conscious reasoning. But does such an autonomous associative reasoning system, or perhaps set of systems, exist? One reason to doubt this is that, in humans at least, even the most basic associative process, those observed in conditioning, seem to be highly responsive to verbal intervention, and hence to processes of reasoning and argument. Thus, for example, consider conditioning experiments in which people learn to associate a cue with a shock. After training, the cue then leads to a galvanic skin response (i.e., an autonomic response which is not under direct cognitive control). But the vast majority of studies indicate that this response is eliminated if people are *told* that the shock will not occur in future, or if the shock electrodes are disconnected or removed (Bridger & Mandel, 1965; Colgan, 1970; Katz, Webb, & Stotland, 1971). An associative System 1, working independently from consciously accessible System 2 reasoning, might be expect to continue to influence autonomic responses—especially as autonomic responses cannot be directly over-ruled by conscious effort. This type of phenomenon is by no means an isolated case—indeed, a number of reviews have suggested that there is currently little empirical support for dissociable processes in human learning in a range of domains (e.g., Boakes, 1989, Brewer, 1974; Chater, in press; Lovibond & Shanks; 2002; Mitchell, de Houwer, & Lovibond, in press; Shanks & St John, 1994).

Now, of course, the associative processes involved in conditioning may be even more basic than those thought to be involved in System 1 reasoning; but if these apparently elementary processes are penetrable by high level cognition, then it seems entirely likely that any System 1 processes will be so too. Indeed, such penetrability from conscious high level argument and reasoning (the presumed domain of System 2) would seem inevitably to have a central role in feeding world knowledge to System 1 processes.

How then are we to explain the origin of internal cognitive conflict, rather than as resulting for competition between competing reasoning systems (as in Kahneman & Frederick, 2005). One straightforward approach (Chater, in press) is to propose that internal conflict arises from a 'clash of reasons' rather than a clash of systems. In almost all non-trivial reasoning problems, different lines of argument appear to favour different conclusions. Flipping the switch tends to lead to the expectation that the light will come on; finding that there is a power cut leads to the opposite expectation. Typically, a large quantity of background knowledge is required to resolve such clashes: for example, we may draw on the default assumption that most lights are powered by the mains electricity, rather than by battery; or that most lights are electric rather than powered by oil or gas. Indeed, everyday reasoning may generally be characterized as concerned with resolving clashes between alternatives lines of argument—thus, internal cognitive conflict, within a single reasoning system, may be the norm, rather than the exception.

Moreover, reasons are often not equally persuasive; or equally easy to evaluate. When paying close attention and given sufficient time, it may become evident one reason is valid, and another weak. But when attention is reduced, the weaker reason may nonetheless prevail. Thus, to choose a classic example from probabilistic reasoning, the reasoner may decide that, given background information about Linda's intellectual and political background, it is more likely that she is a feminist bank teller, than that she is a feminist (Tversky & Kahneman's [1983] conjunction fallacy), because there is a better overall match between the former description (for which at least the first part matches), than the second description (which seems entirely incongruous). Considered reflection on probability may, or may not, lead the reasoner to draw the opposite conclusion.

More generally, it seems entirely possible that there will be systematic differences between responses when time and attention are limited, and responses when time and attention are plentiful. Hence, such differences need not necessarily be explained by adverting to the distinction between a rapid, attention-free System 1, and a slow, attention-demanding System 2 (see Cunningham & Zelazo, 2007, for a similar perspective on apparent dissociations between two putative routes underpinning social cognition, as exemplified by, e.g., Bargh & Chartrand, 1999).

These arguments are not, of course, decisive; and they certainly do not show that reasoning is not the product of a range of partially or completely dissociable cognitive mechanisms. They do, we suggest, indicate that the case for multiple systems of reasoning is as yet unproven, both on theoretical grounds: concerning the interaction between the proposed systems and the resolution of conflict); and on empirical grounds: concerning the apparent cognitive penetrability [Pylyshyn, 1980] of what are presumed to be basic, associative reasoning processes, by high level reasoning concerning arbitrary background knowledge. We suspect that the debate between multiple and single process accounts will continue to be a major focus on investigation, both in the domain of reasoning, and across the brain and cognitive sciences more generally, over the coming decades.

Conclusion

Conditional reasoning corresponds to a core cognitive operation: taking one piece of information, and inferring (or evaluating the plausibility) of another. The variety and subtlety of conditionals, ranging from indicative, to counterfactual, to deontic, cases, is no more than a reflection of the subtlety and variety of human cognition itself. The chapters in this book have provided a state-of-the-art overview of the current research on conditionals, combining perspectives from psychology, philosophy and artificial intelligence. These chapters both make important positive proposals, and also highlight key open issues both for the cognitive science of reasoning, and for cognitive science more broadly, some of which we have highlighted in this chapter. We hope that these chapters provide a stimulus for the next generation in the study of conditionals and cognition.

References

Adams, E. (1975). *The logic of conditionals: An application of probability to deductive logic.* Dordrecht: Reidel.

Ali, N., Schlottman, A., Shaw, A., Chater, N., & Oaksford, M. (this volume). Causal Discounting and Conditional Reasoning in Children.

Bargh, J. A. & Chartrand, T. L. (1999). The unbearable automaticity of being. *American Psychologist*, **54**, 462–479.

Barkow, J. H., Cosmides, L., & Tooby, J. (Eds.). *The adapted mind.* New York: Oxford University Press.

Blei, D. M., Jordan, M. I., & Ng, A. Y. (2003). Hierarchical models for applications in information retrieval. In J. M. Bernardo, M. J. Bayarri, J. O. Berger, A. P. Dawid, D. Heckerman, A. F. M. Smith, & M. West (Eds.) *Bayesian Statistics 7* (pp. 25–43). Oxford: Oxford University Press.

Boakes, R. A. (1989). How one might find evidence for conditioning in adult humans. In T. Archer & L.-G. Nilsson (Eds.), *Aversion, avoidance and anxiety: Perspectives on learning and memory* (pp. 381–402). Hillsdale, NJ: Erlbaum.

Brewer, W. F. (1974). There is no convincing evidence for operant or classical conditioning in adult humans. In W. B. Weimer & D. S. Palermo (Eds.), *Cognition and the symbolic processes* (pp. 1–42). Hillsdale, NJ: Erlbaum.

Bridger, W. H. & Mandel, I. J. (1965). Abolition of the PRE by instructions in GSR conditioning. *Journal of Experimental Psychology*, **69**, 476–482.

Chaiken, S. & Trope, Y. (1999). *Dual-process theories in social psychology.* New York: Guilford Press.

Chater, N. (2009). Rational and mechanistic perspectives on reinforcement learning. *Cognition*, **113**, 350–364.

Chater, N. & Oaksford, M. (1999). The probability heuristics model of syllogistic reasoning. *Cognitive Psychology*, **38**, 191–258.

Cheng, P. W. (1997). From covariation to causation: A causal power theory. *Psychological Review*, **104**, 367–405.

Clark, H. H. (1975). Bridging. In R. C. Schank & B. L. Nash-Webber (Eds.), *Theoretical issues in natural language processing* (pp. 188–193). New York: Association for Computing Machinery.

Colgan, D. M. (1970). Effect of instructions on skin resistance response. *Journal of Experimental Psychology*, **86**, 108–112.

Cosmides, L. (1989). The logic of social exchange: Has natural selection shaped how humans reason? Studies with the Wason selection task. *Cognition*, **31**, 187–276.

Cunningham, W. A. & Zelazo, P. D. (2007). Attitudes and evaluations: A social cognitive neuroscience perspective. *Trends in Cognitive Sciences*, **11**, 97–104.

Daw, N. D., O'Doherty, J. P., Dayan, P., Seymour, B., & Dolan, R. J. (2006). Cortical substrates for exploratory decisions in humans. *Nature*, **441**, 876–879.

Dreyfus, H. (1972). *What computers still can't do: The limits of artificial intelligence*. New York: Harper and Row.

Edgington, D. (1995). On conditionals. *Mind*, **104**, 235–329.

Epstein, S. (1994). Integration of the cognitive and psychodynamic unconscious. *American Psychologist*, **49**, 709–724.

Evans, J. St.B. T. (2008). Dual-processing accounts of reasoning, judgment and social cognition. *Annual Review of Psychology*, **59**, 255–278.

Evans, J. St.B. T. & Over, D. E. (1996). *Rationality and Reasoning*. Hove, UK: Psychology Press

Evans, J. St.B. T. & Over, D. E. (2004). *If*. Oxford, England: Oxford University Press.

Evans, J. St.B. T. & Frankish, K. (Eds.) (2009). *In two minds: Dual processes and beyond*. Oxford: Oxford University Press.

Fitting, Melvin (1996). *First-Order Logic and Automated Theorem Proving* (2nd edition). Berlin: Springer

Fodor, J. A. (1983). *The modularity of mind*. Cambridge, MA: MIT Press.

Fürnkranz, J. & Kubat, M. (Eds.) (2001). *Machines that learn to play games*. Huntington, NY: Nova Science Publishers.

Geiger, S. M. & Oberauer, K. (this volume). Toward a reconciliation of mental model theory and probabilistic theories of conditionals.

Gentner, D. & Stevens, A. (1983). *Mental models*. Hillsdale, NJ: Erlbaum.

Girotto, V. & Johnson-Laird, P. N. (this volume). Conditionals and probability.

Gopnik, A. & Schulz, L. (2007). *Causal Learning: Psychology, Philosophy, and Computation*. Oxford: Oxford University Press.

Griffiths, T. & Steyvers, M. (2004). Finding Scientific Topics. *Proceedings of the National Academy of Sciences*, **101**(suppl. 1), 5228–5235.

Grimmett, G. & Stirzaker, D. (2001). *Probability and random processes (3rd ed)*. Oxford: Oxford University Press.

Hahn, U. & Oaksford, M. (2007). The rationality of informal argumentation: A Bayesian approach to reasoning fallacies. *Psychological Review*, **114**, 704–732.

Harman, G. (1986). *Change in view: Principles of reasoning*. Cambridge, MA: MIT Press.

Hirschfeld, L. & Gelman, S. (Eds.) (1994). *Mapping the Mind: Domain Specificity in Cognition and Culture* (pp. 39–67). Cambridge: Cambridge University Press.

Johnson, M, & Riezler, S. (2002). Statistical models of language learning and use. *Cognitive Science* **26**, 239–253.

Johnson-Laird, P. N. (1983). *Mental models*. Cambridge: Cambridge University Press.

Jordan, M. I. (Ed.) (1998). *Learning in Graphical Models*. Cambridge, MA: MIT Press.

Kahneman, D. & Frederick, S. (2002). Representativeness revisited: Attribute substitution in intuitive judgment. In T. Gilovich, D. Griffin & D. Kahneman (Eds), *Heuristics and Biases: The Psychology of Intuitive Judgment* (pp. 49–81). Cambridge, UK: Cambridge University Press.

Kahneman, D. & Frederick, S. (2005). A model of heuristic judgment. In K. J. Holyoak & R. G. Morrison (Eds.) *The Cambridge Handbook of Thinking and Reasoning* (pp. 267–293). Cambridge: Cambridge University Press.

Katz, A., Webb, L. & Stotland, E. (1971). Cogntive influences on the rate of GSR extinction. *Journal of Experimental Research in Personality*, **5**, 208–215.

Kowalski, R. (this volume). Reasoning with conditionals in artificial intelligence.

Liu, I.-m. (2003). Conditional reasoning and conditionalization. *Journal of Experimental Psychology: Learning, Memory, and Cognition*, **29**, 694–709.

Liu, I.-m. (this volume). A successive-conditionalization approach to conditional reasoning.

Lovibond, P. F. & Shanks, D. R. (2002). The Role of Awareness in Pavlovian Conditioning: Empirical Evidence and Theoretical Implications. *Journal of Experimental Psychology: Animal Behavior Processes*, **28**, 3–26.

McCarthy, J. & Hayes, P. J. (1969). Some philosophical problems from the standpoint of artificial intelligence. In B. Meltzer & D. Michie (Eds). *Machine intelligence* **4**, Edinburgh: Edinburgh University Press.

McClure, S. M., Laibson, D. I., Loewenstein, G., & Cohen, J. D. (2004). Separate neural systems value immediate and delayed monetary rewards. *Science*, **306**, 503–507.

McDermott, D. (1987). A critique of pure reason. *Computational Intelligence*, **3**, 151–160.

Minsky, M. (1977). Frame System Theory. In P. N. Johnson-Laird and P. C. Wason (Eds), *Thinking: Readings in Cognitive Science* (pp. 355–376). Cambridge: Cambridge University Press.

Mitchell, C. J., de Houwer, J., & Lovibond, P. F. (in press). The propositional nature of human associative learning. *Behavioral and Brain Sciences*.

Newell, A. J. C. Shaw. & H. A. Simon. (1958). Chess-playing programs and the problem of complexity. *IBM Journal of Research and Development*, **2**, 320–325.

Oaksford, M. & Chater, N. (this volume). Conditional Inference and Constraint Satisfaction: Reconciling Mental Models and the Probabilistic Approach?

Oaksford, M., Chater, N. & Larkin, J. (2000). Probabilities and polarity biases in conditional inference. *Journal of Experimental Psychology: Learning, Memory and Cognition*, **26**, 883–889.

Over, D. E., Evans, J. St.B. T., & Elqayam, S. (this volume). Conditionals and non-constructive reasoning.

Over, D. E., Hadjichristidis, C., Evans, J. St.B. T., Handley, S. J., & Sloman, S. A. (2007). The probability of causal conditionals. *Cognitive Psychology*, **54**, 62–97.

Paris, J. (1992). *The uncertain reasoner's companion: A mathematical perspective*. Cambridge: Cambridge University Press.

Pearl, J. (1988). *Probabilistic Reasoning in Intelligent Systems*, San Mateo, CA: Morgan Kaufmann.

Pearl, J. (2000). *Causality: Models, reasoning and inference*. Cambridge: Cambridge University Press.

Pennington, N. & Hastie, R. (2000). Explanation-based decision making. In T. Connolly, H. R. Arkes & K. R. Hammond (Eds.), *Judgment and Decision Making: An Interdisciplinary Reader (2nd Ed)* (pp. 212–28). Cambridge: Cambridge University Press.

Pfeifer, N. & Kleiter, G. D. (2005). Towards a mental probability logic. *Psychologica Belgica*, **45**, 71–99.

Pfeifer, N. & Kleiter, G. D. (2006). Inference in conditional probability logic. *Kybernetika*, **42**, 391–404.

Pfeifer, N. & Kleiter, G. D. (this volume). The conditional in mental probability logic.

Pylyshyn, Z. W. (1980). *Computation and cognition*. Cambridge, MA: MIT Press.

Pylyshyn, Z. W. (Ed.) (1987). *The robot's dilemma: The frame problem in artificial intelligence*. Norwood, NJ: Ablex.

Quine, W. V. O. & Ullian, J. S. (1978). *The web of belief*. New York, NY: Random House.

Ramsey, F. P. (1990). General propositions and causality (original publication, 1931). In D. H. Mellor (Ed.), *Philosophical papers* (pp.145–163). Cambridge: Cambridge University Press.

Rao, R. P. N., Olshausen, B. A., & Lewicki, M. S. (Eds.) (2002). *Probabilistic models of the brain: Perception and neural function.* Cambridge, MA: MIT Press.

Redington, M., Chater, N., & Finch, S. (1998). Distributional information: A powerful cue for acquiring syntactic categories. *Cognitive Science*, **22**, 425–469.

Rips, L. J. (1994). *The Psychology of proof.* Cambridge, MA: MIT Press.

Russell, S. J. & Norvig, P. (2003). *Artificial Intelligence: A Modern Approach (2nd ed.).* Upper Saddle River, NJ: Prentice Hall.

Shanks, D. R. (1995). *The psychology of associative learning.* Cambridge: Cambridge University Press.

Shanks, D. R. & St. John, M. F. (1994). Characteristics of dissociable human learning systems. *Behavioral and Brain Sciences*, **17**, 367–447.

Sloman, S. A. (1996). The empirical case for two systems of reasoning. *Psychological Bulletin*, **119**, 3–22.

Stanovich, K. E. & West, R. F. (2000). Individual differences in reasoning: Implications for the rationality debate? *Behavioral and Brain Sciences*, **23**, 645–665.

Stanovich, K. E. (2009). Distinguishing the reflective, algorithmic, and autonomous minds: Is it time for a tri-process theory? In J. St.B. T. Evans & K. Frankish (Eds.), *In two minds: Dual processes and beyond.* Oxford: Oxford University Press.

Stenning, K. & van Lambalgen, M. (2004). A little logic goes a long way: Basing experiment on semantic theory in the cognitive science of conditional reasoning. *Cognitive Science*, **28**, 481–530.

Stenning, K. & van Lambalgen, M. (2005). Semantic interpretation as reasoning in nonmonotonic logic: The real meaning of the suppression task. *Cognitive Science*, **29**, 919–960.

Stenning, K. & van Lambalgen, M. (2007). *Human reasoning and cognitive science.* Cambridge, MA: MIT Press.

Stenning, K. & van Lambalgen, M. (this volume) *The logical response to a noisy world.*

Thompson, V. A. (this volume). Towards a metacognitive dual process theory of conditional reasoning

Tversky, A. & Kahneman, D. (1983). Extension versus intuitive reasoning: The conjunction fallacy in probability judgment. *Psychological Review*, **90**, 293–315.

Verschueren, N. & Schaeken, W. (this volume). A multi-layered dual-process approach to conditional reasoning.

Walton, D. N. (1989). *Informal logic.* Cambridge, UK: Cambridge University Press.

Winskel, G. (1993). *The Formal Semantics of Programming Languages: An Introduction.* Cambridge, MA: MIT Press.

Index